monitoring the future

questionnaire responses from the nation's high school seniors

1978

Jerald G. Bachman, Lloyd D. Johnston, and
Patrick M. O'Malley

Survey Research Center • Institute for Social Research
The University of Michigan
Ann Arbor, Michigan

ISR Code Number 4158
ISSN 0190-9185
ISBN 0-87944-238-7

Published in 1980 by:
Institute for Social Research,
The University of Michigan, Ann Arbor, Michigan

Printed in the United States of America

Table of Contents

Preface

This volume is the fourth in a series which presents descriptive statistical results from a national survey of young people entitled Monitoring the Future: A Continuing Study of the Lifestyles and Values of Youth. Each year the study surveys a large sample of high school seniors, located in approximately 125 schools nationwide, and drawn to be representative of all seniors in the coterminous United States. In 1978, the year covered by the present volume, 18,924 seniors in 111 public and 20 private high schools participated in the research.

The first four volumes in this series, dealing with the high school classes of 1975, 1976, 1977, and 1978, are being published simultaneously. Additional volumes are expected to appear on an annual basis. The most important contribution of this series is likely to be the opportunity it provides for the exploration of trends, a process that obviously involves the use of several different volumes. With that in mind, we have kept the format highly consistent from one volume to another, and we have developed an index (described below) which should facilitate the process of matching data across years. It should be noted that the volume presenting 1975 data is different from the others in several respects.*

Although we designed the volumes to fit together as a series, we also saw distinct advantages in having each volume able to stand alone — to be usable without reference to any of the others. For that reason, the introductory material on research design and questionnaire content, the instructions for accessing the data tables, and the appendices on

sampling errors are all included in each volume. Thus, the small price we pay for making each volume self-contained is that much of the text portion is repeated each year.

Purposes of this Series of Publications

Monitoring the Future, which is conducted by the University of Michigan's Institute for Social Research and receives its core funding from the National Institute on Drug Abuse, is an unusually comprehensive research project in several respects: surveys are conducted annually on an ongoing basis; the samples are large and nationally representative; and the subject matter is very broad, encompassing some 1,300 variables per year. Many people — scholars, policy makers, educators, and so on — will have an interest in the results.

The principal investigators are already writing for a number of these audiences and will continue to do so. Because of the limitations in our own time, interests, and expertise, however, there is an enormous amount of valuable information which may never be utilized if the initiative to digest and disseminate all of it must come from us alone. Further, since the project is in part a social indicators series, its value rests to a considerable degree on *timely* dissemination of the results. For these reasons, we wish to share the study's results with others in a number of fields on a rapid and regular basis. We have chosen to provide two major and complemen-

*The 1975 volume does not include comparison data for black and white subgroups, nor does it include data for the subgroups who did and did not plan to complete four years of college. Also, somewhat fewer questionnaire items appear than in the other volumes. These restrictions are the result primarily of missing data problems that occurred only in the 1975 survey. In most respects, however, those seeking to compare different classes of high school seniors will find the 1975 data useful.

tary vehicles for doing this: (a) these annual reference volumes of descriptive results, and (b) machine-readable data archives for direct analysis by others.

We believe that many potential users who would not mount the effort required to conduct computer analyses of archived data will be able to get most of what they want from these volumes of descriptive results. The user of any one of these volumes can estimate — usually with considerable accuracy — a wide variety of characteristics of the high school class described in that volume. To take just one example, the user of the present volume can ascertain that 50.2 percent of seniors in the high school class of 1978 reported using marijuana at least once during the preceding year. Further, by utilizing two or more of these volumes the reader can describe recent trends in any such characteristic. To continue with the same example, the volume describing the high school class of 1975 indicates that 40.0 percent of those seniors reported marijuana use during the preceding year; and when that is combined with the data from the present volume the reader is able to discern a shift of 10.2 percent over the three years between the classes of 1975 and 1978. And if all of the first four volumes in the series are used, one can observe a steady increase in the proportion of high school seniors who report having used marijuana at least once during the twelve months preceding the survey:

    40.0 percent of seniors in 1975
    44.5 percent of seniors in 1976
    47.6 percent of seniors in 1977
    50.2 percent of seniors in 1978

A similar examination of trends can be carried out for over 1,300 different variables dealing with a wide variety of subject areas (listed in Table 2 of the Introduction). A simple indexing system (described below) has been developed which makes it quite straightforward for the reader wishing to do trend analyses to locate the results for a given question for any year of the study. The index in the present volume lists the location of all items included in the surveys for 1976 through 1978 and most items included in 1975.

Analyses such as those illustrated above need not be limited to the total sample. The data provided in these volumes also permit examination of a variety of subgroups (e.g., males, females, those from different regions, those with different levels of drug use experience). The principal investigators have already conducted and reported some analyses in the area of drug use and related attitudes (Johnston, Bachman, and O'Malley, 1977, 1979), but many other areas have not yet been explored extensively.

We recognize that providing ready access to essentially undigested data carries certain risks, particularly the risk of mistaken interpretations based on inadequate controls, lack of awareness of sample limitations, etc. More than offsetting the risks, in our view, are the advantages of prompt and widespread dissemination of these nationally representative survey indicator data. Although we are unable to eliminate the risks, we hope to reduce them by providing the reader with an extensive list of caveats presented at the end of the Introduction section. We ask all who use the data to read these caveats carefully and take them seriously.

A Guide for the Reader

This volume is divided into three main parts: (1) the introductory section, (2) the section giving the descriptive results from the current year's survey, and (3) the cross-time item reference index.

Introductory Section. The introduction contains a description of the study — its purposes, major content areas, design, field procedures, response rates, and methods of publication and data dissemination. Since most of this material remains unchanged from year to year, anyone having read another of the volumes may wish to skim this section. We do, however, suggest reviewing the caveats, located at the end of the introductory section, which deal with interpreting and extrapolating from these data.

Descriptive Results Section. In this section all questions contained in this year's survey are presented along with percentagized frequency distributions of answers for the entire sample and for selected subgroups. The questions in this section are organized according to the number of the questionnaire form in which they were contained (forms one through five) and according to the order in which the questions occurred. There is one important exception, however. A major segment of questions common to all five forms of the questionnaire (dealing with drug use, background characteristics, and some other subjects) is presented only once, at the beginning of the Descriptive Results section, using the data from respondents on all five forms.

The first portion of the descriptive results section contains detailed definitions of all subgroups for whom data are presented. It also describes the statistical conventions used in generating the tables.

Cross-Time Index of Questionnaire Items. This index is intended to serve two purposes.

First it should be useful in locating items dealing with a subject area of interest. The subject area key at the beginning of the cross-time item index shows the alphabetical code assigned to various subject areas (e.g., "politics" or "work and leisure"). Having selected a subject area of interest, one can then scan the Subject Area column in the item index to locate all questions in any of the surveys (through 1978) which deal with that subject. To locate the results for any given question in the Descriptive Results section of this volume, simply look in column two of the item index for its page location.

The cross-time index can also be used to determine in which other years an item was used and where to locate it. If, in reviewing the Descriptive Results section, one locates an interesting item and would like to know in which of the other annual surveys of seniors it has appeared, it may be found in the cross-time index by its unique "item reference number." The index will indicate all years in which that same item appeared and show the questionnaire form, section, and item number for each year. This information thus can be used to decide which other volumes in this series might be of relevance; and the same item may be readily located by its reference number in the index of any other volume.

Sampling Appendices. Appendix A is provided for those wishing to determine the confidence limits around a percentage estimate, or to test the statistical significance of an observed difference between two groups, or to test the significance of a change from one year to another. It gives the necessary procedures and tables for such tests and provides the appropriate factors by which to correct for the fact that the study makes use of a multistage probability sample clustered in a limited number of schools (usually about 125). Appendix B provides further detail on sample design effects and the procedures which were used to derive the sampling error estimates.

Availability of Archived Data

As was mentioned earlier, this series of volumes will be complemented by an archiving of the raw data sets for direct analysis by others not associated with the project. The present volumes should be a considerable help to those wishing to access the archived data since they provide a verbatim statement of items and answer categories, and also because they include basic univariate and bivariate frequency distributions for all items, as well as the missing data rates. The cross-time index of items contained in each of these volumes also provides an efficient way to identify the relevant variables in various content areas, as well as to determine when they were measured and their

questionnaire locations. In fact, we hope that the availability of this series will not only facilitate the use of the archived data but actually stimulate interest in their use.

Two major social science archives will hold the individual level data which are summarized in this volume:

The Interuniversity Consortium for Political and Social Research (ICPSR)
Institute for Social Research
P.O. Box 1248
Ann Arbor, Michigan 48106

The Drug Abuse Epidemiology Data Center (DAEDAC)
Institute for Behavioral Research
Texas Christian University
Fort Worth, Texas 76129

The ICPSR archive will make individual-level data available on tape to interested investigators for analysis at their own facility. However, it is presently planned that these data sets will not contain the drug use or delinquency measures. Because of the sensitivity of the latter measures — that is, those describing the respondent's own use of illicit drugs and other delinquent behaviors — only the data set in the DAEDAC archive will contain those measures. The Monitoring the Future file at DAEDAC will be treated as a "restricted data set," meaning that all analyses must be carried out by the archive staff (under the instructions of the outside investigator). Individual level data will not be released by DAEDAC, thereby ensuring that the answers of an individual respondent cannot be located through pattern recognition (i.e., using various descriptor variables in combination to make a unique identification). While the probability of such identification may seem remote, we feel that the potential seriousness of the consequences is sufficient to justify this high level of caution.

Other Publications from the Study

A number of different forms of publications based on Monitoring the Future data have been developed or are being planned. One series of annual volumes, dealing with trends in drug use and drug-related attitudes and beliefs, is being published by the National Institute on Drug Abuse. The first volume in that series, *Drug Use Among American High School Students 1975-1977* (Johnston, Bachman, and O'Malley), was published in late 1977; and the second, *Drugs and the Class of '78* (Johnston, Bachman, and O'Malley), in 1979.*

---

*Either the full volumes, or abbreviated highlights versions of each, may be ordered without cost from the National Clearinghouse for Drug Abuse Information, National Institute on Drug Abuse, 5600 Fishers Lane, Rockville, Maryland 20857.

An Occasional Papers series has been launched by the project. It includes papers on design and methodological issues as well as special substantive analyses and early, and sometimes more detailed, drafts of articles planned for journal publication. The first occasional paper, "The Monitoring the Future Project Design and Procedures" (Bachman and Johnston, 1978), provides a detailed description of the study and its underlying rationale.

The present series of reference volumes is being published by the Institute for Social Research. A new volume will be added to this series each year.

Articles for academic journals, as well as for journals serving various professionals working with youths, are also being written. In addition, several integrative books based on the Monitoring the Future project are in the planning stages.

To request particular papers, reprints, or periodic notification of publications available from the study, write to Monitoring the Future, Room 2030, Institute for Social Research, The University of Michigan, Box 1248, Ann Arbor, Michigan 48106.

Acknowledgements

A great many people have contributed to the launching and development of this research effort. We are indebted to a number of officials of the National Institute on Drug Abuse and the Special Action Office for Drug Abuse Prevention for their encouragement and advice at the outset — in particular, Richard Bucher, Robert DuPont, William Pollin, and Louise Richards. To the members of our Advisory Panel we also express our thanks for their review and suggestions regarding instrumentation and design. In addition to Drs. Bucher and Richards, the committee members are John Ball, Donald Campbell, Ira Cisin, Wilbur Cohen, O. Dudley Duncan, Dorothy Gilford, Eric Josephson, Robert Kahn, Donald Michael, and Lee Robins.

Our colleagues at the Institute for Social Research and elsewhere who shared their insights, and often their most cherished instrumentation, are too numerous to mention; but their contributions are greatly appreciated. To the director of the Survey Research Center's Sampling Section, Irene Hess, we owe a particular debt for the creativity of her sampling design for the study. The contributions of the SRC Field Section also have been very valuable.

Major contributions to the production of this particular volume were made by staff members Dawn Bare, Deborah Poinier, Maria Sanchez, and Ann Taylor. We would also like to thank the staff of the Publishing Division of the Institute for Social Research for their work in arranging publication.

The present and former members of the project staff (listed below) have, of course, contributed greatly to the building of this large and complex research series.

Finally, we would like to acknowledge the tens of thousands of high school seniors, their teachers, and their principals, whose cooperation and generous contribution of time make the Monitoring the Future project possible.

JERALD G. BACHMAN
LLOYD D. JOHNSTON
PATRICK M. O'MALLEY

Present and Former Members of the Project Staff

Donna Ando	Walter Gruhn	Jim Neveaux
Margaret Bailey	James Hersey	Dorothy Paulette
Dawn Bare	A. Regula Herzog	Sharon Pietila
Ellen Berger	Mark Krell	Joseph Pleck
Mary Lou Bewley	Sally Lawson	Deborah Poinier
Katherine Blatt	Ludmilla Litus	Judith Redmond
Mary Lea Bonucchi	A. Kathryn Loker	Barbara Renaud
Marcy Breslow	Regina Lumbard	Maria Sanchez
Mary Lou Davis	Oksana Malanchuk	Ann Taylor
Mary Dempsy	Wayne McCulloch	Richard Taylor
William Diedrich	Joan McGraw	Lynda Tolen
Karen Donahue	John Miller	Sandra Wronski
Leslie Eveland	Marion Morse	Thelma Wurzelbacher
Halford Fairchild		

Introduction

The Monitoring the Future project is designed to explore changes in many important values, behaviors, and lifestyle orientations of contemporary American youth. Two general types of tasks may be distinguished. The first is to provide a systematic and accurate *description* of the youth population of interest in a given year, and to quantify the direction and rate of the changes taking place among them over time. The second task, more analytic than descriptive, involves the *explanation* of the relationships and trends observed to exist.

The task of description may be subdivided into three parts: (1) the description of static conditions (which may be accomplished through a single cross-sectional study); (2) the description of cross-cohort or, in longer time-spans, generational changes (usually accomplished using repeated cross sections of the same age groups); and (3) the description of changes with aging (usually accomplished by means of longitudinal studies). The Monitoring the Future project has the capacity to provide each of these three types of description, since it incorporates all three types of research design into a single study. (This complex design, in which multiple cohorts are followed longitudinally, has been referred to as a cohort-sequential design.)

The content of this volume exemplifies the first of these types of description in that it contains cross-sectional data on a single high school class. When the data in this volume are used in combination with data from other such volumes in the series, the nature, direction, and rates of change from one cohort of seniors to another also may be described — the type of reporting which is often labeled as the social indicator approach. The third class of description — dealing with the maturational changes which occur during the years after high school — will not be dealt with in this series of volumes but will be reported in other publications from the study.*

The accurate characterization of American young people and the description of important changes occurring among them is but one class of objectives for the study. The second class of objectives involves the development of a greater understanding of what causes these young people to be as they are, and why the changes being documented are occurring. Explanation will be sought through both the analysis of change at the aggregate level and at the individual level. The results of these explorations will be disseminated via the various publications discussed in the Preface.

The merging of the social indicator approach and the analysis of relationships (particularly longitudinal relationships) into a single cohort-sequential design is, in our view, synergistic: the effectiveness of the two approaches combined is greater than if the two were undertaken separately. Because the present series of volumes deals with senior year data only, our remarks here focus primarily on the project's social indicator contributions — the accurate description of high school seniors and the documentation of trends over time. It is worth not-

*Panels of students from each graduating class are being randomly selected and followed longitudinally for six years. Thus it soon will be possible to characterize the changes which seem to take place consistently with aging during the early adult years. Not only will longitudinal development in the years after high school be studied, but once enough of these longitudinal panels have accumulated, it will also be possible to characterize cross-sectionally most American young people aged 18 to 24, (at least the major segment of the population who completed high school — roughly 80-85 percent), and to describe the changing characteristics of that age group each year.

ing, however, that even the limited amount of bivariate data included in the present volumes will suggest promising directions for relational analyses, many of which can be carried out using the archived data tapes from the project.

The Need for Social Indicators

The fundamental argument for developing social indicators is that there are considerable scientific and practical benefits derived from having accurate information about current social realities and the way those realities have been changing. For the scientific community such indicators provide a rich set of information against which existing theory may be tested and from which new theory may be suggested. For the community at large, social indicators permit the "reality testing" of common perceptions and beliefs about the nation and its people. Past experience has demonstrated that widely held conceptions, which themselves may serve to create or exacerbate problems, can be most inaccurate. One example is the exaggerated popular conception of the size and nature of the "gap" between generations (see Adelson, 1970, 1979); another is the mistaken assumption that most young people condone the use of a variety of illegal drugs (Johnston, 1973; Johnston, Bachman, and O'Malley, 1977; 1979).

While deflating exaggerated perceptions, a continual monitoring of indicators on youth also can reveal the beginning of new problems and thus give rise to corrective efforts at a relatively early stage. For instance, most would view with concern the emergence of new types of drug use. Monitoring the Future has already documented and reported a sharp increase in regular marijuana use among high school seniors, and as a result more attention has been paid to the issue by policy makers, the media, and the general public. The discovery of such trends may trigger more intense efforts to discover the causes, consequences, and (when appropriate) preventatives of such behaviors.

Although social indicators seldom translate directly into specific policy decisions, the availability of descriptive information can substantially enhance the decision-making capabilities of policy makers. These data provide considerable insight into the size and nature of problems, the rate of change occurring nationally and in subgroups, and in some instances information about related factors and even the likely impacts of major social interventions (such as changed drug laws, or new incentives for recruitment into the military, to name but two). They also provide the possibility of feedback

on the consequences of some social interventions as well as major historical events.

The particular topics included in our monitoring system are summarized later in this introduction and, of course, they are presented fully in the complete set of data tables. For present purposes, it is enough to indicate that the range of topics is very broad. This breadth is partly due to the wide interests of the principal investigators; but it also reflects our conviction that the concurrent examination of trends in a variety of areas is not only much more cost efficient but also more scientifically productive.

Research Design and Procedures*

The basic research design involves annual data collections from high school seniors during the spring of each year, beginning with the class of 1975. Each data collection takes place in approximately 125 public and private high schools selected to provide an accurate cross section of high school seniors throughout the coterminous United States. The design also provides for the longitudinal study of a subsample from each class of participating seniors; but since the focus of this series of volumes is exclusively on the data collected annually from seniors, the follow-up procedures will not be discussed here.

Reasons for Focusing on High School Seniors. There are several reasons for choosing the senior year of high school as an optimal point for monitoring the behaviors and attitudes of youth. One is that the completion of high school represents the end of an important developmental stage in this society, since it demarcates both the end of universal public education and, for many, the end of living in the parental home. Therefore, it is a logical point at which to take stock of the accumulated influences of these two environments on American youth.

Further, the completion of high school represents the jumping-off point from which young people diverge into widely differing social environments, including college, business firms, military service, and homemaking. But these environmental transitions are not the only important changes which coincide with the end of high school. Most young men and women now reach the formal age of adulthood shortly before or after graduation; more significantly, they begin to assume adult roles, including financial self-support, marriage, and parenthood.

Finally, there are some important practical

---

*A more extensive description of the research design and procedures may be found in Bachman and Johnston (1978).

advantages to building a system of data collections around samples of high school seniors. The last year of high school constitutes the final point at which a reasonably good national sample of an age-specific cohort can be drawn and studied economically. The need for systematically repeated, large-scale samples from which to make reliable estimates of change requires that considerable stress be laid on efficiency and feasibility; the present design meets those requirements.

One limitation in the design is that it does not include in the target population those young men and women who drop out of high school before graduation (or before the last few months of the senior year, to be more precise). This excludes a relatively small proportion of each age cohort — between 15 and 20 percent (Golladay, 1976, 1977) — though not an unimportant segment, since we know that certain behaviors such as illicit drug use (Johnston, 1973) and delinquency (Bachman, O'Malley, and Johnston, 1978) tend to be higher than average in this group. However, the addition of a representative sample of dropouts would increase the cost of the present research enormously, because of their dispersion and generally higher level of resistance to being located and interviewed.

For the purposes of estimating characteristics of the entire age group, the omission of high school dropouts does introduce certain biases; however, their small proportion sets outer limits on the bias (Johnston, O'Malley, and Eveland, 1975, Appendix B). For the purposes of estimating *changes* from one cohort of high school seniors to another, the omission of dropouts represents a problem only if different cohorts have considerably different proportions who drop out. We have no reason to expect dramatic changes in those rates for the foreseeable future, and recently published government statistics indicate a great deal of stability in dropout rates since 1967 (Golladay, 1976, p. 62; 1977, p. 81).

Some may use our high school data to draw conclusions about changes for the entire age group. While we do not encourage such extrapolation, we suspect that the conclusions reached often would be valid, since over 80 percent of the age group is in the surveyed segment of the population *and* since we expect that change among those not in school are very likely to parallel the changes among those who are. Nevertheless, for purposes of characterizing the entire age group we would urge the user to check the results emanating from the present monitoring system against those emerging from other data collection systems using different methods, such as household interviews. (It is encouraging to note that when we have compared drug use data for this age group from the present study with those

from interview studies, the findings have shown a high degree of similarity.)

Sampling Procedures. The procedure for securing a nationwide sample of high school seniors is a multi-stage one. Stage 1 is the selection of particular geographic areas, Stage 2 is the selection of one or more high schools in each area, and Stage 3 is the selection of seniors within each high school.

Stage 1: Geographic Areas. The geographic areas used in this study are the primary sampling units (PSUs) developed by the Sampling Section of the Survey Research Center for use in the Center's nationwide interview studies. These consist of 74 primary areas throughout the coterminous United States — including the 12 largest metropolitan areas, which contain about 30 percent of the nation's population. Of the 62 other primary areas, 10 are in the Northeast, 18 in the North Central area, 24 in the South, and 10 in the West. Because these same PSUs are used for personal interview studies by the Survey Research Center (SRC), local field representatives can be assigned to administer the data collections in practically all schools.

Stage 2: Schools. In the major metropolitan areas more than one high school is often included in the sampling design; in most other sampling areas a single high school is sampled. In all cases, the selections of high schools are made such that the probability of drawing a school is proportionate to the size of its senior class. The larger the senior class (according to recent records), the higher the selection probability assigned to the high school. When a sampled school is unwilling to participate, a replacement school as similar to it as possible is selected from the same geographic area.

Stage 3: Students. Within each selected school, up to about 400 seniors may be included in the data collection. In schools with fewer than 400 seniors, the usual procedure is to include all of them in the data collection. In larger schools, a subset of seniors is selected either by randomly sampling classrooms or by some other random method that is convenient for the school and judged to be unbiased. Sample weights are assigned to each respondent so as to take account of variations in the sizes of samples from one school to another, as well as the (smaller) variations in selection probabilities occurring at the earlier stages of sampling.

The three-stage sampling procedure described above yielded the number of participating schools and students indicated in Table 1.

One other important feature of the base-year sampling procedure should be noted here. All schools (except for half of the initial 1975 sample) are asked to participate in two data collections, thereby permitting replacement of half of the total sample of schools each year. One motivation for

Table 1

Sample Sizes and Student Response Rates

	1975	1976	1977	1978
Number of Public Schools	111	108	108	111
Number of Private Schools	14	15	16	20
Total Number of Schools	125	123	124	131
Actual Number of Participating Students	15792	16678	18436	18924
Number of Weighted Cases (Total)*	15104	15299	15839	18924
Student Response Rate**	78%	77%	79%	83%

* Sample weights are assigned to each respondent to correct for unequal probablities of selection which arise in the multi-stage sampling procedure.

** The student response rate is derived by dividing the attained sample by the target sample (both based on weighted numbers of cases). The target sample is based upon listings provided by schools. Since such listings may fail to take account of recent student attrition, the actual response rate may be slightly underestimated.

requesting that schools participate for two years is administrative efficiency; it is a costly and time-consuming procedure to secure the cooperation of schools, and a two-year period of participation cuts down that effort substantially. Another important advantage is that whenever an appreciable shift in scores from one graduating class to the next is observed, it is possible to check whether the shift might be attributable to some differences in the newly sampled schools. This is done simply by repeating the analysis using only the 60 or so schools which participated both years. Thus far, the half-sample approach has worked quite well; an examination of drug prevalence data from the classes of 1975 and 1976 showed that the half sample of repeat schools yielded drug prevalence trends which were virtually identical to trends based on all schools.

School Recruiting Procedures. Early during the fall semester an initial contact is made with each sampled school. First a letter is sent to the principal describing the study and requesting permission to survey seniors. The letter is followed by a telephone call from a project staff member, who attempts to deal with any questions or problems and (when necessary) makes arrangements to contact and seek permission from other school district officials. Basically the same procedures are followed for schools asked to participate for the second year.

Once the school's agreement to participate is obtained, arrangements are made by phone for

administering the questionnaires. A specific date for the survey is mutually agreed upon and a local SRC representative is assigned to carry out the administration.

Advance Contact with Teachers and Students. The local SRC representative is instructed to visit the school two weeks ahead of the actual date of administration. This visit serves as an occasion to meet the teachers whose classes will be affected and to provide them with a brochure describing the study, a brief set of guidelines about the questionnaire administration, and a supply of flyers to be distributed to the students a week to 10 days in advance of the questionnaire administration. The guidelines to the teachers include a suggested announcement to students at the time the flyers are distributed.

From the students' standpoint, the first information about the study usually consists of the teacher's announcement and the short descriptive flyer. In announcing the study, the teachers are asked to stress that the questionnaires used in the survey are not tests, and that there are no right or wrong answers. The flyer tells students that they will be invited to participate in the study, points out that their participation is strictly voluntary, and stresses confidentiality (including a reference to the fact that the Monitoring the Future project has a special government grant of confidentiality which allows their answers to be protected). The flyer also serves as an informative document which the students can show to their parents.

Questionnaire Administrations. The questionnaire administration in each school is carried out by the local SRC representatives and their assistants, following standardized procedures detailed in a project instruction manual. The questionnaires are administered in classrooms during normal class periods whenever possible, although circumstances in some schools require the use of larger group administrations. Teachers are not asked to do anything more than introduce the SRC staff members and (in most cases) remain in the classroom to help guarantee an orderly atmosphere for the survey. Teachers are urged to avoid walking around the room, so that students may feel free to write their answers without fear of being observed.

The actual process of completing the questionnaires is quite straightforward. Respondents are given sharpened pencils and asked to use them because the questionnaires are designed for automatic scanning. Most respondents can finish within a 45-minute class period; for those who cannot, an effort is made to provide a few minutes of additional time.

Procedures for Protecting Confidentiality. In any study that relies on voluntary reporting of drug use or other illegal acts, it is essential to develop procedures which guarantee the confidentiality of such reports. It is also desirable that these procedures be described adequately to respondents so that they are comfortable about providing honest answers.

We noted that the first information given to students about the survey consists of a descriptive flyer stressing confidentiality and voluntary participation. This theme is repeated at the start of the questionnaire administration. Each participating student is instructed to read the message on the cover of the questionnaire, which stresses the importance and value of the study, notes that answers will be kept strictly confidential, states that the study is completely voluntary, and tells the student "If there is any question you or your parents would find objectionable for any reason, just leave it blank." The instructions then point out that in a few months a summary of nationwide results will be mailed to all participants and also that a follow-up questionnaire will be sent to some students after a year. The cover message explains that these are the reasons for asking that name and address be written on a special form which will be removed from the questionnaire and handed in separately. The message also points out that the two different code numbers (one on the questionnaire and one on the tear-out form) cannot be matched except by a special computer tape at The University of Michigan. (The content of the inside and outside of the standard questionnaire cover, including the tear-out form, may be found in Appendix C.)

Content Areas and Questionnaire Design

Drug use and related attitudes are the topics which receive the most extensive coverage in the Monitoring the Future project; but the questionnaires also deal with a wide range of other subject areas, including attitudes about government, social institutions, race relations, changing roles for women, educational aspirations, occupational aims, and marital and family plans, as well as a variety of background and demographic factors. (Table 2 provides an outline of the 19 general subject areas into which all items are categorized in the Question Index toward the end of this volume.) Given this breadth of content, the study is not presented to respondents as a "drug use study," nor do they tend to view it as such.

Table 2

Measurement Content Areas

A. **Drugs.** Drug use and related attitudes and beliefs, drug availability and exposure, surrounding conditions and social meaning of drug use. Views of significant others regarding drugs.

B. **Education.** Educational lifestyle, values, experiences, and environments. Media usage.

C. **Work and Leisure.** Vocational values, meaning of work and leisure, work and leisure activities, preferences regarding occupational characteristics and type of work setting.

Table 2 (continued)

D. **Sex Roles and Family.** Values, attitudes, and expectations about marriage, family structure, sex roles, and sex discrimination.

E. **Family Plans and Population Concerns.** Values, attitudes, and expectations about personal family plans. Views on sexual mores and concerns about overpopulation.

F. **Conservation, Materialism, Equity, etc.** Values, attitudes, and expectations related to conservation, pollution, materialism, equity, and the sharing of resources. Preferences regarding type of dwelling and urbanicity.

G. **Religion.** Religious affiliation, practices, and views.

H. **Politics.** Political affiliation, activities, and views.

I. **Social Change.** Values, attitudes, and expectations about social change.

J. **Social Problems.** Concern with various social problems facing the nation and the world.

K. **Major Social Institutions.** Confidence in and commitment to various major social institutions (business, unions, branches of government, press, organized religion, military, etc.).

L. **Military.** Views about the armed services and the use of military force. Personal plans for military service.

M. **Interpersonal Relationships.** Qualitative and quantitative characteristics of cross-age and peer relationships. Interpersonal conflict.

N. **Race Relations.** Attitudes toward and experiences with other racial groups.

O. **Concern for Others.** Radius of concern for others; voluntary and charitable activities.

P. **Happiness.** Happiness and life satisfaction, overall and in specific life domains.

Q. **Other Personality Variables.** Attitudes about self (including self-esteem), locus of control, loneliness, optimism, trust in others, somatic symptoms, importance placed on various life goals, counter-culture orientation.

R. **Background and School.** Demographic and family background characteristics, curriculum and grades in high school, victimization in school.

S. **Deviant Behavior and Victimization.** Delinquent behaviors, driving violations and accidents, violations and accidents under the influence of drugs, victimization experiences.

Because many questions are needed to cover all of these topic areas, much of the questionnaire content is divided into five different questionnaire forms which are distributed to participants in an ordered sequence that produces five virtually identical subsamples. About one-third of each questionnaire form consists of key or "core" variables which are common to all forms. All demographic variables and some measures of drug use are included in this "core" set of measures. This use of the full sample for drug and demographic measures provides a more accurate estimation on these dimensions and also makes it possible to link them statistically to all of the other measures which are included in a single form only.*

Representativeness and Validity

The samples for this study are intended to be representative of high school seniors throughout the 48 coterminous states. We have already discussed the fact that this definition of the sample excludes one important portion of the age cohort: those who have dropped out of high school before nearing the end of the senior year. But given the aim of representing high school seniors, it will now be useful to consider the extent to which the obtained samples of schools and students are likely to be representative of all seniors and the degree to which the data obtained are likely to be valid.

We can distinguish at least four ways in which survey data of this sort might fall short of being fully accurate. First, some sampled schools refuse to participate, which could introduce some bias. Second, the failure to obtain questionnaire data from 100 percent of the students sampled in participating schools could also introduce bias. Third, the answers provided by participating students are open to both conscious and unconscious distortions which could reduce validity. Finally, limitations in sample size and/or design could place limits on the accuracy of estimates. Each of these issues is treated extensively elsewhere (Johnston, Bachman, and O'Malley, 1979, especially Appendices A and B), so in this section we will present only the highlights of each of those discussions.

School Participation. As noted in the description of the sampling design, schools are invited to participate in the study for a two-year period. With very few exceptions, each school which has participated for one data collection has agreed to participate for a second. Thus far, from 66 percent to 80 percent of the schools initially invited to participate have agreed to do so each year; for each

school refusal, a similar school (in terms of size, geographic area, urbanicity, etc.) was recruited as a replacement. The selection of replacement schools almost entirely removes problems of bias in region, urbanicity, and the like that might result from certain schools refusing to participate. Other potential biases are more subtle, however. For example, if it turned out that most schools with "drug problems" refused to participate, that could seriously bias the drug estimates derived from the sample. And if any other single factor were dominant in most refusals, that also might suggest a source of serious bias. In fact, however, the reasons for schools' refusals to participate are varied and largely a function of happenstance events of the particular year. Thus, we feel fairly confident that school refusals have not seriously biased the surveys.

Student Participation. Completed questionnaires are obtained from three-fourths to four-fifths of all students sampled. The single most important reason that students are missed is that they are absent from class at the time of data collection, and in most cases it is not workable to schedule a special follow-up data collection for them. Students with fairly high rates of absenteeism also report above-average rates of drug use; therefore, there is some degree of bias introduced by missing the absentees. That bias could be largely corrected through the use of special weighting; however, this course was not chosen because the bias in estimates (for drug use, where the potential effect was hypothesized to be largest) was determined to be quite small and because the necessary weighting procedures would have introduced undesirable complications (see Johnston et al., 1977).

In addition to absenteeism, student nonparticipation occurs because of schedule conflicts with school trips and other activities which tend to be more frequent than usual during the final months of the senior year. Of course, some students refuse to complete or turn in a questionnaire. However, the SRC representatives in the field estimate this proportion to be only about one percent.

Validity of Self-Report Data. Survey measures of delinquency and of drug use depend upon respondents reporting what are, in many cases, illegal acts. Thus, a critical question is whether such self-reports are likely to be valid. Like most studies dealing with these areas, we have no direct, objective validation of the present measures; however, the considerable amount of inferential evidence which exists strongly suggests that the self-report questions produce largely valid data. A number of

*These core variables are the first ones on which data are presented in the Descriptive Results Section.

factors have given us reasonable confidence about the validity of the responses to what are presumably among the most sensitive questions in the study: a low nonresponse on the drug questions; a large proportion admitting to some illicit drug use; the consistency of findings across several years of the present study; strong evidence of construct validity (based on relationships observed between variables); a close match between our data and the findings from other studies using other methods; and the findings from several methodological studies which have used objective validation methods.*

As for others of the measures, a few have a long and venerable history — as scholars of the relevant literatures will recognize — though some of these measures have been modified to fit the present questionnaire format. Many (probably most) questions, however, have been developed specifically for this project through a careful process of question writing, pilot testing, pretesting, and question revision or elimination. Some already have been included in other publications from the study, but many have not; therefore, there currently exists little *empirical* evidence of their validity and reliability. On the other hand, the fact that virtually all results presented in this volume are based on individual items, rather than indexes or abstract concepts, should make it easy for the reader to judge the degree to which each item has "face validity" and also the degree to which there is some evidence of construct validity in the bivariate results.

Accuracy of the Sample. A sample survey never can provide the same level of accuracy as would be obtained if the entire target population were to participate in the survey — in the case of the present study, about three million seniors per year. But perfect accuracy of this sort would be extremely expensive and certainly not worthwhile considering the fact that a high level of accuracy can be provided by a carefully designed probability sample. The accuracy of the sample in this study is affected both by the size of the student sample and by the number of schools in which they are clustered. Appendix B presents a discussion of the ways in which this clustering and other aspects of the sampling design are taken into account in computing the precision or accuracy of the samples. For the purposes of this introduction, it is sufficient to note that virtually all estimates based on the total sample have confidence intervals of ±1.5 percentage points or smaller — sometimes considerably smaller. This means that, had we been able to invite all schools and all seniors in the 48 coterminous states to participate, the results from such a

massive survey would be within an estimated 1.5 percentage points of our present sample findings at least 95 times out of 100. We consider this to be a quite high level of accuracy, and one that permits the detection of fairly small trends from one year to the next.

Consistency and the Measurement of Trends. One other point is worth noting in a discussion of the validity of our findings. The Monitoring the Future project is, by intention, a study designed to be sensitive to changes from one time to another. Accordingly, the measures and procedures have been standardized and applied consistently across each data collection. To the extent that any biases remain because of limits in school and/or student participation, and to the extent that there are distortions (lack of validity) in the responses of some students, it seems very likely that such problems will exist in much the same way from one year to the next. In other words, biases in the survey estimates should tend to be consistent from one year to another, which means that the measurement of *trends* should be affected very little by any such biases.

Caveats to Users of the Data

In attempting to understand and interpret the statistical results contained in this volume, the reader should keep in mind the several considerations discussed below.

Estimation of Sampling Errors. Appendix A provides figures which allow the reader to determine the 95 percent confidence interval around any observed percentage for both the total sample and the several subgroups for which statistics are given. Appendix A also provides tables and guidelines for testing the statistical significance of observed differences between subgroups (e.g., males vs. females) and the significance of year-to-year changes for the entire sample and for the various subgroups on any given variable. Estimates based on subgroups containing relatively few cases (e.g., those who have used heroin) will have substantially larger margins of error than those subgroups with large numbers of cases.

Subgroup Definitions. At the beginning of the Descriptive Results section there is a careful definition of each of the subgroups analyzed in this series of volumes. It is important for the reader to read these definitions so as not to be misled by the

---

*A more detailed discussion of the evidence for validity of the measures of illicit drug use may be found in Johnston et al. (1977), Appendix A.

necessarily abbreviated descriptions given in the column headings of the data tables. For example, the column labeled "4-year college plans" includes data only for seniors who expect to be graduated from a four-year college, which is only a subset of all who expect to receive some college training. To take another example, several column headings in the lifetime illicit drug use index use the term "pills"; however, these categories contain people who indicate that they used any of a number of drugs — including some which usually are not taken in pill form (e.g., cocaine and narcotics other than heroin).

Missing Data Notes. Each column of percentages for a given variable adds to 100 percent (with slight variations due to rounding), whether based on the entire sample or any one of the subgroups being described. Missing data were not included in computing these percentages, so it is up to the reader to determine whether an exceptional level of missing data exists on any given question. This can be done by comparing the weighted number of cases on which those percentages were based (given in italics under each percentage distribution) with the total number of weighted cases who took the questionnaire (given at the top of the same column). As would be expected, the missing data rate tends to rise modestly toward the end of each questionnaire. Occasionally there is an exceptional level of nonresponse for some other reason, the most common being that the respondent has been branched around a question or set of questions which are inappropriate for him or her. In this case the percentages are based only on those for whom the question was appropriate *and* who answered. A footnote has been entered to help call attention to the fact that completing a particular question is contingent upon the answer on a prior question. Most such cases are contained in Form 1 of the questionnaire, which has several sets of detailed questions about drug use which are answered only by those respondents who have used a particular class of drug during the past year.

Characterizing Heroin Users. Because this project places a special emphasis on the study of drug use, one set of columns distinguishes respondents according to the extent to which they have been involved with illicit drugs. The five drug use categories are based on an index of seriousness of involvement. The index has Guttman-like properties — that is, anyone classified at a given level is also very likely to have exhibited any drug-using behaviors which are associated with the lower levels in the index.

The most extreme category in the index is defined in terms of the respondent's ever having used heroin during his or her lifetime. However, any interpretations made about heroin users from these data must be tempered with extreme caution, not only because the small number of cases makes estimation in a given year relatively unreliable, but also because heroin users are probably the most selectively represented of all of the subgroups presented here. Heroin users — especially continuing users — are among those most likely to drop out of high school (Johnston, 1973). Therefore, we feel that heroin users are particularly underrepresented in a sample of high school seniors. Furthermore, most of those included in the study report only very occasional heroin use. Frequent users — addicts, if you will — are not well represented in these data.

Given these problems with the representation of heroin users, the reader may wonder why it was decided to present them as a separate category of drug users. There are two reasons for doing so. First, because even occasional heroin use represents such an extreme point on the continuum of drug involvement, it seems preferable that the heroin users not be mixed in with the next highest category of use (the "more pills" category). It remains quite possible, of course, for anyone to *combine* any two or more categories in the drug use continuum (by computing means of percentages weighted by the number of cases in each category); therefore, those wishing to incorporate heroin users with the next category can do so whenever they wish. The second reason for keeping them separate is that we suspect the data based on high school seniors provide some indication of the characteristics which might be found among heavier heroin users who dropped out of school. Some variables in the study are strongly correlated with the drug use continuum, and the present heroin user category provides both an end point for that continuum and an indication of the direction (further out on the continuum) in which heavier heroin users are likely to lie.

In sum, the reporting of separate percentages for heroin users among high school seniors permits greater clarity in analyzing other levels of drug use and provides data which may be suggestive about the larger population of young heroin users. But the particular data are clearly limited and should be interpreted with these cautions in mind.

Interpreting Racial Differences. Data are given for the two largest racial/ethnic subgroups in the population — those who identify themselves as white or Caucasian and those who identify themselves as black or Afro-American. Data are not given for the other ethnic categories (American Indians, Asian Americans, Mexican Americans, Puerto Ricans, or other Latin Americans) since each of these groups comprises less than three percent of the sample in any given year, which means that their small Ns (in combination with their clustered groupings in a limited number of schools) would yield estimates which would be too unreliable. In fact, even blacks — who constitute approximately 12 percent of each year's sample — are represented by only 350 to 425 respondents per year on any single questionnaire form. Further, because our sample is a stratified clustered sample, it yields less accuracy than would be yielded by a pure random sample of equal size (see Appendix B for details). Therefore, because of the limited number of cases, the margin of sampling error around any statistic describing blacks is larger than for most other subgroups described in this volume.

There exists, however, a quick way to determine the replicability of any finding involving racial comparisons. Since most questions are repeated from year to year, one can readily establish the degree to which a finding is replicated by looking at the results for the same question in prior or subsequent years. Given the relatively small Ns for blacks, the reader is urged to seek such replication before putting much faith in the reliability of any particular racial comparison.

There are factors in addition to unreliability, however, which could be misleading in the interpretation of racial differences. Given the social importance which has been placed on various racial differences reported in the social science literature, we would like to caution the reader to consider the various factors which could account for differences. These factors fall into three categories: differential representation in the sample, differential response tendencies, and the confounding of race with a number of other background and demographic characteristics.

Differential Representation. Census data characterizing American young people in the approximate age range of those in our sample show that somewhat lower proportions of blacks than whites remain in school through the end of twelfth grade (Golladay, 1977, p. 197). Therefore, a slightly different segment of the black population than of the white population resides in our target population of high school seniors. Further, our samples appear to underrepresent slightly those black males who, according to census figures, *are* in high school at the twelfth grade level. Identified black males comprise about 6 percent of our sample, whereas census data suggest that they should comprise around 7 percent (U.S. Bureau of the Census, 1978). Therefore, it appears that we are losing more black males from our target population than white males or females of either race. This may be due to generally poorer attendance rates on the part of some black males and/or an unwillingness on the part of

some to participate in data collections of this sort.

In sum, a smaller segment of the black population than of the white population of high school age is represented by the data contained here. Insofar as any characteristic is associated with being a school dropout or absentee, it is likely to be somewhat disproportionately underrepresented among blacks in our sample.

Differential Response Tendencies. In examining our full range of variables, we have noted certain racial differences in response tendencies. First, the tendency to state agreement in response to agree-disagree questions is generally somewhat greater among blacks than among whites. For example, blacks tend to agree more with the positively worded items in our index of self-esteem, but they also tend to agree more with the negatively worded items. As it happens, that particular index has an equal number of positively and negatively worded items, so that any overall "agreement bias" should be self-cancelling when the index score is computed. Since all data in this volume are based on single items, however, group differences in agreement bias are likely to affect results on questions employing the agree-disagree format. Fortunately, most of our questions are not of that type.

We have also observed a somewhat greater than average tendency for black respondents to select extreme answer categories on attitudinal scales. For example, even if the same proportion of blacks as whites felt positively (or negatively) about some subject, fewer of the whites are likely to say they feel *very* positively (or *very* negatively). We do not have any ready explanations for these differences in response styles, but what seems important for our present purposes is that, in the process of interpreting racial differences, the reader should be aware that differences in responses to particular questions may be related to these more general tendencies.

A somewhat separate issue in response tendency is a respondent's willingness to answer particular questions. The missing data rate, which can be determined by dividing the number responding to a question by the number taking the questionnaire (given at the top of each page), may reflect willingness to answer particular questions. If a particular question or set of questions has a missing data rate higher than is true for the prior or subsequent questions, then presumably more respondents than usual were unwilling (or perhaps unable) to answer it. We have observed such an exaggerated missing data rate for black males on the set of questions dealing with the respondent's own use of illicit drugs. Clearly a respondent's willingness to be candid on such questions depends on his or her trust of the research process and of the researchers themselves. We interpret the exaggerated missing data rates for black males in these sections as possibly reflecting, at least in part, less trust. The reader is advised to check for exceptional levels of missing data when making comparisons on any variable in which candor is likely to be reduced by lower system trust.

Covariance with Other Factors. Some characteristics such as race are highly confounded (correlated) with other variables — variables which may in fact explain some observed racial differences. Put another way, at the aggregate level we might observe a considerable racial difference on some characteristic, but once we control for some background characteristics such as socioeconomic level or region of the country — that is, once we compare the black respondents with whites who come from similar backgrounds — there may be no racial difference at all.

Race happens to be correlated with important background and demographic variables much more than some of the other variables dealt with here (like the respondent's sex). When we compare males and females in this sample we know that observed differences between them are not likely to be explained by differences in their family background (such as the socioeconomic level of their families, the region of the country, or the size of the cities in which they grew up) because males and females on the average come from extremely similar backgrounds. A perusal of Section C of Questionnaire Forms 1 through 5, however, will illustrate that on the average the black subgroup in this sample is quite different from the white subgroup in a number of such respects. A higher proportion of blacks live in the South and a higher proportion grew up in large cities. Blacks are more likely to report low levels of parental education (an indication of a lower socioeconomic background more generally). A greater than average proportion of blacks grew up in families with the father and/or mother absent, and more had mothers who worked while they were growing up. A substantially higher proportion of blacks are Baptists, and blacks tend to attribute more importance to religion in their lives than do whites. Fewer are enrolled in a college-preparatory curriculum (though a higher proportion say they plan to attend some type of college). A slightly higher proportion of black respondents are married and have children, and on the average they are slightly older than the white sample. As was mentioned earlier, black males are more underrepresented in our sample than black females, with the result that

each year roughly 58 percent of our black sample is female versus roughly 51 percent of the white sample.

We note these differences in demographic, background, and ascriptive characteristics because, in any attempt to understand *why* a racial difference exists, one would want to be able to examine the role of these covarying characteristics. It is not possible, given the amount of data contained in this volume, to "factor out" the contribution of most of these covarying characteristics when interpreting racial differences. Therefore, while the data here may provide a relatively accurate *description* of racial differences (keeping in mind our earlier cautions about representativeness and response style), they do not by themselves yield a great deal by way of explanation. However, since the full data sets now reside in two archives, described in the Preface, it is possible for the reader to conduct a more in depth exploration of observed differences — or nondifferences, for that matter. We particularly encourage readers interested in racial comparisons to make further explorations in the data in order to determine the possible role of the other variables discussed here. Users of the data are also encouraged to contact the principal investigators for information on the most recent analyses of racial differences, some of which are already underway.

Given the long list of caveats about interpreting racial differences, one might ask why we chose to publish the statistics for racial subgroups at all. After considerable deliberation among ourselves as well as with colleagues more knowledgeable in the field of race relations, we concluded that the expected benefits of making these data available (along with this cautionary discussion) outweigh the potential costs of having them misused. Unfortunately, because blacks constitute a relatively small proportion of the American population, they constitute too small a number in most surveys to be characterized separately. Because the sample sizes in the present survey are large in comparison to most, we have at least sufficient numbers of cases to consider publishing data on blacks separately. Further, given the iterative nature of the series, we are also able to provide checks for replication of findings on different samples each year. While there may be some risk that findings will be taken out of context or used carelessly in ways that might tend to increase racial misunderstandings, there is substantially greater risk that valuable information concerning the races (and relevant to their well-being) will be lost if it were not included here.

Descriptive Results: 1978

Introduction to the Table Format and Conventions

Univariate and selected bivariate percentage distributions are given in this section for all questions asked of this year's senior class. The definitions of column headings and the source of the standard contents for each table are given below under the numbers indicated in Figure 1.

Definitions of Column Headings

(1) **Questionnaire Form.** The form from which all data on the page were derived is given here. When the designation "Forms 1-5" is used, it indicates that responses from students completing all five questionnaires have been combined; accordingly, the numbers of respondents in each column are five times as large for questions contained in a single form only.

(2) **Total Sample.** Univariate percentage distributions based on the total sample of respondents are given in this column.

(3) **Sex.** Percentage distributions are given separately for males (M) and females (F). Respondents with missing data on the question asking the respondent's sex (Question C03) are omitted from both groupings.

(4) **Race.** Percentage distributions are given separately for those describing themselves as "White or Caucasian" (W) and "Black or Afro-American" (B) in answer to Question C04. Comparable columns for the other racial or ethnic groups (Mexican Americans, Asian Americans, American Indians, etc.) are not shown because of the low number of cases in each group. *Note:* See the caveats regarding the interpretation of racial differences in the Introduction section of this volume.

(5) **Region.** Percentage distributions are given separately for respondents living in each of four mutually exclusive regions of the country. The regional classifications are based on Census categories and are defined as follows:

Northeast (NE): Census classifications of New England and Middle Atlantic states; includes Maine, New Hampshire, Vermont, Massachusetts, Rhode Island, Connecticut, New York, New Jersey, and Pennsylvania.

North Central (NC): Census classifications of East North Central and West North Central states; includes Ohio, Indiana, Illinois, Michigan, Wisconsin, Minnesota, Iowa, Missouri, North Dakota, South Dakota, Nebraska, and Kansas.

South (S): Census classifications of South Atlantic, East South Central, and West South Central states; includes Delaware, Maryland, District of Columbia, Virginia, West Virginia, North Carolina, South Carolina, Georgia, Florida, Kentucky, Tennessee, Alabama, Mississippi, Arkansas, Louisiana, Oklahoma, and Texas.

West (W): Census classifications of Mountain and Pacific states; includes Montana, Idaho, Wyoming, Colorado, New Mexico, Arizona, Utah, Nevada, Washington, Oregon, and California.

(6) **Four-Year College Plans.** Percentage distributions are given separately for (1) respondents who indicate that they "definitely will" or "probably will" graduate from a four-year college program and (2) those who say that they "definitely won't" or "probably won't" graduate from a four-year college program, based on responses to Question C21d. Respondents not answering question C21d are omitted from both columns. (A number of those who do not expect to complete a four-year college program *do* expect to get some post-secondary education, as may be seen in the tables for questions

13

C21a and c.)

(7) **Illicit Drug Use: Lifetime.** Percentage distributions are given separately for five mutually exclusive subgroups differentiated by their degree of involvement with illicit drugs. Eligibility for each category is defined below.

None. This column contains data from those respondents who indicated that they had not used marijuana at any time and did not report use of any of the following illicit drugs in their lifetime: LSD, other psychedelics, cocaine, amphetamines, tranquilizers, methaqualone, barbiturates, heroin, or other narcotics.

Marijuana Only. This column contains data from those respondents who indicated that they had used marijuana (or hashish) but had never used any of the other illicit drugs just listed.

Few Pills. This column contains data from those respondents who indicated having used one or more of the above listed drugs (other than marijuana) but who had not used any one class of them on more than three occasions *and* who had not used heroin at all.

More Pills. This column contains data from respondents who had used any of the above listed drugs (other than marijuana) on more than three occasions but who had never used heroin.

Any Heroin. This column contains data from those respondents who indicated having used heroin on one or more occasions in their lifetime.

(8) **Weighted Number of Cases.** This row contains the number of students who turned in questionnaires in each of the categories indicated by the column headings. The number of cases is stated in terms of the weighted number of respondents rather than the actual number, since all percentages in the tables have been calculated using weighted cases. The actual number of respondents generally is about 15 percent higher than the weighted number for data collected in 1975, 1976, and 1977. (A comparison of weighted and unweighted numbers is provided in Tables B-1 and B-2 in Appendix B.) For data collected in 1978 or later, the actual number of respondents is roughly equal to the weighted number. Weighting is used to improve the accuracy of estimates by correcting for unequal probabilities of selection which arise in the multi-stage sampling procedures.

(9) **Percentage of Weighted Total.** This row indicates the percentage of the total number of respondents who fall into the category indicated by each column heading. Unlike all other percentages on the page, which can be summed vertically, these percentages sum horizontally. To the extent that the subcategories in a column (e.g., Males and Females) fail to sum to 100 percent, cases have been eliminated because of missing data on the variable in question (e.g., Sex), or, in the case of Race, because several subcategories have been omitted intentionally.

Table Contents

(10) **Questions and Answers.** Each question along with its accompanying answer alternatives is presented verbatim. The alphanumeric prefix to the question indicates the section of the questionnaire in which it is located and its sequence within that section. So, for example, a prefix of B12c indicates that the item was question 12c in the B Section of the questionnaire.

(11) **Item Reference Number.** This is a unique identification number permanently assigned to each question. Any question may be located in the cross-time item index of this volume (or any other volume in this series) by using this reference number.

(12) **Percentage Distribution.** Each column of numbers beside a question gives the percentage of each group (defined by the column heading) who chose each answer alternative, rounded to the nearest tenth of a percent. These figures add vertically to 100 percent (with some rounding error). Nonrespondents to the question are excluded from the percentage calculations.

(13) **Number of Weighted Cases Answering (N Wtd.).** The number of students in the relevant group (defined by the column heading) who answered the question is given just below the percentage distribution. The number of nonrespondents may be determined by subtracting this weighted number answering from the weighted number taking the questionnaire, shown at the top of the same column. Nonresponse may be due to the subject not answering the question, even though it pertains to him or her, or to the subject skipping inappropriate questions as instructed on a prior item.

Figure 1
Guide to Table Format

Column annotations: (1) form label · (2) TOTAL · (3) SEX · (4) RACE · (5) REGION · (6) 4YR COLLEGE PLANS · (7) ILLICIT DRUG USE: LIFETIME

QUESTIONNAIRE FORM 1-5 1978	TOTAL	SEX		RACE		REGION				4YR COLLEGE PLANS		ILLICIT DRUG USE: LIFETIME				
		M	F	White	Black	NE	NC	S	W	Yes	No	None	Marijuana Only	Few Pills	More Pills	Any Heroin
(8) Weighted No. of Cases:	18916	8779	9266	14847	2096	4607	5411	6292	2605	8844	8413	6595	5214	2304	3885	302
(9) % of Weighted Total:	100.0	46.4	49.0	78.5	11.1	24.4	28.6	33.3	13.8	46.8	44.5	34.9	27.6	12.2	20.5	1.6

These next questions ask for some background information about yourself.

C01: In what year were you born? (10)

	TOTAL	M	F	White	Black	NE	NC	S	W	Yes	No	None	Mari-juana Only	Few Pills	More Pills	Any Heroin
1. Before '58	.2	.2	.2	.1	.8	.1	.2	.4	.1	.1	.3	.3	.2	.2	.1	.3
2. 1958	1.9	2.5	1.2	1.2	4.1	1.5	1.5	2.6	1.6	.9	2.8	2.0	1.4	1.4	1.6	5.1
3. 1959	22.2	25.8	18.4	21.1	25.0	16.4	25.1	23.9	22.3	18.0	25.7	22.3	21.8	23.2	21.6	25.9
4. 1960	73.3	70.0	76.8	75.7	65.1	78.6	72.1	70.7	72.7	78.2	69.3	73.2	74.0	73.0	74.1	66.6
5. 1961	2.4	1.4	3.3	2.0	4.8	3.4	1.1	2.4	3.1	2.7	1.9	2.2	2.6	2.2	2.6	1.7
6. 1962	*	*	.1	*	.2	*	*	.1	.1	.1	*	.1	*	*	*	
7. 1963	*	*	*	*		*		*		*		*		*		
8. After 1963	*	*	*	*	-	*	*	*	-	*	*	-	*	-	-	-
(11) Item 10 N(Wtd)	18410	8766	9264	14824	2094	4442	5320	6129	2518	8799	8366	6514	5131	2267	3802	293

C02: In what month were you born? (12)

	TOTAL	M	F	White	Black	NE	NC	S	W	Yes	No	None	Mari-juana Only	Few Pills	More Pills	Any Heroin
01. January	8.0	7.9	8.2	7.9	8.6	8.1	8.1	8.0	7.4	8.4	7.5	7.4	8.6	8.0	7.9	6.9
02. February	7.1	7.1	7.1	7.0	7.4	7.5	7.4	6.4	7.8	7.3	7.0	7.4	6.7	6.6	6.9	9.0
03. March	7.9	8.1	7.9	7.9	8.3	7.5	7.7	8.3	8.6	7.7	8.3	7.7	7.8	8.7	8.2	5.9
04. April	8.0	7.8	8.0	8.0	7.2	7.5	8.7	7.5	8.4	8.1	7.9	8.2	7.7	8.3	7.8	9.7
05. May	7.9	7.5	8.3	8.2	7.1	8.3	8.2	7.5	7.8	8.1	7.7	7.9	7.8	8.1	7.9	7.2
06. June	7.7	8.2	7.5	7.7	7.8	7.1	7.5	8.2	8.2	8.0	7.5	7.9	7.5	8.7	7.2	7.2
07. July	8.7	8.8	8.7	8.7	8.9	8.8	8.7	8.9	8.2	8.7	8.7	8.3	8.9	8.6	9.4	8.6
08. August	9.4	9.5	9.4	9.5	8.7	9.5	9.5	9.2	9.5	9.0	9.8	9.6	9.5	9.5	9.3	10.0
09. September	9.2	8.9	9.8	9.2	9.3	9.0	8.8	9.5	9.8	8.9	9.6	9.2	8.9	8.9	10.0	8.6
10. October	8.7	9.1	8.1	8.6	8.7	9.2	8.3	8.7	8.8	8.5	9.0	8.9	8.6	7.8	9.1	9.3
11. November	8.8	8.6	8.5	8.8	9.7	9.1	8.6	9.3	7.4	9.0	8.5	9.1	9.2	8.5	8.2	7.2
12. December	8.4	8.4	8.5	8.4	8.3	8.5	8.5	8.5	8.1	8.4	8.5	8.3	8.7	8.4	8.3	10.7
Item 20 N(Wtd)	18373	8750	9256	14805	2094	4432	5300	6125	2516	8783	8351	6510	5121	2264	3786	290

C03: What is your sex?

	TOTAL	M	F	White	Black	NE	NC	S	W	Yes	No	None	Mari-juana Only	Few Pills	More Pills	Any Heroin
1. Male	48.7	100.0	-	49.1	42.0	49.1	47.4	49.2	49.3	49.7	46.4	43.3	54.7	45.4	50.2	61.2
2. Female	51.4	-	100.0	50.9	58.0	50.9	52.6	50.8	50.7	50.3	53.6	56.7	45.3	54.6	49.8	38.8
(13) Item 30 N(Wtd)	18044	8779	9266	14583	2027	4376	5208	5993	2467	8678	8167	6385	5028	2222	3735	286

C04: How do you describe yourself?

	TOTAL	M	F	White	Black	NE	NC	S	W	Yes	No	None	Mari-juana Only	Few Pills	More Pills	Any Heroin
1. American Indian	1.1	1.2	.9	-	-	1.0	.8	1.3	1.1	.5	1.6	.6	.9	1.2	1.8	1.7
2. Black or Afro-American	11.5	9.8	12.8	-	100.0	6.2	6.7	21.1	7.0	11.3	9.8	13.1	13.2	10.6	4.5	10.0
3. Mexican American or Chicano	2.2	2.1	2.2	-	-	.1	.4	1.9	10.1	1.4	2.6	2.2	2.5	2.2	1.5	2.4
4. Puerto Rican or other Latin American	.9	1.0	.8	-	-	2.1	.2	.5	1.4	1.1	.6	1.1	.7	.8	.8	3.1
5. Oriental or Asian American	.7	.8	.6	-	-	.7	.4	.3	2.4	1.2	.2	1.0	.6	.5	.4	1.7
6. White or Caucasian	81.1	82.1	80.6	100.0	-	86.1	89.3	73.5	73.7	82.5	82.2	79.5	80.1	82.4	87.9	77.2
7. Other	2.6	3.0	2.1	-	-	3.6	2.2	1.3	4.3	1.9	3.0	2.5	2.0	2.3	3.1	3.5
Item 40 N(Wtd)	18299	8723	9207	14847	2096	4405	5291	6107	2496	8764	8311	6494	5105	2245	3772	289

C05: Where did you grow up mostly?

	TOTAL	M	F	White	Black	NE	NC	S	W	Yes	No	None	Mari-juana Only	Few Pills	More Pills	Any Heroin
1. On a farm	8.8	9.8	7.6	9.4	5.4	3.7	13.2	9.7	6.1	6.3	11.5	11.8	7.0	7.3	6.4	10.9
2. In the country not			.5	14.4	18.7	13.5	11.9	19.5	12.2	9.8	20.3	16.7	12.7	13.7	14.6	13.5
3. In a sm...						36.2	27.2	34.2	25.1	30.4	32.6	31.7	31.3	30.9	31.2	
						13.7	10.6	15.1	13.6	12.5	12.4	13.8	13.8			
							4.9	6.9	8.1	5.9	6.2	7.8				

QUESTIONNAIRE FORM 1-5 1978	TOTAL	SEX		RACE		REGION				4YR COLLEGE PLANS		ILLICIT DRUG USE: LIFETIME				
		M	F	White	Black	NE	NC	S	W	Yes	No	None	Mari-juana Only	Few Pills	More Pills	Any Her-oin
Weighted No. of Cases:	18916	8779	9266	14847	2096	4607	5411	6292	2605	8844	8413	6595	5214	2304	3885	302
% of Weighted Total:	100.0	46.4	49.0	78.5	11.1	24.4	28.6	33.3	13.8	46.8	44.5	34.9	27.6	12.2	20.5	1.6

These next questions ask for some background information about yourself.

C01: In what year were you born?

	TOTAL	M	F	White	Black	NE	NC	S	W	Yes	No	None	Mari-juana Only	Few Pills	More Pills	Any Her-oin
1. Before '58	.2	.2	.2	.1	.8	.1	.2	.4	.1	.1	.3	.3	.2	.2	.1	.3
2. 1958	1.9	2.5	1.2	1.2	4.1	1.5	1.5	2.6	1.6	.9	2.8	2.0	1.4	1.4	1.6	5.1
3. 1959	22.2	25.8	18.4	21.1	25.0	16.4	25.1	23.9	22.3	18.0	25.7	22.3	21.8	23.2	21.6	25.9
4. 1960	73.3	70.0	76.8	75.7	65.1	78.6	72.1	70.7	72.7	78.2	69.3	73.2	74.0	73.0	74.1	66.6
5. 1961	2.4	1.4	3.3	2.0	4.8	3.4	1.1	2.4	3.1	2.7	1.9	2.2	2.6	2.2	2.6	1.7
6. 1962	*	*	.1	*	.2	*	*	.1	.1	.1	*	.1	*	*	*	-
7. 1963	*	-	*	-	-	-	*	-	-	*	-	-	-	-	-	-
8. After 1963	*	*	*	-	*	-	-	-	*	-	*	-	*	-	*	-
Item 10 N(Wtd)	18410	8766	9264	14824	2094	4442	5320	6129	2518	8799	8366	6514	5131	2267	3802	293

C02: In what month were you born?

	TOTAL	M	F	White	Black	NE	NC	S	W	Yes	No	None	Mari-juana Only	Few Pills	More Pills	Any Her-oin
01. January	8.0	7.9	8.2	7.9	8.6	8.1	8.1	8.0	7.4	8.4	7.5	7.4	8.6	8.0	7.9	6.9
02. February	7.1	7.1	7.1	7.0	7.4	7.5	7.4	6.4	7.8	7.3	7.0	7.4	6.7	6.6	6.9	9.0
03. March	7.9	8.1	7.9	7.9	8.3	7.5	7.7	8.3	8.6	7.7	8.3	7.7	7.8	8.7	8.2	5.9
04. April	8.0	7.8	8.0	8.0	7.2	7.5	8.7	7.5	8.4	8.1	7.9	8.2	7.7	8.3	7.8	9.7
05. May	7.9	7.5	8.3	8.2	7.1	8.3	8.2	7.5	7.8	8.1	7.7	7.9	7.8	8.1	7.9	7.2
06. June	7.7	8.2	7.5	7.7	7.8	7.1	7.5	8.2	8.2	8.0	7.5	7.9	7.5	8.7	7.2	7.2
07. July	8.7	8.8	8.7	8.7	8.9	8.8	8.7	8.9	8.2	8.7	8.7	8.3	8.9	8.6	9.4	8.6
08. August	9.4	9.5	9.4	9.5	8.7	9.5	9.5	9.2	9.5	9.0	9.8	9.6	9.5	9.5	9.3	10.0
09. September	9.2	8.9	9.8	9.2	9.3	9.0	8.8	9.5	9.8	8.9	9.6	9.2	8.9	8.9	10.0	8.6
10. October	8.7	9.1	8.1	8.6	8.7	9.2	8.3	8.7	8.8	8.5	9.0	8.9	8.6	7.8	9.1	9.3
11. November	8.8	8.6	8.5	8.8	9.7	9.1	8.6	9.3	7.4	9.0	8.5	9.1	9.2	8.5	8.2	7.2
12. December	8.4	8.4	8.5	8.4	8.3	8.5	8.5	8.5	8.1	8.4	8.5	8.3	8.7	8.4	8.3	10.7
Item 20 N(Wtd)	18373	8750	9256	14805	2094	4432	5300	6125	2516	8783	8351	6510	5121	2264	3786	290

C03: What is your sex?

	TOTAL	M	F	White	Black	NE	NC	S	W	Yes	No	None	Mari-juana Only	Few Pills	More Pills	Any Her-oin
1. Male	48.7	100.0	-	49.1	42.0	49.1	47.4	49.2	49.3	49.7	46.4	43.3	54.7	45.4	50.2	61.2
2. Female	51.4	-	100.0	50.9	58.0	50.9	52.6	50.8	50.7	50.3	53.6	56.7	45.3	54.6	49.8	38.8
Item 30 N(Wtd)	18044	8779	9266	14583	2027	4376	5208	5993	2467	8678	8167	6385	5028	2222	3735	286

C04: How do you describe yourself?

	TOTAL	M	F	White	Black	NE	NC	S	W	Yes	No	None	Mari-juana Only	Few Pills	More Pills	Any Her-oin
1. American Indian	1.1	1.2	.9	-	-	1.0	.8	1.3	1.1	.5	1.6	.6	.9	1.2	1.8	1.7
2. Black or Afro-American	11.5	9.8	12.8	-	100.0	6.2	6.7	21.1	7.0	11.3	9.8	13.1	13.2	10.6	4.5	10.0
3. Mexican American or Chicano	2.2	2.1	2.2	-	-	.1	.4	1.9	10.1	1.4	2.6	2.2	2.5	2.2	1.5	2.4
4. Puerto Rican or other Latin American	.9	1.0	.8	-	-	2.1	.2	.5	1.4	1.1	.6	1.1	.7	.8	.8	3.1
5. Oriental or Asian American	.7	.7	.6	-	-	.7	.4	.3	2.4	1.2	.2	1.0	.6	.5	.4	1.7
6. White or Caucasian	81.1	82.1	80.6	100.0	-	86.1	89.3	73.5	73.7	82.5	82.2	79.5	80.1	82.4	87.9	77.2
7. Other	2.6	3.0	2.1	-	-	3.6	2.2	1.3	4.3	1.9	3.0	2.5	2.0	2.3	3.1	3.5
Item 40 N(Wtd)	18299	8723	9207	14847	2096	4405	5291	6107	2496	8764	8311	6494	5105	2245	3772	289

C05: Where did you grow up mostly?

	TOTAL	M	F	White	Black	NE	NC	S	W	Yes	No	None	Mari-juana Only	Few Pills	More Pills	Any Her-oin
1. On a farm	8.8	9.8	7.6	9.4	5.4	3.7	13.2	9.7	6.1	6.3	11.5	11.8	7.0	7.3	6.4	10.9
2. In the country, not on a farm	14.8	15.1	14.5	14.4	18.7	13.5	11.9	19.5	12.2	9.8	20.3	16.7	12.7	13.7	14.6	13.5
3. In a small city or town (under 50,000 people)	31.4	31.8	31.2	32.6	24.8	36.2	27.2	34.2	25.1	30.4	32.6	31.7	31.3	30.9	31.2	34.6
4. In a medium-sized city (50,000 - 100,000)	13.1	12.1	14.0	13.1	12.3	14.7	13.7	10.6	15.1	13.6	12.5	12.4	13.8	13.8	13.6	7.9
5. In a suburb of a medium-sized city	7.0	6.4	7.6	7.3	5.4	8.8	8.0	4.9	6.9	8.1	5.9	6.2	7.8	6.9	7.7	7.1
6. In a large city (100,000 - 500,000)	6.3	5.3	7.1	4.3	16.6	5.7	5.5	5.7	10.4	6.5	5.4	5.7	7.1	6.5	5.8	4.5
7. In a suburb of a large city	8.3	8.3	8.4	9.3	2.9	6.6	10.5	6.9	10.0	10.8	6.1	6.8	8.5	9.4	10.4	8.6
8. In a very large city (over 500,000)	4.8	4.9	4.7	3.3	11.6	6.3	3.1	3.7	8.5	6.0	3.2	4.0	5.4	5.4	4.5	8.6
9. In a suburb of a very large city	5.6	6.3	4.9	6.2	2.1	4.5	7.0	5.0	5.7	8.6	2.5	4.8	6.5	6.1	5.8	4.9
Item 50 N(Wtd)	17135	8163	8565	13798	1958	4176	5023	5627	2309	8237	7785	6083	4801	2100	3513	266

* = less than .05 per cent.

QUESTIONNAIRE FORM 1-5 1978	TOTAL	SEX		RACE		REGION				4YR COLLEGE PLANS		ILLICIT DRUG USE: LIFETIME				
		M	F	White	Black	NE	NC	S	W	Yes	No	None	Marijuana Only	Few Pills	More Pills	Any Heroin
Weighted No. of Cases:	18916	8779	9266	14847	2096	4607	5411	6292	2605	8844	8413	6595	5214	2304	3885	302
% of Weighted Total:	100.0	46.4	49.0	78.5	11.1	24.4	28.6	33.3	13.8	46.8	44.5	34.9	27.6	12.2	20.5	1.6
C06: What is your present marital status?																
1. Married	2.4	2.3	2.5	2.0	5.0	1.5	2.0	3.7	1.9	1.3	3.4	2.4	2.0	3.3	2.1	3.8
2. Engaged	7.0	3.6	10.2	7.1	5.8	5.1	6.9	8.8	6.1	3.0	11.3	5.8	6.6	8.5	8.9	7.2
3. Separated/divorced	.4	.5	.3	.2	1.4	.3	.4	.5	.6	.4	.4	.2	.4	.4	.7	1.4
4. Single	90.2	93.5	87.0	90.8	87.8	93.1	90.7	87.1	91.4	95.4	84.9	91.5	91.0	87.7	88.3	88.0
Item 60 N(Wtd)	18378	8729	9227	14795	2077	4426	5317	6127	2508	8811	8361	6498	5129	2260	3797	292
C07: Which of the following people live in the same household with you? (Mark ALL that apply.)																
A. I live alone	.6	.8	.3	.5	.7	.4	.7	.6	.8	.4	.7	.2	.6	.6	.9	2.7
B. Father (or male guardian)	81.9	82.9	81.3	85.7	58.6	83.2	85.0	78.2	82.3	84.3	80.8	85.4	82.4	80.4	78.3	70.1
C. Mother (or female guardian)	92.3	92.1	92.6	93.8	85.2	94.2	92.8	90.6	92.5	94.4	90.9	94.4	92.7	90.8	90.5	82.8
D. Brother(s) and/or sister(s)	78.3	78.1	78.8	78.9	75.1	82.4	78.5	75.1	78.5	79.5	77.4	81.0	80.2	76.1	73.4	71.5
E. Grandparent(s)	5.4	5.3	5.5	4.7	9.9	6.9	4.1	6.1	3.9	5.4	5.3	5.2	5.7	5.0	5.4	7.2
F. My husband/wife	1.1	.6	1.6	1.1	1.1	.8	1.1	1.6	.6	.4	1.9	.8	.9	1.6	1.5	2.1
G. My children	.9	.3	1.5	.5	4.2	.5	1.1	1.3	.5	.5	1.3	.8	1.1	.5	1.0	2.4
H. Other relative(s)	4.3	3.7	4.9	2.8	12.6	4.1	2.9	5.7	4.0	3.7	4.8	4.0	4.2	4.2	4.2	7.9
I. Non-relative(s)	2.4	2.2	2.6	2.4	1.5	2.2	2.3	1.9	4.1	2.0	2.8	1.5	1.7	2.8	4.3	5.2
Item 80-160 N(Wtd)	18312	8689	9206	14761	2059	4399	5313	6111	2490	8790	8355	6480	5113	2255	3781	291

The next three questions ask about your parents. If you were raised mostly by foster parents, step-parents, or others, answer for them. For example, if you have both a step-father and a natural father, answer for the one that was most important in raising you.

	TOTAL	M	F	White	Black	NE	NC	S	W	Yes	No	None	Marijuana Only	Few Pills	More Pills	Any Heroin
C08: What is the highest level of schooling your father completed?																
1. Completed grade school or less	8.7	7.6	9.8	6.5	17.2	6.7	6.9	12.1	8.1	5.5	11.9	10.2	7.9	7.4	7.7	9.7
2. Some high school	16.4	15.7	17.1	15.6	21.2	18.3	15.8	17.2	11.9	10.3	22.6	16.5	15.3	16.7	16.6	17.6
3. Completed high school	30.8	30.6	30.7	31.9	26.9	33.6	35.8	26.4	26.2	25.6	36.3	31.1	30.8	29.5	31.0	29.7
4. Some college	12.9	13.5	12.4	14.0	7.7	11.4	13.3	12.2	16.3	16.5	9.5	12.3	12.7	14.0	14.2	11.4
5. Completed college	15.7	17.1	14.4	17.5	6.3	15.0	14.9	15.4	18.8	22.3	9.1	14.9	17.4	15.5	15.1	16.6
6. Graduate or professional school after college	9.9	10.4	9.5	10.9	3.8	10.4	8.8	9.4	12.5	16.1	3.5	9.0	10.7	10.5	10.3	9.3
7. Don't know, or does not apply	5.7	5.1	6.1	3.7	17.0	4.5	4.5	7.3	6.2	3.8	7.2	5.9	5.1	6.3	5.1	5.9
Item 310 N(Wtd)	18225	8645	9167	14730	2023	4366	5291	6079	2489	8780	8340	6449	5091	2243	3764	290
C09: What is the highest level of schooling your mother completed?																
1. Completed grade school or less	4.9	4.0	5.6	3.2	7.5	4.1	3.6	5.9	6.4	3.2	6.4	5.9	4.5	4.6	3.6	4.8
2. Some high school	16.3	14.2	18.1	14.3	27.0	15.6	13.4	20.5	13.2	9.7	22.6	16.1	14.4	18.1	17.5	13.7
3. Completed high school	44.0	45.7	42.6	46.2	36.9	47.8	49.7	39.4	36.5	39.9	48.8	44.1	45.0	42.1	43.6	43.6
4. Some college	13.9	13.8	14.1	15.0	10.0	10.8	14.5	13.2	20.0	19.0	8.7	13.6	13.6	13.7	15.6	14.4
5. Completed college	12.5	13.5	11.5	13.5	7.0	12.1	12.0	11.8	15.4	18.3	6.6	12.5	13.4	12.3	11.5	12.7
6. Graduate or professional school after college	5.3	5.5	5.2	5.4	4.5	7.0	4.0	5.2	5.3	8.1	2.5	4.4	6.1	5.9	5.5	6.5
7. Don't know, or does not apply	3.2	3.4	2.9	2.3	7.0	2.7	2.7	3.9	3.1	1.8	4.4	3.4	3.0	3.2	2.6	4.1
Item 320 N(Wtd)	18248	8655	9179	14734	2035	4372	5295	6089	2492	8794	8350	6458	5093	2249	3767	291
C10: Did your mother have a paid job (half-time or more) during the time you were growing up?																
1. No	35.7	36.8	34.7	38.0	19.5	38.1	38.7	31.4	35.8	37.8	33.9	38.5	36.3	33.6	31.9	33.1
2. Yes, some of the time when I was growing up	30.9	31.4	30.5	32.2	23.3	32.2	30.0	29.9	32.9	30.6	31.4	31.3	31.3	31.5	30.5	22.4
3. Yes, most of the time	15.8	15.7	15.8	15.0	21.0	15.9	15.4	16.6	14.6	14.5	17.1	13.4	15.7	17.3	18.7	20.0
4. Yes, all or nearly all of the time	17.5	16.0	19.1	14.8	36.2	13.7	15.8	22.1	16.7	17.1	17.6	16.8	16.7	17.5	18.9	24.5
Item 330 N(Wtd)	18201	8633	9159	14707	2024	4360	5287	6074	2481	8789	8329	6447	5087	2243	3748	290

QUESTIONNAIRE FORM 1-5 1978	TOTAL	SEX		RACE		REGION				4YR COLLEGE PLANS		ILLICIT DRUG USE: LIFETIME				
		M	F	White	Black	NE	NC	S	W	Yes	No	None	Marijuana Only	Few Pills	More Pills	Any Heroin
Weighted No. of Cases:	18916	8779	9266	14847	2096	4607	5411	6292	2605	8844	8413	6595	5214	2304	3885	302
% of Weighted Total:	100.0	46.4	49.0	78.5	11.1	24.4	28.6	33.3	13.8	46.8	44.5	34.9	27.6	12.2	20.5	1.6

C11: How would you describe your political preference?

	TOTAL	M	F	White	Black	NE	NC	S	W	Yes	No	None	Marijuana Only	Few Pills	More Pills	Any Heroin
1. Strongly Republican	5.7	7.0	4.3	6.1	4.0	3.7	6.8	6.2	5.5	6.6	4.7	6.7	5.1	5.1	5.1	4.2
2. Mildly Republican	13.3	14.3	12.4	14.9	4.9	10.6	16.0	12.0	15.7	15.2	11.9	14.6	13.5	13.6	12.0	6.9
3. Mildly Democrat	15.4	15.4	15.4	14.9	18.8	14.5	14.1	17.0	15.8	16.3	14.9	15.8	16.0	14.3	15.1	12.2
4. Strongly Democrat	9.1	9.4	8.7	6.9	24.6	7.1	6.9	12.9	8.0	8.9	8.9	9.2	9.3	9.7	7.7	10.4
5. American Independent Party	1.8	2.0	1.5	1.6	2.2	2.2	1.6	1.5	2.0	1.5	1.9	1.3	1.3	1.9	2.6	4.9
6. No preference, independent	27.1	28.2	26.2	29.0	15.7	30.4	30.4	23.0	24.5	28.5	25.9	23.9	28.0	27.6	31.6	30.9
7. Other	1.2	1.8	.7	1.1	.8	1.8	1.0	1.0	1.5	1.2	1.2	.9	.9	1.1	2.1	4.9
8. Don't know, haven't decided	26.3	21.8	30.8	25.6	28.9	29.8	23.2	26.3	27.1	21.8	30.7	27.7	25.8	26.8	23.9	26.0
Item 340 N(Wtd)	18099	8586	9102	14650	2007	4336	5258	6049	2456	8746	8294	6418	5051	2235	3732	288

C12: How would you describe your political beliefs?

	TOTAL	M	F	White	Black	NE	NC	S	W	Yes	No	None	Marijuana Only	Few Pills	More Pills	Any Heroin
1. Very conservative	2.9	3.5	2.2	2.6	4.6	2.4	2.0	4.1	2.6	2.8	2.9	3.5	2.3	3.0	2.4	3.2
2. Conservative	13.0	16.0	10.3	13.5	10.7	10.0	12.5	15.0	15.0	14.9	11.3	15.3	13.1	12.5	9.4	9.5
3. Moderate	32.1	31.7	32.4	33.3	27.9	28.1	35.1	32.4	31.8	34.2	30.7	34.7	33.2	31.4	27.5	23.7
4. Liberal	18.1	18.6	17.7	18.2	17.9	20.1	19.1	15.1	19.6	21.2	14.7	13.3	18.7	19.9	24.5	21.9
5. Very liberal	3.6	3.5	3.6	3.3	5.3	4.5	3.0	3.4	3.9	4.4	2.8	2.2	3.2	4.3	5.7	9.5
6. Radical	2.6	3.7	1.4	2.3	4.0	3.1	2.4	2.1	3.3	2.4	2.5	1.4	1.8	2.7	5.0	8.1
8. None of the above, or don't know	27.8	23.0	32.4	26.8	29.8	31.8	26.0	28.0	24.0	20.2	35.2	29.5	27.7	26.2	25.5	24.0
Item 350 N(Wtd)	18057	8555	9092	14615	1992	4319	5255	6024	2459	8758	8276	6409	5043	2233	3717	283

C13: The next three questions are about religion.

C13A: What is your religious preference?

	TOTAL	M	F	White	Black	NE	NC	S	W	Yes	No	None	Marijuana Only	Few Pills	More Pills	Any Heroin
01. Baptist	22.2	21.4	22.4	17.6	61.7	6.4	13.7	44.6	12.5	18.9	25.3	25.0	21.2	22.4	16.8	26.3
02. Churches of Christ	5.4	5.6	5.2	5.0	6.6	5.9	4.6	5.0	7.3	4.3	6.4	5.3	5.2	5.7	5.6	4.9
03. Disciples of Christ	.4	.4	.4	.4	.3	.2	.4	.5	.4	.5	.2	.4	.4	.6	.3	-
04. Episcopal	2.1	2.2	2.0	2.3	1.0	2.1	1.1	2.6	2.9	3.0	1.2	1.8	2.4	2.1	2.2	2.5
05. Lutheran	7.2	7.6	6.9	8.5	.4	3.9	14.7	3.5	5.9	7.0	7.5	7.6	7.1	5.9	7.7	5.6
06. Methodist	9.0	8.3	9.7	9.7	8.4	5.8	11.5	11.2	4.0	9.0	9.2	10.1	8.7	8.6	8.0	8.4
07. Presbyterian	3.8	3.8	3.8	4.3	1.1	2.9	3.8	3.9	5.3	5.0	2.7	4.0	4.0	3.9	3.5	3.2
08. United Church of Christ	.9	.8	1.1	1.0	.6	.9	1.7	.5	.5	1.0	.9	1.3	.8	.6	.7	.4
09. Other Protestant	3.7	3.3	4.1	4.1	1.6	4.5	3.7	2.6	5.1	3.6	3.8	4.3	3.4	3.5	3.4	2.5
10. Unitarian	.1	.1	.2	.2	-	.1	.1	.2	.1	.3	*	*	.2	.2	.2	.7
11. Roman Catholic	28.1	27.0	29.3	29.5	6.6	48.3	29.9	12.6	26.8	30.3	25.8	24.6	32.2	28.5	29.6	21.4
12. Eastern Orthodox	.3	.3	.3	.3	-	.7	.2	.1	.2	.4	.1	.3	.2	.2	.2	.7
13. Jewish	1.7	2.0	1.3	1.9	.2	4.6	.6	.5	1.4	2.9	.4	1.1	2.0	2.2	1.9	1.8
14. Other religion	5.4	5.1	5.7	5.1	5.3	3.7	4.2	4.7	12.8	4.6	6.2	7.2	3.4	5.6	4.9	5.6
15. None	9.7	12.0	7.7	9.9	6.3	9.9	9.9	7.5	14.8	9.2	10.2	6.8	8.8	9.9	15.2	16.1
Item 360 N(Wtd)	17990	8517	9071	14556	2007	4283	5235	6045	2427	8727	8243	6377	5033	2215	3709	285

C13B: How often do you attend religious services?

	TOTAL	M	F	White	Black	NE	NC	S	W	Yes	No	None	Marijuana Only	Few Pills	More Pills	Any Heroin
1. Never	9.0	11.3	6.8	9.2	5.4	11.3	8.3	6.1	13.4	6.8	11.1	5.8	8.0	8.9	14.8	20.4
2. Rarely	34.4	37.2	31.7	34.5	31.4	37.4	34.3	31.8	35.7	29.3	39.1	24.7	36.1	39.7	45.1	38.1
3. Once or twice a month	17.2	16.7	17.5	16.0	25.8	15.4	17.0	19.7	14.6	18.1	16.2	16.0	19.0	17.6	16.5	16.3
4. About once a week or more	39.4	34.8	44.0	40.3	37.4	35.9	40.4	42.4	36.2	45.7	33.7	53.6	36.9	33.8	23.6	25.3
Item 370 N(Wtd)	18204	8614	9174	14717	2026	4354	5290	6085	2474	8809	8359	6461	5085	2239	3744	289

C13C: How important is religion in your life?

	TOTAL	M	F	White	Black	NE	NC	S	W	Yes	No	None	Marijuana Only	Few Pills	More Pills	Any Heroin
1. Not important	11.2	14.5	8.2	12.1	4.4	15.4	11.5	6.6	14.8	10.6	11.8	6.8	10.7	12.2	18.5	19.7
2. A little important	27.9	30.9	25.2	29.4	18.1	33.5	30.8	22.1	26.5	25.2	30.8	20.6	30.4	30.4	35.3	33.6
3. Pretty important	33.0	31.1	35.0	33.3	31.7	32.1	34.5	34.3	28.3	33.4	32.9	32.6	35.7	33.3	30.4	28.7
4. Very important	27.8	23.4	31.7	25.3	45.8	19.0	23.2	37.1	30.4	30.8	24.5	40.0	23.1	24.0	15.9	18.0
Item 380 N(Wtd)	18155	8581	9162	14679	2020	4341	5274	6071	2470	8797	8336	6445	5073	2232	3734	289

*=less than .05 per cent.

QUESTIONNAIRE FORM 1-5 1978	TOTAL	SEX		RACE		REGION				4YR COLLEGE PLANS		ILLICIT DRUG USE: LIFETIME				
		M	F	White	Black	NE	NC	S	W	Yes	No	None	Marijuana Only	Few Pills	More Pills	Any Heroin
Weighted No. of Cases:	18916	8779	9266	14847	2096	4607	5411	6292	2605	8844	8413	6595	5214	2304	3885	302
% of Weighted Total:	100.0	46.4	49.0	78.5	11.1	24.4	28.6	33.3	13.8	46.8	44.5	34.9	27.6	12.2	20.5	1.6
C14: When are you most likely to graduate from high school?																
1. By this June	98.2	97.4	99.0	98.6	96.9	98.8	98.6	97.8	97.0	99.0	97.7	98.9	98.9	97.7	96.6	93.5
2. July to January	1.4	2.0	.7	1.1	2.3	.7	1.0	1.8	2.4	.9	1.6	.8	.9	1.7	2.7	4.3
3. After next January	-	-	-	-	-	-	-	-	-	-	-	-	-	-	-	-
6. Don't expect to graduate	.4	.6	.2	.3	.8	.5	.4	.4	.6	.1	.7	.3	.2	.5	.7	2.5
Item 390 N(Wtd)	18118	8560	9114	14652	1977	4337	5262	6057	2462	8829	8397	6452	5058	2226	3722	279
C15: Which of the following best describes your present high school program?																
1. Academic or college prep	42.8	42.7	43.6	45.4	34.5	54.2	39.4	40.4	36.4	68.9	16.5	47.5	46.5	39.7	34.6	26.2
2. General	31.8	30.9	32.6	31.7	29.9	22.1	34.8	33.0	39.9	21.9	42.0	28.9	30.4	34.4	36.6	36.0
3. Vocational, technical, or commercial	16.8	18.5	15.0	16.1	19.2	17.6	17.3	16.5	14.8	5.6	28.1	15.2	15.6	17.0	20.3	26.5
4. Other, or don't know	8.5	7.9	8.8	6.8	16.4	6.1	8.5	10.2	8.9	3.5	13.3	8.4	7.6	8.9	8.5	11.3
Item 400 N(Wtd)	18023	8512	9067	14590	1957	4319	5237	6017	2450	8811	8352	6424	5032	2217	3700	275
C16: Compared with others your age throughout the country, how do you rate yourself on school ability?																
1. Far below average	.6	.8	.5	.5	1.2	.8	.4	.8	.4	.2	1.0	.4	.7	.8	.8	1.1
2. Below average	1.8	2.0	1.4	1.6	2.0	1.6	2.1	1.7	1.3	.8	2.7	1.3	1.6	1.8	2.6	2.6
3. Slightly below average	4.8	5.5	4.1	4.2	6.9	4.6	5.1	4.7	4.7	2.5	7.0	3.4	4.8	5.2	6.4	8.7
4. Average	38.4	36.5	39.7	35.7	51.1	39.0	34.7	42.4	35.5	24.2	52.8	34.4	38.5	40.3	42.1	42.3
5. Slightly above average	23.3	22.9	23.8	24.2	21.2	22.7	24.4	22.1	25.1	25.7	20.9	22.6	24.3	23.8	23.7	21.1
6. Above average	25.5	25.3	26.3	27.8	14.4	25.2	27.8	23.1	27.3	37.1	14.0	30.8	25.1	23.0	20.5	17.7
7. Far above average	5.6	7.1	4.4	6.0	3.1	6.1	5.6	5.2	5.7	9.6	1.6	7.2	5.2	5.0	4.0	6.8
Item 410 N(Wtd)	17634	8380	8821	14298	1894	4229	5112	5909	2384	8668	8169	6285	4941	2175	3602	265
C17: How intelligent do you think you are compared with others your age?																
1. Far below average	.5	.5	.4	.3	1.0	.4	.4	.6	.4	.2	.7	.3	.5	.8	.4	.4
2. Below average	1.0	1.1	.9	1.0	.6	1.2	1.2	.8	1.0	.5	1.7	.9	1.1	1.0	1.0	.7
3. Slightly below average	3.8	3.5	4.1	3.5	4.2	3.8	4.4	3.5	3.4	1.6	6.0	2.9	3.8	4.4	4.7	6.3
4. Average	37.9	34.5	40.7	36.2	44.5	38.2	34.9	41.7	34.6	23.8	52.5	35.3	37.6	38.3	40.9	39.8
5. Slightly above average	23.1	22.8	23.6	24.2	19.5	23.2	24.2	21.8	23.9	25.7	20.6	22.3	24.9	24.2	22.3	23.8
6. Above average	27.6	30.1	25.7	29.2	21.9	27.2	29.1	25.6	30.3	38.9	16.3	31.5	26.4	25.5	25.6	20.8
7. Far above average	6.0	7.6	4.5	5.6	8.3	6.0	5.7	6.0	6.3	9.4	2.3	6.7	5.8	5.8	5.1	7.8
Item 420 N(Wtd)	17702	8347	8919	14391	1874	4233	5171	5894	2403	8700	8222	6306	4960	2174	3638	269
C18: During the LAST FOUR WEEKS, how many whole days of school have you missed...																
C18A: Because of illness																
1. None	58.4	63.6	53.7	59.5	53.7	53.6	59.2	61.4	57.8	61.6	55.6	65.8	58.2	53.2	49.6	52.1
2. 1 day	16.4	15.4	17.5	16.6	15.6	16.8	16.7	15.8	16.6	16.7	16.2	14.6	16.5	19.8	18.1	12.0
3. 2 days	10.6	9.2	11.9	10.4	11.5	12.6	9.8	10.0	10.2	9.9	11.4	8.6	11.2	10.6	12.6	18.7
4. 3 days	6.3	5.4	7.1	6.0	7.2	7.2	6.1	5.7	6.9	5.5	7.0	4.8	6.1	6.7	8.9	7.1
5. 4-5 days	5.3	4.1	6.3	5.0	7.3	5.7	5.3	4.6	5.9	4.3	6.2	4.2	5.3	5.9	6.7	3.7
6. 6-10 days	2.1	1.6	2.6	1.9	2.9	2.8	2.2	1.7	1.9	1.5	2.6	1.6	1.8	3.0	2.7	3.0
7. 11 or more	.9	.7	1.0	.7	1.7	1.2	.7	.8	.7	.5	1.1	.5	.9	.7	1.4	3.4
Item 430 N(Wtd)	17513	8254	8826	14199	1896	4157	5113	5878	2365	8639	8152	6284	4903	2152	3549	267
C18B: Because you skipped or "cut"																
1. None	69.5	66.8	72.2	68.4	82.4	66.2	71.4	71.9	65.3	74.4	64.9	84.8	69.6	62.7	48.8	46.2
2. 1 day	13.3	13.3	13.2	14.2	6.2	14.6	12.8	12.7	13.3	12.6	14.0	8.2	14.9	16.7	17.7	16.5
3. 2 days	6.9	7.8	6.0	7.0	4.8	7.9	6.3	6.2	8.0	5.7	8.1	3.1	6.7	9.4	12.0	10.8
4. 3 days	4.2	4.8	3.6	4.2	3.1	4.5	4.2	3.7	5.3	3.5	4.8	1.9	3.7	5.1	8.0	9.2
5. 4-5 days	3.5	4.2	2.9	3.6	1.8	4.2	3.2	3.0	4.5	2.3	4.7	1.3	2.7	4.1	8.0	5.8
6. 6-10 days	1.6	1.9	1.4	1.7	.8	1.8	1.3	1.5	2.3	.9	2.3	.5	1.4	1.5	3.3	6.5
7. 11 or more	.9	1.2	.6	.8	.8	.8	.8	1.1	1.3	.6	1.2	.2	1.0	.4	2.2	5.4
Item 440 N(Wtd)	16942	8036	8499	13827	1769	4022	4984	5646	2291	8397	7905	6050	4730	2078	3496	260

QUESTIONNAIRE FORM 1-5 1978	TOTAL	SEX		RACE		REGION				4YR COLLEGE PLANS		ILLICIT DRUG USE: LIFETIME				
		M	F	White	Black	NE	NC	S	W	Yes	No	None	Mari-juana Only	Few Pills	More Pills	Any Her-oin
Weighted No. of Cases:	18916	8779	9266	14847	2096	4607	5411	6292	2605	8844	8413	6595	5214	2304	3885	302
% of Weighted Total:	100.0	46.4	49.0	78.5	11.1	24.4	28.6	33.3	13.8	46.8	44.5	34.9	27.6	12.2	20.5	1.6
C18C: For other reasons																
1. None	58.8	59.9	57.9	58.4	63.1	56.5	60.3	60.7	55.1	58.4	59.3	62.9	59.5	55.1	52.8	56.4
2. 1 day	19.1	18.2	20.0	19.7	16.6	20.4	18.8	18.4	18.9	19.8	18.4	19.3	18.8	20.1	19.0	13.6
3. 2 days	10.5	10.0	10.8	10.5	8.5	11.4	9.5	10.4	11.4	10.6	10.4	9.1	10.2	11.7	12.5	12.8
4. 3 days	5.5	5.6	5.3	5.3	5.3	5.2	5.3	5.4	6.5	5.4	5.5	4.2	5.3	6.3	7.2	8.6
5. 4-5 days	3.9	4.1	3.7	3.9	4.1	3.7	4.1	3.4	4.8	3.6	4.0	3.0	4.0	4.2	5.0	4.7
6. 6-10 days	1.6	1.6	1.5	1.6	1.3	2.0	1.5	1.1	2.3	1.5	1.5	1.1	1.6	1.9	2.1	1.9
7. 11 or more	.7	.8	.7	.6	1.1	.8	.6	.6	1.0	.6	.9	.4	.5	.6	1.4	1.6
Item 450 N(Wtd)	17006	8023	8582	13865	1790	4030	5029	5657	2290	8481	7886	6159	4746	2086	3434	257
C19: During the last four weeks, how often have you gone to school, but skipped a class when you weren't supposed to?																
1. Not at all	60.8	56.0	65.4	60.1	70.5	58.5	62.9	65.8	48.2	61.4	60.8	78.6	57.7	54.1	39.8	37.3
2. 1 or 2 times	22.2	23.7	20.7	22.4	19.3	22.2	21.8	20.6	27.1	23.1	21.2	14.8	25.4	27.3	27.6	29.2
3. 3-5 times	10.0	11.5	8.6	10.2	6.3	11.0	9.2	8.0	14.8	9.4	10.4	3.9	10.6	11.5	18.1	16.2
4. 6-10 times	4.0	5.1	3.0	4.4	1.4	4.9	3.5	3.0	6.2	3.8	4.3	1.6	3.5	4.4	8.3	8.9
5. 11-20 times	1.6	2.0	1.3	1.7	.7	2.1	1.5	1.2	2.0	1.5	1.7	.4	1.6	1.7	3.5	5.9
6. More than 20 times	1.3	1.7	1.0	1.1	1.9	1.3	1.0	1.5	1.6	.8	1.7	.7	1.2	1.0	2.6	2.2
Item 460 N(Wtd)	17947	8459	9046	14554	1933	4283	5228	6012	2425	8819	8399	6406	5009	2207	3677	271
C20: Which of the following best describes your average grade so far in high school?																
9. A (93-100)	7.7	6.2	9.4	8.4	4.1	6.2	8.2	8.5	7.4	12.3	3.2	11.9	5.8	6.2	4.7	4.4
8. A- (90-92)	10.8	8.5	13.1	11.5	7.6	9.5	11.2	10.7	12.2	14.9	6.7	14.7	10.2	9.1	6.8	2.2
7. B+ (87-89)	17.5	15.2	19.6	18.2	14.9	18.4	16.0	18.1	17.6	22.1	12.9	21.4	16.1	16.2	14.6	10.7
6. B (83-86)	21.1	20.1	22.2	22.0	16.2	22.7	20.2	19.7	23.5	22.3	20.1	20.6	22.6	22.1	20.1	16.7
5. B- (80-82)	15.5	17.1	13.9	15.0	19.2	14.9	14.8	16.4	16.4	13.8	17.1	12.7	16.8	16.1	17.6	24.4
4. C+ (77-79)	13.4	15.6	11.3	12.1	20.4	14.7	13.2	13.7	11.2	8.7	17.9	9.0	15.1	15.8	16.0	18.1
3. C (73-76)	8.7	10.5	7.0	8.2	10.7	8.5	10.5	8.0	7.3	4.4	13.2	6.3	8.7	8.7	12.2	14.8
2. C- (70-72)	3.8	5.0	2.5	3.4	5.1	3.6	4.2	3.7	3.3	1.1	6.4	2.6	3.5	4.1	5.8	6.3
1. D (69 or below)	1.4	1.8	.9	1.2	1.8	1.4	1.8	1.2	1.0	.3	2.5	.9	1.2	1.8	2.2	1.9
Item 470 N(Wtd)	17843	8422	8985	14479	1918	4241	5196	5987	2420	8787	8345	6379	4976	2196	3647	270
C21: How likely is it that you will do each of the following things after high school?																
C21A: Attend a technical or vocational school																
1. Definitely won't	42.1	38.2	46.2	43.7	34.7	55.0	40.3	38.6	32.2	57.3	27.5	44.6	44.4	39.7	37.7	32.0
2. Probably won't	29.7	30.9	28.4	30.3	25.9	23.8	31.0	30.3	35.5	29.8	30.0	29.7	29.7	28.6	30.6	29.6
3. Probably will	19.3	21.7	16.8	17.9	26.5	13.6	19.6	22.0	22.1	9.4	28.8	17.2	17.4	21.5	23.0	27.7
4. Definitely will	8.9	9.2	8.6	8.2	12.9	7.6	9.1	9.1	10.2	3.6	13.7	8.5	8.6	10.2	8.7	10.3
Item 480 N(Wtd)	17139	8016	8706	13966	1795	4055	5030	5767	2287	8499	8372	6171	4750	2101	3509	253
C21B: Serve in the armed forces																
1. Definitely won't	62.6	48.4	76.3	64.5	52.6	63.5	65.0	59.4	64.2	65.5	60.1	63.1	61.5	64.1	64.1	53.3
2. Probably won't	25.4	32.9	18.2	25.8	20.8	24.6	25.9	26.0	24.4	25.7	25.4	26.1	25.8	24.8	24.5	22.9
3. Probably will	7.6	11.4	3.9	6.3	15.4	7.8	5.7	9.4	6.9	5.8	9.3	6.6	7.9	6.9	8.0	15.4
4. Definitely will	4.4	7.3	1.6	3.4	11.2	4.2	3.4	5.3	4.5	3.0	5.3	4.2	4.9	4.2	3.4	8.3
Item 490 N(Wtd)	16570	7748	8436	13598	1689	3935	4861	5576	2198	8347	8025	5997	4608	2019	3375	240
C21C: Graduate from a two-year college program																
1. Definitely won't	38.1	38.3	38.2	39.6	32.0	44.9	39.5	38.2	22.9	40.6	36.6	40.0	38.1	36.0	36.7	34.9
2. Probably won't	30.8	33.9	28.0	31.6	28.2	26.2	33.6	32.4	29.2	31.5	30.9	31.4	32.1	29.9	29.3	29.8
3. Probably will	20.3	19.0	21.4	18.6	28.9	17.0	18.5	20.5	29.7	17.4	22.6	18.3	19.4	21.7	23.5	26.2
4. Definitely will	10.7	8.7	12.5	10.3	11.0	11.9	8.3	8.9	18.2	10.5	10.0	10.3	10.4	12.3	10.6	9.1
Item 500 N(Wtd)	17096	7980	8708	13946	1787	4053	5017	5734	2293	8475	8358	6144	4751	2091	3512	252

QUESTIONNAIRE FORM 1-5 1978	TOTAL	M	F	White	Black	NE	NC	S	W	Yes	No	None	Mari- juana Only	Few Pills	More Pills	Any Her- oin
Weighted No. of Cases:	18916	8779	9266	14847	2096	4607	5411	6292	2605	8844	8413	6595	5214	2304	3885	302
% of Weighted Total:	100.0	46.4	49.0	78.5	11.1	24.4	28.6	33.3	13.8	46.8	44.5	34.9	27.6	12.2	20.5	1.6
C21D: Graduate from college (four-year program)																
1. Definitely won't	29.7	27.5	31.4	30.0	24.9	31.2	32.0	29.2	23.0	-	60.8	26.8	27.4	32.7	34.8	37.7
2. Probably won't	19.1	19.3	18.6	18.6	20.2	16.7	19.6	19.4	21.4	-	39.2	17.8	18.0	19.1	22.2	23.1
3. Probably will	21.6	22.7	20.6	21.5	22.8	18.8	21.3	21.4	27.9	42.1	-	21.0	23.2	21.5	20.9	19.6
4. Definitely will	29.7	30.4	29.3	29.9	32.2	33.4	27.1	30.0	27.8	57.9	-	34.4	31.4	26.7	22.2	19.6
Item 510 N(Wtd)	17257	8102	8744	14068	1809	4081	5075	5797	2305	8844	8413	6213	4811	2090	3528	260
C21E: Attend graduate or professional school after college																
1. Definitely won't	37.6	35.7	39.2	38.2	32.2	38.0	40.5	37.4	31.0	10.7	65.2	34.1	35.6	39.6	43.9	42.0
2. Probably won't	32.4	33.0	31.7	32.9	30.9	29.0	32.8	33.0	36.2	36.7	28.3	34.1	33.3	30.9	30.1	27.8
3. Probably will	21.3	21.8	21.0	21.1	23.3	22.9	19.8	20.8	22.8	37.7	4.5	22.2	22.7	21.4	18.3	19.6
4. Definitely will	8.7	9.5	8.1	7.8	13.6	10.1	6.9	8.7	10.2	14.8	2.0	9.6	8.4	8.2	7.7	10.2
Item 520 N(Wtd)	17026	7968	8646	13868	1791	4023	5017	5733	2253	8473	8372	6137	4736	2065	3489	255
C22: Suppose you could do just what you'd like and nothing stood in your way. How many of the following things would you WANT to do? (Mark ALL that apply)																
A. Attend a technical or vocational school	28.4	30.6	26.1	27.2	33.9	22.3	30.2	30.5	29.7	13.2	44.8	27.3	25.7	31.5	30.8	34.2
B. Serve in the armed forces	14.0	18.3	9.8	12.2	24.3	14.5	11.6	16.3	12.4	11.3	16.6	14.1	14.3	13.8	12.2	19.6
C. Graduate from a two-year college program	25.5	20.4	30.3	24.5	29.8	23.9	24.5	24.0	34.7	17.4	33.6	25.1	24.1	26.7	27.6	25.4
D. Graduate from college (four year program)	55.2	55.5	55.5	55.9	55.5	54.6	52.3	56.0	60.1	89.5	20.5	59.1	57.1	53.9	48.5	43.8
E. Attend graduate or professional school after college	35.2	35.0	35.7	35.4	35.4	36.9	33.4	34.9	36.8	55.7	13.9	36.2	36.8	34.7	33.2	26.2
F. None of the above	12.1	11.6	12.3	12.6	6.4	13.8	13.2	11.0	9.5	2.5	22.2	10.8	11.3	11.7	15.0	17.3
Item 530-580 N(Wtd)	17442	8180	8885	14159	1865	4105	5115	5874	2848	8710	8178	6255	4875	2186	8547	260
C23: On the average over the school year, how many hours per week do you work in a paid or unpaid job?																
1. None	22.0	18.1	25.7	18.9	42.7	22.7	18.1	25.3	21.4	22.6	21.2	27.3	20.3	18.9	17.0	14.9
2. 5 or less hours	9.3	9.2	9.6	9.2	10.9	9.1	8.7	9.3	11.0	11.6	7.0	10.7	8.8	10.6	6.9	6.0
3. 6 to 10 hours	9.9	9.8	9.9	9.7	11.2	9.7	9.4	9.8	11.7	11.0	8.9	11.7	10.0	8.4	7.7	7.8
4. 11 to 15 hours	10.0	9.1	10.9	10.6	6.1	11.3	10.3	8.6	10.5	11.3	8.7	10.3	9.9	10.0	9.8	9.7
5. 16 to 20 hours	15.1	14.4	15.9	16.3	8.9	15.8	16.8	13.7	13.8	16.1	14.3	14.0	16.3	17.1	14.8	13.1
6. 21 to 25 hours	12.6	12.8	12.2	13.5	6.9	13.4	14.6	10.5	12.1	11.9	13.3	9.8	13.8	13.0	15.7	11.6
7. 26 to 30 hours	9.1	10.6	7.6	9.5	5.4	9.2	9.5	9.1	7.7	7.6	10.5	6.4	9.7	10.5	11.7	14.6
8. More than 30 hours	12.0	16.0	8.1	12.3	7.9	8.8	12.6	13.7	11.9	7.9	16.1	9.8	11.2	11.7	16.4	22.8
Item 590 N(Wtd)	17614	8264	8913	14344	1859	4155	5176	5914	2369	8753	8289	6315	4907	2164	3593	268
C24: During an average week, how much money do you get from...																
C24A: A job or other work																
1. None	23.8	19.4	28.0	21.4	40.9	24.0	20.8	26.4	23.6	25.8	21.8	30.3	21.2	22.2	17.2	14.5
2. $1-5	5.3	4.4	6.2	5.5	5.1	5.0	5.5	4.8	6.3	5.5	5.2	6.8	4.9	4.6	3.8	2.7
3. $6-10	4.8	4.7	4.8	4.8	5.2	4.2	4.6	4.6	6.7	5.2	4.2	5.6	4.3	4.6	3.9	5.5
4. $11-20	6.8	6.8	6.7	7.0	5.6	6.6	6.9	6.5	7.8	7.6	6.0	7.3	7.1	6.2	6.0	3.5
5. $21-35	12.8	10.9	14.5	13.2	10.7	14.9	13.2	11.2	12.0	13.9	11.6	12.8	13.1	13.4	12.4	11.7
6. $36-50	17.7	16.5	18.9	18.8	11.4	19.1	19.5	16.2	15.0	18.1	17.4	15.8	18.8	18.3	19.1	20.7
7. $51 +	28.9	37.3	20.8	29.4	21.3	26.2	29.6	30.3	28.6	23.9	33.7	21.4	30.5	30.7	37.6	41.4
Item 600 N(Wtd)	16714	7927	8381	13728	1681	3942	4944	5579	2249	8356	7848	5994	4694	2053	3392	256

QUESTIONNAIRE FORM 1-5 1978	TOTAL	SEX		RACE		REGION				4YR COLLEGE PLANS		ILLICIT DRUG USE: LIFETIME				
		M	F	White	Black	NE	NC	S	W	Yes	No	None	Mari-juana Only	Few Pills	More Pills	Any Her-oin
Weighted No. of Cases:	18916	8779	9266	14847	2096	4607	5411	6292	2605	8844	8413	6595	5214	2304	3885	302
% of Weighted Total:	100.0	46.4	49.0	78.5	11.1	24.4	28.6	33.3	13.8	46.8	44.5	34.9	27.6	12.2	20.5	1.6

C24B: Other sources (allowances, etc.)

	TOTAL	M	F	White	Black	NE	NC	S	W	Yes	No	None	Mari-juana Only	Few Pills	More Pills	Any Her-oin
1. None	40.5	42.4	38.7	41.8	29.2	43.7	42.5	37.1	38.8	37.3	43.7	40.8	40.8	40.8	39.6	36.1
2. $1-5	26.4	22.9	29.9	27.3	23.0	26.0	27.4	25.1	28.1	28.7	24.2	29.7	26.4	25.1	22.3	17.4
3. $6-10	16.2	16.0	16.2	15.8	20.1	15.4	15.3	17.0	17.7	17.4	14.9	15.0	17.2	15.8	17.5	13.7
4. $11-20	9.1	10.1	8.2	8.4	12.7	8.0	8.1	11.1	7.9	9.1	9.0	8.3	8.5	10.2	10.5	10.4
5. $21-35	3.6	3.7	3.4	3.1	6.5	3.2	2.7	4.8	3.0	3.6	3.6	3.1	3.4	3.8	4.3	5.0
6. $36-50	1.5	1.6	1.4	1.2	3.7	1.2	1.4	1.8	1.7	1.6	1.4	1.1	1.3	1.4	2.2	3.3
7. $51 +	2.7	3.2	2.3	2.3	4.8	2.4	2.6	3.1	2.8	2.3	3.2	1.9	2.3	3.0	3.6	14.5
Item 610 N(Wtd)	16254	7578	8298	13334	1655	3814	4812	5451	2177	8257	7559	5867	4552	1969	3312	241

C25: During a typical week, on how many evenings do you go out for fun and recreation?

	TOTAL	M	F	White	Black	NE	NC	S	W	Yes	No	None	Mari-juana Only	Few Pills	More Pills	Any Her-oin
1. Less than one	7.1	5.8	8.2	6.0	12.6	6.6	6.1	7.7	8.7	6.5	7.5	11.6	4.8	5.9	3.2	3.0
2. One	12.2	10.8	13.6	11.5	16.0	11.3	11.3	11.9	16.5	13.4	11.0	17.6	9.7	10.6	7.5	7.2
3. Two	27.6	27.3	27.8	28.0	25.6	26.7	27.9	27.7	27.9	30.6	24.4	31.3	30.3	25.7	19.9	11.4
4. Three	27.1	26.4	27.7	27.9	22.9	26.2	28.3	27.8	23.9	27.4	27.1	23.9	31.1	29.3	25.6	20.1
5. Four or five	17.8	19.4	16.2	18.6	13.5	18.6	18.5	17.3	15.8	16.3	19.4	11.5	17.4	20.4	27.1	33.3
6. Six or seven	8.3	10.2	6.5	8.1	9.3	10.6	7.8	7.5	7.3	5.9	10.7	4.1	6.7	7.9	16.7	25.4
Item 620 N(Wtd)	17564	8216	8912	14304	1849	4132	5169	5904	2358	8743	8246	6303	4901	2153	3576	264

C26: On the average, how often do you go out with a date (or your spouse, if you are married)?

	TOTAL	M	F	White	Black	NE	NC	S	W	Yes	No	None	Mari-juana Only	Few Pills	More Pills	Any Her-oin
1. Never	13.6	13.4	13.8	12.1	20.5	15.5	13.0	11.9	15.8	13.4	13.6	21.4	10.0	9.6	7.3	9.7
2. Once a month or less	18.8	20.2	17.5	19.3	15.9	19.5	20.0	16.6	20.8	22.1	15.5	21.3	19.2	17.4	15.7	9.4
3. 2 or 3 times a month	18.2	20.7	16.0	18.1	19.8	15.9	17.7	19.4	20.1	20.3	15.9	16.9	18.8	20.0	18.7	17.6
4. Once a week	15.5	17.4	13.7	15.2	18.7	14.3	15.9	15.8	16.2	15.7	15.3	15.0	16.7	14.8	15.0	17.6
5. 2 or 3 times a week	22.4	20.2	24.5	23.4	17.7	20.8	22.2	25.5	18.0	21.1	24.2	18.4	24.5	25.0	24.9	28.8
6. Over 3 times a week	11.4	8.1	14.6	11.9	7.4	14.0	11.2	10.7	9.1	7.4	15.5	7.1	10.8	13.2	18.4	16.5
Item 630 N(Wtd)	17358	8108	8819	14163	1812	4046	5139	5854	2320	8632	8125	6220	4858	2133	3524	267

C27: During an average week, how much do you usually drive a car, truck, or motorcycle?

	TOTAL	M	F	White	Black	NE	NC	S	W	Yes	No	None	Mari-juana Only	Few Pills	More Pills	Any Her-oin
1. Not at all	12.9	7.4	18.0	8.8	37.6	19.8	8.4	11.9	13.3	11.5	13.8	15.2	11.4	12.6	10.8	9.3
2. 1 to 10 miles	13.0	9.1	16.6	11.6	21.8	16.0	12.2	11.9	12.1	12.2	13.6	15.5	12.4	12.0	9.4	11.9
3. 11 to 50 miles	29.5	24.6	33.9	30.8	21.8	29.5	33.2	25.2	31.7	32.5	26.5	32.8	29.2	29.9	25.2	20.0
4. 51 to 100 miles	21.2	24.6	18.1	23.0	10.2	17.6	22.0	22.7	21.9	22.5	20.1	19.4	23.0	21.1	22.4	19.6
5. 100 to 200 miles	14.9	20.8	9.4	16.7	5.2	10.9	15.5	17.7	13.8	14.3	15.7	11.5	15.8	14.9	19.3	19.3
6. More than 200 miles	8.5	13.5	4.0	9.0	3.5	6.2	8.6	10.6	7.2	7.0	10.2	5.6	8.2	9.5	12.9	20.4
Item 640 N(Wtd)	17526	8199	8892	14289	1838	4104	5183	5892	2347	8698	8208	6298	4887	2152	3556	270

C28: Within the LAST 12 MONTHS, how many times, if any, have you received a ticket (OR been stopped and warned) for moving violations such as speeding, running a stop light, or improper passing?

	TOTAL	M	F	White	Black	NE	NC	S	W	Yes	No	None	Mari-juana Only	Few Pills	More Pills	Any Her-oin
0. None--GO TO Q.C30	73.2	62.1	83.6	71.3	87.5	81.3	70.5	71.1	70.0	74.7	71.7	82.8	71.2	69.1	62.6	52.9
1. Once	16.6	21.6	12.1	17.6	8.8	12.5	18.2	17.3	18.7	16.6	16.6	12.4	17.9	17.9	21.3	22.6
2. Twice	5.8	9.0	2.7	6.2	2.6	3.4	6.6	6.5	6.4	5.0	6.5	3.1	6.3	7.3	8.3	13.6
3. Three times	2.4	3.8	.9	2.6	.8	1.3	2.5	3.0	2.5	2.1	2.7	1.0	2.6	2.8	4.2	3.9
4. Four or more times	2.1	3.6	.6	2.3	.4	1.5	2.3	2.1	2.4	1.6	2.4	.7	2.1	2.8	3.7	6.6
Item 650 N(Wtd)	17100	7987	8694	14047	1718	3976	5081	5744	2299	8560	7959	6176	4777	2113	3449	257

C29: How many of these tickets or warnings occurred after you were...

QUESTIONNAIRE FORM 1-5 1978	TOTAL	SEX		RACE		REGION				4YR COLLEGE PLANS		ILLICIT DRUG USE: LIFETIME				
		M	F	White	Black	NE	NC	S	W	Yes	No	None	Mari- juana Only	Few Pills	More Pills	Any Her- oin
Weighted No. of Cases:	18916	8779	9266	14847	2096	4607	5411	6292	2605	8844	8413	6595	5214	2304	3885	302
% of Weighted Total:	100.0	46.4	49.0	78.5	11.1	24.4	28.6	33.3	13.8	46.8	44.5	34.9	27.6	12.2	20.5	1.6
C29A: Drinking alcoholic beverages?																
0. None	82.4	79.5	88.5	81.7	93.6	83.0	78.5	83.9	86.7	85.3	80.2	92.0	84.4	83.6	72.9	61.0
1. One	13.4	15.2	9.6	14.1	5.0	12.3	16.7	12.3	10.3	11.6	14.5	6.6	12.4	12.9	19.9	22.0
2. Two	3.0	3.6	1.5	3.0	.5	4.0	2.9	3.0	2.3	2.3	3.6	.8	2.3	2.0	5.5	11.9
3. Three	.7	.9	.3	.7	.9	.5	1.1	.4	.6	.5	.9	.3	.6	.6	1.0	2.5
4. Four or more	.5	.7	.1	.5	-	.3	.8	.5	.1	.3	.7	.2	.4	.8	.7	2.5
Item 660 N(Wtd) ★	4533	2982	1423	3973	220	729	1481	1641	682	2142	2221	1068	1372	641	1259	118
C29B: Smoking marijuana or hashish?																
0. None	89.6	87.9	93.7	89.3	93.4	86.5	87.9	91.4	92.3	91.9	87.9	100.0	96.0	90.6	76.0	60.7
1. One	7.4	8.6	4.7	7.7	5.2	9.1	8.4	6.4	5.8	6.1	8.2	-	3.2	7.4	16.8	23.0
2. Two	2.0	2.5	1.0	2.0	1.4	3.3	2.4	1.4	1.0	1.4	2.6	-	.6	1.1	4.8	10.7
3. Three	.4	.5	.3	.5	-	.5	.7	.1	.4	.3	.5	-	.1	.3	1.0	2.5
4. Four or more	.6	.6	.4	.5	-	.7	.6	.6	.6	.3	.7	-	.1	.3	1.4	3.3
Item 670 N(Wtd) ★	4466	2931	1408	3922	212	728	1441	1624	672	2118	2182	1045	1335	638	1252	122
C29C: Using other illegal drugs?																
0. None	97.7	97.3	98.7	97.9	98.6	96.6	97.0	98.1	99.1	98.5	97.1	100.0	100.0	99.0	94.4	79.3
1. One	1.6	1.8	.9	1.5	-	2.2	2.3	1.1	.6	1.1	2.0	-	-	.8	4.3	9.5
2. Two	.4	.6	.1	.4	-	.8	.4	.4	.2	.4	.5	-	-	.2	.7	6.9
3. Three	.2	.1	.3	.1	1.4	.1	.1	.2	-	-	.2	-	-	-	.3	2.6
4. Four or more	.1	.2	-	.1	-	.1	.2	.1	-	*	.2	-	-	.2	.2	1.7
Item 680 N(Wtd) ★	4406	2890	1394	3865	213	714	1425	1610	658	2095	2152	1045	1322	624	1224	116
C30: We are interested in any accidents which occurred while you were driving a car, truck, or motorcycle. ("Accidents" means a collision involving property damage or personal injury--not bumps or scratches in parking lots.) During the LAST 12 MONTHS, how many accidents have you had while you were driving (whether or not you were responsible)?																
0. None--GO TO Q.C32	73.6	68.1	78.8	71.5	88.8	76.2	69.7	74.7	74.8	74.0	73.2	81.1	72.3	69.7	64.9	60.1
1. One	19.8	23.0	16.7	21.2	9.6	17.7	21.9	19.6	19.0	19.6	19.9	15.9	21.3	22.5	23.1	21.8
2. Two	4.9	6.3	3.3	5.3	1.1	4.3	6.0	4.3	4.7	4.7	5.0	2.4	4.5	5.7	8.6	11.9
3. Three	1.3	1.8	.8	1.4	.5	1.4	1.7	1.0	1.2	1.1	1.5	.5	1.4	1.5	2.2	4.5
4. Four or more	.5	.7	.3	.6	-	.4	.8	.4	.3	.6	.4	.1	.5	.4	1.2	1.6
Item 690 N(Wtd)	16810	7857	8549	13851	1667	3880	5021	5648	2261	8453	7781	6100	4690	2074	3383	243
C31: How many of these accidents occurred after you were...																
C31A: Drinking alcoholic beverages?																
0. None	86.5	82.8	91.6	86.3	91.1	86.5	84.4	88.2	87.4	87.8	85.6	95.1	89.0	85.4	77.3	70.2
1. One	11.6	14.1	7.8	11.7	8.3	10.7	13.4	10.6	10.5	10.7	11.9	4.4	10.1	12.9	18.7	24.5
2. Two	1.5	2.4	.4	1.6	-	2.4	1.7	.8	1.6	1.1	2.0	.3	.8	1.4	3.1	5.3
3. Three	.2	.4	.1	.3	-	.2	.3	.1	.2	.3	.2	.2	.2	-	.5	-
4. Four or more	.2	.3	-	.1	-	.1	.1	.2	.3	.1	.1	-	-	.5	.4	-
Item 700 N(Wtd) ★	4408	2488	1798	3910	192	904	1502	1429	573	2186	2061	1162	1288	622	1168	94
C31B: Smoking marijuana or hashish?																
0. None	92.4	90.4	95.2	92.6	93.3	90.2	91.3	94.1	94.6	94.1	91.2	100.0	96.8	93.2	80.7	75.0
1. One	6.0	7.5	4.2	5.9	5.6	6.4	7.2	5.2	4.5	5.1	6.6	-	2.8	5.3	15.0	20.7
2. Two	1.2	1.7	.6	1.1	1.1	2.7	1.2	.6	.5	.6	1.7	-	.3	1.2	3.2	4.3
3. Three	.2	.2	.1	.2	-	.4	.2	.1	.2	.2	.2	-	.1	-	.7	-
4. Four or more	.1	.2	-	.1	-	.1	.1	.1	.4	*	.2	-	-	.5	.3	-
Item 710 N(Wtd) ★	4318	2426	1778	3842	179	900	1466	1392	560	2154	2017	1142	1263	607	1150	92

★ = excludes respondents for whom question was inappropriate.   * = less than .05 per cent.

QUESTIONNAIRE FORM 1-5 1978	TOTAL	SEX		RACE		REGION				4YR COLLEGE PLANS		ILLICIT DRUG USE: LIFETIME				
		M	F	White	Black	NE	NC	S	W	Yes	No	None	Marijuana Only	Few Pills	More Pills	Any Heroin
Weighted No. of Cases:	18916	8779	9266	14847	2096	4607	5411	6292	2605	8844	8413	6595	5214	2304	3885	302
% of Weighted Total:	100.0	46.4	49.0	78.5	11.1	24.4	28.6	33.3	13.8	46.8	44.5	34.9	27.6	12.2	20.5	1.6
C31C: Using other illegal drugs?																
0. None	98.2	97.5	99.3	98.4	98.3	97.9	97.8	98.5	98.7	98.7	97.7	100.0	100.0	99.2	94.9	87.8
1. One	1.4	1.8	.7	1.2	1.7	1.1	1.9	1.2	.7	1.0	1.6	-	-	.3	3.9	10.0
2. Two	.3	.4	-	.3	-	.7	.1	.1	.2	.2	.3	-	-	-	.8	2.2
3. Three	-	-	-	-	-	-	-	-	-	-	-	-	-	-	-	-
4. Four or more	.2	.3	-	.2	-	.3	.1	.1	.4	*	.3	-	-	.5	.5	-
Item 720 N(Wtd) ★	4273	2395	1765	3806	176	889	1448	1377	559	2128	2004	1141	1254	595	1130	90
C32: If you have not entered military service, and do not expect to enter, GO TO PART D. What is, or will be, your branch of service?																
1. Army	21.4	20.1	23.1	17.6	35.3	19.6	17.6	26.6	15.1	18.1	23.6	23.2	21.7	18.6	18.5	29.9
2. Navy	18.9	19.9	17.2	21.0	12.2	19.8	21.1	15.5	23.8	16.6	19.5	19.6	18.8	18.6	19.8	4.5
3. Marine Corps	10.3	11.4	6.6	10.3	9.1	11.3	10.7	10.2	8.0	9.3	11.2	7.3	10.7	10.8	12.9	17.9
4. Air Force	29.5	29.2	31.5	30.3	27.4	30.4	28.0	29.7	30.9	35.2	26.9	29.5	30.5	33.3	28.3	16.4
5. Coast Guard	4.0	4.7	2.0	4.6	1.4	4.5	4.0	2.8	7.4	4.9	3.8	4.2	4.6	1.3	3.5	10.4
6. Uncertain	15.8	14.7	19.6	16.2	14.8	14.5	18.6	15.2	15.1	15.9	15.0	16.0	13.6	17.6	16.9	19.4
Item 730 N(Wtd) ★	2491	1787	603	1725	485	550	607	1023	311	927	1408	833	719	306	480	67
C33: Do you expect to be an officer?																
1. No	18.3	16.2	23.5	18.1	17.2	15.2	24.1	17.0	16.8	10.3	22.4	18.5	17.1	17.3	18.8	20.0
2. Uncertain	44.3	44.0	46.2	46.3	38.7	48.7	45.7	41.4	43.4	33.0	52.1	38.3	47.1	52.4	46.9	46.2
3. Yes	37.4	39.8	30.3	35.6	44.2	36.0	30.3	41.5	39.5	56.7	25.5	43.2	35.8	30.3	34.3	35.4
Item 740 N(Wtd) ★	2499	1795	604	1727	489	558	598	1034	309	923	1418	840	712	307	490	65
C34: Do you expect to have a career in the Armed Forces?																
1. No	29.1	29.7	26.0	30.2	23.2	27.7	35.0	26.2	29.6	29.4	28.2	26.8	27.9	29.4	33.9	26.6
2. Uncertain	50.0	51.0	47.8	53.5	41.5	52.1	49.2	48.5	52.9	49.0	51.4	48.0	54.5	49.5	49.1	50.0
3. Yes	21.0	19.2	26.1	16.4	35.2	20.2	15.9	25.3	17.5	21.6	20.4	25.1	17.5	21.1	17.0	25.0
Item 750 N(Wtd) ★	2496	1790	605	1726	491	555	597	1030	314	916	1419	837	714	313	487	64
The following questions are about CIGARETTE SMOKING.																
B01: Have you ever smoked cigarettes?																
1. Never	24.7	25.6	24.4	24.6	28.5	23.7	23.2	24.1	31.3	30.7	19.7	48.9	13.2	13.8	8.2	5.5
2. Once or twice	27.1	29.3	25.1	26.4	32.0	24.3	26.5	28.1	30.8	30.1	24.3	33.6	31.5	24.4	13.9	10.2
3. Occasionally but not regularly	16.2	15.2	17.2	16.3	15.4	14.2	16.7	18.0	14.4	16.6	15.8	10.0	22.8	20.6	14.9	11.3
4. Regularly in the past	9.1	8.8	9.3	9.2	7.9	9.7	9.3	8.8	8.3	8.2	9.9	3.4	10.2	12.0	14.6	18.8
5. Regularly now	22.8	21.1	24.0	23.5	16.3	28.0	24.3	20.9	15.2	14.4	30.2	4.1	22.3	29.2	48.4	54.3
Item 760 N(Wtd)	18465	8628	9110	14660	2005	4486	5308	6136	2535	8714	8260	6459	5157	2278	3839	293
B02: How frequently have you smoked cigarettes during the past 30 days?																
1. Not at all - incl. (1) in B01	63.3	65.5	61.9	63.0	68.5	59.4	61.0	64.3	72.7	72.6	55.4	88.5	59.9	52.9	35.3	31.2
2. Less than one cigarette per day	9.2	8.6	9.8	9.2	9.3	8.1	10.4	9.3	8.2	9.1	9.4	5.8	11.8	12.2	9.6	6.1
3. One to five cigarettes per day	8.8	7.0	10.2	8.0	12.6	8.9	8.8	9.4	6.9	7.2	9.7	2.8	11.6	12.3	11.9	8.5
4. About one-half pack per day	9.0	8.1	9.7	9.1	7.1	10.8	9.5	8.7	5.7	5.8	11.6	1.7	9.1	11.6	18.7	17.6
5. About one pack per day	7.7	8.7	6.5	8.4	2.1	10.2	8.0	6.8	4.9	4.3	10.9	1.0	6.3	8.8	19.0	26.4
6. About one and one-half packs per day	1.7	1.8	1.6	1.9	.2	2.2	2.0	1.3	1.4	.8	2.5	.2	1.0	2.1	4.7	7.8
7. Two packs or more per day	.3	.4	.2	.3	.1	.5	.3	.2	.2	.2	.4	*	.2	.1	.8	2.4
Item 780 N(Wtd)	18440	8615	9101	14643	2005	4473	5301	6130	2536	8706	8252	6449	5152	2276	3835	295

* = less than .05 per cent.   ★ = excludes respondents for whom question was inappropriate.

QUESTIONNAIRE FORM 1-5 1978	TOTAL	SEX		RACE		REGION				4YR COLLEGE PLANS		ILLICIT DRUG USE: LIFETIME				
		M	F	White	Black	NE	NC	S	W	Yes	No	None	Mari-juana Only	Few Pills	More Pills	Any Heroin
Weighted No. of Cases:	18916	8779	9266	14847	2096	4607	5411	6292	2605	8844	8413	6595	5214	2304	3885	302
% of Weighted Total:	100.0	46.4	49.0	78.5	11.1	24.4	28.6	33.3	13.8	46.8	44.5	34.9	27.6	12.2	20.5	1.6

B03: Next we want to ask you about drinking alcoholic beverages, including beer, wine, and liquor.

Have you ever had any beer, wine, or liquor to drink?

	TOTAL	M	F	White	Black	NE	NC	S	W	Yes	No	None	Mari-juana Only	Few Pills	More Pills	Any Heroin
1. No	6.8	5.7	7.7	5.6	13.2	4.3	5.0	8.8	10.0	6.9	6.6	16.8	.8	2.3	.7	.8
2. Yes	93.2	94.3	92.3	94.4	86.9	95.7	95.0	91.2	90.0	93.1	93.4	83.2	99.2	97.7	99.3	99.2
Item 790 N(Wtd) ‡	14295	6714	7119	11504	1485	3501	4117	4715	1962	6846	6499	5062	4001	1803	2978	243

B04: On how many occasions have you had alcoholic beverages to drink...

B04A: ...in your lifetime?

	TOTAL	M	F	White	Black	NE	NC	S	W	Yes	No	None	Mari-juana Only	Few Pills	More Pills	Any Heroin
1. 0 occasions - incl. (1) in B03	6.9	5.6	8.1	5.7	14.5	4.3	5.0	9.3	10.2	7.0	6.8	17.1	1.0	2.4	.7	.7
2. 1-2	7.0	5.4	8.4	5.7	15.9	4.6	5.6	9.6	7.9	6.3	7.3	15.1	3.0	3.7	1.1	.7
3. 3-5	7.4	5.9	8.9	6.3	15.1	5.9	6.2	8.9	8.8	7.6	7.3	13.1	5.4	6.0	1.6	.7
4. 6-9	8.1	6.5	9.7	7.5	12.2	7.4	8.1	8.2	8.7	8.4	8.0	12.5	7.1	6.9	3.1	2.9
5. 10-19	12.2	10.0	14.3	12.2	13.0	12.8	11.7	12.1	12.5	12.9	11.7	14.8	14.1	12.0	6.2	4.3
6. 20-39	13.2	11.7	14.8	13.8	9.2	14.6	13.9	11.6	13.1	14.2	12.7	10.8	17.7	15.5	10.2	9.4
7. 40 or more	45.2	55.0	35.9	48.7	20.3	50.4	49.6	40.2	38.9	43.5	46.2	16.6	51.8	53.6	77.2	81.5
Item 810 N(Wtd)	17581	8227	8722	14218	1748	4312	5113	5713	2442	8487	7778	6167	4978	2149	3705	276

B04B: ...during the last 12 months?

	TOTAL	M	F	White	Black	NE	NC	S	W	Yes	No	None	Mari-juana Only	Few Pills	More Pills	Any Heroin
1. 0 occasions - incl. (1) in B03	12.3	10.0	14.3	10.0	27.4	7.5	9.0	16.8	17.2	12.4	12.0	27.6	4.4	5.4	2.1	2.5
2. 1-2	12.3	9.6	15.0	10.6	24.3	10.8	11.1	13.6	14.4	12.0	12.6	21.8	8.7	9.8	3.5	3.9
3. 3-5	11.4	9.2	13.4	10.7	16.6	10.9	10.4	12.0	13.0	11.6	11.3	15.5	11.4	10.0	5.7	6.4
4. 6-9	11.6	10.4	12.7	11.8	9.9	12.5	11.6	11.1	10.9	12.2	11.1	12.0	13.5	13.1	7.7	7.5
5. 10-19	16.3	16.5	16.2	17.4	9.7	17.6	17.7	14.4	15.3	17.1	15.8	11.3	21.6	19.8	15.6	11.7
6. 20-39	14.7	14.9	14.5	16.1	6.3	16.4	16.0	13.0	13.0	15.4	14.1	6.7	18.9	17.4	20.6	17.1
7. 40 or more	21.5	29.3	14.0	23.5	5.9	24.4	24.2	19.1	16.2	19.4	23.0	5.2	21.5	24.4	44.9	51.2
Item 820 N(Wtd)	17508	8190	8692	14152	1746	4308	5086	5691	2423	8447	7742	6126	4956	2149	3696	281

B04C: ...during the last 30 days?

	TOTAL	M	F	White	Black	NE	NC	S	W	Yes	No	None	Mari-juana Only	Few Pills	More Pills	Any Heroin
1. 0 occasions - incl. (1) in B03	27.9	22.5	32.9	24.4	53.0	22.0	22.8	33.0	36.9	28.5	27.3	52.4	17.7	17.5	8.9	8.8
2. 1-2	21.8	18.9	24.7	21.3	25.1	21.9	21.6	21.8	22.0	22.8	20.8	24.8	24.8	21.8	13.7	9.9
3. 3-5	18.9	20.2	17.7	20.5	9.7	20.7	20.2	16.9	17.4	20.4	17.6	12.1	24.5	23.3	19.9	14.1
4. 6-9	14.4	16.3	12.4	15.6	5.5	16.3	15.8	12.9	11.3	14.3	14.4	6.2	17.2	18.9	21.0	15.8
5. 10-19	11.4	13.8	9.1	12.2	4.9	12.8	12.6	10.4	8.6	9.9	12.7	3.3	11.5	12.5	22.8	30.6
6. 20-39	3.5	4.7	2.3	3.8	.7	3.9	4.2	3.0	2.1	2.6	4.3	.7	2.7	3.7	8.4	9.9
7. 40 or more	2.3	3.6	.9	2.3	1.1	2.4	2.8	2.0	1.6	1.5	3.0	.5	1.7	2.2	5.3	11.3
Item 830 N(Wtd)	17543	8222	8682	14192	1740	4318	5099	5699	2427	8477	7738	6102	4966	2165	3728	284

B05: On the occasions that you drink alcoholic beverages, how often do you drink enough to feel pretty high?

	TOTAL	M	F	White	Black	NE	NC	S	W	Yes	No	None	Mari-juana Only	Few Pills	More Pills	Any Heroin
1. On none of the occasions	23.6	18.7	28.1	20.9	41.6	22.2	20.5	25.5	28.6	20.3	28.6	52.0	13.5	14.2	6.1	2.9
2. On few of the occasions	32.1	29.3	34.6	31.4	35.9	31.9	32.3	33.1	30.9	32.5	31.6	30.4	38.0	35.7	25.0	21.9
3. On about half of the occasions	17.8	19.4	16.4	19.2	10.2	18.3	19.3	16.8	16.1	18.4	17.4	8.8	21.0	21.0	23.9	17.7
4. On most of the occasions	17.4	21.2	14.0	19.1	7.0	18.4	18.9	15.7	15.5	18.2	16.7	5.9	18.6	20.9	28.5	28.1
5. On nearly all of the occasions	9.1	11.4	6.9	9.4	5.3	9.2	9.0	8.9	8.9	10.6	7.6	2.9	8.9	8.2	16.5	29.4
Item 840 N(Wtd) ★‡	13152	6316	6836	10938	1420	3586	4119	3890	1990	5825	6796	4168	4136	1829	3050	238

B06: Think back over the LAST TWO WEEKS. How many times have you had five or more drinks in a row? (A "drink" is a glass of wine, a bottle of beer, a shot glass of liquor, or a mixed drink.)

	TOTAL	M	F	White	Black	NE	NC	S	W	Yes	No	None	Mari-juana Only	Few Pills	More Pills	Any Heroin
1. None - incl. (1) in B03	59.7	48.6	70.4	57.1	80.7	56.5	54.7	63.6	66.7	64.1	55.7	83.9	54.7	51.5	33.3	24.1
2. Once	12.5	13.8	11.4	13.5	7.0	13.4	13.4	12.0	10.2	13.1	11.9	7.5	16.3	15.8	14.2	8.9
3. Twice	10.2	12.8	7.9	10.7	5.9	11.4	11.1	8.9	9.6	9.0	11.5	4.4	12.3	13.0	15.2	14.2
4. Three to five times	12.0	16.3	7.8	13.0	4.2	12.7	14.5	10.5	9.5	10.0	13.8	3.4	12.2	14.4	24.1	22.8
5. Six to nine times	3.3	5.0	1.7	3.6	1.1	3.7	4.1	2.7	2.3	2.4	4.2	0.6	2.6	3.1	8.4	14.6
6. Ten or more times	2.2	3.6	0.9	2.2	1.1	2.3	2.2	2.3	1.7	1.3	3.0	0.3	1.8	2.2	4.9	15.5
Item 850 N(Wtd)	17512	8171	8720	14176	1735	4308	5086	5575	2424	8469	7713	6157	4924	2163	3689	274

★ = excludes respondents for whom question was inappropriate.   ‡ This question appeared in Forms 2 through 5 only.

QUESTIONNAIRE FORM 1-5 1978	TOTAL	SEX		RACE		REGION				4YR COLLEGE PLANS		ILLICIT DRUG USE: LIFETIME				
		M	F	White	Black	NE	NC	S	W	Yes	No	None	Mari-juana Only	Few Pills	More Pills	Any Her-oin
Weighted No. of Cases:	18916	8779	9266	14847	2096	4607	5411	6292	2605	8844	8413	6595	5214	2304	3885	302
% of Weighted Total:	100.0	46.4	49.0	78.5	11.1	24.4	28.6	33.3	13.8	46.8	44.5	34.9	27.6	12.2	20.5	1.6

The next major section of this questionnaire deals with various other drugs. There is a lot of talk these days about this subject, but very little accurate information. Therefore, we still have a lot to learn about the actual experiences and attitudes of people your age.

We hope that you can answer all questions; but if you find one which you feel you cannot answer honestly, we would prefer that you leave it blank.

Remember that your answers will be kept strictly confidential: they are never connected with your name or your class.

B07: On how many occasions (if any) have you used marijuana (grass, pot) or hashish (hash, hash oil)...

B07A: ...in your lifetime?

	TOTAL	M	F	White	Black	NE	NC	S	W	Yes	No	None	Mari-juana Only	Few Pills	More Pills	Any Her-oin
1. 0 occasions	40.8	35.6	46.1	39.8	49.6	33.3	39.4	47.6	41.0	44.5	38.6	100.0	-	22.1	7.7	2.1
2. 1-2	9.1	9.1	9.1	8.5	12.7	7.6	9.4	9.4	10.0	9.0	9.1	-	25.8	8.6	2.7	1.1
3. 3-5	6.1	6.3	6.0	6.2	5.6	5.8	6.5	6.0	6.4	6.5	5.9	-	16.5	6.9	2.5	2.1
4. 6-9	4.8	4.8	4.7	4.8	4.8	4.6	5.6	4.4	4.4	5.0	4.4	-	12.2	5.3	2.8	2.8
5. 10-19	6.4	6.3	6.6	6.6	5.8	6.7	7.0	6.0	5.8	6.4	6.6	-	14.1	10.3	5.1	2.8
6. 20-39	6.2	5.6	6.7	6.5	4.9	7.0	6.2	5.3	6.5	6.2	6.3	-	11.2	10.3	7.7	3.5
7. 40 or more	26.6	32.3	20.8	27.6	16.7	35.1	26.0	21.3	25.8	22.4	29.0	-	20.1	36.5	71.5	85.6
Item 860 N(Wtd)	18090	8459	8992	14512	1906	4417	5227	5966	2480	8640	8076	6595	5157	2232	3771	285

B07B: ...during the last 12 months?

	TOTAL	M	F	White	Black	NE	NC	S	W	Yes	No	None	Mari-juana Only	Few Pills	More Pills	Any Her-oin
1. 0 occasions	49.8	44.1	55.7	48.4	61.1	40.8	48.4	57.3	50.9	52.9	48.4	100.0	23.1	31.8	12.3	6.4
2. 1-2	8.9	9.1	8.6	8.8	9.0	7.9	9.6	8.2	10.5	9.2	8.5	-	22.8	10.2	4.8	4.3
3. 3-5	6.5	6.8	6.1	6.4	6.9	6.8	7.0	5.7	6.8	6.7	6.2	-	15.2	8.0	5.3	2.5
4. 6-9	5.4	5.4	5.5	5.6	4.2	5.8	5.9	5.1	4.6	5.6	5.4	-	11.2	8.1	5.6	5.0
5. 10-19	6.1	6.0	6.3	6.5	4.2	8.2	6.2	4.7	5.4	6.1	6.1	-	10.3	11.0	8.0	6.7
6. 20-39	5.8	5.9	5.8	5.9	5.5	7.3	5.3	5.2	5.8	5.5	5.9	-	7.4	9.6	10.9	14.2
7. 40 or more	17.5	22.8	12.0	18.3	9.1	23.2	17.6	13.8	16.1	14.2	19.5	-	9.9	21.2	53.0	61.0
Item 870 N(Wtd)	18011	8421	8957	14477	1888	4409	5212	5921	2469	8628	8026	6595	5108	2217	3761	282

B07C: ...during the last 30 days?

	TOTAL	M	F	White	Black	NE	NC	S	W	Yes	No	None	Mari-juana Only	Few Pills	More Pills	Any Her-oin
1. 0 occasions	62.9	57.4	68.7	62.1	71.4	53.3	62.2	69.4	65.7	66.8	60.8	100.0	53.9	48.5	22.7	13.2
2. 1-2	9.2	9.5	8.7	9.2	8.8	10.1	9.8	7.9	8.9	9.4	8.8	-	20.3	12.0	8.5	5.6
3. 3-5	6.0	6.0	6.0	6.2	4.8	7.2	6.1	5.1	5.7	5.9	6.0	-	9.8	10.9	8.4	6.3
4. 6-9	4.6	5.1	4.1	4.6	4.4	5.8	4.3	3.8	4.7	4.4	4.5	-	6.2	7.4	8.3	8.0
5. 10-19	6.7	7.9	5.4	6.8	5.7	9.2	6.1	5.2	6.8	6.1	7.1	-	6.1	10.3	16.1	18.8
6. 20-39	5.4	6.7	4.1	5.7	2.7	7.0	6.1	4.1	4.2	4.1	6.2	-	2.1	6.4	17.9	17.0
7. 40 or more	5.3	7.4	3.0	5.4	2.2	7.4	5.3	4.3	4.0	3.3	6.5	-	1.5	4.5	18.2	31.6
Item 880 N(Wtd)	18020	8431	8958	14489	1886	4404	5215	5938	2463	8630	8037	6595	5099	2224	3771	288

B08: On how many occasions (if any) have you used LSD ("acid")...

B08A: ...during your lifetime?

	TOTAL	M	F	White	Black	NE	NC	S	W	Yes	No	None	Mari-juana Only	Few Pills	More Pills	Any Her-oin
1. 0 occasions	90.3	88.4	92.5	89.7	97.3	88.3	88.7	93.6	89.6	93.0	88.6	100.0	100.0	92.6	63.3	28.8
2. 1-2	4.4	5.1	3.8	4.8	1.8	5.4	4.7	3.4	4.7	3.3	5.4	-	-	7.4	15.5	19.2
3. 3-5	2.0	2.5	1.4	2.2	.4	2.5	2.2	1.3	2.3	1.4	2.3	-	-	-	8.9	10.3
4. 6-9	1.2	1.5	.9	1.3	.1	1.3	1.6	.7	1.4	.9	1.3	-	-	-	4.9	12.3
5. 10-19	1.1	1.4	.7	1.1	.1	1.3	1.4	.6	1.1	.7	1.4	-	-	-	4.3	10.6
6. 20-39	.5	.5	.4	.6	-	.6	.6	.3	.6	.4	.5	-	-	-	1.8	8.6
7. 40 or more	.5	.5	.3	.4	.2	.6	.7	.2	.4	.3	.5	-	-	-	1.4	10.6
Item 890 N(Wtd)	18346	8611	9097	14651	2009	4466	5294	6073	2513	8706	8247	6560	5191	2272	3817	292

QUESTIONNAIRE FORM 1-5 1978	TOTAL	SEX		RACE		REGION				4YR COLLEGE PLANS		ILLICIT DRUG USE: LIFETIME				
		M	F	White	Black	NE	NC	S	W	Yes	No	None	Mari-juana Only	Few Pills	More Pills	Any Her-oin
Weighted No. of Cases:	18916	8779	9266	14847	2096	4607	5411	6292	2605	8844	8413	6595	5214	2304	3885	302
% of Weighted Total:	100.0	46.4	49.0	78.5	11.1	24.4	28.6	33.3	13.8	46.8	44.5	34.9	27.6	12.2	20.5	1.6

B08B: ...during the last 12 months?

	TOTAL	M	F	White	Black	NE	NC	S	W	Yes	No	None	Mari-juana Only	Few Pills	More Pills	Any Her-oin
1. 0 occasions	93.7	92.2	95.5	93.3	98.6	92.0	92.1	96.3	94.2	95.4	92.8	100.0	100.0	96.6	76.1	45.6
2. 1-2	3.7	4.5	2.9	4.1	.8	4.5	4.4	2.4	4.0	2.7	4.4	-	-	3.4	14.3	19.7
3. 3-5	1.2	1.6	.8	1.2	.2	1.7	1.7	.6	.9	.8	1.5	-	-	-	5.0	12.2
4. 6-9	.7	.9	.4	.7	.1	.8	.9	.6	.4	.5	.7	-	-	-	2.7	8.8
5. 10-19	.4	.6	.2	.4	.1	.6	.7	.1	.3	.4	.5	-	-	-	1.4	8.5
6. 20-39	.1	.1	.1	.1	.2	.1	.3	.1	*	.1	.1	-	-	-	.4	4.1
7. 40 or more	.1	.1	*	*	-	.1	*	*	.1	*	.1	-	-	-	.2	1.0
Item 900 N(Wtd)	18341	8610	9092	14642	2011	4462	5289	6076	2514	8707	8244	6560	5194	2275	3803	294

B08C: ...during the last 30 days?

	TOTAL	M	F	White	Black	NE	NC	S	W	Yes	No	None	Mari-juana Only	Few Pills	More Pills	Any Her-oin
1. 0 occasions	97.9	97.3	98.6	97.9	99.6	97.1	97.3	98.9	98.3	98.6	97.5	100.0	100.0	99.1	92.7	71.1
2. 1-2	1.4	1.9	.9	1.5	.1	2.2	1.6	.8	1.3	1.0	1.8	-	-	.9	5.3	14.6
3. 3-5	.4	.5	.3	.4	.1	.4	.7	.2	.2	.3	.4	-	-	-	1.4	7.1
4. 6-9	.2	.2	.1	.1	*	.2	.3	.1	.1	.2	.2	-	-	-	.4	4.1
5. 10-19	.1	.1	.1	*	.1	.1	.1	*	*	*	*	-	-	-	.1	2.4
6. 20-39	*	*	-	*	-	*	-	*	.1	-	*	-	-	-	.1	.3
7. 40 or more	*	*	-	-	-	*	-	*	*	-	*	-	-	-	*	.3
Item 910 N(Wtd)	18336	8605	9095	14641	2012	4461	5286	6072	2517	8706	8243	6561	5195	2270	3802	294

B09: On how many occasions (if any) have you used psychedelics other than LSD (like mescaline, peyote, psilocybin, PCP)...

B09A: ...in your lifetime?

	TOTAL	M	F	White	Black	NE	NC	S	W	Yes	No	None	Mari-juana Only	Few Pills	More Pills	Any Her-oin
1. 0 occasions	88.4	86.3	90.7	87.6	97.4	84.8	87.5	92.2	87.4	91.0	86.8	100.0	100.0	88.3	56.8	27.2
2. 1-2	5.0	5.8	4.1	5.4	1.2	6.5	5.0	3.4	6.0	4.2	5.4	-	-	11.7	15.8	13.9
3. 3-5	2.5	3.2	1.9	2.8	.6	3.2	2.9	1.7	2.7	1.9	3.0	-	-	-	11.0	15.3
4. 6-9	1.4	1.7	1.1	1.4	.5	1.7	1.4	1.1	1.8	1.2	1.5	-	-	-	5.9	11.6
5. 10-19	1.2	1.4	.9	1.3	.2	1.5	1.3	.9	1.1	.9	1.4	-	-	-	4.9	10.5
6. 20-39	.7	.7	.7	.7	-	1.2	.9	.3	.6	.4	.9	-	-	-	3.0	7.1
7. 40 or more	.8	.9	.5	.8	.3	1.2	1.0	.4	.4	.4	1.0	-	-	-	2.7	13.9
Item 920 N(Wtd)	18279	8574	9077	14605	1996	4438	5273	6060	2508	8703	8205	6548	5151	2269	3802	294

B09B: ...during the last 12 months?

	TOTAL	M	F	White	Black	NE	NC	S	W	Yes	No	None	Mari-juana Only	Few Pills	More Pills	Any Her-oin
1. 0 occasions	92.7	91.2	94.5	92.2	98.5	89.7	92.4	95.2	92.8	94.3	91.9	100.0	100.0	94.8	72.3	43.4
2. 1-2	3.9	4.6	3.1	4.2	.8	5.6	3.8	2.4	4.4	3.2	4.2	-	-	5.2	14.2	17.6
3. 3-5	1.7	2.1	1.2	1.8	.4	2.0	1.9	1.3	1.5	1.3	1.8	-	-	-	6.8	16.3
4. 6-9	.8	.9	.6	.8	.2	1.1	.9	.5	.7	.5	.9	-	-	-	3.1	9.2
5. 10-19	.6	.6	.4	.6	.1	1.0	.6	.4	.3	.4	.7	-	-	-	2.2	7.1
6. 20-39	.2	.3	.2	.3	.1	.5	.2	.1	.2	.1	.4	-	-	-	.9	2.7
7. 40 or more	.2	.2	.1	.2	-	.2	.2	.2	.1	.1	.2	-	-	-	.6	3.7
Item 930 N(Wtd)	18256	8564	9065	14589	1997	4435	5261	6054	2506	8700	8194	6548	5152	2269	3776	295

B09C: ...during the last 30 days?

	TOTAL	M	F	White	Black	NE	NC	S	W	Yes	No	None	Mari-juana Only	Few Pills	More Pills	Any Her-oin
1. 0 occasions	97.3	96.6	98.1	97.2	99.3	96.0	96.9	98.2	98.0	98.0	97.0	100.0	100.0	98.9	89.8	70.6
2. 1-2	1.9	2.4	1.3	2.0	.6	2.8	2.1	1.2	1.4	1.4	2.1	-	-	1.1	7.2	15.4
3. 3-5	.5	.6	.3	.5	-	.8	.4	.3	.3	.4	.4	-	-	-	1.7	7.5
4. 6-9	.2	.3	.2	.2	-	.3	.3	.2	.2	.2	.2	-	-	-	.8	4.4
5. 10-19	.1	.2	.1	.1	.1	.1	.3	*	*	*	.2	-	-	-	.5	1.7
6. 20-39	*	*	-	*	-	-	-	*	*	-	*	-	-	-	.1	.3
7. 40 or more	*	*	*	*	-	*	-	*	*	-	*	-	-	-	.1	.3
Item 940 N(Wtd)	18246	8558	9063	14581	1997	4430	5260	6053	2504	8699	8187	6548	5153	2269	3768	293

B10: On how many occasions (if any) have you use cocaine (sometimes called "coke")...

* = less than .05 per cent.

QUESTIONNAIRE FORM 1-5 1978	TOTAL	SEX		RACE		REGION				4YR COLLEGE PLANS		ILLICIT DRUG USE: LIFETIME				
		M	F	White	Black	NE	NC	S	W	Yes	No	None	Mari- juana Only	Few Pills	More Pills	Any Her- oin
Weighted No. of Cases:	18916	8779	9266	14847	2096	4607	5411	6292	2605	8844	8413	6595	5214	2304	3885	302
% of Weighted Total:	100.0	46.4	49.0	78.5	11.1	24.4	28.6	33.3	13.8	46.8	44.5	34.9	27.6	12.2	20.5	1.6
B10A: ...in your lifetime?																
1. 0 occasions	87.1	84.4	90.1	87.1	91.3	84.0	87.8	89.5	85.7	89.6	85.8	100.0	100.0	81.7	55.6	18.3
2. 1-2	6.7	8.0	5.3	6.6	5.3	8.3	6.3	5.9	6.6	5.4	7.5	-	-	18.3	19.3	23.1
3. 3-5	2.5	2.9	2.0	2.5	1.4	3.3	2.3	1.9	2.4	2.0	2.7	-	-	-	10.7	14.6
4. 6-9	1.4	1.7	1.1	1.3	1.2	1.8	1.3	.9	2.0	1.2	1.5	-	-	-	5.7	11.9
5. 10-19	1.0	1.4	.7	1.0	.4	1.2	1.1	.7	1.5	.9	1.0	-	-	-	4.2	9.5
6. 20-39	.6	.7	.4	.6	.3	.7	.5	.5	.8	.4	.6	-	-	-	2.1	8.8
7. 40 or more	.7	1.0	.5	.8	.1	.8	.6	.7	1.1	.5	.8	-	-	-	2.5	13.9
Item 950 N(Wtd)	18230	8588	9059	14608	1987	4413	5278	6040	2499	8700	8198	6532	5135	2258	3801	295
B10B: ...during the last 12 months?																
1. 0 occasions	91.0	88.6	93.5	90.7	95.4	88.2	91.5	93.2	89.4	92.3	90.5	100.0	100.0	91.2	66.4	39.9
2. 1-2	5.1	6.3	3.7	5.2	3.2	6.7	4.8	3.9	5.7	4.3	5.4	-	-	8.8	17.7	19.3
3. 3-5	1.7	2.2	1.3	1.8	.9	2.3	1.7	1.3	1.9	1.5	1.9	-	-	-	7.4	11.1
4. 6-9	.9	1.2	.6	.9	.4	1.1	.8	.7	1.3	.9	.8	-	-	-	3.7	10.1
5. 10-19	.7	1.0	.4	.8	.1	1.0	.7	.6	.7	.5	.9	-	-	-	2.7	10.5
6. 20-39	.3	.3	.3	.3	.1	.5	.2	.2	.5	.2	.4	-	-	-	1.3	2.7
7. 40 or more	.3	.3	.2	.3	-	.3	.2	.2	.5	.3	.2	-	-	-	.8	6.4
Item 960 N(Wtd)	18208	8577	9049	14596	1986	4404	5275	6038	2491	8696	8186	6535	5136	2250	3783	296
B10C: ...during the last 30 days?																
1. 0 occasions	96.1	95.0	97.4	96.1	98.5	94.3	96.6	97.3	95.1	96.7	96.0	100.0	100.0	97.3	85.3	66.3
2. 1-2	2.5	3.1	1.7	2.5	1.2	3.8	2.2	1.6	3.1	2.2	2.6	-	-	2.7	9.4	13.9
3. 3-5	.8	1.0	.5	.7	.2	1.0	.6	.6	.9	.6	.7	-	-	-	3.1	7.1
4. 6-9	.4	.5	.2	.3	-	.6	.3	.3	.3	.3	.4	-	-	-	1.3	5.8
5. 10-19	.2	.3	.1	.2	.1	.2	.1	.1	.3	.1	.2	-	-	-	.6	3.4
6. 20-39	.1	.1	*	.1	-	*	.1	*	.2	.1	*	-	-	-	.2	.7
7. 40 or more	.1	.1	*	*	-	.1	.1	*	.1	*	*	-	-	-	.1	2.4
Item 970 N(Wtd)	18206	8569	9052	14593	1987	4403	5274	6037	2491	8692	8189	6533	5137	2252	3781	294
B11: Amphetamines are sometimes prescribed by doctors to help people lose weight or to give people more energy. They are sometimes called uppers, ups, speed, bennies, dexies, pep pills, and diet pills. On how many occasions (if any) have you taken amphetamines on your own--that is, without a doctor telling you to take them...																
B11A: ...in your lifetime?																
1. 0 occasions	77.1	77.7	76.8	75.2	91.7	74.5	75.8	80.9	75.3	81.6	73.3	100.0	100.0	60.0	20.6	16.6
2. 1-2	7.1	6.2	7.8	7.6	4.1	7.5	6.7	6.6	8.2	6.2	7.7	-	-	40.0	9.5	7.4
3. 3-5	4.1	4.3	3.9	4.3	1.6	4.0	4.5	3.6	4.3	3.8	4.3	-	-	-	18.5	11.5
4. 6-9	2.8	3.2	2.4	3.0	.7	3.5	2.7	2.5	2.6	2.3	3.3	-	-	-	12.8	8.1
5. 10-19	3.0	3.0	3.1	3.4	.8	3.5	3.3	2.5	3.0	2.4	3.6	-	-	-	13.6	11.8
6. 20-39	2.4	2.2	2.6	2.6	.6	2.9	2.9	1.6	2.7	1.6	3.1	-	-	-	10.7	12.8
7. 40 or more	3.5	3.3	3.6	3.9	.4	4.2	4.2	2.2	3.7	2.1	4.7	-	-	-	14.2	31.8
Item 980 N(Wtd)	18174	8560	9063	14566	2007	4401	5252	6026	2494	8674	8169	6505	5087	2253	3792	296
B11B: ...during the last 12 months?																
1. 0 occasions	82.9	83.1	82.9	81.3	96.0	80.4	81.8	86.0	82.2	86.3	80.0	100.0	100.0	80.5	34.8	27.7
2. 1-2	6.5	6.3	6.6	7.1	1.7	6.6	6.4	5.9	7.9	5.7	7.1	-	-	19.5	18.6	14.5
3. 3-5	3.4	3.7	3.2	3.7	.9	3.9	3.3	3.3	2.9	3.1	3.8	-	-	-	15.5	11.5
4. 6-9	2.3	2.5	2.1	2.5	.7	3.0	2.2	1.8	2.4	1.7	2.7	-	-	-	10.1	12.5
5. 10-19	2.2	2.2	2.2	2.4	.3	2.7	3.0	1.3	1.9	1.4	3.0	-	-	-	9.8	11.5
6. 20-39	1.3	1.2	1.5	1.5	.2	1.8	1.7	.8	1.1	.8	1.8	-	-	-	5.7	9.5
7. 40 or more	1.3	1.1	1.5	1.4	.1	1.6	1.6	.9	1.5	1.1	1.6	-	-	-	5.5	12.2
Item 990 N(Wtd)	18129	8535	9046	14538	2001	4397	5244	6010	2478	8663	8147	6506	5089	2231	3763	296

* = less than .05 per cent.

QUESTIONNAIRE FORM 1-5 1978	TOTAL	SEX		RACE		REGION				4YR COLLEGE PLANS		ILLICIT DRUG USE: LIFETIME				
		M	F	White	Black	NE	NC	S	W	Yes	No	None	Mari-juana Only	Few Pills	More Pills	Any Her-oin
Weighted No. of Cases:	18916	8779	9266	14847	2096	4607	5411	6292	2605	8844	8413	6595	5214	2304	3885	302
% of Weighted Total:	100.0	46.4	49.0	78.5	11.1	24.4	28.6	33.3	13.8	46.8	44.5	34.9	27.6	12.2	20.5	1.6
B11C: ...during the last 30 days?																
1. 0 occasions	91.3	91.4	91.4	90.6	97.8	89.3	90.4	93.1	92.3	93.5	89.4	100.0	100.0	95.5	64.4	51.9
2. 1-2	4.3	4.4	4.0	4.5	1.2	4.7	4.5	3.6	4.4	3.5	4.8	-	-	4.5	16.6	15.6
3. 3-5	1.9	2.1	1.7	2.1	.6	2.7	1.9	1.7	1.2	1.3	2.5	-	-	-	8.4	12.9
4. 6-9	1.2	1.1	1.3	1.4	.3	1.5	1.5	.9	1.0	.8	1.6	-	-	-	5.4	6.8
5. 10-19	.8	.7	.9	.9	.2	1.1	1.0	.5	.7	.5	1.1	-	-	-	3.1	10.8
6. 20-39	.3	.2	.4	.4	.1	.3	.5	.2	.2	.2	.4	-	-	-	1.5	.7
7. 40 or more	.2	.1	.2	.2	.1	.3	.1	*	.3	.1	.2	-	-	-	.7	1.7
Item 1000 N(Wtd)	18115	8528	9041	14529	1999	4391	5242	6002	2480	8657	8140	6505	5090	2223	3757	295
B12: On how many occasions (if any) have you used quaaludes (quads, soapers, methaqualone) on your own--that is, without a doctor telling you to take them...																
B12A: ...in your lifetime?																
1. 0 occasions	92.1	90.9	93.4	91.6	97.7	90.8	93.6	91.1	93.6	93.6	91.2	100.0	100.0	94.2	70.4	37.3
2. 1-2	3.5	3.7	3.2	3.8	1.5	4.3	3.0	3.5	3.0	3.0	3.8	-	-	5.8	11.9	17.3
3. 3-5	1.5	1.9	1.3	1.7	.2	1.9	1.1	1.8	1.2	1.4	1.6	-	-	-	6.8	7.5
4. 6-9	1.0	1.3	.7	1.0	.1	1.3	.6	1.3	.6	.7	1.1	-	-	-	3.9	11.2
5. 10-19	.8	.9	.7	.8	.2	.7	.8	.8	.8	.6	.9	-	-	-	2.9	9.8
6. 20-39	.5	.6	.4	.5	.1	.5	.3	.7	.4	.3	.7	-	-	-	1.9	6.1
7. 40 or more	.6	.8	.4	.6	.3	.4	.6	.8	.4	.5	.7	-	-	-	2.1	10.8
Item 1010 N(Wtd)	18159	8565	9061	14578	1993	4395	5248	6019	2497	8664	8176	6490	5098	2263	3770	295
B12B: ...during the last 12 months?																
1. 0 occasions	95.1	94.0	96.1	94.8	98.7	94.2	96.2	94.4	95.8	95.7	94.9	100.0	100.0	97.4	81.0	58.8
2. 1-2	2.5	3.1	2.0	2.7	.9	2.8	2.2	2.6	2.4	2.3	2.5	-	-	2.6	9.6	12.6
3. 3-5	1.1	1.3	.8	1.1	.2	1.5	.5	1.3	.7	1.0	1.0	-	-	-	4.4	8.5
4. 6-9	.6	.8	.4	.6	.1	.8	.3	.7	.5	.4	.7	-	-	-	2.2	8.8
5. 10-19	.4	.4	.3	.3	.1	.4	.3	.4	.4	.3	.4	-	-	-	1.5	2.0
6. 20-39	.2	.2	.1	.2	-	.1	.1	.3	.2	.1	.2	-	-	-	.6	3.7
7. 40 or more	.2	.3	.1	.2	.2	.2	.3	.2	.1	.1	.3	-	-	-	.6	5.4
Item 1020 N(Wtd)	18150	8563	9057	14575	1992	4388	5251	6014	2497	8663	8169	6490	5099	2261	3762	294
B12C: ...during the last 30 days?																
1. 0 occasions	98.1	97.7	98.6	98.1	99.4	97.5	98.7	97.9	98.6	98.6	97.9	100.0	100.0	99.3	93.2	76.1
2. 1-2	1.2	1.4	.9	1.2	.3	1.6	.8	1.3	1.0	1.0	1.2	-	-	.7	4.4	10.9
3. 3-5	.3	.4	.2	.3	.3	.5	.2	.3	.3	.2	.3	-	-	-	1.0	7.2
4. 6-9	.2	.3	.1	.2	-	.3	.2	.3	.1	.1	.3	-	-	-	.9	3.4
5. 10-19	.1	.1	.1	.1	-	.1	.1	.1	-	*	.1	-	-	-	.3	2.0
6. 20-39	*	*	-	*	-	-	*	*	*	*	*	-	-	-	*	-
7. 40 or more	*	.1	*	*	.1	-	.1	*	*	.1	*	-	-	-	.1	.7
Item 1030 N(Wtd)	18149	8560	9056	14569	1994	4389	5249	6015	2496	8660	8174	6490	5100	2260	3760	293
B13: Barbiturates are sometimes prescribed by doctors to help people relax or get to sleep. They are sometimes called downs, downers, goofballs, yellows, reds, blues, rainbows. On how many occasions (if any) have you taken barbiturates on your own--that is, without a doctor telling you to take them...																
B13A: ...in your lifetime?																
1. 0 occasions	86.3	85.7	87.0	85.4	93.5	84.5	86.5	86.9	87.4	89.0	84.0	100.0	100.0	83.2	50.0	21.8
2. 1-2	5.3	5.3	5.3	5.6	3.5	5.8	5.1	5.3	5.3	4.4	6.1	-	-	16.8	14.4	16.6
3. 3-5	2.9	3.1	2.6	3.2	1.1	3.4	3.2	2.4	2.7	2.3	3.3	-	-	-	13.0	11.1
4. 6-9	1.7	1.8	1.6	1.9	.7	1.7	1.8	1.7	1.8	1.5	1.9	-	-	-	7.5	11.4
5. 10-19	1.5	1.4	1.5	1.6	.6	1.8	1.3	1.5	1.2	1.1	1.9	-	-	-	6.2	12.1
6. 20-39	1.1	1.2	1.0	1.2	.3	1.5	1.0	1.2	.6	.9	1.2	-	-	-	4.8	8.3
7. 40 or more	1.2	1.4	1.0	1.2	.4	1.3	1.2	1.1	1.1	.7	1.5	-	-	-	4.2	18.7
Item 1040 N(Wtd)	18133	8572	9043	14576	1989	4387	5250	6010	2486	8685	8157	6492	5085	2248	3778	289

* = less than .05 per cent.

QUESTIONNAIRE FORM 1-5 1978	TOTAL	SEX		RACE		REGION				4YR COLLEGE PLANS		ILLICIT DRUG USE: LIFETIME				
		M	F	White	Black	NE	NC	S	W	Yes	No	None	Mari-juana Only	Few Pills	More Pills	Any Her-oin
Weighted No. of Cases:	18916	8779	9266	14847	2096	4607	5411	6292	2605	8844	8413	6595	5214	2304	3885	302
% of Weighted Total:	100.0	46.4	49.0	78.5	11.1	24.4	28.6	33.3	13.8	46.8	44.5	34.9	27.6	12.2	20.5	1.6

B13B: ...during the last 12 months?

	TOTAL	M	F	White	Black	NE	NC	S	W	Yes	No	None	Mari-juana Only	Few Pills	More Pills	Any Her-oin
1. 0 occasions	91.9	91.6	92.3	91.3	97.1	90.4	92.1	92.2	93.4	93.2	90.9	100.0	100.0	94.6	68.3	44.9
2. 1-2	3.8	3.9	3.7	4.1	1.4	4.3	3.8	3.7	3.3	3.4	4.1	-	-	5.5	13.9	14.7
3. 3-5	1.8	1.8	1.7	2.0	.6	2.2	1.9	1.4	1.5	1.5	2.0	-	-	-	7.8	9.5
4. 6-9	1.1	1.3	.8	1.1	.5	1.2	1.0	1.2	.9	.9	1.2	-	-	-	4.3	11.9
5. 10-19	.8	.8	.8	.8	.2	1.2	.6	.8	.3	.7	.8	-	-	-	3.2	8.1
6. 20-39	.4	.4	.4	.4	.1	.4	.3	.5	.3	.2	.6	-	-	-	1.5	4.9
7. 40 or more	.3	.3	.3	.3	.2	.3	.3	.3	.3	.1	.5	-	-	-	1.0	6.3
Item 1050 N(Wtd)	18108	8559	9032	14563	1984	4380	5248	5996	2484	8680	8141	6492	5088	2239	3763	285

B13C: ...during the last 30 days?

	TOTAL	M	F	White	Black	NE	NC	S	W	Yes	No	None	Mari-juana Only	Few Pills	More Pills	Any Her-oin
1. 0 occasions	96.8	96.6	97.0	96.7	98.6	95.7	97.1	96.8	97.8	97.5	96.3	100.0	100.0	98.7	87.5	69.9
2. 1-2	1.8	1.8	1.7	1.9	.9	2.3	1.7	1.6	1.4	1.5	1.9	-	-	1.3	7.0	9.9
3. 3-5	.7	.7	.6	.7	.3	1.0	.5	.7	.4	.5	.7	-	-	-	2.6	7.1
4. 6-9	.4	.4	.4	.4	.1	.4	.5	.5	.1	.3	.5	-	-	-	1.6	6.7
5. 10-19	.2	.3	.2	.2	-	.4	.2	.3	.2	.1	.3	-	-	-	.9	3.9
6. 20-39	.1	.1	.1	.1	-	.1	*	.2	.1	.1	.1	-	-	-	.4	.7
7. 40 or more	*	*	.1	*	.2	*	.1	-	*	-	*	-	-	-	.1	1.8
Item 1060 N(Wtd)	18103	8563	9026	14559	1982	4382	5241	5994	2486	8678	8140	6492	5090	2236	3762	282

B14: Tranquilizers are sometimes prescribed by doctors to calm people down, quiet their nerves, or relax their muscles. Librium, Valium, and Miltown are all tranquilizers. On how many occasions (if any) have you taken tranquilizers on your own--that is, without a doctor telling you to take them...

B14A: ...in your lifetime?

	TOTAL	M	F	White	Black	NE	NC	S	W	Yes	No	None	Mari-juana Only	Few Pills	More Pills	Any Her-oin
1. 0 occasions	83.0	83.6	82.4	81.9	92.0	81.7	84.6	82.5	82.7	85.4	80.5	100.0	100.0	65.1	44.5	31.1
2. 1-2	7.7	6.9	8.5	8.1	4.4	8.3	6.8	7.7	8.4	6.8	8.6	-	-	34.9	14.9	14.2
3. 3-5	3.7	3.8	3.6	4.0	1.0	3.7	3.4	3.6	4.1	3.3	4.1	-	-	-	16.8	9.8
4. 6-9	1.9	1.8	2.0	2.0	1.0	2.1	1.9	2.0	1.6	1.6	2.2	-	-	-	8.7	8.4
5. 10-19	1.7	1.8	1.6	1.8	.9	1.7	1.4	2.0	1.5	1.5	1.9	-	-	-	7.0	14.9
6. 20-39	.9	.7	1.1	1.0	.2	1.2	.8	.9	.7	.7	1.2	-	-	-	3.9	6.8
7. 40 or more	1.1	1.3	.9	1.2	.6	1.2	1.0	1.2	1.1	.8	1.4	-	-	-	4.3	15.2
Item 1070 N(Wtd)	18123	8589	9032	14577	1987	4384	5253	6004	2482	8679	8164	6470	5084	2253	3778	296

B14B: ...during the last 12 months?

	TOTAL	M	F	White	Black	NE	NC	S	W	Yes	No	None	Mari-juana Only	Few Pills	More Pills	Any Her-oin
1. 0 occasions	90.1	90.3	89.9	89.3	96.1	89.0	91.2	89.5	91.1	91.4	88.9	100.0	100.0	87.1	63.9	51.4
2. 1-2	5.3	5.2	5.6	5.9	2.1	5.9	4.6	5.6	5.2	4.8	5.7	-	-	12.9	17.1	11.0
3. 3-5	2.1	2.0	2.1	2.3	.8	2.2	2.0	2.2	1.7	1.8	2.4	-	-	-	9.1	10.3
4. 6-9	1.0	1.0	1.0	1.1	.4	1.2	.8	1.3	.6	.9	1.1	-	-	-	4.2	10.3
5. 10-19	.8	.8	.8	.8	.3	.9	.7	.8	.7	.7	1.0	-	-	-	3.2	8.6
6. 20-39	.4	.3	.4	.4	.2	.4	.3	.4	.4	.3	.5	-	-	-	1.4	4.5
7. 40 or more	.3	.3	.2	.3	.1	.3	.3	.3	.2	.1	.4	-	-	-	1.1	3.8
Item 1080 N(Wtd)	18092	8574	9021	14558	1977	4374	5246	5995	2477	8673	8143	6472	5086	2230	3770	292

B14C: ...during the last 30 days?

	TOTAL	M	F	White	Black	NE	NC	S	W	Yes	No	None	Mari-juana Only	Few Pills	More Pills	Any Her-oin
1. 0 occasions	96.6	96.8	96.3	96.3	98.9	95.8	97.0	96.5	97.0	97.2	95.9	100.0	100.0	97.3	87.1	73.2
2. 1-2	2.1	1.8	2.4	2.3	.7	2.7	1.7	2.1	1.6	1.8	2.3	-	-	2.7	7.5	11.3
3. 3-5	.7	.6	.7	.7	.1	.6	.7	.6	.8	.5	.7	-	-	-	2.8	5.5
4. 6-9	.4	.5	.3	.4	.1	.4	.4	.5	.1	.3	.5	-	-	-	1.5	5.2
5. 10-19	.2	.2	.2	.2	.1	.3	.1	.3	.3	.1	.4	-	-	-	.9	4.5
6. 20-39	*	*	*	*	-	.1	-	*	*	-	.1	-	-	-	.1	.7
7. 40 or more	*	*	*	*	.1	*	.1	-	-	*	*	-	-	-	.1	-
Item 1090 N(Wtd)	18079	8564	9018	14550	1978	4374	5244	5989	2472	8672	8138	6471	5086	2222	3764	291

* = less than .05 per cent.

QUESTIONNAIRE FORM 1-5 1978	TOTAL	SEX		RACE		REGION				4YR COLLEGE PLANS		ILLICIT DRUG USE: LIFETIME				
		M	F	White	Black	NE	NC	S	W	Yes	No	None	Mari-juana Only	Few Pills	More Pills	Any Heroin
Weighted No. of Cases:	18916	8779	9266	14847	2096	4607	5411	6292	2605	8844	8413	6595	5214	2304	3885	302
% of Weighted Total:	100.0	46.4	49.0	78.5	11.1	24.4	28.6	33.3	13.8	46.8	44.5	34.9	27.6	12.2	20.5	1.6

B15: On how many occasions (if any) have you used heroin (smack, horse, skag)...

B15A: ...in your lifetime?

	TOTAL	M	F	White	Black	NE	NC	S	W	Yes	No	None	Mari-juana Only	Few Pills	More Pills	Any Heroin
1. 0 occasions	98.4	98.0	98.8	98.5	98.6	98.7	98.6	97.9	98.4	98.8	98.1	100.0	100.0	100.0	100.0	-
2. 1-2	1.1	1.1	.9	1.0	.6	.9	.9	1.3	1.1	.7	1.3	-	-	-	-	63.9
3. 3-5	.3	.4	.1	.2	.3	.1	.2	.4	.3	.2	.3	-	-	-	-	15.4
4. 6-9	.1	.1	.1	.1	.1	-	.1	.2	.1	.1	.1	-	-	-	-	6.7
5. 10-19	.1	.1	*	.1	-	*	.1	.1	-	.1	.1	-	-	-	-	4.0
6. 20-39	.1	.1	.1	.1	.1	*	.1	.1	.1	.1	.1	-	-	-	-	5.0
7. 40 or more	.1	.1	*	.1	.2	.1	*	.1	*	.1	.1	-	-	-	-	5.0
Item 1100 N(Wtd)	18173	8602	9094	14628	2003	4387	5264	6030	2491	8703	8201	6492	5098	2256	3784	299

B15B: ...during the last 12 months?

	TOTAL	M	F	White	Black	NE	NC	S	W	Yes	No	None	Mari-juana Only	Few Pills	More Pills	Any Heroin
1. 0 occasions	99.2	98.9	99.4	99.2	99.3	99.4	99.2	98.9	99.2	99.4	99.0	100.0	100.0	100.0	100.0	48.1
2. 1-2	.5	.6	.4	.5	.3	.4	.5	.6	.6	.3	.7	-	-	-	-	32.0
3. 3-5	.1	.2	.1	.1	.1	*	.1	.2	.1	.1	.1	-	-	-	-	6.7
4. 6-9	.1	.1	*	*	-	-	.1	.1	*	.1	*	-	-	-	-	3.7
5. 10-19	.1	.1	.1	.1	.2	.1	.1	.1	*	.1	.1	-	-	-	-	5.7
6. 20-39	*	*	-	*	*	*	*	*	-	*	*	-	-	-	-	1.3
7. 40 or more	*	.1	*	*	-	.1	*	*	*	*	.1	-	-	-	-	2.7
Item 1110 N(Wtd)	18175	8605	9094	14630	2003	4387	5267	6032	2489	8705	8203	6492	5099	2256	3786	297

B15C: ...during the last 30 days?

	TOTAL	M	F	White	Black	NE	NC	S	W	Yes	No	None	Mari-juana Only	Few Pills	More Pills	Any Heroin
1. 0 occasions	99.7	99.4	99.9	99.7	99.7	99.7	99.8	99.5	99.7	99.8	99.6	100.0	100.0	100.0	100.0	78.7
2. 1-2	.2	.3	.1	.2	.2	.2	.1	.2	.1	.1	.2	-	-	-	-	10.5
3. 3-5	.1	.1	*	.1	-	*	.1	.1	.1	*	.1	-	-	-	-	4.1
4. 6-9	*	.1	*	*	-	*	*	.1	-	*	*	-	-	-	-	2.4
5. 10-19	*	.1	-	*	.1	-	-	.1	-	*	.1	-	-	-	-	2.4
6. 20-39	*	*	-	-	-	*	-	-	-	-	*	-	-	-	-	.3
7. 40 or more	*	*	*	*	-	*	*	*	*	*	*	-	-	-	-	1.7
Item 1120 N(Wtd)	18176	8608	9094	14633	2004	4387	5265	6034	2490	8702	8205	6492	5099	2256	3787	296

B16: There are a number of narcotics other than heroin, such as methadone, opium, morphine, codeine, demerol, paregoric, talwin, and laudanum. These are sometimes prescribed by doctors. On how many occasions (if any) have you taken narcotics other than heroin on your own--that is, without a doctor telling you to take them...

B16A: ...in your lifetime?

	TOTAL	M	F	White	Black	NE	NC	S	W	Yes	No	None	Mari-juana Only	Few Pills	More Pills	Any Heroin
1. 0 occasions	90.1	88.8	91.4	89.5	95.8	89.0	89.1	92.0	89.3	91.8	88.7	100.0	100.0	87.1	65.4	29.0
2. 1-2	4.7	5.0	4.4	4.9	2.5	5.4	5.1	3.9	4.2	4.1	5.1	-	-	13.0	13.2	20.3
3. 3-5	2.1	2.3	1.8	2.3	.6	2.1	2.5	1.7	2.3	1.9	2.3	-	-	-	9.1	12.8
4. 6-9	1.1	1.3	.9	1.2	.4	1.3	1.1	.9	1.3	.9	1.3	-	-	-	4.5	9.3
5. 10-19	.9	1.1	.7	1.0	.5	.9	1.1	.7	1.1	.7	1.1	-	-	-	3.6	10.0
6. 20-39	.5	.5	.3	.5	.1	.5	.5	.3	.7	.2	.6	-	-	-	1.7	6.6
7. 40 or more	.7	1.0	.5	.7	.2	.9	.6	.5	1.2	.4	1.0	-	-	-	2.6	11.7
Item 1130 N(Wtd)	18029	8550	9048	14549	1995	4346	5233	5982	2469	8658	8144	6458	5068	2239	3733	290

B16B: ...during the last 12 months?

	TOTAL	M	F	White	Black	NE	NC	S	W	Yes	No	None	Mari-juana Only	Few Pills	More Pills	Any Heroin
1. 0 occasions	94.0	93.1	94.9	93.5	98.0	93.2	93.3	95.5	93.3	95.1	93.2	100.0	100.0	95.2	77.7	50.9
2. 1-2	3.2	3.5	2.9	3.6	1.0	3.8	4.0	2.2	3.2	3.0	3.5	-	-	4.8	11.2	19.2
3. 3-5	1.2	1.5	1.0	1.3	.4	1.4	1.2	1.1	1.4	1.0	1.4	-	-	-	5.2	9.6
4. 6-9	.7	.8	.5	.7	.4	.6	.7	.6	.9	.5	.7	-	-	-	2.7	6.5
5. 10-19	.4	.6	.3	.5	.1	.6	.4	.3	.7	.3	.6	-	-	-	1.7	5.8
6. 20-39	.2	.3	.2	.2	.2	.3	.2	.2	.3	.1	.3	-	-	-	.8	3.8
7. 40 or more	.2	.3	.1	.2	.1	.3	.2	.1	.3	.1	.3	-	-	-	.7	3.8
Item 1140 N(Wtd)	18015	8543	9043	14539	1991	4342	5229	5977	2466	8656	8136	6459	5068	2231	3724	291

* = less than .05 per cent.

QUESTIONNAIRE FORM 1-5 1978	TOTAL	SEX		RACE		REGION				4YR COLLEGE PLANS		ILLICIT DRUG USE: LIFETIME				
		M	F	White	Black	NE	NC	S	W	Yes	No	None	Mari-juana Only	Few Pills	More Pills	Any Her-oin
Weighted No. of Cases:	18916	8779	9266	14847	2096	4607	5411	6292	2605	8844	8413	6595	5214	2304	3885	302
% of Weighted Total:	100.0	46.4	49.0	78.5	11.1	24.4	28.6	33.3	13.8	46.8	44.5	34.9	27.6	12.2	20.5	1.6

B16C: ...during the last 30 days?

	TOTAL	M	F	White	Black	NE	NC	S	W	Yes	No	None	Mari-juana Only	Few Pills	More Pills	Any Heroin
1. 0 occasions	97.9	97.5	98.3	97.8	99.3	97.5	97.7	98.3	97.6	98.4	97.4	100.0	100.0	99.2	91.8	79.1
2. 1-2	1.2	1.4	1.0	1.3	.5	1.3	1.5	1.0	1.3	1.1	1.4	-	-	.8	4.9	8.0
3. 3-5	.5	.6	.4	.5	.1	.6	.5	.3	.6	.3	.6	-	-	-	1.9	5.9
4. 6-9	.2	.2	.2	.2	.1	.3	.2	.2	.1	.1	.3	-	-	-	.8	2.8
5. 10-19	.1	.2	.1	.1	.1	.1	.1	.1	.2	*	.2	-	-	-	.4	3.5
6. 20-39	*	.1	*	.1	-	.1	*	.1	.1	*	.1	-	-	-	.2	.3
7. 40 or more	*	.1	-	*	.1	*	*	-	.1	-	*	-	-	-	.1	.7
Item 1150 N(Wtd)	18007	8535	9042	14532	1992	4342	5225	5977	2463	8654	8132	6459	5069	2226	3724	287

B17: On how many occasions (if any) have you sniffed glue, or breathed the contents of aerosol spray cans, or inhaled any other gases or sprays in order to get high...

B17A: ...in your lifetime?

	TOTAL	M	F	White	Black	NE	NC	S	W	Yes	No	None	Mari-juana Only	Few Pills	More Pills	Any Heroin
1. 0 occasions	88.0	85.3	90.7	87.5	94.3	87.6	87.3	88.6	88.9	90.8	85.2	97.6	92.4	86.2	70.5	43.4
2. 1-2	7.0	8.4	5.7	7.3	3.8	7.2	7.0	7.0	6.9	5.7	8.4	1.8	5.8	9.7	14.4	25.1
3. 3-5	2.0	2.5	1.6	2.2	.9	2.2	2.3	1.8	1.7	1.5	2.5	.2	.8	2.2	6.1	9.2
4. 6-9	1.1	1.3	.9	1.1	.4	1.3	1.1	1.0	.8	.8	1.3	.1	.5	.9	3.2	6.8
5. 10-19	.8	1.1	.5	.9	.2	1.0	.9	.6	.8	.5	1.1	.1	.2	.6	2.6	5.2
6. 20-39	.4	.5	.3	.4	.4	.2	.8	.3	.3	.3	.6	*	.1	.3	1.6	2.0
7. 40 or more	.6	.9	.3	.6	.1	.6	.6	.7	.5	.4	.8	.2	.2	.2	1.5	8.0
Item 1160 N(Wtd) ‡	14677	6977	7357	11808	1647	3561	4228	4876	2012	7005	6748	5215	4072	1863	3082	251

B17B: ...during the last 12 months?

	TOTAL	M	F	White	Black	NE	NC	S	W	Yes	No	None	Mari-juana Only	Few Pills	More Pills	Any Heroin
1. 0 occasions	95.9	94.4	97.2	95.5	98.4	95.6	95.2	96.4	96.4	96.6	95.1	99.3	98.0	95.0	89.0	78.8
2. 1-2	2.3	3.1	1.6	2.5	.8	2.2	2.7	2.1	2.2	1.9	2.7	.4	1.5	3.5	5.6	6.0
3. 3-5	.8	1.1	.4	.8	.4	.9	.9	.7	.5	.7	.9	.1	.2	.7	2.2	6.8
4. 6-9	.4	.5	.4	.5	.4	.5	.6	.4	.2	.3	.5	.1	.1	.4	1.2	4.8
5. 10-19	.3	.3	.2	.3	-	.4	.2	.1	.4	.2	.3	-	.1	.3	.9	.8
6. 20-39	.1	.2	.1	.1	-	.1	.1	.1	.1	.1	.1	*	*	.1	.4	1.6
7. 40 or more	.2	.4	.1	.3	.1	.3	.4	.1	.1	.2	.3	.1	*	.1	.7	1.6
Item 1170 N(Wtd) ‡	14648	6966	7346	11796	1639	3549	4226	4865	2008	7002	6733	5213	4067	1853	3071	250

B17C: ...during the last 30 days?

	TOTAL	M	F	White	Black	NE	NC	S	W	Yes	No	None	Mari-juana Only	Few Pills	More Pills	Any Heroin
1. 0 occasions	98.5	97.9	99.1	98.4	99.2	98.4	98.4	98.6	98.8	99.0	98.0	99.6	99.5	98.7	95.7	92.3
2. 1-2	.9	1.1	.6	.9	.5	.9	.9	1.0	.5	.6	1.2	.3	.3	.8	2.5	3.6
3. 3-5	.3	.4	.1	.3	.2	.3	.3	.2	.2	.2	.3	*	*	.5	.6	2.0
4. 6-9	.1	.2	.1	.1	-	.1	.1	*	.3	.1	.2	*	.1	-	.4	.8
5. 10-19	.1	.2	*	.2	-	.2	.1	.1	.1	.1	.2	.1	*	-	.4	.8
6. 20-39	*	*	*	*	-	.1	*	*	-	*	*	-	*	.1	.1	-
7. 40 or more	.1	.1	*	.1	.1	.1	.2	*	-	*	.1	-	-	-	.3	.4
Item 1180 N(Wtd) ‡	14641	6960	7344	11790	1640	3549	4223	4862	2007	7002	6728	5213	4068	1848	3070	248

* = less than .05 per cent. ‡ This question appeared in Forms 2 through 5 only.

QUESTIONNAIRE FORM 1 1978	TOTAL	SEX		RACE		REGION				4YR COLLEGE PLANS		ILLICIT DRUG USE: LIFETIME				
		M	F	White	Black	NE	NC	S	W	Yes	No	None	Marijuana Only	Few Pills	More Pills	Any Heroin
Weighted No. of Cases:	3799	1740	1842	2962	411	922	1096	1257	524	1758	1571	1301	1086	411	760	46
% of Weighted Total:	100.0	45.8	48.5	78.0	10.8	24.3	28.8	33.1	13.8	46.3	41.3	34.3	28.6	10.8	20.0	1.2

A001: Taking all things together, how would you say things are these days--would you say you're very happy, pretty happy, or not too happy these days?

	TOTAL	M	F	White	Black	NE	NC	S	W	Yes	No	None	Marijuana Only	Few Pills	More Pills	Any Heroin
3. Very happy	19.7	16.4	22.5	21.1	12.4	16.8	20.6	20.0	21.9	22.6	16.8	22.0	19.0	18.6	15.6	29.2
2. Pretty happy	68.1	71.9	65.8	69.3	63.8	68.3	67.3	68.5	68.5	66.8	70.6	65.8	69.1	71.5	71.1	52.9
1. Not too happy	12.2	11.6	11.7	9.6	23.8	14.9	12.1	11.5	9.6	10.7	12.5	12.2	11.9	9.8	13.4	18.0
Item 1190 N(Wtd)	3781	1733	1836	2951	411	915	1092	1252	522	1751	1565	1298	1084	408	758	46

A002: How much do you agree or disagree with each of the following statements?

A002A: The nation needs much more long-range planning and coordination to be prepared for the future

	TOTAL	M	F	White	Black	NE	NC	S	W	Yes	No	None	Marijuana Only	Few Pills	More Pills	Any Heroin
1. Disagree	2.2	2.0	2.1	1.6	4.1	2.5	2.3	2.2	1.6	1.4	3.0	2.3	2.3	1.6	1.4	4.2
2. Mostly disagree	3.9	3.9	3.6	3.6	5.2	4.0	3.8	3.8	4.4	3.6	4.0	3.4	4.7	3.0	3.4	7.7
3. Neither	7.9	7.6	8.0	8.0	3.2	7.7	9.6	5.6	9.9	7.0	8.3	7.1	8.3	8.1	8.9	10.3
4. Mostly agree	41.7	39.4	45.0	43.5	37.0	38.6	45.2	40.3	43.2	41.9	43.2	44.3	41.6	40.9	40.1	42.5
5. Agree	44.3	47.2	41.2	43.3	50.4	47.3	39.0	48.1	40.9	46.1	41.5	42.9	43.1	46.4	46.1	35.3
Item 1200 N(Wtd)	3736	1723	1808	2924	406	904	1081	1237	514	1741	1547	1287	1071	404	746	45

A002B: I enjoy the fast pace and changes of today's world

	TOTAL	M	F	White	Black	NE	NC	S	W	Yes	No	None	Marijuana Only	Few Pills	More Pills	Any Heroin
1. Disagree	15.6	15.2	15.4	14.2	21.8	13.3	12.2	20.6	15.2	12.9	18.2	16.6	13.4	20.8	11.6	20.4
2. Mostly disagree	19.9	18.2	21.1	20.5	17.8	19.8	22.8	17.9	18.4	19.3	20.2	21.7	20.6	14.7	19.4	24.0
3. Neither	18.9	22.5	16.0	20.1	10.3	20.1	21.6	15.5	18.8	18.9	20.3	18.1	21.0	19.8	17.8	16.8
4. Mostly agree	29.8	28.1	31.6	30.6	27.4	28.8	29.9	28.9	33.2	32.8	26.1	30.3	29.9	28.9	31.0	27.2
5. Agree	15.9	16.0	15.9	14.6	22.7	17.9	13.6	17.0	14.3	16.1	15.2	13.4	15.1	15.9	20.2	11.6
Item 1210 N(Wtd)	3757	1724	1822	2939	403	913	1086	1238	520	1748	1551	1297	1072	406	753	45

A002C: Things change too quickly in today's world

	TOTAL	M	F	White	Black	NE	NC	S	W	Yes	No	None	Marijuana Only	Few Pills	More Pills	Any Heroin
1. Disagree	13.4	13.9	12.7	12.7	17.1	15.4	11.2	14.5	12.0	12.8	13.3	11.0	13.8	12.0	16.5	17.5
2. Mostly disagree	19.6	20.3	19.5	21.1	11.6	20.1	21.3	17.7	20.1	21.9	17.1	17.5	20.4	22.4	23.1	17.3
3. Neither	17.5	19.3	16.4	18.7	11.9	17.2	20.0	15.0	18.8	21.0	15.0	18.0	19.4	15.6	16.5	18.0
4. Mostly agree	24.8	24.0	25.9	25.7	23.0	23.0	27.9	23.7	24.1	25.2	25.5	27.6	24.6	22.6	22.5	21.2
5. Agree	24.7	22.4	25.5	21.7	36.3	24.4	19.6	29.1	25.0	19.1	29.1	26.0	21.7	27.4	21.4	25.9
Item 1220 N(Wtd)	3746	1724	1816	2937	403	911	1083	1237	515	1744	1548	1291	1072	406	749	45

A002D: I think the times ahead for me will be tougher and less fun than things are now

	TOTAL	M	F	White	Black	NE	NC	S	W	Yes	No	None	Marijuana Only	Few Pills	More Pills	Any Heroin
1. Disagree	20.7	20.1	21.2	20.9	19.9	21.9	19.8	20.7	20.5	20.7	20.4	20.4	20.2	19.0	22.2	20.9
2. Mostly disagree	20.0	18.3	22.3	21.6	12.9	19.9	21.9	16.9	23.3	22.0	18.5	19.9	20.9	19.5	20.1	30.5
3. Neither	11.6	11.0	11.8	11.9	8.2	11.2	12.9	10.7	11.4	12.2	10.3	11.0	12.5	11.5	11.9	9.2
4. Mostly agree	21.8	23.2	20.8	22.1	21.0	21.0	21.9	22.1	21.9	21.6	22.9	23.2	19.8	24.4	21.5	21.4
5. Agree	26.0	27.4	23.9	23.6	38.0	26.0	23.4	29.6	22.9	23.4	27.8	25.5	26.6	25.7	24.3	18.1
Item 1230 N(Wtd)	3756	1726	1822	2941	404	913	1087	1235	520	1746	1553	1295	1074	406	752	46

A003: Of all the time you spend with other people, about how much is spent with people over 30?

	TOTAL	M	F	White	Black	NE	NC	S	W	Yes	No	None	Marijuana Only	Few Pills	More Pills	Any Heroin
1. Very little	22.6	24.3	19.6	18.8	40.7	25.0	20.5	23.6	20.7	19.5	23.2	16.4	26.4	21.0	24.3	18.1
2. Some	42.0	44.3	40.8	44.5	28.5	43.0	45.3	40.2	37.8	47.1	37.4	39.9	44.4	43.7	44.1	41.7
3. About half	28.9	26.8	31.7	30.5	23.6	27.6	28.7	29.0	31.7	28.1	31.7	36.2	24.4	28.6	25.3	38.6
4. Most	5.3	4.2	6.3	5.4	4.8	3.3	4.9	5.8	8.0	4.3	6.6	6.0	4.1	5.8	5.2	1.6
5. Nearly all	1.1	.4	1.7	.8	2.4	1.1	.6	1.3	1.8	1.0	1.1	1.5	.7	.9	1.2	-
Item 1240 N(Wtd)	3794	1738	1842	2961	411	922	1093	1255	524	1757	1570	1301	1084	411	760	46

QUESTIONNAIRE FORM 1 1978	TOTAL	SEX		RACE		REGION				4YR COLLEGE PLANS		ILLICIT DRUG USE: LIFETIME				
		M	F	White	Black	NE	NC	S	W	Yes	No	None	Mari-juana Only	Few Pills	More Pills	Any Her-oin
Weighted No. of Cases:	3799	1740	1842	2962	411	922	1096	1257	524	1758	1571	1301	1086	411	760	46
% of Weighted Total:	100.0	45.8	48.5	78.0	10.8	24.3	28.8	33.1	13.8	46.3	41.3	34.3	28.6	10.8	20.0	1.2

A004: Would you like to spend more time, or less time, with people over 30 if you could?

	TOTAL	M	F	White	Black	NE	NC	S	W	Yes	No	None	Marijuana Only	Few Pills	More Pills	Any Heroin
1. Much less time	2.9	2.7	2.9	2.3	4.7	4.3	2.1	2.9	2.5	1.5	3.9	2.2	2.1	3.4	4.3	3.1
2. Somewhat less time	7.5	7.8	7.5	7.4	7.4	6.9	8.3	7.5	6.8	6.9	7.7	6.9	6.1	7.7	10.4	7.5
3. About the same as now	68.0	69.3	67.7	71.0	55.4	70.1	67.4	66.3	69.3	69.2	68.9	68.7	71.2	66.1	65.9	62.1
4. Somewhat more time	18.7	18.1	18.8	17.3	25.7	16.4	19.8	20.0	17.5	19.9	17.2	19.1	18.1	19.9	16.7	25.8
5. Much more time	2.9	2.0	3.1	2.0	6.7	2.3	2.4	3.2	4.0	2.5	2.4	3.1	2.5	2.9	2.6	1.6
Item 1250 N(Wtd)	3792	1736	1841	2959	411	921	1093	1255	522	1756	1569	1301	1083	411	760	46

A005: Would you like to spend more time, or less time, working with or helping younger children?

	TOTAL	M	F	White	Black	NE	NC	S	W	Yes	No	None	Marijuana Only	Few Pills	More Pills	Any Heroin
1. Much less time	4.5	6.2	2.7	4.4	2.3	6.3	3.9	4.1	3.7	2.9	4.8	3.3	3.5	5.1	6.4	17.0
2. Somewhat less time	5.3	7.4	3.0	5.3	4.8	4.5	4.9	5.5	7.2	4.7	5.4	5.5	4.3	6.6	4.8	4.1
3. About the same as now	34.1	45.0	24.1	35.7	23.6	31.8	37.5	31.3	37.8	34.5	33.1	30.4	35.8	34.3	38.7	27.8
4. Somewhat more time	34.6	30.3	39.5	35.5	31.2	35.9	35.5	34.2	31.3	36.9	35.1	38.8	35.3	32.0	32.0	23.2
5. Much more time	21.5	11.1	30.8	19.1	38.0	21.5	18.2	24.9	20.0	21.0	21.6	22.0	21.0	22.0	18.1	27.9
Item 1260 N(Wtd)	3782	1728	1840	2954	408	919	1090	1250	523	1751	1565	1296	1083	411	759	46

A006: The next questions ask how satisfied or dissatisfied you are with several aspects of your life. For each question, mark the circle that shows best how you feel. If you are neutral about something, or are just as satisfied as you are dissatisfied, mark the middle answer.

How satisfied are you with...

A006A: Your job? (If you have no job, leave blank)

	TOTAL	M	F	White	Black	NE	NC	S	W	Yes	No	None	Marijuana Only	Few Pills	More Pills	Any Heroin
7. Completely satisfied	22.0	22.1	22.5	21.8	20.9	19.9	19.9	25.6	22.2	20.7	24.1	21.2	20.1	26.6	21.2	27.2
6.	19.7	21.5	18.4	21.5	5.6	18.3	22.8	17.4	20.8	22.1	18.9	21.9	19.2	15.3	20.8	10.6
5.	12.8	13.9	11.9	13.7	8.4	12.3	13.7	12.1	13.6	14.9	11.4	14.8	10.4	12.6	14.3	10.4
4. Neutral	27.3	25.1	28.6	25.0	46.4	27.7	24.6	31.6	22.8	22.6	30.7	27.9	30.2	27.2	21.9	28.2
3.	6.2	6.3	6.5	7.1	1.5	7.1	8.0	3.8	5.9	7.3	5.0	5.5	6.8	4.8	7.4	12.1
2.	4.4	4.2	4.5	4.5	3.7	6.8	4.1	2.8	4.2	5.3	3.3	4.1	4.2	5.2	5.2	2.4
1. Completely dissatisfied	7.6	6.9	7.7	6.4	13.4	7.9	6.9	6.8	10.4	7.1	6.6	4.8	8.9	8.2	9.2	9.1
Item 1270 N(Wtd)	2464	1246	1085	2016	191	598	759	773	335	1140	1018	773	710	270	558	31

A006B: The neighborhood where you live?

	TOTAL	M	F	White	Black	NE	NC	S	W	Yes	No	None	Marijuana Only	Few Pills	More Pills	Any Heroin
7. Completely satisfied	33.8	35.4	32.9	33.8	33.4	28.3	30.6	39.2	37.1	32.9	35.1	37.3	34.5	33.7	26.7	19.8
6.	16.7	18.0	16.1	18.8	8.1	15.9	21.5	12.5	17.8	19.2	15.6	17.1	17.4	16.0	16.9	16.0
5.	9.4	11.1	7.8	9.9	4.4	9.8	10.7	8.3	8.5	10.7	7.6	10.2	9.2	7.7	10.7	3.7
4. Neutral	23.6	18.5	27.7	21.4	35.3	25.9	22.0	24.0	22.1	20.1	26.5	20.5	24.2	25.9	26.1	23.0
3.	5.4	5.7	5.2	6.1	2.1	5.6	7.0	4.1	5.0	6.4	4.7	5.4	4.2	6.2	6.6	16.0
2.	4.1	4.4	3.8	4.1	4.4	6.3	3.6	3.4	3.1	4.9	3.4	3.5	3.5	4.0	5.5	9.4
1. Completely dissatisfied	7.0	6.8	6.5	6.0	12.3	8.2	4.5	8.5	6.4	5.8	7.2	6.0	7.0	6.4	7.4	12.0
Item 1280 N(Wtd)	3780	1734	1837	2957	406	919	1089	1250	522	1755	1565	1295	1081	411	758	46

A006C: Your personal safety in your neighborhood, on your job, and in your school--safety from being attacked and injured in some way?

	TOTAL	M	F	White	Black	NE	NC	S	W	Yes	No	None	Marijuana Only	Few Pills	More Pills	Any Heroin
7. Completely satisfied	41.9	46.1	38.4	43.2	35.2	41.1	43.8	43.6	35.3	41.7	42.1	41.0	42.9	40.9	43.3	32.7
6.	20.1	21.1	19.8	22.2	12.1	17.7	24.2	17.0	23.1	23.2	18.6	21.1	20.6	16.0	21.0	21.8
5.	8.4	8.5	8.3	9.2	4.7	10.9	8.2	6.6	9.2	9.5	7.7	9.1	7.3	11.1	8.6	6.2
4. Neutral	19.5	15.8	22.0	16.9	27.0	20.0	15.7	21.5	21.6	14.7	22.9	18.9	20.2	17.8	17.9	25.4
3.	3.5	2.9	4.2	3.4	4.8	4.5	3.1	3.2	3.5	4.5	2.5	4.5	2.7	5.0	2.5	1.6
2.	2.1	1.6	2.6	2.1	3.0	1.8	1.8	2.3	2.8	2.6	1.6	1.7	1.8	2.5	2.5	3.6
1. Completely dissatisfied	4.5	3.9	4.7	3.1	13.2	3.9	3.2	5.9	4.5	3.8	4.6	3.6	4.5	6.7	4.1	8.7
Item 1290 N(Wtd)	3780	1735	1833	2956	404	919	1091	1247	524	1754	1565	1294	1084	411	759	46

QUESTIONNAIRE FORM 1 1978	TOTAL	SEX		RACE		REGION				4YR COLLEGE PLANS		ILLICIT DRUG USE: LIFETIME				
		M	F	White	Black	NE	NC	S	W	Yes	No	None	Marijuana Only	Few Pills	More Pills	Any Heroin
Weighted No. of Cases:	3799	1740	1842	2962	411	922	1096	1257	524	1758	1571	1301	1086	411	760	46
% of Weighted Total:	100.0	45.8	48.5	78.0	10.8	24.3	28.8	33.1	13.8	46.3	41.3	34.3	28.6	10.8	20.0	1.2

A006D: The safety of things you own from being stolen or destroyed in your neighborhood, on your job, and in your school?

	TOTAL	M	F	White	Black	NE	NC	S	W	Yes	No	None	Mar.	Few	More	Her.
7. Completely satisfied	19.7	20.0	19.7	18.9	23.5	16.5	20.5	23.2	15.3	17.7	22.2	19.1	19.2	20.3	19.0	26.0
6.	19.0	19.2	19.7	21.5	7.2	17.8	23.2	16.2	18.7	22.5	16.6	20.6	18.0	19.0	19.9	9.0
5.	12.4	12.7	12.5	13.3	8.7	12.1	14.4	9.7	15.2	13.5	11.9	12.1	13.7	11.5	12.4	6.5
4. Neutral	21.3	18.3	22.9	19.3	25.8	21.4	17.9	23.5	22.6	17.6	23.1	19.8	22.3	20.8	20.7	32.8
3.	9.4	10.9	8.3	10.0	7.6	11.5	8.2	8.8	9.6	10.5	8.7	10.1	8.3	10.1	9.9	12.4
2.	6.0	6.4	5.9	6.3	5.2	5.6	6.5	5.5	7.0	7.6	4.6	5.8	5.8	7.7	6.6	4.1
1. Completely dissatisfied	12.3	12.4	11.0	10.6	22.1	15.1	9.3	13.1	11.6	10.6	12.8	12.4	12.7	10.7	11.6	9.1
Item 1300 N(Wtd)	3774	1735	1831	2958	402	917	1091	1245	521	1754	1560	1292	1082	411	756	46

A006E: Your educational experiences?

	TOTAL	M	F	White	Black	NE	NC	S	W	Yes	No	None	Mar.	Few	More	Her.
7. Completely satisfied	19.6	18.8	21.0	18.6	26.8	17.9	17.2	23.8	17.7	19.6	19.3	22.3	17.4	21.5	16.9	10.6
6.	22.0	22.7	22.2	24.0	16.5	19.5	26.3	20.1	21.8	28.0	18.0	26.7	22.2	18.9	16.9	20.3
5.	15.9	17.7	14.5	17.2	9.5	15.5	20.1	12.7	15.4	17.5	15.2	15.6	15.5	17.0	17.1	27.0
4. Neutral	25.2	23.1	26.3	23.5	29.9	27.1	21.6	26.5	26.6	18.5	31.0	21.6	29.6	22.0	25.4	29.6
3.	7.0	7.4	6.7	7.4	4.4	7.9	7.3	5.5	8.2	7.4	6.6	6.5	5.4	7.0	10.9	2.4
2.	4.1	3.8	4.1	4.1	3.7	5.2	3.8	4.0	3.3	4.3	3.2	2.7	4.1	6.8	5.3	3.1
1. Completely dissatisfied	6.1	6.4	5.2	5.2	9.2	7.0	3.7	7.3	6.9	4.6	6.8	4.6	5.8	6.9	7.4	7.0
Item 1310 N(Wtd)	3763	1727	1829	2948	400	914	1086	1245	518	1748	1562	1289	1080	409	754	46

A006F: Your friends and other people you spend time with?

	TOTAL	M	F	White	Black	NE	NC	S	W	Yes	No	None	Mar.	Few	More	Her.
7. Completely satisfied	46.3	42.5	50.2	46.1	48.1	44.8	42.6	51.6	43.9	41.8	51.0	46.5	48.1	46.5	41.1	52.2
6.	26.1	29.3	23.9	28.4	15.6	26.3	29.5	21.8	28.7	30.0	23.6	27.3	25.4	24.3	28.0	25.7
5.	9.5	10.7	8.4	10.0	6.8	9.4	12.4	7.3	8.7	11.5	7.6	8.1	9.1	12.2	11.7	4.8
4. Neutral	12.9	12.1	12.3	10.4	23.3	13.0	10.4	14.9	13.1	11.0	13.1	13.3	12.9	10.8	12.2	7.4
3.	2.4	2.5	2.2	2.5	1.6	2.9	2.8	1.6	2.2	2.5	2.1	2.4	1.8	3.0	3.1	2.1
2.	1.5	1.6	1.4	1.5	1.3	1.9	1.1	1.5	1.3	1.8	1.2	1.2	1.5	1.9	1.5	4.5
1. Completely dissatisfied	1.5	1.4	1.5	1.1	3.3	1.6	1.2	1.3	2.2	1.4	1.4	1.2	1.2	1.3	2.3	3.3
Item 1320 N(Wtd)	3783	1738	1836	2957	408	918	1092	1252	521	1755	1568	1299	1084	411	758	45

A006G: The way you get along with your parents?

	TOTAL	M	F	White	Black	NE	NC	S	W	Yes	No	None	Mar.	Few	More	Her.
7. Completely satisfied	36.1	35.2	36.8	34.5	44.3	33.9	33.2	39.0	39.1	34.3	37.3	42.3	35.6	37.0	26.2	13.5
6.	20.3	22.4	19.1	22.7	10.2	22.4	22.5	16.7	20.7	23.8	18.6	21.2	20.3	23.6	18.7	7.5
5.	10.3	12.3	8.7	11.2	6.6	10.0	12.5	9.5	8.0	12.0	9.2	9.2	11.1	10.8	11.8	11.7
4. Neutral	17.9	17.0	18.4	16.8	22.4	16.7	15.2	20.3	19.3	14.9	20.0	15.3	18.2	14.9	20.0	46.1
3.	5.2	4.7	5.5	5.5	3.6	5.9	5.9	3.5	6.6	6.0	4.1	3.7	4.9	5.3	9.1	4.4
2.	4.1	3.9	4.5	4.1	4.2	2.8	5.3	4.3	3.2	3.9	4.6	3.3	4.3	3.2	5.6	10.2
1. Completely dissatisfied	6.1	4.5	7.1	5.3	8.6	8.2	5.3	6.5	3.0	5.1	6.1	5.0	5.6	5.3	8.6	6.6
Item 1330 N(Wtd)	3773	1727	1836	2950	406	913	1090	1247	523	1755	1561	1295	1082	410	753	46

A006H: Yourself?

	TOTAL	M	F	White	Black	NE	NC	S	W	Yes	No	None	Mar.	Few	More	Her.
7. Completely satisfied	29.9	32.4	27.1	25.6	52.0	27.8	24.4	35.3	32.1	25.7	31.4	30.2	30.8	28.6	25.5	30.4
6.	25.1	25.7	25.7	27.6	15.2	24.6	30.4	20.9	25.4	29.1	23.0	25.9	24.9	28.6	23.2	26.5
5.	13.3	13.8	13.4	15.0	5.4	13.4	16.0	10.9	13.1	16.4	11.5	14.3	12.2	15.7	14.2	13.7
4. Neutral	21.9	19.2	23.3	21.5	19.3	22.6	21.4	21.9	21.6	17.8	25.8	21.4	22.8	18.3	22.7	17.3
3.	4.9	4.8	5.0	5.5	2.6	6.2	4.7	4.7	3.6	6.5	3.4	4.5	4.9	4.8	6.6	5.4
2.	1.9	1.7	2.0	2.0	.9	2.0	1.8	2.1	1.5	1.9	1.9	1.3	1.8	1.4	3.5	-
1. Completely dissatisfied	2.9	2.3	3.5	2.8	4.5	3.3	1.4	4.2	2.6	2.6	3.0	2.3	2.6	2.6	4.3	6.6
Item 1340 N(Wtd)	3770	1733	1832	2954	405	918	1087	1247	518	1753	1563	1292	1081	408	757	46

A006I: Your standard of living--the things you have like housing, car, furniture, recreation, and the like?

	TOTAL	M	F	White	Black	NE	NC	S	W	Yes	No	None	Mar.	Few	More	Her.
7. Completely satisfied	36.9	38.9	35.5	37.0	32.3	36.8	34.2	38.4	39.3	37.1	36.7	39.4	37.6	38.1	30.8	42.5
6.	23.5	25.7	22.5	26.3	12.3	23.5	25.9	20.5	25.8	28.0	20.7	24.0	23.1	22.9	24.6	27.1
5.	12.3	11.4	13.3	13.1	8.8	13.4	16.0	8.9	10.6	12.6	12.5	10.4	12.9	13.0	15.2	8.0
4. Neutral	15.9	13.6	16.5	13.4	28.6	15.4	13.0	19.1	14.8	11.3	18.3	16.0	15.1	15.9	15.3	13.8
3.	5.0	4.8	5.5	5.2	5.3	4.7	5.5	5.7	3.2	5.5	4.9	4.9	4.8	4.1	6.6	2.3
2.	2.6	2.5	2.5	2.3	3.9	2.9	2.1	2.6	3.0	2.9	2.3	1.8	3.0	2.7	3.2	4.5
1. Completely dissatisfied	3.8	3.0	4.1	2.8	8.9	3.4	3.2	4.8	3.3	2.4	4.6	3.5	3.4	3.3	4.3	1.9
Item 1350 N(Wtd)	3784	1734	1839	2956	409	917	1092	1252	524	1757	1567	1298	1083	411	758	46

QUESTIONNAIRE FORM 1 1978	TOTAL	SEX		RACE		REGION				4YR COLLEGE PLANS		ILLICIT DRUG USE: LIFETIME				
		M	F	White	Black	NE	NC	S	W	Yes	No	None	Mari-juana Only	Few Pills	More Pills	Any Her-oin
Weighted No. of Cases:	3799	1740	1842	2962	411	922	1096	1257	524	1758	1571	1301	1086	411	760	46
% of Weighted Total:	100.0	45.8	48.5	78.0	10.8	24.3	28.8	33.1	13.8	46.3	41.3	34.3	28.6	10.8	20.0	1.2

A006J: The amount of time you have for doing things you want to do?

7. Completely satisfied	16.3	17.5	14.9	15.1	22.6	15.6	14.1	17.9	18.1	14.8	17.3	15.9	17.6	13.7	14.8	14.9
6.	15.6	16.5	15.2	17.0	8.1	15.0	18.0	13.2	17.6	17.9	14.7	17.3	15.8	14.7	14.6	16.2
5.	14.4	16.0	13.0	15.6	8.9	13.8	15.7	12.4	17.7	16.9	12.1	15.4	14.4	16.5	13.5	8.8
4. Neutral	18.6	17.4	19.9	16.9	26.8	18.6	17.9	19.0	19.5	15.2	21.1	18.5	18.6	17.8	17.7	23.9
3.	13.3	12.6	14.2	14.8	6.5	13.7	15.9	12.0	10.0	14.9	12.2	13.7	12.7	14.0	13.7	11.0
2.	8.0	8.2	7.9	8.6	6.7	9.9	8.8	6.8	5.7	9.2	6.8	6.8	7.4	9.8	9.7	11.2
1. Completely dissatisfied	13.8	11.7	15.0	12.0	20.4	13.5	9.7	18.6	11.4	11.0	15.8	12.3	13.4	13.5	16.0	13.9
Item 1360 N(Wtd)	3773	1727	1835	2950	405	917	1089	1245	522	1752	1560	1296	1083	410	753	43

A006K: The way you spend your leisure time--recreation, relaxation, and so on?

7. Completely satisfied	32.7	33.6	31.5	31.4	36.7	30.4	29.4	38.9	28.9	28.2	36.2	33.5	32.6	32.5	30.5	44.4
6.	20.6	22.6	19.0	22.4	12.9	21.9	24.9	15.0	22.7	24.1	18.0	20.8	19.6	23.1	22.0	14.2
5.	13.0	13.7	12.8	14.7	6.7	12.7	16.6	9.7	13.5	15.4	11.6	12.3	13.8	14.9	12.1	14.0
4. Neutral	17.6	15.9	18.8	16.2	23.3	16.5	15.6	19.8	18.0	15.3	19.3	18.0	18.1	15.1	16.2	15.4
3.	7.2	6.5	7.9	7.8	5.1	7.5	7.3	6.5	8.0	9.0	5.7	6.9	6.9	7.4	9.2	3.7
2.	3.6	2.9	4.3	3.4	4.3	4.4	2.4	4.4	3.1	3.7	3.6	3.6	3.5	2.9	4.2	3.6
1. Completely dissatisfied	5.3	4.7	5.6	4.0	11.0	6.5	3.7	5.7	5.7	4.3	5.7	4.8	5.5	4.1	5.7	4.7
Item 1370 N(Wtd)	3778	1733	1837	2956	405	918	1092	1248	521	1752	1567	1296	1082	410	757	46

A006L: Your life as a whole these days?

7. Completely satisfied	21.0	21.2	20.6	19.9	26.1	18.2	18.0	24.9	23.0	19.3	21.9	22.4	20.8	21.9	17.5	26.1
6.	27.3	28.8	26.8	30.1	15.6	25.5	31.4	23.2	31.6	33.6	22.6	30.1	26.5	27.5	25.6	19.5
5.	15.5	17.1	14.5	17.2	8.2	15.7	19.9	12.4	13.3	17.3	14.3	13.7	17.4	16.8	15.7	23.3
4. Neutral	24.6	21.9	26.1	21.8	33.5	25.7	22.2	27.1	21.4	18.6	29.5	23.6	24.7	23.4	25.2	18.2
3.	5.0	5.0	4.9	5.5	3.1	6.5	4.5	4.2	5.3	5.6	4.3	4.2	3.7	5.7	8.4	-
2.	3.0	3.2	2.9	2.9	3.2	4.6	1.8	3.2	2.6	3.1	2.9	2.6	2.9	3.4	3.3	11.4
1. Completely dissatisfied	3.6	2.8	4.3	2.6	10.3	3.8	2.3	5.0	2.8	2.4	4.5	3.3	4.0	1.3	4.3	1.5
Item 1380 N(Wtd)	3774	1730	1835	2949	409	915	1089	1252	518	1752	1563	1297	1080	410	753	46

A006M: The way our national government is operating?

7. Completely satisfied	2.0	2.3	1.3	1.0	5.9	1.2	1.1	3.1	2.4	1.4	2.0	2.1	1.5	1.7	1.9	1.7
6.	2.8	3.0	2.6	2.8	1.7	2.9	3.6	2.1	3.1	3.1	2.1	3.1	3.0	2.7	2.5	-
5.	9.6	10.8	8.7	10.5	6.9	7.4	11.8	8.5	11.3	11.6	8.1	11.0	9.9	9.4	8.7	3.4
4. Neutral	39.1	33.1	45.6	38.4	41.6	39.7	37.1	41.2	37.2	35.2	44.1	40.0	40.2	36.1	37.3	32.0
3.	14.9	16.3	14.2	16.8	7.6	14.6	17.2	12.1	17.4	18.8	11.4	15.6	15.4	15.2	14.5	15.7
2.	11.9	12.3	11.8	12.6	9.3	12.1	12.2	11.4	11.9	13.8	10.3	10.1	12.6	13.9	12.7	6.7
1. Completely dissatisfied	19.7	22.3	15.8	17.9	27.0	22.2	16.9	21.6	16.6	16.2	22.0	18.0	17.4	20.9	22.4	40.6
Item 1390 N(Wtd)	3775	1733	1833	2948	410	918	1087	1250	519	1753	1563	1297	1080	409	755	46

A006N: The amount of fun you are having?

7. Completely satisfied	26.8	24.7	28.3	26.1	30.3	23.5	23.7	33.0	24.1	24.1	28.7	27.4	27.1	27.3	23.8	30.9
6.	23.1	25.2	21.6	25.2	13.3	23.6	25.3	19.7	25.6	25.3	22.0	23.7	22.3	24.5	23.3	25.2
5.	17.9	19.5	16.7	19.6	9.9	18.9	22.6	13.6	16.5	20.4	15.8	17.5	17.5	20.3	19.2	14.5
4. Neutral	18.9	18.3	19.5	17.2	26.8	20.1	16.4	19.5	20.9	16.5	20.7	19.2	20.6	14.9	17.6	18.2
3.	5.5	5.3	5.7	5.6	5.7	5.4	5.6	5.3	6.0	6.8	4.3	5.2	5.1	5.9	7.0	4.2
2.	3.0	3.3	2.9	3.0	3.3	4.0	2.5	2.5	3.2	3.4	2.7	2.9	2.6	2.2	3.9	1.9
1. Completely dissatisfied	4.8	3.7	5.3	3.3	10.6	4.6	3.9	6.3	3.6	3.5	5.7	4.1	4.8	5.0	5.2	5.0
Item 1400 N(Wtd)	3785	1735	1839	2958	409	918	1092	1253	522	1757	1566	1299	1084	410	757	46

A007: How important is each of the following to you in your life?

A007A: Being successful in my line of work

1. Not important	1.2	1.8	.4	1.0	1.9	1.3	.9	1.5	1.1	.9	1.0	.9	1.3	.6	1.8	3.3
2. Somewhat important	10.1	8.5	10.9	9.6	9.6	9.5	10.8	10.2	9.5	7.0	12.7	11.3	9.3	7.3	9.2	17.3
3. Quite important	32.9	31.5	34.4	34.8	22.0	33.4	37.6	29.2	31.0	30.1	36.8	32.7	33.6	31.5	32.6	41.2
4. Extremely important	55.8	58.2	54.2	54.6	66.4	55.9	50.7	59.1	58.4	62.0	49.5	55.1	55.7	60.7	56.4	38.2
Item 1410 N(Wtd)	3752	1721	1819	2935	401	908	1087	1240	517	1742	1551	1288	1070	408	754	46

QUESTIONNAIRE FORM 1 1978	TOTAL	SEX		RACE		REGION				4YR COLLEGE PLANS		ILLICIT DRUG USE: LIFETIME				
		M	F	White	Black	NE	NC	S	W	Yes	No	None	Marijuana Only	Few Pills	More Pills	Any Heroin
Weighted No. of Cases:	3799	1740	1842	2962	411	922	1096	1257	524	1758	1571	1301	1086	411	760	46
% of Weighted Total:	100.0	45.8	48.5	78.0	10.8	24.3	28.8	33.1	13.8	46.3	41.3	34.3	28.6	10.8	20.0	1.2

A007B: Having a good marriage and family life

1. Not important	4.0	5.1	2.8	3.5	6.4	4.7	4.0	3.9	3.3	3.4	4.1	2.2	3.4	4.4	6.9	18.6
2. Somewhat important	7.2	9.5	4.5	6.9	7.6	8.3	7.5	5.8	8.1	6.7	6.4	5.8	6.4	7.5	10.1	16.3
3. Quite important	13.9	15.6	12.2	14.4	12.0	15.5	14.7	12.5	13.2	13.7	14.1	13.1	12.4	15.4	15.4	16.5
4. Extremely important	74.8	69.9	80.4	75.3	74.0	71.6	73.8	77.7	75.4	76.2	75.3	78.9	77.8	72.7	67.6	48.6
Item 1420 N(Wtd)	3734	1706	1821	2918	404	903	1081	1234	515	1737	1548	1284	1067	406	746	46

A007C: Having lots of money

1. Not important	9.2	6.8	11.2	9.6	5.5	9.2	9.1	9.6	8.6	8.7	10.2	10.9	8.0	8.2	8.2	18.8
2. Somewhat important	42.0	35.2	49.3	44.5	33.3	43.1	45.2	39.9	38.2	44.8	40.6	46.5	41.9	43.4	36.3	38.2
3. Quite important	32.0	36.3	28.6	31.7	34.2	30.3	32.0	32.3	34.2	32.3	32.1	30.3	32.3	34.6	33.7	25.3
4. Extremely important	16.8	21.7	10.9	14.2	27.0	17.4	13.6	18.2	19.0	14.2	17.1	12.4	17.7	13.7	21.8	17.8
Item 1430 N(Wtd)	3764	1724	1829	2942	408	911	1091	1247	515	1747	1559	1290	1075	409	757	46

A007D: Having plenty of time for recreation and hobbies

1. Not important	2.6	1.9	3.1	2.0	5.3	2.1	2.2	3.6	2.1	1.8	3.6	2.8	2.8	2.8	1.5	6.6
2. Somewhat important	31.1	25.3	36.8	30.5	37.6	29.0	30.3	33.1	31.6	27.9	34.7	34.4	29.6	32.5	27.7	27.1
3. Quite important	42.4	42.5	43.1	43.9	35.8	43.2	45.6	39.9	40.6	46.6	38.9	41.5	43.1	41.7	43.3	38.0
4. Extremely important	23.9	30.3	17.0	23.6	21.3	25.7	21.9	23.5	25.7	23.7	22.8	21.3	24.4	23.0	27.4	28.3
Item 1440 N(Wtd)	3765	1725	1827	2943	406	914	1089	1245	517	1747	1558	1293	1076	408	757	46

A007E: Having strong friendships

1. Not important	1.3	1.0	1.2	.5	3.3	1.7	.7	1.6	.9	.6	1.3	1.1	1.2	.4	1.7	1.6
2. Somewhat important	8.3	6.9	8.6	5.4	22.0	7.5	7.0	9.6	9.0	6.2	9.3	8.6	8.2	8.5	5.7	14.0
3. Quite important	27.1	29.1	25.5	26.9	32.5	25.5	29.5	27.2	24.7	25.5	29.4	29.7	27.0	24.1	25.1	16.3
4. Extremely important	63.4	63.0	64.7	67.1	42.2	65.3	62.8	61.6	65.4	67.7	60.0	60.6	63.6	67.0	67.4	68.1
Item 1450 N(Wtd)	3766	1727	1827	2944	405	915	1088	1247	515	1747	1559	1294	1076	407	755	46

A007F: Being able to find steady work

1. Not important	1.4	1.9	.7	1.3	1.3	1.3	1.3	1.5	1.3	1.0	1.5	.7	1.6	.9	1.8	5.9
2. Somewhat important	6.7	5.0	8.0	6.5	4.0	6.6	7.0	6.4	7.2	7.1	5.4	7.1	5.5	6.6	7.1	8.3
3. Quite important	27.3	26.1	29.2	29.7	15.1	27.5	31.6	24.9	24.0	28.2	28.3	28.2	26.2	29.1	26.2	34.4
4. Extremely important	64.5	67.0	62.2	62.5	79.7	64.6	60.1	67.1	67.5	63.7	64.7	64.0	66.7	63.4	64.9	51.4
Item 1460 N(Wtd)	3760	1723	1825	2936	407	910	1089	1245	516	1746	1555	1294	1071	409	754	46

A007G: Making a contribution to society

1. Not important	7.5	7.4	7.3	7.3	5.9	7.6	9.7	6.1	6.2	6.4	8.1	6.3	6.4	9.2	9.7	9.8
2. Somewhat important	39.8	40.5	38.8	39.9	36.1	38.6	42.0	38.3	40.7	31.9	47.4	37.8	40.6	38.2	43.3	34.9
3. Quite important	34.6	34.1	36.2	35.0	37.2	35.5	33.3	33.9	37.3	37.7	32.8	36.2	35.7	32.8	31.7	45.2
4. Extremely important	18.1	18.0	17.7	17.7	20.8	18.2	14.9	21.7	15.8	24.0	11.7	19.6	17.3	19.7	15.3	10.2
Item 1470 N(Wtd)	3757	1721	1825	2937	407	909	1088	1246	514	1743	1556	1292	1073	407	752	46

A007H: Being a leader in my community

1. Not important	37.9	32.6	43.1	38.7	28.9	41.5	40.0	33.7	37.2	28.4	47.0	34.5	34.1	40.2	45.9	60.9
2. Somewhat important	39.1	41.3	37.0	39.5	38.8	37.5	40.6	37.7	42.3	41.0	37.7	38.8	43.3	37.5	36.9	27.3
3. Quite important	15.8	18.6	13.5	15.1	22.0	13.9	13.5	20.0	13.8	20.6	11.3	18.5	14.2	17.5	12.0	9.5
4. Extremely important	7.2	7.5	6.4	6.7	10.3	7.1	5.9	8.6	6.7	10.1	4.0	8.2	8.4	4.7	5.3	2.2
Item 1480 N(Wtd)	3756	1718	1827	2937	406	910	1088	1244	514	1741	1557	1286	1074	408	755	45

A007I: Being able to give my children better opportunities than I've had

1. Not important	3.0	2.8	3.0	3.4	.1	2.9	3.2	2.8	2.9	3.3	2.5	2.4	2.5	5.3	3.5	7.8
2. Somewhat important	13.0	13.3	13.1	14.4	5.0	15.0	15.2	9.8	12.8	15.0	10.7	13.7	12.7	10.0	13.9	14.9
3. Quite important	31.9	32.2	32.1	35.2	14.8	31.3	38.5	26.8	31.4	33.4	31.6	32.0	32.1	30.9	32.8	31.1
4. Extremely important	52.1	51.6	51.8	47.0	80.1	50.8	43.1	60.7	52.9	48.3	55.2	51.9	52.6	53.8	49.8	46.3
Item 1490 N(Wtd)	3717	1704	1808	2904	406	896	1082	1229	509	1724	1542	1280	1058	405	743	45

QUESTIONNAIRE FORM 1 1978	TOTAL	SEX		RACE		REGION				4YR COLLEGE PLANS		ILLICIT DRUG USE: LIFETIME				
		M	F	White	Black	NE	NC	S	W	Yes	No	None	Mari- juana Only	Few Pills	More Pills	Any Her- oin
Weighted No. of Cases:	3799	1740	1842	2962	411	922	1096	1257	524	1758	1571	1301	1086	411	760	46
% of Weighted Total:	100.0	45.8	48.5	78.0	10.8	24.3	28.8	33.1	13.8	46.3	41.3	34.3	28.6	10.8	20.0	1.2

A007J: Living close to parents and relatives

1. Not important	30.5	32.3	28.6	30.1	34.0	30.8	29.9	32.5	26.4	30.2	30.7	23.7	29.3	32.4	41.8	52.8
2. Somewhat important	42.0	40.9	43.7	43.0	40.6	41.0	46.0	38.9	42.7	43.7	40.8	43.8	43.1	41.0	39.4	29.6
3. Quite important	19.1	19.0	19.1	19.3	14.9	19.2	17.2	20.1	20.7	18.1	20.1	22.4	19.4	19.1	13.1	10.6
4. Extremely important	8.4	7.7	8.6	7.6	10.5	9.0	6.8	8.6	10.2	8.1	8.4	10.1	8.1	7.4	5.7	7.0
Item 1500 N(Wtd)	3752	1716	1826	2929	408	909	1085	1243	514	1742	1554	1288	1069	409	755	43

A007K: Getting away from this area of the country

1. Not important	54.6	56.4	54.2	57.4	43.3	50.1	51.9	58.5	59.1	56.9	55.4	62.4	55.7	55.5	42.5	33.6
2. Somewhat important	23.7	21.8	25.4	23.1	26.0	24.7	25.2	21.8	23.0	22.0	24.6	21.2	23.8	22.4	26.8	31.3
3. Quite important	10.7	10.7	10.0	10.0	13.1	12.0	11.0	9.9	9.8	10.9	9.5	9.9	10.3	10.7	12.7	12.8
4. Extremely important	11.0	11.1	10.3	9.5	17.5	13.1	11.9	9.8	8.1	10.2	10.5	6.6	10.2	11.4	18.0	22.3
Item 1510 N(Wtd)	3764	1725	1828	2942	407	912	1090	1247	515	1745	1559	1289	1077	408	756	46

A007L: Working to correct social and economic inequalities

1. Not important	21.1	24.9	18.1	22.7	11.8	21.2	23.6	19.3	20.0	17.8	25.4	19.6	21.0	18.3	25.2	29.3
2. Somewhat important	45.9	45.1	47.5	47.8	39.0	45.1	47.3	44.5	47.8	45.9	46.1	46.9	47.1	46.6	42.9	42.9
3. Quite important	23.6	21.6	25.0	21.5	34.3	22.9	21.6	25.4	24.4	25.3	21.5	24.8	22.5	24.8	22.1	16.8
4. Extremely important	9.4	8.4	9.5	8.0	14.9	10.7	7.5	10.8	7.7	10.9	6.9	8.7	9.4	10.3	9.8	11.0
Item 1520 N(Wtd)	3737	1715	1813	2924	408	905	1082	1240	510	1742	1544	1281	1069	407	751	46

A007M: Discovering new ways to experience things

1. Not important	8.3	8.3	8.5	8.1	8.5	4.7	9.9	9.9	7.7	7.5	9.5	10.1	7.1	8.4	5.5	16.7
2. Somewhat important	33.9	35.9	32.8	35.8	29.3	30.8	36.4	35.8	29.2	33.7	36.1	37.4	34.5	30.1	30.5	27.7
3. Quite important	38.5	39.0	38.1	38.0	40.6	41.3	36.3	36.0	44.4	38.2	39.0	37.1	40.1	39.8	38.9	31.9
4. Extremely important	19.3	16.9	20.6	18.1	21.6	23.2	17.4	18.3	18.8	20.7	15.4	15.4	18.4	21.8	25.2	23.7
Item 1530 N(Wtd)	3758	1727	1821	2938	406	911	1089	1241	518	1739	1561	1289	1074	409	752	46

A007N: Finding purpose and meaning in my life

1. Not important	1.6	2.8	.3	1.8	-	1.6	2.0	1.5	.9	1.1	1.8	1.3	1.2	1.7	2.0	5.2
2. Somewhat important	8.1	11.3	5.4	8.2	7.7	8.2	8.6	7.0	9.5	7.5	8.4	7.4	9.6	7.8	7.1	3.9
3. Quite important	24.9	29.3	20.3	25.5	18.1	23.5	29.4	22.1	24.5	22.2	27.6	25.8	25.2	23.5	23.0	22.2
4. Extremely important	65.4	56.6	74.0	64.6	74.2	66.7	59.9	69.3	65.2	69.2	62.1	65.4	64.0	67.0	67.9	68.7
Item 1540 N(Wtd)	3766	1725	1830	2946	407	912	1091	1246	517	1746	1559	1291	1076	409	757	46

A008: Generally speaking, would you say that most people can be trusted or that you can't be too careful in dealing with people?

3. Most people can be trusted	31.3	31.8	31.8	35.1	15.5	28.8	38.3	26.0	33.2	36.6	28.1	33.5	31.8	29.7	29.3	33.2
2. Don't know, undecided	28.2	27.4	29.0	27.8	23.9	28.6	26.9	27.8	31.1	26.5	29.1	28.8	28.8	29.8	25.4	22.9
1. Can't be too careful	40.6	40.8	39.2	37.1	60.6	42.5	34.8	46.2	35.7	36.9	42.8	37.7	39.4	40.6	45.2	43.9
Item 1550 N(Wtd)	3683	1686	1800	2891	393	886	1069	1217	511	1721	1525	1264	1061	402	730	44

A009: Would you say that most of the time people try to be helpful or that they are mostly just looking out for themselves?

3. Try to be helpful	33.0	29.1	37.4	34.1	29.2	32.0	36.5	31.2	31.6	34.7	32.3	37.6	33.8	31.6	26.5	21.7
2. Don't know, undecided	31.0	31.3	30.4	31.5	27.0	30.8	31.7	30.2	31.9	29.7	31.9	28.3	31.4	33.3	32.7	46.5
1. Just looking out for themselves	36.0	39.7	32.3	34.4	43.8	37.3	31.8	38.5	36.5	35.6	35.8	34.1	34.8	35.1	40.8	31.8
Item 1560 N(Wtd)	3754	1723	1827	2939	408	909	1087	1241	516	1741	1559	1287	1076	409	753	46

QUESTIONNAIRE FORM 1 1978	TOTAL	SEX		RACE		REGION				4YR COLLEGE PLANS		ILLICIT DRUG USE: LIFETIME				
		M	F	White	Black	NE	NC	S	W	Yes	No	None	Mari-juana Only	Few Pills	More Pills	Any Her-oin
Weighted No. of Cases:	3799	1740	1842	2962	411	922	1096	1257	524	1758	1571	1301	1086	411	760	46
% of Weighted Total:	100.0	45.8	48.5	78.0	10.8	24.3	28.8	33.1	13.8	46.3	41.3	34.3	28.6	10.8	20.0	1.2

A010: Do you think most people would try to take advantage of you if they got a chance or would they try to be fair?

	TOTAL	M	F	White	Black	NE	NC	S	W	Yes	No	None	Mari-juana Only	Few Pills	More Pills	Any Her-oin
3. Would try to be fair	30.1	27.6	33.5	32.7	15.8	30.5	32.4	27.0	32.2	32.2	28.0	32.5	28.7	28.0	29.6	29.5
2. Don't know, undecided	33.1	33.4	33.2	35.1	19.3	30.8	37.2	30.2	35.6	34.0	33.8	32.6	33.0	35.4	34.0	42.7
1. Would try to take advantage of you	36.7	39.0	33.3	32.2	64.9	38.7	30.4	42.8	32.2	33.8	38.2	34.9	38.2	36.7	36.4	27.8
Item 1570 N(Wtd)	3755	1725	1828	2942	408	910	1087	1242	516	1743	1559	1287	1077	410	752	46

A011: These next questions ask your opinions about a number of different topics. How much do you agree or disagree with each statement below?

A011A: I feel that you cant be a good citizen unless you always obey the law

	TOTAL	M	F	White	Black	NE	NC	S	W	Yes	No	None	Mari-juana Only	Few Pills	More Pills	Any Her-oin
1. Disagree	20.2	22.7	17.1	18.9	28.5	23.6	19.4	19.7	17.4	18.2	20.5	14.6	21.6	23.4	25.1	31.7
2. Mostly disagree	16.8	17.6	16.0	17.7	13.6	17.7	18.0	14.0	19.3	16.3	17.2	11.7	17.0	21.0	23.7	11.5
3. Neither	17.0	16.2	18.1	18.4	8.1	18.1	19.6	13.9	17.1	16.4	18.0	13.0	19.3	17.7	19.8	26.4
4. Mostly agree	34.2	32.2	36.7	35.4	30.0	31.8	34.7	36.3	32.7	38.2	32.0	44.2	31.3	29.5	26.7	14.9
5. Agree	11.7	11.3	12.0	9.7	19.7	8.8	8.3	16.2	13.5	10.9	12.3	16.5	10.8	8.4	4.7	15.4
Item 1580 N(Wtd)	3762	1727	1827	2943	407	912	1089	1245	517	1747	1557	1291	1075	409	756	46

A011B: I feel a good citizen should go along with whatever the government does even if he disagrees with it

	TOTAL	M	F	White	Black	NE	NC	S	W	Yes	No	None	Mari-juana Only	Few Pills	More Pills	Any Her-oin
1. Disagree	43.2	42.9	43.2	41.7	51.6	48.7	41.8	42.1	39.5	44.8	40.6	38.4	44.3	46.8	48.5	45.1
2. Mostly disagree	24.0	24.3	24.5	25.6	17.0	24.4	26.7	21.5	24.0	26.2	22.8	24.8	23.0	26.2	24.3	19.4
3. Neither	15.9	15.2	16.8	16.7	12.0	13.8	16.4	15.8	18.6	13.1	19.3	16.2	17.6	12.7	14.4	26.4
4. Mostly agree	12.7	13.6	11.7	12.9	11.3	9.7	13.0	13.8	14.4	13.0	12.2	15.2	11.7	10.5	10.5	3.8
5. Agree	4.2	4.0	3.8	3.1	8.1	3.5	2.0	6.9	3.6	2.9	5.0	5.4	3.5	3.8	2.3	5.3
Item 1590 N(Wtd)	3761	1727	1826	2941	407	908	1091	1245	517	1742	1560	1289	1077	409	755	46

A011C: I feel a good citizen tries to change the government policies he disagrees with

	TOTAL	M	F	White	Black	NE	NC	S	W	Yes	No	None	Mari-juana Only	Few Pills	More Pills	Any Her-oin
1. Disagree	6.4	5.3	7.0	5.0	13.8	6.1	4.9	8.2	5.6	4.4	7.7	5.8	6.0	6.0	4.9	11.9
2. Mostly disagree	7.8	6.6	8.3	6.5	12.4	8.2	6.8	8.8	6.6	7.1	7.7	7.9	8.5	8.5	6.3	2.6
3. Neither	20.0	18.8	21.5	20.1	17.8	17.7	20.1	20.4	23.1	16.7	24.0	20.5	20.0	18.8	21.3	16.7
4. Mostly agree	32.1	32.5	32.3	34.2	22.4	34.9	34.5	26.5	35.3	33.9	31.7	31.3	34.4	33.6	31.0	38.5
5. Agree	33.8	36.8	30.9	34.2	33.6	33.1	33.8	36.0	29.4	37.9	28.9	34.4	31.2	33.1	36.5	30.3
Item 1600 N(Wtd)	3756	1726	1824	2939	406	909	1089	1241	517	1744	1560	1288	1077	409	754	46

A011D: The way people vote has a major impact on how things are run in this country

	TOTAL	M	F	White	Black	NE	NC	S	W	Yes	No	None	Mari-juana Only	Few Pills	More Pills	Any Her-oin
1. Disagree	9.0	10.3	8.0	9.3	8.4	11.0	9.7	7.3	8.2	9.5	7.9	6.9	8.7	11.1	10.9	18.6
2. Mostly disagree	12.8	14.2	11.6	13.5	9.0	15.7	13.0	9.9	14.7	15.6	10.3	11.1	14.2	11.0	14.7	25.3
3. Neither	14.7	15.3	14.2	15.6	8.3	15.2	18.0	11.4	14.8	13.6	15.6	14.4	13.6	14.5	17.0	18.6
4. Mostly agree	29.2	26.6	31.5	29.7	25.1	27.3	31.9	28.1	29.6	30.5	27.9	29.4	29.5	28.8	29.2	27.9
5. Agree	34.2	33.6	34.8	31.9	49.1	31.0	27.3	43.3	32.8	30.8	38.2	38.1	34.1	34.5	28.1	9.5
Item 1610 N(Wtd)	3758	1724	1827	2940	405	911	1090	1243	514	1746	1556	1291	1076	407	754	46

A011E: People who get together in citizen action groups to influence government policies can have a real effect

	TOTAL	M	F	White	Black	NE	NC	S	W	Yes	No	None	Mari-juana Only	Few Pills	More Pills	Any Her-oin
1. Disagree	4.3	4.8	3.5	4.2	4.4	5.4	4.6	3.7	3.3	3.1	4.8	3.3	4.0	6.2	4.5	12.9
2. Mostly disagree	9.8	10.2	9.1	10.0	6.0	12.3	9.9	7.2	11.2	9.9	9.2	8.3	9.6	7.6	13.1	3.8
3. Neither	24.7	25.0	25.3	26.4	16.4	24.3	25.4	23.4	26.6	23.5	26.5	21.3	26.3	30.0	26.3	32.1
4. Mostly agree	39.2	39.4	40.0	40.3	37.1	38.2	40.0	39.3	38.7	39.9	40.4	42.2	40.0	34.4	37.2	38.4
5. Agree	22.1	20.5	22.2	19.0	36.1	19.8	20.0	26.4	20.2	23.5	19.1	24.9	20.0	21.9	18.8	12.9
Item 1620 N(Wtd)	3735	1718	1814	2921	405	900	1083	1238	513	1738	1546	1286	1068	406	751	45

QUESTIONNAIRE FORM 1 1978	TOTAL	SEX		RACE		REGION				4YR COLLEGE PLANS		ILLICIT DRUG USE: LIFETIME				
		M	F	White	Black	NE	NC	S	W	Yes	No	None	Mari- juana Only	Few Pills	More Pills	Any Her- oin
Weighted No. of Cases:	3799	1740	1842	2962	411	922	1096	1257	524	1758	1571	1301	1086	411	760	46
% of Weighted Total:	100.0	45.8	48.5	78.0	10.8	24.3	28.8	33.1	13.8	46.3	41.3	34.3	28.6	10.8	20.0	1.2

A011F: Despite its many faults, our system of doing things is still the best in the world

	TOTAL	M	F	White	Black	NE	NC	S	W	Yes	No	None	Mari-juana Only	Few Pills	More Pills	Any Heroin
1. Disagree	6.9	6.0	7.1	5.2	14.9	9.8	5.5	7.1	4.3	4.9	8.0	6.0	5.9	6.3	8.1	10.3
2. Mostly disagree	7.0	5.7	8.0	6.3	11.1	9.1	7.3	6.0	5.1	5.8	7.5	4.5	7.7	8.4	8.5	5.8
3. Neither	21.4	18.8	24.3	20.6	21.7	24.0	22.9	17.7	22.8	18.8	23.7	18.9	23.4	22.7	21.9	31.3
4. Mostly agree	31.3	29.9	33.3	32.7	28.1	29.2	32.9	30.9	32.3	32.4	32.2	34.1	29.7	31.8	30.5	37.4
5. Agree	33.3	39.6	27.3	35.1	24.2	27.8	31.3	38.2	35.5	38.2	28.7	36.6	33.3	30.8	31.0	15.1
Item 1630 N(Wtd)	3748	1724	1823	2933	407	906	1089	1242	512	1744	1555	1287	1072	407	756	46

A011G: America needs growth to survive, and that is going to require some increase in pollution

	TOTAL	M	F	White	Black	NE	NC	S	W	Yes	No	None	Mari-juana Only	Few Pills	More Pills	Any Heroin
1. Disagree	36.6	37.6	36.3	37.8	35.1	40.0	35.3	36.4	34.2	41.0	32.6	34.9	35.6	39.9	39.0	42.7
2. Mostly disagree	21.2	21.4	21.4	23.0	11.6	20.0	22.3	19.8	23.8	22.9	20.5	22.7	21.3	20.4	20.3	24.1
3. Neither	19.4	17.9	20.9	19.1	17.4	16.9	20.9	19.5	20.6	16.5	22.3	19.7	20.2	16.8	19.2	18.3
4. Mostly agree	14.1	14.9	12.8	13.4	19.5	15.2	13.8	13.9	13.2	12.4	15.9	13.4	14.5	13.6	14.4	8.4
5. Agree	8.7	8.2	8.5	6.7	16.4	8.0	7.7	10.4	8.3	7.2	8.8	9.3	8.3	9.3	7.1	6.5
Item 1640 N(Wtd)	3734	1721	1811	2924	404	904	1084	1233	513	1739	1546	1283	1067	404	752	46

A011H: If we just leave things to God, they will turn out for the best

	TOTAL	M	F	White	Black	NE	NC	S	W	Yes	No	None	Mari-juana Only	Few Pills	More Pills	Any Heroin
1. Disagree	22.4	25.8	19.5	24.0	11.3	29.4	23.5	15.1	25.4	25.5	18.4	16.0	22.1	29.1	30.7	31.5
2. Mostly disagree	14.1	14.6	13.8	15.1	7.8	16.9	15.6	9.8	16.4	14.6	13.6	12.2	15.2	18.2	14.7	11.2
3. Neither	24.8	26.0	23.6	25.5	18.1	27.3	27.0	21.3	23.9	24.5	25.2	21.3	29.6	21.1	26.1	28.0
4. Mostly agree	17.1	16.0	18.2	16.8	20.1	14.6	16.8	19.8	15.7	16.9	18.3	20.3	15.2	14.8	15.5	12.8
5. Agree	21.5	17.7	24.9	18.7	42.7	11.7	17.0	34.0	18.5	18.5	24.6	30.2	18.0	16.8	13.1	16.6
Item 1650 N(Wtd)	3732	1714	1813	2921	402	905	1082	1232	513	1735	1546	1281	1070	404	751	44

A011I: Going to school has been an enjoyable experience for me

	TOTAL	M	F	White	Black	NE	NC	S	W	Yes	No	None	Mari-juana Only	Few Pills	More Pills	Any Heroin
1. Disagree	7.6	8.2	6.8	7.3	7.5	10.5	7.7	6.5	5.1	4.2	10.5	4.1	6.5	6.6	13.9	18.8
2. Mostly disagree	7.2	6.9	7.3	7.2	5.1	7.0	8.1	6.8	6.8	5.0	8.3	4.6	6.2	8.1	12.2	13.3
3. Neither	13.8	14.6	12.1	14.3	8.7	17.5	14.3	9.9	15.3	13.0	14.8	11.7	14.4	14.5	16.5	9.6
4. Mostly agree	38.6	39.3	39.1	40.9	33.4	35.3	40.2	39.5	39.0	40.0	39.1	40.9	39.7	39.5	34.9	36.1
5. Agree	32.7	30.3	34.7	30.3	45.2	29.6	29.6	37.2	33.9	37.8	27.3	38.7	33.2	31.2	22.5	22.2
Item 1660 N(Wtd)	3756	1726	1824	2939	405	907	1090	1243	516	1744	1558	1290	1074	407	756	46

A011J: Doing well in school is important for getting a good job

	TOTAL	M	F	White	Black	NE	NC	S	W	Yes	No	None	Mari-juana Only	Few Pills	More Pills	Any Heroin
1. Disagree	2.6	3.6	1.5	2.5	1.8	4.4	2.7	1.6	1.3	2.1	3.0	1.7	2.1	3.3	3.7	6.9
2. Mostly disagree	4.6	5.0	3.9	4.7	4.1	5.7	3.4	4.4	5.5	2.6	6.6	2.9	4.8	4.7	6.6	13.8
3. Neither	8.5	9.8	6.9	8.5	5.2	8.2	10.2	6.2	10.9	6.2	10.2	5.3	10.3	10.6	10.2	13.5
4. Mostly agree	32.6	32.9	32.7	34.9	21.7	32.0	37.9	28.6	31.6	33.4	32.0	32.7	32.1	30.0	35.4	37.8
5. Agree	51.8	48.6	55.0	49.5	67.3	49.7	45.8	59.1	50.8	55.8	48.2	57.5	50.8	51.3	44.1	28.0
Item 1670 N(Wtd)	3760	1727	1828	2940	408	909	1089	1246	516	1749	1557	1293	1077	408	754	46

The following questions are about CIGARETTE SMOKING.

B001: Have you ever smoked cigarettes?

	TOTAL	M	F	White	Black	NE	NC	S	W	Yes	No	None	Mari-juana Only	Few Pills	More Pills	Any Heroin
1. Never--GO TO Q.B006	25.1	25.6	25.4	25.6	25.9	23.4	24.3	24.4	31.7	32.3	19.7	50.9	12.2	17.2	7.6	-
2. Once or twice	26.2	28.1	25.0	25.2	33.2	24.0	26.0	26.8	28.9	27.5	25.5	33.1	29.6	22.2	12.6	12.8
3. Occasionally but not regularly	16.4	15.6	17.6	16.7	16.5	15.3	14.8	19.6	13.8	17.6	15.8	8.4	24.7	20.8	14.9	10.2
4. Regularly in the past	8.7	8.6	8.5	8.6	7.9	8.7	9.9	8.2	6.9	8.3	8.9	3.7	8.8	9.4	15.1	25.8
5. Regularly now	23.6	22.1	23.6	23.9	16.4	28.6	25.0	20.9	18.6	14.4	30.1	3.9	24.8	30.5	49.7	51.1
Item 760 N(Wtd)	3728	1712	1813	2924	401	902	1084	1234	508	1730	1546	1270	1074	407	754	45

QUESTIONNAIRE FORM 1 1978	TOTAL	SEX		RACE		REGION				4YR COLLEGE PLANS		ILLICIT DRUG USE: LIFETIME				
		M	F	White	Black	NE	NC	S	W	Yes	No	None	Mari-juana Only	Few Pills	More Pills	Any Her-oin
Weighted No. of Cases:	3799	1740	1842	2962	411	922	1096	1257	524	1758	1571	1301	1086	411	760	46
% of Weighted Total:	100.0	45.8	48.5	78.0	10.8	24.3	28.8	33.1	13.8	46.3	41.3	34.3	28.6	10.8	20.0	1.2

B002: When did you first smoke cigarettes on a daily basis?†

	TOTAL	M	F	White	Black	NE	NC	S	W	Yes	No	None	Mari-juana Only	Few Pills	More Pills	Any Her-oin
0. Never smoked daily	42.3	45.5	41.4	43.9	40.4	37.7	41.5	43.7	49.8	53.7	37.0	69.4	46.0	35.1	19.2	13.0
1. Grade 6 or earlier	5.6	7.1	3.9	5.6	4.9	4.9	5.8	5.7	6.7	4.3	6.5	5.4	3.8	6.5	7.0	27.0
2. Grade 7 or 8	15.8	14.7	15.8	16.3	9.9	18.7	14.5	15.7	12.9	12.8	17.0	6.7	12.3	17.7	26.7	24.2
3. Grade 9 (Freshman)	13.8	12.8	14.6	13.5	13.4	17.2	14.7	11.1	12.3	10.5	15.4	5.8	12.5	16.5	21.9	15.0
4. Grade 10 (Sophomore)	10.0	9.4	10.4	9.1	12.9	11.2	8.7	11.0	8.4	7.3	11.1	4.9	10.9	11.0	12.9	1.4
5. Grade 11 (Junior)	8.4	7.4	9.1	8.1	11.9	8.0	10.9	7.0	6.9	7.2	9.0	3.9	10.0	9.4	8.6	19.4
6. Grade 12 (Senior)	4.0	3.1	4.8	3.5	6.5	2.2	3.9	5.9	3.0	4.2	4.0	3.9	4.5	3.7	3.6	-
Item 1680　N(Wtd) ★	2778	1265	1345	2159	295	686	817	930	345	1164	1234	620	938	334	695	45

B003: How frequently have you smoked cigarettes during the past 30 days?

	TOTAL	M	F	White	Black	NE	NC	S	W	Yes	No	None	Mari-juana Only	Few Pills	More Pills	Any Her-oin
1. Not at all	51.5	54.3	50.6	51.2	58.8	46.6	50.0	53.8	58.5	58.9	47.9	79.8	52.4	43.0	30.4	37.7
2. Less than one cigarette per day	11.7	10.7	12.8	11.7	13.9	10.5	11.6	12.9	10.8	15.1	9.6	9.5	14.2	15.4	8.6	4.7
3. One to five cigarettes per day	11.7	9.5	13.8	10.7	17.4	12.3	13.0	11.5	7.8	10.4	12.2	5.7	11.7	13.6	14.1	7.3
4. About one-half pack per day	11.3	10.7	11.1	11.4	7.8	13.8	11.8	10.4	7.8	7.5	13.1	2.5	11.8	14.1	17.5	7.5
5. About one pack per day	10.8	11.6	8.9	11.7	1.6	13.8	9.8	8.8	12.3	6.7	13.1	1.7	7.7	10.8	23.1	32.1
6. About one and one-half packs per day	2.7	2.8	2.4	2.9	.3	2.5	3.1	2.3	2.6	1.0	3.7	.7	2.0	2.5	5.4	9.0
7. Two packs or more per day	.4	.4	.4	.4	.2	.5	.6	.2	.3	.4	.4	-	.2	.6	.7	1.7
Item 780　N(Wtd) ★	2786	1266	1350	2169	295	687	818	934	346	1171	1237	625	939	336	695	45

B004: Have you ever tried to stop smoking and found that you could not?

	TOTAL	M	F	White	Black	NE	NC	S	W	Yes	No	None	Mari-juana Only	Few Pills	More Pills	Any Her-oin
1. Yes	20.5	18.1	21.3	19.4	23.5	21.8	21.7	20.5	15.0	14.4	23.7	10.2	15.8	21.1	32.9	26.2
2. No	79.5	81.9	78.7	80.6	76.5	78.2	78.2	79.5	85.0	85.6	76.3	89.8	84.1	78.9	67.1	73.8
Item 1690　N(Wtd) ★	2629	1198	1269	2061	269	652	774	882	321	1093	1175	555	890	324	683	45

B005: Do you want to stop smoking now?

	TOTAL	M	F	White	Black	NE	NC	S	W	Yes	No	None	Mari-juana Only	Few Pills	More Pills	Any Her-oin
1. Yes	19.9	19.2	19.6	19.4	24.0	24.1	21.4	18.1	13.3	15.2	22.1	6.9	18.8	22.6	29.6	29.9
2. No	21.7	20.4	22.1	22.0	12.6	23.2	21.6	20.6	21.8	16.0	25.6	7.0	21.3	22.9	35.0	30.5
8. Don't smoke now	58.4	60.4	58.3	58.6	63.4	52.7	57.0	61.4	64.9	68.8	52.3	86.1	60.0	54.5	35.4	39.6
Item 1700　N(Wtd) ★	2711	1235	1313	2117	284	668	797	910	336	1132	1213	601	917	320	686	44

B006: Do you think you will be smoking cigarettes five years from now?

	TOTAL	M	F	White	Black	NE	NC	S	W	Yes	No	None	Mari-juana Only	Few Pills	More Pills	Any Her-oin
1. I definitely will	.6	.9	.3	.6	.3	.7	.8	.4	.7	.5	.5	.2	.5	.8	1.2	3.9
2. I probably will	16.6	14.5	18.4	16.8	12.8	18.9	17.6	16.8	9.9	10.5	23.0	4.3	18.7	18.2	33.2	26.5
3. I probably will not	28.2	28.4	28.2	27.7	32.3	27.6	28.6	29.0	26.3	25.9	30.3	22.4	31.6	33.4	30.6	31.6
4. I definitely will not	54.5	56.2	53.1	54.9	54.7	52.7	52.9	53.7	63.1	63.1	46.2	73.2	49.2	47.6	35.0	38.0
Item 1710　N(Wtd)	3717	1700	1812	2909	401	897	1079	1232	509	1725	1540	1274	1065	406	747	46

The different questionnaire forms used in this study tend to emphasize somewhat different topics. The next major section in this form deals with alcohol and various other drugs. There is a lot of talk these days about these subjects, but very little accurate information. Therefore, we still have a lot to learn about the actual experiences and attitudes of people your age.

We hope that you can answer all questions; but if you find one which you feel you cannot answer honestly, we would prefer that you leave it blank.

† Wording changed from previous year.　　★ = excludes respondents for whom question was inappropriate.

QUESTIONNAIRE FORM 1 1978	TOTAL	SEX		RACE		REGION				4YR COLLEGE PLANS		ILLICIT DRUG USE: LIFETIME				
		M	F	White	Black	NE	NC	S	W	Yes	No	None	Mari-juana Only	Few Pills	More Pills	Any Her-oin
Weighted No. of Cases:	3799	1740	1842	2962	411	922	1096	1257	524	1758	1571	1301	1086	411	760	46
% of Weighted Total:	100.0	45.8	48.5	78.0	10.8	24.3	28.8	33.1	13.8	46.3	41.3	34.3	28.6	10.8	20.0	1.2

Remember that your answers will be strictly confidential. We never connect them with your name or your class.

The next questions are about ALCOHOLIC BEVERAGES, including beer, wine, and liquor.

B007: On how many occasions (if any) have you had alcohol to drink...

B007A: ...in your lifetime?

	TOTAL	M	F	White	Black	NE	NC	S	W	Yes	No	None	Mari-juana Only	Few Pills	More Pills	Any Her-oin
1. 0 occasions	6.9	4.7	8.8	5.6	15.3	3.6	4.7	9.9	10.4	7.4	6.6	16.5	1.7	2.5	.5	-
2. 1-2	7.7	5.5	9.8	6.2	17.1	4.9	6.9	10.8	7.1	7.3	8.0	17.2	2.9	3.0	1.2	-
3. 3-5	7.5	7.2	8.1	6.5	14.9	5.6	5.5	10.2	8.5	7.4	8.0	13.9	5.4	4.9	.6	-
4. 6-9	7.6	6.9	8.6	7.0	12.1	8.6	6.5	7.3	9.1	7.8	8.2	11.5	7.8	7.2	1.5	-
5. 10-19	12.7	10.0	15.3	12.8	14.2	14.1	10.5	13.7	12.2	13.3	12.4	14.8	15.1	11.8	6.8	5.5
6. 20-39	13.5	12.5	14.7	14.2	11.1	15.5	13.9	11.8	13.4	15.5	12.4	9.5	17.9	17.0	11.9	11.5
7. 40 or more	44.1	53.2	34.7	47.8	15.2	47.7	52.0	36.4	39.2	41.1	44.4	16.6	49.2	53.6	77.4	82.9
Item 810 N(Wtd)	3566	1639	1746	2835	363	866	1041	1170	489	1698	1460	1247	1029	382	722	42

B007B: ...during the last 12 months?

	TOTAL	M	F	White	Black	NE	NC	S	W	Yes	No	None	Mari-juana Only	Few Pills	More Pills	Any Her-oin
1. 0 occasions	13.5	10.1	16.2	10.6	30.1	7.7	9.3	20.1	16.9	13.6	13.5	29.7	6.2	5.0	1.8	-
2. 1-2	11.9	10.0	14.2	10.2	24.3	11.2	10.4	13.5	12.4	12.6	11.6	22.1	8.5	8.7	1.8	-
3. 3-5	12.1	10.2	13.8	11.4	17.6	12.7	9.9	12.9	13.7	11.2	13.6	14.7	13.2	10.4	6.6	12.3
4. 6-9	11.8	11.1	12.9	12.8	8.1	11.7	12.6	11.0	12.3	12.4	11.8	11.5	13.2	13.3	10.0	10.2
5. 10-19	15.8	17.0	15.1	17.1	9.5	16.4	18.8	12.7	16.1	16.8	15.7	10.0	21.8	21.8	13.7	14.4
6. 20-39	14.3	13.8	14.9	15.8	4.7	15.9	15.1	13.0	12.6	15.1	12.9	6.7	16.7	15.7	22.0	12.9
7. 40 or more	20.6	27.8	12.8	22.0	5.6	24.4	23.9	16.8	16.0	18.2	20.8	5.3	20.3	24.9	44.1	50.2
Item 820 N(Wtd)	3544	1631	1735	2820	362	864	1042	1157	482	1680	1456	1232	1020	385	723	45

B007C: ...during the last 30 days?

	TOTAL	M	F	White	Black	NE	NC	S	W	Yes	No	None	Mari-juana Only	Few Pills	More Pills	Any Her-oin
1. 0 occasions	28.9	23.1	34.4	25.0	55.3	22.1	22.9	36.5	35.5	29.2	29.4	53.7	21.4	15.5	7.5	14.6
2. 1-2	22.4	20.6	24.4	22.5	24.2	22.4	22.6	22.3	22.2	22.9	22.6	24.4	23.5	24.9	16.2	14.5
3. 3-5	19.4	21.1	18.0	21.1	9.8	21.1	20.5	16.9	20.0	21.0	18.5	11.3	25.9	23.3	20.6	9.8
4. 6-9	13.1	14.9	11.4	14.4	4.7	15.5	14.3	11.4	9.9	13.2	12.4	5.9	13.6	19.3	20.9	12.9
5. 10-19	10.8	12.8	8.6	11.4	3.5	12.1	12.9	8.9	8.6	9.7	10.6	3.2	11.5	12.0	21.1	35.6
6. 20-39	3.2	4.4	2.0	3.4	1.0	3.4	4.5	2.4	2.0	2.5	3.9	.8	2.1	2.9	8.8	6.4
7. 40 or more	2.2	3.0	1.1	2.2	1.3	3.3	2.2	1.5	1.7	1.5	2.6	.7	1.9	2.1	4.8	6.3
Item 830 N(Wtd)	3556	1643	1728	2833	359	866	1045	1161	484	1694	1441	1217	1025	391	738	45

IF YOU HAVE NOT HAD ANY BEER, WINE, OR LIQUOR IN THE LAST TWELVE MONTHS, GO TO Q.B017.

B008: When you used alcohol during the last year, how often did you use it in each of the following situations?

B008A: When you were alone

	TOTAL	M	F	White	Black	NE	NC	S	W	Yes	No	None	Mari-juana Only	Few Pills	More Pills	Any Her-oin
1. Not at all	68.2	61.3	77.5	69.2	66.9	70.5	67.8	64.0	74.4	71.8	67.3	82.3	70.6	63.4	52.7	50.2
2. A few of the times	24.3	28.7	19.0	24.4	24.3	24.9	24.6	25.7	19.5	22.5	25.0	14.2	22.8	29.0	35.2	27.9
3. Some of the times	6.3	8.6	2.8	5.4	5.8	3.7	7.0	8.6	4.4	4.9	6.1	2.6	5.8	6.2	10.3	18.9
4. Most of the times	1.0	1.2	.6	.8	2.7	.7	.6	1.4	1.5	.6	1.4	.5	.5	1.3	1.8	1.4
5. Every time	.2	.2	.1	.2	.3	.1	-	.4	.2	.2	.1	.3	.2	-	-	1.7
Item 1720 N(Wtd) ★	3113	1483	1473	2548	253	808	939	945	421	1470	1269	858	977	380	720	45

B008B: With just 1 or 2 other people

	TOTAL	M	F	White	Black	NE	NC	S	W	Yes	No	None	Mari-juana Only	Few Pills	More Pills	Any Her-oin
1. Not at all	12.3	8.1	17.0	11.4	18.7	15.1	11.2	10.3	14.0	14.6	10.9	26.1	9.4	8.0	4.2	1.5
2. A few of the times	29.6	24.8	34.7	28.6	39.6	31.1	27.2	28.5	34.4	31.5	28.8	33.0	31.7	27.9	23.1	28.5
3. Some of the times	28.0	31.9	23.8	29.4	17.1	29.6	28.2	27.1	26.9	27.1	28.6	18.5	27.6	31.5	35.9	47.7
4. Most of the times	24.0	27.9	19.5	24.6	16.4	20.4	28.2	25.4	18.5	21.6	24.4	15.6	24.8	27.1	32.1	20.9
5. Every time	6.0	7.4	5.0	5.9	8.1	3.8	5.1	8.8	6.1	5.2	7.3	6.8	6.5	5.6	4.7	1.4
Item 1730 N(Wtd) ★	3113	1485	1473	2552	254	808	945	940	419	1468	1270	858	973	380	723	45

★ = excludes respondents for whom question was inappropriate.

QUESTIONNAIRE FORM 1 1978	TOTAL	SEX		RACE		REGION				4YR COLLEGE PLANS		ILLICIT DRUG USE: LIFETIME				
		M	F	White	Black	NE	NC	S	W	Yes	No	None	Mari-juana Only	Few Pills	More Pills	Any Her-oin
Weighted No. of Cases:	3799	1740	1842	2962	411	922	1096	1257	524	1758	1571	1301	1086	411	760	46
% of Weighted Total:	100.0	45.8	48.5	78.0	10.8	24.3	28.8	33.1	13.8	46.3	41.3	34.3	28.6	10.8	20.0	1.2

B008C: At a party

1. Not at all	12.0	12.8	11.7	11.8	17.7	9.1	12.3	13.1	14.5	12.0	13.4	24.3	8.9	8.3	4.1	1.5
2. A few of the times	19.9	18.3	21.2	18.9	25.3	18.7	17.5	21.0	25.2	20.9	18.3	27.6	19.7	20.7	11.3	4.6
3. Some of the times	18.6	18.3	19.2	18.5	20.1	19.0	19.6	18.5	15.7	18.9	18.4	13.9	20.3	18.7	21.2	23.9
4. Most of the times	30.4	31.6	29.3	31.7	22.1	33.9	30.3	28.0	29.3	32.2	29.8	21.7	31.5	32.9	36.7	36.4
5. Every time	19.1	19.0	18.6	19.1	14.9	19.3	20.4	19.4	15.2	16.0	20.1	12.5	19.6	19.3	26.7	33.6
Item 1740 N(Wtd) ★	3119	1484	1477	2551	257	808	950	946	416	1470	1269	860	976	378	724	45

B008D: When your date or spouse was present

1. Not at all	30.5	34.7	26.7	28.9	45.5	30.4	27.8	31.4	35.2	33.6	29.1	50.2	29.2	21.8	13.1	29.3
2. A few of the times	27.3	28.6	26.3	27.0	31.9	26.7	26.7	28.1	28.2	28.3	27.0	24.9	32.1	28.7	23.9	12.9
3. Some of the times	19.7	20.7	18.3	20.1	13.0	20.1	22.1	16.4	21.1	19.5	18.2	11.2	19.1	23.5	28.4	21.3
4. Most of the times	16.5	12.7	19.9	17.5	7.2	18.2	16.7	16.9	11.6	14.2	17.8	8.4	14.8	18.7	27.0	26.3
5. Every time	5.9	3.3	8.7	6.5	2.4	4.5	6.6	7.2	3.9	4.4	7.9	5.3	4.7	7.2	7.6	10.2
Item 1750 N(Wtd) ★	3072	1457	1459	2513	253	799	930	934	409	1445	1253	851	954	377	714	44

B008E: When people over age 30 were present

1. Not at all	25.8	25.6	26.3	24.2	45.0	20.9	22.4	32.6	27.4	25.9	25.3	31.6	28.7	24.2	14.8	17.8
2. A few of the times	39.3	39.3	39.9	39.9	33.0	41.6	39.1	37.8	38.7	40.7	38.6	33.4	42.0	39.2	42.8	52.1
3. Some of the times	22.1	23.0	19.8	22.6	12.4	22.7	25.0	19.9	19.3	20.9	22.4	15.1	20.5	25.8	30.8	23.1
4. Most of the times	8.8	9.2	8.9	9.0	6.4	10.9	8.8	6.7	9.8	7.7	10.2	10.9	7.0	6.8	9.6	4.4
5. Every time	4.0	3.0	5.1	4.3	3.3	3.9	4.7	3.1	4.8	4.9	3.5	8.9	1.7	3.9	1.9	2.6
Item 1760 N(Wtd) ★	3118	1487	1473	2553	253	808	948	940	422	1470	1269	861	975	379	724	45

B008F: During the daytime (before 4:00 p.m.)

1. Not at all	57.3	48.3	68.3	56.7	68.5	59.0	57.1	56.5	56.1	61.6	55.0	74.6	59.4	54.6	36.1	26.4
2. A few of the times	32.7	39.1	25.4	33.5	24.8	31.6	32.6	34.0	32.0	30.5	34.3	20.6	34.0	36.8	43.1	42.7
3. Some of the times	8.4	10.7	5.3	8.2	5.5	7.5	8.2	8.5	10.5	6.9	8.8	3.1	5.5	8.1	17.9	24.9
4. Most of the times	1.2	1.4	.9	1.1	1.1	1.5	1.6	1.0	.5	.6	1.7	.8	1.0	.5	2.6	2.7
5. Every time	.4	.6	.2	.5	-	.4	.5	.1	.9	.4	.3	.9	.1	-	.4	3.3
Item 1770 N(Wtd) ★	3106	1483	1471	2549	253	805	944	939	418	1467	1266	855	974	379	724	45

B008G: At your home (or apartment or dorm)

1. Not at all	35.3	34.8	37.0	35.5	38.3	32.1	30.0	42.6	36.7	36.1	35.7	46.2	38.1	29.7	21.8	21.9
2. A few of the times	36.5	35.4	37.1	36.4	38.8	38.6	37.3	34.5	35.0	36.7	36.7	31.5	37.3	41.4	39.3	33.5
3. Some of the times	17.9	18.9	16.2	18.2	10.7	19.9	20.7	14.7	15.1	17.5	17.0	9.6	17.8	21.0	25.9	29.1
4. Most of the times	7.9	9.0	6.9	7.5	9.5	7.0	9.8	5.8	9.9	7.0	8.6	8.0	6.0	7.1	10.4	10.7
5. Every time	2.4	2.0	2.8	2.4	2.6	2.5	2.2	2.3	3.2	2.7	2.0	4.6	.8	.7	2.5	4.7
Item 1780 N(Wtd) ★	3110	1484	1472	2548	254	808	944	939	418	1466	1268	858	973	380	724	45

B008H: At school

1. Not at all	85.3	80.5	91.2	85.9	84.4	86.4	86.2	84.6	82.8	88.5	83.1	94.6	87.4	81.9	73.8	63.8
2. A few of the times	11.4	15.5	6.7	11.2	11.5	11.1	9.7	11.8	14.6	9.6	12.7	3.7	10.1	15.8	19.7	23.8
3. Some of the times	2.6	3.0	1.7	2.2	3.0	1.7	3.1	3.0	2.2	1.2	3.5	1.1	2.2	1.8	5.1	7.4
4. Most of the times	.6	.8	.3	.6	.3	.5	.8	.4	.4	.6	.5	.3	.3	.5	1.2	3.0
5. Every time	.2	.2	.1	.1	.7	.3	.2	.2	-	-	.3	.3	-	-	.1	2.0
Item 1790 N(Wtd) ★	3111	1483	1475	2549	255	809	944	939	420	1469	1267	858	974	380	724	45

B008I: In a car

1. Not at all	30.2	23.3	38.4	28.3	45.5	34.7	26.9	24.7	41.5	34.9	26.8	53.0	25.2	23.2	15.0	16.9
2. A few of the times	24.6	23.8	25.4	24.0	33.8	22.5	22.2	28.7	25.2	25.1	24.9	21.2	27.7	24.4	24.4	31.9
3. Some of the times	24.9	28.1	21.5	27.0	10.0	25.1	25.4	25.9	21.1	24.6	23.6	13.1	26.2	29.2	34.8	22.3
4. Most of the times	17.4	21.5	12.7	18.0	8.7	15.5	21.8	17.6	11.0	14.0	20.9	10.8	18.2	19.3	22.5	20.9
5. Every time	2.8	3.5	2.0	2.7	2.1	2.3	3.6	3.1	1.2	1.4	3.8	1.9	2.7	3.8	3.3	7.9
Item 1810 N(Wtd) ★	3114	1485	1474	2551	255	810	948	938	419	1466	1272	859	974	380	725	45

★ = excludes respondents for whom question was inappropriate.

QUESTIONNAIRE FORM 1 1978	TOTAL	SEX		RACE		REGION				4YR COLLEGE PLANS		ILLICIT DRUG USE: LIFETIME				
		M	F	White	Black	NE	NC	S	W	Yes	No	None	Mari-juana Only	Few Pills	More Pills	Any Her-oin
Weighted No. of Cases:	3799	1740	1842	2962	411	922	1096	1257	524	1758	1571	1301	1086	411	760	46
% of Weighted Total:	100.0	45.8	48.5	78.0	10.8	24.3	28.8	33.1	13.8	46.3	41.3	34.3	28.6	10.8	20.0	1.2

B009: What have been the most important reasons for your drinking alcoholic beverages? (Mark all that apply.)

	TOTAL	M	F	White	Black	NE	NC	S	W	Yes	No	None	Mari-juana Only	Few Pills	More Pills	Any Her-oin
A. To experiment--to see what it's like	37.4	35.0	40.3	36.2	54.6	35.6	35.8	41.8	34.7	39.0	37.1	45.8	37.1	34.1	30.3	22.3
B. To relax or relieve tension	39.5	37.5	41.0	41.2	20.5	43.6	39.0	37.9	36.5	39.8	38.8	26.1	37.4	44.4	54.6	42.4
C. To feel good or get high	53.6	59.3	47.0	54.7	44.9	59.7	53.8	49.0	52.4	52.0	52.6	23.6	58.2	63.2	75.2	72.6
D. To seek deeper insights and understanding	3.9	4.8	2.6	3.6	4.1	5.7	2.8	3.4	4.4	3.5	3.7	1.9	3.9	3.5	5.8	9.0
E. To have a good time with my friends	68.7	73.9	63.7	70.3	56.4	69.9	71.7	64.4	68.9	68.3	69.0	56.1	73.9	68.9	75.8	72.8
F. To fit in with a group I like	11.2	13.6	9.2	12.0	5.7	8.5	13.3	12.3	9.4	12.0	11.3	13.9	11.1	8.6	8.8	19.3
G. To get away from my problems or troubles	16.9	16.0	17.5	16.8	10.7	19.6	16.1	17.2	13.2	15.0	18.6	11.2	15.8	17.2	23.5	32.8
H. Because of boredom, nothing else to do	21.7	22.7	20.6	21.8	22.3	24.8	22.3	22.1	13.4	21.3	22.4	14.0	21.6	22.3	30.4	31.3
I. Because of anger or frustration	14.3	13.2	14.7	14.6	8.3	16.5	14.2	14.7	9.5	12.9	15.7	10.3	12.5	14.3	20.1	27.3
J. To get through the day	1.8	2.2	1.2	1.6	2.1	3.1	1.1	1.7	.9	1.1	2.3	.7	.9	1.7	3.9	1.6
K. To increase the effects of some other drug(s)	8.3	9.2	6.0	8.0	8.2	11.8	6.4	7.4	7.6	6.8	7.0	-	3.2	7.8	23.0	32.0
L. To decrease (offset) the effects of some other drug(s)	1.2	1.0	1.0	1.1	.3	1.9	1.3	.9	.5	.7	1.2	-	.7	1.2	2.5	10.5
M. To get to sleep	6.1	7.0	4.6	5.9	6.7	6.7	4.7	6.6	6.8	6.1	5.6	4.7	5.4	4.3	9.6	6.6
N. Because it tastes good	51.2	52.4	50.9	54.3	34.5	51.3	54.9	47.7	50.4	53.6	50.0	48.7	47.0	53.8	59.3	49.9
O. Because I am "hooked"--I feel I have to drink	.5	.6	.4	.5	.7	.5	.7	.5	-	.4	.7		.1	.3	1.0	3.7
Item 1820-1960 N(Wtd) ★	3030	1461	1422	2482	249	773	933	922	402	1430	1239	805	968	368	720	45

B010: When you drink alcoholic beverages, how high do you usually get?

	TOTAL	M	F	White	Black	NE	NC	S	W	Yes	No	None	Mari-juana Only	Few Pills	More Pills	Any Her-oin
1. Not at all high	19.1	13.5	25.4	18.4	27.8	16.3	18.0	22.1	20.2	22.3	17.6	45.0	9.2	12.7	5.4	7.3
2. A little high	33.9	33.3	35.3	33.1	42.3	34.4	33.8	33.5	34.1	33.5	35.6	36.1	39.7	33.3	24.8	25.0
3. Moderately high	39.9	44.8	34.5	41.9	25.4	40.2	42.5	37.8	37.7	39.3	39.5	17.5	45.7	45.6	55.3	45.4
4. Very high	7.1	8.4	4.7	6.6	4.5	9.0	5.6	6.5	8.0	5.0	7.3	1.4	5.4	8.3	14.4	22.3
Item 1970 N(Wtd) ★	3097	1480	1469	2542	252	804	945	937	411	1456	1273	846	980	378	720	45

B011: When you drink alcoholic beverages, how long do you usually stay high?

	TOTAL	M	F	White	Black	NE	NC	S	W	Yes	No	None	Mari-juana Only	Few Pills	More Pills	Any Her-oin
1. Usually don't get high	21.3	15.5	27.6	20.2	33.6	18.3	20.6	24.5	21.5	24.6	19.5	48.4	11.8	14.1	6.9	3.7
2. One to two hours	39.8	39.5	40.5	40.0	39.4	39.7	39.1	41.0	38.7	41.2	39.1	33.9	49.1	42.1	32.5	40.3
3. Three to six hours	35.7	41.6	29.4	36.8	24.6	38.1	37.4	31.4	36.8	31.9	38.0	17.0	37.1	40.4	54.1	46.9
4. Seven to 24 hours	3.1	3.2	2.5	2.8	2.4	3.9	2.9	2.8	3.1	2.3	3.2	.5	2.1	3.4	6.5	5.4
5. More than 24 hours	.1	.2	-	.1	-	-	-	.3	-	-	.2	.1	-	-	-	3.6
Item 1980 N(Wtd) ★	3073	1473	1455	2528	246	799	940	925	409	1444	1263	832	979	375	716	45

The following questions ask about how much you have to drink on the occasions when you drink alcoholic beverages. For these questions, a "drink" means any of the following: A 12-ounce can (or bottle) of beer, a 4-ounce glass of wine, a mixed drink or shot glass of liquor.

B012: Think back over the LAST TWO WEEKS. How many times have you had five or more drinks in a row?

	TOTAL	M	F	White	Black	NE	NC	S	W	Yes	No	None	Mari-juana Only	Few Pills	More Pills	Any Her-oin
1. None	59.4	47.6	72.4	57.9	79.4	56.5	55.6	63.1	65.2	62.5	58.9	79.3	58.0	56.2	40.4	36.9
2. Once	13.8	16.2	11.7	14.4	10.7	12.7	14.5	14.7	12.1	15.3	12.3	10.9	15.5	14.9	14.3	10.2
3. Twice	10.5	13.6	7.3	10.7	5.7	12.0	10.7	9.4	9.9	9.0	11.5	5.5	13.3	10.8	12.7	11.4
4. 3 to 5 times	12.2	16.7	6.8	12.8	3.0	13.2	14.6	10.1	9.1	10.0	13.0	3.7	10.2	14.2	22.9	27.9
5. 6 to 9 times	2.9	4.2	1.4	3.0	1.2	3.6	3.4	2.0	2.7	2.3	3.3	.4	2.0	2.4	7.2	10.4
6. 10 or more times	1.2	1.7	.5	1.1	-	2.0	1.2	.7	1.0	.9	1.0	.2	1.0	1.5	2.5	3.2
Item 850 N(Wtd) ★	3076	1461	1464	2519	251	801	943	920	413	1454	1254	848	967	377	716	42

★ = excludes respondents for whom question was inappropriate.

QUESTIONNAIRE FORM 1 1978	TOTAL	SEX		RACE		REGION				4YR COLLEGE PLANS		ILLICIT DRUG USE: LIFETIME				
		M	F	White	Black	NE	NC	S	W	Yes	No	None	Mari- juana Only	Few Pills	More Pills	Any Her- oin
Weighted No. of Cases:	3799	1740	1842	2962	411	922	1096	1257	524	1758	1571	1301	1086	411	760	46
% of Weighted Total:	100.0	45.8	48.5	78.0	10.8	24.3	28.8	33.1	13.8	46.3	41.3	34.3	28.6	10.8	20.0	1.2

B013: During the last two weeks, how many times have you had 3 or 4 drinks in a row (but no more than that)? †

1. None	55.4	47.1	64.3	53.1	78.4	53.6	52.8	56.6	62.0	57.6	54.9	78.8	55.1	49.6	31.2	48.0
2. Once	19.0	20.7	18.0	20.2	14.6	20.6	18.8	18.9	16.7	20.4	18.8	12.5	21.4	20.8	23.6	9.2
3. Twice	13.5	16.8	9.6	13.9	4.5	13.8	14.3	13.4	11.8	12.1	13.5	5.0	14.2	17.9	20.7	19.4
4. 3 to 5 times	9.2	11.5	6.6	9.9	1.8	8.4	10.8	8.9	7.4	7.6	10.1	2.4	7.9	8.9	17.9	13.8
5. 6 to 9 times	1.8	2.6	.9	2.0	-	2.2	1.9	1.8	.9	1.4	1.7	1.0	.8	2.0	3.8	8.0
6. 10 or more times	1.0	1.3	.6	.9	.7	1.4	1.3	.3	1.2	.9	1.0	.3	.6	.8	2.8	1.6
Item 1990 N(Wtd) ★	3074	1465	1464	2522	253	797	939	921	417	1457	1255	845	971	377	714	42

B014: During the last two weeks, how many times have you had two drinks in a row (but no more than that)? †

1. None	52.3	49.0	56.1	50.7	65.2	51.5	52.4	50.2	58.1	53.3	52.8	69.3	49.9	47.5	38.9	45.6
2. Once	21.8	21.8	22.1	22.5	16.8	24.1	23.0	19.8	19.6	22.3	21.5	19.6	23.3	21.3	23.1	20.3
3. Twice	13.4	14.6	12.0	13.9	11.7	12.2	12.1	16.1	13.0	12.4	14.3	6.6	15.5	16.5	16.3	13.0
4. 3 to 5 times	8.8	9.5	7.8	9.3	4.8	8.6	8.5	10.2	7.1	8.8	7.9	3.2	8.6	11.7	14.0	11.9
5. 6 to 9 times	2.4	3.6	1.3	2.5	1.1	2.1	3.1	2.8	.8	2.2	2.6	.9	2.1	2.3	4.8	5.7
6. 10 to 19 times	.7	.9	.5	.7	-	.7	.6	.9	.4	.7	.4	.2	.6	.8	1.1	1.6
7. 20 or more times	.5	.5	.2	.3	.4	.7	.4	.1	1.0	.3	.4	.1	-	-	1.7	1.8
Item 2000 N(Wtd) ★	3022	1436	1445	2473	250	776	927	909	410	1442	1232	841	955	365	703	42

B015: During the last two weeks, how many times have you had just one drink?

1. None	49.4	47.9	51.8	49.8	51.7	49.9	48.2	48.7	53.0	50.5	50.0	60.3	47.9	41.8	43.1	49.9
2. Once	27.6	26.9	28.7	27.3	31.6	25.3	29.0	27.3	29.1	26.9	28.7	26.3	29.7	31.9	25.0	17.7
3. Twice	11.6	12.2	10.6	11.1	10.7	13.9	10.5	12.1	8.8	11.0	11.3	7.6	11.3	14.6	14.9	5.1
4. 3 to 5 times	8.2	8.9	7.0	8.7	3.8	7.8	9.0	7.9	7.9	8.6	6.8	4.7	8.6	8.3	10.6	21.1
5. 6 to 9 times	2.1	3.0	1.2	2.2	1.8	1.7	2.0	3.4	.3	2.1	2.2	.7	1.7	2.2	4.1	4.2
6. 10 to 19 times	.6	.8	.4	.7	.3	.8	.8	.4	.4	.6	.6	.2	.7	.8	1.0	-
7. 20 or more times	.4	.3	.3	.3	-	.7	.6	.1	.5	.3	.4	.1	.1	.3	1.3	1.9
Item 2010 N(Wtd) ★	2963	1410	1416	2438	238	758	913	880	412	1410	1204	816	937	353	707	39

B016: Have you ever tried to stop using alcoholic beverages and found that you couldn't stop?

1. Yes	2.5	3.2	1.7	2.2	4.3	2.0	2.3	3.7	1.4	1.6	3.5	2.5	2.0	1.2	2.4	3.9
2. No	97.5	96.8	98.3	97.8	95.7	98.0	97.7	96.3	98.6	98.4	96.5	97.5	98.0	98.8	97.6	96.1
Item 2020 N(Wtd) ★	3021	1458	1417	2483	244	784	919	912	406	1430	1230	796	962	376	725	45

B017: Do you think you will be drinking alcoholic beverages five years from now?

1. I definitely will	15.0	18.1	12.2	17.2	2.3	21.9	17.4	9.3	11.4	17.5	12.9	7.6	17.2	19.9	22.8	23.2
2. I probably will	55.8	57.8	54.2	58.7	38.0	57.2	61.2	50.2	55.6	55.0	55.7	43.5	61.6	58.1	67.1	62.5
3. I probably will not	15.3	13.5	17.2	13.5	26.8	12.5	12.3	19.3	17.2	14.7	16.5	22.8	12.7	14.3	6.2	9.1
4. I definitely will not	13.8	10.6	16.4	10.6	32.8	8.5	9.1	21.1	15.8	12.8	14.9	26.1	8.5	7.7	3.9	5.3
Item 2030 N(Wtd)	3732	1718	1816	2930	404	901	1081	1235	514	1735	1552	1287	1073	406	753	46

The next questions are about MARIJUANA and HASHISH.

Marijuana is sometimes called: grass, pot, dope.

Hashish is sometimes called: hash, hash oil.

† Wording changed from previous year.   ★ = excludes respondents for whom question was inappropriate.

QUESTIONNAIRE FORM 1 1978	TOTAL	SEX		RACE		REGION				4YR COLLEGE PLANS		ILLICIT DRUG USE: LIFETIME				
		M	F	White	Black	NE	NC	S	W	Yes	No	None	Marijuana Only	Few Pills	More Pills	Any Heroin
Weighted No. of Cases:	3799	1740	1842	2962	411	922	1096	1257	524	1758	1571	1301	1086	411	760	46
% of Weighted Total:	100.0	45.8	48.5	78.0	10.8	24.3	28.8	33.1	13.8	46.3	41.3	34.3	28.6	10.8	20.0	1.2

B018: On how many occasions (if any) have you used hashish...

B018A: ...in your lifetime?

	TOTAL	M	F	White	Black	NE	NC	S	W	Yes	No	None	Marijuana Only	Few Pills	More Pills	Any Heroin
1. 0 occasions	67.0	62.2	73.6	65.4	87.0	57.1	67.7	74.4	65.5	72.3	67.3	100.0	67.3	49.1	22.1	3.7
2. 1-2	11.3	12.7	9.7	11.9	7.6	12.3	10.6	11.2	11.4	11.0	11.1	-	21.4	18.4	12.5	3.9
3. 3-5	5.4	6.1	4.9	6.1	1.6	7.2	4.9	4.0	6.6	5.0	5.9	-	5.4	12.4	10.7	14.5
4. 6-9	3.5	3.0	3.6	3.6	.3	4.9	3.2	2.8	3.2	2.5	3.7	-	2.8	6.6	8.8	5.1
5. 10-19	4.2	5.0	3.3	4.4	1.1	4.8	5.2	2.9	4.4	3.3	3.7	-	1.3	6.3	13.7	25.4
6. 20-39	2.8	3.5	1.9	2.9	1.0	4.5	3.2	1.7	1.7	2.0	3.0	-	.8	2.8	10.5	11.5
7. 40 or more	5.7	7.6	3.0	5.7	1.4	9.2	5.1	3.1	7.1	4.0	5.3	-	1.0	4.3	21.8	36.0
Item 2040 N(Wtd)	3644	1679	1778	2877	383	894	1060	1186	504	1716	1502	1301	1081	398	743	43

B018B: ...during the last 12 months?

	TOTAL	M	F	White	Black	NE	NC	S	W	Yes	No	None	Marijuana Only	Few Pills	More Pills	Any Heroin
1. 0 occasions	76.0	71.2	82.2	74.8	91.7	66.2	76.5	83.5	74.9	79.7	77.7	100.0	81.9	66.7	33.4	16.1
2. 1-2	9.4	10.8	8.2	10.1	4.7	11.8	8.3	8.2	10.1	9.7	8.2	-	12.6	15.7	17.2	9.7
3. 3-5	4.8	5.7	3.7	5.2	2.2	6.2	5.9	2.8	5.2	3.8	5.1	-	3.7	7.8	13.1	17.9
4. 6-9	3.2	3.8	1.8	3.2	.5	4.4	3.5	1.7	3.8	2.2	2.5	-	.8	2.6	11.6	21.5
5. 10-19	3.0	3.8	2.0	3.0	.4	5.3	2.1	2.0	2.8	2.1	3.0	-	.4	3.1	11.6	11.7
6. 20-39	1.5	1.4	1.3	1.4	.3	2.0	2.1	.6	1.2	1.2	1.6	-	.2	2.4	4.8	12.7
7. 40 or more	2.1	3.2	.7	2.2	.2	4.1	1.6	1.2	2.0	1.4	1.9	-	.2	1.7	8.3	10.5
Item 2050 N(Wtd)	3618	1676	1765	2864	381	887	1054	1177	500	1713	1487	1301	1068	397	737	43

B018C: ...during the last 30 days?

	TOTAL	M	F	White	Black	NE	NC	S	W	Yes	No	None	Marijuana Only	Few Pills	More Pills	Any Heroin
1. 0 occasions	89.2	86.5	92.7	88.7	96.9	84.0	88.2	93.3	90.6	91.2	90.1	100.0	95.5	87.3	64.7	39.5
2. 1-2	5.3	6.4	3.9	5.7	2.1	6.3	6.4	3.5	5.2	4.5	5.0	-	3.4	7.2	14.7	28.8
3. 3-5	2.0	2.4	1.4	2.0	.8	2.6	1.7	1.7	2.2	1.8	1.6	-	.9	1.7	6.9	10.8
4. 6-9	1.4	1.8	.9	1.4	-	2.5	1.6	.5	.8	1.0	1.3	-	-	.9	5.8	7.8
5. 10-19	1.0	1.1	.7	1.0	-	2.0	1.2	.4	.3	.8	.7	-	.2	1.7	3.5	3.2
6. 20-39	.5	.9	.2	.6	-	1.0	.5	.4	.2	.3	.6	-	-	.7	1.9	5.7
7. 40 or more	.7	.9	.3	.6	.2	1.5	.4	.2	.6	.3	.6	-	.1	.5	2.5	4.3
Item 2060 N(Wtd)	3613	1673	1763	2861	379	888	1054	1173	497	1713	1487	1301	1069	393	736	43

B019: On how many occasions (if any) have you used marijuana...

B019A: ...in your lifetime?

	TOTAL	M	F	White	Black	NE	NC	S	W	Yes	No	None	Marijuana Only	Few Pills	More Pills	Any Heroin
1. 0 occasions	39.5	35.8	44.8	39.2	47.4	32.2	38.3	46.4	39.0	44.2	39.1	100.0	.5	19.0	6.3	2.3
2. 1-2	9.2	9.1	9.3	8.7	12.8	7.9	10.0	9.0	10.0	9.5	8.8	-	24.8	7.7	2.7	-
3. 3-5	6.1	6.3	6.3	6.4	5.4	5.7	6.7	6.1	5.8	6.6	6.0	-	16.0	6.9	2.1	5.1
4. 6-9	5.6	5.7	5.6	5.8	5.1	3.3	7.2	5.2	6.9	6.3	5.2	-	13.3	5.4	3.3	1.4
5. 10-19	6.0	6.3	5.9	6.0	5.5	7.3	5.9	6.1	3.5	6.6	5.9	-	12.7	10.5	4.0	-
6. 20-39	6.1	5.1	7.0	6.3	6.2	6.4	6.0	5.5	7.2	5.5	7.2	-	11.7	10.4	6.2	3.8
7. 40 or more	27.5	31.7	21.1	27.7	17.6	37.2	25.9	21.7	27.7	21.3	27.8	-	21.0	40.1	75.5	87.4
Item 2070 N(Wtd)	3616	1672	1763	2864	375	881	1055	1179	500	1708	1491	1301	1074	397	736	43

B019B: ...during the last 12 months?

	TOTAL	M	F	White	Black	NE	NC	S	W	Yes	No	None	Marijuana Only	Few Pills	More Pills	Any Heroin
1. 0 occasions	48.9	44.3	55.2	48.1	59.4	40.4	47.1	56.2	51.0	53.1	49.3	100.0	23.2	28.2	11.3	5.0
2. 1-2	9.0	9.6	8.6	9.1	9.5	8.3	11.4	7.7	8.1	10.0	8.3	-	24.1	7.9	3.1	-
3. 3-5	6.9	7.4	6.8	7.2	6.4	6.4	9.4	5.1	7.2	7.1	7.0	-	14.5	8.6	6.8	6.6
4. 6-9	5.6	5.4	5.7	5.7	6.1	6.0	5.4	6.3	3.9	6.1	5.3	-	11.3	9.6	4.9	5.7
5. 10-19	5.4	5.8	5.3	5.6	4.1	6.8	4.9	5.0	5.2	5.3	5.7	-	9.2	13.0	5.3	2.7
6. 20-39	6.5	6.0	6.6	6.7	5.3	9.1	5.2	5.3	7.3	5.3	6.8	-	7.8	10.2	13.2	24.5
7. 40 or more	17.6	21.5	11.8	17.6	9.3	23.0	16.6	14.5	17.3	13.0	17.5	-	9.8	22.5	55.3	55.5
Item 2080 N(Wtd)	3574	1653	1746	2849	362	879	1043	1158	493	1700	1464	1301	1046	393	731	43

B019C: ...during the last 30 days?

	TOTAL	M	F	White	Black	NE	NC	S	W	Yes	No	None	Marijuana Only	Few Pills	More Pills	Any Heroin
1. 0 occasions	62.6	57.8	69.7	62.6	70.3	53.8	62.7	68.8	63.7	67.4	63.7	100.0	54.5	47.1	20.8	16.4
2. 1-2	9.6	10.8	8.4	9.9	9.2	9.1	11.5	9.4	7.0	10.4	8.8	-	20.2	12.1	9.0	10.4
3. 3-5	5.5	5.6	5.2	5.7	3.9	6.2	5.5	4.4	6.6	5.4	5.0	-	8.5	9.8	8.4	3.1
4. 6-9	4.6	5.0	4.4	4.6	5.4	6.0	3.9	3.6	6.2	4.6	4.3	-	6.3	10.0	7.4	4.4
5. 10-19	6.4	7.8	4.5	6.4	5.6	9.3	5.9	4.7	6.3	5.6	6.5	-	6.2	9.0	16.1	16.5
6. 20-39	4.8	5.1	3.8	4.7	2.5	6.0	4.2	4.1	5.6	3.1	4.9	-	1.9	5.9	16.1	19.8
7. 40 or more	6.5	7.9	3.9	6.1	3.2	9.7	6.2	5.0	4.6	3.4	6.7	-	2.4	6.2	22.2	29.4
Item 2090 N(Wtd)	3577	1657	1745	2851	362	879	1043	1162	493	1700	1463	1301	1052	394	735	43

QUESTIONNAIRE FORM 1 1978	TOTAL	SEX		RACE		REGION				4YR COLLEGE PLANS		ILLICIT DRUG USE: LIFETIME				
		M	F	White	Black	NE	NC	S	W	Yes	No	None	Marijuana Only	Few Pills	More Pills	Any Heroin
Weighted No. of Cases:	3799	1740	1842	2962	411	922	1096	1257	524	1758	1571	1301	1086	411	760	46
% of Weighted Total:	100.0	45.8	48.5	78.0	10.8	24.3	28.8	33.1	13.8	46.3	41.3	34.3	28.6	10.8	20.0	1.2

IF YOU HAVE NOT USED MARIJUANA OR HASHISH IN THE LAST TWELVE MONTHS, GO TO Q.B028.

B020: When you used marijuana or hashish during the last year, how often did you use it in each of the following situations?

B020A: When you were alone

	TOTAL	M	F	White	Black	NE	NC	S	W	Yes	No	None	Mari- juana Only	Few Pills	More Pills	Any Her- oin
1. Not at all	59.2	53.8	69.2	62.6	51.4	59.8	60.9	57.5	57.5	65.6	60.5	-	77.7	63.7	35.7	27.4
2. A few of the times	25.1	27.9	20.6	23.5	30.6	23.5	22.7	27.8	28.1	22.3	25.2	-	17.5	22.3	35.6	34.0
3. Some of the times	12.9	15.1	8.6	12.2	11.3	14.2	13.4	11.7	12.0	10.8	11.4	-	3.8	11.6	24.6	28.5
4. Most of the times	1.9	2.4	1.2	1.2	6.1	1.5	2.3	2.5	.9	.9	2.4	-	1.0	2.3	2.5	4.1
5. Every time	.9	.9	.4	.5	.6	1.0	.8	.5	1.6	.4	.5	-	.1	.1	1.6	5.9
Item 2100 N(Wtd) ★	1852	920	805	1481	161	524	556	527	246	798	755	-	813	287	652	41

B020B: With just 1 or 2 other people

	TOTAL	M	F	White	Black	NE	NC	S	W	Yes	No	None	Mari- juana Only	Few Pills	More Pills	Any Her- oin
1. Not at all	5.3	5.5	5.3	5.5	3.3	4.3	6.6	3.8	7.4	7.0	4.1	-	8.9	3.5	1.8	-
2. A few of the times	27.8	24.9	33.0	27.5	38.7	29.3	25.8	27.3	30.6	27.7	31.2	-	38.0	27.8	15.8	7.9
3. Some of the times	22.1	22.5	21.4	21.6	22.1	24.4	21.3	20.8	21.4	22.2	23.5	-	17.7	25.8	25.6	31.0
4. Most of the times	35.7	37.9	31.4	36.1	27.5	34.7	36.7	37.5	31.4	34.0	33.1	-	24.1	36.6	48.6	52.0
5. Every time	9.2	9.2	9.0	9.2	8.4	7.3	9.6	10.6	9.2	9.1	8.1	-	11.4	6.3	8.2	9.1
Item 2110 N(Wtd) ★	1863	929	806	1496	158	531	560	527	245	803	758	-	819	286	656	41

B020C: At a party

	TOTAL	M	F	White	Black	NE	NC	S	W	Yes	No	None	Mari- juana Only	Few Pills	More Pills	Any Her- oin
1. Not at all	20.4	19.3	21.9	20.5	29.7	15.8	20.0	25.1	20.8	22.3	21.2	-	32.9	15.4	7.6	2.4
2. A few of the times	19.9	20.3	19.9	19.9	21.6	17.3	23.8	19.7	17.4	23.4	17.7	-	25.7	22.0	12.4	13.1
3. Some of the times	20.0	20.5	19.8	20.2	16.9	21.6	19.6	18.8	19.9	19.6	20.4	-	16.3	23.6	23.8	14.0
4. Most of the times	21.6	21.8	21.6	22.4	16.1	24.4	20.5	17.0	27.7	21.8	22.5	-	15.8	23.8	26.8	35.8
5. Every time	18.1	18.1	16.7	17.0	15.7	20.9	16.0	19.4	14.3	12.9	18.1	-	9.3	15.2	29.4	34.7
Item 2120 N(Wtd) ★	1845	922	800	1485	156	527	551	520	247	795	753	-	809	286	651	41

B020D: When your date or spouse was present

	TOTAL	M	F	White	Black	NE	NC	S	W	Yes	No	None	Mari- juana Only	Few Pills	More Pills	Any Her- oin
1. Not at all	39.3	46.5	32.6	39.5	50.3	35.0	42.5	40.1	39.0	45.1	37.3	-	56.5	35.9	17.8	34.0
2. A few of the times	21.8	21.8	22.1	21.7	23.1	21.9	21.3	21.5	23.4	22.2	21.3	-	22.1	22.6	21.7	15.5
3. Some of the times	15.5	16.2	14.2	15.5	12.4	17.8	14.0	14.4	16.5	15.1	15.6	-	8.9	20.8	21.6	23.2
4. Most of the times	14.5	10.2	18.5	14.4	10.3	16.8	14.1	13.0	14.2	11.0	16.0	-	6.2	15.2	24.8	14.7
5. Every time	8.9	5.3	12.6	8.9	3.9	8.4	8.1	11.0	6.9	6.5	9.8	-	6.2	5.4	14.1	12.5
Item 2130 N(Wtd) ★	1834	916	795	1474	158	519	553	521	241	789	749	-	803	284	647	41

B020E: When people over age 30 were present

	TOTAL	M	F	White	Black	NE	NC	S	W	Yes	No	None	Mari- juana Only	Few Pills	More Pills	Any Her- oin
1. Not at all	64.6	61.6	71.8	66.3	65.8	65.3	67.9	63.8	57.5	70.2	65.0	-	82.3	64.1	43.7	27.7
2. A few of the times	21.7	23.3	18.1	21.5	20.4	20.9	20.6	22.0	25.5	20.2	21.2	-	12.3	23.3	32.2	46.5
3. Some of the times	10.4	12.1	7.4	10.0	8.6	10.8	8.6	11.2	11.5	7.5	11.3	-	3.9	9.9	18.8	16.1
4. Most of the times	2.2	2.1	1.7	1.5	4.1	1.7	2.1	2.2	3.3	1.7	1.9	-	1.1	2.3	3.3	6.1
5. Every time	1.1	.9	1.0	.7	1.2	1.2	.8	.7	2.2	.5	.6	-	.4	.3	2.1	3.7
Item 2140 N(Wtd) ★	1847	924	798	1486	157	525	556	521	245	799	756	-	814	285	648	41

B020F: During the daytime (before 4:00 p.m.)

	TOTAL	M	F	White	Black	NE	NC	S	W	Yes	No	None	Mari- juana Only	Few Pills	More Pills	Any Her- oin
1. Not at all	31.1	28.9	36.5	31.8	36.8	28.2	35.4	30.4	29.1	38.6	29.1	-	47.4	30.2	11.4	12.0
2. A few of the times	25.6	24.4	27.6	25.8	28.1	21.0	26.0	28.5	27.9	26.4	26.4	-	28.4	28.6	20.2	18.6
3. Some of the times	28.0	31.7	22.7	28.2	21.5	30.8	24.2	28.1	30.3	26.6	27.7	-	18.6	28.7	40.3	39.4
4. Most of the times	11.6	11.3	10.3	11.0	10.0	14.5	11.8	9.6	9.0	6.7	13.2	-	4.3	10.5	20.4	24.1
5. Every time	3.8	3.8	2.9	3.2	3.7	5.5	2.5	3.3	3.6	1.8	3.6	-	1.3	2.0	7.6	6.0
Item 2150 N(Wtd) ★	1849	922	803	1487	157	525	559	518	247	796	757	-	814	284	652	41

★ = excludes respondents for whom question was inappropriate.

QUESTIONNAIRE FORM 1 1978	TOTAL	SEX		RACE		REGION				4YR COLLEGE PLANS		ILLICIT DRUG USE: LIFETIME				
		M	F	White	Black	NE	NC	S	W	Yes	No	None	Marijuana Only	Few Pills	More Pills	Any Heroin
Weighted No. of Cases:	3799	1740	1842	2962	411	922	1096	1257	524	1758	1571	1301	1086	411	760	46
% of Weighted Total:	100.0	45.8	48.5	78.0	10.8	24.3	28.8	33.1	13.8	46.3	41.3	34.3	28.6	10.8	20.0	1.2
B020G: At your home (or apartment or dorm)																
1. Not at all	51.6	51.1	55.5	54.1	46.4	49.5	55.4	53.5	43.9	57.8	51.5	-	69.5	53.0	29.9	23.9
2. A few of the times	22.4	21.6	23.0	21.7	28.0	20.7	22.3	24.6	21.2	21.6	23.4	-	17.8	26.8	26.8	11.8
3. Some of the times	15.1	15.9	12.2	14.6	13.7	18.0	13.1	12.1	19.7	13.7	13.6	-	8.9	13.2	23.7	27.9
4. Most of the times	7.8	8.1	6.5	7.2	8.7	7.9	6.9	6.9	11.5	5.4	7.9	-	2.6	5.4	14.0	23.0
5. Every time	3.1	3.3	2.8	2.4	3.2	3.9	2.3	2.9	3.7	1.5	3.6	-	1.2	1.6	5.5	13.3
Item 2160 N(Wtd) ★	1848	924	802	1490	155	524	557	521	246	799	756	-	813	284	653	41
B020H: At school																
1. Not at all	53.9	50.0	61.9	56.5	49.0	44.2	59.8	58.5	51.2	60.9	52.6	-	71.7	52.5	32.5	37.8
2. A few of the times	19.9	20.0	19.4	19.5	21.8	20.3	19.8	20.5	18.4	19.7	20.2	-	16.0	27.9	21.9	12.5
3. Some of the times	14.5	18.0	9.4	13.4	16.3	17.0	12.3	12.4	18.6	12.3	15.3	-	8.3	12.5	22.8	27.2
4. Most of the times	7.4	7.3	6.1	6.7	8.6	11.6	4.6	5.6	8.5	4.6	7.9	-	2.8	4.7	13.9	15.3
5. Every time	4.3	4.8	3.1	3.9	4.3	6.9	3.5	3.0	3.4	2.5	3.9	-	1.2	2.4	8.8	7.1
Item 2170 N(Wtd) ★	1852	923	804	1488	158	526	559	521	246	799	755	-	814	286	653	41
B020I: In a car																
1. Not at all	14.7	13.2	17.3	14.5	19.8	13.5	13.2	12.7	24.7	18.9	12.4	-	22.5	10.4	7.1	1.7
2. A few of the times	22.6	20.3	25.6	22.6	25.5	19.7	26.1	20.1	26.2	24.0	22.6	-	29.8	20.5	13.9	16.0
3. Some of the times	24.7	27.1	22.4	24.3	25.1	27.3	20.2	26.5	25.8	25.2	25.2	-	23.1	27.9	25.5	33.4
4. Most of the times	29.8	30.0	28.7	30.7	24.4	30.4	31.2	33.2	18.0	26.0	32.2	-	19.1	35.6	41.3	29.7
5. Every time	8.2	9.4	6.0	7.9	5.2	9.1	9.3	7.5	5.2	5.9	7.6	-	5.4	5.5	12.1	19.2
Item 2190 N(Wtd) ★	1851	925	801	1489	157	524	557	523	247	799	755	-	813	286	654	41
B021: How many of the times when you used marijuana or hashish during the last year did you use it along with alcohol--that is, so that their effects overlapped?																
1. Not at all	28.1	24.8	32.4	26.3	46.3	23.5	30.5	30.0	28.2	30.1	27.7	-	41.0	26.1	11.8	17.5
2. A few of the times	28.4	27.8	30.1	29.2	25.9	27.5	25.5	30.5	32.9	29.7	29.1	-	31.2	34.6	22.8	23.0
3. Some of the times	24.5	26.3	21.2	25.3	15.4	29.2	23.3	22.6	21.0	24.0	23.5	-	15.7	24.7	36.0	30.5
4. Most of the times	14.8	16.0	12.5	14.7	10.7	15.0	16.3	13.0	14.5	13.5	13.6	-	9.0	10.8	23.5	22.4
5. Every time	4.3	5.1	3.7	4.5	1.7	4.8	4.4	3.9	3.4	2.7	6.2	-	3.1	3.8	5.9	6.6
Item 2200 N(Wtd) ★	1813	903	793	1469	152	513	553	510	237	793	736	-	797	283	635	40
B022: What have been the most important reasons for your using marijuana or hashish? (Mark all that apply.)																
A. To experiment--to see what it's like	61.6	60.4	64.2	62.3	67.0	56.0	63.2	66.4	59.4	67.0	60.9	-	72.1	59.5	51.5	41.4
B. To relax or relieve tension	42.8	41.7	43.6	44.5	28.5	42.6	39.2	45.2	46.3	40.0	44.4	-	25.3	44.3	63.4	64.6
C. To feel good or get high	76.4	77.8	74.5	77.4	69.2	81.2	73.9	74.4	76.0	74.7	76.9	-	65.3	81.3	88.4	92.0
D. To seek deeper insights and understanding	16.4	18.8	14.0	17.0	11.4	17.9	16.5	15.2	15.6	14.7	15.0	-	7.5	15.1	25.9	45.0
E. To have a good time with my friends	63.3	67.1	59.2	64.6	56.1	67.4	61.5	59.4	67.1	61.9	64.6	-	54.3	65.1	74.2	81.0
F. To fit in with a group I like	13.2	15.7	10.4	14.5	7.0	12.5	12.3	14.9	13.1	13.5	14.1	-	15.2	10.9	10.4	26.1
G. To get away from my problems or troubles	17.7	16.1	19.6	17.7	17.1	20.3	16.2	20.0	11.1	15.8	20.0	-	11.9	18.2	23.2	37.7
H. Because of boredom, nothing else to do	26.6	27.9	24.8	26.8	24.6	33.4	23.4	25.2	22.4	24.5	26.9	-	17.3	30.0	35.9	45.7
I. Because of anger or frustration	13.2	11.3	14.9	12.7	13.0	14.4	12.8	12.9	12.6	11.8	14.0	-	9.7	8.1	18.8	28.0
J. To get through the day	7.8	7.9	6.9	7.6	8.5	12.4	4.2	7.2	7.7	5.7	9.0	-	2.6	4.6	15.2	19.6
K. To increase the effects of some other drug(s)	11.3	12.7	8.4	11.0	7.7	15.1	9.3	10.1	10.3	10.1	9.5	-	3.3	5.9	22.7	36.0
L. To decrease (offset) the effects of some other drug(s)	2.1	1.8	1.9	2.0	2.1	2.5	2.3	1.2	2.5	1.3	2.1	-	.4	1.4	3.9	14.3
M. Because I am "hooked"--I have to have it	3.2	3.4	2.3	2.8	3.2	3.6	3.7	2.4	3.2	2.1	3.0	-	.9	.7	6.5	17.7
Item 2210-2330 N(Wtd) ★	1855	928	803	1490	160	523	559	526	247	799	759	-	816	287	656	41

★ = excludes respondents for whom question was inappropriate.

QUESTIONNAIRE FORM 1 1978	TOTAL	SEX		RACE		REGION				4YR COLLEGE PLANS		ILLICIT DRUG USE: LIFETIME				
		M	F	White	Black	NE	NC	S	W	Yes	No	None	Mari- juana Only	Few Pills	More Pills	Any Her- oin
Weighted No. of Cases:	3799	1740	1842	2962	411	922	1096	1257	524	1758	1571	1301	1086	411	760	46
% of Weighted Total:	100.0	45.8	48.5	78.0	10.8	24.3	28.8	33.1	13.8	46.3	41.3	34.3	28.6	10.8	20.0	1.2

B023: When you use marijuana or hashish how high do you usually get?

	TOTAL	M	F	White	Black	NE	NC	S	W	Yes	No	None	Mari- juana Only	Few Pills	More Pills	Any Her- oin
1. Not at all high	6.3	5.2	7.5	5.9	8.2	4.4	8.3	6.4	5.4	7.7	5.6	-	12.2	2.3	.7	-
2. A little high	20.3	19.3	23.3	20.7	22.1	19.1	23.0	17.7	22.2	23.9	19.0	-	31.0	15.7	9.2	4.4
3. Moderately high	46.8	48.7	44.1	47.4	43.2	45.1	45.5	49.1	48.2	45.7	49.4	-	42.0	53.4	49.5	45.3
4. Very high	26.6	26.8	25.1	26.0	26.6	31.4	23.2	26.8	24.1	22.7	26.0	-	14.8	28.5	40.6	50.2
Item 2340 N(Wtd) ★	1843	926	795	1486	158	518	559	524	242	794	752	-	815	284	650	41

B024: When you use marijuana or hashish, how long do you usually stay high?

	TOTAL	M	F	White	Black	NE	NC	S	W	Yes	No	None	Mari- juana Only	Few Pills	More Pills	Any Her- oin
1. Usually don't get high	8.0	6.4	9.6	7.2	12.0	5.7	10.7	8.0	6.5	9.3	7.0	-	14.8	3.3	1.3	-
2. One to two hours	47.4	47.5	47.0	48.7	33.7	50.1	48.3	43.2	48.5	48.9	45.8	-	53.1	47.4	40.9	32.3
3. Three to six hours	39.0	40.4	37.6	39.0	44.4	37.7	34.7	43.5	42.1	36.2	41.9	-	28.9	44.6	49.5	50.5
4. Seven to 24 hours	5.1	4.8	5.6	4.7	9.5	5.9	5.7	5.1	1.9	5.3	4.9	-	2.8	4.5	7.4	15.0
5. More than 24 hours	.5	.7	.1	.5	.4	.6	.6	.1	1.0	.2	.4	-	.3	.2	.9	2.2
Item 2350 N(Wtd) ★	1842	925	800	1489	157	517	559	521	245	798	755	-	814	285	653	41

B025: During the LAST MONTH, about how many marijuana cigarettes (joints, reefers), or the equivalent, did you smoke a day, on the average? (If you shared them with other people, count only the amount YOU smoked.)

	TOTAL	M	F	White	Black	NE	NC	S	W	Yes	No	None	Mari- juana Only	Few Pills	More Pills	Any Her- oin
1. None	31.1	27.0	38.8	33.0	25.2	27.9	34.3	31.0	31.3	37.2	30.3	-	47.1	30.4	13.3	14.2
2. Less than 1 a day	33.3	35.3	31.0	34.5	30.1	31.8	33.4	34.6	33.9	38.2	30.7	-	37.6	35.9	28.2	23.1
3. 1 a day	11.1	13.2	8.8	11.3	8.7	13.9	8.9	9.5	13.8	9.7	11.1	-	5.9	13.3	15.7	16.3
4. 2 - 3 a day	15.0	14.9	13.6	13.2	24.7	13.5	16.2	17.0	11.7	10.0	17.0	-	6.9	15.2	24.9	12.7
5. 4 - 6 a day	5.5	4.7	5.9	5.1	5.0	7.5	5.3	4.7	3.5	3.1	7.0	-	1.2	3.1	10.6	23.2
6. 7 - 10 a day	1.9	2.4	1.0	1.4	3.8	2.4	.9	2.1	2.6	1.1	1.7	-	.6	.4	4.0	4.7
7. 11 or more a day	1.9	2.4	1.0	1.5	2.6	3.1	.9	1.1	3.2	.7	2.2	-	.7	1.7	3.3	5.8
Item 2360 N(Wtd) ★	1746	876	757	1416	144	501	524	493	228	763	701	-	750	272	639	41

B026: Do you know how much marijuana you have used (in ounces) during the LAST MONTH?

	TOTAL	M	F	White	Black	NE	NC	S	W	Yes	No	None	Mari- juana Only	Few Pills	More Pills	Any Her- oin
8. Don't know	18.9	12.8	26.1	17.5	30.2	18.8	18.7	19.5	17.9	16.8	22.4	-	22.4	17.2	14.8	8.3
1. None	28.5	26.0	33.8	29.8	27.5	26.6	31.0	29.2	25.2	32.1	29.3	-	43.1	27.2	12.7	16.2
2. Less than 1/2 ounce	18.3	20.8	15.3	18.9	17.8	18.0	19.6	16.5	19.7	23.0	13.2	-	21.1	20.7	14.9	1.6
3. About 1/2 ounce	8.6	10.4	7.0	9.1	6.8	8.1	8.3	8.6	10.1	8.6	9.7	-	5.0	12.6	11.7	4.3
4. About 1 ounce	11.0	11.6	8.2	10.2	9.9	12.8	9.0	10.5	12.3	10.2	9.6	-	4.5	11.7	17.8	27.4
5. About 2 ounces	8.4	10.5	5.4	8.1	4.4	9.9	8.8	7.3	6.5	5.2	8.7	-	2.3	6.2	16.2	14.9
6. 3 to 5 ounces	4.8	5.7	3.5	5.1	2.8	4.4	3.7	6.2	5.2	3.6	5.2	-	.9	3.6	9.0	18.6
7. 6 or more ounces	1.7	2.2	.7	1.3	.6	1.4	.8	2.2	3.0	.6	1.8	-	.7	.8	2.8	8.6
Item 2370 N(Wtd) ★	1750	880	758	1421	145	501	525	492	232	765	704	-	748	273	642	41

B027: Have you ever tried to stop using marijuana or hashish and found that you couldn't stop?

	TOTAL	M	F	White	Black	NE	NC	S	W	Yes	No	None	Mari- juana Only	Few Pills	More Pills	Any Her- oin
1. Yes	4.0	4.1	2.9	3.4	4.9	3.8	3.9	3.7	5.4	3.5	3.2	-	2.0	4.0	5.5	18.4
2. No	96.0	95.9	97.1	96.6	95.1	96.2	96.1	96.3	94.6	96.5	96.8	-	98.0	96.0	94.5	81.6
Item 2380 N(Wtd) ★	1826	915	795	1479	155	515	553	516	242	792	748	-	797	286	654	41

B028: Do you think you will be using marijuana or hashish five years from now?

	TOTAL	M	F	White	Black	NE	NC	S	W	Yes	No	None	Mari- juana Only	Few Pills	More Pills	Any Her- oin
1. I definitely will	6.5	7.6	4.7	6.4	2.7	9.3	6.7	4.4	6.2	4.7	6.4	.2	2.8	6.4	21.4	31.1
2. I probably will	21.0	24.3	17.2	21.3	17.5	24.9	19.5	18.6	23.0	18.6	20.8	1.2	23.3	33.0	43.9	46.5
3. I probably will not	23.0	23.6	21.9	23.9	18.9	25.3	25.9	20.0	19.7	24.4	22.0	12.3	36.4	28.3	18.6	9.8
4. I definitely will not	49.6	44.5	56.1	48.5	60.8	40.5	47.9	57.0	51.2	52.3	50.8	86.3	37.6	32.3	16.2	12.7
Item 2390 N(Wtd)	3659	1688	1794	2887	397	880	1069	1204	506	1712	1528	1263	1068	402	746	46

★ = excludes respondents for whom question was inappropriate.

QUESTIONNAIRE FORM 1 1978	TOTAL	SEX		RACE		REGION				4YR COLLEGE PLANS		ILLICIT DRUG USE: LIFETIME				
		M	F	White	Black	NE	NC	S	W	Yes	No	None	Marijuana Only	Few Pills	More Pills	Any Heroin
Weighted No. of Cases:	3799	1740	1842	2962	411	922	1096	1257	524	1758	1571	1301	1086	411	760	46
% of Weighted Total:	100.0	45.8	48.5	78.0	10.8	24.3	28.8	33.1	13.8	46.3	41.3	34.3	28.6	10.8	20.0	1.2

The next questions are about LSD, the psychedelic drug which is sometimes called "acid".

B029: On how many occasions (if any) have you taken LSD...

B029A: ...in your lifetime?

	TOTAL	M	F	White	Black	NE	NC	S	W	Yes	No	None	Marijuana Only	Few Pills	More Pills	Any Heroin
1. 0 occasions	90.3	89.6	92.6	90.2	98.7	88.2	89.0	93.9	88.7	93.8	91.1	100.0	100.0	93.1	61.8	19.5
2. 1-2	4.2	4.3	3.8	4.4	.7	4.5	4.0	3.5	5.9	3.2	3.8	-	-	6.9	15.5	21.3
3. 3-5	2.1	2.8	1.3	2.3	.3	2.9	2.4	1.1	2.5	1.3	2.0	-	-	-	9.5	10.4
4. 6-9	1.3	1.1	1.2	1.2	-	1.4	2.1	.6	.7	.7	1.0	-	-	-	5.2	16.1
5. 10-19	1.0	1.1	.6	.9	.2	1.7	1.3	.5	.6	.5	1.3	-	-	-	4.2	12.1
6. 20-39	.4	.4	.1	.3	-	.2	.7	.1	.9	.3	.2	-	-	-	1.7	5.5
7. 40 or more	.6	.7	.4	.6	-	1.1	.6	.3	.7	.2	.6	-	-	-	2.1	15.2
Item 890 N(Wtd)	3587	1662	1758	2857	374	875	1052	1163	496	1697	1486	1278	1071	397	741	45

B029B: ...during the last 12 months?

	TOTAL	M	F	White	Black	NE	NC	S	W	Yes	No	None	Marijuana Only	Few Pills	More Pills	Any Heroin
1. 0 occasions	93.5	92.5	95.6	93.6	99.0	90.9	92.2	96.3	94.1	96.2	94.0	100.0	100.0	96.4	73.9	38.9
2. 1-2	3.7	4.3	2.8	3.8	1.0	5.0	3.7	2.2	4.5	2.5	3.3	-	-	3.6	14.5	22.1
3. 3-5	1.4	1.6	.9	1.3	-	2.2	1.7	.8	.4	.5	1.7	-	-	-	5.4	19.5
4. 6-9	1.0	.8	.6	.9	-	1.0	1.6	.6	.4	.4	.6	-	-	-	4.0	10.5
5. 10-19	.4	.7	-	.3	-	.5	.6	-	.6	.3	.3	-	-	-	1.7	4.3
6. 20-39	.1	.1	.1	.1	-	.1	.2	.1	-	.1	-	-	-	-	.4	2.3
7. 40 or more	*	.1	-	*	-	.2	-	-	-	-	.1	-	-	-	.1	2.3
Item 900 N(Wtd)	3582	1661	1756	2854	374	873	1049	1163	497	1695	1487	1278	1072	397	735	45

B029C: ...during the last 30 days?

	TOTAL	M	F	White	Black	NE	NC	S	W	Yes	No	None	Marijuana Only	Few Pills	More Pills	Any Heroin
1. 0 occasions	97.6	97.2	98.6	97.9	100.0	96.1	97.1	98.8	98.6	98.7	97.8	100.0	100.0	99.3	90.5	70.6
2. 1-2	1.6	2.0	1.1	1.5	-	3.1	1.7	.8	.9	1.0	1.6	-	-	.7	6.7	13.4
3. 3-5	.5	.4	.3	.4	-	.4	.7	.3	.5	.1	.4	-	-	-	1.9	8.4
4. 6-9	.2	.3	-	.1	-	.1	.5	-	-	.1	.1	-	-	-	.6	3.0
5. 10-19	*	-	.1	*	-	.1	-	-	-	.1	-	-	-	-	-	2.3
6. 20-39	*	*	-	*	-	.1	-	.1	-	-	*	-	-	-	.2	-
7. 40 or more	*	.1	-	-	-	.1	-	-	-	-	.1	-	-	-	-	2.3
Item 910 N(Wtd)	3580	1660	1755	2851	376	872	1046	1165	497	1695	1487	1280	1072	395	733	45

IF YOU HAVE NOT TAKEN LSD IN THE LAST TWELVE MONTHS, GO TO Q.B037.

B030: When you used LSD during the last year, how often did you use it in each of the following situations?

B030A: When you were alone

	TOTAL	M	F	White	Black	NE	NC	S	W	Yes	No	None	Marijuana Only	Few Pills	More Pills	Any Heroin
1. Not at all	79.1	79.3	82.5	82.4	55.7	81.8	78.6	72.3	82.1	74.3	89.2	-	-	90.4	80.8	59.8
2. A few of the times	13.6	14.5	12.1	12.3	44.3	11.5	17.2	9.4	15.1	18.7	5.7	-	-	9.6	13.6	16.7
3. Some of the times	2.7	3.1	-	2.0	-	4.6	3.1	-	-	1.6	1.2	-	-	-	2.8	4.1
4. Most of the times	1.4	-	4.1	1.9	-	-	-	8.5	-	3.8	.8	-	-	-	-	12.2
5. Every time	3.1	3.1	1.3	1.4	-	2.1	1.1	9.8	2.8	1.6	3.1	-	-	-	2.9	7.1
Item 2400 N(Wtd) ★	218	110	77	168	2	78	76	37	27	65	84	-	-	14	177	25

B030B: With just 1 or 2 other people

	TOTAL	M	F	White	Black	NE	NC	S	W	Yes	No	None	Marijuana Only	Few Pills	More Pills	Any Heroin
1. Not at all	18.9	19.4	20.5	20.5	-	26.8	10.8	20.7	18.6	22.6	22.2	-	-	30.0	18.4	14.7
2. A few of the times	39.2	43.0	35.1	37.0	100.0	33.5	47.1	43.5	25.7	39.9	44.6	-	-	60.4	37.5	39.3
3. Some of the times	16.4	13.6	18.1	15.5	-	7.5	24.8	17.3	15.0	17.4	7.8	-	-	-	15.4	33.4
4. Most of the times	16.7	14.6	17.5	17.4	-	21.3	11.5	13.5	23.3	14.5	16.8	-	-	-	18.7	12.6
5. Every time	8.8	9.3	8.8	9.5	-	10.9	5.7	5.0	17.4	5.5	8.5	-	-	9.5	10.1	-
Item 2410 N(Wtd) ★	223	115	79	175	2	77	81	37	27	64	87	-	-	14	182	25

* = less than .05 per cent.　★ = excludes respondents for whom question was inappropriate.

QUESTIONNAIRE FORM 1 1978	TOTAL	SEX		RACE		REGION				4YR COLLEGE PLANS		ILLICIT DRUG USE: LIFETIME				
		M	F	White	Black	NE	NC	S	W	Yes	No	None	Mari- juana Only	Few Pills	More Pills	Any Her- oin
Weighted No. of Cases:	3799	1740	1842	2962	411	922	1096	1257	524	1758	1571	1301	1086	411	760	46
% of Weighted Total:	100.0	45.8	48.5	78.0	10.8	24.3	28.8	33.1	13.8	46.3	41.3	34.3	28.6	10.8	20.0	1.2
B030C: At a party																
1. Not at all	31.4	30.6	34.1	33.1	19.5	30.3	26.3	28.1	53.7	35.0	32.5	-	-	29.2	31.9	27.5
2. A few of the times	24.6	32.5	18.0	24.9	44.3	25.9	32.2	13.4	14.7	25.9	32.0	-	-	35.2	24.6	17.4
3. Some of the times	18.4	15.0	20.4	16.3	36.2	14.4	20.0	27.6	11.4	14.4	14.2	-	-	-	18.5	28.3
4. Most of the times	13.2	9.4	15.6	12.5	-	13.2	10.8	16.3	15.6	10.1	11.4	-	-	19.8	12.5	14.8
5. Every time	12.5	12.4	12.0	13.3	-	16.1	10.6	14.7	4.6	14.6	9.9	-	-	15.8	12.4	11.9
Item 2420 N(Wtd) ★	224	117	77	176	2	78	80	39	27	64	87	-	-	14	182	26
B030D: When your date or spouse was present																
1. Not at all	56.0	67.8	49.5	59.8	19.5	58.0	51.1	62.3	56.4	70.3	55.6	-	-	71.9	54.2	57.5
2. A few of the times	20.2	16.1	23.1	18.9	-	12.7	28.0	16.3	23.6	10.2	26.7	-	-	20.1	19.2	29.2
3. Some of the times	5.5	4.3	3.0	3.6	-	6.2	4.5	6.6	4.9	4.3	1.2	-	-	-	5.3	9.9
4. Most of the times	9.4	6.3	11.1	8.1	80.5	12.2	10.7	6.1	2.4	4.4	8.5	-	-	-	11.1	3.4
5. Every time	8.9	5.5	13.3	9.6	-	11.0	5.7	8.7	12.6	10.9	8.0	-	-	8.0	10.2	-
Item 2430 N(Wtd) ★	222	114	79	174	2	77	82	37	27	63	87	-	-	14	181	25
B030E: When people over age 30 were present																
1. Not at all	70.9	72.5	75.8	74.0	19.5	74.2	66.7	74.3	68.8	68.0	77.6	-	-	87.3	71.7	55.3
2. A few of the times	18.1	16.4	16.1	16.3	36.2	14.4	20.9	19.8	18.2	18.7	15.4	-	-	-	17.5	32.6
3. Some of the times	6.6	7.9	3.1	5.3	44.3	7.0	7.7	3.7	6.1	5.9	4.4	-	-	-	6.7	9.2
4. Most of the times	2.1	-	3.9	1.8	-	3.2	1.2	-	4.1	1.5	2.5	-	-	-	2.5	-
5. Every time	2.4	3.2	1.2	2.6	-	1.2	3.5	2.1	2.8	5.9	-	-	-	12.7	1.6	2.9
Item 2440 N(Wtd) ★	221	112	79	172	2	78	79	37	27	64	85	-	-	13	181	25
B030F: During the daytime (before 4:00 p.m.)																
1. Not at all	48.2	48.1	51.0	50.3	19.5	43.7	47.9	71.1	31.4	57.6	50.8	-	-	82.8	48.4	27.6
2. A few of the times	27.5	28.4	24.9	26.3	36.2	26.6	30.9	15.2	36.7	28.2	25.4	-	-	7.6	26.2	47.5
3. Some of the times	14.4	17.1	11.4	13.7	44.3	17.6	13.3	4.8	21.6	8.8	9.8	-	-	9.6	14.7	16.3
4. Most of the times	7.8	3.4	12.7	7.2	-	8.1	7.2	8.9	7.4	2.9	11.6	-	-	-	8.8	5.6
5. Every time	2.0	2.9	-	2.5	-	4.0	.7	-	2.8	2.5	2.4	-	-	-	2.0	3.0
Item 2450 N(Wtd) ★	223	114	79	174	2	78	81	37	27	64	87	-	-	14	182	25
B030G: At your home (or apartment or dorm)																
1. Not at all	48.2	52.8	47.8	51.6	19.5	46.5	50.2	48.3	46.5	57.6	54.5	-	-	61.4	49.2	33.2
2. A few of the times	29.2	26.0	33.1	28.0	36.2	24.3	32.5	26.2	37.9	22.4	28.8	-	-	34.3	27.0	41.6
3. Some of the times	11.9	13.0	5.6	10.3	-	14.3	11.0	11.6	8.0	12.8	4.0	-	-	-	12.8	13.0
4. Most of the times	3.7	2.3	5.3	3.8	44.3	3.9	5.7	1.8	-	4.1	4.9	-	-	-	4.2	2.4
5. Every time	7.0	5.9	8.2	6.4	-	11.0	.6	12.1	7.7	3.1	7.8	-	-	4.3	6.9	9.8
Item 2460 N(Wtd) ★	225	115	79	175	2	78	82	37	27	64	87	-	-	14	183	25
B030H: At school																
1. Not at all	65.3	66.3	70.7	69.5	63.8	60.1	60.9	87.1	63.8	79.7	67.1	-	-	90.4	64.7	53.6
2. A few of the times	21.8	19.7	21.9	20.1	36.2	24.1	27.0	4.2	24.4	13.4	24.9	-	-	9.6	21.7	30.5
3. Some of the times	6.5	8.6	5.2	5.9	-	9.2	6.4	1.8	5.7	3.2	4.7	-	-	-	6.1	13.4
4. Most of the times	4.1	2.6	2.1	2.7	-	4.6	3.7	2.6	6.1	2.9	2.1	-	-	-	4.7	2.4
5. Every time	2.1	2.8	-	1.8	-	2.0	2.0	4.3	-	.9	1.3	-	-	-	2.6	-
Item 2470 N(Wtd) ★	224	115	79	175	2	78	81	37	27	64	87	-	-	14	183	25
B030I: In a car																
1. Not at all	47.5	45.4	58.2	51.2	19.5	44.5	39.1	67.8	52.0	53.2	51.8	-	-	64.7	45.7	50.2
2. A few of the times	29.5	29.0	24.5	25.4	80.5	29.4	34.6	13.3	37.4	27.7	33.5	-	-	29.2	29.6	28.5
3. Some of the times	10.8	7.5	12.8	9.5	-	10.8	11.8	10.9	7.3	9.7	10.1	-	-	-	11.6	11.2
4. Most of the times	6.4	10.5	2.1	7.8	-	5.9	10.3	1.8	3.3	3.9	2.2	-	-	-	7.2	4.9
5. Every time	5.8	7.5	2.4	6.0	-	9.4	4.1	6.2	-	5.5	2.4	-	-	6.2	6.0	5.1
Item 2490 N(Wtd) ★	224	116	78	176	2	78	80	38	27	64	88	-	-	14	182	26

★ = excludes respondents for whom question was inappropriate.

QUESTIONNAIRE FORM 1 1978	TOTAL	SEX		RACE		REGION				4YR COLLEGE PLANS		ILLICIT DRUG USE: LIFETIME				
		M	F	White	Black	NE	NC	S	W	Yes	No	None	Marijuana Only	Few Pills	More Pills	Any Heroin
Weighted No. of Cases:	3799	1740	1842	2962	411	922	1096	1257	524	1758	1571	1301	1086	411	760	46
% of Weighted Total:	100.0	45.8	48.5	78.0	10.8	24.3	28.8	33.1	13.8	46.3	41.3	34.3	28.6	10.8	20.0	1.2

B031: How many of the times when you used LSD during the last year did you use it along with each of the following drugs--that is, so that their effects overlapped?

B031A: With alcohol

	TOTAL	M	F	White	Black	NE	NC	S	W	Yes	No	None	Marijuana Only	Few Pills	More Pills	Any Heroin
1. Not at all	32.6	33.5	35.5	35.8	19.5	28.3	28.7	37.2	50.7	39.1	32.9	-	-	46.6	31.2	32.7
2. A few of the times	31.9	31.8	31.7	30.5	36.2	28.1	40.3	22.8	30.2	28.0	33.3	-	-	43.7	31.8	27.1
3. Some of the times	7.8	5.9	10.1	7.9	-	4.9	10.6	13.1	-	10.1	9.3	-	-	-	6.5	20.9
4. Most of the times	9.9	11.5	6.4	8.7	44.3	15.1	8.1	1.8	12.0	6.1	7.1	-	-	4.3	10.7	7.7
5. Every time	17.8	17.3	16.3	17.2	-	23.6	12.3	25.2	7.1	16.7	17.3	-	-	5.4	19.8	11.6
Item 2500 N(Wtd) ★	225	116	78	176	2	78	82	38	27	65	86	-	-	14	184	26

B031B: With marijuana

	TOTAL	M	F	White	Black	NE	NC	S	W	Yes	No	None	Marijuana Only	Few Pills	More Pills	Any Heroin
1. Not at all	13.4	11.7	14.0	14.1	19.5	14.6	11.1	14.0	15.6	19.8	12.0	-	-	32.2	10.9	18.3
2. A few of the times	24.6	23.3	29.6	25.3	-	21.3	26.7	29.2	21.4	29.5	28.0	-	-	62.2	22.6	19.7
3. Some of the times	9.7	10.6	11.1	10.8	-	8.5	9.6	12.7	9.1	16.0	9.2	-	-	-	9.2	18.9
4. Most of the times	18.5	23.0	15.6	18.3	44.3	14.5	24.4	11.3	22.7	8.1	19.2	-	-	-	20.3	16.5
5. Every time	33.8	31.4	29.7	31.4	36.2	41.1	28.2	32.8	31.2	26.6	31.6	-	-	5.6	37.0	26.6
Item 2510 N(Wtd) ★	224	115	78	175	2	78	82	37	27	65	85	-	-	14	185	25

B032: What have been the most important reasons for your taking LSD? (Mark all that apply.)

	TOTAL	M	F	White	Black	NE	NC	S	W	Yes	No	None	Marijuana Only	Few Pills	More Pills	Any Heroin
A. To experiment--to see what it's like	79.2	81.4	77.8	80.8	55.7	79.7	82.0	72.5	78.2	83.2	80.6	-	-	94.4	80.9	58.9
B. To relax or relieve tension	15.9	14.7	19.9	16.9	-	13.7	19.1	20.3	6.1	22.3	8.7	-	-	7.1	12.0	47.4
C. To feel good or get high	72.5	72.1	71.1	72.2	36.2	72.3	75.0	67.3	72.3	65.8	74.4	-	-	35.5	73.8	81.9
D. To seek deeper insights and understanding	29.9	28.0	26.8	27.2	36.2	30.3	26.6	31.0	37.4	34.4	20.3	-	-	11.6	29.0	46.5
E. To have a good time with my friends	50.7	53.6	44.8	50.9	36.2	48.9	57.7	37.7	51.7	52.8	45.4	-	-	17.5	52.8	52.0
F. To fit in with a group I like	4.7	5.9	3.5	5.4	-	4.7	4.1	9.3	-	7.6	2.9	-	-	-	4.4	9.1
G. To get away from my problems or troubles	14.4	9.7	19.9	13.3	44.3	11.9	17.9	18.7	4.4	19.7	12.9	-	-	-	11.9	38.5
H. Because of boredom, nothing else to do	19.0	15.3	19.5	16.5	36.2	25.2	15.8	15.6	16.9	20.6	13.6	-	-	4.8	17.7	35.8
I. Because of anger or frustration	5.2	2.0	8.8	4.6	-	2.4	5.9	10.4	4.0	6.4	1.2	-	-	-	4.4	13.9
J. To get through the day	4.6	4.1	4.1	2.6	-	4.5	5.8	2.7	4.0	4.6	3.8	-	-	4.5	3.5	12.8
K. To increase the effects of some other drug(s)	8.9	10.7	3.1	6.6	44.3	15.4	5.3	2.1	11.3	10.1	5.0	-	-	5.6	8.1	16.4
L. To decrease (offset) the effects of some other drug(s)	2.0	1.3	3.7	2.5	-	2.1	3.5	-	-	3.0	1.1	-	-	-	1.4	7.3
M. Because I am "hooked"--I have to have it	3.0	4.0	1.4	2.7	44.3	3.7	4.6	-	-	4.3	.7	-	-	-	3.0	4.0
Item 2520-2640 N(Wtd) ★	221	115	77	174	2	74	83	37	27	63	85	-	-	14	180	26

B033: When you take LSD how high do you usually get?

	TOTAL	M	F	White	Black	NE	NC	S	W	Yes	No	None	Marijuana Only	Few Pills	More Pills	Any Heroin
1. Not at all high	.5	.5	.8	.7	-	-	1.5	-	-	-	.7	-	-	4.3	.3	-
2. A little high	4.9	4.6	6.4	5.8	-	2.5	3.9	5.7	14.1	8.7	5.5	-	-	10.5	3.8	10.0
3. Moderately high	24.7	22.7	30.0	24.0	19.5	21.9	32.4	13.9	23.4	22.8	26.2	-	-	42.7	22.2	29.9
4. Very high	69.9	72.2	62.8	69.4	80.5	75.5	62.3	80.3	62.5	68.5	67.6	-	-	42.5	73.7	60.1
Item 2650 N(Wtd) ★	223	116	77	177	2	77	83	37	26	63	87	-	-	14	182	26

B034: When you take LSD how long do you usually stay high?

	TOTAL	M	F	White	Black	NE	NC	S	W	Yes	No	None	Marijuana Only	Few Pills	More Pills	Any Heroin
1. Usually don't get high	.5	.5	.8	.7	-	-	1.5	-	-	-	.7	-	-	4.3	.3	-
2. One to two hours	3.9	2.4	5.5	4.0	-	-	4.3	7.5	8.7	7.2	2.8	-	-	10.5	2.5	10.0
3. Three to six hours	31.9	30.7	35.6	33.5	19.5	32.3	35.7	30.2	21.1	44.3	26.7	-	-	54.9	29.9	31.4
4. Seven to 24 hours	58.5	61.7	52.3	57.9	-	57.1	55.7	62.4	65.7	43.8	63.5	-	-	26.9	63.6	41.1
5. More than 24 hours	5.3	4.7	5.8	3.9	80.5	10.6	2.9	-	4.6	4.8	6.2	-	-	3.4	3.7	17.5
Item 2660 N(Wtd) ★	224	116	78	178	2	77	83	37	27	64	87	-	-	14	183	26

★ = excludes respondents for whom question was inappropriate.

QUESTIONNAIRE FORM 1 1978	TOTAL	SEX		RACE		REGION				4YR COLLEGE PLANS		ILLICIT DRUG USE: LIFETIME				
		M	F	White	Black	NE	NC	S	W	Yes	No	None	Marijuana Only	Few Pills	More Pills	Any Heroin
Weighted No. of Cases:	3799	1740	1842	2962	411	922	1096	1257	524	1758	1571	1301	1086	411	760	46
% of Weighted Total:	100.0	45.8	48.5	78.0	10.8	24.3	28.8	33.1	13.8	46.3	41.3	34.3	28.6	10.8	20.0	1.2

B035: Have you ever had a "bad trip" on LSD?

	TOTAL	M	F	White	Black	NE	NC	S	W	Yes	No	None	Marijuana Only	Few Pills	More Pills	Any Heroin
1. No	73.0	78.7	71.4	75.4	100.0	67.8	81.9	52.8	88.8	72.1	76.1	-	-	95.7	73.1	57.6
2. Yes, once	21.6	16.3	22.7	21.4	-	26.7	14.8	36.2	7.2	23.2	19.4	-	-	4.3	23.4	20.1
3. Yes, more than once	5.4	5.0	5.9	3.2	-	5.5	3.3	11.0	4.0	4.7	4.5	-	-	-	3.5	22.3
Item 2670 N(Wtd) ★	226	117	80	178	3	77	83	38	27	66	88	-	-	14	183	26

B036: Have you ever tried to stop using LSD and found that you couldn't stop?

	TOTAL	M	F	White	Black	NE	NC	S	W	Yes	No	None	Marijuana Only	Few Pills	More Pills	Any Heroin
1. Yes	4.0	4.3	3.7	4.3	-	4.6	2.4	9.1	-	9.3	2.9	-	-	-	3.0	12.9
2. No	96.0	95.7	96.3	95.7	100.0	95.4	97.6	90.9	99.9	90.7	97.1	-	-	100.0	97.0	87.1
Item 2680 N(Wtd) ★	223	116	78	177	2	77	81	37	27	64	87	-	-	14	182	26

B037: Do you think you will be using LSD five years from now?

	TOTAL	M	F	White	Black	NE	NC	S	W	Yes	No	None	Marijuana Only	Few Pills	More Pills	Any Heroin
1. I definitely will	.9	.8	.6	.7	.7	1.0	1.2	.5	.9	.7	1.1	.3	1.2	1.0	.8	8.5
2. I probably will	1.7	1.7	1.3	1.6	.7	2.7	2.0	.8	1.5	1.1	1.5	-	.5	.5	7.2	4.7
3. I probably will not	10.6	11.6	9.2	11.0	7.2	11.8	12.6	9.0	8.4	7.7	11.9	3.4	7.0	11.7	28.0	30.6
4. I definitely will not	86.8	85.9	88.9	86.7	91.4	84.5	84.2	89.7	89.2	90.5	85.5	96.3	91.3	86.8	64.0	56.2
Item 2690 N(Wtd)	3499	1599	1744	2771	384	826	1028	1157	489	1654	1462	1260	1000	384	685	46

The next questions are about PSYCHEDELICS OTHER THAN LSD.

This group would include the following drugs: mescaline, peyote, psilocybin, PCP

B038: On how many occasions (if any) have you taken psychedelics other than LSD...

B038A: ...in your lifetime?

	TOTAL	M	F	White	Black	NE	NC	S	W	Yes	No	None	Marijuana Only	Few Pills	More Pills	Any Heroin
1. 0 occasions	86.4	85.5	88.8	85.9	97.7	82.9	85.4	90.0	86.2	90.4	86.7	100.0	100.0	83.8	47.7	10.7
2. 1-2	5.3	5.6	4.9	5.9	.3	6.1	5.4	4.7	5.3	4.3	5.5	-	-	16.2	16.7	10.1
3. 3-5	2.7	2.9	2.2	2.8	1.2	3.2	3.4	1.8	2.1	1.9	2.2	-	-	-	11.8	19.3
4. 6-9	1.6	1.9	1.2	1.6	.7	1.8	1.8	1.0	2.4	1.3	1.5	-	-	-	6.9	16.8
5. 10-19	1.7	2.0	1.1	1.7	.2	2.0	1.6	1.5	2.0	1.1	1.8	-	-	-	7.8	8.9
6. 20-39	1.2	.8	1.1	1.1	-	2.2	1.3	.2	1.5	.4	1.1	-	-	-	4.8	18.2
7. 40 or more	1.1	1.2	.5	1.0	-	1.8	1.1	.7	.6	.5	1.2	-	-	-	4.3	16.1
Item 920 N(Wtd)	3505	1619	1733	2808	358	845	1030	1144	487	1683	1443	1271	1028	391	715	45

B038B: ...during the last 12 months?

	TOTAL	M	F	White	Black	NE	NC	S	W	Yes	No	None	Marijuana Only	Few Pills	More Pills	Any Heroin
1. 0 occasions	90.8	90.1	93.1	90.8	98.2	87.0	90.7	93.5	91.5	94.0	91.0	100.0	100.0	92.7	62.9	29.2
2. 1-2	4.2	4.2	3.7	4.4	.9	5.7	3.7	3.5	4.2	3.3	4.0	-	-	7.3	15.8	17.9
3. 3-5	2.2	2.7	1.5	2.3	.9	2.3	3.2	1.3	2.2	1.5	1.8	-	-	-	9.3	27.2
4. 6-9	1.2	1.4	.7	1.1	-	1.9	1.0	.9	1.2	.7	1.4	-	-	-	5.6	6.4
5. 10-19	.9	.9	.6	.8	-	2.2	.7	.4	.5	.3	.9	-	-	-	3.8	13.2
6. 20-39	.3	.4	.2	.3	-	.6	.4	-	.3	.1	.5	-	-	-	1.4	3.1
7. 40 or more	.3	.3	.1	.2	-	.3	.3	.4	-	.1	.3	-	-	-	1.2	2.9
Item 930 N(Wtd)	3492	1614	1726	2796	359	842	1021	1142	486	1681	1439	1271	1028	391	701	45

B038C: ...during the last 30 days?

	TOTAL	M	F	White	Black	NE	NC	S	W	Yes	No	None	Marijuana Only	Few Pills	More Pills	Any Heroin
1. 0 occasions	95.7	95.1	97.0	95.9	98.8	93.5	94.7	97.5	97.5	97.9	95.3	100.0	100.0	98.0	82.3	59.9
2. 1-2	2.7	3.2	2.1	2.8	1.2	3.4	3.9	1.7	1.2	1.3	3.1	-	-	2.0	11.2	18.6
3. 3-5	.9	1.0	.3	.8	-	2.1	.5	.4	.7	.5	.8	-	-	-	3.4	15.4
4. 6-9	.4	.3	.3	.3	-	.7	.3	.2	.5	.2	.3	-	-	-	1.8	3.2
5. 10-19	.3	.3	.2	.3	-	.2	.6	.1	-	.1	.4	-	-	-	1.1	3.0
6. 20-39	-	-	-	-	-	-	-	-	-	-	-	-	-	-	-	-
7. 40 or more	*	*	-	*	-	.1	-	.1	-	-	*	-	-	-	.2	-
Item 940 N(Wtd)	3488	1613	1724	2793	358	841	1021	1141	485	1681	1438	1271	1028	391	699	45

★ = excludes respondents for whom question was inappropriate.   * = less than .05 per cent.

QUESTIONNAIRE FORM 1 1978	TOTAL	SEX		RACE		REGION				4YR COLLEGE PLANS		ILLICIT DRUG USE: LIFETIME				
		M	F	White	Black	NE	NC	S	W	Yes	No	None	Mari- juana Only	Few Pills	More Pills	Any Her- oin
Weighted No. of Cases:	3799	1740	1842	2962	411	922	1096	1257	524	1758	1571	1301	1086	411	760	46
% of Weighted Total:	100.0	45.8	48.5	78.0	10.8	24.3	28.8	33.1	13.8	46.3	41.3	34.3	28.6	10.8	20.0	1.2

IF YOU HAVE NOT TAKEN ANY PSYCHEDELICS OTHER THAN LSD IN THE LAST TWELVE MONTHS, GO TO Q.B042.

B039: When you take psychedelics other than LSD how high do you usually get?

	TOTAL	M	F	White	Black	NE	NC	S	W	Yes	No	None	Mari. only	Few Pills	More Pills	Any Heroin
1. Not at all high	1.2	1.4	1.3	1.5	-	2.2	.6	1.0	-	.6	1.7	-	-	2.8	.9	2.0
2. A little high	8.3	6.9	9.8	7.3	56.0	7.3	9.7	7.2	9.2	9.8	6.4	-	-	2.2	9.5	2.2
3. Moderately high	36.3	35.7	38.4	38.0	15.1	31.7	42.6	28.6	47.5	30.7	42.1	-	-	24.8	36.4	45.7
4. Very high	54.3	56.0	50.5	53.2	28.9	58.8	47.0	63.2	43.3	58.9	49.8	-	-	70.2	53.2	50.2
Item 2700 N(Wtd) ★	326	163	122	264	6	113	100	74	40	99	135	-	-	28	266	31

B040: When you take psychedelics other than LSD how long do you usually stay high?

	TOTAL	M	F	White	Black	NE	NC	S	W	Yes	No	None	Mari. only	Few Pills	More Pills	Any Heroin
1. Usually don't get high	1.3	1.5	1.3	1.6	-	1.4	1.1	1.9	-	1.1	1.5	-	-	2.8	1.2	-
2. One to two hours	8.4	6.5	11.7	8.2	37.6	6.1	8.1	8.6	14.8	14.1	5.5	-	-	2.2	8.7	11.3
3. Three to six hours	47.7	47.7	48.7	50.9	18.5	44.9	43.3	53.7	55.5	45.2	50.6	-	-	55.7	46.2	53.5
4. Seven to 24 hours	41.1	42.8	36.1	37.5	44.0	45.4	44.9	35.8	29.7	39.5	39.3	-	-	39.3	42.4	32.3
5. More than 24 hours	1.5	1.5	2.2	1.9	-	2.2	2.6	-	-	-	3.0	-	-	-	1.6	2.8
Item 2710 N(Wtd) ★	326	163	122	263	6	111	100	75	40	100	134	-	-	28	267	31

B041: What psychedelics other than LSD have you taken during the last year? (Mark all that apply.)

	TOTAL	M	F	White	Black	NE	NC	S	W	Yes	No	None	Mari. only	Few Pills	More Pills	Any Heroin
A. Mescaline	54.3	54.7	58.2	56.5	18.5	54.2	69.1	39.9	45.2	48.4	62.1	-	-	21.5	55.6	72.9
B. Peyote	16.1	17.1	9.5	13.4	-	12.7	12.3	14.4	38.2	15.4	13.4	-	-	-	16.6	26.7
C. Psilocybin	14.4	19.9	9.1	14.9	-	13.2	9.4	14.5	30.1	24.5	9.5	-	-	4.8	14.5	22.3
D. PCP	48.5	52.6	40.5	46.2	61.5	45.3	44.1	58.8	49.2	45.0	45.3	-	-	53.6	45.0	73.0
E. Concentrated THC	57.2	62.5	52.5	56.5	38.5	74.2	49.6	52.4	37.1	47.6	61.2	-	-	50.5	59.2	47.0
F. Other	37.0	33.3	40.3	36.0	38.5	29.7	43.5	37.0	41.2	32.1	37.3	-	-	9.7	38.3	50.6
G. Don't know the names of some I have used	16.5	12.5	24.3	16.2	46.1	20.8	12.5	20.7	6.7	12.7	18.8	-	-	14.4	15.2	29.9
Item 2720-2780 N(Wtd) ★	322	162	119	262	5	110	98	75	39	99	132	-	-	28	263	31

The next questions are about AMPHETAMINES, which doctors sometimes prescribe to help people lose weight or to give people more energy. Drugstores are not supposed to sell them without a prescription.

Amphetamines are sometimes called: uppers, ups, speed, bennies, dexies, pep pills, diet pills. They include the following drugs: Benzedrine, Dexedrine, Methedrine, Ritalin, Preludin, Dexamyl, Methamphetamine.

B042: Have you ever taken amphetamines because a doctor told you to use them?

	TOTAL	M	F	White	Black	NE	NC	S	W	Yes	No	None	Mari. only	Few Pills	More Pills	Any Heroin
1. No	85.7	86.6	84.9	84.6	91.6	86.4	86.2	85.0	85.1	86.6	84.3	92.7	87.3	77.8	76.8	73.0
2. Yes, but I had already tried them on my own	3.6	2.6	4.1	3.7	1.2	3.9	3.7	3.2	3.6	2.5	4.2	-	-	5.1	12.5	16.5
3. Yes, and it was the first time I took any	10.7	10.7	11.0	11.7	7.1	9.7	10.1	11.9	11.4	10.9	11.5	7.3	12.5	17.1	10.7	10.5
Item 2790 N(Wtd)	3502	1611	1742	2804	361	841	1028	1150	483	1662	1460	1250	1005	393	732	46

B043: On how many occasions (if any) have you taken amphetamines on your own--that is, without a doctor telling you to take them...

★=excludes respondents for whom question was inappropriate.

QUESTIONNAIRE FORM 1 1978	TOTAL	SEX		RACE		REGION				4YR COLLEGE PLANS		ILLICIT DRUG USE: LIFETIME				
		M	F	White	Black	NE	NC	S	W	Yes	No	None	Marijuana Only	Few Pills	More Pills	Any Heroin
Weighted No. of Cases:	3799	1740	1842	2962	411	922	1096	1257	524	1758	1571	1301	1086	411	760	46
% of Weighted Total:	100.0	45.8	48.5	78.0	10.8	24.3	28.8	33.1	13.8	46.3	41.3	34.3	28.6	10.8	20.0	1.2
B043A: ...in your lifetime?																
1. 0 occasions	78.4	79.1	79.2	76.8	93.4	75.2	77.8	81.9	77.2	82.9	77.8	100.0	100.0	65.8	20.3	10.1
2. 1-2	5.9	5.9	5.5	6.2	3.2	5.9	5.9	5.5	6.5	5.5	5.7	-	-	34.2	9.6	4.0
3. 3-5	3.8	3.3	4.3	4.2	1.5	3.6	4.1	3.3	4.8	3.6	3.9	-	-	-	17.5	13.6
4. 6-9	2.6	3.9	1.4	2.8	.7	4.0	2.1	2.1	2.3	2.2	2.7	-	-	-	11.8	12.3
5. 10-19	2.8	3.0	2.4	3.0	.6	3.0	2.9	2.6	2.6	2.6	2.4	-	-	-	12.1	22.1
6. 20-39	2.7	1.9	3.2	2.9	.5	3.2	3.5	1.7	2.7	1.5	3.2	-	-	-	12.6	7.9
7. 40 or more	3.7	2.8	4.1	4.2	-	5.0	3.7	2.8	3.9	1.7	4.4	-	-	-	16.1	30.0
Item 980 N(Wtd)	3476	1597	1731	2790	356	838	1023	1132	483	1663	1442	1262	1008	390	726	43
B043B: ...during the last 12 months?																
1. 0 occasions	83.5	84.4	84.1	82.2	96.9	80.4	83.3	86.4	82.6	87.7	82.8	100.0	100.0	83.0	33.7	22.9
2. 1-2	5.9	6.1	5.4	6.4	1.7	6.0	5.9	5.0	8.0	4.8	6.1	-	-	17.0	18.3	21.2
3. 3-5	3.1	3.1	3.0	3.4	.1	4.2	2.5	3.2	2.1	3.3	2.4	-	-	-	14.2	11.1
4. 6-9	2.2	2.5	1.7	2.3	.6	3.1	2.2	1.3	3.1	1.2	2.5	-	-	-	9.4	25.4
5. 10-19	2.1	1.8	2.3	2.4	.5	2.1	3.2	1.4	1.7	1.3	2.6	-	-	-	10.2	3.4
6. 20-39	1.6	1.4	1.7	1.8	-	1.9	1.7	1.3	1.6	.9	1.9	-	-	-	7.5	7.6
7. 40 or more	1.5	.8	1.8	1.6	-	2.3	1.2	1.3	.9	.9	1.6	-	-	-	6.7	8.4
Item 990 N(Wtd)	3458	1582	1728	2778	352	838	1018	1121	482	1656	1435	1262	1010	385	711	43
B043C: ...during the last 30 days?																
1. 0 occasions	91.4	92.5	91.6	91.1	98.4	88.8	91.7	92.9	91.6	93.8	91.6	100.0	100.0	95.7	63.3	52.3
2. 1-2	3.8	3.5	3.5	3.9	.7	4.4	3.2	3.6	4.7	3.1	3.4	-	-	4.3	14.6	27.4
3. 3-5	2.0	1.9	1.8	2.0	.5	3.5	1.6	1.2	1.8	1.3	1.9	-	-	-	9.1	7.8
4. 6-9	1.3	1.3	1.2	1.5	.4	.9	2.0	1.1	1.0	1.0	1.3	-	-	-	6.1	4.9
5. 10-19	.9	.6	1.0	.9	-	1.3	1.4	.3	.6	.4	1.1	-	-	-	4.0	7.6
6. 20-39	.3	.1	.4	.4	-	.4	.1	.6	-	.3	.3	-	-	-	1.4	-
7. 40 or more	.3	.1	.5	.3	-	.8	-	.2	.2	.1	.4	-	-	-	1.4	-
Item 1000 N(Wtd)	3457	1582	1727	2777	352	838	1018	1118	483	1654	1436	1262	1010	382	711	43

IF YOU HAVE NOT TAKEN AMPHETAMINES IN THE LAST TWELVE MONTHS, GO TO Q.B052.

THE FOLLOWING QUESTIONS REFER ONLY TO TAKING AMPHETAMINES WITHOUT A DOCTOR'S ORDERS. IF YOU HAVE NOT DONE THIS IN THE LAST TWELVE MONTHS, GO TO Q.B052

B044: When you used amphetamines during the last year, how often did you use them in each of the following situations?

B044A: When you were alone

	TOTAL	M	F	White	Black	NE	NC	S	W	Yes	No	None	Marijuana Only	Few Pills	More Pills	Any Heroin
1. Not at all	50.6	62.8	41.2	50.5	44.6	48.1	50.4	49.4	58.6	56.7	46.1	-	-	68.9	48.6	42.6
2. A few of the times	25.0	21.6	27.3	24.5	35.7	26.3	24.6	23.5	26.3	19.0	28.7	-	-	22.1	25.3	26.2
3. Some of the times	12.7	9.8	15.0	12.4	3.9	14.7	13.7	12.8	6.1	11.4	13.1	-	-	-	13.9	21.1
4. Most of the times	6.9	3.3	10.4	7.4	7.9	7.0	6.5	7.6	6.1	4.3	8.5	-	-	-	7.8	8.1
5. Every time	4.8	2.5	6.1	5.1	7.9	3.9	4.7	6.7	2.8	8.5	3.6	-	-	9.1	4.4	2.0
Item 2800 N(Wtd) ★	551	236	265	473	12	160	164	151	76	195	238	-	-	63	457	31

B044B: With just 1 or 2 other people

	TOTAL	M	F	White	Black	NE	NC	S	W	Yes	No	None	Marijuana Only	Few Pills	More Pills	Any Heroin
1. Not at all	17.5	17.7	16.7	17.4	21.8	18.2	14.3	20.9	15.9	22.8	16.3	-	-	28.0	16.1	16.0
2. A few of the times	37.7	42.6	33.0	37.0	55.7	39.3	38.2	36.3	36.4	38.5	36.4	-	-	43.1	37.0	38.2
3. Some of the times	25.4	23.1	28.1	26.0	18.5	25.5	28.1	23.5	23.4	21.3	25.7	-	-	6.7	27.9	27.1
4. Most of the times	14.4	12.7	16.1	14.3	3.9	12.9	16.0	17.1	8.8	11.5	18.1	-	-	9.4	15.0	16.4
5. Every time	4.9	4.0	6.1	5.4	-	4.0	3.3	2.1	15.4	5.9	3.5	-	-	12.7	4.0	2.3
Item 2810 N(Wtd) ★	552	240	262	474	12	159	162	152	78	193	241	-	-	63	458	31

★=excludes respondents for whom question was inappropriate.

QUESTIONNAIRE FORM 1 1978	TOTAL	SEX		RACE		REGION				4YR COLLEGE PLANS		ILLICIT DRUG USE: LIFETIME				
		M	F	White	Black	NE	NC	S	W	Yes	No	None	Marijuana Only	Few Pills	More Pills	Any Heroin
Weighted No. of Cases:	3799	1740	1842	2962	411	922	1096	1257	524	1758	1571	1301	1086	411	760	46
% of Weighted Total:	100.0	45.8	48.5	78.0	10.8	24.3	28.8	33.1	13.8	46.3	41.3	34.3	28.6	10.8	20.0	1.2
B044C: At a party																
1. Not at all	41.1	38.4	44.2	42.0	63.7	32.9	34.1	52.5	50.5	51.3	38.1	-	-	62.6	39.4	22.9
2. A few of the times	22.6	25.6	20.6	23.1	20.5	26.6	27.1	15.2	19.3	19.9	25.8	-	-	16.7	22.8	30.9
3. Some of the times	16.2	17.6	13.5	15.1	15.7	18.0	16.9	16.7	9.9	15.6	14.1	-	-	7.2	16.9	24.3
4. Most of the times	13.4	12.3	13.9	12.9	-	14.8	15.3	8.5	16.1	7.0	16.6	-	-	4.2	14.8	11.0
5. Every time	6.8	6.2	7.8	6.9	-	7.7	6.7	7.1	4.3	6.1	5.4	-	-	9.2	6.1	10.8
Item 2820 N(Wtd) ★	546	237	260	468	12	160	160	151	74	192	238	-	-	62	452	32
B044D: When your date or spouse was present																
1. Not at all	50.5	60.1	42.5	51.9	67.7	49.8	50.0	45.6	62.7	62.2	48.5	-	-	74.1	47.6	45.4
2. A few of the times	23.1	22.5	23.3	22.9	21.1	23.6	24.8	24.1	16.1	23.6	20.4	-	-	10.9	24.5	27.0
3. Some of the times	13.2	11.7	14.0	12.9	7.3	13.8	15.7	12.9	7.0	7.2	14.3	-	-	4.3	14.1	17.4
4. Most of the times	7.3	3.8	10.3	6.6	3.9	9.8	4.8	6.9	8.2	2.6	9.3	-	-	5.4	7.7	4.7
5. Every time	6.0	1.9	9.9	5.7	-	3.0	4.7	10.5	6.1	4.4	7.4	-	-	5.3	6.1	5.4
Item 2830 N(Wtd) ★	546	237	261	469	12	158	163	150	75	195	236	-	-	62	453	31
B044E: When people over age 30 were present																
1. Not at all	57.1	59.3	55.0	58.3	54.6	56.6	54.8	60.2	57.5	66.4	52.7	-	-	80.4	54.9	44.6
2. A few of the times	24.3	22.9	26.0	23.7	20.3	25.9	25.5	20.1	26.6	18.6	27.9	-	-	10.0	25.4	35.9
3. Some of the times	12.5	12.0	12.9	12.6	11.2	11.1	13.9	15.3	6.7	8.8	12.4	-	-	4.4	13.7	10.1
4. Most of the times	4.2	4.3	3.9	4.0	-	5.0	4.8	2.2	5.1	3.4	5.8	-	-	3.9	4.1	6.1
5. Every time	1.9	1.5	2.2	1.4	13.9	1.4	1.0	2.2	4.1	2.8	1.1	-	-	1.3	1.9	3.4
Item 2840 N(Wtd) ★	547	239	261	471	12	159	162	150	76	193	241	-	-	61	455	31
B044F: During the daytime (before 4:00 p.m.)																
1. Not at all	21.3	24.7	17.2	19.8	35.7	19.7	21.8	25.6	15.2	23.9	18.0	-	-	50.9	16.7	32.4
2. A few of the times	30.3	35.8	26.1	30.9	14.9	31.8	25.7	32.2	33.2	36.9	28.0	-	-	24.0	31.4	25.2
3. Some of the times	18.5	19.9	17.6	18.8	15.7	21.1	17.1	18.2	17.0	15.9	18.3	-	-	8.0	20.0	17.4
4. Most of the times	17.5	13.5	21.6	17.8	7.9	18.6	21.5	12.7	16.1	11.0	23.9	-	-	7.1	19.3	10.6
5. Every time	12.4	6.2	17.6	12.6	25.8	8.8	13.9	11.3	18.6	12.3	11.8	-	-	10.0	12.6	14.4
Item 2850 N(Wtd) ★	554	240	265	478	12	159	166	150	79	198	241	-	-	60	462	31
B044G: At your home (or apartment or dorm)																
1. Not at all	36.8	49.0	27.4	38.1	45.3	33.0	34.6	42.5	38.5	44.0	34.4	-	-	67.7	33.0	33.2
2. A few of the times	26.1	24.8	27.5	26.1	19.3	27.2	27.4	25.3	22.7	23.1	28.6	-	-	21.7	26.8	23.8
3. Some of the times	18.4	15.7	19.4	17.8	19.7	19.7	22.4	15.0	14.3	13.7	19.9	-	-	-	20.9	17.7
4. Most of the times	10.9	8.0	14.4	10.5	7.9	13.7	12.4	6.6	10.3	9.2	10.3	-	-	-	12.0	15.5
5. Every time	7.7	2.6	11.3	7.5	7.9	6.4	3.3	10.6	14.2	10.0	6.7	-	-	10.5	7.2	9.9
Item 2860 N(Wtd) ★	544	236	260	467	12	158	160	150	77	192	240	-	-	60	453	31
B044H: At school																
1. Not at all	38.7	40.7	38.5	40.0	37.8	35.3	36.6	47.5	32.8	40.4	44.3	-	-	76.5	33.3	43.7
2. A few of the times	27.7	28.8	26.3	27.0	24.6	27.8	22.7	30.6	32.5	32.7	23.1	-	-	20.0	29.4	18.1
3. Some of the times	15.0	15.6	13.6	14.8	19.7	16.0	17.6	9.9	18.0	13.4	12.8	-	-	1.7	16.6	18.0
4. Most of the times	13.9	11.5	15.7	14.1	3.9	14.8	17.4	10.3	11.9	9.9	15.3	-	-	-	15.7	14.8
5. Every time	4.6	3.3	5.8	4.2	13.9	6.1	5.8	1.7	4.9	3.5	4.5	-	-	1.8	5.0	5.4
Item 2880 N(Wtd) ★	546	238	260	469	12	159	162	150	75	193	238	-	-	61	454	31
B044I: In a car																
1. Not at all	45.2	43.6	48.7	45.5	84.0	46.2	43.7	42.6	51.8	53.6	43.2	-	-	75.4	41.8	35.6
2. A few of the times	24.1	25.8	21.3	22.8	8.7	23.0	20.9	27.9	25.3	22.0	24.8	-	-	11.4	24.9	37.0
3. Some of the times	16.3	18.3	14.1	16.8	7.3	14.4	19.0	16.1	15.1	15.6	15.4	-	-	5.7	17.2	24.2
4. Most of the times	10.8	9.7	11.2	11.3	-	11.7	13.9	9.2	5.1	6.8	12.7	-	-	2.2	12.5	3.3
5. Every time	3.6	2.6	4.7	3.6	-	4.7	2.4	4.1	2.8	2.1	3.8	-	-	5.4	3.6	-
Item 2890 N(Wtd) ★	542	237	258	467	12	156	160	151	75	193	238	-	-	61	449	32

★ = excludes respondents for whom question was inappropriate.

QUESTIONNAIRE FORM 1 1978	TOTAL	SEX		RACE		REGION				4YR COLLEGE PLANS		ILLICIT DRUG USE: LIFETIME				
		M	F	White	Black	NE	NC	S	W	Yes	No	None	Marijuana Only	Few Pills	More Pills	Any Heroin
Weighted No. of Cases:	3799	1740	1842	2962	411	922	1096	1257	524	1758	1571	1301	1086	411	760	46
% of Weighted Total:	100.0	45.8	48.5	78.0	10.8	24.3	28.8	33.1	13.8	46.3	41.3	34.3	28.6	10.8	20.0	1.2

B045: How many of the times when you used amphetamines during the last year did you use them along with each of the following drugs--that is, so that their effects overlapped?

B045A: With alcohol

1. Not at all	41.3	43.1	42.6	42.5	66.1	34.1	36.0	48.5	53.4	51.1	38.9	-	-	61.2	39.1	36.0
2. A few of the times	28.4	25.8	27.4	26.9	18.5	30.4	30.7	28.1	20.2	25.9	28.6	-	-	24.0	29.4	22.3
3. Some of the times	12.1	14.0	10.4	11.9	15.5	12.5	11.1	9.7	18.2	9.1	13.8	-	-	2.2	13.1	17.3
4. Most of the times	12.5	10.4	14.2	12.8	-	15.0	15.6	10.8	4.0	8.6	14.6	-	-	9.6	12.5	17.1
5. Every time	5.6	6.7	5.3	5.8	-	8.0	6.6	2.9	4.2	5.2	4.2	-	-	3.1	5.8	7.4
Item 2900 N(Wtd) ★	549	239	263	473	12	155	166	151	77	196	239	-	-	60	457	32

B045B: With marijuana

1. Not at all	28.5	26.0	31.9	29.9	31.1	21.1	30.0	31.1	35.5	35.5	28.2	-	-	52.0	25.4	30.9
2. A few of the times	24.1	26.2	22.3	23.7	49.0	24.8	21.2	24.3	28.1	24.1	24.8	-	-	28.3	24.3	12.3
3. Some of the times	16.7	16.1	17.2	16.1	8.2	14.9	18.3	16.5	17.1	15.9	17.9	-	-	4.0	18.0	20.4
4. Most of the times	17.5	18.0	17.1	18.5	4.1	20.4	19.8	17.8	5.9	16.3	16.2	-	-	12.1	18.0	19.4
5. Every time	13.3	13.7	11.5	11.7	7.6	18.7	10.6	10.2	13.4	8.2	12.8	-	-	3.5	14.3	17.0
Item 2910 N(Wtd) ★	547	240	260	472	11	159	167	144	77	197	234	-	-	58	459	30

B045C: With LSD

1. Not at all	96.1	93.9	99.1	96.7	100.0	95.3	94.4	97.9	98.1	97.5	96.3	-	-	100.0	96.6	82.8
2. A few of the times	2.2	3.6	.5	1.8	-	2.2	3.7	.7	1.9	1.3	2.1	-	-	-	1.8	11.7
3. Some of the times	1.1	1.8	-	.9	-	1.8	1.4	.7	-	1.3	.7	-	-	-	1.4	-
4. Most of the times	.1	.3	-	.2	-	-	.5	-	-	-	-	-	-	-	-	2.4
5. Every time	.4	.4	.4	.4	-	.7	-	.7	-	-	.8	-	-	-	.2	3.2
Item 2920 N(Wtd) ★	527	227	255	454	11	149	162	143	73	184	233	-	-	58	438	31

B045D: With psychedelics other than LSD

1. Not at all	89.9	89.6	93.7	92.2	100.0	89.4	86.5	94.0	90.7	95.7	88.7	-	-	100.0	89.4	78.7
2. A few of the times	6.4	6.8	4.1	4.8	-	4.8	8.6	5.3	7.1	2.8	8.2	-	-	-	6.7	14.1
3. Some of the times	2.9	2.8	1.4	2.2	-	3.2	5.0	.7	2.2	.6	2.4	-	-	-	3.0	7.3
4. Most of the times	.4	.5	.4	.5	-	1.4	-	-	-	.7	.3	-	-	-	.5	-
5. Every time	.3	.3	.4	.3	-	1.1	-	-	-	.3	.4	-	-	-	.4	-
Item 2930 N(Wtd) ★	529	227	255	454	11	150	162	143	75	184	233	-	-	58	440	31

B046: What have been the most important reasons for your taking amphetamines without a doctor's orders? (Mark all that apply.)

A. To experiment--to see what it's like	58.5	65.6	51.0	58.9	61.4	60.1	61.4	55.6	54.9	59.2	58.5	-	-	63.9	57.9	56.9
B. To relax or relieve tension	19.6	17.8	21.9	19.6	15.2	20.3	21.9	21.8	9.2	14.3	23.2	-	-	9.2	20.3	29.3
C. To feel good or get high	58.7	63.6	53.3	57.4	47.2	65.3	58.6	57.8	46.9	50.4	59.1	-	-	34.5	61.4	64.4
D. To seek deeper insights and understanding	7.5	8.1	6.0	6.2	11.2	7.8	9.4	7.7	2.7	5.1	6.4	-	-	1.5	7.6	17.2
E. To have a good time with my friends	37.1	42.2	30.2	35.6	34.6	37.8	35.5	40.1	33.0	33.4	35.2	-	-	23.8	37.8	52.5
F. To fit in with a group I like	3.8	3.8	3.2	3.7	-	2.7	4.7	3.9	4.2	4.1	3.1	-	-	8.8	3.2	3.8
G. To get away from my problems or troubles	11.4	6.0	17.2	12.2	-	11.2	10.1	17.3	2.6	10.6	14.6	-	-	5.4	11.5	20.6
H. Because of boredom, nothing else to do	15.1	16.3	12.4	14.0	11.2	25.4	11.9	11.0	8.8	11.4	16.1	-	-	6.2	15.7	23.9
I. Because of anger or frustration	7.0	3.9	10.0	7.4	-	5.5	6.8	11.8	1.0	8.8	6.4	-	-	-	7.7	10.3
J. To get through the day	21.4	21.9	19.7	21.0	16.3	21.2	28.6	15.6	18.0	20.0	23.3	-	-	2.6	23.4	27.8
K. To increase the effects of some other drug(s)	8.5	10.4	6.7	7.6	22.2	10.2	9.4	7.2	5.1	7.2	8.2	-	-	2.7	8.9	12.9
L. To decrease (offset) the effects of some other drug(s)	2.0	1.9	1.1	1.3	-	1.2	3.0	2.1	1.5	1.4	.7	-	-	-	2.0	6.0
M. To stay awake	54.0	51.6	56.8	55.0	27.6	58.0	55.2	51.5	48.3	51.8	57.5	-	-	25.5	58.4	44.8
N. To get more energy	63.4	60.7	66.8	64.0	34.2	65.0	65.1	60.0	63.5	61.9	64.7	-	-	38.1	68.0	45.8
O. To help me lose weight	30.4	8.2	52.0	31.4	31.7	37.5	33.8	23.8	21.7	24.7	38.3	-	-	27.1	31.8	17.2
P. Because I am "hooked"--I feel I have to have them	1.6	.8	1.6	1.2	-	1.0	.8	3.3	.9	2.4	.7	-	-	-	1.5	5.2
Item 2940-3090 N(Wtd) ★	552	240	264	477	12	159	163	153	77	197	240	-	-	61	459	32

★=excludes respondents for whom question was inappropriate.

QUESTIONNAIRE FORM 1 1978	TOTAL	SEX		RACE		REGION				4YR COLLEGE PLANS		ILLICIT DRUG USE: LIFETIME				
		M	F	White	Black	NE	NC	S	W	Yes	No	None	Marijuana Only	Few Pills	More Pills	Any Heroin
Weighted No. of Cases:	3799	1740	1842	2962	411	922	1096	1257	524	1758	1571	1301	1086	411	760	46
% of Weighted Total:	100.0	45.8	48.5	78.0	10.8	24.3	28.8	33.1	13.8	46.3	41.3	34.3	28.6	10.8	20.0	1.2

B047: When you take amphetamines, how high do you usually get?

	TOTAL	M	F	White	Black	NE	NC	S	W	Yes	No	None	Marijuana Only	Few Pills	More Pills	Any Heroin
1. Not at all high	6.2	8.2	4.8	5.7	29.6	3.9	7.5	6.0	8.8	7.9	4.8	-	-	19.6	5.0	-
2. A little high	25.9	28.7	23.5	26.3	19.9	26.1	24.4	27.4	25.6	30.1	23.1	-	-	31.4	25.4	22.7
3. Moderately high	40.2	38.9	40.8	41.0	19.1	42.4	38.4	41.8	36.2	33.4	46.0	-	-	28.7	42.4	29.6
4. Very high	13.0	12.8	13.3	11.8	19.4	15.5	11.4	14.5	8.7	12.6	11.1	-	-	4.7	12.8	31.4
5. I don't take them to get high	14.7	11.4	17.6	15.2	12.0	12.0	18.4	10.2	20.7	16.0	15.0	-	-	15.6	14.4	16.3
Item 3100 N(Wtd) ★	542	240	257	470	12	154	169	147	72	190	240	-	-	58	452	32

B048: When you take amphetamines how long do you usually stay high?

	TOTAL	M	F	White	Black	NE	NC	S	W	Yes	No	None	Marijuana Only	Few Pills	More Pills	Any Heroin
1 Usually don't get high	14.5	12.5	16.5	14.1	44.8	13.6	14.5	14.3	16.7	16.4	13.3	-	-	35.7	12.4	5.3
2. One to two hours	17.0	16.4	17.3	17.2	18.8	12.8	23.6	13.8	20.0	16.2	-	-	-	18.9	15.3	39.8
3. Three to six hours	39.5	45.5	35.4	41.5	8.0	37.8	41.3	37.4	43.6	36.6	42.6	-	-	29.8	41.4	30.3
4. Seven to 24 hours	27.1	23.6	29.1	25.6	18.0	33.6	27.3	20.8	25.9	24.0	27.4	-	-	13.3	29.0	24.5
5. More than 24 hours	1.9	1.8	1.6	1.5	10.4	2.3	.7	3.9	-	3.0	.5	-	-	2.2	2.0	-
Item 3110 N(Wtd) ★	546	240	260	473	13	154	163	152	77	196	237	-	-	58	458	30

B049: What amphetamines have you taken during the last year without a doctor's orders? (Mark all that apply.)

	TOTAL	M	F	White	Black	NE	NC	S	W	Yes	No	None	Marijuana Only	Few Pills	More Pills	Any Heroin
A. Benzedrine	23.7	24.5	23.2	23.5	11.2	22.6	25.1	23.8	22.8	23.5	24.3	-	-	11.2	23.9	42.4
B. Dexedrine	23.7	30.6	19.0	24.9	7.3	30.4	21.8	17.0	27.1	22.2	24.1	-	-	3.5	24.7	45.2
C. Methedrine	24.5	22.7	26.1	23.3	22.2	27.6	25.9	22.4	18.7	23.1	23.3	-	-	14.1	24.1	47.6
D. Ritalin	3.7	5.1	1.8	3.3	-	2.4	3.2	2.4	9.8	3.1	5.3	-	-	1.7	3.8	5.4
E. Preludin	6.9	7.3	5.8	6.5	-	5.1	5.6	12.8	1.8	5.5	7.6	-	-	-	6.7	20.9
F. Dexamyl	7.0	5.9	8.9	6.9	-	11.1	5.2	6.0	4.4	5.8	10.1	-	-	-	6.8	21.4
G. Methamphetamine	14.3	12.2	15.5	13.1	15.9	14.1	20.0	10.2	10.2	12.4	13.9	-	-	1.7	14.6	32.8
H. Other	41.0	38.0	41.7	40.8	36.7	45.0	39.5	41.6	35.3	35.8	43.7	-	-	37.6	41.2	44.8
I. Don't know the names of some amphetamines I have used	42.9	40.2	46.4	44.3	25.8	49.5	40.3	44.1	32.4	43.7	41.6	-	-	42.7	42.8	44.4
Item 3120-3200 N(Wtd) ★	541	239	259	469	12	156	165	145	75	195	233	-	-	55	453	32

B050: What methods have you used for taking amphetamines? (Mark all that apply.)

	TOTAL	M	F	White	Black	NE	NC	S	W	Yes	No	None	Marijuana Only	Few Pills	More Pills	Any Heroin
A. By mouth	97.9	97.4	99.1	98.6	84.7	98.5	99.0	95.5	99.2	99.5	98.1	-	-	95.1	98.3	97.7
B. Injection	3.2	4.0	1.6	2.3	6.9	4.4	3.6	2.5	1.0	1.6	3.1	-	-	-	2.4	19.3
C. Other	18.8	22.1	14.9	17.8	32.5	26.2	15.6	11.8	24.4	15.0	16.9	-	-	7.1	19.7	26.8
Item 3210-3230 N(Wtd) ★	557	244	267	484	13	159	169	154	76	201	242	-	-	59	465	32

B051: Have you ever tried to stop using amphetamines and found that you couldn't stop?

	TOTAL	M	F	White	Black	NE	NC	S	W	Yes	No	None	Marijuana Only	Few Pills	More Pills	Any Heroin
1. Yes	1.9	2.2	1.9	2.1	-	1.7	2.6	1.9	.9	1.4	2.5	-	-	3.9	1.8	-
2. No	98.1	97.7	98.1	97.9	100.0	98.3	97.4	98.1	99.1	98.6	97.5	-	-	96.1	98.2	100.0
Item 3240 N(Wtd) ★	557	244	267	482	13	159	167	153	77	201	242	-	-	60	463	32

B052: Do you think you will be using amphetamines without a doctor's orders five years from now?

	TOTAL	M	F	White	Black	NE	NC	S	W	Yes	No	None	Marijuana Only	Few Pills	More Pills	Any Heroin
1. I definitely will	.8	.9	.7	.8	.5	1.7	.8	.3	.3	.5	1.0	.3	.5	-	2.3	4.8
2. I probably will	5.9	5.1	6.1	5.9	3.2	6.8	7.4	4.5	4.5	3.4	7.0	.1	1.2	3.5	22.8	26.0
3. I probably will not	21.6	22.7	20.1	22.0	16.0	23.0	20.9	20.9	22.3	19.5	22.7	10.3	16.3	28.3	45.2	30.6
4. I definitely will not	71.7	71.3	73.2	71.2	80.2	68.5	70.9	74.2	73.0	76.5	69.3	89.3	82.0	68.2	29.7	38.6
Item 3250 N(Wtd)	3483	1600	1739	2780	370	824	1022	1146	490	1652	1465	1242	982	385	707	46

★ = excludes respondents for whom question was inappropriate.

QUESTIONNAIRE FORM 1 1978	TOTAL	SEX		RACE		REGION				4YR COLLEGE PLANS		ILLICIT DRUG USE: LIFETIME				
		M	F	White	Black	NE	NC	S	W	Yes	No	None	Marijuana Only	Few Pills	More Pills	Any Heroin
Weighted No. of Cases:	3799	1740	1842	2962	411	922	1096	1257	524	1758	1571	1301	1086	411	760	46
% of Weighted Total:	100.0	45.8	48.5	78.0	10.8	24.3	28.8	33.1	13.8	46.3	41.3	34.3	28.6	10.8	20.0	1.2

The next questions are about QUAALUDES (Methaqualone), which are sometimes prescribed by doctors. Drugstores are not supposed to sell them without a prescription.

Quaaludes are sometimes called: soapers, quads.

B053: On how many occasions (if any) have you taken quaaludes on your own--that is, without a doctor telling you to take them...

B053A: ...in your lifetime?

	TOTAL	M	F	White	Black	NE	NC	S	W	Yes	No	None	Mari. Only	Few Pills	More Pills	Heroin
1. 0 occasions	92.6	92.1	93.7	92.3	98.6	91.0	94.2	91.9	93.5	94.2	93.0	100.0	100.0	94.8	71.3	18.9
2. 1-2	3.2	3.7	2.5	3.6	.6	3.6	2.6	3.6	3.0	2.6	2.9	-	-	5.2	11.3	26.8
3. 3-5	1.2	1.3	1.2	1.3	.2	1.5	.7	1.7	.8	1.4	.9	-	-	-	5.3	12.8
4. 6-9	1.1	1.0	.9	.9	-	2.0	.7	.6	1.3	.7	1.2	-	-	-	4.4	15.1
5. 10-19	.8	.8	.7	.9	.3	.8	.6	1.0	.8	.5	.8	-	-	-	2.6	18.9
6. 20-39	.5	.2	.5	.3	-	.4	.3	.7	.4	.1	.6	-	-	-	2.3	-
7. 40 or more	.7	.8	.5	.7	.2	.7	.9	.5	.2	.6	.6	-	-	-	2.8	7.4
Item 1010 N(Wtd)	3452	1611	1706	2791	345	823	1025	1121	483	1666	1428	1261	1014	390	694	45

B053B: ...during the last 12 months?

	TOTAL	M	F	White	Black	NE	NC	S	W	Yes	No	None	Mari. Only	Few Pills	More Pills	Heroin
1. 0 occasions	95.3	94.8	96.0	95.1	99.7	93.8	96.5	95.2	95.4	96.0	95.7	100.0	100.0	98.2	80.8	48.9
2. 1-2	2.3	2.7	1.8	2.5	-	2.1	2.2	2.0	3.2	1.8	2.1	-	-	1.7	8.7	24.8
3. 3-5	1.0	.9	1.0	1.0	.3	1.6	.3	1.2	.7	1.4	.3	-	-	-	4.4	6.6
4. 6-9	.9	1.0	.8	1.0	-	1.8	.4	.9	.2	.4	1.2	-	-	-	3.4	14.9
5. 10-19	.3	.2	.2	.1	-	.3	.1	.4	.2	.1	.3	-	-	-	1.2	1.5
6. 20-39	.2	.2	.1	.2	-	.1	.3	.2	.2	.2	.1	-	-	-	.9	3.2
7. 40 or more	.1	.1	.1	.1	-	.2	.2	-	-	*	.1	-	-	-	.5	-
Item 1020 N(Wtd)	3451	1611	1706	2792	345	822	1024	1121	484	1668	1427	1261	1014	389	695	45

B053C: ...during the last 30 days?

	TOTAL	M	F	White	Black	NE	NC	S	W	Yes	No	None	Mari. Only	Few Pills	More Pills	Heroin
1. 0 occasions	98.0	97.8	98.3	98.0	99.7	96.4	98.6	98.0	99.4	98.3	98.2	100.0	100.0	99.7	91.8	74.3
2. 1-2	1.1	.8	1.3	1.2	-	1.8	.7	1.2	.4	1.2	.8	-	-	.3	4.8	6.9
3. 3-5	.6	.9	.2	.5	.3	1.3	.1	.7	.2	.4	.7	-	-	-	2.0	15.7
4. 6-9	.2	.3	*	.1	-	.4	.2	.1	-	-	.3	-	-	-	.8	1.8
5. 10-19	.1	.1	.1	.1	-	.2	.2	-	-	.1	.1	-	-	-	.5	1.4
6. 20-39	-	-	-	-	-	-	-	-	-	-	-	-	-	-	-	-
7. 40 or more	*	.1	-	*	-	-	.1	-	-	-	-	-	-	-	.1	-
Item 1030 N(Wtd)	3447	1609	1706	2789	345	822	1024	1119	483	1665	1427	1261	1014	389	692	45

IF YOU HAVE NOT TAKEN QUAALUDES IN THE LAST TWELVE MONTHS, GO TO Q.B056.

THE FOLLOWING QUESTIONS REFER ONLY TO TAKING QUAALUDES WITHOUT A DOCTOR'S ORDERS. IF YOU HAVE NOT DONE THIS IN THE LAST TWELVE MONTHS, GO TO Q.B056.

B054: When you take quaaludes how high do you usually get?

	TOTAL	M	F	White	Black	NE	NC	S	W	Yes	No	None	Mari. Only	Few Pills	More Pills	Heroin
1. Not at all high	2.0	3.8	-	2.4	-	1.9	6.0	-	-	1.7	3.4	-	-	-	2.4	-
2. A little high	12.4	11.6	13.4	12.2	46.2	10.2	10.7	17.6	8.7	12.2	14.0	-	-	49.0	10.6	10.9
3. Moderately high	32.3	32.3	35.0	35.1	-	33.8	27.5	35.1	30.4	29.1	33.2	-	-	24.1	32.5	34.3
4. Very high	48.7	48.0	45.8	45.6	-	46.7	54.1	47.3	47.5	48.6	47.3	-	-	26.9	50.1	47.6
5. I don't take them to get high	4.6	4.3	5.9	4.7	53.8	7.5	1.8	-	13.3	8.4	2.1	-	-	-	4.4	7.3
Item 3260 N(Wtd) ★	163	84	67	136	2	52	37	52	22	66	63	-	-	8	133	23

* = less than .05 per cent.   ★ = excludes respondents for whom question was inappropriate.

QUESTIONNAIRE FORM 1 1978	TOTAL	SEX		RACE		REGION				4YR COLLEGE PLANS		ILLICIT DRUG USE: LIFETIME				
		M	F	White	Black	NE	NC	S	W	Yes	No	None	Marijuana Only	Few Pills	More Pills	Any Heroin
Weighted No. of Cases:	3799	1740	1842	2962	411	922	1096	1257	524	1758	1571	1301	1086	411	760	46
% of Weighted Total:	100.0	45.8	48.5	78.0	10.8	24.3	28.8	33.1	13.8	46.3	41.3	34.3	28.6	10.8	20.0	1.2

B055: When you take quaaludes how long do you usually stay high?

1. Usually don't get high	1.3	2.1	.6	1.6	-	-	4.7	-	1.9	2.3	-	-	-	5.4	1.3	-
2. One to two hours	14.1	11.0	17.9	13.3	46.2	12.2	13.8	13.0	22.8	15.4	12.7	-	-	13.2	13.5	18.2
3. Three to six hours	50.3	57.0	44.8	54.6	53.8	56.2	38.3	53.7	48.5	44.7	66.9	-	-	81.4	51.0	37.0
4. Seven to 24 hours	33.0	27.5	36.8	29.8	-	27.8	43.2	33.3	26.9	37.7	18.6	-	-	-	33.5	40.2
5. More than 24 hours	1.2	2.4	-	.7	-	3.8	-	-	-	-	1.7	-	-	-	.7	4.6
Item 3270 N(Wtd) ★	161	83	66	134	2	52	37	52	20	64	61	-	-	7	132	23

The next questions are about BARBITURATES, which doctors sometimes prescribe to help people relax or get to sleep. Drugstores are not supposed to sell them without a prescription.

Barbiturates are sometimes called: downs, downers, goofballs, yellows, reds, blues, rainbows.

They include the following drugs: Phenobarbitol, Seconal, Tuinal, Nembutal, Luminal, Desbutal, Amytal.

B056: Have you ever taken barbiturates because a doctor told you to use them?

1. No	87.6	86.6	88.8	86.8	92.0	88.4	88.8	86.6	86.0	87.5	88.1	94.1	88.3	83.3	77.8	76.5
2. Yes, but I had already tried them on my own.	2.7	2.4	2.4	2.8	1.0	3.1	1.9	2.9	3.5	1.8	2.8	-	-	3.4	10.6	13.2
3. Yes, and it was the first time I took any	9.6	11.0	8.8	10.4	7.0	8.4	9.3	10.5	10.5	10.7	9.2	5.9	11.6	13.3	11.6	10.3
Item 3280 N(Wtd)	3421	1589	1706	2773	346	816	1014	1121	469	1656	1423	1243	992	376	703	44

B057: On how many occasions (if any) have you taken barbiturates on your own--that is, without a doctor telling you to take them...

B057A: ...in your lifetime?

1. 0 occasions	87.6	87.9	88.2	87.0	94.0	85.1	88.2	88.2	88.9	91.3	86.0	100.0	100.0	87.7	51.2	15.2
2. 1-2	4.0	3.8	4.3	4.3	3.6	4.1	3.9	3.8	4.7	3.0	5.0	-	-	12.3	12.2	13.4
3. 3-5	2.5	2.8	2.3	2.9	.3	3.5	2.4	2.4	1.4	2.0	2.5	-	-	-	11.2	19.0
4. 6-9	2.0	2.2	1.4	2.0	.8	2.4	1.7	1.9	2.0	1.6	1.9	-	-	-	8.9	12.1
5. 10-19	1.5	1.3	1.5	1.5	.5	1.6	1.5	1.5	1.2	.9	1.9	-	-	-	6.4	15.7
6. 20-39	1.2	1.0	.9	1.1	-	1.9	1.0	.9	1.0	.8	.9	-	-	-	5.1	10.3
7. 40 or more	1.2	1.0	1.4	1.2	.8	1.3	1.2	1.3	.8	.5	1.7	-	-	-	4.9	14.4
Item 1040 N(Wtd)	3438	1608	1701	2787	346	821	1023	1122	473	1671	1422	1255	1006	382	704	44

B057B: ...during the last 12 months?

1. 0 occasions	92.0	92.7	92.4	91.8	97.4	89.8	92.7	92.5	93.3	94.4	91.6	100.0	100.0	95.1	66.6	48.3
2. 1-2	3.4	3.2	3.4	3.6	1.6	4.2	3.2	3.3	3.1	2.9	3.4	-	-	4.9	13.5	9.6
3. 3-5	1.7	1.8	1.5	1.9	.3	2.6	1.8	.8	2.1	1.3	1.6	-	-	-	7.6	12.4
4. 6-9	1.2	1.2	.8	1.2	.2	1.3	.8	1.6	.9	.7	1.2	-	-	-	5.0	15.5
5. 10-19	.9	.5	1.1	.7	.6	1.2	.8	1.1	.1	.5	1.1	-	-	-	3.9	7.5
6. 20-39	.5	.4	.4	.5	-	.3	.5	.6	.4	.2	.5	-	-	-	1.9	6.7
7. 40 or more	.3	.2	.4	.3	-	.5	.3	.2	-	.1	.5	-	-	-	1.4	-
Item 1050 N(Wtd)	3432	1607	1697	2784	345	819	1021	1117	476	1670	1418	1255	1008	380	701	41

B057C: ...during the last 30 days?

1. 0 occasions	96.6	96.8	96.9	96.7	98.9	94.7	97.0	96.7	99.0	97.5	96.7	100.0	100.0	98.5	85.9	68.8
2. 1-2	1.9	1.9	1.6	1.9	.5	2.6	1.6	1.9	.7	1.4	1.6	-	-	1.5	7.3	17.3
3. 3-5	.6	.5	.7	.6	.3	1.2	.4	.6	.1	.6	.5	-	-	-	2.9	6.0
4. 6-9	.5	.4	.4	.3	.3	.6	.7	.5	.2	.1	.7	-	-	-	2.3	5.2
5. 10-19	.2	.3	.2	.3	-	.4	.3	.1	-	.2	.3	-	-	-	1.0	2.6
6. 20-39	.1	.1	.2	.2	-	.5	-	.1	-	.1	.2	-	-	-	.7	-
7. 40 or more	-	-	-	-	-	-	-	-	-	-	-	-	-	-	-	-
Item 1060 N(Wtd)	3428	1605	1695	2780	345	818	1018	1117	475	1670	1415	1255	1008	378	699	40

★ = excludes respondents for whom question was inappropriate.

QUESTIONNAIRE FORM 1 1978	TOTAL	SEX		RACE		REGION				4YR COLLEGE PLANS		ILLICIT DRUG USE: LIFETIME				
		M	F	White	Black	NE	NC	S	W	Yes	No	None	Mari-juana Only	Few Pills	More Pills	Any Her-oin
Weighted No. of Cases:	3799	1740	1842	2962	411	922	1096	1257	524	1758	1571	1301	1086	411	760	46
% of Weighted Total:	100.0	45.8	48.5	78.0	10.8	24.3	28.8	33.1	13.8	46.3	41.3	34.3	28.6	10.8	20.0	1.2

IF YOU HAVE NOT TAKEN BARBITURATES IN THE LAST TWELVE MONTHS, GO TO Q.B065.

THE FOLLOWING QUESTIONS REFER ONLY TO TAKING BARBITURATES WITHOUT A DOCTOR'S ORDERS. IF YOU HAVE NOT DONE THIS IN THE LAST TWELVE MONTHS, GO TO Q.B065

B058: When you used barbiturates during the last year, how often did you use them in each of the following situations?

B058A: When you were alone

	TOTAL	M	F	White	Black	NE	NC	S	W	Yes	No	None	Mari-juana Only	Few Pills	More Pills	Any Her-oin
1. Not at all	50.0	56.5	48.3	51.1	46.4	58.2	42.7	48.7	48.2	52.0	48.7	-	-	51.0	51.5	28.1
2. A few of the times	24.5	20.6	24.4	21.4	37.0	26.2	23.7	18.2	38.8	20.6	23.2	-	-	23.1	24.2	31.7
3. Some of the times	10.6	10.4	9.3	10.6	9.6	5.8	20.0	7.8	8.3	8.3	11.2	-	-	-	10.9	16.8
4. Most of the times	9.7	8.6	10.4	10.5	7.0	5.1	8.4	19.2	-	8.8	13.0	-	-	6.6	8.9	20.8
5. Every time	5.2	3.9	7.5	6.3	-	4.7	5.2	6.0	4.7	10.4	4.0	-	-	19.3	4.5	2.6
Item 3290 N(Wtd) ★	263	108	128	218	10	82	72	81	30	88	117	-	-	17	219	23

B058B: With just 1 or 2 other people

	TOTAL	M	F	White	Black	NE	NC	S	W	Yes	No	None	Mari-juana Only	Few Pills	More Pills	Any Her-oin
1. Not at all	21.7	20.1	27.8	22.8	40.6	21.1	25.0	21.5	15.9	34.6	19.0	-	-	45.7	20.2	8.8
2. A few of the times	38.4	45.1	32.3	36.3	48.8	34.5	37.4	38.4	50.9	31.8	38.8	-	-	46.9	37.2	48.6
3. Some of the times	22.6	15.9	21.5	21.3	10.6	29.6	16.9	22.1	19.4	17.1	21.8	-	-	-	25.5	13.7
4. Most of the times	12.8	15.5	12.0	14.3	-	9.0	16.9	13.2	11.2	9.7	17.2	-	-	-	12.1	28.8
5. Every time	4.6	3.3	6.4	5.4	-	5.7	3.7	4.9	2.6	6.9	3.2	-	-	7.4	4.9	-
Item 3300 N(Wtd) ★	259	107	125	213	9	77	71	82	29	87	115	-	-	15	217	23

B058C: At a party

	TOTAL	M	F	White	Black	NE	NC	S	W	Yes	No	None	Mari-juana Only	Few Pills	More Pills	Any Her-oin
1. Not at all	45.6	40.8	54.6	47.4	60.5	33.8	46.1	54.6	50.5	57.2	44.1	-	-	83.2	44.2	23.0
2. A few of the times	16.9	20.9	9.3	15.7	28.9	18.6	11.3	21.7	12.1	13.4	17.6	-	-	11.0	15.4	36.9
3. Some of the times	21.6	14.7	26.2	20.1	10.6	28.6	21.9	12.9	27.6	13.7	24.5	-	-	-	24.1	18.0
4. Most of the times	6.8	9.7	5.1	7.5	-	3.2	11.3	5.4	9.8	3.2	6.5	-	-	5.7	6.4	12.5
5. Every time	9.1	13.9	5.0	9.4	-	15.8	9.5	5.4	-	12.4	7.3	-	-	-	9.9	9.6
Item 3310 N(Wtd) ★	261	107	127	216	9	79	71	84	28	88	116	-	-	16	216	24

B058D: When your date or spouse was present

	TOTAL	M	F	White	Black	NE	NC	S	W	Yes	No	None	Mari-juana Only	Few Pills	More Pills	Any Her-oin
1. Not at all	55.2	60.5	52.9	58.1	79.6	49.8	62.1	55.0	53.5	63.9	59.0	-	-	82.1	53.0	50.1
2. A few of the times	20.3	22.8	14.9	16.8	9.9	21.8	20.4	21.3	13.1	14.5	15.6	-	-	6.3	20.2	33.6
3. Some of the times	10.1	11.0	8.6	9.0	10.6	12.2	9.3	6.7	16.4	8.2	9.8	-	-	-	11.5	6.1
4. Most of the times	6.9	3.2	10.5	7.2	-	6.1	6.5	5.2	14.5	6.3	7.3	-	-	11.6	6.7	5.7
5. Every time	7.5	2.5	13.0	8.9	-	10.2	1.6	11.7	2.5	7.1	8.3	-	-	-	8.5	4.5
Item 3320 N(Wtd) ★	259	106	126	214	9	79	71	82	28	87	115	-	-	16	216	23

B058E: When people over age 30 were present

	TOTAL	M	F	White	Black	NE	NC	S	W	Yes	No	None	Mari-juana Only	Few Pills	More Pills	Any Her-oin
1. Not at all	64.8	66.9	65.2	67.9	60.5	64.2	67.7	60.7	70.1	71.2	65.6	-	-	76.8	62.9	69.1
2. A few of the times	17.5	14.7	17.8	15.8	29.6	22.0	10.2	19.7	16.3	17.1	12.7	-	-	15.9	18.1	14.4
3. Some of the times	9.5	10.0	7.3	8.2	-	7.9	11.3	10.0	7.7	6.4	11.3	-	-	-	10.3	8.8
4. Most of the times	4.5	5.0	4.9	5.0	9.9	1.2	9.8	4.6	-	1.0	8.5	-	-	-	4.6	6.2
5. Every time	3.8	3.3	4.8	3.2	-	4.7	.9	4.9	5.9	4.3	2.0	-	-	7.4	3.9	1.5
Item 3330 N(Wtd) ★	262	108	127	216	9	79	71	82	30	88	115	-	-	15	220	23

B058F: During the daytime (before 4:00 p.m.)

	TOTAL	M	F	White	Black	NE	NC	S	W	Yes	No	None	Mari-juana Only	Few Pills	More Pills	Any Her-oin
1. Not at all	41.3	44.8	42.8	41.7	62.3	40.1	43.2	40.6	41.5	47.2	40.5	-	-	56.3	40.6	28.6
2. A few of the times	27.7	26.7	26.6	27.0	27.1	30.8	18.4	29.1	38.9	27.0	25.9	-	-	23.4	28.5	27.6
3. Some of the times	19.0	19.4	13.9	17.4	10.6	19.4	23.4	16.1	14.8	12.7	20.1	-	-	4.5	18.9	32.5
4. Most of the times	9.0	8.4	11.0	10.7	-	7.0	12.0	9.9	4.8	9.2	9.7	-	-	6.6	9.4	8.7
5. Every time	3.0	.6	5.7	3.2	-	2.7	3.0	4.4	-	4.0	3.8	-	-	9.1	2.6	2.6
Item 3340 N(Wtd) ★	261	107	127	215	9	80	72	81	28	87	116	-	-	17	217	23

★ = excludes respondents for whom question was inappropriate.

QUESTIONNAIRE FORM 1 1978	TOTAL	SEX		RACE		REGION				4YR COLLEGE PLANS		ILLICIT DRUG USE: LIFETIME				
		M	F	White	Black	NE	NC	S	W	Yes	No	None	Mari- juana Only	Few Pills	More Pills	Any Her- oin
Weighted No. of Cases:	3799	1740	1842	2962	411	922	1096	1257	524	1758	1571	1301	1086	411	760	46
% of Weighted Total:	100.0	45.8	48.5	78.0	10.8	24.3	28.8	33.1	13.8	46.3	41.3	34.3	28.6	10.8	20.0	1.2
B058G: At your home (or apartment or dorm)																
1. Not at all	31.3	36.8	27.2	31.4	52.5	37.1	32.7	26.2	27.2	31.9	31.2	-	-	43.7	30.8	19.6
2. A few of the times	29.0	21.6	32.0	28.2	27.1	27.8	25.5	28.0	43.5	28.0	29.9	-	-	27.5	29.3	27.8
3. Some of the times	16.6	19.4	14.8	15.0	10.6	16.5	15.8	19.2	11.6	16.6	15.8	-	-	-	18.2	16.3
4. Most of the times	13.8	11.0	16.6	15.2	9.9	11.6	14.5	17.6	7.0	10.7	14.8	-	-	-	12.9	33.7
5. Every time	9.3	11.1	9.4	10.1	-	7.0	11.5	9.1	10.7	12.9	8.2	-	-	28.8	8.7	2.6
Item 3350　N(Wtd) ★	263	108	128	217	9	79	72	83	29	89	117	-	-	16	219	23
B058H: At school																
1. Not at all	56.5	55.6	64.8	61.9	60.5	46.9	65.5	57.2	58.1	67.1	58.0	-	-	80.9	53.5	59.9
2. A few of the times	16.5	22.0	10.5	13.7	19.1	19.7	12.9	15.5	19.7	13.0	16.7	-	-	11.8	18.5	4.5
3. Some of the times	17.8	13.6	14.9	15.2	10.6	22.6	12.9	20.3	9.4	12.4	17.4	-	-	7.4	18.2	24.2
4. Most of the times	7.3	7.8	6.6	6.9	9.9	5.3	7.8	7.0	12.9	3.2	7.9	-	-	-	7.9	8.7
5. Every time	1.9	1.0	3.1	2.3	-	5.5	.9	-	-	4.3	-	-	-	-	2.0	2.6
Item 3360　N(Wtd) ★	260	107	126	215	9	79	71	83	28	89	115	-	-	15	217	23
B058I: In a car																
1. Not at all	55.6	51.1	62.8	59.1	87.8	47.2	58.9	59.2	60.1	66.9	58.0	-	-	84.9	55.5	30.2
2. A few of the times	21.7	23.0	17.3	18.8	12.2	23.8	22.3	21.8	13.8	14.7	18.0	-	-	7.3	23.4	18.1
3. Some of the times	14.0	10.9	15.5	12.3	-	21.1	9.7	8.5	20.2	10.9	13.3	-	-	-	12.5	38.6
4. Most of the times	7.8	14.4	2.7	8.6	-	5.3	9.1	9.7	6.0	6.4	10.1	-	-	7.8	7.4	13.1
5. Every time	1.0	.6	1.6	1.2	-	2.6	-	.8	-	1.2	.6	-	-	-	1.2	-
Item 3380　N(Wtd) ★	259	105	127	215	8	79	70	81	28	88	112	-	-	15	217	23
B059: How many of the times when you used barbiturates during the last year did you use them along with each of the following drugs- -that is, so that their effects overlapped?																
B059A: With alcohol																
1. Not at all	49.8	54.0	48.3	49.5	83.9	42.5	46.3	57.1	58.0	54.2	52.5	-	-	76.5	48.6	32.1
2. A few of the times	23.9	18.6	26.0	23.6	16.1	25.1	27.6	22.2	16.2	22.4	25.1	-	-	17.8	26.8	7.3
3. Some of the times	12.5	11.0	12.9	12.5	-	11.4	11.5	14.5	12.2	8.5	11.7	-	-	-	12.0	27.8
4. Most of the times	8.6	9.2	8.6	8.8	-	11.9	9.6	3.7	11.1	10.3	5.7	-	-	-	7.3	27.1
5. Every time	5.2	7.2	4.3	5.6	-	9.1	5.0	2.5	2.6	4.6	5.0	-	-	5.8	5.2	5.6
Item 3390　N(Wtd) ★	260	110	124	217	10	80	70	82	27	87	118	-	-	15	215	24
B059B: With marijuana																
1. Not at all	30.9	30.0	34.2	31.3	79.6	20.3	35.8	37.7	29.4	41.5	31.7	-	-	78.5	29.2	-
2. A few of the times	21.6	23.3	18.0	20.5	20.4	26.5	13.8	21.6	27.5	15.0	25.4	-	-	14.3	22.6	22.3
3. Some of the times	15.9	11.8	20.1	15.6	-	7.5	19.7	20.8	15.8	12.6	16.9	-	-	7.1	14.0	44.0
4. Most of the times	16.6	17.2	15.0	16.8	-	25.0	14.5	9.0	20.5	14.6	12.9	-	-	-	18.0	18.0
5. Every time	14.9	17.6	12.6	15.7	-	20.7	16.1	10.8	6.8	16.2	13.1	-	-	-	16.2	15.7
Item 3400　N(Wtd) ★	258	110	123	216	9	80	70	81	26	87	117	-	-	15	216	22
B059C: With LSD																
1. Not at all	99.0	98.3	100.0	99.1	100.0	98.7	98.0	99.9	99.9	100.0	99.1	-	-	100.0	99.5	93.6
2. A few of the times	.7	1.0	-	.5	-	1.3	.9	-	-	-	.9	-	-	-	.5	2.9
3. Some of the times	.3	.7	-	.4	-	-	1.1	-	-	-	-	-	-	-	-	3.5
4. Most of the times	-	-	-	-	-	-	-	-	-	-	-	-	-	-	-	-
5. Every time	-	-	-	-	-	-	-	-	-	-	-	-	-	-	-	-
Item 3410　N(Wtd) ★	251	103	122	209	9	78	70	77	26	85	112	-	-	15	210	21
B059D: With psychedelics other than LSD																
1. Not at all	93.2	94.4	91.6	92.9	100.0	91.9	86.9	97.9	99.9	94.1	91.9	-	-	100.0	93.5	85.2
2. A few of the times	4.7	4.0	6.0	4.9	-	4.4	12.2	-	-	4.8	4.9	-	-	-	4.3	12.0
3. Some of the times	2.1	1.6	2.4	2.2	-	3.7	.9	2.1	-	1.1	3.2	-	-	-	2.2	2.8
4. Most of the times	-	-	-	-	-	-	-	-	-	-	-	-	-	-	-	-
5. Every time	-	-	-	-	-	-	-	-	-	-	-	-	-	-	-	-
Item 3420　N(Wtd) ★	249	104	121	206	9	78	68	78	26	85	112	-	-	15	208	22

★ = excludes respondents for whom question was inappropriate.

QUESTIONNAIRE FORM 1 1978	TOTAL	SEX		RACE		REGION				4YR COLLEGE PLANS		ILLICIT DRUG USE: LIFETIME				
		M	F	White	Black	NE	NC	S	W	Yes	No	None	Mari-juana Only	Few Pills	More Pills	Any Her-oin
Weighted No. of Cases:	3799	1740	1842	2962	411	922	1096	1257	524	1758	1571	1301	1086	411	760	46
% of Weighted Total:	100.0	45.8	48.5	78.0	10.8	24.3	28.8	33.1	13.8	46.3	41.3	34.3	28.6	10.8	20.0	1.2

B059E: With amphetamines

	TOTAL	M	F	White	Black	NE	NC	S	W	Yes	No	None	Mari.	Few Pills	More Pills	Any Heroin
1. Not at all	87.3	90.2	85.9	88.1	90.1	89.9	79.5	88.3	97.3	93.5	85.4	-	-	100.0	87.0	79.4
2. A few of the times	8.5	6.9	8.3	8.1	-	6.7	13.2	8.0	2.7	2.7	9.4	-	-	-	9.0	11.3
3. Some of the times	2.7	.6	4.6	1.9	9.9	2.8	3.9	2.4	-	2.7	3.5	-	-	-	2.9	2.8
4. Most of the times	1.0	1.4	.8	1.2	-	-	2.1	1.3	-	1.2	1.3	-	-	-	.5	6.6
5. Every time	.6	.9	.4	.7	-	.6	1.3	-	-	-	.4	-	-	-	.7	-
Item 3430 N(Wtd) ★	253	106	122	210	9	78	70	78	26	85	113	-	-	15	212	22

B059F: With quaaludes

	TOTAL	M	F	White	Black	NE	NC	S	W	Yes	No	None	Mari.	Few Pills	More Pills	Any Heroin
1. Not at all	91.2	92.6	89.3	91.2	100.0	91.3	87.2	94.8	91.0	93.4	90.0	-	-	100.0	93.2	64.5
2. A few of the times	5.9	4.2	8.0	5.6	-	6.3	8.7	1.9	9.0	5.5	7.2	-	-	-	4.0	29.3
3. Some of the times	1.3	1.6	.8	1.3	-	1.2	.9	2.1	-	1.1	1.5	-	-	-	1.2	2.8
4. Most of the times	.9	.7	1.2	1.0	-	-	1.8	1.1	-	-	.5	-	-	-	.7	3.4
5. Every time	.7	.9	.8	.9	-	1.2	1.3	-	-	-	.8	-	-	-	.9	-
Item 3440 N(Wtd) ★	253	105	122	210	9	78	70	78	26	85	114	-	-	15	210	22

B060: What are the most important reasons for your taking barbiturates without a doctor's orders? (Mark all that apply.)

	TOTAL	M	F	White	Black	NE	NC	S	W	Yes	No	None	Mari.	Few Pills	More Pills	Any Heroin
A. To experiment--to see what it's like	51.5	59.3	44.3	52.3	64.8	48.4	59.7	50.4	43.0	47.1	57.1	-	-	45.5	51.5	55.4
B. To relax or relieve tension	59.3	48.7	67.1	59.1	29.6	52.5	64.7	61.4	58.8	58.6	57.9	-	-	32.3	61.8	55.7
C. To feel good or get high	54.2	59.0	47.8	53.4	21.1	59.1	41.4	56.9	64.5	53.0	48.7	-	-	27.1	53.6	78.0
D. To seek deeper insights and understanding	6.4	7.6	5.5	3.7	-	8.5	10.6	1.3	4.5	6.9	2.8	-	-	-	5.9	14.7
E. To have a good time with my friends	30.7	34.6	22.1	29.8	-	27.7	35.4	28.6	33.1	28.8	28.4	-	-	19.6	30.9	36.7
F. To fit in with a group I like	3.5	4.8	3.0	3.2	-	2.5	.9	6.5	3.7	7.1	2.4	-	-	7.1	3.6	-
G. To get away from my problems or troubles	25.4	18.0	30.1	24.2	32.4	23.3	26.4	30.5	14.4	26.5	26.2	-	-	20.7	24.3	38.1
H. Because of boredom, nothing else to do	15.5	14.7	17.2	14.6	46.3	19.8	18.1	14.8	-	16.0	14.8	-	-	10.8	14.8	24.7
I. Because of anger or frustration	17.6	8.8	21.4	17.0	-	19.2	19.0	18.0	8.6	23.2	11.4	-	-	3.9	17.3	29.2
J. To get through the day	9.9	8.0	7.7	7.0	12.6	7.8	6.4	16.1	7.1	11.5	7.4	-	-	-	10.0	16.1
K. To increase the effects of some other drug(s)	8.6	11.5	6.4	8.9	-	11.8	9.2	7.5	2.4	9.1	8.0	-	-	-	9.6	5.6
L. To decrease (offset) the effects of some other drug(s)	4.5	4.2	4.4	5.1	-	4.4	10.0	1.5	-	3.8	4.2	-	-	-	3.9	13.4
M. To get to sleep	46.3	36.8	54.0	46.6	35.5	45.8	47.5	46.4	44.3	52.9	41.1	-	-	26.5	47.6	48.1
N. To relieve physical pain§	36.3	32.9	34.2	36.0	17.6	35.0	37.4	39.8	28.0	40.2	30.6	-	-	13.3	38.0	37.0
O. Because I am "hooked"--I have to have them	.6	-	1.3	.7	-	-	.9	1.2	-	1.9	-	-	-	-	.5	2.5
Item 3450-3580 N(Wtd) ★	258	108	125	217	8	77	71	81	30	86	117	-	-	17	217	24

B061: When you take barbiturates how high do you usually get?

	TOTAL	M	F	White	Black	NE	NC	S	W	Yes	No	None	Mari.	Few Pills	More Pills	Any Heroin
1. Not at all high	7.3	8.2	7.0	7.6	12.6	10.7	7.2	5.3	3.9	4.6	10.8	-	-	19.2	7.3	-
2. A little high	18.9	19.9	20.3	20.8	19.5	16.1	29.7	15.3	10.5	17.2	23.9	-	-	35.0	17.4	23.1
3. Moderately high	42.4	40.9	42.6	43.4	22.5	49.6	33.7	45.6	34.9	40.2	43.1	-	-	13.3	46.0	32.2
4. Very high	18.6	22.3	13.6	15.9	10.8	13.3	19.5	18.4	31.2	20.3	12.5	-	-	7.1	17.9	33.6
5. I don't take them to get high	12.8	8.6	16.5	12.3	34.5	10.2	9.9	15.3	19.6	17.7	9.7	-	-	25.4	11.3	11.1
Item 3590 N(Wtd) ★	256	107	125	215	9	76	70	82	28	85	117	-	-	16	214	24

B062: When you take barbiturates how long do you usually stay high?

	TOTAL	M	F	White	Black	NE	NC	S	W	Yes	No	None	Mari.	Few Pills	More Pills	Any Heroin
1. Usually don't get high	17.4	15.5	19.1	16.8	37.0	20.5	17.0	15.4	16.1	18.1	17.3	-	-	45.1	15.5	10.3
2. One to two hours	17.2	20.5	16.6	17.5	47.1	8.7	18.2	24.9	14.4	17.2	21.1	-	-	22.7	16.6	19.4
3. Three to six hours	52.0	47.9	52.3	53.2	15.9	53.0	48.6	51.1	60.6	48.6	52.2	-	-	25.1	54.4	52.7
4. Seven to 24 hours	13.4	16.0	12.1	12.5	-	17.8	16.2	8.5	8.9	16.1	9.4	-	-	7.1	13.5	17.7
5. More than 24 hours	-	-	-	-	-	-	-	-	-	-	-	-	-	-	-	-
Item 3600 N(Wtd) ★	255	106	125	213	9	75	70	82	28	84	115	-	-	16	213	24

★ = excludes respondents for whom question was inappropriate.   § = category added in this data collection.

QUESTIONNAIRE FORM 1 1978	TOTAL	SEX		RACE		REGION				4YR COLLEGE PLANS		ILLICIT DRUG USE: LIFETIME				
		M	F	White	Black	NE	NC	S	W	Yes	No	None	Mari- juana Only	Few Pills	More Pills	Any Her- oin
Weighted No. of Cases:	3799	1740	1842	2962	411	922	1096	1257	524	1758	1571	1301	1086	411	760	46
% of Weighted Total:	100.0	45.8	48.5	78.0	10.8	24.3	28.8	33.1	13.8	46.3	41.3	34.3	28.6	10.8	20.0	1.2

B063: What barbiturates have you taken during the last year without a doctor's orders? (Mark all that apply.)

	TOTAL	M	F	White	Black	NE	NC	S	W	Yes	No	None	Mari-juana Only	Few Pills	More Pills	Any Heroin
A. Phenobarbital	29.3	33.1	29.1	30.2	12.1	27.9	42.5	23.2	17.3	31.7	29.9	-	-	13.7	29.1	42.9
B. Seconal	32.3	33.7	29.5	31.6	11.9	25.3	38.9	30.3	41.3	29.1	28.4	-	-	15.0	31.8	48.8
C. Tuinal	10.6	11.8	8.9	9.7	-	7.7	9.9	14.2	9.7	15.2	5.9	-	-	-	11.1	14.0
D. Nembutal	12.6	12.9	13.3	12.6	-	6.3	22.3	11.5	8.2	20.6	8.2	-	-	14.6	9.8	36.0
E. Luminal	8.8	10.3	8.7	8.6	-	9.9	12.3	7.6	-	6.4	11.8	-	-	-	8.7	15.3
F. Desbutal	6.0	10.5	2.3	6.0	-	5.6	10.2	4.7	-	3.3	6.3	-	-	-	5.3	16.0
G. Amytal	6.5	5.5	6.8	6.6	-	7.6	12.0	2.0	2.6	5.6	8.4	-	-	6.1	6.3	8.5
H. Adrenocal	5.9	7.0	6.1	5.6	11.9	8.3	8.1	3.8	-	5.3	6.9	-	-	-	5.2	16.6
I. Other	47.5	38.1	54.3	48.0	41.2	53.9	47.5	42.7	44.5	48.8	47.1	-	-	29.6	48.9	44.2
J. Don't know the names of some that I have used	41.3	38.5	42.9	39.7	46.7	43.7	31.2	47.5	41.8	36.5	46.7	-	-	41.9	40.7	48.7
Item 3610-3700 N(Wtd) ★	254	104	127	214	8	76	70	82	26	85	113	-	-	15	213	24

B064: Have you ever tried to stop using barbiturates and found that you couldn't stop?

	TOTAL	M	F	White	Black	NE	NC	S	W	Yes	No	None	Mari-juana Only	Few Pills	More Pills	Any Heroin
1. Yes	3.3	4.1	2.7	3.0	22.8	.9	5.5	3.8	3.1	2.4	2.3	-	-	4.5	3.0	-
2. No	96.7	95.9	97.3	97.0	77.2	99.1	94.5	99.9	99.9	97.6	97.7	-	-	95.5	97.0	100.0
Item 3710 N(Wtd) ★	259	108	127	217	9	77	70	83	29	85	117	-	-	16	217	24

B065: Do you think you will be using barbiturates without a doctor's prescription five years from now?

	TOTAL	M	F	White	Black	NE	NC	S	W	Yes	No	None	Mari-juana Only	Few Pills	More Pills	Any Heroin
1. I definitely will	.6	.5	.6	.6	.5	1.1	.6	.4	.4	.6	.6	.4	.5	.3	1.0	6.5
2. I probably will	2.9	2.9	2.3	2.8	1.4	3.1	2.6	3.0	2.8	2.1	2.9	.2	.2	3.2	10.8	21.1
3. I probably will not	20.8	21.7	19.7	20.7	19.0	22.1	22.7	19.8	17.0	18.4	21.7	9.2	16.2	24.9	46.6	37.6
4. I definitely will not	75.7	74.9	77.4	75.9	79.1	73.7	74.1	76.8	79.8	78.9	74.8	90.2	83.1	71.6	41.6	34.8
Item 3720 N(Wtd)	3502	1619	1754	2809	376	827	1024	1168	484	1676	1476	1259	1010	388	680	45

The next questions are about TRANQUILIZERS, which doctors sometimes prescribe to calm people down, quiet their nerves, or relax their muscles.

They include the following drugs: Librium, Valium, Miltown, Equanil, Meprobamate, Serax, Atarax, Tranxene, Vistaril.

B066: Have you ever taken tranquilizers because a doctor told you to use them?

	TOTAL	M	F	White	Black	NE	NC	S	W	Yes	No	None	Mari-juana Only	Few Pills	More Pills	Any Heroin
1. No	83.5	84.0	83.1	82.7	89.0	84.2	84.8	83.1	80.5	84.2	82.8	91.5	85.8	70.6	73.3	70.4
2. Yes, but I had already tried them on my own.	2.8	2.6	2.6	2.7	1.6	3.9	2.3	2.5	2.7	2.4	2.5	.1	.4	3.6	10.1	13.9
3. Yes, and it was the first time I took any	13.7	13.4	14.3	14.6	9.5	11.9	12.9	14.5	16.8	13.4	14.7	8.3	13.8	25.8	16.6	15.7
Item 3730 N(Wtd)	3465	1629	1722	2821	353	822	1034	1139	470	1682	1445	1256	1013	385	700	43

B067: On how many occasions (if any) have you taken tranquilizers on your own--that is, without a doctor telling you to take them...

B067A: ...in your lifetime?

	TOTAL	M	F	White	Black	NE	NC	S	W	Yes	No	None	Mari-juana Only	Few Pills	More Pills	Any Heroin
1. 0 occasions	84.7	86.4	83.4	83.5	94.2	83.7	85.4	84.4	85.4	87.1	83.9	100.0	100.0	65.6	47.8	33.2
2. 1-2	6.9	6.6	7.3	7.4	3.5	7.1	7.1	6.2	7.4	5.9	7.2	-	-	34.4	14.0	12.7
3. 3-5	3.3	2.8	3.6	3.7	.3	3.8	2.8	3.5	3.1	3.2	3.1	-	-	-	15.5	11.5
4. 6-9	1.8	1.7	1.7	1.8	.8	1.5	1.5	2.4	1.5	1.4	1.8	-	-	-	8.5	4.6
5. 10-19	1.6	1.4	1.7	1.7	.5	1.6	1.6	1.9	1.2	1.3	1.8	-	-	-	6.3	26.5
6. 20-39	.7	.5	.9	.8	.3	1.1	.5	.6	.9	.5	.8	-	-	-	3.3	4.9
7. 40 or more	1.0	.6	1.4	1.1	.3	1.3	1.0	1.0	.5	.6	1.4	-	-	-	4.5	6.6
Item 1070 N(Wtd)	3445	1617	1711	2802	348	823	1025	1125	472	1674	1431	1257	1013	385	699	44

★=excludes respondents for whom question was inappropriate.

QUESTIONNAIRE FORM 1 1978	TOTAL	SEX		RACE		REGION				4YR COLLEGE PLANS		ILLICIT DRUG USE: LIFETIME				
		M	F	White	Black	NE	NC	S	W	Yes	No	None	Marijuana Only	Few Pills	More Pills	Any Heroin
Weighted No. of Cases:	3799	1740	1842	2962	411	922	1096	1257	524	1758	1571	1301	1086	411	760	46
% of Weighted Total:	100.0	45.8	48.5	78.0	10.8	24.3	28.8	33.1	13.8	46.3	41.3	34.3	28.6	10.8	20.0	1.2

B067B: ...during the last 12 months?

	TOTAL	M	F	White	Black	NE	NC	S	W	Yes	No	None	Marijuana Only	Few Pills	More Pills	Any Heroin
1. 0 occasions	91.3	92.6	90.3	90.4	98.1	89.7	93.0	90.2	93.1	91.7	92.1	100.0	100.0	90.1	65.6	52.3
2. 1-2	4.7	4.6	4.9	5.3	.8	5.5	3.6	5.3	4.6	5.2	3.7	-	-	9.9	17.5	9.7
3. 3-5	1.6	1.1	2.1	1.8	.5	2.4	1.2	1.7	1.1	1.4	1.6	-	-	-	7.5	8.5
4. 6-9	1.1	1.0	1.1	1.1	.3	.9	.9	1.6	.9	1.0	1.0	-	-	-	4.4	18.0
5. 10-19	.6	.4	.7	.6	-	.4	.8	.7	.1	.5	.7	-	-	-	2.6	4.9
6. 20-39	.3	-	.6	.3	.1	.4	.2	.3	.1	.2	.3	-	-	-	1.1	4.6
7. 40 or more	.3	.3	.3	.3	.3	.6	.4	.1	-	.1	.6	-	-	-	1.2	2.0
Item 1080 N(Wtd)	3434	1613	1706	2797	345	817	1022	1121	474	1674	1420	1257	1013	377	696	44

B067C: ...during the last 30 days?

	TOTAL	M	F	White	Black	NE	NC	S	W	Yes	No	None	Marijuana Only	Few Pills	More Pills	Any Heroin
1. 0 occasions	96.5	97.5	95.6	96.2	99.1	95.4	97.0	96.1	98.3	96.7	96.3	100.0	100.0	97.6	86.0	67.5
2. 1-2	2.1	1.4	2.8	2.3	.6	3.0	1.5	2.6	1.1	2.4	1.7	-	-	2.4	8.4	14.4
3. 3-5	.5	.4	.6	.5	-	.3	.5	.7	.6	.4	.6	-	-	-	2.5	3.1
4. 6-9	.5	.5	.5	.5	-	.4	.6	.5	-	.3	.6	-	-	-	1.6	10.1
5. 10-19	.2	.1	.4	.3	-	.6	.2	.1	-	*	.5	-	-	-	.9	3.4
6. 20-39	*	-	.1	.1	-	.2	-	-	-	-	.1	-	-	-	.1	1.6
7. 40 or more	.1	.1	*	.1	.3	.1	.2	-	-	.1	.1	-	-	-	.4	-
Item 1090 N(Wtd)	3434	1609	1710	2797	346	817	1022	1124	470	1675	1421	1257	1013	377	693	44

IF YOU HAVE NOT TAKEN TRANQUILIZERS IN THE LAST TWELVE MONTHS, GO TO Q.B075.

THE FOLLOWING QUESTIONS REFER ONLY TO TAKING TRANQUILIZERS WITHOUT A DOCTOR'S ORDERS. IF YOU HAVE NOT DONE THIS IN THE LAST TWELVE MONTHS, GO TO Q.B075.

B068: When you used tranquilizers during the last year, how often did you use them in each of the following situations?

B068A: When you were alone

	TOTAL	M	F	White	Black	NE	NC	S	W	Yes	No	None	Marijuana Only	Few Pills	More Pills	Any Heroin
1. Not at all	42.2	43.7	42.5	41.4	64.4	50.3	32.2	45.4	32.8	40.5	38.6	-	-	52.0	42.1	15.2
2. A few of the times	25.7	28.5	23.9	27.5	12.7	21.4	29.5	25.2	29.3	27.0	27.8	-	-	23.6	27.1	20.0
3. Some of the times	11.6	12.6	8.8	11.1	3.7	9.9	15.7	11.9	4.7	6.5	14.1	-	-	11.8	9.4	36.4
4. Most of the times	8.3	3.7	11.6	8.3	3.7	6.5	10.9	3.6	24.1	10.7	7.0	-	-	-	8.7	17.9
5. Every time	12.3	11.5	13.3	11.7	15.7	11.9	11.7	13.9	9.1	15.3	12.5	-	-	12.6	12.7	10.5
Item 3740 N(Wtd) ★	277	113	150	241	13	74	68	107	28	123	111	-	-	31	220	21

B068B: With just 1 or 2 other people

	TOTAL	M	F	White	Black	NE	NC	S	W	Yes	No	None	Marijuana Only	Few Pills	More Pills	Any Heroin
1. Not at all	30.4	23.7	37.0	29.0	62.9	31.2	30.0	30.4	29.4	35.3	29.9	-	-	54.3	27.4	10.0
2. A few of the times	35.4	42.6	30.9	37.2	-	39.3	32.3	32.9	42.0	35.9	37.0	-	-	29.0	37.4	32.6
3. Some of the times	17.5	15.9	16.7	17.7	11.4	11.2	21.5	22.7	4.7	12.9	19.2	-	-	3.1	17.6	42.1
4. Most of the times	11.4	13.1	9.9	11.2	11.1	11.5	14.4	7.2	20.2	10.7	11.3	-	-	8.2	11.9	13.5
5. Every time	5.3	4.7	5.5	4.9	14.6	6.8	1.8	6.9	3.6	5.1	2.7	-	-	5.4	5.7	1.7
Item 3750 N(Wtd) ★	270	110	148	236	12	71	64	106	28	123	109	-	-	30	215	20

B068C: At a party

	TOTAL	M	F	White	Black	NE	NC	S	W	Yes	No	None	Marijuana Only	Few Pills	More Pills	Any Heroin
1. Not at all	65.9	56.5	75.0	66.0	85.3	66.8	54.6	69.1	77.5	73.3	63.5	-	-	97.0	63.1	39.4
2. A few of the times	14.3	20.4	8.5	13.7	14.7	12.2	17.4	17.6	-	13.0	15.7	-	-	3.0	14.6	31.0
3. Some of the times	10.9	14.2	7.7	11.1	-	6.8	14.6	8.9	20.1	10.1	8.9	-	-	-	12.2	16.1
4. Most of the times	4.4	3.8	4.2	4.4	-	8.0	5.3	1.9	2.5	2.0	5.4	-	-	-	4.3	13.5
5. Every time	4.6	5.1	4.5	4.8	-	6.2	8.1	2.5	-	1.7	6.5	-	-	-	5.7	-
Item 3760 N(Wtd) ★	272	112	148	238	12	73	65	105	28	123	110	-	-	31	216	20

* = less than .05 per cent.   ★ = excludes respondents for whom question was inappropriate.

QUESTIONNAIRE FORM 1 1978	TOTAL	SEX		RACE		REGION				4YR COLLEGE PLANS		ILLICIT DRUG USE: LIFETIME				
		M	F	White	Black	NE	NC	S	W	Yes	No	None	Marijuana Only	Few Pills	More Pills	Any Heroin
Weighted No. of Cases:	3799	1740	1842	2962	411	922	1096	1257	524	1758	1571	1301	1086	411	760	46
% of Weighted Total:	100.0	45.8	48.5	78.0	10.8	24.3	28.8	33.1	13.8	46.3	41.3	34.3	28.6	10.8	20.0	1.2
B068D: When your date or spouse was present																
1. Not at all	68.0	77.4	64.6	68.9	84.0	73.5	62.8	64.9	78.0	84.1	58.1	–	–	88.4	65.3	59.1
2. A few of the times	14.8	13.8	13.5	14.5	–	7.3	22.4	15.8	12.1	7.7	19.1	–	–	–	15.9	28.2
3. Some of the times	8.0	3.1	10.0	7.0	7.2	9.3	8.3	7.1	7.4	3.0	9.4	–	–	–	9.4	7.6
4. Most of the times	4.2	2.9	4.9	4.4	–	4.9	4.9	3.8	2.5	.7	7.2	–	–	8.2	3.9	3.5
5. Every time	4.9	2.8	6.9	5.2	8.8	5.0	1.7	8.3	–	4.5	6.2	–	–	3.3	5.6	1.7
Item 3770 N(Wtd) ★	270	110	148	236	12	72	65	105	28	122	109	–	–	30	215	20
B068E: When people over age 30 were present																
1. Not at all	56.7	68.0	48.8	57.0	61.9	54.6	52.9	58.6	63.4	59.1	56.1	–	–	52.3	56.3	61.1
2. A few of the times	19.8	17.9	19.8	19.7	5.8	21.0	27.0	19.1	3.9	21.2	17.6	–	–	22.0	19.4	26.1
3. Some of the times	7.1	5.6	8.2	7.4	7.8	9.6	6.4	6.0	6.1	4.5	7.7	–	–	–	8.3	7.4
4. Most of the times	6.1	2.3	9.2	6.4	–	3.8	7.0	7.1	6.5	4.4	9.3	–	–	7.8	6.3	3.7
5. Every time	10.2	6.2	14.0	9.4	24.6	10.9	6.7	9.2	20.1	10.7	9.3	–	–	17.8	9.8	1.7
Item 3780 N(Wtd) ★	275	111	152	240	12	74	66	105	30	124	111	–	–	31	219	20
B068F: During the daytime (before 4:00 p.m.)																
1. Not at all	42.3	42.0	44.0	41.3	64.7	41.0	41.2	39.1	60.2	51.8	32.8	–	–	58.7	38.9	38.8
2. A few of the times	28.0	31.4	25.8	29.8	11.6	26.1	28.6	31.9	17.3	23.2	36.1	–	–	26.6	28.9	27.6
3. Some of the times	16.6	15.1	15.6	15.6	7.2	18.5	16.0	15.0	18.7	16.4	13.3	–	–	11.2	16.8	27.1
4. Most of the times	6.4	6.3	7.0	6.9	7.8	6.6	8.3	6.8	–	3.0	10.5	–	–	–	8.1	–
5. Every time	6.7	5.2	7.5	6.4	8.8	7.8	5.9	7.2	3.9	5.6	7.2	–	–	3.6	7.3	6.5
Item 3790 N(Wtd) ★	274	112	151	240	12	75	65	105	28	123	112	–	–	31	218	20
B068G: At your home (or apartment or dorm)																
1. Not at all	29.8	38.1	24.2	28.6	41.2	31.6	28.4	30.0	27.6	29.9	29.3	–	–	28.7	30.0	11.6
2. A few of the times	23.1	24.4	21.8	23.4	24.4	14.9	27.9	27.9	17.0	26.3	21.2	–	–	42.0	19.2	43.9
3. Some of the times	13.0	10.2	15.5	14.3	–	15.6	15.7	9.4	12.8	9.7	13.8	–	–	–	15.3	10.1
4. Most of the times	11.6	11.6	10.1	11.5	3.9	13.5	12.7	8.8	14.1	11.1	11.3	–	–	2.0	12.1	22.9
5. Every time	22.5	15.8	28.4	22.2	30.6	24.3	15.3	23.9	28.5	22.9	24.5	–	–	27.2	23.4	11.6
Item 3800 N(Wtd) ★	278	113	153	244	12	76	65	106	30	124	112	–	–	31	222	20
B068H: At school																
1. Not at all	67.4	62.1	73.7	68.0	80.1	68.1	67.9	67.8	62.5	72.4	67.8	–	–	84.7	63.9	70.3
2. A few of the times	16.3	19.8	12.7	16.2	3.9	14.8	16.2	15.8	22.4	14.4	14.8	–	–	11.4	17.7	13.1
3. Some of the times	10.2	10.0	9.1	9.6	7.2	13.5	9.0	9.5	7.6	6.7	12.1	–	–	–	11.6	13.5
4. Most of the times	3.4	6.0	1.6	3.9	–	.5	4.6	3.5	7.5	4.2	2.7	–	–	–	4.2	–
5. Every time	2.7	2.0	2.9	2.3	8.8	3.1	2.2	3.5	–	2.3	2.5	–	–	3.9	2.6	3.0
Item 3810 N(Wtd) ★	272	111	148	237	12	73	66	105	28	122	110	–	–	31	216	20
B068I: In a car																
1. Not at all	63.6	58.7	70.3	64.2	80.1	61.7	59.4	63.9	77.7	73.5	60.8	–	–	88.6	60.9	45.1
2. A few of the times	16.9	20.7	11.4	15.9	3.9	16.7	21.1	17.8	3.5	13.3	16.7	–	–	7.8	18.4	17.9
3. Some of the times	13.2	9.9	14.8	13.1	7.2	13.8	11.0	14.6	11.7	8.8	16.8	–	–	–	14.1	26.8
4. Most of the times	3.3	5.4	1.9	3.8	–	4.8	4.6	2.3	–	.6	4.2	–	–	–	3.8	3.5
5. Every time	3.0	5.3	1.6	3.0	8.8	2.9	3.9	1.5	7.1	3.8	1.5	–	–	3.6	2.7	6.7
Item 3830 N(Wtd) ★	270	111	147	236	12	73	65	104	28	121	110	–	–	31	214	20
B069: How many of the times when you used tranquilizers during the last year did you use them along with each of the following drugs--that is, so that their effects overlapped?																

★=excludes respondents for whom question was inappropriate.

QUESTIONNAIRE FORM 1 1978	TOTAL	SEX M	F	RACE White	Black	REGION NE	NC	S	W	4YR COLLEGE PLANS Yes	No	ILLICIT DRUG USE: LIFETIME None	Marijuana Only	Few Pills	More Pills	Any Heroin
Weighted No. of Cases:	3799	1740	1842	2962	411	922	1096	1257	524	1758	1571	1301	1086	411	760	46
% of Weighted Total:	100.0	45.8	48.5	78.0	10.8	24.3	28.8	33.1	13.8	46.3	41.3	34.3	28.6	10.8	20.0	1.2
B069A: With alcohol																
1. Not at all	61.1	54.5	68.2	61.1	71.6	58.1	54.6	62.8	79.1	70.9	57.9	-	-	94.7	57.6	39.3
2. A few of the times	17.7	21.7	13.3	16.9	22.4	18.0	24.5	15.9	7.2	15.8	17.1	-	-	2.1	20.2	18.5
3. Some of the times	10.1	11.1	8.8	10.7	-	6.8	10.2	13.3	7.3	7.2	12.6	-	-	-	11.0	18.1
4. Most of the times	5.9	5.7	6.2	6.1	-	11.4	6.5	1.3	6.4	2.2	8.6	-	-	-	6.2	12.8
5. Every time	5.1	7.0	3.5	5.2	5.9	5.7	4.2	6.7	-	3.9	3.8	-	-	3.1	4.9	11.4
Item 3840 N(Wtd) ★	276	113	150	240	12	76	68	103	28	124	111	-	-	33	218	21
B069B: With marijuana																
1. Not at all	49.6	38.9	61.3	49.3	71.9	50.5	51.4	42.6	68.9	61.8	46.9	-	-	91.6	44.8	29.3
2. A few of the times	18.0	22.2	13.5	18.4	9.6	17.5	11.4	26.4	4.6	15.3	18.0	-	-	3.3	21.7	4.5
3. Some of the times	12.4	14.8	10.3	12.8	4.2	8.8	14.0	14.7	9.9	10.7	14.2	-	-	5.1	11.2	38.2
4. Most of the times	8.8	12.3	5.4	8.3	7.9	8.3	14.4	5.5	8.7	7.9	7.7	-	-	-	9.2	19.4
5. Every time	11.1	11.8	9.5	11.2	6.3	14.8	8.9	10.8	7.9	4.3	13.3	-	-	-	13.1	8.6
Item 3850 N(Wtd) ★	274	112	150	239	11	74	68	103	28	124	110	-	-	31	218	21
B069C: With LSD																
1. Not at all	98.2	98.1	98.6	98.2	100.0	98.7	94.3	99.9	99.9	98.9	99.1	-	-	100.0	99.0	87.1
2. A few of the times	1.6	1.9	1.4	1.8	-	1.3	4.8	-	-	1.1	.9	-	-	-	1.0	10.0
3. Some of the times	.2	-	-	-	-	-	.9	-	-	-	-	-	-	-	-	2.9
4. Most of the times	-	-	-	-	-	-	-	-	-	-	-	-	-	-	-	-
5. Every time	-	-	-	-	-	-	-	-	-	-	-	-	-	-	-	-
Item 3860 N(Wtd) ★	269	108	148	234	11	74	67	99	28	122	108	-	-	31	213	21
B069D: With psychedelics other than LSD																
1. Not at all	96.7	95.4	98.0	97.4	100.0	96.9	94.9	96.7	99.9	100.0	93.3	-	-	100.0	96.3	94.8
2. A few of the times	1.4	1.6	.7	.7	-	2.6	2.7	-	-	-	2.6	-	-	-	1.7	-
3. Some of the times	1.0	2.3	.2	.9	-	.5	1.3	1.6	-	-	2.6	-	-	-	1.2	1.7
4. Most of the times	.3	.7	-	.3	-	-	1.1	-	-	-	-	-	-	-	-	3.5
5. Every time	.6	-	1.1	.7	-	-	-	1.7	-	-	1.5	-	-	-	.8	-
Item 3870 N(Wtd) ★	271	109	150	236	11	74	66	102	28	123	109	-	-	31	215	21
B069E: With amphetamines																
1. Not at all	92.9	92.4	93.2	92.4	100.0	91.8	89.1	94.1	99.9	96.2	89.2	-	-	100.0	91.9	91.2
2. A few of the times	6.0	6.0	6.5	6.3	-	7.5	9.5	4.2	-	3.8	8.8	-	-	-	6.7	8.8
3. Some of the times	1.1	1.6	.3	1.3	-	.7	1.4	1.7	-	-	2.0	-	-	-	1.4	-
4. Most of the times	-	-	-	-	-	-	-	-	-	-	-	-	-	-	-	-
5. Every time	-	-	-	-	-	-	-	-	-	-	-	-	-	-	-	-
Item 3880 N(Wtd) ★	267	108	147	234	10	73	66	100	28	121	108	-	-	31	212	21
B069F: With quaaludes																
1. Not at all	94.4	95.6	93.6	95.2	82.5	94.0	92.0	96.3	94.1	94.4	94.3	-	-	100.0	95.7	72.2
2. A few of the times	4.1	1.9	5.4	3.4	7.9	3.5	8.0	1.4	5.9	4.7	2.8	-	-	-	2.9	23.0
3. Some of the times	1.6	2.5	1.0	1.3	9.6	2.5	-	2.3	-	.9	2.9	-	-	-	1.5	4.8
4. Most of the times	-	-	-	-	-	-	-	-	-	-	-	-	-	-	-	-
5. Every time	-	-	-	-	-	-	-	-	-	-	-	-	-	-	-	-
Item 3890 N(Wtd) ★	270	109	148	235	11	74	67	100	28	123	108	-	-	31	214	21
B069G: With barbiturates																
1. Not at all	90.3	90.9	89.5	90.0	92.1	89.5	84.5	94.1	92.8	94.1	87.6	-	-	100.0	89.7	79.2
2. A few of the times	7.0	5.4	8.2	6.8	7.9	7.3	11.8	3.4	7.2	5.2	6.9	-	-	-	7.4	14.7
3. Some of the times	2.7	3.6	2.3	3.1	-	3.2	3.6	2.5	-	.6	5.4	-	-	-	2.8	6.1
4. Most of the times	-	-	-	-	-	-	-	-	-	-	-	-	-	-	-	-
5. Every time	-	-	-	-	-	-	-	-	-	-	-	-	-	-	-	-
Item 3900 N(Wtd) ★	263	105	147	229	11	73	65	97	28	122	103	-	-	30	212	18

★ = excludes respondents for whom question was inappropriate.

QUESTIONNAIRE FORM 1 1978	TOTAL	SEX		RACE		REGION				4YR COLLEGE PLANS		ILLICIT DRUG USE: LIFETIME				
		M	F	White	Black	NE	NC	S	W	Yes	No	None	Mari- juana Only	Few Pills	More Pills	Any Her- oin
Weighted No. of Cases:	3799	1740	1842	2962	411	922	1096	1257	524	1758	1571	1301	1086	411	760	46
% of Weighted Total:	100.0	45.8	48.5	78.0	10.8	24.3	28.8	33.1	13.8	46.3	41.3	34.3	28.6	10.8	20.0	1.2

B070: What have been the most important reasons for your taking tranquilizers without a doctor's orders? (Mark all that apply.)

	TOTAL	M	F	White	Black	NE	NC	S	W	Yes	No	None	Marijuana Only	Few Pills	More Pills	Any Heroin
A. To experiment--to see what it's like	36.0	54.5	21.1	37.4	43.8	31.3	43.0	37.5	27.4	38.0	35.6	-	-	19.8	36.3	53.7
B. To relax or relieve tension	68.3	59.0	76.7	69.2	57.7	65.3	77.7	65.0	67.6	69.3	67.3	-	-	58.0	67.8	86.8
C. To feel good or get high	37.7	52.9	24.3	38.0	14.9	31.1	42.7	42.8	25.9	29.1	41.0	-	-	12.7	38.8	59.0
D. To seek deeper insights and understanding	7.1	8.3	5.8	6.8	6.0	7.6	4.6	6.2	14.2	5.8	5.3	-	-	-	6.2	25.9
E. To have a good time with my friends	18.6	23.8	13.2	18.7	-	17.4	21.7	18.5	15.7	15.1	17.6	-	-	-	20.5	24.2
F. To fit in with a group I like	2.2	4.4	.7	1.7	11.7	-	1.4	4.9	-	1.5	3.7	-	-	3.2	2.3	-
G. To get away from my problems or troubles	21.2	13.9	25.5	21.1	29.1	16.5	28.5	23.4	9.7	20.3	22.8	-	-	11.0	20.9	37.4
H. Because of boredom, nothing else to do	13.7	16.5	10.9	13.7	23.1	19.3	10.9	13.8	4.0	16.1	11.4	-	-	4.2	14.5	17.6
I. Because of anger or frustration	18.6	11.3	24.9	19.4	29.1	14.4	30.2	17.3	9.5	23.0	17.8	-	-	7.2	20.1	18.4
J. To get through the day	7.7	8.6	6.8	8.4	6.0	5.6	3.3	14.0	-	5.7	12.0	-	-	10.0	6.7	14.6
K. To increase the effects of some other drug(s)	7.3	10.7	4.6	7.1	6.0	7.9	9.4	7.6	-	6.7	7.6	-	-	-	8.3	6.5
L. To decrease (offset) the effects of some other drug(s)	2.0	-	3.7	2.3	-	1.9	4.9	1.0	-	3.4	.4	-	-	-	1.6	9.1
M. To get to sleep	45.8	37.1	53.3	45.9	36.4	44.5	53.9	40.8	49.6	52.0	41.0	-	-	51.3	43.5	61.6
N. To relieve physical pain§	26.8	28.5	25.2	26.2	8.9	26.7	29.7	23.0	34.6	25.1	28.3	-	-	27.0	25.9	36.5
O. Because I am "hooked"--I have to have them	.2	-	.4	.3	-	-	1.0	-	-	.5	-	-	-	-	-	2.9
Item 3910-4040 N(Wtd) ★	268	111	145	239	8	76	62	102	28	118	110	-	-	28	219	21

B071: When you take tranquilizers how high do you usually get?

	TOTAL	M	F	White	Black	NE	NC	S	W	Yes	No	None	Marijuana Only	Few Pills	More Pills	Any Heroin
1. Not at all high	14.0	13.1	14.8	12.9	26.1	16.5	18.4	9.6	13.5	16.2	12.5	-	-	32.7	12.0	8.3
2. A little high	27.0	31.7	24.7	28.4	16.7	28.5	17.0	33.8	20.5	20.2	33.4	-	-	13.8	29.3	22.9
3. Moderately high	29.1	35.7	23.3	29.0	37.4	28.4	37.1	25.7	24.4	30.8	26.0	-	-	9.9	30.4	42.8
4. Very high	6.8	5.6	6.5	6.5	-	3.7	6.6	9.3	7.2	2.7	8.5	-	-	-	8.1	3.3
5. I don't take them to get high	23.0	14.0	30.7	23.2	19.8	23.0	20.9	21.6	34.4	30.1	19.6	-	-	43.7	20.2	22.7
Item 4050 N(Wtd) ★	267	112	143	238	8	76	64	101	25	118	110	-	-	30	215	21

B072: When you take tranquilizers how long do you usually stay high?

	TOTAL	M	F	White	Black	NE	NC	S	W	Yes	No	None	Marijuana Only	Few Pills	More Pills	Any Heroin
1. Usually don't get high	32.7	21.3	41.9	31.5	37.4	40.6	31.3	22.9	47.7	35.4	30.3	-	-	69.8	27.6	34.3
2. One to two hours	26.0	29.3	25.2	25.9	35.7	24.5	23.3	29.2	22.0	23.6	32.4	-	-	16.6	27.8	19.5
3. Three to six hours	32.3	38.7	25.4	33.6	8.4	22.8	36.4	37.6	30.2	30.2	33.1	-	-	13.6	34.0	39.7
4. Seven to 24 hours	8.7	9.9	7.5	8.6	18.5	10.9	9.0	9.3	-	10.0	4.2	-	-	-	10.1	6.4
5. More than 24 hours	.4	.9	-	.4	-	-	-	1.0	-	.8	-	-	-	-	.4	-
Item 4060 N(Wtd) ★	269	112	145	239	8	77	66	97	29	121	108	-	-	29	219	21

B073: What tranquilizers have you taken during the last year without a doctor's orders? (Mark all that apply.)

	TOTAL	M	F	White	Black	NE	NC	S	W	Yes	No	None	Marijuana Only	Few Pills	More Pills	Any Heroin
A. Librium	31.0	28.7	33.3	31.5	15.3	42.7	37.4	19.4	25.8	32.4	31.1	-	-	8.5	32.7	43.7
B. Valium	76.3	75.0	78.7	78.4	53.1	77.2	73.3	79.3	70.7	84.9	69.0	-	-	52.6	79.7	72.6
C. Miltown	1.8	.8	1.9	1.5	-	.5	3.0	2.6	-	3.0	-	-	-	-	1.9	3.2
D. Equanil	8.4	4.4	12.1	8.5	-	6.8	19.3	3.8	3.8	6.4	12.8	-	-	-	8.7	15.7
E. Meprobamate	5.2	7.5	3.8	5.8	-	7.9	3.2	5.9	-	6.2	4.2	-	-	-	6.0	3.2
F. Serax	.9	.8	1.1	.7	-	1.3	2.3	-	-	1.3	.8	-	-	-	.8	2.9
G. Atarax	1.2	1.8	.9	.5	28.5	2.2	-	1.6	-	1.4	1.4	-	-	3.3	.8	3.2
H. Tranxene	4.0	5.9	2.9	3.9	-	6.9	2.8	2.1	5.0	5.2	2.7	-	-	-	3.7	11.5
I. Vistaril	5.1	4.0	6.3	5.3	-	5.4	4.0	7.1	-	4.4	7.9	-	-	-	5.4	8.2
J. Don't know the names of some tranquilizers I have used	34.8	29.6	37.4	32.3	33.7	32.2	35.2	36.6	34.3	27.1	43.4	-	-	44.2	33.4	36.4
Item 4070-4160 N(Wtd) ★	266	109	145	239	7	76	64	98	29	121	105	-	-	28	218	21

§ = category added in this data collection.   ★ = excludes respondents for whom question was inappropriate.

QUESTIONNAIRE FORM 1 1978	TOTAL	SEX		RACE		REGION				4YR COLLEGE PLANS		ILLICIT DRUG USE: LIFETIME				
		M	F	White	Black	NE	NC	S	W	Yes	No	None	Marijuana Only	Few Pills	More Pills	Any Heroin
Weighted No. of Cases:	3799	1740	1842	2962	411	922	1096	1257	524	1758	1571	1301	1086	411	760	46
% of Weighted Total:	100.0	45.8	48.5	78.0	10.8	24.3	28.8	33.1	13.8	46.3	41.3	34.3	28.6	10.8	20.0	1.2

B074: Have you ever tried to stop using tranquilizers and found that you couldn't stop?

	TOTAL	M	F	White	Black	NE	NC	S	W	Yes	No	None	Marijuana Only	Few Pills	More Pills	Any Heroin
1. Yes	2.5	3.7	1.7	2.6	5.7	.6	5.2	1.9	3.1	1.1	4.1	-	-	7.6	2.0	-
2. No	97.5	96.3	98.3	97.4	94.3	99.4	94.7	98.1	96.9	98.9	95.9	-	-	92.4	98.0	100.0
Item 4170 N(Wtd) ★	270	112	147	241	8	77	66	98	29	121	107	-	-	31	217	21

B075: Do you think you will be using tranquilizers without a doctor's orders five years from now?

	TOTAL	M	F	White	Black	NE	NC	S	W	Yes	No	None	Marijuana Only	Few Pills	More Pills	Any Heroin
1. I definitely will	.5	.6	.3	.4	-	.5	.6	.5	-	.2	.7	.7	.1	-	.5	5.8
2. I probably will	3.7	2.9	4.3	3.7	2.6	4.4	3.1	3.7	4.0	2.6	4.7	.5	.7	3.9	13.5	24.3
3. I probably will not	28.8	29.7	28.0	29.6	23.1	30.1	30.9	26.5	27.3	27.8	29.0	17.7	23.5	38.2	52.8	27.5
4. I definitely will not	67.0	66.8	67.4	66.2	74.3	64.9	65.4	69.4	68.6	69.3	65.6	81.1	75.6	57.9	33.1	42.4
Item 4180 N(Wtd)	3436	1596	1730	2774	366	806	1012	1141	476	1659	1453	1249	993	377	657	44

The next questions are about COCAINE, which is sometimes called "coke".

B076: On how many occasions (if any) have you taken cocaine...

B076A: ...in your lifetime?

	TOTAL	M	F	White	Black	NE	NC	S	W	Yes	No	None	Marijuana Only	Few Pills	More Pills	Any Heroin
1. 0 occasions	86.4	84.2	89.6	86.4	92.2	82.6	87.5	89.0	84.6	89.9	86.9	100.0	100.0	74.7	53.4	13.8
2. 1-2	6.6	7.2	5.7	6.7	5.4	8.8	5.2	6.2	6.5	5.1	6.7	-	-	25.3	17.7	7.8
3. 3-5	2.8	3.3	1.8	2.7	1.0	4.0	2.0	2.3	3.7	2.1	2.4	-	-	-	12.8	13.3
4. 6-9	1.3	1.4	1.1	1.2	1.0	1.4	1.5	.5	2.4	.9	1.2	-	-	-	4.7	25.6
5. 10-19	1.3	2.1	.6	1.4	.3	1.2	1.9	.7	1.8	1.1	1.2	-	-	-	5.6	12.6
6. 20-39	.8	1.0	.5	.7	.2	.8	1.0	.8	.5	.4	.9	-	-	-	3.0	14.4
7. 40 or more	.7	.8	.6	.8	-	1.2	.8	.6	.3	.4	.7	-	-	-	2.8	12.4
Item 950 N(Wtd)	3493	1645	1735	2838	358	834	1046	1136	478	1693	1455	1269	1021	389	720	45

B076B: ...during the last 12 months?

	TOTAL	M	F	White	Black	NE	NC	S	W	Yes	No	None	Marijuana Only	Few Pills	More Pills	Any Heroin
1. 0 occasions	89.9	87.6	93.2	89.9	96.1	86.0	91.3	92.1	88.7	92.2	91.0	100.0	100.0	84.5	63.7	33.8
2. 1-2	5.7	6.9	4.0	5.9	2.5	8.2	4.5	4.8	6.3	4.5	5.3	-	-	15.5	18.7	12.7
3. 3-5	1.9	2.2	1.4	1.8	1.4	2.9	1.8	1.1	2.5	1.5	1.6	-	-	-	8.2	16.9
4. 6-9	1.0	1.6	.3	1.0	-	.5	1.3	.6	1.8	1.0	.6	-	-	-	3.8	13.7
5. 10-19	.7	1.0	.4	.7	-	1.1	.6	.6	.5	.3	.9	-	-	-	2.7	12.0
6. 20-39	.4	.4	.3	.4	-	.8	.3	.4	-	.3	.4	-	-	-	1.8	1.7
7. 40 or more	.3	.3	.2	.3	-	.6	.2	.3	.2	.2	.2	-	-	-	1.0	9.1
Item 960 N(Wtd)	3491	1644	1733	2836	357	832	1045	1135	479	1693	1452	1269	1021	388	719	45

B076C: ...during the last 30 days?

	TOTAL	M	F	White	Black	NE	NC	S	W	Yes	No	None	Marijuana Only	Few Pills	More Pills	Any Heroin
1. 0 occasions	95.3	94.0	97.0	95.4	98.7	91.8	96.0	96.8	96.1	96.3	96.1	100.0	100.0	96.5	81.7	57.4
2. 1-2	3.1	4.0	2.0	3.0	1.3	5.7	2.5	1.9	2.8	2.6	2.6	-	-	3.5	12.3	14.6
3. 3-5	.9	1.2	.6	.9	-	1.1	1.0	.8	.6	.7	.5	-	-	-	3.7	10.4
4. 6-9	.4	.5	.3	.3	-	.7	.5	.2	.3	.2	.5	-	-	-	1.7	4.1
5. 10-19	.2	.3	.1	.2	-	.4	-	.3	-	.2	.2	-	-	-	.5	6.8
6. 20-39	*	-	*	*	-	-	-	.1	-	-	*	-	-	-	-	1.5
7. 40 or more	.1	*	.1	.1	-	.2	.1	-	.2	.1	-	-	-	-	.1	5.4
Item 970 N(Wtd)	3490	1643	1733	2835	357	832	1045	1135	478	1693	1452	1269	1021	388	718	45

IF YOU HAVE NOT TAKEN COCAINE IN THE LAST TWELVE MONTHS, GO TO Q.B084.

B077: When you used cocaine during the Last year, how often did you use it in each of the following situations?

★ = excludes respondents for whom question was inappropriate.   * = less than .05 per cent.

QUESTIONNAIRE FORM 1 1978	TOTAL	SEX		RACE		REGION				4YR COLLEGE PLANS		ILLICIT DRUG USE: LIFETIME				
		M	F	White	Black	NE	NC	S	W	Yes	No	None	Mari-juana Only	Few Pills	More Pills	Any Her-oin
Weighted No. of Cases:	3799	1740	1842	2962	411	922	1096	1257	524	1758	1571	1301	1086	411	760	46
% of Weighted Total:	100.0	45.8	48.5	78.0	10.8	24.3	28.8	33.1	13.8	46.3	41.3	34.3	28.6	10.8	20.0	1.2
B077A: When you were alone																
1. Not at all	81.5	79.4	85.0	83.7	87.1	84.3	72.2	83.0	88.4	81.6	82.7	-	-	95.1	82.2	49.5
2. A few of the times	12.2	13.8	8.5	9.5	6.6	11.6	21.7	4.5	10.1	12.0	9.4	-	-	3.2	13.1	21.9
3. Some of the times	3.1	2.5	4.7	3.3	-	3.2	2.2	6.0	-	4.3	3.1	-	-	-	2.9	11.0
4. Most of the times	1.7	2.6	.6	2.0	-	.9	1.0	4.5	-	.8	3.6	-	-	-	.7	12.9
5. Every time	1.5	1.7	1.3	1.4	6.3	-	3.0	1.9	1.4	1.2	1.3	-	-	1.7	1.0	4.7
Item 4190 N(Wtd) ★	332	189	117	274	15	111	85	83	53	126	127	-	-	55	246	29
B077B: With just 1 or 2 other people																
1. Not at all	13.9	14.3	12.4	14.8	15.4	16.2	12.4	10.7	16.8	13.7	15.6	-	-	24.1	11.8	7.8
2. A few of the times	39.0	39.5	39.2	37.3	40.8	41.7	41.6	37.7	31.1	37.9	39.8	-	-	48.9	37.9	31.2
3. Some of the times	14.1	12.8	15.4	13.7	4.7	8.9	16.6	19.7	11.8	14.1	13.2	-	-	.9	15.9	24.0
4. Most of the times	15.0	16.7	12.7	15.4	15.8	14.8	17.5	10.2	19.2	16.1	12.2	-	-	-	16.7	29.6
5. Every time	18.0	16.6	20.2	18.8	23.4	18.4	12.0	21.7	21.2	18.2	19.2	-	-	26.1	17.6	7.5
Item 4200 N(Wtd) ★	338	195	117	280	14	111	87	86	54	128	127	-	-	55	252	29
B077C: At a party																
1. Not at all	38.3	33.7	46.1	39.1	44.8	39.5	29.1	44.4	41.4	44.2	34.5	-	-	68.7	34.0	15.5
2. A few of the times	19.9	23.8	14.1	18.5	25.8	20.4	19.3	19.6	20.4	16.5	22.1	-	-	6.8	22.2	25.8
3. Some of the times	16.1	17.8	14.0	14.9	23.1	14.3	20.0	15.0	15.1	13.8	16.7	-	-	3.4	17.9	25.4
4. Most of the times	10.6	10.9	8.8	11.0	-	9.8	12.6	9.0	11.7	9.9	12.8	-	-	4.2	12.0	11.4
5. Every time	15.0	13.8	17.1	16.5	6.3	16.0	19.0	11.9	11.4	15.6	13.9	-	-	16.9	13.9	22.0
Item 4210 N(Wtd) ★	339	195	119	282	14	109	89	87	53	128	129	-	-	54	253	30
B077D: When your date or spouse was present																
1. Not at all	55.1	64.6	40.2	54.9	60.0	50.2	49.6	64.9	59.1	61.5	58.9	-	-	86.3	47.7	59.1
2. A few of the times	15.8	12.8	18.5	14.9	7.9	19.1	22.0	8.8	9.3	12.6	13.2	-	-	5.2	19.0	8.8
3. Some of the times	9.5	11.3	4.4	8.7	12.6	9.5	12.8	7.0	7.5	7.2	8.0	-	-	1.9	11.0	10.6
4. Most of the times	5.4	4.8	7.6	6.6	-	7.2	4.5	2.8	7.5	5.8	5.0	-	-	-	6.2	9.3
5. Every time	14.2	6.5	29.3	14.8	19.5	14.0	11.0	16.4	16.6	12.8	15.0	-	-	6.6	16.2	12.2
Item 4220 N(Wtd) ★	330	191	114	272	14	108	88	81	52	127	123	-	-	52	247	29
B077E: When people over age 30 were present																
1. Not at all	73.8	75.0	71.5	74.5	57.8	72.5	70.2	74.9	80.9	73.1	74.9	-	-	88.5	71.7	65.0
2. A few of the times	12.4	11.9	14.3	12.7	13.4	13.8	10.2	15.4	8.5	14.5	9.7	-	-	4.2	13.6	17.4
3. Some of the times	8.5	9.3	6.3	7.7	19.1	7.5	13.3	6.5	5.6	7.6	9.3	-	-	1.8	9.3	14.3
4. Most of the times	4.0	3.3	5.3	3.6	9.8	3.9	5.2	3.2	3.7	3.8	4.6	-	-	5.6	3.9	2.1
5. Every time	1.2	.5	2.7	1.5	-	2.3	1.1	-	1.2	.9	1.6	-	-	-	1.5	1.2
Item 4230 N(Wtd) ★	332	191	116	275	14	108	87	84	53	128	125	-	-	53	249	29
B077F: During the daytime (before 4:00 p.m.)																
1. Not at all	57.9	57.0	58.4	56.6	77.7	61.3	50.5	65.4	51.2	59.9	57.7	-	-	84.0	57.1	17.2
2. A few of the times	23.9	22.7	26.2	24.4	7.9	25.2	31.0	14.9	23.4	25.6	21.6	-	-	8.9	25.5	39.1
3. Some of the times	11.3	14.2	6.9	11.1	14.4	7.9	11.3	14.4	13.7	9.4	13.4	-	-	1.7	10.3	38.7
4. Most of the times	3.6	2.5	4.8	3.8	-	2.7	3.9	4.1	4.3	2.7	4.3	-	-	-	4.2	2.4
5. Every time	3.3	3.6	3.6	4.0	-	2.9	3.4	1.2	7.4	2.4	3.0	-	-	5.4	3.0	2.6
Item 4240 N(Wtd) ★	332	192	116	275	14	109	87	83	53	128	125	-	-	54	248	29
B077G: At your home (or apartment or dorm)																
1. Not at all	59.9	56.0	67.7	62.9	45.3	69.2	50.1	64.7	49.5	61.4	61.2	-	-	83.2	59.0	23.8
2. A few of the times	17.7	18.9	14.7	14.6	25.9	16.8	18.8	12.4	25.9	15.3	17.8	-	-	10.6	18.1	28.0
3. Some of the times	9.7	12.8	4.7	9.9	12.6	3.7	12.0	12.8	13.5	8.8	9.0	-	-	-	10.3	23.3
4. Most of the times	6.4	6.6	5.2	6.9	-	6.0	10.4	2.8	6.2	6.0	6.7	-	-	-	6.7	15.5
5. Every time	6.3	5.7	7.7	5.8	16.3	4.3	8.7	7.2	4.8	8.6	5.3	-	-	6.2	5.9	9.4
Item 4250 N(Wtd) ★	330	190	116	273	14	107	87	83	53	127	125	-	-	53	247	29

★ = excludes respondents for whom question was inappropriate.

QUESTIONNAIRE FORM 1 1978	TOTAL	SEX		RACE		REGION				4YR COLLEGE PLANS		ILLICIT DRUG USE: LIFETIME				
		M	F	White	Black	NE	NC	S	W	Yes	No	None	Mari- juana Only	Few Pills	More Pills	Any Her- oin
Weighted No. of Cases:	3799	1740	1842	2962	411	922	1096	1257	524	1758	1571	1301	1086	411	760	46
% of Weighted Total:	100.0	45.8	48.5	78.0	10.8	24.3	28.8	33.1	13.8	46.3	41.3	34.3	28.6	10.8	20.0	1.2

B077H: At school

1. Not at all	80.1	75.6	87.5	81.8	78.7	76.9	82.0	86.6	73.3	88.2	80.6	–	–	94.7	77.9	71.9
2. A few of the times	12.6	14.7	10.2	11.1	15.3	17.1	9.6	10.2	12.2	9.3	12.9	–	–	4.3	15.2	5.9
3. Some of the times	4.3	5.9	.6	4.0	6.0	3.2	3.1	1.9	12.0	2.0	3.0	–	–	-	3.5	18.9
4. Most of the times	1.2	1.5	.3	.9	-	1.2	2.4	-	.9	-	2.6	–	–	.9	1.2	1.2
5. Every time	1.8	2.3	1.4	2.2	-	1.4	2.9	1.2	1.6	.5	.8	–	–	-	2.2	2.1
Item 4260 N(Wtd) ★	331	191	116	274	14	108	87	83	53	127	125	–	–	53	248	29

B077I: In a car

1. Not at all	57.4	56.1	60.5	58.7	68.7	53.0	54.2	62.5	63.4	68.8	53.7	–	–	72.9	55.9	39.8
2. A few of the times	23.2	24.2	20.6	20.8	20.6	25.9	23.3	20.8	21.5	18.1	25.5	–	–	11.5	24.4	35.7
3. Some of the times	9.7	10.1	8.6	9.8	6.0	6.9	15.7	7.1	9.9	7.3	10.9	–	–	-	11.1	15.8
4. Most of the times	2.8	2.1	4.0	2.9	4.7	3.3	3.1	3.1	.9	2.7	2.9	–	–	.9	3.0	4.6
5. Every time	6.8	7.4	6.3	7.8	-	10.9	3.6	6.5	4.4	3.1	7.0	–	–	14.6	5.5	4.1
Item 4280 N(Wtd) ★	334	191	118	277	14	108	88	85	53	127	128	–	–	53	251	29

B078: How many of the times when you used cocaine during the last year did you use it along with each of the following drugs-- that is, so that their effects overlapped?

B078A: With alcohol

1. Not at all	38.4	40.2	37.1	37.5	56.5	37.7	25.9	43.7	52.6	42.3	34.9	–	–	61.3	35.4	22.7
2. A few of the times	31.4	30.2	32.1	29.8	31.7	28.6	35.3	33.7	26.3	32.3	34.6	–	–	27.6	30.3	46.5
3. Some of the times	8.1	9.7	3.7	8.3	5.7	5.0	14.3	6.5	6.2	5.3	7.5	–	–	-	9.3	12.2
4. Most of the times	6.5	6.1	7.4	6.6	6.2	4.4	11.3	4.3	6.3	6.6	3.8	–	–	-	8.0	6.7
5. Every time	15.6	13.8	19.8	17.7	-	24.3	13.0	11.8	8.6	13.6	19.2	–	–	11.1	17.0	11.9
Item 4290 N(Wtd) ★	325	188	115	270	15	102	87	84	51	123	126	–	–	53	242	30

B078B: With marijuana

1. Not at all	25.0	25.4	25.5	26.0	26.6	25.9	18.9	30.7	24.0	25.5	29.1	–	–	55.1	20.3	10.2
2. A few of the times	20.4	20.0	20.5	19.0	30.4	17.7	24.3	21.5	17.8	21.1	22.3	–	–	20.6	19.0	31.5
3. Some of the times	13.8	16.7	10.0	14.9	6.9	8.2	13.2	16.3	22.2	13.9	12.0	–	–	1.4	15.0	25.7
4. Most of the times	11.0	13.4	6.7	11.3	6.7	10.0	19.1	6.4	7.0	12.7	7.6	–	–	-	12.3	19.9
5. Every time	29.8	24.5	37.3	28.8	29.4	38.2	24.5	25.1	29.0	26.8	29.0	–	–	22.9	33.4	12.7
Item 4300 N(Wtd) ★	333	194	115	280	13	108	87	86	52	127	125	–	–	54	249	30

B078C: With LSD

1. Not at all	96.8	96.6	97.9	97.4	94.0	97.6	91.6	99.1	99.9	97.2	97.6	–	–	100.0	97.9	85.8
2. A few of the times	2.3	2.6	.8	2.2	-	.9	6.6	.9	-	1.1	1.7	–	–	-	1.9	9.2
3. Some of the times	.4	.5	.4	.2	6.0	.5	1.0	-	-	.4	.7	–	–	-	.2	2.8
4. Most of the times	.3	-	.9	-	-	1.0	-	-	-	.8	-	–	–	-	-	-
5. Every time	.2	.3	-	.2	-	-	.8	-	-	.5	-	–	–	-	-	2.2
Item 4310 N(Wtd) ★	320	185	114	267	14	103	83	84	51	124	123	–	–	52	237	30

B078D: With psychedelics other than LSD

1. Not at all	98.4	98.0	99.2	98.2	100.0	96.6	98.1	99.9	99.9	99.0	99.2	–	–	100.0	98.2	97.8
2. A few of the times	.3	-	.8	.4	-	.9	-	-	-	-	.8	–	–	-	.4	-
3. Some of the times	.4	.5	-	.4	-	.4	1.1	-	-	-	-	–	–	-	.5	-
4. Most of the times	-	-	-	-	-	-	-	-	-	-	-	–	–	-	-	-
5. Every time	.9	1.5	-	1.0	-	2.1	.8	-	-	1.0	-	–	–	-	.9	2.2
Item 4320 N(Wtd) ★	320	186	114	268	14	102	84	84	51	123	123	–	–	52	238	30

B078E: With amphetamines

1. Not at all	94.4	93.2	95.7	93.9	100.0	93.3	94.0	98.0	90.9	96.2	95.9	–	–	100.0	94.9	80.5
2. A few of the times	3.7	4.3	3.0	3.8	-	4.9	4.9	.9	4.1	2.3	3.0	–	–	-	3.5	11.5
3. Some of the times	.6	.5	1.0	.8	-	.5	1.1	-	1.4	-	.4	–	–	-	.6	2.3
4. Most of the times	.6	1.0	-	.7	-	-	-	-	3.6	-	.4	–	–	-	.2	4.5
5. Every time	.7	1.0	.3	.8	-	1.3	-	1.1	-	1.5	.3	–	–	-	.8	1.2
Item 4330 N(Wtd) ★	322	187	114	270	14	102	85	85	51	124	123	–	–	52	240	30

★ = excludes respondents for whom question was inappropriate.

QUESTIONNAIRE FORM 1 1978	TOTAL	SEX		RACE		REGION				4YR COLLEGE PLANS		ILLICIT DRUG USE: LIFETIME				
		M	F	White	Black	NE	NC	S	W	Yes	No	None	Mari- juana Only	Few Pills	More Pills	Any Her- oin
Weighted No. of Cases:	3799	1740	1842	2962	411	922	1096	1257	524	1758	1571	1301	1086	411	760	46
% of Weighted Total:	100.0	45.8	48.5	78.0	10.8	24.3	28.8	33.1	13.8	46.3	41.3	34.3	28.6	10.8	20.0	1.2

B078F: With quaaludes

	TOTAL	M	F	White	Black	NE	NC	S	W	Yes	No	None	Mari-juana Only	Few Pills	More Pills	Any Heroin
1. Not at all	95.8	95.5	97.7	97.1	100.0	93.2	97.5	95.4	98.8	97.1	94.7	-	-	96.9	96.8	85.9
2. A few of the times	2.8	2.5	1.9	1.7	-	3.8	.7	4.6	1.2	1.5	4.1	-	-	3.1	1.3	14.1
3. Some of the times	1.2	1.7	.4	1.0	-	3.0	1.1	-	-	1.0	1.2	-	-	-	1.7	-
4. Most of the times	-	-	-	-	-	-	-	-	-	-	-	-	-	-	-	-
5. Every time	.2	.3	-	.2	-	-	.7	-	-	.4	-	-	-	-	.2	-
Item 4340 N(Wtd) ★	319	185	114	268	14	100	84	84	50	123	123	-	-	52	237	30

B078G: With barbiturates

	TOTAL	M	F	White	Black	NE	NC	S	W	Yes	No	None	Mari-juana Only	Few Pills	More Pills	Any Heroin
1. Not at all	97.8	98.5	97.1	98.1	100.0	97.7	95.2	99.9	98.6	100.0	96.4	-	-	100.0	98.0	91.7
2. A few of the times	1.6	1.0	2.5	1.4	-	1.5	3.7	-	1.4	-	3.2	-	-	-	1.2	8.3
3. Some of the times	.6	.5	.4	.5	-	.8	1.1	-	-	-	.4	-	-	-	.8	-
4. Most of the times	-	-	-	-	-	-	-	-	-	-	-	-	-	-	-	-
5. Every time	-	-	-	-	-	-	-	-	-	-	-	-	-	-	-	-
Item 4350 N(Wtd) ★	318	184	114	268	14	100	84	84	50	123	122	-	-	52	237	29

B078H: With tranquilizers

	TOTAL	M	F	White	Black	NE	NC	S	W	Yes	No	None	Mari-juana Only	Few Pills	More Pills	Any Heroin
1. Not at all	97.7	99.6	95.3	97.7	100.0	97.7	95.0	98.8	99.9	99.1	97.4	-	-	100.0	97.9	91.7
2. A few of the times	1.9	.4	4.3	2.1	-	1.1	5.0	1.2	-	.9	2.2	-	-	-	1.6	8.3
3. Some of the times	.4	-	.4	.2	-	1.2	-	-	-	-	.4	-	-	-	.5	-
4. Most of the times	-	-	-	-	-	-	-	-	-	-	-	-	-	-	-	-
5. Every time	-	-	-	-	-	-	-	-	-	-	-	-	-	-	-	-
Item 4360 N(Wtd) ★	317	183	114	267	14	99	84	84	50	123	122	-	-	52	236	29

B079: What have been the most important reasons for your taking cocaine? (Mark all that apply.)

	TOTAL	M	F	White	Black	NE	NC	S	W	Yes	No	None	Mari-juana Only	Few Pills	More Pills	Any Heroin
A. To experiment--to see what it's like	73.0	75.8	69.5	74.0	92.1	72.8	73.4	74.8	69.8	73.2	74.7	-	-	83.5	71.2	68.5
B. To relax or relieve tension	28.6	30.5	24.8	28.5	12.7	27.8	40.4	20.9	23.6	23.7	26.5	-	-	12.5	27.8	63.9
C. To feel good or get high	74.0	75.3	71.5	73.7	53.4	72.4	79.7	67.6	78.5	68.3	72.5	-	-	47.3	78.1	88.6
D. To seek deeper insights and understanding	18.1	22.2	12.2	18.6	6.5	20.0	20.6	15.0	15.2	16.6	13.7	-	-	4.4	18.6	39.1
E. To have a good time with my friends	44.5	47.1	36.0	44.0	32.9	44.0	45.3	39.9	51.7	48.3	36.1	-	-	34.9	44.9	58.0
F. To fit in with a group I like	4.1	5.1	3.3	4.6	6.4	5.5	2.7	3.1	5.2	6.7	2.5	-	-	3.9	3.3	11.2
G. To get away from my problems or troubles	8.2	8.2	6.1	6.9	14.6	5.1	14.7	10.3	-	7.6	9.8	-	-	-	6.9	33.1
H. Because of boredom, nothing else to do	12.5	12.6	10.7	11.1	20.6	17.3	14.7	7.5	7.1	13.1	10.1	-	-	1.4	13.5	24.0
I. Because of anger or frustration	4.1	2.8	5.1	3.4	8.3	1.0	6.5	4.7	5.8	5.6	2.2	-	-	-	3.1	20.5
J. To get through the day	2.5	2.7	2.2	2.4	-	3.5	2.3	1.2	3.0	1.9	2.3	-	-	-	1.6	15.0
K. To increase the effects of some other drug(s)	9.7	11.2	7.1	9.8	12.4	7.5	13.2	9.2	9.1	12.0	6.8	-	-	2.9	10.7	13.8
L. To decrease (offset) the effects of some other drug(s)	1.7	1.3	2.3	1.5	6.5	1.8	4.2	-	-	1.5	.6	-	-	-	1.5	6.4
M. To stay awake	11.4	9.9	15.1	11.0	20.5	10.2	18.3	7.2	9.3	9.8	13.5	-	-	5.7	10.4	29.4
N. To get more energy	23.1	20.4	28.4	24.1	16.0	18.7	26.3	22.6	27.9	24.0	25.4	-	-	14.6	23.6	34.8
O. Because I am "hooked"--I have to have it	1.2	1.3	.9	.9	-	2.0	1.4	-	1.5	1.3	-	-	-	-	.7	8.1
Item 4370-4510 N(Wtd) ★	331	194	115	278	15	108	86	85	52	128	126	-	-	54	247	30

B080: When you take cocaine how high do you usually get?

	TOTAL	M	F	White	Black	NE	NC	S	W	Yes	No	None	Mari-juana Only	Few Pills	More Pills	Any Heroin
1. Not at all high	5.5	3.4	8.6	5.3	17.3	6.6	5.5	5.9	2.6	7.5	4.4	-	-	15.3	3.8	2.1
2. A little high	17.6	16.6	20.1	17.6	25.5	19.6	14.9	13.2	25.4	16.0	19.6	-	-	15.9	19.8	2.9
3. Moderately high	38.2	40.6	33.7	39.5	31.6	34.8	44.4	33.1	43.4	40.1	33.8	-	-	39.2	37.1	45.4
4. Very high	38.6	39.4	37.6	37.6	25.7	39.0	35.1	47.7	28.6	36.5	42.2	-	-	29.6	39.3	49.7
5. I don't take it to get high	-	-	-	-	-	-	-	-	-	-	-	-	-	-	-	-
Item 4520 N(Wtd) ★	335	196	117	280	15	110	86	86	52	128	128	-	-	55	250	30

★ = excludes respondents for whom question was inappropriate.

QUESTIONNAIRE FORM 1 1978	TOTAL	SEX		RACE		REGION				4YR COLLEGE PLANS		ILLICIT DRUG USE: LIFETIME				
		M	F	White	Black	NE	NC	S	W	Yes	No	None	Marijuana Only	Few Pills	More Pills	Any Heroin
Weighted No. of Cases:	3799	1740	1842	2962	411	922	1096	1257	524	1758	1571	1301	1086	411	760	46
% of Weighted Total:	100.0	45.8	48.5	78.0	10.8	24.3	28.8	33.1	13.8	46.3	41.3	34.3	28.6	10.8	20.0	1.2

B081: When you take cocaine how long do you usually stay high?

	TOTAL	M	F	White	Black	NE	NC	S	W	Yes	No	None	Marijuana Only	Few Pills	More Pills	Any Heroin
1. Usually don't get high	5.8	4.0	9.1	5.6	15.3	6.0	6.1	6.1	4.5	8.0	5.2	-	-	15.4	3.9	4.9
2. One to two hours	33.2	36.2	28.8	34.7	34.6	31.6	38.4	23.0	44.5	35.6	32.5	-	-	38.1	33.3	23.7
3. Three to six hours	39.6	39.9	37.5	39.0	34.8	40.9	33.0	45.3	38.5	38.0	41.7	-	-	30.5	40.6	46.9
4. Seven to 24 hours	20.9	19.9	23.0	20.0	15.3	21.5	22.5	23.5	12.6	18.4	19.2	-	-	16.0	21.4	24.5
5. More than 24 hours	.5	-	1.6	.6	-	-	-	2.1	-	-	1.4	-	-	-	.7	-
Item 4530 N(Wtd) ★	331	194	115	277	15	108	86	85	52	127	127	-	-	53	248	30

B082: Have you ever tried to stop using cocaine and found that you couldn't stop?

	TOTAL	M	F	White	Black	NE	NC	S	W	Yes	No	None	Marijuana Only	Few Pills	More Pills	Any Heroin
1. Yes	2.3	2.3	2.4	2.6	-	1.8	3.8	2.2	1.5	1.7	2.6	-	-	.9	2.4	4.6
2. No	97.7	97.7	97.6	97.4	100.0	98.2	96.2	97.8	98.5	98.3	97.4	-	-	99.1	97.6	95.4
Item 4540 N(Wtd) ★	330	193	115	277	15	110	86	83	51	127	125	-	-	53	247	30

B083: What methods have you used for taking cocaine? (Mark all that apply.)

	TOTAL	M	F	White	Black	NE	NC	S	W	Yes	No	None	Marijuana Only	Few Pills	More Pills	Any Heroin
A. Sniffing or "snorting"	95.3	95.9	93.9	94.6	95.4	98.5	94.3	92.2	95.2	93.4	96.3	-	-	84.3	97.6	95.8
B. Smoking	20.4	18.4	24.2	18.5	26.5	12.6	22.7	25.6	24.5	18.5	23.3	-	-	22.7	18.7	30.5
C. Injection	4.3	4.9	3.3	4.1	-	2.8	7.1	6.2	-	2.3	7.5	-	-	-	3.2	21.8
D. By mouth	24.9	21.6	28.7	24.8	5.7	24.7	33.0	21.4	18.0	19.1	25.9	-	-	6.5	26.5	45.0
E. Other	3.6	3.9	2.8	3.1	4.6	5.7	4.1	1.6	2.1	3.5	3.1	-	-	1.3	2.9	14.2
Item 4550-4590 N(Wtd) ★	335	196	117	280	15	110	86	86	52	128	128	-	-	55	250	30

B084: Do you think you will be using cocaine five years from now?

	TOTAL	M	F	White	Black	NE	NC	S	W	Yes	No	None	Marijuana Only	Few Pills	More Pills	Any Heroin
1. I definitely will	1.5	1.9	.8	1.4	-	2.4	1.5	.6	1.8	1.3	1.4	.6	.3	.5	4.5	18.2
2. I probably will	6.3	8.0	4.5	6.7	2.4	8.7	5.2	5.5	6.6	4.8	5.7	*	1.9	6.1	23.9	28.0
3. I probably will not	17.6	21.2	14.1	18.1	14.4	19.6	17.6	16.6	16.7	16.5	17.6	6.0	16.3	26.6	36.1	25.6
4. I definitely will not	74.6	69.0	80.6	73.8	83.2	69.3	75.7	77.3	74.9	77.4	75.4	93.4	81.5	66.9	35.6	28.2
Item 4600 N(Wtd)	3513	1649	1759	2846	376	834	1035	1165	480	1697	1480	1262	1012	390	687	46

The next questions are about HEROIN.

Heroin is sometimes called: smack, horse, skag.

B085: On how many occasions (if any) have you taken heroin...

B085A: ...in your lifetime?

	TOTAL	M	F	White	Black	NE	NC	S	W	Yes	No	None	Marijuana Only	Few Pills	More Pills	Any Heroin
1. 0 occasions	98.7	98.4	99.0	98.6	99.8	99.0	98.5	98.6	98.4	99.1	98.7	100.0	100.0	100.0	100.0	-
2. 1-2	.9	1.0	.8	1.0	.2	.7	1.1	.7	1.5	.7	.7	-	-	-	-	70.3
3. 3-5	.2	.2	.1	.2	-	.1	.3	.1	.2	.1	.1	-	-	-	-	13.2
4. 6-9	-	-	-	-	-	-	-	-	-	-	-	-	-	-	-	-
5. 10-19	*	.1	-	-	-	-	-	.1	-	.1	-	-	-	-	-	2.1
6. 20-39	.1	.2	-	.1	-	-	.1	.3	-	-	.3	-	-	-	-	8.6
7. 40 or more	.1	.2	-	.1	-	.1	-	.1	-	-	.2	-	-	-	-	5.8
Item 1100 N(Wtd)	3447	1626	1726	2817	355	814	1028	1130	476	1682	1441	1261	1018	383	692	46

B085B: ...during the last 12 months?

	TOTAL	M	F	White	Black	NE	NC	S	W	Yes	No	None	Marijuana Only	Few Pills	More Pills	Any Heroin
1. 0 occasions	99.3	99.2	99.5	99.3	100.0	99.5	99.3	99.4	99.2	99.4	99.3	100.0	100.0	100.0	100.0	51.9
2. 1-2	.4	.3	.5	.4	-	.4	.6	.1	.6	.5	.2	-	-	-	-	28.6
3. 3-5	.1	.1	*	.1	-	-	.1	.1	.2	.1	.1	-	-	-	-	6.7
4. 6-9	-	-	-	-	-	-	-	-	-	-	-	-	-	-	-	-
5. 10-19	.1	.2	-	.1	-	-	-	.3	-	-	.2	-	-	-	-	6.8
6. 20-39	-	-	-	-	-	-	-	-	-	-	-	-	-	-	-	-
7. 40 or more	.1	.2	-	.1	-	.1	-	.1	-	-	.2	-	-	-	-	6.0
Item 1110 N(Wtd)	3446	1624	1726	2816	355	814	1028	1130	474	1682	1441	1261	1018	383	692	45

★ = excludes respondents for whom question was inappropriate.   * = less than .05 per cent.

QUESTIONNAIRE FORM 1 1978	TOTAL	SEX		RACE		REGION				4YR COLLEGE PLANS		ILLICIT DRUG USE: LIFETIME				
		M	F	White	Black	NE	NC	S	W	Yes	No	None	Mari- juana Only	Few Pills	More Pills	Any Her- oin
Weighted No. of Cases:	3799	1740	1842	2962	411	922	1096	1257	524	1758	1571	1301	1086	411	760	46
% of Weighted Total:	100.0	45.8	48.5	78.0	10.8	24.3	28.8	33.1	13.8	46.3	41.3	34.3	28.6	10.8	20.0	1.2
B085C: ...during the last 30 days?																
1. 0 occasions	99.6	99.3	99.9	99.6	100.0	99.6	99.9	99.5	99.5	99.9	99.4	100.0	100.0	100.0	100.0	73.6
2. 1-2	.1	.2	.1	.1	-	.3	.1	-	.3	.1	.1	-	-	-	-	8.8
3. 3-5	.1	.1	*	.1	-	-	*	.1	.2	*	.1	-	-	-	-	5.1
4. 6-9	-	-	-	-	-	-	-	-	-	-	-	-	-	-	-	-
5. 10-19	.1	.2	-	.1	-	-	-	.3	-	-	.2	-	-	-	-	6.6
6. 20-39	*	.1	-	-	-	.1	-	-	-	-	.1	-	-	-	-	2.3
7. 40 or more	.1	.1	-	.1	-	-	-	.1	-	-	.1	-	-	-	-	3.6
Item 1120 N(Wtd)	3447	1626	1726	2817	355	814	1028	1130	476	1682	1441	1261	1018	383	692	46

IF YOU HAVE NOT TAKEN HEROIN IN THE LAST TWELVE MONTHS, GO TO Q.B093.

B086: When you used heroin during the last year, how often did you use it in each of the following situations?

B086A: When you were alone

	TOTAL	M	F	White	Black	NE	NC	S	W	Yes	No	None	Mari- juana Only	Few Pills	More Pills	Any Her- oin
1. Not at all	44.3	38.6	42.4	44.7	-	42.3	66.1	33.0	45.7	52.9	38.4	-	-	-	-	42.2
2. A few of the times	8.4	6.3	13.3	10.1	-	16.0	18.6	-	-	12.9	-	-	-	-	-	9.6
3. Some of the times	12.9	8.9	21.3	4.0	-	41.7	-	-	-	12.0	11.2	-	-	-	-	9.3
4. Most of the times	20.1	25.9	15.2	24.1	-	-	-	43.6	33.3	14.7	32.8	-	-	-	-	22.8
5. Every time	14.3	20.3	7.8	17.1	-	-	15.3	23.4	99.9	7.5	17.6	-	-	-	-	16.1
Item 4610 N(Wtd) ★	21	12	8	18	-	7	4	7	4	8	9	-	-	-	-	19

B086B: With just 1 or 2 other people

	TOTAL	M	F	White	Black	NE	NC	S	W	Yes	No	None	Mari- juana Only	Few Pills	More Pills	Any Her- oin
1. Not at all	24.4	22.6	32.6	27.8	-	35.8	-	13.9	54.3	31.3	20.5	-	-	-	-	26.3
2. A few of the times	6.9	11.8	-	7.9	-	-	34.8	-	-	9.1	-	-	-	-	-	7.4
3. Some of the times	23.8	34.8	10.2	21.3	-	31.5	-	43.6	-	-	44.0	-	-	-	-	25.7
4. Most of the times	7.3	-	-	-	-	26.5	-	-	-	-	-	-	-	-	-	-
5. Every time	37.6	30.8	57.2	43.0	-	6.2	65.2	42.5	45.7	59.6	35.5	-	-	-	-	40.6
Item 4620 N(Wtd) ★	20	12	7	18	-	6	4	7	4	7	9	-	-	-	-	19

B086C: At a party

	TOTAL	M	F	White	Black	NE	NC	S	W	Yes	No	None	Mari- juana Only	Few Pills	More Pills	Any Her- oin
1. Not at all	49.5	31.6	80.1	52.4	-	34.1	65.2	23.4	99.9	81.6	28.3	-	-	-	-	49.5
2. A few of the times	28.4	39.3	9.7	30.1	-	23.0	16.2	53.1	-	18.4	42.8	-	-	-	-	28.4
3. Some of the times	5.6	8.9	-	-	-	25.7	-	-	-	-	11.2	-	-	-	-	5.6
4. Most of the times	-	-	-	-	-	-	-	-	-	-	-	-	-	-	-	-
5. Every time	16.5	20.2	10.2	17.5	-	17.2	18.6	23.5	-	-	17.7	-	-	-	-	16.5
Item 4630 N(Wtd) ★	19	12	7	18	-	4	4	7	4	7	9	-	-	-	-	19

B086D: When your date or spouse was present

	TOTAL	M	F	White	Black	NE	NC	S	W	Yes	No	None	Mari- juana Only	Few Pills	More Pills	Any Her- oin
1. Not at all	80.3	71.7	95.0	85.0	-	65.9	83.8	76.6	99.9	90.9	67.4	-	-	-	-	80.3
2. A few of the times	3.5	5.5	-	3.7	-	-	16.2	-	-	9.1	-	-	-	-	-	3.5
3. Some of the times	5.6	8.9	-	-	-	25.6	-	-	-	-	11.2	-	-	-	-	5.6
4. Most of the times	-	-	-	-	-	-	-	-	-	-	-	-	-	-	-	-
5. Every time	10.6	13.9	5.0	11.3	-	8.5	-	23.4	-	-	21.4	-	-	-	-	10.6
Item 4640 N(Wtd) ★	19	12	7	18	-	4	4	7	4	7	9	-	-	-	-	19

B086E: When people over age 30 were present

	TOTAL	M	F	White	Black	NE	NC	S	W	Yes	No	None	Mari- juana Only	Few Pills	More Pills	Any Her- oin
1. Not at all	69.0	70.9	80.6	78.9	-	54.6	81.4	57.5	99.9	90.7	64.0	-	-	-	-	74.5
2. A few of the times	3.3	-	9.7	3.8	-	-	-	9.5	-	-	7.2	-	-	-	-	3.6
3. Some of the times	19.5	15.2	9.7	8.0	-	45.4	18.6	9.5	-	9.3	11.2	-	-	-	-	13.1
4. Most of the times	-	-	-	-	-	-	-	-	-	-	-	-	-	-	-	-
5. Every time	8.2	13.9	-	9.3	-	-	-	23.5	-	-	17.6	-	-	-	-	8.8
Item 4650 N(Wtd) ★	20	12	7	18	-	6	4	7	4	7	9	-	-	-	-	19

* = less than .05 per cent.　★ = excludes respondents for whom question was inappropriate.

QUESTIONNAIRE FORM 1 1978	TOTAL	SEX		RACE		REGION				4YR COLLEGE PLANS		ILLICIT DRUG USE: LIFETIME				
		M	F	White	Black	NE	NC	S	W	Yes	No	None	Marijuana Only	Few Pills	More Pills	Any Heroin
Weighted No. of Cases:	3799	1740	1842	2962	411	922	1096	1257	524	1758	1571	1301	1086	411	760	46
% of Weighted Total:	100.0	45.8	48.5	78.0	10.8	24.3	28.8	33.1	13.8	46.3	41.3	34.3	28.6	10.8	20.0	1.2
B086F: During the daytime (before 4:00 p.m.)																
1. Not at all	40.1	38.6	51.2	45.8	-	35.8	81.4	23.4	33.3	62.4	31.2	-	-	-	-	43.2
2. A few of the times	8.8	6.3	15.2	10.2	-	18.8	18.6	-	-	14.6	-	-	-	-	-	9.6
3. Some of the times	16.7	8.9	33.6	13.1	-	18.8	-	9.5	45.7	23.0	18.4	-	-	-	-	18.0
4. Most of the times	22.5	25.9	-	17.3	-	26.6	-	43.6	-	-	32.8	-	-	-	-	16.4
5. Every time	11.9	20.3	-	13.6	-	-	-	23.5	21.0	-	17.6	-	-	-	-	12.8
Item 4660 N(Wtd) ★	20	12	7	18	-	6	4	7	4	7	9	-	-	-	-	19
B086G: At your. home (or apartment or dorm)																
1. Not at all	33.5	33.1	41.3	38.3	-	16.9	49.9	13.9	79.0	58.5	27.5	-	-	-	-	36.1
2. A few of the times	15.4	11.8	24.9	17.6	-	18.8	34.8	9.5	-	23.6	7.2	-	-	-	-	16.6
3. Some of the times	30.9	34.8	9.7	21.1	-	45.4	-	53.1	-	9.3	44.0	-	-	-	-	25.5
4. Most of the times	3.5	-	10.2	4.0	-	12.7	-	-	-	-	-	-	-	-	-	3.8
5. Every time	16.7	20.3	13.9	19.0	-	6.2	15.3	23.5	21.0	8.6	21.3	-	-	-	-	18.0
Item 4670 N(Wtd) ★	20	12	7	18	-	6	4	7	4	7	9	-	-	-	-	19
B086H: At school																
1. Not at all	76.3	77.2	91.1	87.2	-	54.6	84.7	76.6	99.9	91.5	71.1	-	-	-	-	82.3
2. A few of the times	-	-	-	-	-	-	-	-	-	-	-	-	-	-	-	-
3. Some of the times	5.2	8.9	-	-	-	18.8	-	-	-	-	11.2	-	-	-	-	5.6
4. Most of the times	7.3	-	-	-	-	26.6	-	-	-	-	-	-	-	-	-	-
5. Every time	11.2	13.9	8.9	12.8	-	-	15.3	23.4	-	8.5	17.7	-	-	-	-	12.1
Item 4680 N(Wtd) ★	20	12	7	18	-	6	4	7	4	7	9	-	-	-	-	19
B086I: In a car																
1. Not at all	54.8	34.4	80.1	54.3	-	68.5	50.1	23.4	99.9	62.8	38.4	-	-	-	-	51.2
2. A few of the times	13.2	16.9	9.7	15.1	-	-	49.9	9.5	-	37.2	-	-	-	-	-	14.3
3. Some of the times	8.7	8.9	10.2	4.0	-	31.5	-	-	-	-	11.2	-	-	-	-	9.3
4. Most of the times	15.1	25.9	-	17.3	-	-	-	43.6	-	-	32.8	-	-	-	-	16.4
5. Every time	8.2	13.9	-	9.3	-	-	-	23.5	-	-	17.6	-	-	-	-	8.8
Item 4700 N(Wtd) ★	20	12	7	18	-	6	4	7	4	7	9	-	-	-	-	19
B087: How many of the times when you used heroin during the last year did you use it along with each of the following drugs--that is, so that their effects overlapped?																
B087A: With alcohol																
1. Not at all	46.9	21.0	80.1	45.3	-	51.6	33.9	23.4	99.9	62.8	21.4	-	-	-	-	42.7
2. A few of the times	23.0	39.3	-	26.3	-	16.9	16.2	43.6	-	9.1	42.8	-	-	-	-	24.9
3. Some of the times	5.2	8.9	-	-	-	18.8	-	-	-	-	11.2	-	-	-	-	5.6
4. Most of the times	6.8	-	19.9	7.8	-	12.7	-	9.5	-	9.3	-	-	-	-	-	7.3
5. Every time	18.1	30.8	-	20.6	-	-	49.9	23.5	-	18.8	24.6	-	-	-	-	19.5
Item 4710 N(Wtd) ★	20	12	7	18	-	6	4	7	4	7	9	-	-	-	-	19
B087B: With marijuana																
1. Not at all	18.8	7.0	41.5	21.7	-	18.8	15.3	-	54.3	39.8	-	-	-	-	-	20.4
2. A few of the times	8.8	15.5	-	10.1	-	16.9	18.6	-	-	-	11.3	-	-	-	-	9.5
3. Some of the times	29.9	37.9	23.9	28.2	-	18.8	-	50.6	45.7	23.0	49.1	-	-	-	-	32.4
4. Most of the times	21.7	6.0	29.6	16.1	-	39.2	16.2	22.2	-	18.4	8.0	-	-	-	-	15.2
5. Every time	20.8	33.6	5.0	23.9	-	6.3	49.9	27.2	-	18.8	31.6	-	-	-	-	22.5
Item 4720 N(Wtd) ★	19	11	7	17	-	6	4	6	4	7	8	-	-	-	-	18

★=excludes respondents for whom question was inappropriate.

QUESTIONNAIRE FORM 1 1978	TOTAL	SEX		RACE		REGION				4YR COLLEGE PLANS		ILLICIT DRUG USE: LIFETIME				
		M	F	White	Black	NE	NC	S	W	Yes	No	None	Marijuana Only	Few Pills	More Pills	Any Heroin
Weighted No. of Cases:	3799	1740	1842	2962	411	922	1096	1257	524	1758	1571	1301	1086	411	760	46
% of Weighted Total:	100.0	45.8	48.5	78.0	10.8	24.3	28.8	33.1	13.8	46.3	41.3	34.3	28.6	10.8	20.0	1.2
B087C: With LSD																
1. Not at all	73.6	66.4	100.0	85.2	-	54.6	65.2	81.8	99.9	90.9	73.7	-	-	-	-	80.0
2. A few of the times	12.8	23.3	-	14.8	-	-	34.8	18.2	-	9.1	12.7	-	-	-	-	13.9
3. Some of the times	13.6	10.3	-	-	-	45.4	-	-	-	-	13.6	-	-	-	-	6.1
4. Most of the times	-	-	-	-	-	-	-	-	-	-	-	-	-	-	-	-
5. Every time	-	-	-	-	-	-	-	-	-	-	-	-	-	-	-	-
Item 4730 N(Wtd) ★	19	10	7	16	-	6	4	5	4	7	8	-	-	-	-	17
B087D: With psychedelics other than LSD																
1. Not at all	83.6	75.9	95.0	89.1	-	65.9	83.8	99.9	99.9	90.9	81.9	-	-	-	-	83.6
2. A few of the times	5.8	6.4	5.0	6.2	-	8.5	16.2	-	-	9.1	4.5	-	-	-	-	5.8
3. Some of the times	6.1	10.3	-	-	-	25.6	-	-	-	-	13.6	-	-	-	-	6.1
4. Most of the times	-	-	-	-	-	-	-	-	-	-	-	-	-	-	-	-
5. Every time	4.5	7.4	-	4.7	-	-	-	-	21.0	-	-	-	-	-	-	4.5
Item 4740 N(Wtd) ★	17	10	7	16	-	4	4	5	4	7	8	-	-	-	-	17
B087E: With amphetamines																
1. Not at all	91.8	89.7	95.0	97.8	-	65.9	99.9	99.9	99.9	100.0	81.9	-	-	-	-	91.8
2. A few of the times	-	-	-	-	-	-	-	-	-	-	-	-	-	-	-	-
3. Some of the times	6.2	10.3	-	-	-	25.6	-	-	-	-	13.6	-	-	-	-	6.2
4. Most of the times	2.0	-	5.0	2.2	-	8.5	-	-	-	-	4.5	-	-	-	-	2.0
5. Every time	-	-	-	-	-	-	-	-	-	-	-	-	-	-	-	-
Item 4750 N(Wtd) ★	17	10	7	16	-	4	4	5	4	7	8	-	-	-	-	17
B087F: With quaaludes																
1. Not at all	91.8	89.7	95.0	97.8	-	65.9	99.9	99.9	99.9	100.0	81.9	-	-	-	-	91.8
2. A few of the times	2.0	-	5.0	2.2	-	8.5	-	-	-	-	4.5	-	-	-	-	2.0
3. Some of the times	6.2	10.3	-	-	-	25.6	-	-	-	-	13.6	-	-	-	-	6.2
4. Most of the times	-	-	-	-	-	-	-	-	-	-	-	-	-	-	-	-
5. Every time	-	-	-	-	-	-	-	-	-	-	-	-	-	-	-	-
Item 4760 N(Wtd) ★	17	10	7	16	-	4	4	5	4	7	8	-	-	-	-	17
B087G: With barbiturates																
1. Not at all	93.5	88.6	100.0	100.0	-	74.4	99.9	99.9	99.9	100.0	84.4	-	-	-	-	93.5
2. A few of the times	-	-	-	-	-	-	-	-	-	-	-	-	-	-	-	-
3. Some of the times	6.5	11.4	-	-	-	25.6	-	-	-	-	15.6	-	-	-	-	6.5
4. Most of the times	-	-	-	-	-	-	-	-	-	-	-	-	-	-	-	-
5. Every time	-	-	-	-	-	-	-	-	-	-	-	-	-	-	-	-
Item 4770 N(Wtd) ★	16	9	7	15	-	4	4	4	4	7	7	-	-	-	-	16
B087H: With tranquilizers																
1. Not at all	95.1	90.9	100.0	95.1	-	100.0	81.4	99.9	99.9	100.0	100.0	-	-	-	-	95.1
2. A few of the times	4.9	9.1	-	4.9	-	-	18.6	-	-	-	-	-	-	-	-	4.9
3. Some of the times	-	-	-	-	-	-	-	-	-	-	-	-	-	-	-	-
4. Most of the times	-	-	-	-	-	-	-	-	-	-	-	-	-	-	-	-
5. Every time	-	-	-	-	-	-	-	-	-	-	-	-	-	-	-	-
Item 4780 N(Wtd) ★	15	8	7	15	-	3	4	4	4	7	6	-	-	-	-	15
B087I: With cocaine																
1. Not at all	62.9	65.2	59.9	67.3	-	23.0	65.2	84.8	79.0	67.0	79.2	-	-	-	-	62.9
2. A few of the times	8.8	8.1	9.7	9.4	-	-	18.6	15.2	-	9.3	-	-	-	-	-	8.8
3. Some of the times	17.4	11.4	25.4	11.6	-	68.5	-	-	-	14.6	15.6	-	-	-	-	17.4
4. Most of the times	6.2	7.1	5.0	6.6	-	8.5	16.2	-	-	9.1	5.2	-	-	-	-	6.2
5. Every time	4.7	8.2	-	5.1	-	-	-	-	21.0	-	-	-	-	-	-	4.7
Item 4790 N(Wtd) ★	16	9	7	15	-	4	4	4	4	7	7	-	-	-	-	16

★ = excludes respondents for whom question was inappropriate.

QUESTIONNAIRE FORM 1 1978	TOTAL	SEX		RACE		REGION				4YR COLLEGE PLANS		ILLICIT DRUG USE: LIFETIME				
		M	F	White	Black	NE	NC	S	W	Yes	No	None	Mari-juana Only	Few Pills	More Pills	Any Her-oin
Weighted No. of Cases:	3799	1740	1842	2962	411	922	1096	1257	524	1758	1571	1301	1086	411	760	46
% of Weighted Total:	100.0	45.8	48.5	78.0	10.8	24.3	28.8	33.1	13.8	46.3	41.3	34.3	28.6	10.8	20.0	1.2

B088: What have been the most important reasons for your taking heroin? (Mark all that apply.)

	TOTAL	M	F	White	Black	NE	NC	S	W	Yes	No	None	Mari-juana Only	Few Pills	More Pills	Any Her-oin
A. To experiment--to see what it's like	57.8	68.9	51.2	66.1	-	35.8	99.9	53.1	54.3	77.0	49.8	-	-	-	-	62.4
B. To relax or relieve tension	37.0	52.0	19.1	36.3	-	31.5	66.3	43.6	-	17.6	50.9	-	-	-	-	39.9
C. To feel good or get high	65.8	69.8	72.9	69.2	-	56.6	99.9	53.1	66.7	73.9	61.8	-	-	-	-	71.0
D. To seek deeper insights and understanding	18.4	31.4	-	21.0	-	-	16.2	43.6	-	-	39.7	-	-	-	-	19.8
E. To have a good time with my friends	13.8	20.6	5.0	9.8	-	25.1	34.8	-	-	9.1	14.9	-	-	-	-	14.9
F. To fit in with a group I like	5.9	-	17.4	6.8	-	-	-	-	33.3	16.7	-	-	-	-	-	6.4
G. To get away from my problems or troubles	31.4	48.5	8.9	30.0	-	18.8	31.5	57.5	-	8.5	61.4	-	-	-	-	33.9
H. Because of boredom, nothing else to do	18.8	32.2	-	21.5	-	-	18.6	43.6	-	-	32.8	-	-	-	-	20.3
I. Because of anger or frustration	3.0	-	8.9	3.5	-	-	15.3	-	-	8.5	-	-	-	-	-	3.3
J. To get through the day	21.4	15.1	15.2	10.1	-	64.2	18.6	-	-	14.6	11.2	-	-	-	-	15.2
K. To increase the effects of some other drug(s)	3.7	6.3	-	4.2	-	-	18.6	-	-	-	-	-	-	-	-	4.0
L. To decrease (offset) the effects of some other drug(s)	-	-	-	-	-	-	-	-	-	-	-	-	-	-	-	-
M. Because I am "hooked"--I have to have it	18.5	22.8	15.2	15.2	-	37.7	-	23.4	-	14.6	28.9	-	-	-	-	20.0
Item 4800-4920 N(Wtd) ★	20	12	7	18	-	6	4	7	4	7	9	-	-	-	-	19

B089: When you take heroin how high do you usually get?

	TOTAL	M	F	White	Black	NE	NC	S	W	Yes	No	None	Mari-juana Only	Few Pills	More Pills	Any Her-oin
1. Not at all high	8.8	13.9	-	9.3	-	-	-	23.4	-	-	17.6	-	-	-	-	8.8
2. A little high	12.1	-	32.8	12.8	-	-	15.3	-	45.7	31.5	-	-	-	-	-	12.1
3. Moderately high	17.8	13.5	25.4	18.9	-	65.9	16.2	-	-	23.6	10.1	-	-	-	-	17.8
4. Very high	56.1	64.3	41.9	53.5	-	34.1	68.5	62.7	54.3	44.8	61.8	-	-	-	-	56.1
5. I don't take it to get high	5.2	8.3	-	5.5	-	-	-	13.9	-	-	10.5	-	-	-	-	5.2
Item 4930 N(Wtd) ★	19	12	7	18	-	4	4	7	4	7	9	-	-	-	-	19

B090: When you take heroin how long do you usually stay high?

	TOTAL	M	F	White	Black	NE	NC	S	W	Yes	No	None	Mari-juana Only	Few Pills	More Pills	Any Her-oin
1. Usually don't get high	-	-	-	-	-	-	-	-	-	-	-	-	-	-	-	-
2. One to two hours	8.8	-	23.9	9.3	-	-	-	-	45.7	23.0	-	-	-	-	-	8.8
3. Three to six hours	42.7	47.6	34.3	45.2	-	65.9	31.5	57.5	-	32.2	53.3	-	-	-	-	42.7
4. Seven to 24 hours	30.1	23.3	41.9	31.9	-	8.5	49.9	19.1	54.3	44.8	17.9	-	-	-	-	30.1
5. More than 24 hours	18.4	29.1	-	13.5	-	25.6	18.6	23.4	-	-	28.9	-	-	-	-	18.4
Item 4940 N(Wtd) ★	19	12	7	18	-	4	4	7	4	7	9	-	-	-	-	19

B091: Have you ever tried to stop using heroin and found that you couldn't stop?

	TOTAL	M	F	White	Black	NE	NC	S	W	Yes	No	None	Mari-juana Only	Few Pills	More Pills	Any Her-oin
1. Yes	5.0	8.3	-	5.5	-	-	-	12.5	-	-	10.5	-	-	-	-	5.2
2. No	95.0	91.7	100.0	94.5	-	100.0	99.9	87.5	99.9	100.0	89.5	-	-	-	-	94.8
Item 4950 N(Wtd) ★	20	12	8	18	-	4	4	8	4	8	9	-	-	-	-	19

B092: What methods have you used for taking heroin? (Mark all that apply.)

	TOTAL	M	F	White	Black	NE	NC	S	W	Yes	No	None	Mari-juana Only	Few Pills	More Pills	Any Her-oin
A. Sniffing or "snorting"	53.2	59.6	42.3	50.5	-	74.4	49.9	53.1	33.3	35.5	71.9	-	-	-	-	53.2
B. Smoking	26.7	14.4	47.9	22.4	-	51.3	31.5	-	45.7	55.2	11.2	-	-	-	-	26.7
C. Injection	40.5	52.6	19.9	37.0	-	42.9	33.7	53.1	21.0	18.8	51.2	-	-	-	-	40.5
D. By mouth	31.1	26.5	38.8	27.0	-	59.8	67.5	9.5	-	51.3	14.9	-	-	-	-	31.1
E. Other	23.7	37.5	-	19.1	-	25.6	-	37.3	21.0	-	39.3	-	-	-	-	23.7
Item 4960-5000 N(Wtd) ★	19	12	7	18	-	4	4	7	4	7	9	-	-	-	-	19

★ = excludes respondents for whom question was inappropriate.

QUESTIONNAIRE FORM 1 1978	TOTAL	SEX		RACE		REGION				4YR COLLEGE PLANS		ILLICIT DRUG USE: LIFETIME				
		M	F	White	Black	NE	NC	S	W	Yes	No	None	Mari- juana Only	Few Pills	More Pills	Any Her- oin
Weighted No. of Cases:	3799	1740	1842	2962	411	922	1096	1257	524	1758	1571	1301	1086	411	760	46
% of Weighted Total:	100.0	45.8	48.5	78.0	10.8	24.3	28.8	33.1	13.8	46.3	41.3	34.3	28.6	10.8	20.0	1.2

B093: Do you think you will be using heroin five years from now?

	TOTAL	M	F	White	Black	NE	NC	S	W	Yes	No	None	Mari- juana Only	Few Pills	More Pills	Any Her- oin
1. I definitely will	.6	.9	.2	.4	.3	.8	.6	.3	.8	.3	.8	.6	.3	.5	.5	9.0
2. I probably will	.4	.6	.1	.3	.5	.4	.1	.7	-	.1	.6	-	.1	.2	.7	11.9
3. I probably will not	7.5	8.4	6.6	7.3	8.9	7.4	8.1	8.3	4.2	5.2	8.8	3.7	6.4	9.7	14.4	15.8
4. I definitely will not	91.6	90.1	93.2	91.9	90.3	91.4	91.2	90.7	95.0	94.3	89.8	95.7	93.2	89.6	84.3	63.4
Item 5010 N(Wtd)	3416	1605	1720	2767	370	795	1013	1138	470	1648	1457	1241	993	383	644	42

The next questions are about NARCOTICS OTHER THAN HEROIN, which are sometimes prescribed by doctors. Drugstores are not supposed to sell them without a prescription.

These include: Methadone, Opium, Morphine, Codeine, Demerol, Paregoric, Talwin, Laudanum.

B094: Have you ever taken any narcotics other than heroin because a doctor told you to use them?

	TOTAL	M	F	White	Black	NE	NC	S	W	Yes	No	None	Mari- juana Only	Few Pills	More Pills	Any Her- oin
1. No	84.1	85.2	83.4	82.5	93.9	83.8	85.4	84.6	80.7	82.0	85.9	90.8	84.9	73.6	76.3	82.0
2. Yes, but I had already tried them on my own.	1.8	1.9	1.5	2.0	.3	2.0	2.3	1.2	1.6	1.3	1.9	-	-	.9	7.4	12.9
3. Yes, and it was the first time I took any	14.1	12.9	15.0	15.6	5.8	14.2	12.3	14.2	17.7	16.7	12.2	9.1	15.1	25.5	16.3	5.1
Item 5020 N(Wtd)	3391	1595	1711	2785	344	791	1024	1117	459	1663	1423	1231	1000	376	681	42

B095: On how many occasions (if any) have you taken narcotics other than heroin on your own--that is, without a doctor telling you to take them...

B095A: ...in your lifetime?

	TOTAL	M	F	White	Black	NE	NC	S	W	Yes	No	None	Mari- juana Only	Few Pills	More Pills	Any Her- oin
1. 0 occasions	90.3	90.3	90.5	89.5	97.3	88.4	88.9	93.0	90.4	92.0	90.3	100.0	100.0	83.3	66.3	16.0
2. 1-2	4.7	4.6	4.9	5.0	1.5	6.1	5.4	3.2	4.3	4.2	4.4	-	-	16.7	12.9	19.0
3. 3-5	1.8	1.5	1.9	1.8	.8	2.0	2.5	1.2	1.2	1.7	1.7	-	-	-	8.5	5.7
4. 6-9	1.4	1.4	1.3	1.5	.4	1.6	1.5	.8	1.9	1.0	1.3	-	-	-	5.4	21.4
5. 10-19	.9	1.2	.5	1.0	-	1.2	.9	.7	.6	.6	1.0	-	-	-	3.5	11.8
6. 20-39	.6	.5	.5	.7	-	.5	.4	.7	1.0	.3	.6	-	-	-	2.0	16.2
7. 40 or more	.4	.4	.4	.4	-	.2	.4	.4	.5	.2	.7	-	-	-	1.3	10.0
Item 1130 N(Wtd)	3379	1591	1703	2769	346	791	1017	1110	461	1660	1417	1239	997	378	678	43

B095B: ...during the last 12 months?

	TOTAL	M	F	White	Black	NE	NC	S	W	Yes	No	None	Mari- juana Only	Few Pills	More Pills	Any Her- oin
1. 0 occasions	94.4	94.9	94.1	93.7	99.1	93.1	93.9	95.5	95.0	95.1	94.6	100.0	100.0	93.4	79.2	44.3
2. 1-2	2.9	2.3	3.5	3.3	.5	3.4	3.6	2.2	2.1	2.8	2.5	-	-	6.6	9.8	15.7
3. 3-5	1.2	1.3	1.1	1.3	.1	2.2	1.1	.8	1.1	1.0	1.2	-	-	-	5.4	12.7
4. 6-9	.7	.8	.6	.9	.3	.7	.7	.8	.6	.6	.7	-	-	-	3.1	8.7
5. 10-19	.5	.6	.5	.7	-	.4	.3	.6	1.1	.4	.6	-	-	-	2.0	12.1
6. 20-39	.1	.1	.1	.1	-	.1	.2	-	.1	*	.2	-	-	-	.4	2.5
7. 40 or more	.1	.1	-	*	-	.1	.1	-	-	*	.1	-	-	-	.1	4.0
Item 1140 N(Wtd)	3374	1588	1701	2764	345	789	1014	1110	460	1660	1414	1239	997	376	674	43

B095C: ...during the last 30 days?

	TOTAL	M	F	White	Black	NE	NC	S	W	Yes	No	None	Mari- juana Only	Few Pills	More Pills	Any Her- oin
1. 0 occasions	97.5	97.6	97.5	97.2	99.6	97.5	97.3	97.9	96.9	98.0	97.2	100.0	100.0	98.7	90.4	64.9
2. 1-2	1.6	1.6	1.6	1.8	.4	1.6	2.0	1.1	2.2	1.6	1.6	-	-	1.3	6.5	14.5
3. 3-5	.6	.6	.5	.7	-	.7	.5	.6	.6	.4	.7	-	-	-	2.4	8.1
4. 6-9	.1	-	.1	.1	-	.2	-	.1	-	-	.1	-	-	-	.2	1.6
5. 10-19	.2	.2	.2	.2	-	*	.2	.3	.3	-	.4	-	-	-	.4	10.9
6. 20-39	-	-	-	-	-	-	-	-	-	-	-	-	-	-	-	-
7. 40 or more	-	-	-	-	-	-	-	-	-	-	-	-	-	-	-	-
Item 1150 N(Wtd)	3373	1587	1701	2765	345	787	1016	1110	460	1660	1414	1239	997	376	675	42

* = less than .05 per cent.

QUESTIONNAIRE FORM 1 1978	TOTAL	SEX		RACE		REGION				4YR COLLEGE PLANS		ILLICIT DRUG USE: LIFETIME				
		M	F	White	Black	NE	NC	S	W	Yes	No	None	Marijuana Only	Few Pills	More Pills	Any Heroin
Weighted No. of Cases:	3799	1740	1842	2962	411	922	1096	1257	524	1758	1571	1301	1086	411	760	46
% of Weighted Total:	100.0	45.8	48.5	78.0	10.8	24.3	28.8	33.1	13.8	46.3	41.3	34.3	28.6	10.8	20.0	1.2

IF YOU HAV$ NOT TAKEN NARCOTICS OTHER THAN HEROIN IN THE LAST TWELVE MONTHS, GO TO Q.B104.

THE FOLLOWING QUESTIONS REFER ONLY TO TAKING NARCOTICS OTHER THAN HEROIN WITHOUT A DOCTOR'S ORDERS. IF YOU HAVE NOT DONE THIS IN THE LAST TWELVE MONTHS, GO TO Q.B104.

B096: When you used narcotics other than heroin during the last year, how often did you use them in each of the following situations?

B096A: When you were alone

	TOTAL	M	F	White	Black	NE	NC	S	W	Yes	No	None	Marij. Only	Few Pills	More Pills	Any Heroin
1. Not at all	54.0	54.3	54.3	53.7	45.9	52.0	55.0	58.5	45.5	48.5	56.1	–	–	79.2	49.7	50.1
2. A few of the times	22.9	27.5	19.2	22.4	54.1	23.9	28.1	16.0	22.1	26.3	20.1	–	–	11.2	24.7	25.5
3. Some of the times	7.4	6.7	6.8	7.4	–	4.8	5.5	12.5	6.7	5.0	6.9	–	–	–	8.8	6.6
4. Most of the times	6.8	7.9	6.6	7.1	–	5.9	3.6	9.7	10.8	7.6	8.8	–	–	–	6.8	14.8
5. Every time	9.0	3.5	13.0	9.5	–	13.4	7.8	3.3	14.9	12.5	8.1	–	–	9.6	10.0	3.0
Item 5030 N(Wtd) ★	179	81	87	162	5	51	58	49	22	78	70	–	–	23	134	21

B096B: With just 1 or 2 other people

	TOTAL	M	F	White	Black	NE	NC	S	W	Yes	No	None	Marij. Only	Few Pills	More Pills	Any Heroin
1. Not at all	26.2	24.7	27.1	26.1	–	34.2	22.8	27.9	12.6	35.1	18.6	–	–	45.8	24.1	19.1
2. A few of the times	32.5	33.2	33.5	32.1	79.4	28.9	30.2	31.7	50.3	32.7	36.2	–	–	33.7	32.1	34.0
3. Some of the times	19.7	23.0	16.4	20.1	–	9.5	26.5	25.0	12.4	12.6	26.2	–	–	–	22.3	23.6
4. Most of the times	12.1	8.2	16.1	12.6	20.6	14.9	14.1	5.5	14.4	8.6	11.1	–	–	2.2	13.7	12.1
5. Every time	9.5	10.9	6.9	9.2	–	12.5	6.4	10.0	10.3	11.1	7.8	–	–	18.3	7.8	11.1
Item 5040 N(Wtd) ★	178	79	89	161	2	50	60	47	20	77	71	–	–	22	134	22

B096C: At a party

	TOTAL	M	F	White	Black	NE	NC	S	W	Yes	No	None	Marij. Only	Few Pills	More Pills	Any Heroin
1. Not at all	47.7	40.8	53.8	46.5	41.3	57.2	35.1	54.9	44.3	64.2	35.5	–	–	90.3	46.1	15.0
2. A few of the times	16.3	19.1	13.0	15.7	58.7	16.2	16.0	14.7	20.8	14.0	16.1	–	–	4.5	17.1	23.2
3. Some of the times	13.9	15.5	11.0	14.2	–	2.3	19.4	15.6	22.6	6.9	19.4	–	–	3.5	13.8	25.3
4. Most of the times	11.2	12.7	11.1	12.3	–	9.5	17.6	6.2	8.6	8.8	12.5	–	–	1.7	13.6	6.1
5. Every time	10.8	11.9	11.0	11.3	–	14.8	11.9	8.5	3.6	6.2	16.4	–	–	–	9.4	30.4
Item 5050 N(Wtd) ★	177	79	89	161	2	50	59	47	21	78	69	–	–	22	133	22

B096D: When your date or spouse was present

	TOTAL	M	F	White	Black	NE	NC	S	W	Yes	No	None	Marij. Only	Few Pills	More Pills	Any Heroin
1. Not at all	57.3	67.0	49.4	58.5	41.3	67.0	52.0	57.0	49.7	68.6	54.9	–	–	90.3	53.3	49.4
2. A few of the times	13.6	12.7	13.3	12.8	58.7	10.8	15.6	12.5	16.5	11.9	13.9	–	–	4.4	14.9	14.0
3. Some of the times	12.1	10.0	12.7	11.9	–	7.8	18.4	11.0	6.6	9.6	12.9	–	–	5.3	13.3	11.2
4. Most of the times	8.1	5.5	11.4	9.0	–	7.1	10.7	3.6	13.5	2.0	8.0	–	–	–	8.2	15.6
5. Every time	8.9	4.8	13.3	7.9	–	7.4	3.3	15.8	13.8	8.0	10.3	–	–	–	10.2	9.9
Item 5060 N(Wtd) ★	177	79	88	161	2	50	60	46	20	77	70	–	–	21	134	22

B096E: When people over age 30 were present

	TOTAL	M	F	White	Black	NE	NC	S	W	Yes	No	None	Marij. Only	Few Pills	More Pills	Any Heroin
1. Not at all	66.8	67.4	63.5	65.7	20.6	68.8	60.4	70.2	72.2	58.5	70.3	–	–	78.5	65.0	65.5
2. A few of the times	14.9	16.9	14.2	15.4	38.2	12.7	19.5	14.1	8.6	17.9	12.1	–	–	4.5	14.8	26.2
3. Some of the times	4.4	5.9	3.6	4.8	–	3.9	4.9	6.4	–	4.5	6.3	–	–	–	5.3	3.2
4. Most of the times	6.3	2.1	10.7	5.9	41.3	5.1	5.5	4.3	15.9	6.6	8.8	–	–	5.1	7.5	–
5. Every time	7.6	7.7	7.9	8.1	–	9.4	9.7	5.0	3.2	12.6	2.6	–	–	11.9	7.3	5.1
Item 5070 N(Wtd) ★	179	79	90	163	2	49	60	47	22	78	71	–	–	22	136	21

★ = excludes respondents for whom question was inappropriate.

QUESTIONNAIRE FORM 1 1978	TOTAL	SEX		RACE		REGION				4YR COLLEGE PLANS		ILLICIT DRUG USE: LIFETIME				
		M	F	White	Black	NE	NC	S	W	Yes	No	None	Mari-juana Only	Few Pills	More Pills	Any Her-oin
Weighted No. of Cases:	3799	1740	1842	2962	411	922	1096	1257	524	1758	1571	1301	1086	411	760	46
% of Weighted Total:	100.0	45.8	48.5	78.0	10.8	24.3	28.8	33.1	13.8	46.3	41.3	34.3	28.6	10.8	20.0	1.2

B096F: During the daytime (before 4:00 p.m.)

	TOTAL	M	F	White	Black	NE	NC	S	W	Yes	No	None	Mari-juana Only	Few Pills	More Pills	Any Her-oin
1. Not at all	40.4	40.1	39.2	37.1	58.7	44.6	35.0	50.5	24.1	40.0	34.1	-	-	47.1	40.1	35.3
2. A few of the times	29.7	23.8	34.5	30.2	41.3	27.7	32.7	26.6	32.3	28.8	34.5	-	-	24.6	30.4	30.3
3. Some of the times	15.7	18.0	15.3	17.2	-	12.0	15.8	16.9	21.3	16.1	16.1	-	-	7.5	15.7	24.7
4. Most of the times	7.3	11.6	4.2	8.0	-	3.9	10.2	3.6	14.7	5.6	10.7	-	-	-	9.1	3.1
5. Every time	6.9	6.3	6.8	7.6	-	11.7	6.3	2.4	7.6	9.5	4.6	-	-	20.8	4.7	6.6
Item 5080 N(Wtd) ★	179	80	91	164	2	49	61	47	22	78	72	-	-	22	136	21

B096G: At your home (or apartment or dorm)

	TOTAL	M	F	White	Black	NE	NC	S	W	Yes	No	None	Mari-juana Only	Few Pills	More Pills	Any Her-oin
1. Not at all	42.6	41.2	43.5	41.6	58.7	36.1	42.0	53.2	36.0	34.7	46.1	-	-	80.0	36.0	45.9
2. A few of the times	22.9	25.3	20.9	24.4	-	22.7	31.4	15.1	16.5	25.4	22.7	-	-	10.1	25.5	19.8
3. Some of the times	12.5	16.0	8.8	12.6	-	14.5	5.3	18.4	15.2	9.9	13.2	-	-	-	13.2	21.3
4. Most of the times	7.0	6.5	8.2	6.7	41.3	5.2	7.7	6.9	9.7	6.8	8.3	-	-	-	8.8	3.4
5. Every time	14.9	10.9	18.6	14.6	-	21.4	13.6	6.4	22.6	23.3	9.7	-	-	9.9	16.5	9.6
Item 5090 N(Wtd) ★	179	80	90	163	2	49	61	47	21	77	72	-	-	22	136	21

B096H: At school

	TOTAL	M	F	White	Black	NE	NC	S	W	Yes	No	None	Mari-juana Only	Few Pills	More Pills	Any Her-oin
1. Not at all	74.9	69.6	80.4	73.9	100.0	74.4	79.9	78.6	53.4	78.8	71.1	-	-	87.1	73.6	70.3
2. A few of the times	10.9	12.3	8.8	12.0	-	13.1	5.8	11.6	18.8	8.6	15.5	-	-	7.8	11.1	13.2
3. Some of the times	9.2	8.9	8.8	8.7	-	6.5	6.8	8.2	24.1	7.3	9.1	-	-	5.1	9.7	9.8
4. Most of the times	2.7	6.1	-	2.9	-	3.9	3.5	1.6	-	1.0	4.3	-	-	-	3.6	-
5. Every time	2.3	3.0	1.9	2.5	-	2.0	4.0	-	3.6	4.3	-	-	-	2.0	6.6
Item 5100 N(Wtd) ★	178	78	90	162	2	50	60	47	21	78	70	-	-	22	135	21

B096I: In a car

	TOTAL	M	F	White	Black	NE	NC	S	W	Yes	No	None	Mari-juana Only	Few Pills	More Pills	Any Her-oin
1. Not at all	55.2	55.9	57.7	56.4	41.3	59.9	49.3	57.7	55.2	61.7	56.0	-	-	66.0	54.8	46.0
2. A few of the times	18.1	22.8	13.1	16.4	58.7	13.7	14.7	23.8	25.5	19.3	18.7	-	-	8.0	17.3	34.2
3. Some of the times	12.6	8.3	14.8	12.2	-	11.2	18.1	5.7	15.8	10.1	14.1	-	-	-	14.6	13.0
4. Most of the times	5.3	7.4	4.0	5.8	-	5.8	6.5	5.7	-	2.1	7.7	-	-	-	6.5	3.1
5. Every time	8.8	5.7	10.4	9.2	-	9.3	11.5	7.2	3.5	6.8	3.5	-	-	26.0	6.8	3.7
Item 5120 N(Wtd) ★	180	80	91	164	2	50	61	47	22	79	72	-	-	22	137	21

B097: How many of the times when you used narcotics other than heroin during the last year did you use them along with each of the following drugs--that is, so that their effects overlapped?

B097A: With alcohol

	TOTAL	M	F	White	Black	NE	NC	S	W	Yes	No	None	Mari-juana Only	Few Pills	More Pills	Any Her-oin
1. Not at all	48.9	44.7	53.8	47.5	47.2	57.8	38.7	54.3	42.7	59.3	39.2	-	-	74.7	48.6	21.6
2. A few of the times	24.7	24.8	22.7	25.2	29.1	25.5	22.0	22.7	34.2	25.3	24.6	-	-	14.0	25.3	32.9
3. Some of the times	12.9	15.5	11.0	14.2	-	3.1	20.2	13.7	15.0	3.8	20.9	-	-	-	11.7	35.5
4. Most of the times	8.0	8.2	7.4	8.1	23.6	8.6	9.7	6.0	6.3	4.0	9.7	-	-	7.4	7.8	10.0
5. Every time	5.5	6.8	5.1	5.0	-	5.1	9.2	3.3	1.8	7.6	5.6	-	-	3.9	6.7	-
Item 5130 N(Wtd) ★	174	76	90	159	3	50	56	47	21	75	70	-	-	23	131	20

B097B: With marijuana

	TOTAL	M	F	White	Black	NE	NC	S	W	Yes	No	None	Mari-juana Only	Few Pills	More Pills	Any Her-oin
1. Not at all	29.2	23.5	34.8	29.9	41.2	23.1	24.7	32.7	47.7	38.7	23.2	-	-	42.7	29.3	14.7
2. A few of the times	17.5	17.3	17.3	17.7	-	23.3	12.9	21.7	6.9	14.9	23.3	-	-	27.2	14.2	27.6
3. Some of the times	13.9	17.5	10.7	14.7	20.6	11.6	15.8	14.3	13.5	11.5	16.7	-	-	-	14.7	23.9
4. Most of the times	16.3	20.8	12.6	17.0	-	16.9	18.2	14.1	14.4	10.8	20.6	-	-	4.5	17.4	21.6
5. Every time	23.1	20.9	24.6	20.7	38.2	25.1	28.4	17.2	17.5	24.1	16.2	-	-	25.6	24.4	12.2
Item 5140 N(Wtd) ★	174	75	90	159	2	49	57	47	21	74	70	-	-	22	131	21

★=excludes respondents for whom question was inappropriate.

QUESTIONNAIRE FORM 1 1978	TOTAL	SEX		RACE		REGION				4YR COLLEGE PLANS		ILLICIT DRUG USE: LIFETIME				
		M	F	White	Black	NE	NC	S	W	Yes	No	None	Marijuana Only	Few Pills	More Pills	Any Heroin
Weighted No. of Cases:	3799	1740	1842	2962	411	922	1096	1257	524	1758	1571	1301	1086	411	760	46
% of Weighted Total:	100.0	45.8	48.5	78.0	10.8	24.3	28.8	33.1	13.8	46.3	41.3	34.3	28.6	10.8	20.0	1.2

B097C: With LSD

1. Not at all	96.6	94.4	98.2	96.4	100.0	100.0	91.1	97.9	99.9	93.7	98.5	-	-	100.0	97.9	85.3
2. A few of the times	3.0	5.6	1.1	3.2	-	-	7.7	2.1	-	5.5	1.5	-	-	-	1.6	14.7
3. Some of the times	.4	-	.7	.4	-	-	1.2	-	-	.8	-	-	-	-	.5	-
4. Most of the times	-	-	-	-	-	-	-	-	-	-	-	-	-	-	-	-
5. Every time	-	-	-	-	-	-	-	-	-	-	-	-	-	-	-	-
Item 5150 N(Wtd) ★	169	73	88	157	2	48	52	47	21	75	65	-	-	22	126	20

B097D: With psychedelics other than LSD

1. Not at all	94.6	90.6	97.5	94.8	58.7	97.3	88.5	96.5	99.9	95.8	92.5	-	-	100.0	94.7	88.4
2. A few of the times	2.9	4.1	2.1	2.5	41.3	2.0	7.4	-	-	2.7	2.8	-	-	-	2.2	9.9
3. Some of the times	1.8	3.8	.4	2.0	-	.7	2.0	3.5	-	1.5	3.0	-	-	-	2.2	1.7
4. Most of the times	.7	1.5	-	.7	-	-	2.1	-	-	-	1.7	-	-	-	.9	-
5. Every time	-	-	-	-	-	-	-	-	-	-	-	-	-	-	-	-
Item 5160 N(Wtd) ★	170	73	88	157	2	48	53	47	21	75	66	-	-	22	127	20

B097E: With amphetamines

1. Not at all	89.2	87.2	89.9	88.9	58.7	86.1	87.2	94.3	90.4	91.1	86.7	-	-	100.0	86.4	94.8
2. A few of the times	5.5	7.5	4.4	5.4	41.3	10.6	3.6	2.1	6.3	7.4	4.4	-	-	-	7.4	-
3. Some of the times	4.6	3.8	5.7	5.0	-	3.3	7.1	3.6	3.3	1.5	7.2	-	-	-	5.3	5.2
4. Most of the times	.7	1.5	-	.7	-	-	2.1	-	-	-	1.7	-	-	-	.9	-
5. Every time	-	-	-	-	-	-	-	-	-	-	-	-	-	-	-	-
Item 5170 N(Wtd) ★	169	73	87	156	2	48	53	46	21	75	65	-	-	22	126	20

B097F: With quaaludes

1. Not at all	95.1	91.8	97.5	94.8	100.0	92.5	95.7	95.1	99.9	97.0	92.8	-	-	100.0	95.2	89.1
2. A few of the times	3.3	4.6	2.5	3.5	-	5.5	4.3	1.4	-	3.0	3.2	-	-	-	2.7	10.9
3. Some of the times	1.0	2.3	-	1.1	-	-	-	3.5	-	-	2.5	-	-	-	1.3	-
4. Most of the times	-	-	-	-	-	-	-	-	-	-	-	-	-	-	-	-
5. Every time	.6	1.3	-	.6	-	2.0	-	-	-	-	1.5	-	-	-	.8	-
Item 5180 N(Wtd) ★	169	73	88	157	1	49	52	47	21	74	66	-	-	22	128	20

B097G: With barbiturates

1. Not at all	92.8	93.1	92.3	93.1	33.3	96.0	87.0	94.4	96.7	95.6	89.7	-	-	100.0	91.3	94.6
2. A few of the times	5.4	4.6	6.2	5.0	66.7	3.3	11.1	2.1	3.3	4.4	5.7	-	-	-	6.6	3.6
3. Some of the times	1.8	2.3	1.5	1.9	-	.7	1.9	3.5	-	-	4.6	-	-	-	2.1	1.8
4. Most of the times	-	-	-	-	-	-	-	-	-	-	-	-	-	-	-	-
5. Every time	-	-	-	-	-	-	-	-	-	-	-	-	-	-	-	-
Item 5190 N(Wtd) ★	168	72	88	156	1	48	52	47	21	74	65	-	-	22	127	20

B097H: With tranquilizers

1. Not at all	95.3	97.7	93.3	95.2	100.0	97.2	90.7	96.5	99.9	97.2	91.7	-	-	100.0	93.7	100.0
2. A few of the times	3.1	-	5.6	3.1	-	2.8	7.4	-	-	2.8	4.3	-	-	-	4.2	-
3. Some of the times	1.6	2.3	1.1	1.7	-	-	1.9	3.5	-	-	4.0	-	-	-	2.1	-
4. Most of the times	-	-	-	-	-	-	-	-	-	-	-	-	-	-	-	-
5. Every time	-	-	-	-	-	-	-	-	-	-	-	-	-	-	-	-
Item 5200 N(Wtd) ★	166	71	86	155	1	48	52	47	19	72	65	-	-	22	124	20

B097I: With cocaine

1. Not at all	93.8	91.2	95.8	93.6	100.0	88.6	94.3	97.0	98.2	95.2	94.4	-	-	100.0	93.7	88.1
2. A few of the times	2.1	5.0	-	2.3	-	5.9	1.2	-	-	3.5	1.5	-	-	-	2.3	3.2
3. Some of the times	2.6	2.2	3.0	2.7	-	4.1	3.1	1.5	-	.8	2.6	-	-	-	3.4	-
4. Most of the times	1.1	1.1	.8	.9	-	.7	1.4	1.5	-	-	1.0	-	-	-	.3	7.0
5. Every time	.4	.5	.4	.5	-	.7	-	-	1.8	.5	.5	-	-	-	.3	1.7
Item 5210 N(Wtd) ★	168	71	88	156	2	49	53	45	20	74	65	-	-	22	125	20

★ = excludes respondents for whom question was inappropriate.

QUESTIONNAIRE FORM 1 1978	TOTAL	SEX		RACE		REGION				4YR COLLEGE PLANS		ILLICIT DRUG USE: LIFETIME				
		M	F	White	Black	NE	NC	S	W	Yes	No	None	Marijuana Only	Few Pills	More Pills	Any Heroin
Weighted No. of Cases:	3799	1740	1842	2962	411	922	1096	1257	524	1758	1571	1301	1086	411	760	46
% of Weighted Total:	100.0	45.8	48.5	78.0	10.8	24.3	28.8	33.1	13.8	46.3	41.3	34.3	28.6	10.8	20.0	1.2

B097J: With heroin

	TOTAL	M	F	White	Black	NE	NC	S	W	Yes	No	None	Mari-juana Only	Few Pills	More Pills	Any Heroin
1. Not at all	99.2	98.1	100.0	99.1	100.0	100.0	97.4	99.9	99.9	99.1	100.0	–	–	100.0	100.0	93.1
2. A few of the times	.8	1.9	–	.9	–	–	2.6	–	–	.9	–	–	–	–	–	6.9
3. Some of the times	–	–	–	–	–	–	–	–	–	–	–	–	–	–	–	–
4. Most of the times	–	–	–	–	–	–	–	–	–	–	–	–	–	–	–	–
5. Every time	–	–	–	–	–	–	–	–	–	–	–	–	–	–	–	–
Item 5220 N(Wtd) ★	169	73	88	157	2	48	53	47	20	74	66	–	–	22	126	20

B098: What have been the most important reasons for your using narcotics other than heroin without a doctor's orders? (Mark all that apply.)

	TOTAL	M	F	White	Black	NE	NC	S	W	Yes	No	None	Mari-juana Only	Few Pills	More Pills	Any Heroin
A. To experiment--to see what it's like	55.4	60.9	50.1	56.3	29.1	56.6	51.5	59.5	54.8	54.0	52.7	–	–	68.0	50.2	75.0
B. To relax or relieve tension	36.8	35.2	38.3	37.6	76.4	28.1	31.5	50.5	42.3	42.8	36.0	–	–	5.4	38.8	56.4
C. To feel good or get high	59.2	68.8	49.5	60.4	44.9	60.5	49.9	64.2	70.5	59.5	57.2	–	–	24.2	62.4	74.5
D. To seek deeper insights and understanding	12.8	22.6	3.7	12.1	60.6	6.0	18.7	7.1	23.8	13.5	11.6	–	–	–	11.3	35.1
E. To have a good time with my friends	31.8	39.9	23.9	31.2	44.9	27.8	34.4	29.6	38.3	34.1	30.2	–	–	31.4	29.9	44.1
F. To fit in with a group I like	2.8	4.9	1.2	3.1	–	–	5.7	2.3	2.2	4.7	.7	–	–	2.3	.9	14.9
G. To get away from my problems or troubles	14.3	16.7	13.5	14.4	31.5	4.0	22.0	19.5	5.7	13.6	19.4	–	–	14.2	12.2	27.5
H. Because of boredom, nothing else to do	14.1	17.8	10.6	14.3	60.6	13.9	14.0	17.9	6.8	11.2	20.0	–	–	5.5	12.5	32.2
I. Because of anger or frustration	7.9	5.5	9.9	7.1	39.4	7.2	12.3	3.8	5.7	10.3	5.9	–	–	13.3	6.7	9.5
J. To get through the day	6.5	3.3	9.8	6.3	–	3.5	10.1	4.4	7.7	6.6	7.9	–	–	–	7.0	9.7
K. To increase the effects of some other drug(s)	10.5	16.1	6.5	11.0	29.1	12.3	8.3	9.4	14.6	12.1	10.1	–	–	4.6	11.0	13.1
L. To decrease (offset) the effects of some other drug(s)	–	–	–	–	–	–	–	–	–	–	–	–	–	–	–	–
M. To get to sleep	17.8	14.7	20.7	18.3	31.5	13.7	18.5	11.6	37.2	16.2	20.9	–	–	–	19.8	22.9
N. As a substitute for heroin	.6	–	1.3	.7	–	–	1.9	–	–	–	1.6	–	–	–	.9	–
O. To relieve physical pain§	27.3	25.9	29.6	28.7	31.5	19.1	28.2	26.3	44.9	32.4	25.4	–	–	17.5	29.6	22.7
P. To control coughing§	26.6	26.2	25.4	27.0	–	22.8	27.5	21.8	42.5	28.2	29.2	–	–	32.2	28.5	9.8
Q. Because I am "hooked"--I have to have it	–	–	–	–	–	–	–	–	–	–	–	–	–	–	–	–
Item 5230-5370 N(Wtd) ★	170	76	86	154	3	47	57	44	22	74	69	–	–	21	128	21

B099: When you take narcotics other than heroin how high do you usually get?

	TOTAL	M	F	White	Black	NE	NC	S	W	Yes	No	None	Mari-juana Only	Few Pills	More Pills	Any Heroin
1. Not at all high	5.9	2.4	6.9	6.1	23.6	4.0	5.5	11.1	–	5.5	5.5	–	–	7.3	5.9	4.7
2. A little high	17.5	16.6	17.1	16.1	29.1	22.0	14.8	9.4	33.3	12.5	21.5	–	–	10.9	18.9	15.5
3. Moderately high	41.4	41.4	43.0	41.5	31.5	41.2	37.1	46.5	42.5	43.5	38.9	–	–	26.1	45.2	32.2
4. Very high	24.8	31.1	19.9	24.8	15.7	21.7	29.5	27.7	12.5	22.2	26.7	–	–	31.7	20.2	47.5
5. I don't take it to get high	10.4	8.6	13.1	11.5	–	11.1	13.3	5.4	11.7	16.3	7.4	–	–	24.0	9.8	–
Item 5380 N(Wtd) ★	179	78	89	161	3	50	60	48	21	75	71	–	–	22	136	21

B100: When you take narcotics other than heroin how long do you usually stay high?

	TOTAL	M	F	White	Black	NE	NC	S	W	Yes	No	None	Mari-juana Only	Few Pills	More Pills	Any Heroin
1. Usually don't get high	14.6	10.3	17.0	15.3	23.6	10.6	16.9	15.9	14.4	20.3	8.3	–	–	22.4	15.1	3.4
2. One to two hours	19.3	13.6	25.0	18.5	29.1	23.4	17.5	15.2	23.9	18.3	21.0	–	–	19.7	18.8	22.1
3. Three to six hours	50.2	53.5	46.9	51.4	47.2	47.6	45.2	60.5	45.8	42.3	54.7	–	–	48.0	48.9	60.6
4. Seven to 24 hours	15.9	22.6	11.1	14.7	–	18.4	20.3	8.4	15.9	19.2	16.0	–	–	10.0	17.3	13.9
5. More than 24 hours	–	–	–	–	–	–	–	–	–	–	–	–	–	–	–	–
Item 5390 N(Wtd) ★	173	78	86	160	3	47	56	48	22	76	68	–	–	22	130	21

B101: What narcotics other than heroin have you taken during the last year without a doctor's orders? (Mark all that apply.)

	TOTAL	M	F	White	Black	NE	NC	S	W	Yes	No	None	Mari-juana Only	Few Pills	More Pills	Any Heroin
A. Methadone	16.5	13.2	21.3	17.1	31.5	12.2	21.3	18.2	9.7	10.6	19.5	–	–	4.7	16.8	26.2
B. Opium	48.9	51.5	46.8	46.3	44.9	50.7	53.1	39.3	53.7	43.8	51.8	–	–	27.3	49.2	69.0
C. Morphine	13.5	11.6	16.8	14.2	–	13.6	16.8	14.0	3.2	13.5	15.7	–	–	10.3	13.3	18.1
D. Codeine	58.0	59.7	59.9	59.1	60.6	49.1	48.4	66.9	85.8	72.2	55.1	–	–	49.6	61.7	42.8
E. Demerol	21.8	19.9	24.5	22.2	31.5	16.0	15.6	31.1	32.1	19.9	20.3	–	–	6.1	24.3	21.4
F. Paregoric	5.1	5.3	5.4	5.6	–	6.3	4.2	7.2	–	4.3	5.0	–	–	7.9	3.8	10.3
G. Talwin	2.6	4.5	1.3	2.9	–	2.4	–	2.0	11.4	4.5	1.6	–	–	–	3.4	–
H. Laudanum	3.8	2.9	3.4	3.2	–	2.9	3.8	4.0	5.2	2.3	5.0	–	–	–	4.6	3.2
I. Other	25.7	27.4	23.4	26.8	–	15.8	34.4	22.6	32.6	19.8	28.0	–	–	21.3	26.6	24.9
J. Don't know the names of some I have used	10.7	9.5	10.2	10.3	23.6	16.6	7.4	7.2	13.0	9.9	11.1	–	–	12.2	10.6	9.5
Item 5400-5490 N(Wtd) ★	176	77	89	159	3	50	58	46	22	76	69	–	–	21	134	21

★=excludes respondents for whom question was inappropriate.   §=category added in this data collection.

QUESTIONNAIRE FORM 1 1978	TOTAL	SEX		RACE		REGION				4YR COLLEGE PLANS		ILLICIT DRUG USE: LIFETIME				
		M	F	White	Black	NE	NC	S	W	Yes	No	None	Mari-juana Only	Few Pills	More Pills	Any Her-oin
Weighted No. of Cases:	3799	1740	1842	2962	411	922	1096	1257	524	1758	1571	1301	1086	411	760	46
% of Weighted Total:	100.0	45.8	48.5	78.0	10.8	24.3	28.8	33.1	13.8	46.3	41.3	34.3	28.6	10.8	20.0	1.2

B102: Have you ever tried to stop using narcotics other than heroin and found that you couldn't stop?

	TOTAL	M	F	White	Black	NE	NC	S	W	Yes	No	None	Mari-juana Only	Few Pills	More Pills	Any Her-oin
1. Yes	2.5	1.3	2.2	1.9	-	4.8	1.9	2.0	-	-	4.3	-	-	-	2.6	4.7
2. No	97.5	98.7	97.8	98.1	100.0	95.2	98.1	98.0	99.9	100.0	95.7	-	-	100.0	97.4	95.3
Item 5500 N(Wtd) ★	179	77	91	162	3	50	57	49	22	76	71	-	-	22	135	21

B103: What methods have you used for taking any of these narcotics other than heroin? (Mark all that apply.)

	TOTAL	M	F	White	Black	NE	NC	S	W	Yes	No	None	Mari-juana Only	Few Pills	More Pills	Any Her-oin
A. Sniffing or "snorting"	32.3	39.7	29.3	33.0	60.6	24.9	41.7	29.3	31.2	24.7	40.4	-	-	7.4	33.0	52.1
B. Smoking	47.0	46.0	45.8	44.2	44.9	53.7	55.3	28.1	50.2	43.2	47.2	-	-	43.2	47.2	43.9
C. Injection	5.1	7.5	3.6	5.1	29.1	4.1	4.4	9.3	-	2.8	8.7	-	-	-	2.8	25.8
D. By mouth	70.4	68.2	74.7	72.3	60.6	60.8	64.1	82.7	84.1	81.4	62.9	-	-	64.0	74.6	52.7
E. Other	8.0	6.2	9.8	7.9	52.8	5.6	9.2	9.0	8.7	6.3	9.6	-	-	3.2	7.5	12.5
Item 5510-5550 N(Wtd) ★	181	79	91	164	3	53	59	48	22	78	72	-	-	22	136	21

B104: Do you think you will be using any narcotics other than heroin without a doctor's orders five years from now?

	TOTAL	M	F	White	Black	NE	NC	S	W	Yes	No	None	Mari-juana Only	Few Pills	More Pills	Any Her-oin
1. I definitely will	.5	.7	.3	.4	.4	.8	.6	.4	.3	.2	.9	.6	.3	.2	.8	3.9
2. I probably will	2.7	2.7	2.7	3.0	1.2	2.6	3.5	2.0	2.6	2.0	3.3	.1	.2	3.3	9.1	35.7
3. I probably will not	17.8	19.7	15.9	18.4	14.9	19.1	18.3	18.2	13.6	15.1	19.2	9.1	13.2	25.0	37.8	18.7
4. I definitely will not	79.0	76.9	81.1	78.2	83.5	77.5	77.6	79.4	83.5	82.7	76.6	90.2	86.3	71.5	52.3	41.7
Item 5560 N(Wtd)	3492	1642	1759	2844	376	810	1033	1166	482	1698	1484	1257	1013	387	672	43

B105: When (if ever) did you FIRST do each of the following things? Don't count anything you took because a doctor told you to.

B105A: Smoke cigarettes on a daily basis

	TOTAL	M	F	White	Black	NE	NC	S	W	Yes	No	None	Mari-juana Only	Few Pills	More Pills	Any Her-oin
8. Never	54.4	56.1	52.9	54.5	55.9	49.8	54.1	54.2	63.5	65.4	44.7	83.9	48.4	40.7	20.9	12.6
1. Grade 6 or below	5.3	6.5	3.9	5.4	3.3	4.9	5.4	5.3	5.6	4.3	6.1	2.3	5.3	6.5	8.4	31.3
2. Grade 7 or 8	13.2	12.3	14.1	13.6	8.7	15.9	12.2	14.0	8.7	10.3	15.7	4.8	12.1	19.2	25.1	23.4
3. Grade 9 (Freshman)	10.4	10.0	10.8	10.2	10.1	13.1	11.3	8.6	7.6	7.3	13.0	2.9	12.0	11.5	21.1	14.6
4. Grade 10 (Sophomore)	7.5	7.2	7.8	7.3	9.1	8.2	6.3	7.9	7.6	5.1	9.2	2.3	10.2	9.2	12.0	1.6
5. Grade 11 (Junior)	6.5	6.0	6.8	6.3	8.8	6.4	7.9	5.9	4.7	4.8	8.1	2.2	8.1	9.3	8.9	16.4
6. Grade 12 (Senior)	2.9	1.9	3.6	2.6	4.0	1.7	2.8	4.1	2.3	2.9	3.2	1.5	3.8	3.6	3.6	-
Item 5570 N(Wtd)	3285	1571	1652	2747	307	796	982	1068	439	1617	1399	1177	946	362	663	40

B105B: Try an alcoholic beverage-- more than just a few sips

	TOTAL	M	F	White	Black	NE	NC	S	W	Yes	No	None	Mari-juana Only	Few Pills	More Pills	Any Her-oin
8. Never	6.8	4.8	8.6	5.9	13.7	3.4	4.4	9.5	11.9	6.9	7.0	17.8	1.0	2.4	.4	-
1. Grade 6 or below	9.0	10.5	7.2	8.7	6.9	9.5	10.4	7.4	8.6	8.6	9.2	6.3	6.1	13.3	13.7	35.8
2. Grade 7 or 8	24.0	26.9	21.2	24.9	17.0	29.7	24.4	20.1	22.4	22.9	24.4	11.5	25.7	32.4	37.0	26.0
3. Grade 9 (Freshman)	23.7	24.5	22.8	24.9	16.1	24.1	24.9	22.6	22.7	22.8	24.5	17.3	27.8	24.6	26.3	26.9
4. Grade 10 (Sophomore)	17.8	17.1	18.9	18.1	19.6	16.8	18.4	19.2	15.3	19.3	16.8	17.5	22.5	13.8	14.9	9.6
5. Grade 11 (Junior)	13.0	11.9	14.4	12.8	16.1	11.4	12.2	15.2	12.7	14.0	12.4	18.5	13.3	10.0	5.7	1.7
6. Grade 12 (Senior)	5.6	4.3	6.9	4.7	10.6	5.1	5.4	6.0	6.3	5.5	5.6	11.0	3.5	3.5	1.9	-
Item 5580 N(Wtd)	3168	1514	1594	2664	286	773	956	1018	420	1556	1347	1045	956	366	672	37

B105C: Try marijuana or hashish

	TOTAL	M	F	White	Black	NE	NC	S	W	Yes	No	None	Mari-juana Only	Few Pills	More Pills	Any Her-oin
8. Never	40.4	35.8	44.9	39.2	48.7	32.1	39.2	47.0	41.9	44.7	38.8	100.0	-	18.1	6.2	2.4
1. Grade 6 or below	1.7	2.7	.6	1.5	1.9	1.9	1.6	1.0	3.1	1.0	2.1	-	1.4	2.0	3.7	22.0
2. Grade 7 or 8	12.9	14.7	11.1	13.5	7.0	14.4	12.9	11.9	12.4	11.5	12.5	-	12.1	17.5	33.5	44.5
3. Grade 9 (Freshman)	15.4	15.4	15.1	15.6	12.7	19.3	14.2	14.0	14.4	13.2	17.1	-	21.4	23.9	28.8	22.5
4. Grade 10 (Sophomore)	14.3	15.5	13.3	15.0	12.3	18.2	13.8	11.7	14.5	13.8	14.1	-	25.9	21.3	19.8	4.3
5. Grade 11 (Junior)	10.6	10.7	10.7	10.7	12.0	9.1	13.2	9.6	10.1	11.1	10.6	-	26.5	12.2	6.3	1.5
6. Grade 12 (Senior)	4.7	5.1	4.3	4.6	5.4	5.0	5.0	4.7	3.5	4.7	4.9	-	12.7	5.0	1.6	2.6
Item 5590 N(Wtd)	3290	1565	1667	2755	312	794	989	1064	443	1635	1383	1194	936	364	669	40

★ = excludes respondents for whom question was inappropriate.

QUESTIONNAIRE FORM 1 1978	TOTAL	SEX		RACE		REGION				4YR COLLEGE PLANS		ILLICIT DRUG USE: LIFETIME				
		M	F	White	Black	NE	NC	S	W	Yes	No	None	Marijuana Only	Few Pills	More Pills	Any Heroin
Weighted No. of Cases:	3799	1740	1842	2962	411	922	1096	1257	524	1758	1571	1301	1086	411	760	46
% of Weighted Total:	100.0	45.8	48.5	78.0	10.8	24.3	28.8	33.1	13.8	46.3	41.3	34.3	28.6	10.8	20.0	1.2

B105D: Try LSD

	TOTAL	M	F	White	Black	NE	NC	S	W	Yes	No	None	Marijuana Only	Few Pills	More Pills	Any Heroin
8. Never	92.2	90.9	93.5	91.5	99.0	90.7	90.4	95.5	91.1	94.7	92.0	100.0	100.0	94.8	66.9	20.0
1. Grade 6 or below	.1	.1	.1	.1	-	.3	-	.1	.2	-	.2	-	-	.1	.5	1.8
2. Grade 7 or 8	.9	.8	1.0	1.0	.3	.9	1.2	.5	1.6	.7	1.0	-	-	.9	3.6	14.6
3. Grade 9 (Freshman)	1.8	2.5	1.3	2.0	.1	1.6	2.3	1.2	2.6	1.1	2.0	-	-	.5	7.8	26.7
4. Grade 10 (Sophomore)	1.9	2.8	1.2	2.2	.6	2.7	2.5	.8	2.0	1.5	2.0	-	-	.7	8.2	25.7
5. Grade 11 (Junior)	1.7	1.7	1.6	1.9	-	2.5	1.9	1.0	1.4	1.2	1.3	-	-	.5	8.4	4.0
6. Grade 12 (Senior)	1.2	1.3	1.2	1.3	-	1.3	1.7	.9	1.0	.8	1.5	-	-	2.5	4.7	7.3
Item 5600 N(Wtd)	3300	1574	1665	2736	326	788	983	1081	448	1631	1401	1205	965	375	625	38

B105E: Try any psychedelic other than LSD

	TOTAL	M	F	White	Black	NE	NC	S	W	Yes	No	None	Marijuana Only	Few Pills	More Pills	Any Heroin
8. Never	90.7	89.6	92.1	89.9	98.8	88.0	90.0	93.3	90.8	93.1	90.6	100.0	100.0	92.6	57.6	14.0
1. Grade 6 or below	.1	.1	.1	.1	-	.3	-	-	.3	-	.2	-	-	-	.5	-
2. Grade 7 or 8	.8	.7	.9	.9	-	.9	.8	.8	.5	.8	.7	-	-	1.1	3.0	12.4
3. Grade 9 (Freshman)	1.9	2.1	1.7	2.0	.2	1.6	2.5	1.2	3.0	1.4	1.9	-	-	.6	8.5	32.9
4. Grade 10 (Sophomore)	2.5	3.5	1.7	2.8	.8	4.2	2.5	1.7	1.4	1.8	2.6	-	-	1.7	12.7	6.5
5. Grade 11 (Junior)	3.0	2.9	2.8	3.3	.3	4.3	2.9	2.1	2.9	2.1	3.1	-	-	2.6	13.4	27.6
6. Grade 12 (Senior)	1.0	1.2	.8	1.0	-	.7	1.3	.8	1.1	.8	1.0	-	-	1.3	4.3	6.7
Item 5610 N(Wtd)	3223	1522	1640	2668	325	764	956	1065	438	1608	1358	1208	971	343	570	36

B105F: Try amphetamines

	TOTAL	M	F	White	Black	NE	NC	S	W	Yes	No	None	Marijuana Only	Few Pills	More Pills	Any Heroin
8. Never	83.6	83.7	83.7	81.8	95.8	81.2	83.0	85.7	83.7	86.5	82.9	100.0	100.0	80.3	23.5	7.6
1. Grade 6 or below	.1	.2	-	.1	-	.1	-	.3	-	-	.2	-	-	-	.2	8.6
2. Grade 7 or 8	1.2	1.0	1.6	1.4	-	1.1	1.7	.9	1.2	1.0	1.5	-	-	.7	4.8	25.3
3. Grade 9 (Freshman)	3.5	3.4	3.6	3.9	.7	3.8	3.4	2.8	5.2	2.6	3.6	-	-	1.5	17.7	22.7
4. Grade 10 (Sophomore)	4.4	4.4	4.4	4.8	1.6	5.7	4.8	3.5	3.1	3.4	4.6	-	-	4.0	21.3	21.4
5. Grade 11 (Junior)	4.5	4.6	4.3	5.1	1.2	4.9	4.6	4.8	3.2	3.7	4.9	-	-	6.2	21.7	10.6
6. Grade 12 (Senior)	2.7	2.8	2.4	2.9	.6	3.2	2.5	2.0	3.6	2.8	2.3	-	-	7.2	10.8	3.9
Item 5620 N(Wtd)	3178	1508	1611	2632	317	754	944	1050	430	1585	1341	1205	971	319	556	36

B105G: Try quaaludes

	TOTAL	M	F	White	Black	NE	NC	S	W	Yes	No	None	Marijuana Only	Few Pills	More Pills	Any Heroin
8. Never	93.9	93.5	94.2	93.5	98.9	92.0	95.4	93.5	94.5	94.7	94.7	100.0	100.0	96.0	73.5	22.2
1. Grade 6 or below	.1	.1	-	*	-	.2	-	-	-	-	.1	-	-	-	.3	-
2. Grade 7 or 8	.6	.5	.7	.7	-	*	.7	.7	1.0	.4	.3	-	-	.4	2.2	14.6
3. Grade 9 (Freshman)	1.0	.9	1.0	1.1	.3	.9	.6	1.5	.9	1.0	.8	-	-	.4	4.5	11.2
4. Grade 10 (Sophomore)	1.8	1.9	1.7	1.8	.5	2.2	1.5	1.7	1.9	1.4	1.9	-	-	1.0	8.1	17.9
5. Grade 11 (Junior)	1.7	1.8	1.5	1.9	-	2.8	1.2	1.7	.5	1.3	1.6	-	-	1.5	6.9	22.4
6. Grade 12 (Senior)	1.0	1.2	.8	1.1	.3	1.9	.5	.8	1.1	1.2	.5	-	-	.7	4.5	11.6
Item 5630 N(Wtd)	3291	1559	1675	2734	326	794	979	1072	447	1635	1393	1207	972	369	621	29

B105H: Try barbiturates

	TOTAL	M	F	White	Black	NE	NC	S	W	Yes	No	None	Marijuana Only	Few Pills	More Pills	Any Heroin
8. Never	90.4	90.5	90.7	89.6	97.6	88.2	90.5	90.9	93.1	93.8	88.6	100.0	100.0	92.7	56.3	17.4
1. Grade 6 or below	.2	.2	.1	.2	-	.1	.2	.3	-	*	.3	-	-	-	.5	8.8
2. Grade 7 or 8	1.3	1.0	1.5	1.4	-	1.4	1.5	1.0	.9	.9	1.3	-	-	.9	5.6	13.9
3. Grade 9 (Freshman)	1.9	2.1	1.8	2.0	.4	2.1	1.8	2.1	1.6	1.0	2.4	-	-	1.2	8.5	25.2
4. Grade 10 (Sophomore)	2.7	2.6	2.8	2.9	.9	3.2	3.1	2.2	2.3	2.1	2.7	-	-	1.9	12.4	26.9
5. Grade 11 (Junior)	2.1	2.2	1.9	2.3	.7	3.9	1.2	2.0	1.3	1.4	2.4	-	-	1.7	10.5	1.2
6. Grade 12 (Senior)	1.4	1.4	1.2	1.5	.3	1.0	1.8	1.5	.8	.7	2.3	-	-	1.6	6.2	6.5
Item 5640 N(Wtd)	3239	1530	1650	2692	316	771	965	1067	436	1606	1370	1207	971	352	583	35

B105I: Try tranquilizers

	TOTAL	M	F	White	Black	NE	NC	S	W	Yes	No	None	Marijuana Only	Few Pills	More Pills	Any Heroin
8. Never	88.4	89.5	87.3	87.3	95.6	87.1	89.7	87.4	89.9	89.8	88.0	100.0	100.0	79.1	50.9	35.1
1. Grade 6 or below	.5	.5	.4	.5	-	.3	.5	.5	.6	.5	.4	-	-	1.1	1.5	9.4
2. Grade 7 or 8	1.4	1.2	1.6	1.6	.3	1.2	1.4	1.4	1.6	1.3	1.3	-	-	2.3	5.7	11.8
3. Grade 9 (Freshman)	2.6	2.0	3.3	2.9	1.1	3.0	2.4	2.2	3.4	2.2	3.0	-	-	3.9	11.4	17.0
4. Grade 10 (Sophomore)	2.7	2.8	2.7	3.0	.3	2.6	2.2	3.5	2.1	2.7	2.4	-	-	2.7	12.4	20.6
5. Grade 11 (Junior)	3.0	2.7	3.2	3.2	2.2	3.6	2.7	3.7	1.3	2.4	3.3	-	-	7.5	12.4	4.2
6. Grade 12 (Senior)	1.4	1.3	1.5	1.5	.6	2.1	1.2	1.2	1.1	1.2	1.5	-	-	3.5	5.7	1.9
Item 5650 N(Wtd)	3172	1513	1600	2625	319	756	943	1044	429	1583	1338	1201	964	306	576	33

* = less than .05 per cent.

QUESTIONNAIRE FORM 1 1978	TOTAL	SEX		RACE		REGION				4YR COLLEGE PLANS		ILLICIT DRUG USE: LIFETIME				
		M	F	White	Black	NE	NC	S	W	Yes	No	None	Marijuana Only	Few Pills	More Pills	Any Heroin
Weighted No. of Cases:	3799	1740	1842	2962	411	922	1096	1257	524	1758	1571	1301	1086	411	760	46
% of Weighted Total:	100.0	45.8	48.5	78.0	10.8	24.3	28.8	33.1	13.8	46.3	41.3	34.3	28.6	10.8	20.0	1.2
B105J: Try cocaine																
8. Never	88.3	85.7	91.0	87.7	94.3	85.1	89.1	90.7	86.3	90.6	88.7	100.0	100.0	79.7	56.2	15.6
1. Grade 6 or below	.2	.3	-	.2	-	.2	*	.3	-	-	.3	-	-	-	.4	7.9
2. Grade 7 or 8	.5	.5	.6	.6	-	.5	.5	.3	1.3	.4	.6	-	-	.2	1.8	15.6
3. Grade 9 (Freshman)	1.1	1.6	.7	1.2	.2	1.3	1.4	.9	.8	.8	1.0	-	-	1.1	4.3	13.8
4. Grade 10 (Sophomore)	1.9	1.9	1.8	1.9	.7	2.1	1.8	1.8	2.3	1.4	1.6	-	-	1.6	8.4	11.4
5. Grade 11 (Junior)	4.2	5.4	3.0	4.4	2.9	4.9	4.1	3.5	4.8	3.3	4.7	-	-	7.0	16.5	19.0
6. Grade 12 (Senior)	3.7	4.6	3.0	4.0	1.8	5.9	3.1	2.4	4.6	3.5	3.1	-	-	10.3	12.5	16.6
Item 5660 N(Wtd)	3311	1569	1681	2754	324	792	986	1084	449	1637	1406	1205	973	359	643	39
B105K: Try heroin																
8. Never	98.9	98.7	99.1	98.9	99.7	99.2	98.9	98.7	99.0	99.2	99.0	100.0	100.0	100.0	100.0	-
1. Grade 6 or below	.1	.3	-	.2	-	-	-	.4	-	-	.3	-	-	-	-	13.3
2. Grade 7 or 8	.1	-	.2	.1	-	-	-	.2	.2	.1	-	-	-	-	-	8.8
3. Grade 9 (Freshman)	.2	.2	.2	.1	-	-	.2	.2	.3	.1	.1	-	-	-	-	16.0
4. Grade 10 (Sophomore)	.2	.1	.3	.2	-	.4	.3	-	-	.2	.1	-	-	-	-	16.4
5. Grade 11 (Junior)	.3	.5	.2	.3	.3	.3	.3	.4	.4	.3	.4	-	-	-	-	32.1
6. Grade 12 (Senior)	.1	.3	*	.1	-	.1	.3	-	.2	.1	.1	-	-	-	-	13.4
Item 5670 N(Wtd)	3318	1565	1693	2757	327	790	982	1092	454	1640	1413	1205	972	377	636	36
B105L: Try any narcotic other than heroin																
8. Never	92.8	92.4	93.2	92.3	98.4	91.7	91.2	94.9	93.0	94.3	92.8	100.0	100.0	91.2	71.0	18.5
1. Grade 6 or below	.4	.5	.2	.4	-	.3	.3	.5	.3	.2	.5	-	-	.3	1.2	7.8
2. Grade 7 or 8	.8	.9	.8	1.0	-	.4	.9	.7	1.8	1.1	.5	-	-	-	3.3	19.5
3. Grade 9 (Freshman)	1.0	1.1	.9	1.0	.3	.9	1.1	.6	1.7	.4	1.3	-	-	.5	4.2	11.6
4. Grade 10 (Sophomore)	1.6	1.7	1.4	1.7	.3	2.2	1.9	1.1	.9	1.2	1.4	-	-	.3	6.9	21.1
5. Grade 11 (Junior)	2.1	1.9	2.2	2.1	1.0	2.6	2.5	1.7	1.3	1.9	1.8	-	-	3.6	9.0	5.7
6. Grade 12 (Senior)	1.4	1.5	1.3	1.5	-	2.0	2.0	.6	1.0	1.0	1.6	-	-	4.1	4.3	15.8
Item 5680 N(Wtd)	3237	1539	1640	2686	319	763	963	1070	441	1601	1373	1205	965	341	594	39

The next questions are about your experiences in school.

	TOTAL	M	F	White	Black	NE	NC	S	W	Yes	No	None	Marijuana Only	Few Pills	More Pills	Any Heroin
D001: Some people like school very much. Others don't. How do you feel about going to school?																
5. I like school very much	14.3	13.7	14.4	12.4	25.8	10.9	13.0	16.5	17.0	17.9	10.3	18.5	11.8	10.6	10.3	15.2
4. I like school quite a lot	31.9	31.1	33.2	32.6	32.4	28.7	33.1	33.0	32.0	39.6	23.7	38.1	32.3	30.1	21.4	22.9
3. I like school some	38.9	41.2	36.7	39.6	33.3	40.5	37.4	39.4	38.4	33.5	45.1	34.9	41.9	41.3	41.3	38.7
2. I don't like school very much	10.7	10.1	11.0	11.2	6.2	14.3	11.4	8.3	8.9	7.1	14.2	6.1	10.9	12.1	18.1	15.0
1. I don't like school at all	4.2	3.9	4.6	4.2	2.2	5.6	5.0	2.9	3.7	1.9	6.7	2.3	3.1	5.9	8.9	8.1
Item 7630 N(Wtd)	3346	1573	1718	2756	354	748	1019	1138	442	1721	1493	1225	984	370	594	36
D002: How often do you feel that the school work you are assigned is meaningful and important?																
5. Almost always	10.8	9.3	11.9	8.6	23.2	7.3	8.2	15.3	11.0	13.1	8.3	13.7	10.7	7.9	6.4	6.8
4. Often	26.3	27.5	25.4	25.7	29.4	25.8	26.6	25.4	28.6	30.0	22.3	30.0	25.4	26.4	19.7	19.1
3. Sometimes	42.7	40.8	44.2	44.5	36.6	41.1	43.8	42.3	43.9	41.6	44.0	43.7	43.5	40.8	41.3	50.1
2. Seldom	17.9	19.8	16.4	19.0	9.8	21.8	18.6	15.7	15.2	14.4	21.7	11.7	18.4	22.3	27.8	12.0
1. Never	2.4	2.7	2.1	2.2	1.1	3.9	2.9	1.3	1.4	1.0	3.6	.8	2.1	2.6	4.7	12.0
Item 5700 N(Wtd)	3341	1573	1715	2749	355	745	1018	1139	440	1717	1491	1225	981	370	593	36
D003: How interesting are most of your courses to you?																
5. Very exciting and stimulating	3.9	3.0	4.6	3.0	9.1	3.9	2.6	4.3	6.1	4.7	3.0	4.6	3.9	3.8	2.0	2.9
4. Quite interesting	28.7	28.3	29.2	27.4	37.2	23.3	30.3	30.3	30.1	33.1	24.1	34.8	26.5	30.2	20.2	19.2
3. Fairly interesting	46.4	44.7	47.9	47.5	40.4	47.5	46.3	46.7	44.2	45.4	47.7	45.7	48.3	44.9	45.0	53.7
2. Slightly dull	16.4	18.8	14.5	17.7	9.6	17.5	16.2	15.8	16.5	14.0	18.8	12.2	16.6	17.9	24.4	11.3
1. Very dull	4.5	5.1	3.9	4.4	3.7	7.7	4.7	2.9	3.1	2.7	6.4	2.7	4.6	3.2	8.4	13.0
Item 5710 N(Wtd)	3335	1568	1713	2746	354	746	1015	1138	437	1717	1487	1221	983	368	591	36

* = less than .05 per cent.

QUESTIONNAIRE FORM 1 1978	TOTAL	SEX		RACE		REGION				4YR COLLEGE PLANS		ILLICIT DRUG USE: LIFETIME				
		M	F	White	Black	NE	NC	S	W	Yes	No	None	Mari- juana Only	Few Pills	More Pills	Any Her- oin
Weighted No. of Cases:	3799	1740	1842	2962	411	922	1096	1257	524	1758	1571	1301	1086	411	760	46
% of Weighted Total:	100.0	45.8	48.5	78.0	10.8	24.3	28.8	33.1	13.8	46.3	41.3	34.3	28.6	10.8	20.0	1.2
D004: How important do you think the things you are learning in school are going to be for your later life?																
5. Very important	18.9	18.6	19.0	15.3	43.9	14.0	15.1	25.7	18.2	21.2	16.2	22.1	18.1	11.7	16.2	20.0
4. Quite important	29.2	29.3	29.2	29.6	26.9	25.7	28.5	31.3	31.4	31.6	26.6	33.8	26.7	32.0	22.9	17.9
3. Fairly important	32.6	32.2	32.8	34.8	18.0	35.2	36.6	27.0	33.5	32.1	33.3	31.0	33.1	34.9	35.9	47.7
2. Slightly important	16.4	17.6	15.7	17.6	8.1	20.4	16.8	13.9	15.0	13.7	19.5	11.8	19.3	17.6	19.5	5.1
1. Not at all important	2.9	2.3	3.3	2.8	3.0	4.7	3.0	2.1	1.8	1.5	4.4	1.2	2.8	3.9	5.5	9.3
Item 5720　N(Wtd)	3338	1568	1712	2746	355	747	1016	1140	435	1715	1490	1228	983	367	591	36
D005: How much competition for grades is there among students at your school?																
1. None	7.0	6.4	7.5	6.2	9.3	7.4	6.1	7.3	8.0	4.2	9.8	5.3	7.5	5.1	10.7	11.7
2. A little	22.1	21.8	22.3	23.4	16.5	22.4	23.7	19.8	24.3	19.1	25.5	20.0	23.1	22.9	24.7	31.5
3. Some	34.6	36.5	32.9	35.6	26.1	32.7	35.3	34.8	35.9	33.4	35.4	34.1	35.8	35.4	33.1	17.1
4. Quite a bit	26.6	26.3	27.3	25.8	35.0	26.2	27.0	27.0	25.5	30.5	23.1	29.8	23.4	27.5	24.3	26.3
5. A great deal	9.6	9.0	10.0	9.0	13.0	11.4	7.9	11.2	6.3	12.8	6.3	10.7	10.2	9.1	7.2	13.4
Item 5730　N(Wtd)	3328	1554	1710	2731	354	742	1010	1138	438	1708	1465	1227	971	369	594	38
D006: How do you think most of the students in your classes would feel if you cheated on a test?																
1. They would like it very much	1.8	2.2	1.1	1.4	3.1	2.2	1.4	1.8	1.8	1.0	2.5	2.3	.8	1.5	2.1	3.7
2. They would like it	2.1	2.4	1.7	2.0	2.6	3.6	1.6	1.8	1.7	1.7	2.4	1.4	2.2	1.5	3.5	4.9
3. They would not care	75.2	74.8	76.2	75.9	72.7	77.4	74.5	75.1	73.5	72.9	77.7	68.1	77.7	81.2	82.3	71.7
4. They would dislike it	16.6	17.0	16.1	17.1	13.4	13.6	19.6	15.2	18.0	19.6	13.8	21.6	15.6	12.8	10.7	14.2
5. They would dislike it very much	4.3	3.5	4.9	3.6	8.2	3.1	2.9	6.0	5.0	4.8	3.5	6.6	3.6	3.0	1.4	5.4
Item 5740　N(Wtd)	3340	1565	1711	2736	357	748	1006	1144	441	1710	1475	1227	970	369	601	38
D007: How do you think most of the students in your classes would feel if you intentionally did things to make your teachers angry?																
1. They would like it very much	3.7	5.2	2.0	3.1	6.7	4.3	3.5	4.3	2.0	3.0	4.5	4.3	2.7	3.3	2.7	7.8
2. They would like it	10.8	14.4	7.5	10.5	14.4	13.4	11.2	9.5	9.1	10.7	11.3	9.3	12.0	11.2	13.1	-
3. They would not care	43.5	42.7	44.4	43.0	46.8	46.3	40.5	46.1	39.3	38.7	48.9	38.1	45.6	44.7	50.7	53.3
4. They would dislike it	34.9	32.0	37.8	36.6	24.2	29.9	37.4	32.8	42.7	40.8	28.4	39.1	33.9	35.6	28.6	19.4
5. They would dislike it very much	7.0	5.6	8.3	6.7	7.9	6.2	7.3	7.3	6.9	6.8	6.9	9.1	5.8	5.3	5.0	19.6
Item 5750　N(Wtd)	3325	1559	1703	2731	350	740	1007	1138	440	1702	1472	1223	965	369	594	38
D008: How often do you find that your friends encourage you to do things which your teachers wouldn't like?																
1. Never	35.2	23.4	46.3	32.4	54.4	34.4	32.0	36.1	41.3	33.6	36.7	35.7	35.9	36.8	30.2	41.1
2. Seldom	36.3	38.6	34.2	38.1	26.7	36.9	37.1	35.8	34.8	39.8	32.8	37.8	37.1	33.0	36.5	28.4
3. Sometimes	22.7	29.3	16.6	23.5	15.2	22.3	23.5	22.9	21.2	21.9	23.6	20.8	21.7	23.9	27.7	19.0
4. Often	4.7	7.1	2.2	5.1	2.3	5.6	6.2	3.7	2.2	4.0	5.7	4.3	4.6	5.7	4.8	4.4
5. Almost always	1.1	1.5	.6	1.0	1.5	.8	1.1	1.5	.6	.7	1.3	1.4	.6	.5	.9	7.2
Item 5760　N(Wtd)	3330	1561	1706	2730	354	740	1006	1143	441	1705	1474	1226	967	370	594	38
D009: Have you ever been in a work-study program--that is, a program where you work on a job as part of your schooling?																
1. No, not ever	75.7	76.8	75.0	77.2	69.2	82.7	79.2	72.1	65.3	83.9	67.3	79.6	76.4	75.6	68.2	72.1
2. Yes, for a half year or less	8.5	8.9	8.1	7.8	12.0	7.1	6.9	8.0	15.7	6.1	10.9	6.9	8.6	9.9	10.9	1.9
3. Yes, for about a year	11.7	10.0	13.2	11.3	13.7	7.5	11.2	14.1	13.8	6.9	16.8	10.8	10.0	11.2	15.8	13.0
4. Yes, for about two years	3.0	3.0	3.0	2.8	3.6	1.6	1.9	4.8	3.2	2.4	3.5	1.8	3.6	2.7	4.1	7.4
5. Yes, for more than two years	1.1	1.4	.8	.8	1.5	1.1	.7	1.1	2.0	.7	1.4	.9	1.4	.5	1.0	5.6
Item 5770　N(Wtd)	3328	1556	1708	2729	353	741	1007	1142	438	1702	1477	1228	964	370	593	38

QUESTIONNAIRE FORM 1 1978	TOTAL	SEX		RACE		REGION				4YR COLLEGE PLANS		ILLICIT DRUG USE: LIFETIME				
		M	F	White	Black	NE	NC	S	W	Yes	No	None	Mari-juana Only	Few Pills	More Pills	Any Her-oin
Weighted No. of Cases:	3799	1740	1842	2962	411	922	1096	1257	524	1758	1571	1301	1086	411	760	46
% of Weighted Total:	100.0	45.8	48.5	78.0	10.8	24.3	28.8	33.1	13.8	46.3	41.3	34.3	28.6	10.8	20.0	1.2

These last questions are about you and the counselors in your school.

D010: How many times this school year have you seen a counselor individually?

1. No times	13.5	13.3	13.3	13.6	13.6	12.0	13.0	15.6	11.5	8.2	18.8	15.4	12.3	11.7	11.8	14.0
2. 1 time	13.4	12.5	14.0	13.6	9.7	12.6	14.4	13.6	11.6	10.1	16.9	11.3	14.5	16.8	13.0	8.1
3. 2 times	18.8	17.9	19.8	19.0	18.5	19.0	19.8	18.8	16.3	17.1	21.7	18.6	18.3	21.5	18.2	23.0
4. 3 or 4 times	29.9	30.9	28.9	29.6	27.2	28.1	29.9	28.8	35.8	33.4	25.8	30.2	29.9	28.9	31.4	27.2
5. 5 - 7 times	13.7	13.8	13.8	14.0	15.6	15.7	13.2	13.3	12.5	17.4	9.5	13.6	14.0	13.4	14.6	4.8
6. 8 - 10 times	5.7	5.4	6.0	5.6	6.7	6.6	5.5	5.1	6.4	7.0	4.3	6.2	5.6	3.7	6.1	9.1
7. 11 or more times	5.0	6.1	4.1	4.6	8.7	6.1	4.2	4.7	5.9	6.8	3.0	4.6	5.3	4.0	4.9	13.9
Item 5780 N(Wtd)	3323	1553	1706	2727	351	737	1008	1141	437	1703	1472	1225	963	369	592	38

D011: How many times this school year have you seen a counselor as a part of a group of other students?

1. No times	55.4	53.1	57.6	57.1	46.5	57.4	59.4	52.8	50.0	51.7	59.1	54.9	56.1	54.8	56.1	56.3
2. 1 time	15.8	15.3	16.6	15.8	18.7	16.4	16.2	14.9	16.2	15.5	16.4	15.5	15.8	16.4	16.8	13.7
3. 2 times	13.5	14.8	12.0	12.7	15.7	14.3	12.4	13.1	15.2	15.3	11.7	13.8	13.0	16.6	12.4	5.6
4. 3 or 4 times	10.8	11.4	10.2	10.3	12.7	7.5	8.2	14.6	12.5	11.3	10.3	11.3	10.6	10.0	8.8	19.9
5. 5 - 7 times	2.4	2.6	2.2	2.0	4.4	1.6	2.3	2.9	2.5	3.2	1.2	2.7	2.3	1.2	2.6	-
6. 8 - 10 times	.7	.9	.6	.7	1.2	.8	.3	.8	1.4	1.0	.5	.5	.8	.5	1.3	-
7. 11 or more times	1.4	2.0	.8	1.4	.9	2.0	1.1	.9	2.2	2.0	.8	1.2	1.4	.5	2.0	4.5
Item 5790 N(Wtd)	3323	1558	1702	2729	351	738	1011	1140	434	1704	1472	1225	965	367	594	38

D012: Would you have preferred to see a counselor more or less often than you have during the past year?

5. Much more often	9.1	8.9	9.1	7.6	17.5	10.7	7.0	10.1	8.8	9.5	8.2	7.4	10.5	9.4	8.4	8.5
4. A little more often	23.6	22.7	24.2	23.5	22.3	23.1	23.1	22.7	27.8	24.9	22.2	26.0	21.8	24.6	20.6	18.7
3. About as often	52.7	53.7	52.3	55.0	44.0	47.5	55.3	53.5	53.0	54.8	51.1	54.2	53.2	52.8	53.5	38.4
2. A little less often	4.6	4.7	4.3	3.9	7.8	4.9	3.7	5.7	3.0	3.9	5.3	4.1	4.6	4.8	4.4	6.1
1. Much less often	10.1	10.0	10.1	10.0	8.4	13.7	11.0	8.0	7.5	7.0	13.2	8.3	9.9	8.3	13.1	28.3
Item 5800 N(Wtd)	3277	1542	1672	2690	346	726	1002	1119	429	1681	1452	1204	954	364	585	36

D013: How helpful have your sessions with a counselor been to you?

5. Extremely helpful	10.2	10.9	9.5	8.4	23.7	6.4	10.0	12.8	10.1	11.0	9.1	10.2	11.5	10.7	6.7	9.2
4. Quite helpful	22.9	23.3	22.9	21.6	28.9	19.3	21.0	25.1	27.7	25.9	19.6	23.9	24.6	22.3	19.0	11.9
3. Somewhat helpful	25.1	26.0	23.9	25.6	20.2	26.1	25.7	23.5	25.9	26.3	23.8	24.3	24.9	26.6	26.4	19.0
2. A little helpful	19.3	18.2	20.3	20.6	12.4	19.6	20.0	18.3	20.0	19.3	19.8	22.0	17.0	18.2	19.9	18.7
1. Not at all helpful	13.6	13.9	13.4	14.1	9.4	19.7	14.1	10.2	11.0	12.7	14.7	9.6	13.6	14.3	20.5	29.7
8. Did not see a counselor this year	9.0	7.7	10.0	9.7	5.4	8.9	9.3	10.1	5.2	5.0	12.9	10.0	8.4	7.9	7.6	11.4
Item 5810 N(Wtd)	3297	1540	1695	2705	348	728	1001	1134	433	1700	1452	1214	955	362	593	37

QUESTIONNAIRE FORM 2 1978	TOTAL	SEX		RACE		REGION				4YR COLLEGE PLANS		ILLICIT DRUG USE: LIFETIME				
		M	F	White	Black	NE	NC	S	W	Yes	No	None	Mari- juana Only	Few Pills	More Pills	Any Her- oin
Weighted No. of Cases:	3785	1737	1867	2960	430	931	1083	1266	505	1790	1657	1363	1005	474	760	68
% of Weighted Total:	100.0	45.9	49.3	78.2	11.4	24.6	28.6	33.4	13.3	47.3	43.8	36.0	26.6	12.5	20.1	1.8

A01: Taking all things together, how would you say things are these days--would you say you're very happy, pretty happy, or not too happy these days?

3. Very happy	21.2	19.3	23.4	21.9	18.0	17.9	19.3	24.3	23.5	24.5	18.5	24.9	20.7	17.5	17.3	19.7
2. Pretty happy	67.1	70.4	64.3	68.7	61.3	66.5	71.1	64.6	65.6	65.7	68.3	64.6	70.7	70.6	66.4	62.1
1. Not too happy	11.7	10.3	12.3	9.4	20.9	15.6	9.5	11.1	10.9	9.8	13.2	10.5	8.6	11.9	16.5	18.2
Item 1190 N(Wtd)	3677	1680	1835	2885	416	904	1050	1238	485	1751	1611	1336	977	463	735	66

A02: The next questions ask about the kinds of things you might do. † How often do you do each of the following?

A02A: Watch TV

5. Almost everyday	70.1	70.8	69.6	68.9	79.8	67.9	69.7	75.1	62.4	67.7	73.2	75.0	71.1	67.7	62.4	58.7
4. At least once a week	24.3	24.2	24.2	25.3	17.1	26.3	24.8	20.3	29.6	25.7	22.3	21.3	23.7	26.7	28.8	28.6
3. Once or twice a month	3.8	3.3	4.1	3.9	1.7	4.3	3.5	2.9	5.4	4.9	2.5	2.3	4.1	3.6	5.4	7.9
2. A few times a year	1.4	1.2	1.4	1.5	.5	1.3	1.5	1.3	1.6	1.2	1.5	1.0	.8	1.1	2.8	1.6
1. Never	.5	.4	.6	.4	1.0	.2	.6	.5	1.0	.5	.6	.3	.2	.9	.7	4.8
Item 5820 N(Wtd)	3754	1722	1861	2947	421	925	1081	1248	500	1782	1643	1361	995	468	757	63

A02B: Go to movies

5. Almost everyday	.2	.2	.2	.1	.5	.1	.1	.3	-	.1	.2	.2	.1	.4	-	-
4. At least once a week	11.2	10.0	12.5	10.5	13.3	9.5	10.4	13.2	11.4	8.1	14.7	9.8	11.4	12.0	13.1	10.6
3. Once or twice a month	53.9	52.5	55.4	56.7	40.0	50.4	57.7	51.8	57.0	56.1	52.2	50.4	60.5	55.9	51.2	53.0
2. A few times a year	32.0	34.4	29.5	30.5	41.0	38.5	29.0	31.0	29.1	33.7	29.6	34.6	27.0	30.6	34.0	34.8
1. Never	2.7	3.0	2.4	2.2	5.5	1.4	2.9	3.6	2.4	2.0	3.2	4.9	1.0	1.1	1.6	1.5
Item 5830 N(Wtd)	3754	1721	1859	2944	420	923	1081	1248	502	1780	1643	1358	997	467	754	66

A02C: Attend art shows, musical performances, or theater plays

5. Almost everyday	.4	.6	.1	.2	.9	.4	.2	.6	.2	.2	.4	.4	.1	.4	.3	3.0
4. At least once a week	1.7	2.0	1.4	1.2	3.8	1.9	1.1	1.9	2.0	2.4	1.0	1.1	1.4	3.0	1.8	7.6
3. Once or twice a month	10.4	11.0	10.1	10.5	11.3	11.1	10.1	9.9	11.1	14.2	6.1	8.0	10.3	12.3	12.7	21.2
2. A few times a year	55.4	52.5	58.9	57.3	49.6	56.0	56.5	52.9	58.8	63.8	46.9	56.9	57.9	50.6	54.4	42.4
1. Never	32.1	33.9	29.6	30.8	34.3	30.6	32.1	34.8	28.2	19.5	45.6	33.6	30.3	33.6	30.7	24.2
Item 5840 N(Wtd)	3766	1725	1866	2952	423	929	1078	1256	503	1784	1652	1358	1001	470	758	66

A02D: Ride around in a car (or motorcycle) just for fun

5. Almost everyday	38.4	43.5	33.0	38.2	36.6	36.1	37.9	42.1	34.7	29.4	47.7	26.3	36.3	44.3	55.1	75.0
4. At least once a week	31.6	31.1	32.1	32.2	30.2	30.5	32.7	32.2	29.9	32.9	30.3	31.8	35.9	31.3	28.6	16.2
3. Once or twice a month	14.4	12.6	16.8	14.9	13.5	14.1	15.3	13.1	16.0	19.0	10.1	16.5	15.8	15.0	9.5	2.9
2. A few times a year	9.1	7.8	10.3	8.9	11.6	10.7	8.4	7.9	11.1	10.7	7.5	15.2	6.9	4.5	4.5	4.4
1. Never	6.5	5.0	7.6	5.8	8.1	8.6	5.8	4.7	8.3	7.9	4.5	10.1	5.2	4.9	2.5	1.5
Item 5850 N(Wtd)	3764	1728	1861	2951	421	926	1077	1257	505	1783	1649	1354	1003	467	759	68

A02E: Participate in community affairs or volunteer work

5. Almost everyday	2.9	3.0	2.9	2.2	6.9	3.0	1.9	3.3	4.0	3.4	2.1	3.5	2.4	4.5	1.8	-
4. At least once a week	7.5	7.3	7.8	7.4	8.1	6.8	7.3	8.2	7.4	9.4	5.6	8.4	7.5	7.0	5.3	12.3
3. Once or twice a month	12.6	11.0	14.3	12.5	15.8	11.3	11.6	14.8	11.4	14.7	11.0	15.3	12.1	13.0	8.3	13.8
2. A few times a year	47.5	46.6	48.5	49.4	40.0	44.1	48.4	47.8	50.6	51.4	44.1	48.4	48.2	44.7	47.4	41.5
1. Never	29.6	32.1	26.5	28.5	29.2	34.8	30.9	25.9	26.7	21.1	37.2	24.3	29.9	30.9	37.2	33.8
Item 5860 N(Wtd)	3751	1724	1855	2944	418	922	1078	1249	502	1778	1648	1352	998	470	759	65

† Wording changed from previous year.

QUESTIONNAIRE FORM 2 1978	TOTAL	SEX		RACE		REGION				4YR COLLEGE PLANS		ILLICIT DRUG USE: LIFETIME				
		M	F	White	Black	NE	NC	S	W	Yes	No	None	Marijuana Only	Few Pills	More Pills	Any Heroin
Weighted No. of Cases:	3785	1737	1867	2960	430	931	1083	1266	505	1790	1657	1363	1005	474	760	68
% of Weighted Total:	100.0	45.9	49.3	78.2	11.4	24.6	28.6	33.4	13.3	47.3	43.8	36.0	26.6	12.5	20.1	1.8
A02F: Play a musical instrument or sing																
5. Almost everyday	30.0	25.5	34.0	29.7	32.3	28.3	30.0	32.1	28.0	35.0	24.1	32.4	26.8	30.1	29.7	36.4
4. At least once a week	11.6	10.2	13.0	11.2	13.4	9.9	10.4	12.7	14.1	12.6	10.9	13.4	10.8	9.9	10.3	7.6
3. Once or twice a month	5.3	5.4	5.7	5.2	6.9	4.5	5.3	6.2	4.6	6.2	4.5	5.5	5.2	5.6	5.3	4.5
2. A few times a year	11.6	11.7	11.5	11.7	10.0	11.1	12.9	10.6	12.1	11.6	11.7	12.0	12.0	11.2	10.6	10.6
1. Never	41.5	47.3	35.8	42.2	37.6	46.2	41.4	38.5	41.1	34.6	48.8	36.7	45.0	43.4	44.3	40.9
Item 5870 N(Wtd)	3748	1720	1856	2945	418	925	1075	1251	496	1779	1641	1353	996	465	758	66
A02G: Do creative writing																
5. Almost everyday	5.4	4.6	6.3	4.6	8.6	5.1	4.7	5.8	6.6	6.6	4.2	4.7	5.9	6.0	5.7	6.1
4. At least once a week	9.2	8.1	10.3	9.2	11.0	9.3	8.9	8.9	10.5	11.7	6.3	9.4	7.6	11.6	9.0	16.7
3. Once or twice a month	16.6	14.1	19.6	17.5	14.1	18.4	15.9	15.4	17.7	21.9	11.3	15.6	18.4	16.7	17.1	15.2
2. A few times a year	29.4	29.3	30.1	30.0	28.4	28.8	29.5	29.2	30.6	33.4	25.3	32.6	28.6	26.4	27.5	19.7
1. Never	39.4	43.9	33.6	38.7	37.9	38.5	40.9	40.8	34.6	26.4	52.9	37.7	39.4	39.1	40.7	43.9
Item 5880 N(Wtd)	3754	1725	1856	2948	419	927	1074	1250	503	1783	1642	1358	997	466	759	66
A02H: Actively participate in sports, athletics or exercising																
5. Almost everyday	45.6	53.2	37.9	45.4	44.7	49.1	42.1	44.0	50.7	53.2	36.6	44.5	50.2	42.2	44.1	33.8
4. At least once a week	25.4	25.2	26.0	26.0	26.0	25.4	24.1	26.5	25.4	25.0	25.4	24.9	24.6	25.4	25.4	29.4
3. Once or twice a month	12.3	9.2	15.7	12.9	11.1	10.3	14.2	13.0	10.1	11.2	14.2	12.2	12.6	11.8	12.9	16.2
2. A few times a year	11.0	7.9	13.8	10.4	12.8	8.6	13.7	11.0	9.3	8.1	14.8	12.2	8.1	13.1	11.1	16.2
1. Never	5.7	4.6	6.5	5.3	5.4	6.6	5.8	5.5	4.4	2.5	9.0	6.1	4.5	6.4	6.5	4.4
Item 5890 N(Wtd)	3765	1725	1864	2950	423	925	1078	1258	503	1787	1646	1357	1003	467	759	68
A02I: Do art or craft work																
5. Almost everyday	14.2	12.6	15.3	13.9	11.2	12.6	16.6	10.9	20.1	13.4	14.9	12.7	11.5	13.9	20.3	16.9
4. At least once a week	11.0	9.9	12.0	11.0	10.5	11.9	11.1	10.1	11.6	11.8	10.2	11.3	8.3	13.4	12.5	12.3
3. Once or twice a month	18.1	16.7	19.8	19.6	10.2	18.4	17.7	17.8	18.9	19.0	17.3	17.7	20.2	19.0	16.6	15.4
2. A few times a year	29.8	29.2	30.6	30.4	28.3	29.4	30.7	29.5	29.3	33.0	26.7	30.3	32.7	29.0	24.4	32.3
1. Never	26.9	31.5	22.3	25.1	39.8	27.7	23.9	31.7	20.1	22.8	30.9	28.0	27.3	24.5	26.1	21.5
Item 5900 N(Wtd)	3758	1725	1860	2949	420	925	1079	1253	502	1782	1646	1359	997	469	758	65
A02J: Work around the house, yard, garden, car, etc.																
5. Almost everyday	41.4	32.2	50.4	39.1	57.9	38.1	42.8	43.8	38.9	36.8	45.8	45.3	39.2	38.9	39.3	39.4
4. At least once a week	38.7	45.2	32.4	40.6	27.9	41.4	35.7	38.4	40.9	41.0	36.5	36.7	38.9	41.1	41.1	33.3
3. Once or twice a month	14.6	16.9	12.3	15.2	8.0	14.0	16.5	13.4	14.7	16.9	12.3	14.0	16.3	14.3	13.3	18.2
2. A few times a year	4.2	4.3	4.2	4.2	4.5	5.2	4.1	3.4	4.6	4.4	4.2	3.2	4.9	4.3	5.1	6.1
1. Never	1.1	1.4	.6	.9	1.7	1.3	.9	1.0	1.0	1.0	1.2	.7	.7	1.7	1.3	4.5
Item 5910 N(Wtd)	3774	1732	1867	2959	423	930	1082	1258	504	1788	1654	1362	1003	470	760	66
A02K: Get together with friends, informally																
5. Almost everyday	51.6	54.6	48.2	51.3	53.4	55.5	49.9	51.6	48.1	50.3	52.1	39.9	51.7	55.6	67.9	66.7
4. At least once a week	36.1	35.7	36.9	37.2	31.2	33.1	38.3	36.1	37.2	38.1	34.8	41.5	39.6	33.5	25.8	21.2
3. Once or twice a month	9.1	6.9	11.6	9.0	9.5	8.4	9.4	8.5	11.5	8.9	9.8	13.3	7.1	8.8	4.9	9.1
2. A few times a year	2.5	2.0	2.8	2.0	4.0	2.3	2.0	3.0	2.6	2.2	2.5	4.1	1.3	1.5	1.1	3.0
1. Never	.7	.8	.6	.5	1.9	.8	.5	.9	.6	.4	.9	1.1	.4	.9	.3	1.5
Item 5920 N(Wtd)	3753	1714	1861	2938	423	925	1073	1251	503	1778	1643	1356	996	466	759	66
A02L: Go shopping or window-shopping																
5. Almost everyday	3.4	1.9	4.8	2.4	7.6	3.9	2.3	4.2	3.0	2.1	4.3	2.5	3.2	5.1	4.0	1.5
4. At least once a week	35.6	22.0	48.4	34.6	46.1	38.4	34.7	36.1	31.3	34.5	37.7	37.8	35.5	37.9	30.6	35.4
3. Once or twice a month	43.7	45.6	42.1	45.4	36.5	41.1	45.6	41.6	49.9	47.2	40.2	43.5	43.4	45.0	44.5	41.5
2. A few times a year	12.9	21.8	4.4	13.3	6.9	11.8	13.5	13.4	12.5	13.5	12.1	12.7	13.2	8.8	14.8	13.8
1. Never	4.4	8.7	.2	4.2	2.9	5.0	3.9	4.7	3.2	2.7	5.7	3.5	4.5	3.2	6.1	7.7
Item 5930 N(Wtd)	3756	1723	1858	2946	419	925	1075	1250	505	1784	1644	1357	997	467	759	65

QUESTIONNAIRE FORM 2 1978	TOTAL	SEX		RACE		REGION				4YR COLLEGE PLANS		ILLICIT DRUG USE: LIFETIME				
		M	F	White	Black	NE	NC	S	W	Yes	No	None	Mari-juana Only	Few Pills	More Pills	Any Her-oin
Weighted No. of Cases:	3785	1737	1867	2960	430	931	1083	1266	505	1790	1657	1363	1005	474	760	68
% of Weighted Total:	100.0	45.9	49.3	78.2	11.4	24.6	28.6	33.4	13.3	47.3	43.8	36.0	26.6	12.5	20.1	1.8

A02M: Spend at least an hour of leisure time alone

5. Almost everyday	43.1	40.6	45.6	41.5	54.0	45.7	39.5	44.4	42.8	45.0	40.9	42.1	42.5	41.8	47.9	35.4
4. At least once a week	35.1	35.6	34.8	36.8	25.4	34.1	38.2	33.9	33.5	37.8	32.9	36.4	36.8	36.2	31.1	35.4
3. Once or twice a month	11.4	11.2	11.6	11.9	6.4	10.6	11.5	10.7	14.1	10.5	12.1	10.6	10.7	14.1	11.7	10.8
2. A few times a year	5.8	7.2	4.3	6.0	5.0	5.0	6.8	5.5	6.4	4.4	7.3	6.2	6.1	3.6	5.1	7.7
1. Never	4.6	5.4	3.6	3.8	9.0	4.7	4.0	5.5	3.4	2.4	6.8	4.7	4.0	4.5	4.3	12.3
Item 5940 N(Wtd)	3769	1729	1867	2957	422	927	1082	1258	502	1788	1650	1362	1002	469	760	65

A02N: Read books, magazines, or newspapers

5. Almost everyday	58.4	59.1	58.8	59.0	57.7	62.3	60.6	53.7	58.2	66.9	50.2	60.2	59.5	59.7	55.9	42.4
4. At least once a week	26.7	25.5	27.6	26.7	26.1	25.2	25.3	28.8	27.1	23.1	30.3	26.3	27.2	25.1	26.0	34.8
3. Once or twice a month	10.4	10.5	10.1	10.4	10.7	8.2	9.9	11.7	12.2	7.9	12.7	8.7	10.4	10.8	12.9	13.6
2. A few times a year	3.2	3.5	2.6	3.0	3.1	2.9	3.0	4.0	2.2	1.6	4.6	3.6	2.1	3.6	3.4	4.5
1. Never	1.3	1.4	.9	1.0	2.4	1.3	1.1	1.8	.4	.6	2.1	1.2	.9	.8	1.8	4.5
Item 5950 N(Wtd)	3768	1728	1864	2953	421	928	1082	1256	502	1787	1650	1363	1001	471	759	66

A02O: Go to taverns, bars or nightclubs

5. Almost everyday	2.9	4.4	1.3	2.8	1.9	3.1	3.3	2.8	1.6	1.4	4.3	1.5	1.9	3.0	6.3	7.6
4. At least once a week	20.8	24.8	16.9	21.3	18.8	26.0	23.0	20.2	8.3	18.7	22.6	8.7	25.5	27.3	30.4	40.9
3. Once or twice a month	20.9	23.1	18.6	21.6	18.1	21.6	20.8	23.3	13.5	21.9	19.2	13.6	25.5	24.5	25.7	22.7
2. A few times a year	18.0	16.9	19.4	18.4	17.1	18.3	19.5	16.1	19.2	19.4	16.5	16.9	22.2	15.9	17.1	10.6
1. Never	37.4	30.8	43.9	35.8	43.9	31.1	33.3	37.7	57.3	38.5	37.4	59.4	24.8	29.4	20.5	18.2
Item 5960 N(Wtd)	3774	1731	1865	2956	426	928	1082	1260	504	1788	1652	1361	1003	473	760	66

A02P: Go to parties or other social affairs

5. Almost everyday	3.3	4.6	2.0	3.4	2.8	4.4	3.0	2.6	3.8	1.9	4.8	.7	1.7	3.2	9.5	15.2
4. At least once a week	31.2	33.7	28.7	30.9	28.2	34.2	34.6	27.1	29.0	32.1	29.9	17.7	35.8	37.6	43.2	50.0
3. Once or twice a month	37.1	35.2	38.9	38.3	36.7	35.5	39.2	36.6	36.8	40.1	34.4	37.5	42.7	36.8	31.2	24.2
2. A few times a year	24.4	22.6	26.4	23.8	27.3	22.4	20.2	28.6	26.6	23.4	25.6	37.0	18.0	20.3	13.7	6.1
1. Never	4.0	3.9	4.0	3.6	4.9	3.7	3.1	5.1	4.0	2.5	5.3	7.1	1.8	2.3	2.4	1.5
Item 5970 N(Wtd)	3773	1728	1867	2955	425	928	1081	1260	503	1787	1650	1361	1003	473	759	66

A03: How much do you agree or disagree with each of the following statements?

A03A: In the United States, we put too much emphasis on making profits and not enough on human well-being

1. Disagree	4.3	6.1	2.5	4.1	4.6	3.3	2.7	6.1	5.3	5.1	3.1	5.2	4.4	3.4	3.1	3.0
2. Mostly disagree	9.0	10.8	7.5	9.0	8.2	7.0	9.5	9.8	9.5	9.4	8.5	8.9	10.2	8.5	8.6	7.6
3. Neither	13.2	15.9	10.9	14.3	8.6	12.7	14.2	12.8	13.3	13.7	13.5	12.3	13.5	15.8	12.5	13.6
4. Mostly agree	44.3	40.8	48.1	46.0	36.2	44.5	46.6	41.4	46.1	46.9	41.7	44.2	45.4	46.2	44.9	28.8
5. Agree	29.2	26.5	30.9	26.5	42.4	32.5	27.0	29.9	26.1	25.0	33.3	29.3	26.5	26.1	31.1	47.0
Item 5990 N(Wtd)	3741	1725	1848	2941	417	922	1075	1249	495	1782	1642	1355	993	468	753	66

A03B: People are too much concerned with material things these days

1. Disagree	3.6	4.5	2.7	3.1	8.3	4.0	2.0	4.3	4.2	3.1	4.1	3.3	3.4	4.5	3.3	3.0
2. Mostly disagree	5.6	7.4	3.6	5.7	5.5	5.3	6.0	5.3	6.1	5.3	5.6	4.9	6.3	4.9	6.6	3.0
3. Neither	9.4	13.1	5.9	10.0	5.7	9.6	11.1	7.9	8.9	8.5	9.9	8.0	9.5	10.8	11.1	10.4
4. Mostly agree	38.0	38.0	38.7	39.2	31.1	37.8	40.0	35.1	41.6	39.5	37.4	37.6	39.7	39.5	36.5	32.8
5. Agree	43.5	37.0	49.1	41.9	49.4	43.3	40.8	47.6	39.2	43.5	43.1	46.2	41.1	40.3	42.3	50.7
Item 6000 N(Wtd)	3748	1720	1851	2941	421	919	1077	1257	495	1778	1643	1358	990	471	756	67

QUESTIONNAIRE FORM 2 1978	TOTAL	SEX		RACE		REGION				4YR COLLEGE PLANS		ILLICIT DRUG USE: LIFETIME				
		M	F	White	Black	NE	NC	S	W	Yes	No	None	Marijuana Only	Few Pills	More Pills	Any Heroin
Weighted No. of Cases:	3785	1737	1867	2960	430	931	1083	1266	505	1790	1657	1363	1005	474	760	68
% of Weighted Total:	100.0	45.9	49.3	78.2	11.4	24.6	28.6	33.4	13.3	47.3	43.8	36.0	26.6	12.5	20.1	1.8

A03C: Since it helps the economy to grow, people should be encouraged to buy more

1. Disagree	23.2	20.7	24.8	21.0	35.5	22.5	17.7	28.4	22.8	18.8	27.3	22.2	21.2	24.4	24.2	41.2
2. Mostly disagree	24.8	20.1	29.9	25.8	17.7	23.5	26.6	23.7	25.8	25.7	24.4	25.3	25.5	25.9	24.4	20.6
3. Neither	27.6	27.4	28.0	29.4	19.7	28.9	31.4	23.2	27.6	32.0	23.5	27.6	30.4	26.7	26.2	14.7
4. Mostly agree	16.1	19.4	12.8	16.5	13.7	16.6	16.4	15.8	15.1	15.8	16.5	17.0	14.1	15.2	17.0	17.6
5. Agree	8.4	12.3	4.4	7.3	13.2	8.3	7.8	8.9	8.5	7.7	8.3	8.0	8.9	7.9	8.2	5.9
Item 6010 N(Wtd)	3736	1719	1848	2934	417	913	1075	1253	496	1775	1636	1353	993	468	747	68

A03D: There is nothing wrong with advertising that gets people to buy things they don't really need

1. Disagree	42.9	42.2	44.2	43.2	43.3	46.1	39.6	43.8	42.2	43.2	44.1	44.0	41.2	42.3	45.1	39.7
2. Mostly disagree	21.8	20.8	22.6	23.4	14.8	22.2	24.2	20.1	20.1	22.7	21.1	21.4	22.6	21.9	22.6	13.2
3. Neither	13.1	12.7	14.0	13.8	9.3	10.9	16.6	11.1	14.9	13.7	11.7	13.2	13.4	11.7	13.8	13.2
4. Mostly agree	10.9	12.0	9.7	10.1	13.4	9.8	10.9	11.6	11.6	10.9	11.1	11.0	11.4	11.5	9.4	10.3
5. Agree	11.2	12.4	9.5	9.5	19.1	11.0	8.8	13.4	11.2	9.4	12.0	10.3	11.5	12.6	9.3	23.5
Item 6020 N(Wtd)	3756	1722	1859	2949	418	926	1078	1253	498	1784	1645	1360	995	470	756	68

A03E: There will probably be more shortages in the future, so Americans will have to learn how to be happy with fewer "things"

1. Disagree	6.7	8.2	4.9	6.5	5.0	8.5	6.7	5.7	6.2	6.5	6.4	5.2	7.7	7.9	7.4	8.8
2. Mostly disagree	7.8	9.1	6.4	8.0	6.9	8.2	6.5	7.9	10.0	8.4	7.2	7.7	8.3	5.5	8.4	10.3
3. Neither	9.8	9.0	10.3	10.5	4.3	10.1	11.6	7.4	11.4	10.5	9.0	9.9	11.0	6.8	9.4	11.8
4. Mostly agree	26.9	27.3	26.6	28.3	21.9	29.3	28.6	24.5	24.9	28.6	25.3	26.5	28.5	29.6	25.9	19.1
5. Agree	48.7	46.3	51.7	46.6	61.9	43.9	46.6	54.5	47.4	46.0	52.1	50.7	44.4	50.1	48.8	50.0
Item 6030 N(Wtd)	3758	1724	1862	2950	420	923	1079	1257	498	1787	1645	1359	996	469	758	68

A04: Below are several ways that people have used to protest about serious social issues. How much do you approve or disapprove of these actions?

A04A: Signing petitions

4. Strongly approve	22.8	26.0	20.3	24.5	17.2	25.6	22.7	19.6	25.7	29.7	15.3	23.9	20.6	25.1	24.1	24.2
3. Approve	44.2	43.6	45.1	46.0	35.4	43.7	47.3	40.9	46.1	45.5	43.9	44.5	45.8	41.9	45.9	22.7
2. Disapprove	3.1	3.7	2.5	2.7	5.3	2.5	3.1	3.6	2.8	2.5	3.4	3.0	3.0	2.6	3.4	6.1
1. Strongly disapprove	1.2	1.7	.5	1.1	1.4	1.2	.7	1.5	1.6	.6	1.8	.8	1.2	1.1	1.2	4.5
8. Don't know, or it depends	28.8	25.1	31.6	25.7	40.4	27.0	26.2	34.3	23.6	21.7	35.5	27.8	29.4	29.4	25.4	42.4
Item 6040 N(Wtd)	3749	1719	1859	2948	418	926	1076	1249	499	1785	1643	1354	996	470	756	66

A04B: Boycotting certain products or stores

4. Strongly approve	18.0	22.0	14.6	18.7	16.0	25.5	16.6	14.2	16.6	23.1	12.2	16.5	18.1	18.0	22.0	15.4
3. Approve	36.9	38.8	35.6	38.3	33.8	39.3	37.5	34.5	37.1	40.9	33.4	33.9	41.0	37.4	37.6	33.8
2. Disapprove	14.0	14.0	14.0	13.9	14.8	8.5	16.2	16.1	13.8	11.0	17.4	15.7	12.0	15.3	12.3	21.5
1. Strongly disapprove	3.0	3.1	2.6	2.8	2.4	2.7	3.2	3.1	3.4	1.9	4.0	3.8	2.7	2.3	2.1	1.5
8. Don't know, or it depends	28.1	22.0	33.2	26.4	32.9	23.9	26.4	32.0	29.1	23.2	33.0	30.3	26.2	27.0	26.0	26.2
Item 6050 N(Wtd)	3746	1721	1853	2941	420	924	1071	1252	499	1777	1644	1352	994	471	758	65

A04C: Lawful demonstrations

4. Strongly approve	19.9	23.5	16.6	19.4	23.1	23.6	17.8	19.8	18.1	24.7	14.3	17.6	19.6	23.3	23.2	18.5
3. Approve	44.9	45.1	45.1	47.0	38.8	40.5	50.9	43.1	44.6	47.8	42.8	45.7	48.5	42.5	41.8	32.3
2. Disapprove	9.1	8.7	9.5	9.0	9.7	9.4	8.0	10.7	7.0	7.4	10.6	9.2	9.4	9.7	7.6	13.8
1. Strongly disapprove	3.9	3.9	3.8	3.5	4.6	3.6	3.3	3.5	7.0	2.8	5.0	5.1	3.0	3.0	2.7	7.7
8. Don't know, or it depends	22.2	18.8	24.9	21.1	23.8	23.0	20.0	23.0	23.3	17.2	27.4	22.4	19.4	21.8	24.6	27.7
Item 6060 N(Wtd)	3722	1710	1845	2931	412	917	1069	1238	498	1776	1634	1346	993	464	753	65

QUESTIONNAIRE FORM 2 1978	TOTAL	SEX		RACE		REGION				4YR COLLEGE PLANS		ILLICIT DRUG USE: LIFETIME				
		M	F	White	Black	NE	NC	S	W	Yes	No	None	Mari-juana Only	Few Pills	More Pills	Any Her-oin
Weighted No. of Cases:	3785	1737	1867	2960	430	931	1083	1266	505	1790	1657	1363	1005	474	760	68
% of Weighted Total:	100.0	45.9	49.3	78.2	11.4	24.6	28.6	33.4	13.3	47.3	43.8	36.0	26.6	12.5	20.1	1.8
A04D: Occupying buildings or factories																
4. Strongly approve	3.7	4.1	2.7	3.0	7.5	3.5	3.1	4.7	2.9	2.4	4.5	3.4	2.3	3.9	4.1	15.2
3. Approve	17.6	18.2	16.4	15.8	25.4	14.4	19.7	19.0	15.1	12.8	22.1	15.8	17.6	16.7	20.5	16.7
2. Disapprove	29.3	29.7	29.9	30.4	23.4	29.0	30.2	27.8	31.4	34.1	24.6	31.4	28.8	27.9	28.2	24.2
1. Strongly disapprove	16.9	21.2	13.0	18.4	12.1	15.8	15.6	17.0	21.0	21.3	13.2	19.7	18.1	15.2	12.3	13.6
8. Don't know, or it depends	32.6	26.8	38.1	32.4	31.9	37.3	31.2	31.5	29.6	29.3	35.6	29.7	33.1	36.3	34.8	28.8
Item 6070 N(Wtd)	3713	1706	1841	2918	414	915	1069	1240	490	1766	1631	1345	985	466	747	66
A04E: Wildcat strikes																
4. Strongly approve	3.2	4.9	1.4	3.2	3.2	3.4	2.3	3.7	3.1	2.5	3.9	2.4	3.0	3.4	4.0	12.3
3. Approve	10.5	13.2	7.9	10.5	10.0	9.9	12.7	9.3	9.4	9.9	11.1	8.6	10.0	10.5	14.7	7.7
2. Disapprove	31.8	30.1	33.2	32.4	31.7	31.0	32.6	32.1	30.5	33.4	30.7	31.9	32.5	34.2	28.4	33.8
1. Strongly disapprove	21.3	21.1	21.7	21.5	18.8	18.9	21.9	21.2	24.9	22.9	19.8	26.2	20.9	15.7	17.3	12.3
8. Don't know, or it depends	33.3	30.7	35.7	32.3	36.3	36.8	30.4	33.7	31.9	31.3	34.5	30.9	33.6	36.3	35.5	33.8
Item 6080 N(Wtd)	3691	1702	1824	2903	410	910	1061	1232	489	1752	1626	1335	979	465	744	65
A04F: Blocking traffic																
4. Strongly approve	2.3	2.9	1.7	2.0	4.1	3.5	1.2	2.7	2.0	1.5	3.2	1.9	2.2	1.7	2.6	6.1
3. Approve	3.6	3.9	2.9	3.1	4.9	4.0	4.0	2.9	3.6	3.0	4.0	2.9	3.7	3.2	4.6	3.0
2. Disapprove	39.1	35.8	41.8	38.9	41.7	38.6	40.8	38.9	36.8	39.2	39.1	37.8	40.6	39.8	37.9	36.4
1. Strongly disapprove	44.4	45.0	44.7	46.4	37.8	41.2	44.4	45.5	47.7	47.9	41.2	48.1	44.1	43.2	42.3	27.3
8. Don't know, or it depends	10.6	12.4	9.0	9.5	11.7	12.7	9.7	10.1	10.1	8.4	12.5	9.4	9.3	11.8	12.6	25.8
Item 6090 N(Wtd)	3734	1712	1853	2939	410	920	1075	1243	495	1777	1637	1347	996	465	755	66
A04G: Damaging things																
4. Strongly approve	2.2	2.5	1.6	2.0	1.7	2.1	1.2	2.8	3.0	1.0	3.2	1.6	1.7	.9	2.9	19.1
3. Approve	1.9	2.0	1.7	1.0	6.0	1.9	.8	2.6	1.8	1.4	2.3	1.2	1.8	1.7	2.9	4.4
2. Disapprove	19.5	20.4	17.5	17.8	27.5	19.9	18.4	21.2	17.0	15.7	22.5	16.7	19.7	18.8	22.5	25.0
1. Strongly disapprove	70.9	67.5	75.7	74.8	53.8	69.6	74.9	67.4	73.1	78.5	65.0	76.4	71.6	70.7	65.6	42.6
8. Don't know, or it depends	5.6	7.7	3.5	4.4	11.0	6.6	4.5	6.0	5.1	3.4	7.0	4.1	5.2	7.9	6.1	10.3
Item 6100 N(Wtd)	3751	1725	1858	2949	418	924	1077	1255	495	1780	1648	1357	997	468	756	68
A04H: Personal violence																
4. Strongly approve	2.5	2.7	1.9	2.1	3.1	2.4	1.2	3.5	3.0	1.1	3.5	1.8	1.6	1.3	3.8	14.7
3. Approve	2.7	3.4	1.8	1.9	5.8	2.9	1.5	3.2	3.2	1.0	4.1	1.9	2.0	2.8	4.0	10.3
2. Disapprove	18.3	20.5	15.9	16.7	28.7	18.5	17.4	19.6	16.6	15.6	21.1	15.4	20.8	15.1	20.7	20.6
1. Strongly disapprove	68.6	62.8	75.8	72.8	51.6	67.1	72.4	66.2	69.4	76.6	62.2	74.9	68.1	72.6	61.3	39.7
8. Don't know, or it depends	7.9	10.5	4.6	6.4	10.8	9.1	7.5	7.4	7.8	5.7	9.1	5.9	7.5	8.1	10.2	14.7
Item 6110 N(Wtd)	3752	1722	1859	2950	415	922	1077	1252	500	1781	1647	1357	995	470	757	68
A05: Do you think that you would prefer having a mate for most of your life, or would you prefer not having a mate?																
5. Definitely prefer to have a mate	59.9	54.5	65.2	62.1	53.5	58.4	60.5	61.0	58.9	59.2	62.1	60.7	62.5	55.6	60.1	52.2
4. Probably prefer to have a mate	26.8	30.9	23.2	26.6	24.9	27.1	28.7	24.6	27.6	28.1	24.8	25.5	25.2	30.4	28.1	32.8
3. Not sure	9.8	10.3	8.8	8.3	15.5	11.2	7.5	10.5	10.1	8.9	9.8	10.1	9.4	9.8	8.6	7.5
2. Probably prefer not to have a mate	2.7	3.3	2.1	2.5	4.2	2.6	2.5	2.7	3.0	3.2	2.2	3.2	2.0	3.0	2.4	3.0
1. Definitely prefer not to have a mate	.8	1.1	.6	.5	1.9	.6	.8	1.1	.4	.6	1.2	.4	.8	1.3	.9	4.5
Item 6120 N(Wtd)	3759	1721	1863	2946	426	925	1077	1262	496	1783	1648	1362	999	471	755	67
A06: Which do you think you are most likely to choose in the long run?																
3. Getting married	75.9	72.3	80.1	79.0	66.2	73.2	79.5	75.0	75.5	79.0	75.1	79.4	78.4	73.1	71.8	53.0
2. I have no idea	17.8	21.8	13.1	15.7	22.6	20.0	14.9	18.9	17.0	15.1	17.8	14.8	15.4	20.6	21.5	28.8
1. Not getting married	5.5	5.2	5.7	4.5	10.3	6.3	4.3	5.1	7.4	5.7	5.6	4.8	5.6	5.2	5.8	13.6
8. Am already married	.9	.7	1.1	.8	1.3	.4	1.3	1.1	.4	.3	1.6	.9	.6	1.1	.9	4.5
Item 6130 N(Wtd)	3698	1681	1844	2916	399	910	1073	1226	489	1765	1616	1341	985	461	740	66

QUESTIONNAIRE FORM 2 1978	TOTAL	SEX		RACE		REGION				4YR COLLEGE PLANS		ILLICIT DRUG USE: LIFETIME				
		M	F	White	Black	NE	NC	S	W	Yes	No	None	Mari-juana Only	Few Pills	More Pills	Any Her-oin
Weighted No. of Cases:	3785	1737	1867	2960	430	931	1083	1266	505	1790	1657	1363	1005	474	760	68
% of Weighted Total:	100.0	45.9	49.3	78.2	11.4	24.6	28.6	33.4	13.3	47.3	43.8	36.0	26.6	12.5	20.1	1.8

A07: If you did get married (or are married)...

A07A: How likely do you think it is that you would stay married to the same person for life?

5. Very likely	62.6	56.0	69.9	64.2	58.3	60.6	64.5	62.6	62.1	65.3	62.1	72.9	60.1	61.5	51.1	45.3
4. Fairly likely	21.6	25.7	17.9	22.6	18.5	20.7	23.0	21.5	20.5	22.0	21.0	17.7	24.1	21.4	25.6	25.0
3. Uncertain	13.1	14.7	10.8	11.1	19.7	15.7	9.9	13.3	14.9	10.1	14.3	8.2	13.4	13.4	18.6	26.6
2. Fairly unlikely	1.7	2.4	1.1	1.5	1.9	1.8	1.7	1.6	1.9	2.0	1.6	.7	1.4	2.6	3.5	3.1
1. Very unlikely	.9	1.3	.4	.6	1.7	1.0	.9	.9	.6	.6	.9	.5	1.0	1.1	1.3	1.6
Item 6140 N(Wtd)	*3612*	*1653*	*1792*	*2826*	*417*	*869*	*1041*	*1226*	*477*	*1687*	*1610*	*1316*	*955*	*454*	*720*	*64*

A07B: How likely is it that you would want to have children?

5. Very likely	58.6	57.4	60.7	59.3	57.3	59.9	60.5	56.2	58.3	59.7	58.6	59.6	60.9	55.4	57.7	40.9
4. Fairly likely	20.6	23.5	17.7	20.8	20.4	20.5	19.3	22.6	18.1	20.4	20.3	21.9	19.6	20.8	19.8	19.7
3. Uncertain	12.9	13.6	12.0	12.5	12.0	12.4	13.1	12.6	14.6	12.7	12.5	11.8	12.0	14.7	13.5	27.3
2. Fairly unlikely	2.9	2.2	3.5	2.9	3.1	3.4	2.4	2.8	3.3	2.8	2.7	2.4	2.9	3.5	3.7	1.5
1. Very unlikely	3.9	2.7	4.9	4.0	3.1	3.4	3.5	4.2	4.6	3.8	4.4	3.6	3.5	4.4	4.4	7.6
8. Already have child(ren)	1.1	.7	1.2	.5	4.1	.3	1.1	1.5	1.0	.5	1.5	.7	1.1	1.3	.8	4.5
Item 6150 N(Wtd)	*3636*	*1663*	*1803*	*2843*	*417*	*881*	*1048*	*1228*	*480*	*1704*	*1613*	*1323*	*963*	*457*	*721*	*66*

The questions in the next column ask you to imagine different kinds of married life that you might have. We want you to think about different ways you might share responsibilities for working, taking care of the home, and taking care of children. Please indicate how acceptable for you each of the different arrangements would be.

A08: Imagine you are married and have no children--how would you feel about each of the following working arrangements?

A08A: Husband works full-time, wife doesn't work

1. Not at all acceptable	26.4	14.1	38.4	24.4	39.3	31.2	24.1	24.9	26.6	28.4	24.3	25.9	24.8	29.6	26.9	34.8
2. Somewhat acceptable	33.9	31.2	36.3	34.3	31.7	35.1	36.5	31.7	31.8	31.7	35.5	33.5	34.1	33.8	35.1	27.3
3. Acceptable	31.9	43.9	20.3	33.4	21.7	28.8	32.2	33.1	34.3	32.3	32.2	31.4	34.5	31.5	29.2	33.3
4. Desirable	7.7	10.7	5.0	7.9	7.1	5.1	7.2	10.3	7.3	7.6	8.0	9.2	6.6	5.3	8.8	4.5
Item 6160 N(Wtd)	*3745*	*1716*	*1853*	*2940*	*420*	*921*	*1076*	*1255*	*493*	*1775*	*1644*	*1361*	*991*	*470*	*754*	*66*

A08B: Husband works full-time, wife works about half-time

1. Not at all acceptable	4.5	4.0	4.4	3.4	8.6	5.3	3.1	4.9	4.7	3.8	4.7	4.1	4.7	5.5	3.6	4.6
2. Somewhat acceptable	22.5	18.9	26.3	20.8	35.0	22.7	20.1	25.1	20.6	22.7	21.9	24.0	21.7	20.4	21.9	23.1
3. Acceptable	53.4	57.9	48.9	53.9	46.7	54.4	53.9	53.4	50.8	51.9	55.3	55.2	52.6	54.1	50.3	55.4
4. Desirable	19.6	19.3	20.3	21.9	9.8	17.5	22.9	16.5	24.1	21.7	18.1	16.8	20.9	20.0	24.2	16.9
Item 6170 N(Wtd)	*3746*	*1713*	*1856*	*2938*	*420*	*921*	*1077*	*1253*	*494*	*1775*	*1643*	*1361*	*991*	*471*	*752*	*65*

A08C: Both work full-time

1. Not at all acceptable	18.4	24.4	12.1	17.4	18.9	16.6	17.6	19.4	20.6	14.8	20.9	18.1	18.6	16.1	19.5	21.5
2. Somewhat acceptable	19.4	23.3	15.9	19.8	18.1	17.5	20.0	20.5	18.8	18.0	21.6	20.2	20.0	18.7	18.9	12.3
3. Acceptable	41.9	37.2	45.9	40.9	47.3	41.8	40.6	43.2	41.3	43.8	39.8	41.3	41.1	43.0	41.1	49.2
4. Desirable	20.3	15.2	26.1	21.9	15.8	24.0	21.8	16.9	19.4	23.4	17.7	20.4	20.2	22.4	20.6	18.5
Item 6180 N(Wtd)	*3732*	*1709*	*1853*	*2931*	*419*	*913*	*1074*	*1251*	*494*	*1778*	*1635*	*1355*	*993*	*465*	*747*	*65*

QUESTIONNAIRE FORM 2 1978	TOTAL	SEX		RACE		REGION				4YR COLLEGE PLANS		ILLICIT DRUG USE: LIFETIME				
		M	F	White	Black	NE	NC	S	W	Yes	No	None	Mari- juana Only	Few Pills	More Pills	Any Her- oin
Weighted No. of Cases: % of Weighted Total:	3785 100.0	1737 45.9	1867 49.3	2960 78.2	430 11.4	931 24.6	1083 28.6	1266 33.4	505 13.3	1790 47.3	1657 43.8	1363 36.0	1005 26.6	474 12.5	760 20.1	68 1.8
A08D: Both work about half-time																
1. Not at all acceptable	50.0	52.8	47.0	49.2	57.6	46.9	50.4	54.6	43.4	46.9	53.3	49.6	53.6	50.1	46.1	44.6
2. Somewhat acceptable	26.3	24.4	28.5	27.6	20.3	27.6	25.6	24.6	29.4	28.0	24.8	27.4	25.0	25.6	26.6	29.2
3. Acceptable	15.8	14.6	17.4	15.8	13.8	17.9	16.3	13.2	18.0	17.3	14.3	16.8	14.8	16.1	15.8	15.4
4. Desirable	7.9	8.2	7.1	7.5	8.2	7.7	7.7	7.6	9.2	7.8	7.6	6.2	6.7	8.2	11.5	10.8
Item 6190 N(Wtd)	3710	1703	1837	2915	413	913	1069	1239	489	1760	1634	1348	984	465	747	65
A08E: Husband works about half-time, wife works full-time																
1. Not at all acceptable	65.0	68.9	60.9	64.4	66.8	58.6	63.1	72.0	63.3	59.3	71.5	65.4	67.8	62.7	63.4	48.5
2. Somewhat acceptable	21.0	16.9	25.6	22.2	16.8	24.2	22.9	17.5	19.9	25.5	16.7	21.5	20.1	22.1	21.7	19.7
3. Acceptable	9.9	8.8	11.1	10.3	8.4	13.3	10.5	6.1	12.0	12.9	7.0	9.6	9.6	11.2	9.6	18.2
4. Desirable	4.1	5.3	2.4	3.1	7.7	3.8	3.4	4.4	4.9	2.3	4.8	3.5	2.4	4.1	5.2	13.6
Item 6200 N(Wtd)	3728	1713	1848	2933	416	916	1073	1247	493	1771	1640	1356	989	466	751	66
A08F: Husband doesn't work, wife works full-time																
1. Not at all acceptable	84.5	84.3	85.0	84.8	83.3	83.6	84.0	87.0	81.3	84.2	85.2	85.1	87.6	82.7	82.3	67.7
2. Somewhat acceptable	7.9	6.5	9.2	8.6	5.3	9.5	8.6	5.4	9.9	9.7	6.3	8.6	6.3	8.6	8.4	9.2
3. Acceptable	3.9	4.2	3.7	3.9	4.1	4.0	3.7	3.4	4.9	4.3	3.5	2.9	3.5	5.1	4.3	18.5
4. Desirable	3.7	4.9	2.2	2.7	7.7	2.8	3.6	4.2	4.1	1.8	5.1	3.4	2.5	3.6	5.2	6.2
Item 6210 N(Wtd)	3730	1712	1846	2928	418	918	1069	1251	493	1768	1641	1353	989	467	751	65
A09: Imagine you are married and have one or more pre-school children. How would you feel about each of the following working arrangements?																
A09A: Husband works full-time, wife doesn't work																
1. Not at all acceptable	8.3	5.9	10.2	5.5	23.4	9.0	5.6	9.5	9.5	7.7	7.7	7.8	8.1	8.3	8.3	6.2
2. Somewhat acceptable	15.3	13.1	17.0	13.3	25.6	14.3	13.7	17.8	14.6	13.7	16.4	14.3	15.2	13.7	14.7	35.4
3. Acceptable	37.9	37.5	37.7	37.6	35.4	39.3	37.1	37.5	37.7	34.6	41.5	36.6	36.7	41.2	39.3	27.7
4. Desirable	38.5	43.5	35.1	43.6	15.6	37.4	43.6	35.2	37.9	44.1	34.5	41.2	40.0	36.8	37.6	30.8
Item 6220 N(Wtd)	3743	1715	1856	2942	418	921	1077	1252	493	1777	1645	1359	992	468	755	65
A09B: Husband works full-time, wife works about half-time																
1. Not at all acceptable	14.4	18.9	9.7	14.7	10.8	19.3	12.5	12.9	13.3	14.0	14.5	14.2	15.8	13.7	13.9	10.8
2. Somewhat acceptable	27.4	26.4	28.5	26.5	31.9	27.5	25.7	27.6	30.2	27.7	26.9	28.1	27.5	27.0	26.4	23.1
3. Acceptable	44.7	43.2	46.3	43.9	49.9	40.8	46.5	47.4	41.6	42.9	46.5	44.8	44.1	46.5	41.9	60.0
4. Desirable	13.5	11.6	15.6	14.9	7.4	12.5	15.3	12.2	14.9	15.3	12.0	12.8	12.8	12.6	17.8	6.2
Item 6230 N(Wtd)	3741	1713	1858	2940	417	919	1077	1248	497	1781	1641	1356	996	467	754	65
A09C: Both work full-time																
1. Not at all acceptable	68.6	72.7	65.9	73.2	43.9	74.7	72.3	61.6	67.1	69.9	68.2	69.3	69.4	69.9	69.1	63.1
2. Somewhat acceptable	16.1	13.0	19.2	15.6	19.8	11.0	17.1	19.2	15.9	17.2	15.4	18.0	16.2	15.2	13.9	16.9
3. Acceptable	10.9	9.4	11.3	7.9	26.5	10.1	7.4	14.3	11.6	9.7	11.2	9.4	11.1	9.8	10.9	16.9
4. Desirable	4.4	4.9	3.6	3.3	10.0	4.3	3.1	5.0	5.7	3.3	5.2	3.4	3.3	5.1	6.3	4.6
Item 6240 N(Wtd)	3729	1709	1851	2928	419	913	1074	1251	492	1770	1639	1353	988	468	750	65
A09D: Both work about half-time																
1. Not at all acceptable	52.1	56.1	48.1	51.8	54.7	50.9	52.5	54.6	47.0	49.0	54.6	52.2	53.8	48.2	51.8	46.9
2. Somewhat acceptable	28.7	26.4	30.9	29.7	22.5	28.2	30.6	27.0	29.5	29.8	28.6	28.8	29.5	31.1	27.1	28.1
3. Acceptable	13.2	12.1	14.5	13.2	14.5	14.8	11.5	12.7	15.3	15.4	11.1	13.8	11.6	13.8	13.8	12.5
4. Desirable	6.1	5.4	6.5	5.4	8.2	6.1	5.5	5.7	8.1	5.9	5.6	5.3	5.1	6.9	7.5	10.9
Item 6250 N(Wtd)	3720	1699	1851	2926	413	911	1073	1246	491	1768	1635	1352	987	463	749	64

QUESTIONNAIRE FORM 2 1978	TOTAL	SEX		RACE		REGION				4YR COLLEGE PLANS		ILLICIT DRUG USE: LIFETIME				
		M	F	White	Black	NE	NC	S	W	Yes	No	None	Mari- juana Only	Few Pills	More Pills	Any Her- oin
Weighted No. of Cases:	3785	1737	1867	2960	430	931	1083	1266	505	1790	1657	1363	1005	474	760	68
% of Weighted Total:	100.0	45.9	49.3	78.2	11.4	24.6	28.6	33.4	13.3	47.3	43.8	36.0	26.6	12.5	20.1	1.8

A09E: Husband works about half-time, wife works full-time

	TOTAL	M	F	White	Black	NE	NC	S	W	Yes	No	None	Mari- juana Only	Few Pills	More Pills	Any Her- oin
1. Not at all acceptable	75.2	75.9	74.2	75.7	70.8	73.2	75.1	77.6	73.0	71.5	79.6	76.0	77.2	73.8	73.4	67.2
2. Somewhat acceptable	15.6	14.2	17.6	16.3	14.9	17.5	15.3	14.4	16.0	18.3	12.7	14.7	16.2	17.0	15.8	18.8
3. Acceptable	6.2	6.3	6.1	6.0	7.7	6.2	7.1	5.1	7.1	8.2	4.2	6.2	5.1	7.3	6.5	14.1
4. Desirable	2.9	3.6	2.1	2.0	6.5	3.0	2.5	2.9	3.9	2.1	3.5	3.2	1.5	2.1	4.4	1.6
Item 6260 N(Wtd)	3729	1707	1852	2932	415	913	1073	1251	493	1773	1636	1357	988	466	751	64

A09F: Husband doesn't work, wife works full-time

	TOTAL	M	F	White	Black	NE	NC	S	W	Yes	No	None	Mari- juana Only	Few Pills	More Pills	Any Her- oin
1. Not at all acceptable	83.6	84.0	83.2	83.6	82.4	82.4	81.5	87.1	81.3	81.5	86.0	83.8	86.5	81.2	82.3	71.9
2. Somewhat acceptable	8.5	7.8	9.5	9.0	7.5	9.3	10.4	6.4	8.1	10.7	6.5	8.0	8.1	10.1	8.8	12.5
3. Acceptable	4.9	4.6	5.4	5.1	5.1	5.3	5.4	3.7	6.1	5.9	4.1	5.3	3.5	6.2	5.1	9.4
4. Desirable	3.0	3.7	2.0	2.2	5.1	3.1	2.6	2.8	4.5	2.0	3.4	3.0	2.0	2.6	4.0	7.8
Item 6270 N(Wtd)	3732	1714	1846	2934	414	916	1073	1250	492	1774	1638	1355	989	467	751	64

A10: Imagine you are married and have one or more pre-school children. Imagine also that the husband is working full-time and the wife does not have a job outside the home. How would you feel about each of these arrangements for the day-to-day care of the child(ren)?

A10A: Wife does all child care

	TOTAL	M	F	White	Black	NE	NC	S	W	Yes	No	None	Mari- juana Only	Few Pills	More Pills	Any Her- oin
1. Not at all acceptable	31.9	28.8	34.9	32.5	28.2	33.2	34.4	29.6	29.3	36.8	26.8	33.6	31.4	34.6	28.2	31.3
2. Somewhat acceptable	29.2	29.4	29.0	29.8	27.7	29.5	31.0	27.1	30.3	27.5	31.1	28.5	31.1	26.3	30.1	34.4
3. Acceptable	28.0	28.2	27.6	27.1	32.9	28.6	24.2	30.3	29.1	25.1	30.7	28.4	26.8	26.9	29.1	26.6
4. Desirable	10.9	13.7	8.4	10.7	11.1	8.7	10.4	12.9	11.2	10.7	11.4	9.6	10.8	12.2	12.8	9.4
Item 6280 N(Wtd)	3738	1712	1853	2933	422	916	1076	1256	491	1774	1644	1360	990	468	752	64

A10B: Wife does most of it

	TOTAL	M	F	White	Black	NE	NC	S	W	Yes	No	None	Mari- juana Only	Few Pills	More Pills	Any Her- oin
1. Not at all acceptable	9.0	8.5	9.4	7.7	17.1	8.7	7.5	10.5	8.9	8.3	9.1	10.2	8.8	9.0	7.0	7.8
2. Somewhat acceptable	29.1	27.6	30.0	28.1	27.6	31.8	30.7	27.9	23.4	28.9	29.0	30.6	27.3	30.4	28.5	25.0
3. Acceptable	43.5	43.8	43.5	43.8	47.1	41.2	40.5	44.6	51.5	41.7	46.0	41.2	43.6	43.0	45.9	51.6
4. Desirable	18.4	20.0	17.2	20.3	8.4	18.2	21.3	17.0	16.2	21.0	16.0	18.0	20.3	17.6	18.6	15.6
Item 6290 N(Wtd)	3740	1713	1855	2938	416	917	1077	1252	495	1780	1640	1358	996	467	752	64

A10C: Both do it equally

	TOTAL	M	F	White	Black	NE	NC	S	W	Yes	No	None	Mari- juana Only	Few Pills	More Pills	Any Her- oin
1. Not at all acceptable	6.4	7.1	5.2	5.8	8.2	6.0	5.4	6.9	7.6	5.8	6.3	6.2	6.9	6.2	5.6	7.8
2. Somewhat acceptable	20.4	22.3	18.3	20.8	18.8	21.1	19.7	19.8	22.4	20.7	19.9	18.4	20.5	22.4	22.3	18.8
3. Acceptable	39.2	40.2	37.4	36.8	50.2	38.0	36.7	42.4	38.4	35.1	43.1	39.6	39.6	38.1	37.7	35.9
4. Desirable	34.0	30.4	39.2	36.6	22.8	34.8	38.3	30.9	31.6	38.4	30.7	35.8	33.0	33.3	34.4	37.5
Item 6300 N(Wtd)	3721	1706	1846	2925	416	910	1077	1246	487	1770	1635	1356	985	465	749	64

A10D: Husband does most of it

	TOTAL	M	F	White	Black	NE	NC	S	W	Yes	No	None	Mari- juana Only	Few Pills	More Pills	Any Her- oin
1. Not at all acceptable	60.4	57.0	63.2	60.3	57.6	58.9	57.9	62.3	63.8	59.7	60.7	60.5	60.2	62.9	59.5	54.7
2. Somewhat acceptable	30.2	33.4	27.8	31.7	26.4	31.4	33.8	27.6	26.2	31.8	29.1	29.8	31.2	28.1	30.8	29.7
3. Acceptable	6.7	7.2	6.2	6.1	9.1	6.6	7.1	6.3	6.5	7.1	6.3	6.6	6.8	7.1	5.6	12.5
4. Desirable	2.8	2.5	2.8	1.9	7.0	3.1	1.2	3.7	3.3	1.4	3.8	3.1	1.7	1.7	3.9	4.7
Item 6310 N(Wtd)	3724	1706	1849	2927	417	910	1076	1250	489	1771	1638	1357	986	466	749	64

A10E: Husband does all of it

	TOTAL	M	F	White	Black	NE	NC	S	W	Yes	No	None	Mari- juana Only	Few Pills	More Pills	Any Her- oin
1. Not at all acceptable	89.4	88.5	90.7	91.0	81.3	89.1	90.0	89.1	88.8	90.5	88.7	88.4	90.3	90.4	90.9	82.8
2. Somewhat acceptable	6.3	6.9	5.9	5.9	8.4	6.4	6.6	6.4	5.7	6.5	6.0	7.2	6.1	6.0	4.5	10.9
3. Acceptable	1.7	1.9	1.3	1.3	3.4	1.5	1.5	1.8	2.0	1.4	1.8	1.5	1.5	1.9	1.3	1.6
4. Desirable	2.7	2.8	2.2	1.7	7.2	2.9	2.0	2.7	3.5	1.6	3.5	2.9	2.1	1.5	3.2	3.1
Item 6320 N(Wtd)	3730	1708	1852	2931	417	912	1076	1252	491	1774	1640	1357	987	468	751	64

QUESTIONNAIRE FORM 2 1978	TOTAL	SEX		RACE		REGION				4YR COLLEGE PLANS		ILLICIT DRUG USE: LIFETIME				
		M	F	White	Black	NE	NC	S	W	Yes	No	None	Mari- juana Only	Few Pills	More Pills	Any Her- oin
Weighted No. of Cases:	3785	1737	1867	2960	430	931	1083	1266	505	1790	1657	1363	1005	474	760	68
% of Weighted Total:	100.0	45.9	49.3	78.2	11.4	24.6	28.6	33.4	13.3	47.3	43.8	36.0	26.6	12.5	20.1	1.8

The next section of this questionnaire is about government and public affairs.

A11: Some people think about what's going on in government very often, and others are not that interested. How much of an interest do you take in government and current events?

1. No interest at all	4.8	3.9	5.1	4.1	6.6	6.5	4.6	4.2	3.6	2.4	7.2	3.4	5.5	4.7	5.7	6.3
2. Very little interest	18.1	13.3	22.4	17.8	19.6	21.0	19.2	16.4	14.5	11.6	25.5	16.3	19.4	19.5	18.5	18.8
3. Some interest	49.7	46.8	52.3	49.9	47.9	46.9	51.4	49.5	51.8	48.3	51.2	50.9	49.1	48.8	48.4	51.6
4. A lot of interest	20.1	25.2	16.2	20.7	19.3	19.3	18.3	21.0	23.5	28.2	11.6	21.2	19.9	20.8	20.0	14.1
5. A very great interest	7.2	10.8	3.9	7.5	6.6	6.2	6.4	9.0	6.6	9.5	4.4	8.1	6.2	5.9	7.4	7.8
Item 6330 N(Wtd)	3760	1725	1859	2947	424	923	1078	1261	498	1783	1649	1363	1001	471	756	64

A12: Do you think some of the people running the government are crooked or dishonest?

1. Most of them are crooked or dishonest	13.3	13.9	12.3	11.8	21.0	16.1	11.8	13.2	11.7	9.8	16.7	11.3	13.2	15.1	15.6	18.2
2. Quite a few are	37.0	37.8	36.5	38.1	32.2	38.8	35.2	38.2	34.9	37.6	37.2	34.2	37.9	38.0	40.1	50.0
3. Some are	46.3	44.5	48.7	47.4	42.8	43.1	50.1	44.8	48.0	49.6	43.2	51.3	45.0	44.4	42.6	28.8
4. Hardly any are	2.9	3.5	2.3	2.6	3.3	1.6	2.8	3.3	4.4	2.8	2.8	2.9	3.9	1.9	1.6	1.5
5. None at all are crooked or dishonest	.4	.2	.3	.1	.7	.3	-	.6	.8	.2	.2	.5	-	.6	.1	-
Item 6340 N(Wtd)	3752	1723	1853	2943	423	921	1077	1258	496	1780	1647	1361	999	471	751	66

A13: Do you think the government wastes much of the money we pay in taxes?

1. Nearly all tax money is wasted	7.1	7.9	6.3	6.4	9.9	9.2	6.4	6.1	7.6	4.2	10.0	6.4	6.5	5.3	9.3	13.6
2. A lot of tax money is wasted	48.6	50.3	47.4	50.2	42.1	50.5	50.5	45.4	49.3	50.4	48.2	46.3	51.5	51.4	47.9	51.5
3. Some tax money is wasted	36.2	32.7	39.8	36.5	33.9	34.0	36.2	38.3	35.3	36.9	35.4	38.7	33.7	35.4	36.8	27.3
4. A little tax money wasted	7.0	8.2	5.5	6.3	10.1	6.0	6.5	8.1	7.2	8.1	5.3	7.2	7.8	7.0	5.6	4.5
5. No tax money is wasted	1.0	1.0	.9	.5	4.0	.4	.4	2.1	.6	.5	1.2	1.4	.6	.9	.4	3.0
Item 6350 N(Wtd)	3751	1721	1853	2937	425	921	1071	1260	499	1774	1648	1358	1001	469	751	66

A14: How much of the time do you think you can trust the government in Washington to do what is right?

1. Almost always	7.4	8.6	6.0	7.9	3.8	5.7	7.4	7.9	8.9	7.7	6.3	7.2	7.3	6.8	8.2	1.5
2. Often	36.8	37.8	36.5	39.9	20.6	35.8	38.5	35.4	38.2	43.4	30.6	38.1	37.1	40.0	35.2	19.4
3. Sometimes	41.4	38.5	44.4	40.6	47.6	43.2	41.3	40.9	39.4	38.9	44.7	41.1	42.2	41.5	40.4	44.8
4. Seldom	12.6	13.0	11.4	10.2	24.4	12.5	11.4	14.1	11.5	8.9	15.8	12.5	11.1	10.5	13.9	22.4
5. Never	1.9	2.0	1.6	1.5	3.8	2.7	1.4	1.8	1.8	1.1	2.6	1.1	2.3	1.3	2.3	10.4
Item 6360 N(Wtd)	3747	1719	1854	2939	422	922	1072	1256	497	1776	1645	1358	998	468	753	67

A15: Do you feel that the people running the government are smart people who usually know what they are doing?

1. They almost always know what they are doing	11.8	13.9	9.3	11.5	11.8	10.2	11.8	12.1	14.3	12.5	10.4	11.3	12.1	12.2	11.7	13.4
2. They usually know what they are doing	51.4	51.8	52.6	54.0	39.7	51.7	52.7	50.4	50.3	55.9	47.5	53.6	51.1	51.4	50.5	34.3
3. They sometimes know what they are doing	29.9	26.6	32.3	28.6	37.8	31.3	27.8	30.8	29.5	26.6	33.9	28.9	30.8	30.5	30.1	43.3
4. They seldom know what they are doing	5.7	6.2	5.2	5.0	9.0	5.2	6.7	5.7	4.2	4.3	6.9	5.5	5.3	5.8	5.9	4.5
5. They never know what they are doing	1.0	1.5	.5	.8	1.7	1.5	.8	.8	1.4	.7	1.3	.7	.8	.2	1.9	6.0
Item 6370 N(Wtd)	3747	1721	1852	2937	423	922	1075	1255	495	1777	1645	1358	997	469	751	67

QUESTIONNAIRE FORM 2 1978	TOTAL	SEX		RACE		REGION				4YR COLLEGE PLANS		ILLICIT DRUG USE: LIFETIME				
		M	F	White	Black	NE	NC	S	W	Yes	No	None	Mari-juana Only	Few Pills	More Pills	Any Her-oin
Weighted No. of Cases:	3785	1737	1867	2960	430	931	1083	1266	505	1790	1657	1363	1005	474	760	68
% of Weighted Total:	100.0	45.9	49.3	78.2	11.4	24.6	28.6	33.4	13.3	47.3	43.8	36.0	26.6	12.5	20.1	1.8

A16: Would you say the government is pretty much run for a few big interests looking out for themselves, or is it run for the benefit of all the people?

	TOTAL	M	F	White	Black	NE	NC	S	W	Yes	No	None	Mari-juana Only	Few Pills	More Pills	Any Her-oin
1. Nearly always run for a few big interests	8.7	10.3	6.9	8.2	10.0	9.9	7.7	8.6	9.1	6.9	10.8	9.1	7.5	7.3	10.2	12.1
2. Usually run for a few big interests	20.6	21.7	19.4	20.6	19.3	21.4	20.3	20.0	21.4	20.0	21.6	20.2	21.1	19.5	20.1	30.3
3. Run some for the big interests, some for the people	48.9	45.2	52.7	48.8	52.9	49.1	49.3	48.9	47.3	48.2	49.9	47.5	49.2	53.3	48.3	47.0
4. Usually run for the benefit of all the people	17.9	18.3	17.6	18.7	13.8	16.8	19.3	17.6	17.6	20.7	14.5	18.8	18.5	17.1	17.7	4.5
5. Nearly always run for the benefit of all the people	3.9	4.4	3.4	3.7	4.0	2.7	3.4	4.9	4.6	4.2	3.3	4.5	3.5	3.0	3.6	4.5
Item 6380 N(Wtd)	3731	1715	1844	2929	420	917	1068	1250	495	1772	1637	1359	995	467	745	66

A17: Have you ever done, or do you plan to do, the following things?

A17A: Vote in a public election

	TOTAL	M	F	White	Black	NE	NC	S	W	Yes	No	None	Mari-juana Only	Few Pills	More Pills	Any Her-oin
1. I probably won't do this	3.7	3.5	3.5	2.9	4.7	4.3	2.9	3.4	5.0	2.1	5.1	3.6	3.9	2.4	3.3	10.4
2. Don't know	9.5	7.5	10.9	7.2	15.5	10.5	8.5	9.6	9.4	4.8	13.7	8.5	7.9	9.6	10.8	16.4
3. I probably will do this	82.1	83.0	82.1	85.1	75.4	82.1	81.5	82.8	81.4	88.3	76.6	84.1	83.4	83.3	79.4	73.1
4. I have already done this	4.7	6.0	3.4	4.8	4.5	2.9	7.1	4.2	4.2	4.9	4.7	3.8	4.8	4.7	6.3	1.5
Item 6390 N(Wtd)	3758	1727	1861	2947	426	923	1078	1258	499	1785	1649	1362	998	468	757	67

A17B: Write to public officials

	TOTAL	M	F	White	Black	NE	NC	S	W	Yes	No	None	Mari-juana Only	Few Pills	More Pills	Any Her-oin
1. I probably won't do this	18.7	15.6	21.6	16.8	25.8	20.0	17.3	20.0	16.2	10.4	26.7	16.8	18.2	20.7	20.4	21.2
2. Don't know	43.7	41.5	45.2	44.6	41.4	41.0	44.1	44.8	45.4	40.6	47.2	45.2	44.8	40.4	41.2	42.4
3. I probably will do this	26.2	30.7	22.5	26.1	25.5	28.3	25.7	25.1	26.6	33.1	19.3	26.7	26.8	25.9	25.6	30.3
4. I have already done this	11.3	12.2	10.7	12.5	7.1	10.9	12.9	10.1	11.6	16.1	6.8	11.5	10.2	13.0	12.8	6.1
Item 6400 N(Wtd)	3755	1722	1863	2947	423	920	1077	1258	500	1785	1648	1362	998	468	755	66

A17C: Give money to a political candidate or cause

	TOTAL	M	F	White	Black	NE	NC	S	W	Yes	No	None	Mari-juana Only	Few Pills	More Pills	Any Her-oin
1. I probably won't do this	35.7	36.1	34.8	34.9	36.6	39.8	35.2	32.5	37.8	30.0	42.0	32.8	35.6	32.7	42.6	40.3
2. Don't know	39.3	37.4	41.2	39.5	38.3	38.4	37.3	41.0	41.0	40.4	38.1	42.3	38.5	41.9	33.0	38.8
3. I probably will do this	19.2	18.9	19.6	19.6	21.0	17.4	19.7	21.0	17.1	23.2	14.6	20.2	20.8	17.1	17.4	10.4
4. I have already done this	5.8	7.5	4.5	5.9	4.3	4.6	7.8	5.7	4.2	6.3	5.3	4.7	5.1	8.3	7.0	10.4
Item 6410 N(Wtd)	3749	1723	1859	2942	423	922	1075	1255	498	1783	1644	1359	995	468	754	67

A17D: Work in a political campaign

	TOTAL	M	F	White	Black	NE	NC	S	W	Yes	No	None	Mari-juana Only	Few Pills	More Pills	Any Her-oin
1. I probably won't do this	45.3	46.6	43.2	45.9	36.7	47.4	46.8	41.3	47.9	34.6	56.1	42.5	46.0	43.3	50.1	53.7
2. Don't know	36.1	35.6	36.8	36.2	37.7	35.1	35.0	38.6	34.2	39.4	32.9	39.4	33.7	36.9	32.5	34.3
3. I probably will do this	11.5	10.7	12.6	10.0	21.6	11.4	9.0	14.0	10.9	15.8	6.7	11.3	11.9	12.7	10.3	10.4
4. I have already done this	7.1	7.1	7.3	7.9	4.3	6.1	9.2	6.1	7.0	10.2	4.3	6.8	8.3	7.1	7.0	1.5
Item 6420 N(Wtd)	3748	1722	1859	2945	422	922	1078	1251	497	1782	1646	1359	997	466	756	67

A17E: Participate in a lawful demonstration

	TOTAL	M	F	White	Black	NE	NC	S	W	Yes	No	None	Mari-juana Only	Few Pills	More Pills	Any Her-oin
1. I probably won't do this	35.3	30.3	39.5	34.7	30.9	30.0	35.4	38.4	36.7	26.8	44.8	41.0	33.5	32.3	28.9	34.3
2. Don't know	45.7	47.4	44.8	47.8	43.5	46.3	47.3	44.6	44.6	50.1	41.2	46.2	46.7	45.8	44.9	35.8
3. I probably will do this	16.0	18.2	13.6	14.7	22.6	19.1	14.5	14.6	16.7	19.3	11.9	11.3	17.4	18.0	21.2	17.9
4. I have already done this	3.0	4.0	2.2	2.9	3.1	4.7	2.8	2.3	2.0	3.8	2.1	1.5	2.4	3.9	5.0	13.4
Item 6430 N(Wtd)	3745	1721	1860	2943	421	921	1075	1251	498	1783	1645	1360	996	467	755	67

A17F: Boycott certain products or stores

	TOTAL	M	F	White	Black	NE	NC	S	W	Yes	No	None	Mari-juana Only	Few Pills	More Pills	Any Her-oin
1. I probably won't do this	33.2	28.9	36.8	32.1	35.4	21.9	34.8	39.3	35.6	25.1	42.2	39.5	30.2	32.6	25.6	38.8
2. Don't know	39.0	39.5	39.2	39.6	40.1	40.1	39.8	38.4	36.8	39.6	38.5	38.4	40.3	35.7	39.6	34.3
3. I probably will do this	20.9	23.2	18.6	20.9	20.8	27.9	19.3	17.3	20.3	25.9	15.2	18.0	21.2	23.8	25.8	13.4
4. I have already done this	6.9	8.4	5.4	7.4	3.5	10.1	6.2	4.9	7.4	9.4	4.1	4.0	8.3	7.9	9.0	14.9
Item 6440 N(Wtd)	3749	1720	1858	2942	424	921	1073	1258	497	1784	1641	1361	996	470	755	67

QUESTIONNAIRE FORM 2 1978	TOTAL	SEX		RACE		REGION				4YR COLLEGE PLANS		ILLICIT DRUG USE: LIFETIME				
		M	F	White	Black	NE	NC	S	W	Yes	No	None	Mari-juana Only	Few Pills	More Pills	Any Her-oin
Weighted No. of Cases:	3785	1737	1867	2960	430	931	1083	1266	505	1790	1657	1363	1005	474	760	68
% of Weighted Total:	100.0	45.9	49.3	78.2	11.4	24.6	28.6	33.4	13.3	47.3	43.8	36.0	26.6	12.5	20.1	1.8

A18: How much do you agree or disagree with each of the following statements?

A18A: The U.S. should begin a gradual program of disarming whether other countries do or not

	TOTAL	M	F	White	Black	NE	NC	S	W	Yes	No	None	Mari-juana Only	Few Pills	More Pills	Any Her-oin
1. Disagree	44.5	59.5	30.6	47.1	33.0	44.4	40.3	47.5	46.3	47.0	41.7	44.2	45.1	40.2	49.0	37.3
2. Mostly disagree	18.4	17.6	19.4	18.9	16.4	18.1	20.1	16.9	19.3	19.5	17.3	17.1	19.2	20.7	18.8	14.9
3. Neither	19.8	11.2	28.2	19.3	21.0	20.4	23.4	17.2	17.2	16.6	23.5	19.4	19.8	23.9	18.0	19.4
4. Mostly agree	11.8	7.5	15.4	10.6	16.6	11.6	12.7	10.9	12.4	13.1	10.6	13.6	11.4	9.6	10.1	11.9
5. Agree	5.5	4.1	6.4	4.0	12.8	5.6	3.6	7.4	4.8	3.9	6.9	5.6	4.6	5.9	4.1	16.4
Item 6450 N(Wtd)	3692	1709	1821	2908	415	906	1062	1241	482	1765	1619	1347	985	460	739	67

A18B: There may be times when the U.S. should go to war to protect the rights of other countries

	TOTAL	M	F	White	Black	NE	NC	S	W	Yes	No	None	Mari-juana Only	Few Pills	More Pills	Any Her-oin
1. Disagree	24.3	24.0	24.4	23.5	29.0	28.4	25.0	21.9	21.6	20.3	28.5	22.6	23.9	25.7	27.2	22.4
2. Mostly disagree	24.9	22.9	26.5	25.1	24.5	25.8	23.8	25.5	24.2	26.4	23.8	24.2	23.6	25.5	27.2	25.4
3. Neither	16.4	16.4	16.7	17.0	12.4	17.0	18.5	14.9	14.5	16.4	16.8	15.8	17.9	15.6	15.6	19.4
4. Mostly agree	21.4	21.4	21.7	22.2	18.1	17.7	22.9	21.5	24.8	23.6	18.4	22.8	22.1	22.1	18.4	11.9
5. Agree	13.0	15.3	10.7	12.2	16.4	11.2	9.9	16.2	14.7	13.3	12.5	14.6	12.6	11.1	11.6	20.9
Item 5690 N(Wtd)	3730	1716	1849	2931	420	912	1071	1251	496	1776	1637	1356	992	467	750	67

A18C: The U.S. should be willing to go to war to protect its own economic interests

	TOTAL	M	F	White	Black	NE	NC	S	W	Yes	No	None	Mari-juana Only	Few Pills	More Pills	Any Her-oin
1. Disagree	10.2	9.4	10.6	8.7	15.3	11.2	8.6	10.2	12.1	9.0	11.3	8.9	9.9	11.8	11.2	10.6
2. Mostly disagree	12.6	13.2	12.4	13.0	11.3	16.4	12.9	10.3	11.9	14.2	11.0	13.0	12.9	12.7	12.7	7.6
3. Neither	18.6	16.2	21.4	19.9	12.2	21.1	21.6	14.5	18.0	18.6	18.3	18.9	18.5	17.8	20.0	16.7
4. Mostly agree	30.2	29.1	31.5	31.1	26.1	27.2	33.3	29.5	31.0	32.3	29.1	31.5	31.5	29.2	27.8	24.2
5. Agree	28.3	32.2	24.2	27.3	35.2	24.2	24.1	35.4	26.9	26.0	30.2	27.7	27.1	28.8	28.3	39.4
Item 6460 N(Wtd)	3728	1719	1844	2930	426	913	1070	1251	494	1776	1640	1357	993	466	749	66

A18D: The only good reason for the U.S. to go to war is to defend against an attack on our own country

	TOTAL	M	F	White	Black	NE	NC	S	W	Yes	No	None	Mari-juana Only	Few Pills	More Pills	Any Her-oin
1. Disagree	8.6	9.0	8.0	8.3	8.6	9.2	5.8	10.1	9.7	10.5	6.3	9.7	8.6	7.5	7.3	7.5
2. Mostly disagree	11.7	14.1	10.0	12.3	10.5	10.1	12.9	12.6	10.1	13.8	9.6	11.6	11.8	12.0	11.9	9.0
3. Neither	7.9	7.2	8.3	7.9	6.9	7.8	10.0	6.2	8.3	7.6	8.1	7.8	7.7	6.2	8.3	17.9
4. Mostly agree	31.2	29.3	33.8	32.8	24.8	30.2	35.1	28.6	31.5	32.2	30.8	31.2	31.2	35.5	29.2	35.8
5. Agree	40.5	40.4	39.9	38.7	49.2	42.8	36.0	42.5	40.7	36.0	45.2	39.6	40.7	38.9	43.3	31.3
Item 6470 N(Wtd)	3725	1716	1847	2931	419	912	1068	1250	496	1772	1641	1357	991	465	749	67

A18E: The U.S. does not need to have greater military power than the Soviet Union

	TOTAL	M	F	White	Black	NE	NC	S	W	Yes	No	None	Mari-juana Only	Few Pills	More Pills	Any Her-oin
1. Disagree	38.5	42.4	34.2	36.6	50.2	33.7	33.0	47.6	36.5	36.1	41.1	39.3	38.0	36.3	37.7	45.5
2. Mostly disagree	22.4	21.8	23.1	23.2	17.3	21.1	25.0	20.7	23.2	23.0	22.1	21.9	24.1	21.9	23.5	12.1
3. Neither	18.5	14.2	22.9	19.3	13.5	21.1	21.4	14.0	18.5	18.2	19.3	18.4	19.6	18.5	17.3	15.2
4. Mostly agree	11.2	12.3	10.2	11.4	10.2	11.6	12.1	9.9	11.4	12.7	9.2	11.6	9.8	10.5	11.8	12.1
5. Agree	9.5	9.2	9.7	9.4	8.5	12.7	8.4	7.9	10.6	10.1	8.4	8.7	8.4	13.1	9.7	16.7
Item 6480 N(Wtd)	3713	1713	1838	2921	422	906	1068	1248	491	1769	1636	1351	988	466	746	66

A18F: The U.S. ought to have much more military power than any other nation in the world

	TOTAL	M	F	White	Black	NE	NC	S	W	Yes	No	None	Mari-juana Only	Few Pills	More Pills	Any Her-oin
1. Disagree	14.7	14.9	14.8	15.0	14.8	19.4	13.8	12.4	13.7	17.1	12.3	14.6	15.0	15.1	15.6	12.1
2. Mostly disagree	16.1	16.5	16.1	16.7	12.6	17.4	17.9	13.4	16.5	20.1	11.8	16.6	17.2	14.9	14.2	21.2
3. Neither	25.7	21.1	30.9	27.0	20.5	25.4	31.1	21.2	25.7	23.5	28.7	25.7	23.5	27.4	28.5	19.7
4. Mostly agree	21.1	22.1	19.9	21.2	18.4	19.5	19.0	23.8	21.8	21.2	21.4	20.8	21.1	24.1	20.8	15.2
5. Agree	22.4	25.4	18.4	20.1	33.7	18.3	18.2	29.2	22.0	18.2	25.7	22.4	23.1	18.5	20.9	31.8
Item 6490 N(Wtd)	3711	1713	1835	2920	419	907	1068	1246	490	1767	1633	1353	985	464	745	66

QUESTIONNAIRE FORM 2 1978	TOTAL	SEX		RACE		REGION				4YR COLLEGE PLANS		ILLICIT DRUG USE: LIFETIME				
		M	F	White	Black	NE	NC	S	W	Yes	No	None	Marijuana Only	Few Pills	More Pills	Any Heroin
Weighted No. of Cases:	3785	1737	1867	2960	430	931	1083	1266	505	1790	1657	1363	1005	474	760	68
% of Weighted Total:	100.0	45.9	49.3	78.2	11.4	24.6	28.6	33.4	13.3	47.3	43.8	36.0	26.6	12.5	20.1	1.8

A18G: Our present foreign policy is based on our own narrow economic and power interests

	TOTAL	M	F	White	Black	NE	NC	S	W	Yes	No	None	Mari. Only	Few Pills	More Pills	Any Heroin
1. Disagree	7.2	8.8	6.0	7.2	8.9	8.2	5.4	8.0	7.4	7.8	6.5	7.6	7.6	7.1	6.0	10.9
2. Mostly disagree	12.3	13.2	11.2	13.1	7.7	11.9	13.5	11.2	13.2	14.0	10.2	12.1	12.1	13.3	12.1	15.6
3. Neither	41.4	36.5	46.6	44.2	27.6	39.9	46.3	39.3	38.4	40.6	43.8	41.6	42.1	42.6	42.0	29.7
4. Mostly agree	25.7	27.6	24.2	25.0	30.0	25.6	23.5	26.9	27.9	26.4	25.1	25.6	25.8	25.1	25.9	29.7
5. Agree	13.4	14.0	12.0	10.5	25.9	14.5	11.3	14.6	12.8	11.2	14.4	13.2	12.3	11.8	14.2	14.1
Item 6500 N(Wtd)	3637	1687	1791	2856	417	885	1053	1222	476	1736	1597	1326	968	451	733	64

A18H: Servicemen should obey orders without question

	TOTAL	M	F	White	Black	NE	NC	S	W	Yes	No	None	Mari. Only	Few Pills	More Pills	Any Heroin
1. Disagree	18.0	14.0	21.6	16.4	27.6	18.9	16.7	18.6	17.5	18.1	17.6	18.2	15.9	18.0	20.1	27.7
2. Mostly disagree	21.2	20.1	22.5	21.4	21.1	22.9	21.5	19.1	23.0	22.5	20.4	20.1	21.7	22.5	23.1	13.8
3. Neither	20.4	19.4	21.3	21.9	13.4	19.8	24.5	16.1	23.4	20.6	20.3	20.2	21.3	21.2	18.7	18.5
4. Mostly agree	26.7	29.8	23.9	28.2	17.7	27.2	25.0	28.4	25.8	27.5	26.3	27.7	27.6	26.6	24.8	27.7
5. Agree	13.7	16.6	10.8	12.2	20.6	11.2	12.3	17.9	10.4	11.4	15.5	13.8	13.5	11.6	13.5	12.3
Item 6510 N(Wtd)	3717	1708	1848	2927	417	909	1069	1247	492	1770	1637	1355	992	466	743	65

A19: This section deals with activities which may be against the rules or against the law. We hope you will answer all of these questions. However, if you find a question which you cannot answer honestly, we would prefer that you leave it blank. Remember, your answers will never be connected with your name. During the LAST 12 MONTHS, how often have you...

A19A: Argued or had a fight with either of your parents

	TOTAL	M	F	White	Black	NE	NC	S	W	Yes	No	None	Mari. Only	Few Pills	More Pills	Any Heroin
1. Not at all	12.9	14.9	10.1	8.3	38.4	9.0	8.6	18.1	15.9	11.2	12.9	18.2	10.0	9.4	7.2	7.5
2. Once	10.5	11.6	9.1	9.6	14.9	10.2	9.9	10.7	12.0	10.4	10.1	12.4	9.7	9.2	8.5	9.0
3. Twice	13.1	13.5	13.0	13.8	10.7	11.8	14.7	12.7	13.3	13.6	13.3	15.6	14.2	11.9	8.5	10.4
4. 3 or 4 times	23.8	24.6	23.4	25.3	16.4	23.6	26.1	23.3	20.1	24.1	23.9	22.8	24.8	25.4	24.4	13.4
5. 5 or more times	39.7	35.5	44.4	43.1	19.7	45.4	40.6	35.2	38.6	40.8	39.8	31.0	41.1	44.3	51.4	59.7
Item 6520 N(Wtd)	3720	1717	1843	2923	422	914	1067	1241	498	1769	1640	1353	997	469	751	67

A19B: Hit an instructor or supervisor

	TOTAL	M	F	White	Black	NE	NC	S	W	Yes	No	None	Mari. Only	Few Pills	More Pills	Any Heroin
1. Not at all	96.9	94.6	99.1	97.1	96.4	95.9	97.5	97.3	96.2	98.3	95.5	98.5	98.2	96.6	92.9	89.4
2. Once	2.0	3.5	.5	2.0	2.2	2.6	1.9	1.7	2.0	1.3	2.8	1.0	1.5	2.8	4.0	6.1
3. Twice	.7	1.0	.2	.6	.7	.9	.5	.6	1.0	.2	1.1	.1	.2	.6	2.3	3.0
4. 3 or 4 times	.2	.3	-	.1	.2	.2	.2	.1	.4	.1	.2	.1	-	-	.5	-
5. 5 or more times	.2	.4	.1	.1	.7	.3	-	.3	.4	-	.4	.2	.2	.2	.4	1.5
Item 6530 N(Wtd)	3730	1723	1849	2937	418	917	1069	1248	497	1779	1638	1363	1000	466	750	66

A19C: Gotten into a serious fight in school or at work

	TOTAL	M	F	White	Black	NE	NC	S	W	Yes	No	None	Mari. Only	Few Pills	More Pills	Any Heroin
1. Not at all	85.9	80.6	91.3	86.2	87.4	85.0	85.3	87.5	85.0	88.0	84.8	91.6	85.7	87.0	76.7	70.1
2. Once	8.8	11.6	5.7	8.7	8.5	9.3	10.0	7.4	8.6	7.6	9.2	5.8	9.0	9.4	13.0	13.4
3. Twice	2.8	3.9	1.7	2.7	2.6	3.3	2.3	2.3	3.8	2.5	2.7	1.3	3.1	2.1	5.2	7.5
4. 3 or 4 times	1.8	2.7	1.0	1.8	.9	1.3	2.1	2.2	1.6	1.3	2.3	1.0	1.7	1.3	3.5	3.0
5. 5 or more times	.7	1.2	.3	.6	.5	1.2	.3	.6	1.0	.4	1.0	.4	.4	.2	1.6	4.5
Item 6540 N(Wtd)	3738	1726	1850	2940	422	917	1070	1251	500	1779	1641	1363	1001	470	751	67

A19D: Taken part in a fight where a group of your friends were against another group

	TOTAL	M	F	White	Black	NE	NC	S	W	Yes	No	None	Mari. Only	Few Pills	More Pills	Any Heroin
1. Not at all	85.0	82.0	88.1	85.3	86.6	83.7	85.4	85.7	84.6	87.6	82.7	90.9	86.0	82.0	77.4	61.2
2. Once	9.2	10.3	8.0	9.0	9.3	9.5	9.4	9.1	8.4	8.1	10.1	6.4	10.1	10.3	10.6	19.4
3. Twice	2.9	3.7	2.1	2.9	2.6	3.5	3.1	2.3	3.2	2.4	3.3	1.5	2.3	4.3	4.9	11.9
4. 3 or 4 times	1.9	2.2	1.7	1.9	1.0	2.4	1.4	2.0	2.2	1.0	2.9	.6	1.1	2.6	4.9	4.5
5. 5 or more times	1.0	1.8	.2	.9	.7	1.0	.7	.9	1.6	1.0	.9	.6	.6	.9	2.1	3.0
Item 6550 N(Wtd)	3731	1724	1850	2938	418	918	1068	1246	499	1778	1641	1362	1000	466	752	67

QUESTIONNAIRE FORM 2 1978	TOTAL	SEX		RACE		REGION				4YR COLLEGE PLANS		ILLICIT DRUG USE: LIFETIME				
		M	F	White	Black	NE	NC	S	W	Yes	No	None	Marijuana Only	Few Pills	More Pills	Any Heroin
Weighted No. of Cases:	3785	1737	1867	2960	430	931	1083	1266	505	1790	1657	1363	1005	474	760	68
% of Weighted Total:	100.0	45.9	49.3	78.2	11.4	24.6	28.6	33.4	13.3	47.3	43.8	36.0	26.6	12.5	20.1	1.8

A19E: Hurt someone badly enough to need bandages or a doctor

	TOTAL	M	F	White	Black	NE	NC	S	W	Yes	No	None	Marijuana Only	Few Pills	More Pills	Any Heroin
1. Not at all	90.3	83.3	97.6	91.0	90.2	88.5	89.9	92.3	89.7	93.0	89.0	95.4	92.9	90.4	80.3	68.2
2. Once	6.1	10.4	1.6	5.6	6.9	7.7	5.7	5.3	6.0	4.6	6.5	3.1	5.2	6.9	10.3	22.7
3. Twice	1.8	3.1	.7	1.8	1.9	2.1	2.0	1.2	2.6	1.3	2.6	.5	.8	1.9	5.3	4.5
4. 3 or 4 times	1.0	1.7	.1	1.0	.2	.9	1.7	.5	1.0	.4	1.3	.6	.6	.6	2.4	3.0
5. 5 or more times	.7	1.3	-	.6	.7	.8	.7	.7	.6	.7	.7	.4	.5	.2	1.7	1.5
Item 6560 N(Wtd)	3730	1722	1850	2936	418	917	1069	1247	497	1779	1637	1362	1000	467	750	66

A19F: Used a knife or gun or some other thing (like a club) to get something from a person

	TOTAL	M	F	White	Black	NE	NC	S	W	Yes	No	None	Marijuana Only	Few Pills	More Pills	Any Heroin
1. Not at all	97.2	95.7	99.1	97.5	95.9	97.6	97.8	96.5	97.0	98.3	96.0	99.0	98.0	97.6	93.9	83.6
2. Once	1.4	2.1	.4	1.2	2.4	1.2	1.1	2.2	.6	.9	2.0	.4	1.4	1.3	2.1	13.4
3. Twice	.8	1.2	.5	.9	1.2	.9	.7	1.0	.8	.4	1.3	.2	.5	.6	2.4	3.0
4. 3 or 4 times	.3	.5	.1	.2	.5	.2	.2	.2	.6	.1	.3	.1	-	.4	.9	-
5. 5 or more times	.3	.5	-	.2	-	.2	.3	.1	.8	.2	.3	.2	.1	.2	.5	-
Item 6570 N(Wtd)	3728	1724	1849	2939	417	917	1069	1247	496	1778	1639	1361	1001	466	750	67

A19G: Taken something not belonging to you worth under $50

	TOTAL	M	F	White	Black	NE	NC	S	W	Yes	No	None	Marijuana Only	Few Pills	More Pills	Any Heroin
1. Not at all	69.2	60.6	77.7	68.1	77.3	64.4	66.0	74.2	72.0	70.0	67.7	82.0	67.2	64.7	53.8	40.3
2. Once	13.5	16.2	10.9	13.9	13.2	12.7	14.8	13.8	11.2	13.5	13.2	8.3	15.4	16.2	18.1	13.4
3. Twice	7.0	9.3	4.8	7.4	3.3	9.7	7.6	4.9	5.7	6.9	7.3	5.0	6.9	8.9	8.7	16.4
4. 3 or 4 times	5.2	6.6	3.5	5.3	3.3	5.4	6.1	3.9	6.1	5.3	5.5	2.7	5.4	4.1	10.1	10.4
5. 5 or more times	5.2	7.2	3.1	5.2	2.9	7.8	5.3	3.2	4.9	4.4	6.2	2.1	5.0	5.8	9.4	19.4
Item 6580 N(Wtd)	3705	1716	1835	2918	418	911	1063	1241	490	1762	1634	1353	996	462	746	67

A19H: Taken something not belonging to you worth over $50

	TOTAL	M	F	White	Black	NE	NC	S	W	Yes	No	None	Marijuana Only	Few Pills	More Pills	Any Heroin
1. Not at all	94.4	90.4	98.5	94.8	94.2	92.3	95.3	95.7	93.1	96.3	92.8	98.4	96.0	93.5	88.2	68.2
2. Once	2.6	4.4	.7	2.5	3.1	3.4	2.0	2.2	4.1	1.5	3.4	.7	2.3	4.5	4.6	9.1
3. Twice	1.0	1.9	.2	1.0	1.2	1.1	1.0	1.0	1.0	1.0	1.0	.2	.8	.9	2.3	9.1
4. 3 or 4 times	.8	1.3	.2	.7	.7	.5	.8	.7	1.0	.5	1.1	.5	.3	-	2.3	1.5
5. 5 or more times	1.2	1.9	.4	1.0	.7	2.6	.8	.5	.8	.6	1.6	.2	.6	1.1	2.8	13.6
Item 6590 N(Wtd)	3714	1717	1846	2931	416	913	1066	1242	493	1772	1638	1360	999	465	745	66

A19I: Taken something from a store without paying for it

	TOTAL	M	F	White	Black	NE	NC	S	W	Yes	No	None	Marijuana Only	Few Pills	More Pills	Any Heroin
1. Not at all	69.9	65.2	74.5	70.5	70.4	64.3	67.8	74.9	71.8	73.4	66.5	83.7	68.2	64.5	52.4	47.8
2. Once	12.0	11.9	11.9	11.2	14.7	11.3	13.1	11.8	11.3	10.7	13.3	8.9	13.3	11.9	15.6	11.9
3. Twice	6.6	7.3	5.9	6.8	6.0	7.7	7.3	5.3	6.3	5.8	7.3	3.5	6.6	11.9	8.6	14.9
4. 3 or 4 times	6.1	7.3	5.0	6.1	4.8	7.8	6.2	4.6	6.7	5.4	6.6	1.9	6.6	6.7	12.5	6.0
5. 5 or more times	5.4	8.2	2.7	5.5	4.1	8.6	5.6	3.3	4.0	4.8	6.4	2.0	5.2	5.0	11.0	19.4
Item 6600 N(Wtd)	3707	1715	1838	2923	415	908	1063	1240	496	1765	1634	1358	995	462	744	67

A19J: Taken a car that didn't belong to someone in your family without permission of the owner

	TOTAL	M	F	White	Black	NE	NC	S	W	Yes	No	None	Marijuana Only	Few Pills	More Pills	Any Heroin
1. Not at all	95.7	93.8	97.5	95.8	95.7	95.6	94.8	96.6	96.0	97.0	94.4	98.5	97.0	96.6	90.3	73.1
2. Once	2.4	3.5	1.5	2.2	3.3	2.0	3.3	2.2	2.0	1.7	3.1	.7	2.0	2.6	5.1	13.4
3. Twice	.9	1.0	.7	1.1	.2	1.3	1.0	.6	.8	.7	1.2	.2	.5	.4	2.4	7.5
4. 3 or 4 times	.6	1.0	.2	.5	.7	1.0	.4	.4	.8	.3	.9	.1	.4	.2	1.5	6.0
5. 5 or more times	.3	.6	.1	.4	.2	.2	.7	.2	.2	.4	.4	.4	.1	.2	.8	-
Item 6610 N(Wtd)	3726	1723	1849	2937	418	916	1068	1246	496	1775	1642	1360	999	466	751	67

QUESTIONNAIRE FORM 2 1978	TOTAL	SEX		RACE		REGION				4YR COLLEGE PLANS		ILLICIT DRUG USE: LIFETIME				
		M	F	White	Black	NE	NC	S	W	Yes	No	None	Marijuana Only	Few Pills	More Pills	Any Heroin
Weighted No. of Cases:	3785	1737	1867	2960	430	931	1083	1266	505	1790	1657	1363	1005	474	760	68
% of Weighted Total:	100.0	45.9	49.3	78.2	11.4	24.6	28.6	33.4	13.3	47.3	43.8	36.0	26.6	12.5	20.1	1.8

A19K: Taken part of a car without permission of the owner

1. Not at all	94.0	89.4	98.2	93.7	96.2	91.6	94.7	95.2	93.5	96.1	92.3	98.2	96.0	93.4	85.5	74.2
2. Once	3.3	5.6	1.2	3.4	2.4	4.3	3.4	2.6	3.0	2.1	4.1	.9	2.4	4.5	7.6	10.6
3. Twice	1.5	2.4	.5	1.5	1.2	2.4	.7	1.4	1.8	1.0	1.9	.4	1.2	1.1	3.3	13.6
4. 3 or 4 times	.7	1.5	.1	.8	.2	.9	.9	.5	.4	.4	1.0	.1	.3	.6	2.3	1.5
5. 5 or more times	.5	1.0	.1	.5	-	.9	.3	.3	1.0	.5	.6	.4	.2	.6	1.2	-
Item 6620 N(Wtd)	3723	1722	1849	2935	418	915	1068	1245	496	1776	1640	1360	998	467	751	66

A19L: Gone into some house or building when you weren't supposed to be there

1. Not at all	75.9	68.3	83.1	75.0	82.0	73.4	75.3	78.7	74.9	76.6	75.3	85.5	76.0	70.1	63.4	49.3
2. Once	11.8	14.6	9.0	12.4	9.1	12.0	10.9	12.2	12.3	11.9	12.1	7.5	12.7	15.1	16.0	16.4
3. Twice	5.9	8.0	4.2	6.4	3.4	6.9	6.9	4.4	5.5	5.9	5.9	3.7	5.2	8.6	8.5	16.4
4. 3 or 4 times	3.2	4.7	1.7	3.3	2.2	3.6	3.6	2.7	3.0	2.9	3.2	1.3	3.4	3.7	6.1	3.0
5. 5 or more times	3.2	4.4	2.1	3.0	3.4	4.0	3.3	2.1	4.5	2.7	3.5	1.9	2.6	3.0	5.9	14.9
Item 6630 N(Wtd)	3716	1720	1843	2931	416	915	1065	1241	494	1767	1641	1356	996	465	751	67

A19M: Set fire to someone's property on purpose

1. Not at all	98.3	96.9	99.6	98.5	98.1	98.1	98.4	98.8	97.0	98.7	97.7	99.4	98.7	98.9	95.6	94.0
2. Once	1.0	1.7	.4	.9	1.2	1.1	.7	.9	1.8	.8	1.2	.3	1.0	.9	2.1	3.0
3. Twice	.4	.8	.1	.5	.2	.4	.7	.1	.8	.2	.7	-	.3	-	1.7	-
4. 3 or 4 times	.1	.2	-	.1	.7	.2	-	.2	-	.1	.2	.1	-	.4	-	3.0
5. 5 or more times	.2	.5	-	.2	-	.2	.2	-	.6	.3	.1	.2	-	-	.7	-
Item 6640 N(Wtd)	3725	1722	1849	2935	418	918	1066	1245	496	1779	1637	1361	999	467	751	67

A19N: Damaged school property on purpose

1. Not at all	87.7	82.5	92.9	87.0	92.5	85.7	86.6	90.6	87.2	89.5	86.4	94.4	88.9	85.8	76.6	67.2
2. Once	6.9	9.5	4.5	7.4	4.1	7.1	6.9	6.5	7.3	6.1	7.7	3.8	5.7	9.0	12.7	10.4
3. Twice	2.4	3.5	1.4	2.6	1.4	3.0	3.0	1.6	2.0	2.0	2.8	.8	2.7	2.6	4.1	10.4
4. 3 or 4 times	1.5	2.2	.8	1.5	1.7	2.5	2.0	.6	1.2	1.4	1.3	.5	1.6	1.9	2.5	7.5
5. 5 or more times	1.4	2.4	.4	1.6	-	1.8	1.6	.6	2.2	1.0	1.8	.4	1.1	.6	4.0	6.0
Item 6650 N(Wtd)	3705	1714	1839	2924	414	913	1057	1240	494	1765	1634	1351	996	465	747	67

A19O: Damaged property at work on purpose

1. Not at all	93.8	89.2	98.5	93.5	97.1	93.0	92.6	95.4	94.3	95.0	92.9	97.6	93.8	94.2	88.5	80.6
2. Once	2.9	4.9	.8	2.9	1.9	3.1	2.9	2.9	2.0	2.4	3.3	1.1	3.2	2.2	4.8	9.0
3. Twice	1.6	2.9	.4	1.7	.7	2.2	2.0	1.0	1.2	1.4	2.0	.7	1.6	1.7	2.5	7.5
4. 3 or 4 times	.9	1.6	.1	1.1	-	.5	1.4	.6	1.4	.6	1.2	.3	.7	.4	2.4	1.5
5. 5 or more times	.8	1.5	.1	.8	-	1.2	1.1	.2	1.0	.7	.7	.2	.7	1.3	1.7	3.0
Item 6660 N(Wtd)	3716	1718	1847	2934	416	917	1065	1240	493	1774	1637	1361	998	464	746	67

A19P: Gotten into trouble with police because of something you did

1. Not at all	80.7	70.7	91.0	79.7	89.2	79.8	77.7	84.1	79.9	84.1	77.8	92.5	81.1	76.3	64.1	53.7
2. Once	11.0	15.0	6.8	11.5	6.9	11.8	13.1	8.4	11.6	9.5	11.8	5.3	12.3	14.0	16.9	13.4
3. Twice	4.8	7.5	1.7	5.0	3.3	4.5	5.5	4.4	5.0	4.1	5.8	1.3	4.4	6.0	9.7	19.4
4. 3 or 4 times	2.3	4.5	.4	2.7	.5	2.7	2.0	2.4	2.0	1.4	3.2	.5	1.5	2.4	6.5	7.5
5. 5 or more times	1.2	2.3	.1	1.1	.2	1.2	1.6	.7	1.6	.8	1.4	.4	.8	1.3	2.9	6.0
Item 6670 N(Wtd)	3727	1724	1850	2938	418	918	1068	1243	498	1776	1642	1363	999	465	752	67

A20: The next questions are about some things which may have happened TO YOU. During the LAST 12 MONTHS, how often...

QUESTIONNAIRE FORM 2 1978	TOTAL	SEX		RACE		REGION				4YR COLLEGE PLANS		ILLICIT DRUG USE: LIFETIME				
		M	F	White	Black	NE	NC	S	W	Yes	No	None	Mari-juana Only	Few Pills	More Pills	Any Her-oin
Weighted No. of Cases: % of Weighted Total:	3785 100.0	1737 45.9	1867 49.3	2960 78.2	430 11.4	931 24.6	1083 28.6	1266 33.4	505 13.3	1790 47.3	1657 43.8	1363 36.0	1005 26.6	474 12.5	760 20.1	68 1.8
A20A: Has something of yours (worth under $50) been stolen?																
1. Not at all	57.1	52.5	61.8	56.6	60.2	57.0	56.5	59.5	52.4	54.6	59.8	64.5	56.5	52.4	46.1	53.7
2. Once	24.4	26.5	22.8	24.9	21.3	23.9	23.8	24.1	27.7	24.8	24.2	21.4	25.5	26.2	29.2	17.9
3. Twice	11.4	13.1	9.6	11.5	11.3	12.7	12.4	8.8	13.7	13.2	9.9	9.8	11.2	13.1	14.5	11.9
4. 3 or 4 times	5.2	5.6	4.4	5.2	5.3	4.6	5.4	5.8	4.2	5.7	4.3	3.1	5.2	6.7	7.9	6.0
5. 5 or more times	1.9	2.3	1.4	1.8	1.9	1.9	1.9	1.9	1.8	1.7	1.8	1.2	1.6	1.9	2.4	10.4
Item 6680 N(Wtd)	3718	1720	1846	2933	417	914	1063	1243	498	1773	1638	1356	998	466	751	67
A20B: Has something of yours (worth over $50) been stolen?																
1. Not at all	86.7	83.3	90.8	87.6	83.6	87.1	88.7	86.6	81.9	86.7	87.7	89.3	87.2	84.9	83.3	79.1
2. Once	10.5	12.8	7.6	10.0	11.4	9.6	9.3	10.1	15.5	10.6	9.7	9.2	10.2	11.5	12.4	10.4
3. Twice	2.1	2.6	1.5	1.8	3.6	2.4	1.5	2.6	1.4	2.2	1.6	1.1	1.9	3.0	3.1	7.5
4. 3 or 4 times	.6	1.1	.2	.5	1.2	.8	.5	.6	.8	.4	.8	.4	.8	.6	.8	1.5
5. 5 or more times	.1	.2	.1	.1	-	.1	-	.2	.2	.1	.1	.1	-	-	.3	1.5
Item 6690 N(Wtd)	3725	1720	1850	2937	421	917	1064	1248	496	1778	1637	1361	998	470	750	67
A20C: Has someone deliberately damaged your property (your car, clothing, etc.)?																
1. Not at all	67.9	58.8	76.6	67.5	72.2	68.2	67.8	68.1	66.9	68.5	67.8	73.6	66.8	62.9	62.2	67.2
2. Once	19.1	24.0	14.7	19.5	18.4	18.7	18.3	20.2	18.8	19.0	18.8	16.7	20.4	23.0	19.1	16.4
3. Twice	8.3	10.2	6.2	8.0	6.7	8.3	8.4	7.4	10.1	8.0	8.6	6.6	8.0	9.4	10.8	13.4
4. 3 or 4 times	3.7	5.4	2.2	4.0	1.7	3.8	4.4	3.1	3.4	3.5	3.9	2.4	4.1	3.9	5.9	1.5
5. 5 or more times	1.1	1.6	.3	1.0	.7	.9	1.1	1.1	1.0	1.2	.9	.7	.8	.9	2.0	-
Item 6700 N(Wtd)	3713	1716	1848	2932	418	911	1063	1245	495	1773	1637	1357	997	466	749	67
A20D: Has someone injured you with a weapon (like a knife, gun, or club)?																
1. Not at all	95.4	92.4	98.5	96.0	94.2	95.2	95.6	95.2	95.6	97.6	93.8	97.9	97.6	95.3	90.0	77.6
2. Once	3.1	4.9	1.2	2.9	3.6	3.6	3.0	3.0	2.8	1.6	4.1	1.3	1.7	4.3	6.4	17.9
3. Twice	.7	1.2	.2	.4	1.7	.7	.4	1.0	.8	.4	.8	.3	.4	.6	1.5	1.5
4. 3 or 4 times	.6	1.0	.1	.6	.7	.3	.8	.8	.4	.3	.9	.5	.1	-	1.6	3.0
5. 5 or more times	.2	.3	-	.2	-	.2	.4	.1	.2	-	.4	-	.3	-	.5	-
Item 6710 N(Wtd)	3721	1720	1850	2939	417	916	1066	1243	497	1775	1639	1361	997	467	750	67
A20E: Has someone threatened you with a weapon, but not actually injured you?																
1. Not at all	83.7	77.4	89.8	84.6	80.0	85.8	83.8	81.6	84.7	86.4	81.1	89.6	83.6	83.2	74.2	65.2
2. Once	10.0	12.8	7.0	9.1	13.2	8.5	9.4	11.5	9.9	8.7	11.1	6.6	10.7	11.6	14.2	12.1
3. Twice	3.6	5.8	1.5	3.9	2.9	3.7	4.1	3.4	3.0	2.6	4.4	2.2	4.0	2.6	5.6	15.2
4. 3 or 4 times	1.8	2.0	1.5	1.7	1.7	1.1	2.0	2.2	1.4	1.3	2.3	.9	.9	2.2	4.1	4.5
5. 5 or more times	1.0	2.0	.2	.7	1.9	.9	.7	1.4	1.0	1.0	1.2	.7	.9	.6	1.9	3.0
Item 6720 N(Wtd)	3715	1719	1845	2933	416	913	1064	1242	496	1775	1637	1358	998	465	749	66
A20F: Has someone injured you on purpose without using a weapon?																
1. Not at all	84.6	83.6	85.8	84.8	84.9	83.4	84.9	84.5	86.9	86.4	83.7	90.8	86.7	81.2	74.6	67.2
2. Once	9.5	10.5	8.3	9.2	9.6	10.6	8.7	9.8	8.0	8.6	10.1	6.0	8.4	13.3	13.6	17.9
3. Twice	2.8	3.5	2.0	2.7	3.1	3.0	2.9	2.7	2.6	2.4	3.1	1.3	2.5	3.0	5.6	9.0
4. 3 or 4 times	1.8	1.3	2.3	1.9	1.2	1.8	2.0	1.7	1.8	1.6	1.8	.8	1.3	1.7	4.0	3.0
5. 5 or more times	1.3	1.1	1.6	1.4	1.0	1.4	1.5	1.4	.4	1.1	1.3	1.0	1.1	.9	2.1	3.0
Item 6730 N(Wtd)	3719	1721	1850	2935	418	914	1065	1243	497	1776	1636	1360	998	467	749	67
A20G: Has an unarmed person threatened you with injury, but not actually injured you?																
1. Not at all	72.9	65.4	80.0	72.6	75.8	70.8	71.3	74.4	76.5	73.0	73.4	82.6	73.5	69.2	57.7	58.2
2. Once	12.5	14.1	11.0	12.3	14.1	12.6	12.6	12.8	11.9	12.6	12.0	9.6	12.2	13.5	17.4	11.9
3. Twice	5.8	7.8	3.9	5.9	6.2	6.3	6.8	5.1	4.6	7.1	4.9	3.1	6.4	7.7	8.7	10.4
4. 3 or 4 times	4.4	6.2	2.9	4.9	1.9	5.6	3.9	4.3	3.6	3.3	5.7	2.1	5.0	4.3	7.6	13.4
5. 5 or more times	4.3	6.4	2.1	4.4	1.9	4.8	5.3	3.5	3.4	4.1	4.2	2.6	3.0	5.1	8.7	6.0
Item 6740 N(Wtd)	3718	1720	1850	2937	418	912	1066	1243	497	1776	1637	1360	1000	467	747	67

QUESTIONNAIRE FORM 2 1978	TOTAL	SEX		RACE		REGION				4YR COLLEGE PLANS		ILLICIT DRUG USE: LIFETIME				
		M	F	White	Black	NE	NC	S	W	Yes	No	None	Mari-juana Only	Few Pills	More Pills	Any Her-oin
Weighted No. of Cases:	3785	1737	1867	2960	430	931	1083	1266	505	1790	1657	1363	1005	474	760	68
% of Weighted Total:	100.0	45.9	49.3	78.2	11.4	24.6	28.6	33.4	13.3	47.3	43.8	36.0	26.6	12.5	20.1	1.8

A21: The following questions concern cigarettes, alcohol, and a number of other drugs. How difficult do you think it would be for you to get each of the following types of drugs, if you wanted some?

A21A: Marijuana (pot, grass)

	TOTAL	M	F	White	Black	NE	NC	S	W	Yes	No	None	Mari-juana Only	Few Pills	More Pills	Any Her-oin
1. Probably impossible	5.9	4.3	7.0	3.6	17.3	2.8	3.7	9.9	6.3	4.5	7.2	12.5	.9	4.1	.7	4.5
2. Very difficult	1.9	1.6	2.0	1.2	4.3	.7	1.2	2.8	3.4	2.0	1.7	4.0	.7	1.1	.1	-
3. Fairly difficult	4.4	3.6	5.2	4.3	5.9	3.6	4.2	5.0	4.7	3.9	5.0	8.1	2.5	2.6	1.5	1.5
4. Fairly easy	23.2	22.7	24.2	22.6	27.8	18.9	23.7	27.4	20.0	23.7	23.4	30.6	22.3	20.3	13.5	7.5
5. Very easy	64.5	67.8	61.6	68.3	44.4	74.0	67.1	55.0	65.4	65.9	62.7	45.0	73.6	71.7	84.1	86.6
Item 6750 N(Wtd)	3696	1710	1836	2917	421	906	1065	1231	494	1767	1626	1338	1002	467	747	67

A21B: LSD

	TOTAL	M	F	White	Black	NE	NC	S	W	Yes	No	None	Mari-juana Only	Few Pills	More Pills	Any Her-oin
1. Probably impossible	19.9	18.0	20.8	14.2	51.0	13.9	17.6	26.5	19.5	16.4	22.7	25.1	18.9	19.8	9.0	13.4
2. Very difficult	18.5	18.9	17.5	18.3	19.5	18.1	17.5	20.4	16.5	20.3	16.2	18.9	19.2	18.7	16.9	10.4
3. Fairly difficult	29.4	30.3	29.1	32.3	13.4	31.2	32.4	26.3	27.2	31.3	28.5	27.1	30.6	29.1	34.1	29.9
4. Fairly easy	25.7	25.8	26.7	28.6	12.2	29.6	25.9	22.0	27.6	26.6	25.5	24.2	24.8	25.2	30.9	32.8
5. Very easy	6.5	7.0	5.8	6.6	3.9	7.1	6.7	5.0	9.1	5.4	7.2	4.8	6.6	7.2	8.9	13.4
Item 6760 N(Wtd)	3630	1688	1798	2867	410	890	1046	1208	486	1728	1607	1301	989	460	741	67

A21C: Some other psychedelic(mescaline, peyote, psilocybin, PCP, etc.)

	TOTAL	M	F	White	Black	NE	NC	S	W	Yes	No	None	Mari-juana Only	Few Pills	More Pills	Any Her-oin
1. Probably impossible	22.3	18.7	25.1	16.2	55.8	16.3	18.9	30.6	20.4	19.6	24.4	31.2	20.5	19.5	8.2	16.9
2. Very difficult	19.1	19.0	19.6	19.3	18.3	16.5	19.9	20.7	17.9	19.3	19.1	20.8	21.5	16.4	15.5	6.2
3. Fairly difficult	24.8	24.0	25.5	27.5	11.6	25.1	27.5	23.2	22.7	26.2	24.0	24.4	25.9	28.3	24.2	18.5
4. Fairly easy	25.6	28.3	23.4	28.5	9.1	31.6	25.8	20.5	27.3	26.6	25.2	18.7	25.4	27.0	38.0	32.3
5. Very easy	8.2	9.9	6.4	8.5	5.4	10.5	8.0	5.1	11.7	8.3	7.3	4.9	6.8	8.8	14.2	26.2
Item 6770 N(Wtd)	3598	1672	1785	2846	405	885	1033	1200	480	1715	1592	1288	980	456	740	65

A21D: Amphetamines (uppers, pep pills, bennies, speed)

	TOTAL	M	F	White	Black	NE	NC	S	W	Yes	No	None	Mari-juana Only	Few Pills	More Pills	Any Her-oin
1. Probably impossible	14.0	12.1	15.5	9.0	42.1	10.0	10.1	20.0	14.7	11.5	15.3	22.1	11.8	10.0	2.6	10.6
2. Very difficult	9.6	9.8	8.9	8.7	12.7	7.3	10.1	10.3	11.0	10.8	8.7	12.3	11.3	6.3	4.7	3.0
3. Fairly difficult	17.8	19.1	16.6	19.1	12.7	18.5	20.6	16.6	13.7	19.0	16.7	20.0	19.5	20.6	11.3	10.6
4. Fairly easy	37.4	38.2	37.7	40.6	21.7	40.6	36.8	35.4	37.6	39.6	35.9	32.1	40.7	40.0	42.9	31.8
5. Very easy	21.1	20.8	21.4	22.6	11.2	23.6	22.3	17.7	22.8	19.0	23.4	13.6	16.5	23.2	38.7	45.5
Item 6780 N(Wtd)	3632	1689	1799	2870	411	887	1048	1215	482	1733	1606	1303	989	462	742	66

A21E: Barbiturates (downers, goofballs, reds, yellows, etc.)

	TOTAL	M	F	White	Black	NE	NC	S	W	Yes	No	None	Mari-juana Only	Few Pills	More Pills	Any Her-oin
1. Probably impossible	15.5	13.4	17.1	10.4	43.6	10.8	12.8	21.0	16.1	11.9	18.1	23.6	13.2	13.2	4.7	7.6
2. Very difficult	12.5	13.0	11.4	11.7	15.7	10.0	13.1	13.1	13.8	13.0	12.2	12.0	16.4	11.3	7.9	6.1
3. Fairly difficult	21.4	23.2	19.8	22.9	12.7	23.3	23.5	19.4	18.2	23.5	19.6	21.6	20.3	25.3	21.5	10.6
4. Fairly easy	34.5	34.7	35.5	38.2	17.6	36.3	35.1	32.5	35.3	36.6	33.5	30.7	36.4	34.8	40.6	34.8
5. Very easy	16.1	15.7	16.1	16.8	10.0	19.5	15.6	13.9	16.3	15.0	16.7	12.1	13.7	15.4	25.2	40.9
Item 6790 N(Wtd)	3632	1692	1796	2875	408	888	1046	1214	484	1734	1605	1305	989	462	743	66

A21F: Tranquilizers

	TOTAL	M	F	White	Black	NE	NC	S	W	Yes	No	None	Mari-juana Only	Few Pills	More Pills	Any Her-oin
1. Probably impossible	11.3	10.5	11.4	6.4	36.8	6.8	8.5	17.1	11.3	8.2	13.1	16.6	9.9	8.5	3.4	13.6
2. Very difficult	8.0	8.6	7.2	7.4	10.3	7.1	8.9	7.0	10.1	7.2	8.7	8.9	9.1	8.2	4.3	1.5
3. Fairly difficult	16.4	17.1	15.2	17.5	10.8	17.1	19.9	13.9	13.8	16.2	16.6	15.0	18.0	15.6	17.8	13.6
4. Fairly easy	36.1	38.9	34.9	39.1	21.8	39.3	35.1	35.2	34.4	39.3	34.4	34.7	38.7	37.3	34.7	45.5
5. Very easy	28.2	24.9	31.3	29.6	20.6	29.7	27.6	26.8	30.5	29.0	27.2	24.8	24.4	30.2	39.7	27.3
Item 6800 N(Wtd)	3630	1687	1800	2871	408	885	1048	1211	486	1737	1605	1309	988	461	738	66

QUESTIONNAIRE FORM 2 1978	TOTAL	SEX		RACE		REGION				4YR COLLEGE PLANS		ILLICIT DRUG USE: LIFETIME				
		M	F	White	Black	NE	NC	S	W	Yes	No	None	Mari-juana Only	Few Pills	More Pills	Any Her-oin
Weighted No. of Cases:	3785	1737	1867	2960	430	931	1083	1266	505	1790	1657	1363	1005	474	760	68
% of Weighted Total:	100.0	45.9	49.3	78.2	11.4	24.6	28.6	33.4	13.3	47.3	43.8	36.0	26.6	12.5	20.1	1.8
A21G: Cocaine																
1. Probably impossible	19.3	16.5	21.4	14.6	45.9	12.7	17.5	26.1	18.4	17.0	21.1	28.8	17.1	15.3	6.4	6.0
2. Very difficult	16.9	17.3	16.6	17.5	14.5	14.7	19.6	17.2	14.7	16.4	17.7	20.1	15.8	17.9	12.9	9.0
3. Fairly difficult	26.0	26.3	26.1	28.5	13.5	28.3	29.1	22.9	22.4	26.9	25.5	27.1	27.7	25.3	24.2	20.9
4. Fairly easy	25.3	26.6	24.2	27.1	16.7	29.1	22.9	24.2	26.5	27.4	23.3	17.3	28.8	28.4	33.4	29.9
5. Very easy	12.5	13.3	11.7	12.4	9.6	15.3	10.9	9.6	18.0	12.2	12.4	6.6	10.9	13.3	23.0	34.3
Item 6810 N(Wtd)	3623	1683	1798	2868	407	887	1045	1208	483	1727	1604	1301	984	458	745	67
A21H: Heroin (smack, horse)																
1. Probably impossible	32.1	29.7	33.3	27.6	53.8	26.4	30.5	37.6	32.1	29.5	33.6	36.2	29.3	35.1	25.8	12.1
2. Very difficult	26.3	28.8	24.2	28.2	16.7	28.7	27.2	25.1	23.3	27.9	25.1	23.6	27.0	27.2	31.4	21.2
3. Fairly difficult	25.2	26.0	25.0	27.5	14.0	28.1	27.2	21.8	24.2	27.5	23.6	23.7	27.3	22.7	27.9	24.2
4. Fairly easy	11.2	10.0	12.7	11.7	10.3	11.1	10.1	11.7	12.5	10.9	12.2	11.8	11.8	10.6	9.2	25.8
5. Very easy	5.2	5.6	4.8	5.0	4.9	5.7	5.1	3.7	8.1	4.2	5.6	4.8	4.6	4.6	5.7	18.2
Item 6820 N(Wtd)	3603	1672	1789	2846	407	879	1038	1205	480	1718	1596	1292	985	453	739	66
A21I: Some other narcotic (methadone, opium, codeine, paregoric, etc.)																
1. Probably impossible	25.6	23.2	27.0	20.5	53.1	19.5	24.3	32.1	23.4	22.1	27.7	32.4	23.6	27.6	13.8	9.1
2. Very difficult	22.5	22.3	22.7	23.6	16.6	23.5	22.5	22.2	21.6	23.3	22.6	21.7	25.1	23.2	20.9	19.7
3. Fairly difficult	25.8	28.6	23.6	28.6	13.2	29.6	27.3	22.4	24.3	28.5	23.8	25.1	27.2	22.1	28.6	24.2
4. Fairly easy	17.8	17.4	18.6	19.2	10.2	17.5	17.9	17.1	19.9	18.1	18.0	15.0	17.0	19.5	23.4	24.2
5. Very easy	8.2	8.5	8.1	8.2	6.9	9.8	8.0	6.2	10.8	8.1	7.9	5.8	7.3	7.7	13.1	22.7
Item 6830 N(Wtd)	3602	1671	1788	2848	403	884	1034	1202	482	1718	1596	1289	984	456	740	66

This section asks for your views and feelings about a number of different things.

	TOTAL	M	F	White	Black	NE	NC	S	W	Yes	No	None	Mari-juana Only	Few Pills	More Pills	Any Her-oin
D01: How satisfied are you with your life as a whole these days?																
1. Completely dissatisfied	2.2	2.1	2.4	2.0	3.2	2.3	1.5	2.5	2.9	1.9	2.4	1.9	2.3	1.8	2.3	6.5
2. Quite dissatisfied	9.0	8.7	9.3	8.8	9.1	10.4	8.5	8.6	8.9	9.7	8.7	9.5	8.5	10.3	8.4	6.5
3. Somewhat dissatisfied	11.9	12.1	11.7	11.5	15.0	14.4	10.2	11.8	11.8	11.8	12.0	8.6	12.1	11.9	16.5	24.2
4. Neither, or mixed feelings	11.6	11.3	11.7	11.4	10.2	12.7	12.0	10.6	11.6	9.2	14.3	8.7	11.9	14.4	14.2	14.5
5. Somewhat satisfied	24.0	25.1	23.0	24.3	25.5	22.0	26.6	24.0	22.3	22.3	25.5	24.4	21.4	23.7	26.6	25.8
6. Quite satisfied	34.6	34.9	34.7	36.0	25.7	32.6	35.0	35.1	36.2	39.2	30.0	38.0	37.6	33.6	27.1	21.0
7. Completely satisfied	6.6	5.8	7.2	5.9	11.3	5.9	6.1	7.5	6.7	6.0	7.1	8.8	6.1	4.6	4.8	1.6
Item 6840 N(Wtd)	3485	1600	1790	2828	373	829	1034	1173	448	1747	1598	1292	939	438	702	62
D02: These next questions ask you to guess how well you might do in several different situations. How good do you think you would be...																
D02A: As a husband or wife?																
1. Poor	.7	1.0	.5	.6	1.1	.4	.7	1.0	.7	.6	.9	.2	.4	1.1	1.3	4.8
2. Not so good	1.6	1.6	1.3	1.7	.3	1.8	1.7	1.3	2.0	1.8	1.4	1.4	1.8	1.4	2.0	-
3. Fairly good	10.1	9.2	11.1	10.2	6.5	10.4	8.9	10.7	10.5	8.6	12.0	9.1	9.8	11.7	10.5	14.5
4. Good	39.0	42.1	36.6	40.0	34.3	37.7	38.7	40.9	37.4	38.6	39.2	38.3	38.7	39.1	41.0	38.7
5. Very good	43.4	39.0	47.0	42.2	53.2	42.5	45.7	41.5	44.5	45.5	40.9	45.5	44.5	41.9	39.3	37.1
8. Don't know	5.2	7.1	3.5	5.1	4.6	7.2	4.4	4.7	4.9	4.9	5.5	5.4	4.7	4.8	5.9	4.8
Item 6850 N(Wtd)	3471	1593	1784	2817	370	824	1028	1169	449	1741	1593	1290	937	437	695	62
D02B: As a parent?																
1. Poor	1.4	1.3	1.6	1.5	.8	1.5	1.4	1.6	1.1	1.4	1.6	.9	.9	2.5	2.3	4.8
2. Not so good	3.2	2.7	3.6	3.8	.3	2.8	3.0	3.1	4.9	2.6	4.0	2.6	2.8	3.0	5.2	3.2
3. Fairly good	10.8	11.1	10.7	11.0	5.8	10.0	12.3	10.7	9.4	9.0	12.8	9.6	11.1	14.3	11.0	6.5
4. Good	36.1	36.3	36.0	37.4	29.4	37.5	35.6	36.5	33.6	36.8	35.6	38.0	35.9	36.3	34.1	21.0
5. Very good	41.5	40.5	42.8	39.4	58.0	40.5	40.7	41.3	45.7	43.4	39.1	41.4	43.3	37.9	40.5	51.6
8. Don't know	6.9	8.2	5.4	6.9	6.0	7.8	7.0	6.8	5.3	6.8	7.0	7.5	6.0	6.2	7.1	9.7
Item 6860 N(Wtd)	3462	1589	1782	2817	364	823	1026	1164	449	1737	1590	1287	935	433	694	62

QUESTIONNAIRE FORM 2 1978	TOTAL	SEX		RACE		REGION				4YR COLLEGE PLANS		ILLICIT DRUG USE: LIFETIME				
		M	F	White	Black	NE	NC	S	W	Yes	No	None	Mari- juana Only	Few Pills	More Pills	Any Her- oin
Weighted No. of Cases:	3785	1737	1867	2960	430	931	1083	1266	505	1790	1657	1363	1005	474	760	68
% of Weighted Total:	100.0	45.9	49.3	78.2	11.4	24.6	28.6	33.4	13.3	47.3	43.8	36.0	26.6	12.5	20.1	1.8

D02C: As a worker on a job?

	TOTAL	M	F	White	Black	NE	NC	S	W	Yes	No	None	Mari-juana Only	Few Pills	More Pills	Any Heroin
1. Poor	.3	.4	.2	.2	.5	.1	.2	.5	-	.1	.6	.2	-	.5	.6	-
2. Not so good	.6	.4	.8	.7	-	1.0	.4	.6	.4	.3	.8	.3	.6	.9	.6	4.9
3. Fairly good	4.8	3.5	6.0	4.8	3.8	5.3	4.6	4.9	4.2	3.3	6.4	4.2	3.9	5.3	6.1	6.6
4. Good	35.2	32.0	38.0	36.7	26.3	34.1	35.9	35.7	34.3	32.2	38.8	35.1	34.9	37.9	35.4	21.3
5. Very good	58.1	62.6	54.1	56.6	68.5	58.5	57.9	57.0	60.6	63.3	52.2	58.6	59.9	54.5	56.8	67.2
8. Don't know	1.0	1.1	1.0	.9	.8	.8	1.1	1.1	.7	.7	1.3	1.6	.7	.9	.6	-
Item 6870 N(Wtd)	3461	1588	1783	2814	365	824	1024	1164	449	1736	1590	1286	937	433	692	61

D03: Some people think a lot about the social problems of the nation and the world, and about how they might be solved. Others spend little time thinking about these issues. How much do you think about such things?

	TOTAL	M	F	White	Black	NE	NC	S	W	Yes	No	None	Mari-juana Only	Few Pills	More Pills	Any Heroin
1. Never	5.1	6.2	4.2	4.9	5.5	5.2	4.4	6.0	4.3	2.4	8.2	5.1	5.6	3.2	5.2	10.7
2. Seldom	21.1	18.0	23.4	21.4	19.1	22.7	22.9	19.4	18.6	16.5	26.0	21.5	21.5	21.0	20.1	16.1
3. Sometimes	48.5	49.0	48.1	49.4	43.2	48.9	50.1	46.7	49.4	49.9	47.7	48.7	48.8	48.5	48.5	39.3
4. Quite often	20.4	22.3	18.9	19.9	24.3	17.4	18.7	22.9	22.8	25.2	14.8	20.7	19.7	21.7	18.7	28.6
5. A great deal	4.9	4.4	5.5	4.5	7.9	5.8	4.1	5.0	4.9	5.9	3.2	3.9	4.3	5.5	7.4	5.4
Item 6880 N(Wtd)	3444	1575	1777	2796	366	812	1024	1161	447	1733	1576	1286	927	433	691	56

D04: Now we'd like you to make some ratings of how honest and moral the people are who run the following organizations. To what extent are there problems of dishonesty and immorality in the leadership of...

D04A: Large corporations?

	TOTAL	M	F	White	Black	NE	NC	S	W	Yes	No	None	Mari-juana Only	Few Pills	More Pills	Any Heroin
1. Not at all	3.1	4.3	2.1	2.2	7.4	2.8	2.0	3.9	4.3	2.1	4.3	3.5	2.4	3.1	2.3	10.3
2. Slight	14.6	17.2	12.2	14.3	14.4	13.3	16.2	14.7	13.0	13.3	16.5	14.4	17.0	12.8	12.5	10.3
3. Moderate	30.6	28.8	32.0	32.6	22.1	30.6	33.3	29.2	27.8	30.7	30.3	32.6	28.4	27.3	31.4	34.5
4. Considerable	26.5	27.1	26.3	27.6	19.8	26.8	25.5	26.5	28.7	31.1	21.7	26.1	27.1	29.4	26.6	20.7
5. Great	9.1	10.5	8.0	8.7	13.3	11.2	7.8	8.9	9.1	10.3	7.8	8.4	9.4	8.1	10.4	12.1
8. No opinion	16.0	12.0	19.5	14.7	22.7	15.2	15.3	16.8	17.3	12.6	19.4	14.9	15.7	19.7	16.8	12.1
Item 6890 N(Wtd)	3373	1550	1735	2752	353	784	1019	1132	439	1693	1537	1269	908	422	665	58

D04B: Major labor unions?

	TOTAL	M	F	White	Black	NE	NC	S	W	Yes	No	None	Mari-juana Only	Few Pills	More Pills	Any Heroin
1. Not at all	3.6	5.0	2.3	2.8	6.0	3.2	3.3	3.6	4.6	2.3	4.9	4.6	2.4	2.6	2.9	11.5
2. Slight	13.6	13.8	13.4	13.5	14.7	13.8	14.7	12.7	13.5	12.6	15.3	13.1	14.7	14.0	12.0	21.3
3. Moderate	29.5	29.5	29.6	30.4	24.7	30.5	28.6	30.8	26.9	29.9	28.8	31.0	28.6	27.1	29.4	24.6
4. Considerable	24.5	24.9	23.8	25.3	20.7	24.6	26.5	21.7	26.7	28.6	20.5	24.7	25.9	22.6	24.8	21.3
5. Great	10.6	14.3	7.5	11.0	9.8	11.3	9.9	11.2	9.8	12.0	9.1	10.2	11.2	11.9	9.8	9.8
8. No opinion	18.1	12.5	23.3	17.0	24.1	16.8	16.8	20.0	18.5	14.6	21.5	16.4	17.2	21.9	21.2	11.5
Item 6900 N(Wtd)	3363	1549	1728	2751	348	778	1017	1130	438	1680	1540	1261	903	421	666	61

D04C: The nation's colleges and universities?

	TOTAL	M	F	White	Black	NE	NC	S	W	Yes	No	None	Mari-juana Only	Few Pills	More Pills	Any Heroin
1. Not at all	6.0	7.1	5.2	6.0	5.5	5.3	5.6	6.4	7.6	5.1	7.0	6.4	6.2	6.7	3.9	8.2
2. Slight	30.7	33.0	28.7	32.6	21.7	29.9	32.1	30.0	30.9	37.1	24.2	33.3	29.5	31.3	28.2	26.2
3. Moderate	28.3	28.6	28.4	29.7	21.7	30.6	28.9	27.1	25.8	29.5	26.7	26.9	30.4	25.6	30.8	18.0
4. Considerable	14.5	14.1	14.5	13.3	18.8	15.0	13.1	15.7	13.8	13.4	15.8	14.1	14.3	15.6	14.7	16.4
5. Great	5.0	4.3	5.5	3.9	12.2	4.4	3.0	6.1	7.4	4.6	5.6	5.4	5.0	3.8	3.2	14.8
8. No opinion	15.5	12.9	17.6	14.5	19.7	14.8	17.2	14.8	14.7	10.3	20.7	13.8	14.5	16.7	19.3	18.0
Item 6910 N(Wtd)	3349	1538	1723	2743	345	775	1015	1124	434	1670	1534	1258	898	418	662	61

D04D: The nation's public schools?

	TOTAL	M	F	White	Black	NE	NC	S	W	Yes	No	None	Mari-juana Only	Few Pills	More Pills	Any Heroin
1. Not at all	6.4	8.1	4.9	6.2	4.3	6.7	5.6	6.4	7.4	4.9	8.5	7.4	6.1	5.0	4.7	9.8
2. Slight	31.5	33.1	30.1	33.9	21.3	30.7	34.2	29.7	31.4	36.5	26.5	32.9	31.7	33.5	28.9	24.6
3. Moderate	25.9	25.5	26.1	26.6	23.0	27.0	26.7	24.8	24.5	27.0	24.6	25.9	26.6	22.5	27.4	23.0
4. Considerable	17.8	17.5	17.8	16.9	22.4	17.1	17.2	18.6	18.5	17.4	18.0	16.9	18.2	18.4	18.8	18.0
5. Great	8.4	7.8	9.3	7.0	17.3	7.8	5.9	11.1	8.3	8.2	8.3	8.5	8.4	8.6	7.4	13.1
8. No opinion	9.9	7.9	11.8	9.5	11.6	10.6	10.2	9.2	9.9	6.0	14.0	8.4	9.1	11.7	12.7	11.5
Item 6920 N(Wtd)	3350	1539	1723	2736	352	774	1011	1132	433	1677	1531	1257	903	418	661	61

QUESTIONNAIRE FORM 2 1978	TOTAL	SEX		RACE		REGION				4YR COLLEGE PLANS		ILLICIT DRUG USE: LIFETIME				
		M	F	White	Black	NE	NC	S	W	Yes	No	None	Marijuana Only	Few Pills	More Pills	Any Heroin
Weighted No. of Cases:	3785	1737	1867	2960	430	931	1083	1266	505	1790	1657	1363	1005	474	760	68
% of Weighted Total:	100.0	45.9	49.3	78.2	11.4	24.6	28.6	33.4	13.3	47.3	43.8	36.0	26.6	12.5	20.1	1.8
D04E: Churches and religious organizations?																
1. Not at all	18.6	20.8	16.5	19.9	9.5	19.2	17.9	17.3	22.4	18.6	19.1	18.8	19.9	18.4	17.8	8.3
2. Slight	34.2	33.4	35.0	36.8	20.7	35.2	37.3	31.8	31.6	40.3	28.0	36.3	34.4	32.5	33.3	18.3
3. Moderate	13.7	13.6	14.2	13.4	16.4	14.0	13.0	13.6	15.2	14.3	12.7	13.0	13.0	14.6	14.9	13.3
4. Considerable	11.0	10.1	11.8	10.1	17.0	11.1	11.3	11.0	10.1	9.3	12.7	10.0	11.6	12.0	11.3	18.3
5. Great	9.7	10.7	8.7	7.9	21.6	7.8	7.8	12.9	9.4	8.7	10.7	10.8	9.2	9.6	6.6	26.7
8. No opinion	12.7	11.3	13.8	11.9	15.0	12.8	12.8	13.3	11.3	8.7	16.8	11.2	11.9	13.2	15.8	16.7
Item 6930 N(Wtd)	3345	1542	1715	2734	347	772	1009	1131	434	1673	1528	1254	899	418	663	60
D04F: The national news media (TV, magazines, news services)?																
1. Not at all	3.3	4.6	1.8	2.8	4.3	3.8	1.9	3.4	5.1	2.4	4.0	3.3	3.2	3.1	2.7	8.3
2. Slight	20.8	21.4	20.5	21.6	17.9	20.3	22.2	21.1	17.2	22.0	20.1	22.4	18.8	21.0	21.1	15.0
3. Moderate	29.8	31.2	28.6	31.9	19.4	32.1	31.5	26.9	29.2	32.7	26.7	27.6	31.6	30.9	31.4	30.0
4. Considerable	23.2	21.7	24.7	22.9	22.2	21.4	23.8	23.5	23.9	23.7	22.0	24.1	24.5	21.7	20.4	25.0
5. Great	12.4	12.2	12.6	11.0	21.4	11.7	10.4	13.6	15.3	11.9	13.2	13.0	11.9	11.8	11.8	11.7
8. No opinion	10.6	8.9	11.8	9.7	15.1	10.5	10.1	11.5	9.3	7.3	14.0	9.5	9.9	11.6	12.5	8.3
Item 6940 N(Wtd)	3350	1540	1719	2734	351	772	1012	1135	431	1675	1529	1253	901	424	662	60
D04G: The Presidency and the administration?																
1. Not at all	3.7	5.2	2.3	3.0	5.5	3.2	3.3	3.5	6.0	2.4	5.1	4.2	3.0	3.8	2.6	11.9
2. Slight	19.5	22.6	16.9	20.7	16.5	17.5	21.2	19.4	19.7	21.4	17.2	21.0	20.0	19.1	16.5	18.6
3. Moderate	29.7	32.0	28.1	31.1	23.4	28.5	30.3	30.6	28.1	32.9	26.3	30.3	30.1	28.9	29.7	16.9
4. Considerable	22.3	19.6	24.5	22.8	19.4	24.9	21.2	20.9	23.4	23.7	21.1	22.1	21.7	22.4	24.1	25.4
5. Great	11.6	11.4	11.7	10.5	15.6	13.5	11.1	11.0	11.1	11.1	12.1	9.8	12.4	11.9	13.0	20.3
8. No opinion	13.2	9.3	16.6	11.9	19.7	12.3	13.0	14.6	11.8	8.5	18.1	12.5	12.9	13.8	14.1	8.5
Item 6950 N(Wtd)	3337	1529	1721	2731	346	771	1010	1124	431	1669	1526	1249	898	419	661	59
D04H: Congress--that is, the U.S. Senate and House of Representatives?																
1. Not at all	3.5	5.0	2.0	3.0	5.2	4.0	2.9	3.0	4.9	1.9	5.3	3.1	3.1	3.1	3.0	18.6
2. Slight	16.4	17.6	15.4	16.6	16.1	13.8	16.3	17.9	16.9	17.2	15.5	18.3	16.3	14.6	13.3	10.2
3. Moderate	28.8	30.2	27.8	30.5	23.0	27.0	29.9	28.5	29.7	31.0	26.0	29.0	26.6	31.6	30.1	23.7
4. Considerable	23.9	23.0	24.2	24.5	19.3	26.2	24.4	21.9	23.9	27.7	20.5	24.6	25.1	23.9	22.5	22.0
5. Great	11.4	12.2	11.0	10.6	15.5	12.8	10.3	12.0	10.3	11.2	11.5	9.7	13.9	8.9	12.9	13.6
8. No opinion	16.1	11.9	19.6	14.8	21.0	16.2	16.1	16.7	14.1	11.0	21.2	15.3	15.0	17.7	17.9	11.9
Item 6960 N(Wtd)	3332	1530	1716	2724	348	767	1012	1126	427	1666	1524	1252	892	418	661	59
D04I: The U.S. Supreme Court?																
1. Not at all	10.6	14.7	6.8	10.7	9.5	10.5	10.5	9.5	13.5	12.2	9.0	11.0	11.6	9.4	9.1	10.2
2. Slight	25.2	28.1	22.9	26.7	18.2	24.0	27.3	23.9	26.0	30.4	19.9	25.8	24.6	26.3	24.7	20.3
3. Moderate	24.4	22.1	26.2	25.0	22.0	25.1	24.4	23.8	24.3	25.3	23.0	26.2	23.3	25.1	22.0	25.4
4. Considerable	14.6	14.6	14.5	13.9	17.9	14.1	13.5	15.7	14.7	11.8	17.2	12.6	16.5	12.6	16.5	18.6
5. Great	7.5	7.9	7.2	7.1	9.5	9.1	6.4	7.9	6.4	6.7	8.8	6.7	7.5	7.2	8.2	13.6
8. No opinion	17.7	12.6	22.4	16.6	23.1	17.1	17.9	19.1	15.1	13.5	22.1	17.7	16.5	19.1	19.4	11.9
Item 6970 N(Wtd)	3320	1526	1709	2719	346	772	1006	1120	423	1661	1521	1246	893	414	660	59
D04J: All the courts and the justice system in general?																
1. Not at all	5.3	6.3	4.2	4.7	7.8	6.7	4.4	4.5	6.6	3.9	7.0	5.4	4.7	7.4	3.6	11.9
2. Slight	25.1	27.2	23.3	26.5	18.8	22.3	27.3	24.1	27.3	29.1	20.9	25.0	26.0	25.4	24.4	15.3
3. Moderate	29.8	30.5	29.1	31.0	23.5	29.1	30.7	29.8	28.9	32.8	26.3	31.4	28.4	28.5	29.3	32.2
4. Considerable	17.1	16.9	17.5	16.8	17.4	18.9	16.1	16.5	17.4	16.0	17.9	16.5	19.4	16.8	15.7	18.6
5. Great	6.8	7.6	5.8	6.4	9.0	7.7	6.1	7.1	5.9	7.1	6.9	5.9	6.1	5.5	10.1	11.9
8. No opinion	16.0	11.4	20.0	14.6	23.5	15.3	15.3	17.9	13.9	11.1	21.0	15.7	15.4	16.3	16.5	10.2
Item 6980 N(Wtd)	3328	1531	1710	2722	345	771	1010	1122	425	1665	1521	1251	890	417	661	59

QUESTIONNAIRE FORM 2 1978	TOTAL	SEX		RACE		REGION				4YR COLLEGE PLANS		ILLICIT DRUG USE: LIFETIME				
		M	F	White	Black	NE	NC	S	W	Yes	No	None	Marijuana Only	Few Pills	More Pills	Any Heroin
Weighted No. of Cases:	3785	1737	1867	2960	430	931	1083	1266	505	1790	1657	1363	1005	474	760	68
% of Weighted Total:	100.0	45.9	49.3	78.2	11.4	24.6	28.6	33.4	13.3	47.3	43.8	36.0	26.6	12.5	20.1	1.8

D04K: The police and other law enforcement agencies?

	TOTAL	M	F	White	Black	NE	NC	S	W	Yes	No	None	Marijuana Only	Few Pills	More Pills	Any Heroin
1. Not at all	4.2	4.8	3.4	3.5	7.8	4.5	3.0	4.8	4.9	3.0	5.6	4.4	3.7	4.1	3.3	13.8
2. Slight	21.7	21.2	22.6	23.1	15.3	20.5	23.5	19.6	25.1	22.0	21.2	25.7	19.8	21.7	17.1	19.0
3. Moderate	31.4	33.4	29.7	33.0	25.1	30.3	33.3	30.6	31.0	35.4	27.2	31.4	34.1	30.8	29.7	20.7
4. Considerable	21.5	20.2	22.4	21.7	17.3	22.9	21.4	21.4	19.2	22.4	20.7	20.4	21.3	23.9	22.8	19.0
5. Great	11.3	12.1	10.1†	9.9	19.1	11.0	9.0	13.5	11.0	10.8	11.6	9.0	10.8	10.3	16.2	22.4
8. No opinion	10.0	8.2	11.8	8.7	15.3	10.8	9.9	10.0	8.9	6.4	13.9	9.1	10.3	9.5	10.9	6.9
Item 6990 N(Wtd)	3333	1531	1716	2729	346	770	1013	1123	426	1667	1524	1253	892	419	661	58

D04L: The U.S. military?

	TOTAL	M	F	White	Black	NE	NC	S	W	Yes	No	None	Marijuana Only	Few Pills	More Pills	Any Heroin
1. Not at all	8.5	9.4	7.7	7.8	13.0	8.2	6.6	10.1	9.9	7.8	9.7	9.1	8.4	9.2	6.9	10.3
2. Slight	26.5	28.1	24.9	28.2	17.1	27.1	28.6	24.2	25.9	29.6	23.0	27.8	27.0	25.6	24.6	19.0
3. Moderate	25.9	27.0	24.9	27.0	19.4	26.0	25.5	26.0	26.4	26.9	24.4	24.5	27.1	23.2	28.1	32.8
4. Considerable	13.5	14.0	13.1	13.1	16.8	12.1	13.2	14.8	13.6	14.3	13.3	13.6	13.3	12.6	13.7	19.0
5. Great	6.8	8.9	4.8	6.0	11.8	7.7	5.8	7.3	6.6	6.3	6.8	6.7	6.6	8.2	6.3	10.3
8. No opinion	18.8	12.5	24.7	17.9	22.5	19.0	20.3	17.6	17.9	15.1	22.9	18.5	17.6	21.5	20.2	10.3
Item 7000 N(Wtd)	3323	1532	1705	2719	346	770	1009	1119	425	1660	1522	1246	894	414	662	58

D05: How much do you agree or disagree with each of the following statements?

D05A: There is too much competition in this society

	TOTAL	M	F	White	Black	NE	NC	S	W	Yes	No	None	Marijuana Only	Few Pills	More Pills	Any Heroin
1. Disagree	10.3	13.9	7.1	9.9	14.5	8.2	9.6	12.6	9.8	11.8	8.6	11.0	10.6	8.3	10.6	3.5
2. Mostly disagree	12.2	16.8	8.2	12.9	8.7	11.0	13.1	12.0	12.8	14.5	9.8	12.1	14.2	12.5	9.9	10.5
3. Neither	22.6	24.3	21.3	23.2	17.2	21.0	21.4	24.0	24.7	22.2	22.6	23.2	22.1	21.7	23.2	14.0
4. Mostly agree	33.1	28.2	37.4	33.7	29.9	34.1	36.1	29.0	34.4	31.9	34.3	32.0	32.9	35.2	33.8	36.8
5. Agree	21.9	17.0	26.0	20.2	29.4	25.8	19.8	22.4	18.4	19.6	24.7	21.7	20.3	22.2	22.6	36.8
Item 7010 N(Wtd)	3348	1528	1736	2738	344	776	1019	1123	430	1679	1524	1247	902	423	668	57

D05B: Too many young people are sloppy about their grooming and clothing, and just don't care how they look

	TOTAL	M	F	White	Black	NE	NC	S	W	Yes	No	None	Marijuana Only	Few Pills	More Pills	Any Heroin
1. Disagree	15.0	17.0	13.2	15.0	14.2	15.1	13.7	15.9	15.9	14.7	15.4	10.9	15.9	15.8	20.1	26.3
2. Mostly disagree	23.6	25.3	22.0	24.7	17.7	26.1	25.9	20.6	21.9	26.7	20.1	21.1	25.8	22.4	26.4	19.3
3. Neither	20.1	21.0	19.2	20.9	12.5	19.8	23.5	15.5	24.7	21.1	18.6	18.5	20.3	21.2	21.3	24.6
4. Mostly agree	24.8	23.7	26.1	25.1	27.8	24.3	24.2	26.5	22.6	23.0	26.7	28.9	22.9	26.4	20.1	15.8
5. Agree	16.5	13.1	19.6	14.4	27.8	14.7	12.7	21.5	15.2	14.6	19.2	20.6	15.1	14.2	12.1	15.8
Item 7020 N(Wtd)	3352	1531	1738	2741	345	774	1021	1128	429	1679	1528	1247	903	424	671	57

D05C: There is too much hard rock music on the radio these days

	TOTAL	M	F	White	Black	NE	NC	S	W	Yes	No	None	Marijuana Only	Few Pills	More Pills	Any Heroin
1. Disagree	44.0	46.9	41.5	45.9	37.4	48.2	45.1	41.2	41.3	40.4	47.8	31.3	45.4	47.3	62.0	63.2
2. Mostly disagree	23.8	22.9	24.4	25.1	21.6	21.6	27.7	23.8	18.6	25.3	22.3	25.0	28.2	23.6	16.4	10.5
3. Neither	18.4	17.6	19.6	17.6	16.1	18.5	17.3	18.4	21.2	19.0	17.8	23.0	17.2	17.0	13.4	12.3
4. Mostly agree	7.7	7.5	7.9	7.1	11.1	7.1	5.8	9.3	9.1	8.9	6.2	11.4	4.9	6.6	5.5	8.8
5. Agree	6.0	5.0	6.6	4.4	13.7	4.7	4.1	7.2	9.8	6.4	5.8	9.2	4.3	5.4	2.7	5.3
Item 7030 N(Wtd)	3347	1526	1737	2741	342	774	1018	1125	429	1677	1526	1246	901	423	671	57

D05D: People should do their own thing, even if other people think it's strange

	TOTAL	M	F	White	Black	NE	NC	S	W	Yes	No	None	Marijuana Only	Few Pills	More Pills	Any Heroin
1. Disagree	3.2	4.0	2.4	2.8	4.9	2.6	1.5	4.6	4.5	3.1	3.3	4.6	1.9	2.6	2.4	7.1
2. Mostly disagree	7.1	7.5	6.5	6.9	8.7	5.7	7.2	8.6	5.2	7.7	5.7	9.2	6.2	6.4	4.8	-
3. Neither	11.8	13.2	10.8	12.1	7.3	10.8	11.9	11.3	14.4	12.1	11.2	13.3	11.2	13.0	9.2	10.7
4. Mostly agree	36.3	35.4	37.0	38.7	24.1	33.7	41.5	34.2	34.1	39.5	33.3	36.2	38.6	37.1	35.0	21.4
5. Agree	41.7	40.0	43.4	39.5	54.9	47.1	38.0	41.3	42.1	37.6	46.5	36.7	42.1	40.9	48.6	60.7
Item 7040 N(Wtd)	3330	1515	1727	2726	344	768	1014	1122	425	1672	1517	1237	900	423	665	56

QUESTIONNAIRE FORM 2 1978	TOTAL	SEX		RACE		REGION				4YR COLLEGE PLANS		ILLICIT DRUG USE: LIFETIME				
		M	F	White	Black	NE	NC	S	W	Yes	No	None	Mari-juana Only	Few Pills	More Pills	Any Her-oin
Weighted No. of Cases:	3785	1737	1867	2960	430	931	1083	1266	505	1790	1657	1363	1005	474	760	68
% of Weighted Total:	100.0	45.9	49.3	78.2	11.4	24.6	28.6	33.4	13.3	47.3	43.8	36.0	26.6	12.5	20.1	1.8
D05E: I get a real kick out of doing things that are a little dangerous																
1. Disagree	25.1	15.9	33.4	21.7	50.6	22.3	21.2	32.2	21.0	24.7	25.3	33.9	22.3	22.7	15.8	3.5
2. Mostly disagree	21.4	18.9	23.4	22.4	17.9	21.8	21.7	21.4	20.0	22.7	19.9	22.8	21.4	21.7	18.5	15.8
3. Neither	26.8	29.0	24.7	28.1	16.8	27.6	29.1	23.2	29.2	27.1	26.8	24.3	31.0	24.8	27.6	24.6
4. Mostly agree	18.1	24.0	13.0	19.3	9.4	19.4	19.2	15.8	18.4	18.3	17.5	13.4	18.3	21.2	24.1	31.6
5. Agree	8.7	12.1	5.6	8.5	5.3	8.7	8.8	7.4	11.3	7.1	10.4	5.6	7.1	9.5	13.9	26.3
Item 7050 N(Wtd)	3323	1515	1723	2725	340	767	1015	1118	424	1668	1516	1235	898	419	664	57
D05F: I like to test myself every now and then by doing something a little risky																
1. Disagree	23.1	15.5	29.9	21.5	37.0	22.0	19.1	28.8	19.4	23.7	22.3	33.9	18.0	20.6	12.4	8.9
2. Mostly disagree	18.7	17.1	20.2	19.2	17.5	17.9	19.6	19.5	16.0	18.2	18.7	20.3	18.0	18.6	16.8	8.9
3. Neither	21.8	21.8	21.4	22.6	14.2	22.1	21.8	19.7	26.3	21.3	22.5	18.5	26.3	21.3	22.1	23.2
4. Mostly agree	25.3	30.1	21.1	26.3	19.6	26.4	27.5	22.4	25.1	26.9	23.7	19.5	26.7	28.8	32.5	28.6
5. Agree	11.2	15.5	7.5	10.4	11.7	11.6	11.9	9.5	12.9	9.9	12.9	7.8	10.9	10.9	16.2	30.4
Item 7060 N(Wtd)	3305	1506	1714	2716	332	764	1013	1110	418	1661	1505	1230	896	413	661	56
D06: How many of your friends would you estimate...																
D06A: Smoke cigarettes?																
1. None	6.8	7.5	6.5	6.3	11.4	4.4	5.7	6.9	14.0	8.2	5.4	11.9	4.9	3.8	2.4	3.3
2. A few	27.8	27.3	28.2	28.0	26.2	24.8	29.0	25.2	37.1	32.9	22.3	37.6	28.0	21.9	14.6	13.1
3. Some	33.1	36.9	30.0	33.8	30.8	33.0	32.2	35.7	29.2	35.6	30.6	32.9	38.3	34.1	29.1	16.4
4. Most	29.3	25.8	32.0	29.6	25.6	33.6	30.9	29.1	17.8	21.9	37.1	15.3	27.6	37.2	49.3	45.9
5. All	2.9	2.5	3.2	2.3	6.3	4.1	2.3	3.2	1.9	1.4	4.4	2.2	1.3	3.3	4.7	19.7
Item 7070 N(Wtd)	3360	1533	1735	2747	351	773	1022	1136	428	1675	1536	1239	905	425	680	61
D06B: Smoke marijuana (pot, grass) or hashish?																
1. None	13.9	12.5	15.2	13.1	19.9	7.9	13.3	17.0	17.7	13.8	13.9	30.5	3.8	6.6	2.3	1.6
2. A few	25.3	24.6	26.5	25.4	22.5	20.6	25.7	27.6	27.0	28.6	21.4	37.2	25.1	19.9	9.0	6.6
3. Some	25.6	26.1	25.0	26.0	25.6	22.8	26.8	26.6	25.1	26.6	25.3	22.1	35.4	30.1	17.2	13.1
4. Most	27.8	28.3	26.9	28.6	24.2	36.3	28.4	23.5	22.6	26.6	28.7	8.7	30.2	35.3	52.0	52.5
5. All	7.4	8.5	6.4	6.9	7.8	12.4	5.9	5.4	7.7	4.5	10.7	1.5	5.4	7.6	19.5	24.6
Item 7080 N(Wtd)	3354	1534	1732	2743	347	772	1020	1131	430	1677	1532	1239	904	422	681	61
D06C: Take LSD?																
1. None	70.1	70.0	70.0	68.6	82.6	66.3	70.1	72.2	71.5	75.7	64.1	81.8	79.3	67.2	42.5	22.8
2. A few	20.9	20.9	21.1	22.2	9.9	21.7	21.1	20.4	20.1	18.0	24.1	13.6	17.6	25.6	34.3	35.1
3. Some	7.1	6.7	7.4	7.2	5.2	9.8	7.2	5.6	5.8	5.0	9.2	3.5	2.7	5.5	18.6	29.8
4. Most	1.3	1.4	1.1	1.4	.6	2.1	1.4	.7	1.4	1.0	1.6	.4	.4	1.7	3.5	8.8
5. All	.6	1.0	.3	.5	1.7	.1	.2	1.2	1.4	.4	1.0	.7	-	.2	1.2	5.3
Item 7090 N(Wtd)	3329	1525	1720	2723	344	769	1014	1117	428	1664	1519	1230	899	418	677	57
D06D: Take other psychedelics (mescaline, peyote, PCP, etc.)?																
1. None	70.8	67.8	73.5	69.1	86.6	63.3	71.3	75.2	71.7	74.7	66.5	84.5	80.4	67.5	38.7	19.7
2. A few	20.5	23.2	18.1	21.8	8.5	23.3	20.8	18.0	21.0	19.3	21.9	11.8	17.4	26.7	36.0	34.4
3. Some	6.8	7.0	6.8	7.1	3.2	10.8	6.6	4.6	5.8	4.6	9.2	2.7	1.9	5.3	19.9	27.9
4. Most	1.4	1.1	1.5	1.5	-	2.5	1.0	1.3	.5	1.1	1.5	.2	.3	.5	4.4	13.1
5. All	.6	1.0	.2	.5	1.7	.1	.3	1.0	.9	.4	.9	.8	-	.2	.9	3.3
Item 7100 N(Wtd)	3333	1522	1721	2727	343	768	1012	1125	428	1666	1524	1230	897	419	680	61

QUESTIONNAIRE FORM 2 1978	TOTAL	SEX		RACE		REGION				4YR COLLEGE PLANS		ILLICIT DRUG USE: LIFETIME				
		M	F	White	Black	NE	NC	S	W	Yes	No	None	Mari-juana Only	Few Pills	More Pills	Any Her-oin
Weighted No. of Cases:	3785	1737	1867	2960	430	931	1083	1266	505	1790	1657	1363	1005	474	760	68
% of Weighted Total:	100.0	45.9	49.3	78.2	11.4	24.6	28.6	33.4	13.3	47.3	43.8	36.0	26.6	12.5	20.1	1.8

D06E: Take amphetamines (uppers, pep pills, bennies, speed)?

1. None	59.3	59.7	58.9	57.1	76.3	53.3	60.4	61.2	62.2	64.2	53.9	76.5	69.0	52.6	22.5	9.8
2. A few	25.9	26.3	25.8	27.3	15.2	27.4	25.7	25.7	24.2	25.0	26.7	18.8	26.4	34.3	33.5	32.8
3. Some	10.0	9.1	10.9	10.6	5.3	12.4	9.4	9.0	10.0	7.8	12.7	3.2	4.0	10.5	28.5	31.1
4. Most	3.8	3.6	3.9	4.3	1.5	5.8	4.1	2.7	3.0	2.5	5.3	.8	.7	2.4	13.4	18.0
5. All	.9	1.3	.5	.7	2.0	1.0	.3	1.3	.5	.5	1.4	.7	-	.2	2.2	8.2
Item 7110 N(Wtd)	3327	1518	1721	2723	342	764	1015	1120	429	1662	1522	1226	897	420	677	61

D06F: Take quaaludes (quads, methaqualone)?

1. None	73.1	70.9	74.7	71.7	86.9	70.5	76.3	70.4	76.6	77.2	68.6	86.4	82.4	69.0	42.9	23.0
2. A few	18.1	20.4	16.3	19.1	7.9	18.2	16.9	20.1	15.2	16.1	20.3	10.4	15.1	25.0	31.1	31.1
3. Some	6.6	6.0	7.2	7.0	3.8	8.2	5.5	6.6	6.6	4.6	8.9	2.3	1.9	5.2	20.1	24.6
4. Most	1.6	1.4	1.6	1.8	-	2.5	1.1	1.8	.7	1.7	1.5	.2	.4	.5	5.2	14.8
5. All	.6	1.2	.1	.5	1.2	.5	.1	1.0	.9	.4	.7	.7	-	.2	.9	4.9
Item 7120 N(Wtd)	3318	1517	1714	2717	343	764	1010	1118	427	1660	1517	1221	893	420	678	61

D06G: Take barbiturates (downers, goofballs, reds, yellows, etc.)?

1. None	67.5	67.5	67.5	66.2	80.4	63.2	69.0	67.6	71.0	72.6	61.8	80.8	77.0	63.3	36.5	21.3
2. A few	22.9	23.1	22.9	24.1	12.6	24.9	22.8	22.7	20.4	20.4	25.5	15.0	20.4	30.5	36.2	26.2
3. Some	7.3	6.8	7.5	7.6	4.4	8.8	6.9	6.8	6.6	5.1	9.7	2.9	2.2	4.3	21.2	34.4
4. Most	1.8	1.7	1.7	1.9	.9	2.7	1.3	2.0	.7	1.4	2.2	.4	.3	1.4	5.4	13.1
5. All	.6	.9	.2	.3	1.8	.4	.1	.9	1.2	.5	.7	.8	-	.5	.7	3.3
Item 7130 N(Wtd)	3323	1518	1718	2722	342	764	1015	1118	427	1662	1520	1223	895	420	679	61

D06H: Take tranquilizers?

1. None	65.2	65.7	64.4	63.6	77.5	62.2	67.8	64.0	67.1	68.5	61.3	76.9	74.6	60.1	37.0	28.3
2. A few	25.9	25.0	26.8	27.3	15.5	28.2	24.0	26.6	24.2	24.9	27.2	18.5	22.8	34.6	38.5	26.7
3. Some	7.2	7.0	7.4	7.5	4.7	8.5	6.8	6.7	7.1	5.1	9.5	3.4	2.6	3.3	20.7	28.3
4. Most	1.2	1.4	1.0	1.3	.9	.9	1.2	1.7	.7	1.3	1.2	.5	-	1.4	3.3	11.7
5. All	.5	.9	.2	.4	1.5	.1	.2	.9	.9	.3	.8	.7	-	.2	.6	3.3
Item 7140 N(Wtd)	3315	1509	1718	2714	342	762	1013	1115	425	1661	1513	1223	891	419	676	60

D06I: Take cocaine?

1. None	66.8	65.4	68.0	65.6	78.8	61.3	69.5	68.3	65.7	69.6	63.9	84.8	73.4	61.7	32.5	16.4
2. A few	21.8	22.5	21.1	22.9	12.4	24.0	20.4	21.5	21.4	20.4	23.6	11.9	22.2	27.3	34.3	37.7
3. Some	7.4	7.1	7.8	7.5	5.6	9.6	7.0	6.4	7.3	6.6	8.0	2.1	3.8	9.6	19.7	18.0
4. Most	2.9	3.3	2.5	2.9	1.8	3.9	2.7	2.2	3.5	2.8	3.0	.2	.4	1.4	10.8	16.4
5. All	1.1	1.7	.6	1.1	1.8	1.2	.3	1.4	2.1	.7	1.5	.9	.2	.2	2.7	8.2
Item 7150 N(Wtd)	3314	1513	1714	2717	340	763	1011	1115	426	1656	1514	1222	891	418	676	61

D06J: Take heroin (smack, horse)?

1. None	85.7	85.9	85.3	85.8	88.7	85.5	87.8	83.0	87.8	89.1	82.2	89.0	90.3	86.2	77.4	39.3
2. A few	11.1	10.7	11.6	11.3	5.9	11.0	10.4	12.6	9.2	8.6	13.4	7.9	7.9	10.9	18.8	37.7
3. Some	2.3	2.1	2.5	2.1	3.6	2.5	1.5	3.2	1.9	1.2	3.6	2.1	1.7	1.5	2.8	13.1
4. Most	.4	.5	.3	.4	-	.5	.2	.5	.2	.5	.3	.1	-	1.2	.4	4.9
5. All	.6	.9	.3	.4	1.8	.5	.1	.9	.9	.6	.6	.9	.2	.5	.4	3.3
Item 7160 N(Wtd)	3304	1509	1711	2708	337	761	1010	1107	426	1654	1509	1217	894	413	674	61

D06K: Take other narcotics (methadone, opium, codeine, paregoric, etc.)?

1. None	76.8	74.9	78.6	75.9	88.2	75.0	77.3	77.6	76.7	81.0	72.6	86.8	85.4	76.0	51.3	37.9
2. A few	17.4	19.0	16.1	18.4	7.7	19.1	17.4	16.4	17.4	15.0	19.9	10.1	12.9	19.5	34.3	32.8
3. Some	4.3	4.1	4.4	4.3	2.1	4.7	4.0	4.1	4.7	2.7	6.0	2.1	1.7	2.9	11.3	20.7
4. Most	.9	1.2	.6	1.0	.3	1.2	1.2	.8	-	1.1	.7	.2	-	1.2	2.8	5.2
5. All	.5	.9	.2	.4	1.8	-	.1	1.1	.9	.3	.8	.8	.2	.5	.3	3.4
Item 7170 N(Wtd)	3313	1509	1717	2716	338	760	1011	1117	425	1660	1512	1221	892	416	679	58

QUESTIONNAIRE FORM 2 1978	TOTAL	SEX		RACE		REGION				4YR COLLEGE PLANS		ILLICIT DRUG USE: LIFETIME				
		M	F	White	Black	NE	NC	S	W	Yes	No	None	Marijuana Only	Few Pills	More Pills	Any Heroin
Weighted No. of Cases:	3785	1737	1867	2960	430	931	1083	1266	505	1790	1657	1363	1005	474	760	68
% of Weighted Total:	100.0	45.9	49.3	78.2	11.4	24.6	28.6	33.4	13.3	47.3	43.8	36.0	26.6	12.5	20.1	1.8
D06L: Use inhalants (sniffing glue, aerosols, laughing gas, etc.)?																
1. None	80.0	78.5	81.4	80.0	85.2	80.8	81.0	77.9	82.1	82.2	77.5	83.9	84.3	76.9	70.3	66.7
2. A few	16.0	17.6	14.7	16.4	9.8	15.5	15.6	17.5	13.9	15.0	17.2	12.1	13.7	19.3	23.6	23.3
3. Some	2.9	2.3	3.2	2.6	3.3	2.6	2.9	3.1	2.6	1.8	3.9	2.5	1.5	3.1	5.1	6.7
4. Most	.7	.8	.5	.7	.6	1.1	.6	.6	.5	.7	.7	.7	.5	.7	.9	-
5. All	.4	.7	.1	.3	1.5	-	-	.9	.9	.3	.5	.7	.2	.2	.1	1.7
Item 7180 N(Wtd)	3297	1499	1711	2700	338	756	1004	1112	425	1654	1502	1218	886	415	673	60
D06M: Drink alcoholic beverages (liquor, beer, wine)?																
1. None	5.1	4.7	5.6	3.4	15.6	2.6	3.4	6.9	8.7	4.9	5.3	9.3	2.8	3.6	1.3	-
2. A few	10.6	9.1	12.2	9.1	17.6	8.7	8.5	11.7	16.6	10.2	11.3	20.2	5.4	6.3	2.7	5.0
3. Some	15.4	15.1	15.8	14.8	22.4	14.5	12.4	17.5	18.5	15.8	14.5	21.7	13.4	11.8	9.2	13.3
4. Most	42.0	41.8	42.3	44.0	30.9	36.8	46.2	44.3	35.1	44.4	39.5	35.4	49.6	47.1	41.7	31.7
5. All	26.9	29.4	24.1	28.7	13.8	37.2	29.6	19.5	21.1	24.8	29.4	13.4	28.9	31.5	45.2	48.3
Item 7190 N(Wtd)	3325	1513	1725	2724	340	763	1012	1123	427	1666	1517	1230	894	416	677	60
D06N: Get drunk at least once a week?																
1. None	18.0	14.4	21.1	15.3	35.6	17.0	13.3	20.0	25.9	20.5	15.6	29.1	14.2	10.0	8.5	3.3
2. A few	25.5	24.8	26.6	24.9	31.2	23.5	25.1	27.1	26.4	26.2	25.1	31.7	21.9	29.2	16.6	20.0
3. Some	26.2	28.0	24.5	28.1	15.5	24.2	30.0	25.6	22.7	27.6	24.5	23.4	31.1	27.8	24.4	28.3
4. Most	21.7	22.5	21.0	23.3	13.1	23.7	23.4	20.5	17.3	20.2	23.5	12.2	25.5	23.5	33.1	21.7
5. All	8.5	10.2	6.8	8.5	4.7	11.7	8.2	6.8	7.9	5.8	11.3	3.5	7.4	9.5	17.2	25.0
Item 7200 N(Wtd)	3336	1518	1730	2732	343	763	1018	1127	428	1667	1525	1233	897	421	679	60
E01: What is your best guess about whether your parents think you drink alcoholic beverages (beer, wine, liquor)?																
1. They feel sure I don't drink	26.6	21.8	31.1	24.0	40.4	22.6	20.3	31.5	35.8	28.0	24.5	48.2	13.9	18.1	10.1	13.3
2. They think I probably don't drink	12.4	10.6	13.9	13.1	10.8	11.5	12.3	13.1	12.2	13.4	11.6	13.4	12.0	13.6	10.2	8.3
3. I don't know, or they differ in whether they think I drink	8.1	8.9	7.1	7.3	11.4	7.5	8.2	8.5	8.0	6.8	9.3	6.5	10.0	10.5	6.5	11.7
4. They think I probably drink	16.2	16.1	16.0	16.6	12.0	19.3	16.9	14.0	14.6	16.3	16.4	10.9	21.1	18.6	18.5	10.0
5. They feel sure (or know) that I drink	36.8	42.5	31.9	39.0	25.1	39.2	42.3	33.0	28.9	35.4	38.4	20.9	43.0	39.4	54.8	56.7
Item 7510 N(Wtd)	3324	1516	1717	2720	342	762	1014	1123	425	1658	1520	1235	897	419	664	60
E02: What's your best guess about whether your parents think you smoke marijuana?																
1. They feel sure I don't	64.2	58.4	69.6	64.4	62.7	56.7	64.8	67.0	68.4	67.8	60.6	93.9	56.9	51.4	32.0	16.9
2. They think I probably don't	12.5	13.2	11.9	12.9	10.4	13.8	13.6	10.4	13.2	13.1	12.1	3.5	21.9	16.7	13.3	15.3
3. I don't know, or they differ in whether they think I do	6.6	7.6	5.3	6.1	10.7	7.8	6.4	6.9	4.3	5.5	7.8	1.6	8.5	12.2	9.2	10.2
4. They think I probably do	6.6	7.7	5.4	6.4	7.8	8.7	5.5	6.9	4.5	5.8	7.2	.5	6.6	10.0	14.2	23.7
5. They feel sure (or know) that I do	10.1	13.0	7.8	10.2	8.7	13.0	9.6	8.8	9.6	7.7	12.4	.5	6.1	9.6	31.4	33.9
Item 7520 N(Wtd)	3292	1504	1699	2700	335	755	1007	1112	418	1646	1501	1222	884	418	663	59
E03: What's your best guess about whether your parents think you use any other drugs (uppers, downers, psychedelics, etc.) for non-medical reasons?																
1. They feel sure I don't	86.4	84.4	88.7	86.1	89.5	82.2	88.3	86.4	89.3	90.7	81.9	97.5	92.4	83.1	63.9	45.8
2. They think I probably don't	7.2	7.9	6.4	7.8	3.0	9.7	6.7	6.4	5.6	5.1	9.8	1.1	4.7	11.6	17.1	25.4
3. I don't know, or they differ in whether they think I do	3.4	4.2	2.5	3.3	3.3	4.5	2.4	3.7	2.7	2.0	4.7	.6	1.1	2.7	10.8	15.3
4. They think I probably do	1.6	2.4	.9	1.6	.9	1.5	1.4	2.0	1.2	1.1	2.1	.2	.8	.5	5.2	10.2
5. They feel sure (or know) that I do	1.4	1.2	1.4	1.2	3.3	1.9	1.2	1.4	1.2	1.1	1.5	.5	.9	1.9	3.0	3.4
Item 7530 N(Wtd)	3268	1489	1690	2681	333	749	1003	1105	411	1639	1484	1218	874	414	660	59

QUESTIONNAIRE FORM 2 1978	TOTAL	SEX		RACE		REGION				4YR COLLEGE PLANS		ILLICIT DRUG USE: LIFETIME				
		M	F	White	Black	NE	NC	S	W	Yes	No	None	Mari-juana Only	Few Pills	More Pills	Any Her-oin
Weighted No. of Cases:	3785	1737	1867	2960	430	931	1083	1266	505	1790	1657	1363	1005	474	760	68
% of Weighted Total:	100.0	45.9	49.3	78.2	11.4	24.6	28.6	33.4	13.3	47.3	43.8	36.0	26.6	12.5	20.1	1.8

E04: To what extent are these actions effective when people use them in pressing for changes? Are they usually very effective, somewhat effective, not very effective, or not at all effective?

E04A: Writing to public officials

	TOTAL	M	F	White	Black	NE	NC	S	W	Yes	No	None	Mari-juana Only	Few Pills	More Pills	Any Her-oin
4. Very effective	3.8	4.8	3.0	2.7	13.5	3.0	2.8	5.5	3.5	4.1	3.3	4.3	4.5	3.7	1.9	5.8
3. Somewhat effective	34.3	34.1	35.0	36.6	22.5	32.9	34.8	33.2	38.1	38.9	29.6	37.1	32.2	38.8	29.7	30.8
2. Not very effective	32.8	32.3	33.0	34.1	25.2	33.7	34.3	32.1	29.1	35.7	30.3	33.2	35.5	27.2	32.9	28.8
1. Not at all effective	9.7	11.0	8.3	9.2	10.8	12.7	9.5	8.0	9.3	8.2	11.5	8.1	10.4	8.6	12.3	13.5
8. Don't know, or it depends	19.4	17.8	20.7	17.5	28.0	17.7	18.6	21.0	20.3	13.1	25.4	17.3	17.4	21.7	23.1	21.2
Item 16320 N(Wtd)	3195	1446	1661	2628	325	727	995	1074	399	1604	1458	1204	853	405	636	52

E04B: Working in political campaigns

	TOTAL	M	F	White	Black	NE	NC	S	W	Yes	No	None	Mari-juana Only	Few Pills	More Pills	Any Her-oin
4. Very effective	8.2	7.3	9.4	7.8	13.4	7.8	6.8	10.5	6.8	9.7	6.7	8.6	8.6	9.5	7.1	-
3. Somewhat effective	45.9	42.6	48.8	48.0	37.1	46.8	47.9	43.0	47.0	52.4	39.7	45.2	49.9	47.4	42.4	34.0
2. Not very effective	19.9	23.0	17.4	20.7	13.7	19.7	20.4	20.1	18.7	19.8	19.9	21.2	18.8	16.8	19.6	32.1
1. Not at all effective	7.0	9.7	4.2	6.5	8.4	8.7	6.7	5.3	8.8	5.2	8.6	5.9	6.5	7.3	8.8	13.2
8. Don't know, or it depends	19.1	17.3	20.4	17.0	27.7	17.0	18.3	21.1	19.2	12.9	25.0	19.1	16.1	19.0	21.9	22.6
Item 16330 N(Wtd)	3179	1436	1656	2611	321	722	990	1071	396	1592	1455	1196	851	399	634	53

E04C: Voting in public elections

	TOTAL	M	F	White	Black	NE	NC	S	W	Yes	No	None	Mari-juana Only	Few Pills	More Pills	Any Her-oin
4. Very effective	36.0	33.8	38.2	37.1	36.5	34.5	34.3	40.1	32.0	42.5	29.4	39.5	35.9	36.7	30.3	26.9
3. Somewhat effective	37.0	36.5	37.9	38.5	27.9	36.3	39.7	33.1	42.4	39.2	35.6	37.8	38.8	39.2	34.1	26.9
2. Not very effective	11.2	14.0	8.4	10.9	12.4	12.8	11.3	10.7	9.4	9.7	12.5	10.2	11.2	10.8	12.9	9.6
1. Not at all effective	4.7	5.8	3.7	4.1	7.9	5.4	4.8	4.4	4.1	2.7	6.7	3.2	5.1	3.5	6.9	13.5
8. Don't know, or it depends	11.1	10.0	11.8	9.5	15.2	11.0	9.9	11.8	12.2	6.0	15.8	9.2	9.0	10.1	15.6	23.1
Item 16340 N(Wtd)	3162	1429	1648	2603	315	719	988	1061	394	1586	1444	1196	843	398	627	52

E04D: Signing petitions

	TOTAL	M	F	White	Black	NE	NC	S	W	Yes	No	None	Mari-juana Only	Few Pills	More Pills	Any Her-oin
4. Very effective	11.8	14.6	9.6	11.3	17.6	11.9	10.8	12.6	11.9	12.5	10.5	12.5	12.7	9.6	10.9	3.8
3. Somewhat effective	50.1	45.8	54.2	52.8	37.4	49.8	53.5	46.8	50.9	53.5	47.1	51.4	49.5	53.0	49.0	38.5
2. Not very effective	19.6	20.8	18.5	20.3	13.7	19.9	19.9	19.2	18.7	21.4	17.4	18.6	20.8	20.6	19.3	21.2
1. Not at all effective	5.8	6.9	4.6	5.1	11.5	6.3	4.9	6.8	4.6	4.8	6.9	5.8	5.9	3.8	5.4	13.5
8. Don't know, or it depends	12.8	12.0	13.1	10.6	19.8	12.1	10.8	14.6	14.2	7.7	18.1	11.7	11.1	12.9	15.5	23.1
Item 16350 N(Wtd)	3155	1418	1651	2597	313	717	988	1056	395	1590	1438	1193	845	394	626	52

E04E: Boycotting certain products or stores

	TOTAL	M	F	White	Black	NE	NC	S	W	Yes	No	None	Mari-juana Only	Few Pills	More Pills	Any Her-oin
4. Very effective	16.2	19.7	13.2	16.1	19.5	21.5	15.6	13.3	15.7	20.7	11.0	15.1	18.6	14.8	16.7	13.7
3. Somewhat effective	38.7	37.7	39.7	41.2	25.8	39.6	41.4	36.6	35.9	44.0	33.0	37.4	43.3	37.8	36.1	33.3
2. Not very effective	20.6	20.4	20.5	21.4	16.0	18.5	19.3	22.1	23.5	19.7	21.6	22.3	17.1	24.3	20.7	17.6
1. Not at all effective	7.2	8.8	5.9	6.2	13.2	5.9	7.5	7.7	7.8	5.7	8.9	8.6	6.5	5.0	6.0	13.7
8. Don't know, or it depends	17.4	13.3	20.7	15.1	25.5	14.6	16.3	20.4	16.7	9.9	25.5	16.7	14.4	17.8	20.3	23.5
Item 16360 N(Wtd)	3170	1428	1655	2607	318	717	989	1068	395	1593	1444	1196	849	399	629	51

E04F: Lawful demonstrations

	TOTAL	M	F	White	Black	NE	NC	S	W	Yes	No	None	Mari-juana Only	Few Pills	More Pills	Any Her-oin
4. Very effective	12.8	15.4	10.3	12.2	20.2	16.6	12.0	12.1	9.9	14.9	10.1	10.7	13.8	14.4	15.0	9.8
3. Somewhat effective	44.0	44.3	44.4	46.5	29.7	43.4	46.8	41.5	44.9	51.6	36.6	44.3	47.3	43.1	39.6	47.1
2. Not very effective	18.8	18.6	18.8	19.8	13.6	17.3	20.0	18.0	21.2	17.8	20.0	19.7	18.8	18.4	19.0	9.8
1. Not at all effective	6.7	7.5	6.1	6.3	8.8	6.7	5.4	8.1	6.1	4.9	8.9	8.1	4.9	6.0	6.1	11.8
8. Don't know, or it depends	17.6	14.1	20.4	15.1	28.1	15.8	15.9	20.3	17.6	10.7	24.5	17.1	15.1	18.1	20.4	19.6
Item 16370 N(Wtd)	3163	1425	1652	2601	317	716	992	1063	392	1592	1442	1193	849	397	627	51

E04G: Occupying buildings or factories

	TOTAL	M	F	White	Black	NE	NC	S	W	Yes	No	None	Mari-juana Only	Few Pills	More Pills	Any Her-oin
4. Very effective	6.6	8.6	4.7	6.6	7.6	8.5	7.4	5.0	5.4	7.6	5.5	7.1	6.6	5.0	6.2	9.6
3. Somewhat effective	21.8	20.6	23.4	22.3	19.4	22.5	23.2	20.5	20.7	22.0	22.0	21.1	22.6	25.7	19.8	26.9
2. Not very effective	28.5	30.5	26.9	29.7	23.8	23.1	29.7	30.0	31.6	30.6	26.1	28.5	30.2	25.4	29.4	23.1
1. Not at all effective	18.4	21.8	15.5	18.5	17.8	20.3	16.5	19.6	15.8	20.5	16.4	19.9	18.1	16.6	16.9	15.4
8. Don't know, or it depends	24.7	18.6	29.5	23.0	31.4	25.6	23.3	24.8	26.3	19.1	29.9	23.4	22.6	27.2	27.5	26.9
Item 16380 N(Wtd)	3159	1425	1650	2601	315	715	993	1059	392	1588	1443	1192	847	397	626	52

QUESTIONNAIRE FORM 2 1978	TOTAL	SEX		RACE		REGION				4YR COLLEGE PLANS		ILLICIT DRUG USE: LIFETIME				
		M	F	White	Black	NE	NC	S	W	Yes	No	None	Mari-juana Only	Few Pills	More Pills	Any Her-oin
Weighted No. of Cases:	3785	1737	1867	2960	430	931	1083	1266	505	1790	1657	1363	1005	474	760	68
% of Weighted Total:	100.0	45.9	49.3	78.2	11.4	24.6	28.6	33.4	13.3	47.3	43.8	36.0	26.6	12.5	20.1	1.8

E04H: Wildcat strikes

	TOTAL	M	F	White	Black	NE	NC	S	W	Yes	No	None	Mari-juana Only	Few Pills	More Pills	Any Her-oin
4. Very effective	12.1	16.9	7.7	12.2	11.6	15.3	15.1	8.9	7.4	13.5	10.7	11.5	10.6	10.6	15.2	22.6
3. Somewhat effective	27.1	29.0	26.0	28.9	20.7	24.8	28.4	28.6	24.3	29.2	25.3	25.8	28.7	30.0	27.4	11.3
2. Not very effective	19.9	20.6	19.2	20.9	13.5	16.4	21.0	19.8	23.8	21.4	18.5	19.9	23.6	18.9	16.3	24.5
1. Not at all effective	13.7	13.6	13.8	12.8	19.1	14.2	12.1	14.0	16.1	13.4	13.7	14.2	13.0	13.6	13.1	13.2
8. Don't know, or it depends	27.1	19.9	33.2	25.2	35.1	29.3	23.4	28.8	28.1	22.5	31.8	28.6	24.2	27.0	28.2	26.4
Item 16390 N(Wtd)	3151	1424	1641	2588	319	706	993	1061	391	1578	1445	1189	843	397	625	53

E04I: Blocking traffic

	TOTAL	M	F	White	Black	NE	NC	S	W	Yes	No	None	Mari-juana Only	Few Pills	More Pills	Any Her-oin
4. Very effective	7.4	8.4	6.6	6.7	11.3	10.8	6.6	6.4	6.2	8.3	6.4	7.3	5.6	7.8	8.3	24.5
3. Somewhat effective	16.4	15.8	16.8	16.6	16.3	17.2	16.9	17.0	12.3	17.9	15.1	16.1	19.3	15.8	14.1	11.3
2. Not very effective	29.7	32.0	28.2	31.2	21.6	26.8	31.5	28.8	32.3	32.3	27.2	28.8	33.3	27.8	29.0	18.9
1. Not at all effective	28.9	29.0	28.6	29.5	27.6	26.6	28.4	30.0	31.0	29.0	28.4	30.8	27.0	30.3	26.9	24.5
8. Don't know, or it depends	17.6	14.7	19.8	16.0	22.9	18.7	16.4	17.8	17.9	12.6	22.9	17.0	14.9	18.0	21.6	18.9
Item 16400 N(Wtd)	3159	1424	1650	2599	319	710	993	1067	390	1584	1447	1193	846	399	625	53

E04J: Damaging things

	TOTAL	M	F	White	Black	NE	NC	S	W	Yes	No	None	Mari-juana Only	Few Pills	More Pills	Any Her-oin
4. Very effective	7.2	7.0	7.2	5.9	16.3	8.4	5.7	8.2	6.1	7.1	7.3	8.0	5.2	6.8	7.0	24.1
3. Somewhat effective	10.6	10.6	10.7	10.4	11.2	12.4	10.4	10.1	9.2	10.4	10.7	10.3	11.4	8.5	10.5	13.0
2. Not very effective	20.4	21.5	19.3	21.5	13.8	19.7	21.1	18.8	24.0	23.1	17.8	18.6	24.7	20.9	18.4	16.7
1. Not at all effective	46.9	47.0	47.0	48.9	37.2	44.0	49.2	47.2	45.2	49.7	43.8	50.1	44.7	47.2	44.9	35.2
8. Don't know, or it depends	15.0	13.9	15.7	13.3	21.8	15.5	13.6	15.8	15.6	9.7	20.4	13.0	14.0	16.6	19.0	13.0
Item 16410 N(Wtd)	3156	1428	1642	2599	312	711	990	1063	392	1579	1447	1191	843	398	626	54

E04K: Personal violence

	TOTAL	M	F	White	Black	NE	NC	S	W	Yes	No	None	Mari-juana Only	Few Pills	More Pills	Any Her-oin
4. Very effective	7.8	7.9	7.5	6.7	14.5	8.2	6.9	8.0	8.7	7.3	8.4	8.3	5.3	7.8	8.5	27.8
3. Somewhat effective	10.2	10.2	10.4	9.7	12.6	11.7	9.1	11.0	8.4	10.8	9.9	9.7	11.6	8.6	10.4	3.7
2. Not very effective	18.7	20.9	16.9	19.9	13.5	18.3	19.6	17.9	19.1	20.1	17.3	17.2	22.2	19.9	16.7	13.0
1. Not at all effective	47.7	47.0	48.8	50.1	35.8	45.4	50.6	46.2	49.0	52.1	42.6	50.0	47.7	47.6	45.3	35.2
8. Don't know, or it depends	15.5	14.0	16.5	13.8	23.3	16.4	13.7	16.9	15.1	9.7	21.7	14.8	13.2	16.1	19.1	18.5
Item 16420 N(Wtd)	3161	1430	1646	2599	318	709	994	1066	392	1583	1450	1194	844	397	627	54

E05A: How would you feel if everybody, including you, used car pools or public transportation for daily commuting in order to cut down on the nations's gasoline consumption?

	TOTAL	M	F	White	Black	NE	NC	S	W	Yes	No	None	Mari-juana Only	Few Pills	More Pills	Any Her-oin
1. Very dissatisfied	5.8	7.1	4.7	5.1	9.7	4.5	4.4	8.1	5.0	3.4	8.1	5.9	5.7	3.5	6.4	7.0
2. Mostly dissatisfied	5.8	6.7	5.1	5.3	8.2	4.9	5.7	6.3	6.5	4.6	7.2	5.3	4.4	9.0	6.4	8.8
3. Mixed feelings	32.0	31.6	32.3	31.7	30.1	31.7	32.5	32.2	30.6	30.3	34.1	29.8	30.9	33.8	36.6	28.1
4. Mostly satisfied	29.6	28.4	30.3	30.7	26.0	27.9	31.0	29.2	30.1	32.2	26.7	29.9	32.4	26.9	27.3	31.6
5. Very satisfied	26.9	26.4	27.6	27.2	26.0	31.0	26.4	24.1	27.8	29.4	23.8	29.0	26.5	26.6	23.5	26.3
Item 16430 N(Wtd)	3186	1442	1659	2625	319	714	997	1077	399	1598	1455	1198	854	402	626	57

E05B: How would you feel about cutting down on beef and eating more grains and vegetables, if this would conserve more food?

	TOTAL	M	F	White	Black	NE	NC	S	W	Yes	No	None	Mari-juana Only	Few Pills	More Pills	Any Her-oin
1. Very dissatisfied	13.9	19.2	9.2	13.3	20.9	11.8	13.3	16.1	13.6	12.3	15.6	12.5	14.6	12.5	16.1	17.5
2. Mostly dissatisfied	16.9	21.2	12.9	17.3	15.3	14.8	17.2	19.1	13.9	16.0	17.9	15.4	17.6	18.5	17.0	24.6
3. Mixed feelings	32.3	31.8	33.1	32.3	33.0	33.6	33.0	31.0	31.7	31.8	33.1	33.7	33.1	35.2	27.1	28.1
4. Mostly satisfied	22.2	18.2	25.7	22.6	15.6	21.6	22.9	21.4	23.4	23.6	21.1	23.1	20.8	19.5	25.4	14.0
5. Very satisfied	14.7	9.8	19.2	14.5	15.3	18.1	13.6	12.3	17.1	16.4	12.3	15.2	14.0	14.7	14.4	17.5
Item 16440 N(Wtd)	3186	1442	1659	2626	321	714	997	1079	397	1599	1453	1201	856	401	623	57

QUESTIONNAIRE FORM 2 1978	TOTAL	SEX		RACE		REGION				4YR COLLEGE PLANS		ILLICIT DRUG USE: LIFETIME				
		M	F	White	Black	NE	NC	S	W	Yes	No	None	Mari- juana Only	Few Pills	More Pills	Any Her- oin
Weighted No. of Cases:	3785	1737	1867	2960	430	931	1083	1266	505	1790	1657	1363	1005	474	760	68
% of Weighted Total:	100.0	45.9	49.3	78.2	11.4	24.6	28.6	33.4	13.3	47.3	43.8	36.0	26.6	12.5	20.1	1.8

E05C: How would you feel about having taxes increased by ten percent to allow the government to control pollution and conserve our natural resources?

	TOTAL	M	F	White	Black	NE	NC	S	W	Yes	No	None	Mari- juana Only	Few Pills	More Pills	Any Her- oin
1. Very dissatisfied	29.7	33.5	25.9	28.4	37.7	27.7	27.9	33.2	27.9	24.0	35.8	26.7	31.8	27.1	34.8	35.1
2. Mostly dissatisfied	18.6	17.7	19.5	18.6	19.9	16.3	17.8	19.9	21.6	20.0	17.6	20.0	18.9	20.1	13.8	12.3
3. Mixed feelings	34.8	30.1	39.0	36.2	24.7	38.8	35.8	31.1	35.4	38.1	31.0	37.3	33.3	34.6	33.8	22.8
4. Mostly satisfied	11.0	12.2	10.2	11.6	8.9	11.9	12.8	9.7	8.3	12.1	10.0	11.1	10.8	11.0	11.4	15.8
5. Very satisfied	5.9	6.6	5.4	5.4	9.2	5.5	5.6	6.1	6.8	5.8	5.7	4.9	5.3	7.5	6.0	14.0
Item 16450 N(Wtd)	3171	1432	1654	2614	316	712	992	1068	398	1587	1451	1195	851	399	621	57

E06: Some people like school very much. Others don't. How do you feel about going to school?

	TOTAL	M	F	White	Black	NE	NC	S	W	Yes	No	None	Mari- juana Only	Few Pills	More Pills	Any Her- oin
5. I like school very much	15.1	14.8	15.6	13.2	27.4	11.8	13.7	17.1	19.1	19.0	10.7	22.3	11.4	12.5	8.5	8.9
4. I like school quite a lot	29.9	29.1	31.3	30.5	27.7	25.9	30.7	30.3	34.0	37.7	22.0	36.3	28.2	27.6	22.7	23.2
3. I like school some	36.6	38.6	34.6	36.9	33.8	38.1	38.7	35.8	31.0	31.6	41.5	32.1	41.9	38.9	36.6	32.1
2. I don't like school very much	12.3	11.8	12.5	13.1	6.7	16.3	11.0	11.6	10.2	9.2	15.7	6.8	13.0	14.9	19.6	19.6
1. I don't like school at all	6.0	5.8	6.0	6.4	4.6	7.6	5.9	5.2	5.7	2.5	10.0	2.3	5.5	6.4	12.5	14.3
Item 7630 N(Wtd)	3211	1449	1672	2637	328	719	1002	1088	403	1608	1464	1204	861	409	634	56

E07: About how many hours do you spend in an average week on all your homework including both in school and out of school?

	TOTAL	M	F	White	Black	NE	NC	S	W	Yes	No	None	Mari- juana Only	Few Pills	More Pills	Any Her- oin
1. 0 hours	8.1	11.5	4.6	8.3	6.4	7.2	8.8	8.3	7.5	4.5	12.2	4.9	8.5	6.8	13.6	20.4
2. 1-4 hours	43.4	44.9	42.2	42.4	50.0	46.2	38.6	45.1	46.4	37.3	49.3	41.6	43.4	46.0	45.8	31.5
3. 5-9 hours	23.3	21.2	25.0	24.0	18.3	25.2	23.1	22.7	21.9	27.5	19.0	23.7	26.7	22.7	18.2	25.9
4. 10-14 hours	13.0	12.7	13.3	13.7	10.4	12.3	14.4	12.9	11.2	15.6	10.5	14.7	11.7	12.2	11.8	14.8
5. 15-19 hours	5.4	5.0	5.9	5.2	6.4	3.8	6.3	5.1	6.5	6.5	4.3	6.4	3.9	7.1	4.7	3.7
6. 20-24 hours	3.6	2.1	5.0	3.6	3.7	2.5	5.1	2.8	4.0	4.9	2.1	5.1	3.1	2.7	2.5	1.9
7. 25 or more hours	3.2	2.5	3.9	2.9	4.6	2.8	3.9	3.3	2.2	3.8	2.6	3.7	2.7	2.4	3.3	1.9
Item 7640 N(Wtd)	3211	1451	1671	2638	328	718	1003	1089	401	1612	1458	1204	862	409	633	54

E08: In general, how much say or influence do you feel each of the following has on HOW YOUR SCHOOL IS RUN?

E08A: The principal

	TOTAL	M	F	White	Black	NE	NC	S	W	Yes	No	None	Mari- juana Only	Few Pills	More Pills	Any Her- oin
1. Little or no influence	9.6	10.3	9.0	8.5	15.5	8.6	9.3	10.1	10.9	6.6	12.7	6.4	10.8	9.3	13.6	11.9
2. Some influence	14.1	13.2	14.8	13.1	18.0	14.4	14.2	13.5	14.9	11.8	16.8	12.7	15.6	14.7	13.6	13.6
3. Moderate influence	12.7	12.5	12.9	13.0	9.9	14.0	14.7	10.0	12.6	11.4	13.7	13.7	12.2	12.0	12.3	16.9
4. Considerable influence	25.5	26.2	24.8	27.3	15.2	24.0	29.2	22.0	28.2	27.3	23.6	26.5	25.7	27.8	22.9	15.3
5. A great deal of influence	38.1	37.7	38.6	38.2	41.5	38.8	32.6	44.5	33.2	42.9	33.2	40.7	35.8	36.1	37.5	44.1
Item 7650 N(Wtd)	3199	1450	1657	2625	323	707	998	1091	404	1600	1460	1201	852	407	632	59

E08B: The teachers

	TOTAL	M	F	White	Black	NE	NC	S	W	Yes	No	None	Mari- juana Only	Few Pills	More Pills	Any Her- oin
1. Little or no influence	7.7	8.4	7.1	7.1	11.3	7.8	7.2	8.6	6.2	5.7	9.3	4.9	8.1	8.7	10.0	15.5
2. Some influence	22.0	20.7	23.1	22.0	24.8	20.5	23.0	22.1	22.3	21.1	23.6	21.9	22.4	20.4	23.6	20.7
3. Moderate influence	31.3	33.3	29.8	32.8	20.1	34.5	31.4	28.7	32.3	32.1	30.1	31.4	32.0	30.7	31.7	25.9
4. Considerable influence	29.3	28.9	29.6	30.2	24.5	28.9	29.8	29.6	28.0	31.8	26.7	30.5	31.2	28.9	25.8	24.1
5. A great deal of influence	9.7	8.6	10.4	7.9	19.7	8.3	8.7	11.0	11.2	9.3	10.3	11.3	6.3	11.5	8.9	12.1
Item 7660 N(Wtd)	3189	1446	1653	2619	319	702	1002	1082	403	1595	1459	1200	853	401	628	58

E08C: The students

	TOTAL	M	F	White	Black	NE	NC	S	W	Yes	No	None	Mari- juana Only	Few Pills	More Pills	Any Her- oin
1. Little or no influence	31.6	32.2	31.2	32.5	25.8	32.0	35.2	30.1	26.3	30.4	33.1	27.0	34.2	30.1	38.1	31.0
2. Some influence	27.1	27.6	26.8	28.0	23.6	27.0	27.0	27.0	27.8	29.0	25.9	29.9	25.1	27.8	22.6	32.8
3. Moderate influence	19.0	19.1	18.9	19.5	15.1	21.3	17.0	18.1	22.8	20.3	17.0	19.9	19.2	18.5	18.2	15.5
4. Considerable influence	12.7	12.7	12.8	12.4	13.2	12.2	11.9	13.3	13.8	12.2	13.1	13.4	13.5	12.5	11.8	3.4
5. A great deal of influence	9.6	8.5	10.4	7.6	22.3	7.5	8.9	11.6	9.8	8.2	11.0	9.8	8.0	11.0	9.4	15.5
Item 7670 N(Wtd)	3188	1446	1652	2621	318	704	1000	1084	400	1594	1458	1202	852	399	628	58

QUESTIONNAIRE FORM 2 1978	TOTAL	SEX		RACE		REGION				4YR COLLEGE PLANS		ILLICIT DRUG USE: LIFETIME				
		M	F	White	Black	NE	NC	S	W	Yes	No	None	Marijuana Only	Few Pills	More Pills	Any Heroin
Weighted No. of Cases:	3785	1737	1867	2960	430	931	1083	1266	505	1790	1657	1363	1005	474	760	68
% of Weighted Total:	100.0	45.9	49.3	78.2	11.4	24.6	28.6	33.4	13.3	47.3	43.8	36.0	26.6	12.5	20.1	1.8

E08D: Parents of students

1. Little or no influence	20.8	20.5	21.2	21.0	18.3	24.1	17.6	22.7	18.2	16.8	25.3	19.2	19.7	19.8	25.6	25.9
2. Some influence	31.2	30.1	31.9	32.5	22.7	29.6	34.4	30.0	29.4	30.6	32.3	31.0	30.2	33.5	32.0	27.6
3. Moderate influence	22.2	23.0	21.9	23.2	16.4	25.1	23.5	19.8	20.2	24.3	19.8	22.8	24.6	19.3	19.7	20.7
4. Considerable influence	15.9	16.8	15.3	16.2	12.9	14.0	16.3	16.0	18.0	17.6	14.1	17.4	15.5	18.0	13.4	8.6
5. A great deal of influence	9.9	9.8	9.7	7.1	29.7	7.3	8.1	11.6	14.5	10.8	8.6	9.5	10.0	9.5	9.2	15.5
Item 7680 N(Wtd)	3184	1442	1653	2617	317	702	998	1082	401	1593	1457	1201	851	400	628	58

E09: Have you had any drug education courses or lectures in school?

1. No--GO TO Q.E13	20.7	22.5	19.6	19.8	24.5	21.3	18.9	21.7	21.4	18.0	23.6	23.4	19.2	19.2	17.8	21.8
2. No, and I wish I had-- GO TO Q.E13	4.5	4.3	4.6	4.7	3.4	5.0	4.2	4.7	3.9	4.5	4.5	3.9	5.7	4.4	4.7	-
3. Yes	74.8	73.1	75.8	75.5	72.0	73.6	77.0	73.6	75.0	77.4	72.0	72.8	75.2	76.4	77.5	78.2
Item 7690 N(Wtd)	3000	1336	1587	2516	261	666	954	996	384	1540	1341	1135	814	386	573	55

E10: Would you say that the information about drugs that you received in school classes or programs has...

1. Made you less interested in trying drugs	51.5	47.5	55.1	48.9	72.7	47.0	47.3	58.6	52.2	50.5	52.4	71.4	50.7	44.3	22.1	16.7
2. Not changed your interest in trying drugs	45.2	47.6	43.1	48.1	22.2	49.5	50.1	38.4	42.7	47.5	42.9	27.7	46.6	52.4	70.0	71.4
3. Made you more interested in trying drugs	3.3	4.8	1.8	3.1	5.7	3.5	2.6	3.0	5.1	2.1	4.8	.8	2.6	3.4	7.9	9.5
Item 7840 N(Wtd) ★	2245	978	1203	1885	194	491	730	730	293	1181	970	831	609	296	443	42

E11: How many of the following drug education experiences have you had in high school? (Mark all that apply.)

A. A special course about drugs	24.7	27.5	22.1	24.7	22.4	21.9	23.7	24.7	31.8	26.2	22.6	23.7	27.0	23.5	23.5	31.1
B. Films, lectures, or discussions in one of my regular courses	74.7	74.5	75.8	75.1	72.9	75.6	75.3	71.7	79.2	77.7	71.8	75.5	76.0	73.7	73.1	68.9
C. Films or lectures, outside of my regular courses	25.5	26.5	24.2	25.6	27.6	20.9	25.3	29.7	23.2	27.6	23.5	27.9	24.0	23.2	23.5	33.3
D. Special discussions ("rap" groups) about drugs	25.1	23.8	25.9	24.6	29.7	28.1	24.9	24.3	22.5	25.0	24.8	22.7	24.9	26.0	28.9	31.1
Item 7850-7880 N(Wtd) ★	2227	970	1190	1873	192	488	726	724	289	1169	964	820	603	289	443	45

E12: Overall, how valuable were the experiences to you?

1. Little or no value	18.0	20.1	16.3	18.3	14.0	17.6	20.3	15.8	18.1	18.5	17.3	15.2	16.5	16.2	24.8	38.1
2. Some value	45.7	46.3	45.4	48.1	31.1	48.5	49.2	40.8	44.4	46.4	45.1	38.9	46.6	53.7	52.7	38.1
3. Considerable value	21.6	20.4	22.3	20.9	27.5	21.5	18.3	25.2	21.2	21.1	21.7	24.1	23.1	18.9	17.1	21.4
4. Great value	14.7	13.0	15.9	12.6	27.5	12.3	12.1	18.2	16.3	14.1	16.0	21.9	13.7	11.5	5.6	2.4
Item 7890 N(Wtd) ★	2237	978	1193	1882	193	489	734	726	288	1181	964	822	607	296	444	42

E13: Some people have suggested that there be a standard nationwide test of high school skills in arithmetic, reading, and writing. What do you think about each of the following possible uses of such a test?

E13A: Any student age 16 or older who can pass such a test should be given a high school diploma and be allowed to leave high school early

1. Disagree	33.2	32.8	34.2	34.8	26.1	34.1	34.1	32.9	30.5	37.7	29.1	35.9	34.8	32.2	26.2	43.6
2. Mostly disagree	21.2	21.1	21.6	22.2	17.0	19.1	24.0	20.0	21.3	24.5	17.2	22.6	21.4	21.4	18.8	12.7
3. Neither	14.1	14.4	13.8	14.2	10.4	15.3	15.0	13.4	11.9	13.7	15.1	13.4	14.2	14.1	16.0	10.9
4. Mostly agree	16.8	15.9	17.5	16.5	18.9	16.9	14.5	17.4	20.8	14.3	19.2	15.7	15.3	21.1	18.4	9.1
5. Agree	14.6	15.7	12.9	12.4	27.7	14.7	12.3	16.4	15.5	9.7	19.4	12.6	14.2	11.1	20.4	23.6
Item 7900 N(Wtd)	3141	1417	1633	2577	318	687	991	1069	394	1570	1431	1187	836	398	618	55

★= excludes respondents for whom question was inappropriate.

QUESTIONNAIRE FORM 2 1978	TOTAL	SEX		RACE		REGION				4YR COLLEGE PLANS		ILLICIT DRUG USE: LIFETIME				
		M	F	White	Black	NE	NC	S	W	Yes	No	None	Mari- juana Only	Few Pills	More Pills	Any Her- oin
Weighted No. of Cases:	3785	1737	1867	2960	430	931	1083	1266	505	1790	1657	1363	1005	474	760	68
% of Weighted Total:	100.0	45.9	49.3	78.2	11.4	24.6	28.6	33.4	13.3	47.3	43.8	36.0	26.6	12.5	20.1	1.8
E13B: Any student age 14 or older who can pass such a test should be given a high school diploma and be allowed to leave school early																
1. Disagree	58.9	57.4	60.7	61.1	48.4	57.9	61.2	59.1	54.9	63.9	54.5	62.3	60.7	57.1	52.4	50.9
2. Mostly disagree	21.9	19.8	24.0	21.8	22.0	21.9	21.9	21.0	24.3	21.3	22.2	21.8	20.6	25.8	22.0	18.2
3. Neither	10.7	12.3	9.2	9.9	11.5	11.8	9.7	10.5	11.6	9.1	12.2	8.6	10.9	8.8	15.1	12.7
4. Mostly agree	4.2	5.2	3.4	3.9	6.7	4.4	4.4	3.7	4.8	3.1	5.2	4.2	3.7	3.3	4.9	9.1
5. Agree	4.3	5.3	2.8	3.3	11.1	3.9	2.9	5.7	4.3	2.7	5.8	3.0	4.0	5.1	5.7	7.3
Item 7910 N(Wtd)	3129	1413	1628	2570	314	684	991	1060	395	1567	1425	1181	834	396	617	55
E13C: Before any student (no matter what age) is given a high school diploma, he or she should have to pass such a standard nationwide test																
1. Disagree	28.0	27.9	28.0	27.4	30.9	27.5	28.9	27.7	27.4	22.9	33.1	25.3	29.1	29.1	30.2	37.0
2. Mostly disagree	11.5	10.0	12.8	11.9	8.9	11.5	10.4	12.0	12.9	11.7	11.6	11.7	10.4	12.3	11.9	9.3
3. Neither	15.9	17.3	14.6	16.3	13.1	16.3	17.8	14.4	14.2	13.6	17.8	13.7	16.4	17.0	18.1	24.1
4. Mostly agree	19.6	19.7	19.6	20.0	18.8	20.7	19.8	19.0	18.3	22.3	16.8	20.9	21.1	20.1	15.7	14.8
5. Agree	25.1	24.9	25.1	24.3	28.3	24.2	23.0	26.9	27.2	29.5	20.7	28.5	23.1	21.3	24.1	16.7
Item 7920 N(Wtd)	3134	1415	1630	2575	314	687	993	1061	394	1571	1424	1184	836	399	613	54

QUESTIONNAIRE FORM 3 1978	TOTAL	SEX		RACE		REGION				4YR COLLEGE PLANS		ILLICIT DRUG USE: LIFETIME				
		M	F	White	Black	NE	NC	S	W	Yes	No	None	Mari- juana Only	Few Pills	More Pills	Any Her- oin
Weighted No. of Cases:	3778	1711	1917	2973	417	926	1080	1257	516	1758	1748	1313	1078	451	764	68
% of Weighted Total:	100.0	45.3	50.7	78.7	11.0	24.5	28.6	33.3	13.7	46.5	46.3	34.8	28.5	11.9	20.2	1.8

A01: Taking all things together, how would you say things are these days-would you say you're very happy, pretty happy, or not too happy these days?

	TOTAL	M	F	White	Black	NE	NC	S	W	Yes	No	None	Mar	Few	More	Her
3. Very happy	19.9	18.8	21.4	20.8	13.7	19.9	18.9	20.8	20.2	23.9	16.2	24.0	18.0	19.6	15.4	26.5
2. Pretty happy	67.7	68.6	67.2	69.0	64.2	65.2	71.1	67.6	65.4	65.8	71.1	64.5	70.7	66.6	70.8	61.8
1. Not too happy	12.4	12.6	11.4	10.3	22.1	15.0	10.1	11.7	14.2	10.3	12.7	11.5	11.4	13.8	13.8	11.8
Item 1190 N(Wtd)	3765	1702	1913	2965	416	924	1075	1252	514	1753	1739	1310	1075	449	760	68

A02: Some people think a lot about the social problems of the nation and the world, and about how they might be solved. Others spend little time thinking about these issues. How much do you think about such things?

	TOTAL	M	F	White	Black	NE	NC	S	W	Yes	No	None	Mar	Few	More	Her
1. Never	1.9	2.2	1.5	1.8	1.0	2.2	1.6	1.5	2.7	.8	2.8	1.5	1.3	1.6	3.2	7.4
2. Seldom	15.7	15.3	16.0	16.5	12.1	20.3	14.1	15.0	12.6	13.2	18.4	14.7	15.1	14.1	19.7	16.2
3. Sometimes	51.5	50.1	52.9	52.9	45.7	47.7	55.8	51.2	50.2	49.0	54.3	52.3	53.1	53.3	46.3	54.4
4. Quite often	25.9	26.9	25.0	24.1	32.4	23.4	24.6	27.2	29.8	30.7	21.0	26.1	25.5	26.1	26.3	19.1
5. A great deal	5.1	5.5	4.6	4.7	8.9	6.4	4.1	5.2	4.7	6.3	3.6	5.5	5.0	5.1	4.6	4.4
Item 6880 N(Wtd)	3764	1702	1912	2966	414	924	1074	1250	514	1754	1741	1309	1075	448	761	68

A03: The next questions ask your opinions about a number of different topics. How much do you agree or disagree with each statement below?

A03A: Men and women should be paid the same money if they do the same work

	TOTAL	M	F	White	Black	NE	NC	S	W	Yes	No	None	Mar	Few	More	Her
1. Disagree	2.8	5.0	.7	2.2	4.1	2.7	3.2	3.2	1.6	2.4	2.6	2.6	2.6	2.2	2.8	5.9
2. Mostly disagree	1.2	2.5	.2	1.3	.7	1.8	1.5	.6	.6	1.3	1.1	1.1	1.1	1.6	1.3	1.5
3. Neither	1.5	2.6	.5	1.4	.7	1.3	1.4	1.7	1.6	1.0	1.9	1.1	1.7	1.3	1.4	2.9
4. Mostly agree	14.5	19.5	9.5	15.0	11.8	12.1	16.1	14.7	14.7	13.0	16.2	13.9	16.6	14.0	12.2	19.1
5. Agree	80.1	70.4	89.2	80.0	82.7	82.1	77.8	79.8	81.6	82.4	78.2	81.3	78.0	80.7	82.1	72.1
Item 7930 N(Wtd)	3775	1709	1916	2972	417	926	1079	1255	516	1758	1745	1313	1078	451	761	68

A03B: Women should be considered as seriously as men for jobs as executives or politicians

	TOTAL	M	F	White	Black	NE	NC	S	W	Yes	No	None	Mar	Few	More	Her
1. Disagree	6.1	9.6	2.7	5.6	6.3	6.3	5.6	6.3	6.0	4.6	7.2	6.3	6.1	5.5	5.3	10.3
2. Mostly disagree	4.9	7.7	1.8	4.8	5.3	3.4	5.1	5.5	5.3	4.2	5.6	4.7	5.5	5.1	4.5	2.9
3. Neither	4.5	6.9	2.4	4.6	2.9	3.8	5.0	4.9	3.9	3.5	5.7	4.4	4.5	2.4	5.8	1.5
4. Mostly agree	24.2	29.1	19.7	24.3	25.4	19.7	22.9	28.6	24.6	23.5	25.2	23.8	25.3	23.9	23.2	32.4
5. Agree	60.4	46.7	73.5	60.6	59.9	67.0	61.4	54.7	60.2	64.2	56.2	61.0	58.6	63.0	61.4	54.4
Item 7940 N(Wtd)	3768	1707	1912	2970	414	925	1078	1251	513	1756	1741	1309	1078	451	760	68

A03C: A woman should have exactly the same job opportunities as a man

	TOTAL	M	F	White	Black	NE	NC	S	W	Yes	No	None	Mar	Few	More	Her
1. Disagree	9.6	14.0	5.2	8.6	14.8	9.5	8.9	11.2	7.2	6.4	11.8	10.0	7.9	8.7	9.6	22.4
2. Mostly disagree	7.2	10.6	3.8	7.5	4.4	7.6	6.4	7.2	8.6	5.8	8.7	6.8	7.4	7.4	7.4	7.5
3. Neither	5.9	8.1	3.7	6.1	3.2	5.0	6.7	5.4	7.0	5.8	6.4	6.5	5.9	4.0	6.0	4.5
4. Mostly agree	28.9	28.7	29.9	30.8	20.0	27.6	31.3	27.1	30.7	30.4	28.3	28.1	28.6	33.0	29.9	25.4
5. Agree	48.3	38.7	57.3	47.0	57.3	50.3	46.6	49.0	46.5	51.6	44.8	48.7	50.1	46.9	47.0	38.8
Item 7950 N(Wtd)	3738	1694	1897	2950	405	917	1074	1236	512	1744	1725	1299	1072	446	753	67

A03D: A woman should have exactly the same educational opportunities as a man

	TOTAL	M	F	White	Black	NE	NC	S	W	Yes	No	None	Mar	Few	More	Her
1. Disagree	1.5	2.2	.7	.9	3.4	1.3	1.3	1.8	1.8	1.0	1.6	1.5	.9	1.1	1.3	5.9
2. Mostly disagree	1.1	1.6	.8	1.2	.7	1.2	1.5	1.1	.4	.6	1.6	1.2	.6	1.8	.8	5.9
3. Neither	.9	1.1	.7	.9	.7	.4	1.4	1.0	.8	.5	1.4	1.0	.8	.4	1.2	1.5
4. Mostly agree	9.2	10.9	7.3	8.0	15.9	7.8	9.5	10.9	7.4	6.9	11.0	8.5	10.1	8.9	8.6	8.8
5. Agree	87.2	84.2	90.5	89.0	79.3	89.3	86.3	85.4	89.8	91.0	84.5	87.8	87.5	88.0	88.1	77.9
Item 7960 N(Wtd)	3757	1699	1910	2958	416	918	1075	1252	511	1751	1737	1310	1070	450	757	68

QUESTIONNAIRE FORM 3 1978	TOTAL	SEX		RACE		REGION				4YR COLLEGE PLANS		ILLICIT DRUG USE: LIFETIME				
		M	F	White	Black	NE	NC	S	W	Yes	No	None	Mari-juana Only	Few Pills	More Pills	Any Her-oin
Weighted No. of Cases:	3778	1711	1917	2973	417	926	1080	1257	516	1758	1748	1313	1078	451	764	68
% of Weighted Total:	100.0	45.3	50.7	78.7	11.0	24.5	28.6	33.3	13.7	46.5	46.3	34.8	28.5	11.9	20.2	1.8

A03E: It is usually better for everyone involved if the man is the achiever outside the home and the woman takes care of the home and family

	TOTAL	M	F	White	Black	NE	NC	S	W	Yes	No	None	Mari-juana Only	Few Pills	More Pills	Any Her-oin
1. Disagree	20.3	11.8	28.1	18.2	31.8	22.2	19.1	20.3	19.6	23.1	17.1	18.5	20.3	21.9	21.5	22.1
2. Mostly disagree	15.6	11.9	19.3	16.4	12.4	16.8	16.4	14.2	15.9	17.8	14.1	15.3	14.1	17.0	17.9	22.1
3. Neither	15.2	17.3	13.4	16.0	7.0	14.6	16.5	13.6	17.0	16.5	14.2	14.9	13.9	16.1	17.2	14.7
4. Mostly agree	24.3	24.2	24.4	25.4	19.9	24.2	24.5	24.6	23.1	22.5	26.3	24.6	26.3	23.4	22.6	16.2
5. Agree	24.5	34.8	14.7	23.9	28.9	22.2	23.4	27.2	24.7	20.2	28.2	26.7	25.4	21.4	20.8	25.0
Item 7970 N(Wtd)	3753	1698	1907	2961	412	916	1076	1250	511	1750	1736	1305	1076	448	755	68

A03F: A preschool child is likely to suffer if the mother works

	TOTAL	M	F	White	Black	NE	NC	S	W	Yes	No	None	Mari-juana Only	Few Pills	More Pills	Any Her-oin
1. Disagree	15.7	9.9	20.5	12.2	37.5	15.4	14.5	17.9	13.4	15.1	15.4	15.5	16.6	12.6	15.3	14.7
2. Mostly disagree	13.8	9.1	17.9	13.6	13.6	14.0	12.9	14.9	12.8	15.7	11.9	12.7	12.8	15.2	16.3	10.3
3. Neither	12.3	12.2	12.5	12.6	7.7	12.1	14.8	10.4	12.0	13.8	11.4	11.6	13.0	11.2	13.3	13.2
4. Mostly agree	26.1	27.4	25.4	28.2	16.7	25.7	28.1	24.0	28.0	26.9	25.7	25.8	25.1	28.9	27.4	25.0
5. Agree	32.1	41.4	23.8	33.5	24.5	32.9	29.7	32.7	33.9	28.5	35.6	34.4	32.5	31.8	27.8	35.3
Item 7980 N(Wtd)	3740	1695	1902	2947	413	910	1070	1252	508	1750	1726	1300	1073	446	753	68

A03G: A working mother can establish just as warm and secure a relationship with her children as a mother who does not work

	TOTAL	M	F	White	Black	NE	NC	S	W	Yes	No	None	Mari-juana Only	Few Pills	More Pills	Any Her-oin
1. Disagree	19.1	26.7	11.7	19.1	19.5	18.0	17.1	21.2	20.1	15.6	22.3	20.2	20.2	16.9	15.5	22.4
2. Mostly disagree	17.9	22.2	14.4	19.8	6.5	19.8	17.0	15.8	21.4	19.1	17.0	15.5	20.8	20.5	17.5	16.4
3. Neither	8.3	9.9	7.0	9.0	2.7	7.5	10.1	7.1	8.4	10.0	7.1	9.9	8.0	6.7	7.1	13.4
4. Mostly agree	24.8	19.9	29.1	25.3	22.4	24.6	26.2	23.9	24.2	25.0	24.6	26.2	22.0	27.4	27.1	9.0
5. Agree	30.0	21.4	37.8	26.8	48.9	29.9	29.7	31.9	25.9	30.3	29.0	28.2	28.9	28.5	32.9	37.3
Item 7990 N(Wtd)	3763	1703	1915	2963	415	922	1078	1250	513	1753	1742	1311	1075	449	761	67

A04: The next questions are about pollution and the environment. How much do you agree or disagree with each statement below?

A04A: Pollution of most types has increased in the U.S. in the last ten years

	TOTAL	M	F	White	Black	NE	NC	S	W	Yes	No	None	Mari-juana Only	Few Pills	More Pills	Any Her-oin
1. Disagree	2.9	3.9	2.0	2.6	4.8	2.8	3.5	2.8	2.3	2.6	3.1	2.7	3.3	2.7	2.6	-
2. Mostly disagree	4.5	5.8	3.2	4.7	2.9	4.3	4.8	3.9	5.5	5.6	3.4	4.1	4.9	4.9	4.4	6.0
3. Neither	5.1	5.3	4.9	5.3	3.1	4.1	5.8	4.9	6.0	5.5	4.8	5.5	5.1	5.5	4.2	9.0
4. Mostly agree	22.9	22.6	23.0	23.0	21.0	21.6	24.0	22.9	22.6	22.5	23.2	24.0	22.0	20.2	23.5	16.4
5. Agree	64.7	62.3	66.8	64.3	68.0	67.2	61.9	65.6	63.7	63.8	65.6	63.6	64.6	67.0	65.2	68.7
Item 8000 N(Wtd)	3758	1701	1909	2963	415	922	1071	1252	513	1753	1736	1308	1076	451	756	67

A04B: Government should take steps to deal with our environmental problems, even if it means that most of us pay higher prices or taxes

	TOTAL	M	F	White	Black	NE	NC	S	W	Yes	No	None	Mari-juana Only	Few Pills	More Pills	Any Her-oin
1. Disagree	9.6	11.5	7.8	8.2	15.9	9.6	7.5	12.2	8.4	5.9	12.6	8.7	9.7	9.8	9.4	16.7
2. Mostly disagree	9.0	10.0	8.5	8.5	12.8	9.5	7.9	8.8	11.0	7.8	10.3	8.6	8.7	10.9	9.8	7.6
3. Neither	15.0	13.4	16.7	15.8	9.4	13.2	17.5	14.3	14.3	15.0	15.5	14.4	16.7	16.3	14.0	13.6
4. Mostly agree	37.0	33.5	40.9	39.0	29.7	35.7	39.6	35.8	37.2	40.5	34.7	38.9	37.9	35.2	35.0	33.3
5. Agree	29.3	31.7	26.1	28.5	32.4	32.2	27.5	29.0	29.2	30.7	26.8	29.4	27.2	27.8	31.8	28.8
Item 8010 N(Wtd)	3752	1696	1908	2957	414	919	1073	1250	511	1749	1734	1307	1074	449	758	66

A04C: I would prefer to pay more money for things that will last a long time, rather than have them cost less and break sooner

	TOTAL	M	F	White	Black	NE	NC	S	W	Yes	No	None	Mari-juana Only	Few Pills	More Pills	Any Her-oin
1. Disagree	1.2	1.5	.9	.8	3.1	.7	1.1	1.4	1.8	.6	1.6	1.0	1.3	1.6	.7	2.9
2. Mostly disagree	1.2	1.1	1.3	1.0	1.7	1.4	.8	1.5	1.2	.4	1.9	1.7	.3	1.3	1.3	-
3. Neither	3.3	3.7	2.9	3.3	2.2	4.3	3.4	2.1	4.5	3.3	3.3	3.9	2.7	2.0	3.8	8.8
4. Mostly agree	20.7	20.6	20.8	21.2	16.9	18.5	23.2	20.3	20.3	19.6	21.6	19.3	22.1	22.4	21.3	13.2
5. Agree	73.6	73.1	74.1	73.7	76.1	75.1	71.6	74.8	72.5	76.0	71.6	74.1	73.6	72.7	73.1	75.0
Item 8020 N(Wtd)	3760	1702	1910	2964	414	921	1073	1253	513	1753	1737	1310	1074	451	757	68

	TOTAL	SEX		RACE		REGION				4YR COLLEGE PLANS		ILLICIT DRUG USE: LIFETIME				
QUESTIONNAIRE FORM 3 1978		M	F	White	Black	NE	NC	S	W	Yes	No	None	Mari- juana Only	Few Pills	More Pills	Any Her- oin
Weighted No. of Cases:	3778	1711	1917	2973	417	926	1080	1257	516	1758	1748	1313	1078	451	764	68
% of Weighted Total:	100.0	45.3	50.7	78.7	11.0	24.5	28.6	33.3	13.7	46.5	46.3	34.8	28.5	11.9	20.2	1.8

A04D: I would probably be willing to use a bicycle or mass transit (if available) rather than a car to get to work

	TOTAL	M	F	White	Black	NE	NC	S	W	Yes	No	None	Mari-juana Only	Few Pills	More Pills	Any Heroin
1. Disagree	26.3	31.3	21.5	23.7	43.0	26.0	22.8	30.9	23.0	20.2	30.2	22.6	25.8	28.3	28.9	33.8
2. Mostly disagree	17.7	17.1	18.2	18.0	17.0	16.6	17.5	18.7	17.6	17.1	19.3	17.8	18.2	14.3	19.2	16.2
3. Neither	11.5	11.6	11.5	12.1	6.8	9.7	12.7	12.5	10.2	12.4	10.8	11.9	11.8	12.2	9.6	16.2
4. Mostly agree	24.1	22.1	26.0	25.3	20.4	24.6	25.7	21.7	26.0	27.1	21.0	25.9	24.2	25.4	22.4	16.2
5. Agree	20.4	17.9	22.8	21.0	12.9	23.2	21.5	16.2	23.2	23.1	18.8	21.7	19.9	20.0	20.0	19.1
Item 8030 N(Wtd)	3760	1707	1906	2967	412	922	1076	1250	512	1754	1736	1307	1077	449	760	68

A04E: I would be willing to eat less meat and more grains and vegetables, if it would help provide food for starving people

	TOTAL	M	F	White	Black	NE	NC	S	W	Yes	No	None	Mari-juana Only	Few Pills	More Pills	Any Heroin
1. Disagree	10.6	16.9	4.9	10.9	9.3	9.8	11.0	9.2	14.2	9.4	11.4	9.6	10.3	10.7	10.5	20.6
2. Mostly disagree	7.8	11.4	4.5	8.1	4.6	6.3	9.4	7.7	7.4	8.2	7.5	7.5	8.9	6.7	8.1	4.4
3. Neither	12.6	17.2	8.8	14.1	5.4	13.9	13.4	11.0	12.6	13.6	12.3	12.3	13.8	10.7	13.7	14.7
4. Mostly agree	29.3	28.4	30.2	29.6	27.8	31.0	28.4	29.0	28.8	28.9	30.2	28.8	31.2	29.5	28.0	26.5
5. Agree	39.6	26.2	51.6	37.4	52.9	39.0	37.6	43.0	36.6	39.9	38.6	41.7	35.9	42.6	39.9	35.3
Item 8040 N(Wtd)	3755	1700	1908	2966	410	919	1073	1250	514	1751	1737	1313	1072	448	754	68

A05: In the following list you will find some statements about leisure time and work. Please show whether you agree or disagree with each statement.

A05A: I like the kind of work you can forget about after the work day is over

	TOTAL	M	F	White	Black	NE	NC	S	W	Yes	No	None	Mari-juana Only	Few Pills	More Pills	Any Heroin
1. Disagree	15.9	16.7	14.9	13.3	27.6	17.0	12.6	17.8	16.0	17.3	13.5	17.8	16.2	14.0	10.8	19.4
2. Mostly disagree	15.2	13.9	16.6	16.0	12.7	15.4	15.4	16.0	12.7	20.1	10.9	14.7	17.9	14.7	13.8	11.9
3. Neither	11.5	11.1	12.3	12.5	5.8	10.1	13.4	9.3	15.6	14.2	9.5	12.1	11.0	11.6	11.6	13.4
4. Mostly agree	22.6	22.0	23.0	23.2	21.1	22.9	22.4	21.9	24.0	22.8	22.5	23.6	19.7	23.1	25.5	23.9
5. Agree	34.7	36.2	33.1	35.1	32.9	34.4	36.2	35.0	31.8	25.6	43.7	31.7	35.1	36.7	38.4	32.8
Item 8050 N(Wtd)	3766	1706	1912	2966	417	921	1078	1255	512	1755	1740	1310	1077	450	761	67

A05B: To me, work is nothing more than making a living

	TOTAL	M	F	White	Black	NE	NC	S	W	Yes	No	None	Mari-juana Only	Few Pills	More Pills	Any Heroin
1. Disagree	44.7	41.8	47.9	45.8	39.1	45.0	42.5	46.2	45.0	50.0	39.8	46.4	45.7	43.6	42.4	39.7
2. Mostly disagree	24.4	23.6	25.4	26.7	14.1	25.4	26.3	22.3	23.2	28.0	21.5	26.1	24.1	22.7	23.8	27.9
3. Neither	7.6	8.3	6.9	7.9	5.0	6.5	9.7	6.0	9.2	7.1	8.4	8.0	7.7	8.4	6.7	5.9
4. Mostly agree	11.6	12.9	10.3	10.6	17.3	10.6	10.8	12.6	12.5	8.2	14.6	9.9	10.6	13.6	14.0	16.2
5. Agree	11.8	13.5	9.5	9.0	24.5	12.6	10.6	12.8	10.1	6.7	15.7	9.5	11.8	11.8	13.0	10.3
Item 8060 N(Wtd)	3765	1702	1915	2965	417	923	1077	1253	513	1753	1743	1310	1077	450	759	68

A05C: I expect my work to be a very central part of my life

	TOTAL	M	F	White	Black	NE	NC	S	W	Yes	No	None	Mari-juana Only	Few Pills	More Pills	Any Heroin
1. Disagree	5.1	5.0	5.3	5.2	3.9	7.3	5.5	3.4	4.3	4.2	5.9	4.7	5.1	5.1	5.9	4.4
2. Mostly disagree	8.6	8.6	8.7	9.4	3.1	9.5	8.8	7.1	10.2	7.9	9.5	8.0	9.5	10.6	7.7	11.8
3. Neither	10.8	11.2	10.7	12.0	4.3	11.4	11.9	8.3	13.1	12.2	9.4	10.6	10.8	10.6	11.2	14.7
4. Mostly agree	36.2	33.5	38.6	36.6	34.1	34.3	36.7	36.4	38.0	36.1	36.6	36.1	34.4	36.4	39.5	45.6
5. Agree	39.3	41.7	36.6	36.8	54.6	37.4	36.9	44.7	34.1	39.5	38.5	40.7	40.2	37.3	35.7	25.0
Item 8070 N(Wtd)	3754	1698	1910	2958	414	922	1075	1247	510	1752	1734	1306	1074	451	757	68

A05D: I want to do my best in my job, even if this sometimes means working overtime

	TOTAL	M	F	White	Black	NE	NC	S	W	Yes	No	None	Mari-juana Only	Few Pills	More Pills	Any Heroin
1. Disagree	1.8	2.2	1.5	1.7	1.9	2.7	1.6	1.4	1.6	1.4	2.0	1.3	1.5	2.5	2.5	2.9
2. Mostly disagree	1.9	2.2	1.7	1.8	2.2	2.5	1.1	2.0	2.5	1.4	2.4	1.6	1.9	2.0	2.2	4.4
3. Neither	4.1	4.4	3.6	4.5	.5	5.4	5.3	2.1	3.7	3.9	4.4	3.2	4.4	4.5	5.0	2.9
4. Mostly agree	30.3	29.8	30.7	30.9	27.5	28.4	33.0	27.9	33.9	33.1	27.5	26.5	31.7	35.7	32.4	35.3
5. Agree	61.9	61.2	62.4	61.1	67.9	61.0	59.0	66.6	58.3	60.2	63.7	67.4	60.6	55.1	57.8	54.4
Item 8080 N(Wtd)	3754	1700	1906	2959	414	921	1074	1249	511	1748	1737	1306	1075	448	756	68

QUESTIONNAIRE FORM 3 1978	TOTAL	SEX		RACE		REGION				4YR COLLEGE PLANS		ILLICIT DRUG USE: LIFETIME				
		M	F	White	Black	NE	NC	S	W	Yes	No	None	Mari-juana Only	Few Pills	More Pills	Any Her-oin
Weighted No. of Cases:	3778	1711	1917	2973	417	926	1080	1257	516	1758	1748	1313	1078	451	764	68
% of Weighted Total:	100.0	45.3	50.7	78.7	11.0	24.5	28.6	33.3	13.7	46.5	46.3	34.8	28.5	11.9	20.2	1.8

A05E: I would like to stay in the same job for most of my adult life

1. Disagree	17.1	16.2	17.8	16.0	25.4	16.7	17.6	17.8	14.9	14.3	19.2	12.2	17.5	21.6	20.5	25.0
2. Mostly disagree	12.3	10.8	13.7	12.3	11.6	11.4	13.4	12.2	12.2	13.2	12.0	12.1	11.0	12.7	15.1	8.8
3. Neither	16.1	17.2	15.4	17.6	6.8	18.5	15.9	12.8	20.6	18.9	14.0	14.2	17.4	16.3	17.6	22.1
4. Mostly agree	24.9	24.7	24.9	25.2	23.5	25.0	25.0	24.5	25.3	25.5	24.2	28.1	25.6	22.7	21.1	13.2
5. Agree	29.6	31.2	28.2	28.9	32.7	28.5	28.2	32.6	26.9	28.2	30.6	33.3	28.6	26.9	25.8	30.9
Item 8090 N(Wtd)	3750	1700	1903	2957	413	924	1071	1244	510	1751	1730	1301	1075	449	757	68

A06: If you were to get enough money to live as comfortably as you'd like for the rest of your life, would you want to work?

1. I would want to work	79.8	77.5	81.6	79.8	78.7	75.1	79.7	82.2	82.7	81.8	78.4	82.6	81.7	79.6	72.0	76.6
2. I would not want to work	20.2	22.5	18.4	20.2	21.3	24.9	20.3	17.8	17.3	18.2	21.6	17.4	18.3	20.4	28.0	23.4
Item 8100 N(Wtd)	3661	1639	1884	2904	395	904	1057	1209	491	1713	1691	1278	1042	441	740	64

The next questions are about living or working with people of different races. Please rate each of the statements below using the following terms:

Not at all acceptable: I'd avoid this if I possibly could.

Somewhat acceptable: I could live with this, but not be happy about it.

Acceptable: This would be O.K., or I'd be neutral about this.

Desirable: I'd really like this.

A07: How would you feel about...

A07A: Having close personal friends of another race?

1. Not at all acceptable	2.9	3.4	2.3	2.8	1.7	2.1	3.0	4.1	1.4	1.8	3.8	2.7	2.8	3.6	2.2	7.4
2. Somewhat acceptable	7.6	10.4	5.0	8.3	3.6	5.7	8.3	9.0	6.3	5.2	9.8	6.9	7.4	6.0	9.7	5.9
3. Acceptable	56.4	60.9	52.7	58.6	52.4	59.0	56.9	56.0	51.9	56.2	57.1	54.5	57.2	59.2	57.9	57.4
4. Desirable	33.0	25.2	40.0	30.3	42.5	33.3	31.8	30.9	40.7	36.7	29.3	35.9	32.6	31.3	30.1	29.4
Item 8110 N(Wtd)	3761	1705	1910	2964	416	922	1077	1250	511	1753	1739	1311	1072	448	763	68

A07B: Having a job with a supervisor of a different race?

1. Not at all acceptable	4.0	5.6	2.5	4.4	1.2	3.5	3.8	4.7	3.9	3.4	4.8	3.4	3.9	4.7	4.2	7.4
2. Somewhat acceptable	9.3	11.0	7.8	9.7	8.2	6.9	10.2	12.0	4.5	7.6	11.0	9.3	8.9	10.7	8.8	7.4
3. Acceptable	67.7	69.0	66.4	69.5	64.4	71.0	69.2	65.1	65.2	70.7	64.8	67.2	67.6	66.1	71.4	64.7
4. Desirable	19.0	14.3	23.2	16.5	26.0	18.5	16.7	18.3	26.4	18.3	19.3	20.0	19.5	18.5	15.6	20.6
Item 8120 N(Wtd)	3758	1705	1907	2964	416	922	1076	1251	508	1752	1738	1308	1072	448	762	68

A07C: Having a family of a different race (but same level of education and income) move next door to you?

1. Not at all acceptable	7.2	9.0	5.6	7.5	4.6	6.5	6.4	9.9	3.7	5.1	9.2	7.4	7.6	5.1	6.7	13.4
2. Somewhat acceptable	11.5	14.7	8.7	12.6	6.3	9.8	10.7	15.6	6.3	8.8	14.5	9.9	11.8	13.6	12.8	9.0
3. Acceptable	55.4	56.5	54.6	56.1	58.2	56.4	56.7	53.4	56.4	57.9	52.4	55.3	55.2	53.7	57.0	55.2
4. Desirable	25.8	19.9	31.1	23.8	31.0	27.5	26.1	21.1	33.6	28.0	23.9	27.3	25.2	27.7	23.3	22.4
Item 8130 N(Wtd)	3755	1702	1908	2962	416	921	1077	1248	509	1752	1737	1309	1072	447	763	67

QUESTIONNAIRE FORM 3 1978	TOTAL	SEX		RACE		REGION				4YR COLLEGE PLANS		ILLICIT DRUG USE: LIFETIME				
		M	F	White	Black	NE	NC	S	W	Yes	No	None	Marijuana Only	Few Pills	More Pills	Any Heroin
Weighted No. of Cases:	3778	1711	1917	2973	417	926	1080	1257	516	1758	1748	1313	1078	451	764	68
% of Weighted Total:	100.0	45.3	50.7	78.7	11.0	24.5	28.6	33.3	13.7	46.5	46.3	34.8	28.5	11.9	20.2	1.8

A07D: Having your (future) children's friends be all of your race?

	TOTAL	M	F	White	Black	NE	NC	S	W	Yes	No	None	Marijuana Only	Few Pills	More Pills	Any Heroin
1. Not at all acceptable	20.4	18.4	22.8	19.3	26.8	19.7	17.5	22.5	22.9	21.6	19.0	21.8	19.5	22.4	19.2	23.9
2. Somewhat acceptable	20.5	20.5	20.5	20.0	20.9	21.1	20.3	19.8	21.7	22.1	19.5	19.2	21.1	20.6	22.1	14.9
3. Acceptable	41.3	41.6	40.7	42.3	35.5	44.8	43.5	37.2	40.8	41.3	41.0	41.5	41.5	39.6	41.6	41.8
4. Desirable	17.7	19.5	16.1	18.4	16.8	14.4	18.6	20.5	15.1	14.9	20.6	17.5	17.9	17.4	16.9	19.4
Item 8140 N(Wtd)	3712	1684	1886	2934	411	902	1074	1233	503	1735	1714	1300	1062	442	745	67

A07E: Having some of your (future) children's friends be of other races?

	TOTAL	M	F	White	Black	NE	NC	S	W	Yes	No	None	Marijuana Only	Few Pills	More Pills	Any Heroin
1. Not at all acceptable	3.8	4.5	2.8	3.6	3.6	3.1	3.0	5.5	2.4	2.3	4.7	4.7	2.3	2.7	3.4	8.8
2. Somewhat acceptable	9.4	12.2	6.8	10.0	4.8	7.7	10.1	11.5	5.9	6.5	12.0	8.4	9.5	10.3	10.0	8.8
3. Acceptable	49.7	52.1	47.4	50.5	49.2	53.0	49.5	48.0	48.4	48.9	51.5	47.2	51.8	50.8	51.0	48.5
4. Desirable	37.1	31.3	42.9	35.9	42.4	36.2	37.6	35.0	43.3	42.3	31.9	39.7	36.4	36.2	35.6	33.8
Item 8150 N(Wtd)	3744	1700	1900	2957	415	917	1073	1247	506	1748	1731	1304	1069	447	759	68

A08: How would you feel about having a job where...

A08A: ...all the employees are of your race?

	TOTAL	M	F	White	Black	NE	NC	S	W	Yes	No	None	Marijuana Only	Few Pills	More Pills	Any Heroin
1. Not at all acceptable	7.4	6.4	8.2	4.8	19.2	7.1	6.1	7.9	9.6	7.2	6.6	7.6	7.4	10.1	5.0	5.9
2. Somewhat acceptable	15.2	14.0	15.7	12.4	27.7	15.0	11.9	17.2	18.0	15.3	15.0	13.7	15.5	15.5	15.9	20.6
3. Acceptable	52.9	52.7	53.7	56.3	39.6	54.7	57.3	47.5	53.3	56.0	51.1	53.8	53.7	50.9	54.3	42.6
4. Desirable	24.4	26.9	22.3	26.4	13.6	23.1	24.7	27.4	18.8	21.5	27.3	24.9	23.4	23.4	24.8	30.9
Item 8160 N(Wtd)	3745	1697	1902	2953	412	919	1075	1241	510	1750	1731	1306	1068	444	761	68

A08B: ...some employees are of a different race?

	TOTAL	M	F	White	Black	NE	NC	S	W	Yes	No	None	Marijuana Only	Few Pills	More Pills	Any Heroin
1. Not at all acceptable	1.4	1.6	1.1	1.5	.7	.9	2.1	1.7	.4	.9	1.8	1.3	.9	.7	2.1	2.9
2. Somewhat acceptable	5.7	8.1	3.6	5.6	6.0	5.5	5.5	6.7	3.5	3.7	7.6	5.6	5.6	4.2	6.3	2.9
3. Acceptable	65.4	69.5	61.8	68.4	52.3	66.4	67.3	64.1	63.4	66.2	65.2	64.7	66.0	66.3	65.3	72.1
4. Desirable	27.5	20.7	33.6	24.5	41.2	27.3	25.1	27.5	32.9	29.2	25.4	28.4	27.5	28.6	26.2	23.5
Item 8170 N(Wtd)	3750	1702	1904	2958	415	919	1074	1248	508	1750	1734	1306	1067	448	763	68

A08C: ...most employees are of a different race?

	TOTAL	M	F	White	Black	NE	NC	S	W	Yes	No	None	Marijuana Only	Few Pills	More Pills	Any Heroin
1. Not at all acceptable	15.0	17.7	12.9	17.1	6.6	14.8	14.9	18.0	8.6	14.9	15.4	13.9	14.6	16.0	17.9	10.4
2. Somewhat acceptable	35.0	37.8	32.8	37.5	26.9	35.4	37.1	36.6	26.5	34.4	36.1	35.3	35.8	35.8	33.0	32.8
3. Acceptable	42.1	38.4	45.4	41.0	44.7	43.0	41.0	38.1	52.7	43.6	41.1	42.2	42.1	42.3	43.6	34.3
4. Desirable	7.8	6.2	8.9	4.4	21.8	6.7	7.0	7.4	12.2	7.0	7.3	8.6	7.5	5.6	5.7	20.9
Item 8180 N(Wtd)	3732	1697	1892	2941	412	916	1070	1236	509	1746	1721	1296	1067	444	761	67

A09: How would you feel about living in an area where...

A09A: ...all the neighbors are of your race?

	TOTAL	M	F	White	Black	NE	NC	S	W	Yes	No	None	Marijuana Only	Few Pills	More Pills	Any Heroin
1. Not at all acceptable	4.4	4.1	4.6	2.4	11.4	4.8	3.5	3.8	7.5	3.8	4.4	5.4	3.6	4.7	3.5	2.9
2. Somewhat acceptable	9.4	9.4	8.9	6.9	17.9	9.0	8.1	8.8	14.1	9.5	9.0	9.0	9.1	9.6	9.9	10.3
3. Acceptable	50.7	49.7	52.0	52.5	48.8	55.0	52.4	44.5	54.5	54.7	47.2	51.8	51.1	47.4	51.4	44.1
4. Desirable	35.5	36.8	34.6	38.2	21.7	31.1	36.0	42.9	24.1	32.1	39.6	33.8	36.3	38.3	35.2	42.6
Item 8190 N(Wtd)	3755	1703	1907	2961	414	919	1074	1253	510	1751	1739	1308	1070	449	761	68

A09B: ...some of the neighbors are of other races?

	TOTAL	M	F	White	Black	NE	NC	S	W	Yes	No	None	Marijuana Only	Few Pills	More Pills	Any Heroin
1. Not at all acceptable	2.9	3.4	2.3	3.1	1.5	2.7	2.0	4.7	1.2	2.3	3.3	2.5	3.1	2.2	3.5	1.5
2. Somewhat acceptable	10.3	12.6	8.0	10.6	6.8	7.1	9.5	15.2	5.5	7.7	12.6	8.8	10.1	11.2	10.9	17.6
3. Acceptable	64.5	66.7	62.8	66.6	56.9	67.4	66.4	60.7	64.6	66.0	63.5	63.8	66.3	65.8	63.8	61.8
4. Desirable	22.3	17.2	26.9	19.7	34.9	22.9	22.1	19.4	29.0	23.9	20.5	24.9	20.5	20.9	21.7	20.6
Item 8200 N(Wtd)	3746	1700	1902	2954	413	918	1073	1243	511	1747	1733	1307	1067	445	762	68

QUESTIONNAIRE FORM 3 1978	TOTAL	SEX M	F	RACE White	Black	REGION NE	NC	S	W	4YR COLLEGE PLANS Yes	No	ILLICIT DRUG USE: LIFETIME None	Marijuana Only	Few Pills	More Pills	Any Heroin
Weighted No. of Cases:	3778	1711	1917	2973	417	926	1080	1257	516	1758	1748	1313	1078	451	764	68
% of Weighted Total:	100.0	45.3	50.7	78.7	11.0	24.5	28.6	33.3	13.7	46.5	46.3	34.8	28.5	11.9	20.2	1.8
A09C: ...most of the neighbors are of other races?																
1. Not at all acceptable	24.3	28.4	21.0	27.8	9.5	24.7	21.8	30.6	14.0	23.6	25.0	22.8	24.8	24.7	26.0	35.3
2. Somewhat acceptable	35.5	36.5	34.9	37.4	29.6	34.0	39.0	35.6	30.6	35.8	36.3	35.2	36.1	37.9	35.4	20.6
3. Acceptable	34.3	30.2	37.9	31.4	45.4	36.9	33.7	28.5	45.1	35.6	33.1	34.6	34.0	35.0	34.9	26.5
4. Desirable	5.8	4.9	6.2	3.4	15.5	4.4	5.4	5.2	10.5	5.0	5.6	7.4	5.1	2.7	3.7	17.6
Item 8210 N(Wtd)	3731	1695	1896	2946	412	915	1070	1240	506	1745	1724	1305	1061	446	757	68
A10: How would you feel about having your (future) children go to schools where...																
A10A: ...all the children are of your race?																
1. Not at all acceptable	9.5	8.4	10.4	6.0	25.0	10.2	6.5	10.3	12.4	10.3	7.9	8.5	9.7	12.2	9.6	5.9
2. Somewhat acceptable	12.6	11.9	12.8	10.7	21.1	11.4	10.0	14.0	16.4	13.0	11.9	11.9	11.7	16.7	10.9	16.2
3. Acceptable	47.2	47.7	47.1	49.4	38.3	49.7	50.1	41.8	49.5	49.2	45.7	48.5	47.8	41.6	48.6	44.1
4. Desirable	30.8	32.1	29.7	33.9	15.3	28.6	33.3	33.9	21.9	27.5	34.6	31.0	30.7	29.4	30.9	33.8
Item 8220 N(Wtd)	3749	1699	1904	2961	412	919	1075	1248	507	1751	1736	1306	1068	449	761	68
A10B: ...some of the children are of other races?																
1. Not at all acceptable	1.7	2.1	1.4	1.8	1.9	1.1	2.1	2.3	.6	1.1	2.2	1.8	1.4	1.6	1.8	4.4
2. Somewhat acceptable	7.0	9.8	4.1	6.6	7.2	6.2	6.8	9.4	2.5	4.7	8.6	6.7	7.0	6.7	6.3	8.8
3. Acceptable	61.4	64.2	58.7	63.1	54.1	64.0	62.0	58.2	63.0	60.7	62.9	59.0	63.2	63.5	62.1	63.2
4. Desirable	29.9	23.9	35.8	28.6	36.5	28.6	29.1	30.0	33.9	33.5	26.3	32.6	28.4	28.3	29.7	23.5
Item 8230 N(Wtd)	3748	1700	1904	2955	414	919	1073	1245	511	1750	1733	1307	1068	446	760	68
A10C: ...most of the children are of other races?																
1. Not at all acceptable	27.7	33.1	23.5	31.8	10.4	29.7	25.4	32.5	17.4	26.4	29.1	25.8	28.0	28.3	30.9	35.3
2. Somewhat acceptable	34.1	34.5	34.0	36.8	23.7	32.8	38.3	32.9	30.9	35.2	34.3	33.7	35.3	33.9	34.4	22.1
3. Acceptable	31.8	27.4	35.3	28.0	47.0	32.5	30.5	28.4	42.2	32.4	31.2	32.8	31.4	32.7	30.0	30.9
4. Desirable	6.3	5.1	7.3	3.4	18.9	5.1	5.9	6.2	9.7	6.0	5.4	7.8	5.2	5.2	4.7	11.8
Item 8240 N(Wtd)	3740	1699	1896	2952	413	917	1076	1242	505	1749	1730	1303	1066	446	761	68
A11: What race are your close friends?																
1. All my race	40.3	40.0	40.4	44.2	31.2	37.3	53.7	36.5	26.9	37.7	43.3	41.6	42.9	35.9	38.3	30.9
2. Almost all my race	30.2	30.4	30.5	32.4	22.3	30.7	28.1	31.2	30.8	33.2	28.3	29.6	30.4	31.5	32.1	22.1
3. Mostly my race	18.2	19.4	17.3	17.6	21.1	21.9	11.9	19.0	23.3	19.2	16.8	17.2	15.9	21.4	20.3	25.0
4. About half my race	7.3	6.6	7.6	4.6	14.8	5.6	4.2	9.5	11.9	6.1	8.2	7.1	7.3	7.4	6.5	16.2
5. Mostly other race(s)	2.4	2.0	2.8	.9	5.1	2.8	1.4	2.0	4.9	2.3	2.1	2.5	2.2	2.9	2.0	5.9
6. Almost all other race(s)	1.6	1.7	1.4	.3	5.8	1.8	.8	1.8	2.2	1.5	1.3	2.0	1.3	.7	1.1	1.5
Item 8250 N(Wtd)	3737	1694	1899	2948	413	914	1071	1245	506	1746	1726	1302	1065	448	755	68
A12: What race are the people in your neighborhood?																
1. All my race	55.0	54.6	56.2	60.6	41.1	48.2	66.0	58.9	34.4	54.1	57.9	58.5	56.1	52.7	49.9	48.5
2. Almost all my race	24.0	24.7	23.0	24.4	23.4	27.2	21.5	23.0	26.2	25.9	22.0	21.3	24.7	22.5	29.4	22.1
3. Mostly my race	10.0	10.4	9.7	9.5	11.8	12.2	6.6	8.0	17.9	9.6	10.2	9.8	9.1	10.9	10.3	14.7
4. About half my race	5.6	5.3	5.9	3.8	11.8	5.0	3.4	6.0	10.4	5.3	5.7	5.2	5.9	5.6	5.7	5.9
5. Mostly other race(s)	3.2	3.1	2.8	1.2	5.1	4.4	.9	2.3	7.9	3.4	2.3	3.0	2.6	5.4	2.5	4.4
6. Almost all other race(s)	2.2	1.9	2.4	.5	6.8	2.9	1.5	1.8	3.1	1.7	1.9	2.1	1.5	2.7	2.3	4.4
Item 8260 N(Wtd)	3738	1697	1897	2949	414	917	1071	1242	508	1746	1728	1304	1065	448	755	68
A13: What race were the students in the elementary school where you spent the most time?																
1. All my race	42.4	41.0	43.6	46.2	30.9	43.4	58.1	32.7	31.6	41.0	45.3	43.8	43.7	40.9	40.6	32.4
2. Almost all my race	28.4	29.8	27.8	30.8	16.9	31.2	24.8	29.0	29.4	32.0	25.0	27.5	27.8	27.3	31.4	35.3
3. Mostly my race	12.4	13.8	11.0	12.8	10.4	12.8	8.2	15.0	14.2	12.4	12.1	12.6	12.9	12.5	12.3	8.8
4. About half my race	9.7	9.1	9.9	7.7	17.4	6.0	4.6	15.6	12.6	8.3	10.5	9.8	8.3	9.8	10.5	13.2
5. Mostly other race(s)	4.3	4.4	4.0	1.8	12.6	4.1	2.1	4.8	7.9	3.9	4.2	4.1	4.7	5.8	2.4	4.4
6. Almost all other race(s)	2.8	1.9	3.6	.7	11.6	2.4	2.3	2.7	4.3	2.4	2.9	2.2	2.6	3.6	2.8	5.9
Item 8270 N(Wtd)	3737	1697	1897	2948	414	916	1071	1243	507	1746	1729	1304	1066	447	754	68

QUESTIONNAIRE FORM 3 1978	TOTAL	SEX		RACE		REGION				4YR COLLEGE PLANS		ILLICIT DRUG USE: LIFETIME				
		M	F	White	Black	NE	NC	S	W	Yes	No	None	Mari- juana Only	Few Pills	More Pills	Any Her- oin
Weighted No. of Cases:	3778	1711	1917	2973	417	926	1080	1257	516	1758	1748	1313	1078	451	764	68
% of Weighted Total:	100.0	45.3	50.7	78.7	11.0	24.5	28.6	33.3	13.7	46.5	46.3	34.8	28.5	11.9	20.2	1.8
A14: What race are the students in your present school (if you are in school)?																
1. All my race	16.2	17.2	14.8	17.7	10.6	14.6	27.3	9.4	12.5	14.1	18.2	17.2	16.8	15.6	13.1	13.2
2. Almost all my race	33.8	37.2	31.0	38.2	15.0	33.3	43.4	25.7	34.1	36.2	32.7	33.8	34.5	27.2	37.2	38.2
3. Mostly my race	24.4	24.7	24.6	27.1	12.6	32.1	20.1	23.2	22.8	26.1	22.9	21.3	24.8	29.2	29.0	11.8
4. About half my race	16.5	13.2	19.4	13.7	31.2	12.0	5.0	28.9	18.4	15.4	17.9	18.5	15.4	17.2	13.5	22.1
5. Mostly other race(s)	5.9	5.3	6.2	2.7	16.7	4.8	2.4	8.6	8.7	5.4	5.3	5.9	5.4	7.1	4.6	8.8
6. Almost all other race(s)	3.2	2.4	4.1	.6	13.8	3.4	1.9	4.1	3.6	2.9	3.0	3.4	3.1	3.8	2.5	5.9
Item 8280 N(Wtd)	3736	1694	1898	2947	414	917	1070	1244	505	1742	1730	1302	1065	448	755	68
A15: What race are the people that you work with on your job (if you have a job)?																
i. All my race	45.5	45.8	45.0	51.8	14.0	47.0	60.4	35.3	34.2	44.2	47.6	47.1	47.7	38.4	45.5	32.3
2. Almost all my race	22.3	23.6	21.8	24.3	10.3	23.6	20.8	22.6	23.3	22.9	22.0	19.7	22.8	25.1	24.3	35.5
3. Mostly my race	12.2	11.8	12.7	12.8	9.0	13.3	8.9	12.6	16.5	13.3	11.8	11.2	11.2	18.1	12.2	11.3
4. About half my race	10.6	10.4	10.5	8.3	24.3	8.5	5.0	16.4	12.9	10.1	10.6	10.8	9.9	9.3	11.3	9.7
5. Mostly other race(s)	5.9	5.9	6.0	1.8	28.9	4.7	2.9	8.8	8.3	5.9	5.0	7.5	5.0	5.1	4.1	9.7
6. Almost all other race(s)	3.4	2.6	4.0	1.1	13.3	3.1	2.0	4.3	5.1	3.7	2.8	3.7	3.4	4.0	2.5	1.6
Item 8290 N(Wtd)	3059	1484	1460	2472	301	751	920	975	412	1431	1420	1019	886	375	639	62
A16: How often do you do things (like having a conversation, eating together, playing sports) with people of other races?																
1. Not at all	12.2	11.9	12.1	13.4	7.8	10.1	21.5	7.5	8.0	9.4	14.8	13.6	12.5	10.5	10.1	10.3
2. A little	33.4	34.5	32.7	35.7	22.4	34.3	37.5	31.6	26.8	32.5	34.8	33.5	34.1	28.6	36.1	29.4
3. Some	36.3	36.0	36.6	36.5	39.2	37.2	29.6	39.8	40.6	36.8	35.8	34.0	33.7	42.4	38.5	50.0
4. A lot	18.2	17.6	18.6	14.4	30.7	18.4	11.5	21.1	24.9	21.3	14.5	18.9	19.6	18.5	15.4	10.3
Item 8300 N(Wtd)	3733	1695	1895	2946	411	915	1069	1245	503	1746	1726	1304	1064	448	753	68
A17: Generally, how do you feel about the experiences you have had with people of other races?																
5. Very good	22.4	17.4	26.6	20.3	31.8	21.6	24.0	21.0	23.7	24.4	20.7	26.1	22.5	19.7	16.6	23.5
4. Mostly good	40.5	39.1	41.8	40.7	38.6	42.4	39.8	38.1	44.5	42.2	38.5	39.2	38.0	43.6	44.6	39.7
3. Mixed	33.1	38.1	28.9	34.5	28.9	32.6	31.7	36.5	29.1	30.5	36.0	31.2	34.9	33.1	34.8	33.8
2. Mostly bad	3.1	4.0	2.3	3.5	.5	2.5	3.3	3.7	2.2	2.1	4.0	2.7	3.7	3.1	3.1	2.9
1. Very bad	.9	1.4	.4	1.0	.2	.9	1.3	.7	.6	.7	.9	.8	1.1	.7	.9	-
Item 8310 N(Wtd)	3723	1697	1887	2939	412	912	1064	1240	506	1745	1719	1301	1064	447	751	68
A18: The next questions are about some of your own plans. Are you married or engaged?																
1. Married--SKIP TO Q.A20	.8	.4	1.1	.9	-	.2	1.0	1.3	-	.2	1.2	.5	.7	1.9	.9	1.6
2. Engaged	9.2	5.1	12.8	8.8	9.9	8.1	8.7	11.2	7.4	3.9	14.2	7.4	9.0	9.3	11.9	8.2
3. Neither	90.0	94.5	86.1	90.3	90.4	91.6	90.3	87.4	92.6	95.8	84.6	92.0	90.3	88.8	87.3	90.2
Item 8320 N(Wtd)	3476	1561	1796	2804	343	856	1009	1138	474	1652	1601	1220	1006	418	699	61
A19: If it were just up to you, what would be the ideal time for you to get married?																
1. Within the next year or so	8.8	3.7	13.3	8.7	9.2	7.2	9.5	10.4	6.6	2.5	15.5	7.7	7.0	11.2	11.9	7.0
2. Two or three years from now	22.0	17.5	26.3	22.7	18.1	15.9	26.8	21.7	23.9	12.8	31.9	25.4	19.2	20.5	22.4	10.5
3. Four or five years from now	33.9	33.2	34.5	35.1	27.5	35.3	33.3	33.2	34.6	40.4	27.5	36.3	36.4	31.2	28.5	22.8
4. Over five years from now	30.5	40.4	22.0	30.3	32.8	37.4	26.4	29.2	29.7	40.1	20.2	25.6	33.1	32.4	33.4	49.1
5. I don't want to marry	4.7	5.3	3.8	3.3	12.8	4.1	4.1	5.5	5.0	4.1	4.8	5.0	4.2	5.0	3.6	10.5
Item 8330 N(Wtd) ★	3525	1595	1806	2820	360	872	1013	1158	482	1677	1616	1240	1013	420	713	57

★=excludes respondents for whom question was inappropriate.

QUESTIONNAIRE FORM 3 1978	TOTAL	SEX		RACE		REGION				4YR COLLEGE PLANS		ILLICIT DRUG USE: LIFETIME				
		M	F	White	Black	NE	NC	S	W	Yes	No	None	Mari- juana Only	Few Pills	More Pills	Any Her- oin
Weighted No. of Cases:	3778	1711	1917	2973	417	926	1080	1257	516	1758	1748	1313	1078	451	764	68
% of Weighted Total:	100.0	45.3	50.7	78.7	11.0	24.5	28.6	33.3	13.7	46.5	46.3	34.8	28.5	11.9	20.2	1.8

A20: Have you thought at all about whether you'd like to have children or how many you'd like to have?

	TOTAL	M	F	White	Black	NE	NC	S	W	Yes	No	None	Mari- juana Only	Few Pills	More Pills	Any Her- oin
3. I've thought about it a lot	42.6	28.7	56.0	42.7	46.7	40.0	44.5	43.8	39.9	43.0	42.2	42.8	41.3	41.9	46.5	30.9
2. I've thought about it a little	48.2	56.3	40.3	48.6	42.9	49.2	47.4	47.6	49.9	49.3	47.5	46.4	49.8	49.7	47.8	54.4
1. I haven't thought about it at all	9.2	15.0	3.7	8.7	10.7	10.8	8.1	8.6	10.2	7.7	10.2	10.9	9.0	8.2	5.9	14.7
Item 8340 N(Wtd)	3624	1646	1843	2881	392	882	1045	1207	491	1708	1670	1244	1046	437	734	68

A21: All things considered, if you could have exactly the number of children you want, what number would you choose to have?

	TOTAL	M	F	White	Black	NE	NC	S	W	Yes	No	None	Mari- juana Only	Few Pills	More Pills	Any Her- oin
1. None	3.9	3.3	4.3	3.7	3.9	4.2	3.5	4.1	3.8	4.0	3.6	4.1	4.0	3.4	3.2	7.7
2. One	3.9	3.6	4.0	3.5	7.2	3.0	3.0	5.5	3.4	3.6	4.3	3.8	3.1	4.3	4.9	3.1
3. Two	40.5	42.9	38.8	41.8	36.0	36.9	37.6	40.4	41.9	36.9	44.7	38.5	41.1	44.7	41.2	46.2
4. Three	22.6	23.0	22.2	22.2	24.6	26.5	22.8	20.4	20.5	23.4	21.5	21.3	23.8	22.0	22.8	20.0
5. Four	14.4	12.1	16.6	14.1	17.9	14.2	15.3	13.9	14.5	16.3	12.5	16.0	14.6	12.7	13.3	7.7
6. Five	3.1	2.3	3.6	3.3	2.2	2.8	4.1	2.1	3.6	3.6	2.6	2.8	3.0	3.4	3.5	3.1
7. Six or more	3.2	2.0	4.3	2.9	3.4	3.4	4.5	1.5	4.4	4.0	2.3	4.0	2.5	2.5	3.1	4.6
8. Don't know	8.4	10.7	6.2	8.6	5.1	9.1	9.3	7.5	8.0	8.1	8.4	9.7	7.9	6.8	7.8	7.7
Item 8350 N(Wtd)	3696	1677	1881	2911	414	904	1057	1233	503	1731	1708	1294	1059	441	742	65

A22: If the "population explosion" were NOT a problem, would you choose to have a larger number of children?

	TOTAL	M	F	White	Black	NE	NC	S	W	Yes	No	None	Mari- juana Only	Few Pills	More Pills	Any Her- oin
4. Yes, I'm sure I would want more	6.6	5.5	7.5	6.6	5.4	5.8	7.2	6.4	6.7	6.9	6.2	6.4	4.8	8.5	7.2	10.3
3. I probably would want more	12.0	12.5	11.0	11.6	13.4	12.9	10.5	10.9	15.9	13.3	10.5	12.2	11.7	12.3	11.2	13.2
2. I probably would not want more	36.4	37.1	36.3	37.7	29.4	35.7	39.8	35.7	32.5	36.4	36.9	37.1	36.4	37.7	36.1	27.9
1. I'm sure I would not want more	29.5	28.2	31.2	29.5	35.8	27.6	26.5	33.2	30.6	29.3	30.1	28.2	31.4	29.4	30.4	29.4
8. Don't know, no idea	15.6	16.6	14.0	14.6	16.3	18.0	16.1	13.8	14.1	14.0	16.4	16.1	15.6	12.3	15.1	19.1
Item 8360 N(Wtd)	3740	1694	1905	2953	411	917	1074	1244	504	1746	1731	1298	1069	446	760	68

A23: If it were just up to you, how soon after getting married would you want to have your first child?

	TOTAL	M	F	White	Black	NE	NC	S	W	Yes	No	None	Mari- juana Only	Few Pills	More Pills	Any Her- oin
1. I don't want to have children (or get married)	4.5	3.9	4.8	4.1	6.3	4.6	4.6	4.6	4.0	4.4	4.4	5.1	5.0	3.0	3.8	3.0
2. I wouldn't wait at all	4.2	5.3	3.1	3.5	8.3	4.7	4.4	3.4	4.4	4.2	3.6	3.9	4.2	2.5	5.0	6.0
3. I would wait one year	25.6	28.6	22.4	24.1	32.5	28.2	25.3	22.1	29.8	23.3	27.3	26.8	27.0	25.1	21.0	19.4
4. I would wait two years	31.4	27.9	35.0	32.4	27.9	30.6	31.9	33.1	27.8	33.8	29.8	31.1	33.0	30.1	29.7	43.3
5. I would wait three years	14.8	12.8	16.9	15.7	9.5	12.8	15.2	15.6	15.5	16.0	14.3	15.1	14.0	18.9	15.2	6.0
6. I would wait four or five years	8.4	6.2	10.5	9.5	3.2	7.4	7.2	10.7	7.0	7.8	9.6	6.9	7.2	11.6	11.6	6.0
7. I would wait more than five years	1.7	1.4	1.9	1.8	1.2	1.5	2.1	1.7	1.6	1.3	2.3	1.5	1.8	1.1	2.7	-
8. Don't know, or already have a child	9.4	14.0	5.4	8.8	11.4	10.1	9.3	8.8	9.9	9.2	8.7	9.6	8.1	8.2	11.0	14.9
Item 8370 N(Wtd)	3697	1676	1885	2916	412	908	1058	1228	503	1733	1710	1297	1060	439	743	67

A24: Now we'd like you to make some ratings of how good or bad a job you feel each of the following organizations is doing for the country as a whole. For each one, mark the circle that best describes how you feel. How good or bad a job is being done for the country as a whole by...

A24A: Large corporations?

	TOTAL	M	F	White	Black	NE	NC	S	W	Yes	No	None	Mari- juana Only	Few Pills	More Pills	Any Her- oin
1. Very poor	4.1	5.2	3.1	4.0	4.4	4.7	4.7	3.3	3.4	4.0	4.1	3.5	4.7	4.0	4.1	4.4
2. Poor	10.2	13.9	7.2	11.2	6.4	11.1	11.1	9.1	9.3	12.0	8.2	10.2	10.3	10.8	10.4	7.4
3. Fair	34.7	35.1	34.2	34.0	39.2	34.5	32.6	36.3	35.1	34.6	34.6	32.9	35.6	33.3	37.0	27.9
4. Good	30.2	29.6	30.6	31.4	23.8	28.9	31.4	30.5	29.8	30.0	31.2	31.6	29.3	29.4	29.6	32.4
5. Very good	6.9	7.6	6.5	6.3	9.1	7.2	6.5	7.3	6.3	6.5	7.1	7.0	7.2	6.5	5.9	16.2
8. No opinion	14.0	8.5	18.6	13.1	17.2	13.6	13.7	13.6	16.2	12.8	14.8	14.8	12.9	16.2	13.0	10.3
Item 8380 N(Wtd)	3727	1700	1891	2950	408	915	1067	1238	507	1744	1732	1296	1070	445	759	68

QUESTIONNAIRE FORM 3 1978	TOTAL	SEX		RACE		REGION				4YR COLLEGE PLANS		ILLICIT DRUG USE: LIFETIME				
		M	F	White	Black	NE	NC	S	W	Yes	No	None	Mari-juana Only	Few Pills	More Pills	Any Her-oin
Weighted No. of Cases:	3778	1711	1917	2973	417	926	1080	1257	516	1758	1748	1313	1078	451	764	68
% of Weighted Total:	100.0	45.3	50.7	78.7	11.0	24.5	28.6	33.3	13.7	46.5	46.3	34.8	28.5	11.9	20.2	1.8
A24B: Major labor unions?																
1. Very poor	7.1	10.7	4.3	8.3	1.7	5.6	9.0	7.8	4.5	7.7	7.1	8.4	6.8	4.5	6.7	8.8
2. Poor	16.2	18.7	13.7	17.5	9.0	15.5	17.4	16.6	14.2	18.8	13.8	15.5	16.6	18.6	17.1	5.9
3. Fair	32.0	30.9	33.2	31.5	36.6	31.9	32.0	31.3	34.1	31.9	32.1	33.5	32.4	32.3	28.7	32.4
4. Good	24.7	24.6	24.8	24.3	25.6	28.1	23.1	23.4	25.0	24.5	24.9	21.9	25.9	24.0	27.9	25.0
5. Very good	6.0	6.8	5.1	5.3	10.2	6.0	5.7	5.9	6.5	5.6	6.3	5.9	5.9	3.4	7.1	10.3
8. No opinion	14.0	8.4	18.8	13.1	16.8	12.9	12.9	15.0	15.4	11.5	16.0	14.8	12.3	17.0	12.5	16.2
Item 8390 N(Wtd)	3726	1699	1891	2949	410	912	1069	1237	508	1742	1730	1298	1069	446	760	68
A24C: The nation's colleges and universities?																
1. Very poor	.9	.9	.7	.9	.2	1.4	.8	.8	-	.5	1.1	.8	.8	-	1.5	1.5
2. Poor	2.5	2.5	2.4	2.2	4.1	3.8	1.2	2.9	2.0	1.9	3.0	2.6	2.5	2.2	2.2	3.0
3. Fair	17.0	19.1	15.0	16.4	20.0	19.8	17.4	15.6	14.6	14.5	18.5	15.6	17.5	19.1	17.5	20.9
4. Good	43.1	42.8	43.5	43.5	42.1	42.4	43.9	44.0	40.4	43.1	44.1	44.5	43.6	43.3	39.3	40.3
5. Very good	31.1	28.8	33.2	31.9	26.3	27.2	30.6	32.2	36.5	36.4	26.4	31.8	30.9	30.5	31.7	23.9
8. No opinion	5.4	5.8	4.9	5.0	7.3	5.4	5.9	4.5	6.5	3.4	7.0	4.6	4.6	5.2	7.7	10.4
Item 8400 N(Wtd)	3731	1700	1895	2953	411	915	1068	1241	507	1748	1728	1303	1071	446	756	67
A24D: The nation's public schools?																
1. Very poor	6.6	7.1	6.3	6.7	7.1	8.0	7.0	5.2	6.3	6.1	6.5	5.1	7.0	5.9	8.1	14.7
2. Poor	17.1	18.5	15.9	17.5	15.4	18.0	15.7	16.5	20.2	19.5	14.8	15.4	17.4	18.6	19.8	10.3
3. Fair	33.5	32.8	33.9	34.1	27.8	35.2	33.9	31.6	34.6	36.2	31.4	33.4	35.0	31.2	34.5	26.5
4. Good	30.6	30.1	31.4	30.9	32.7	28.8	31.2	32.3	28.7	28.0	34.2	32.8	29.1	31.9	27.7	36.8
5. Very good	9.1	8.4	9.6	8.4	12.0	7.5	9.3	10.8	7.3	8.4	9.2	10.7	8.8	9.5	6.5	4.4
8. No opinion	3.1	3.1	2.9	2.3	5.1	2.4	3.0	3.6	3.0	1.8	3.9	2.5	2.8	3.2	3.6	10.3
Item 8410 N(Wtd)	3729	1700	1894	2955	410	912	1072	1239	506	1752	1721	1303	1074	442	754	68
A24E: Churches and religious organizations?																
1. Very poor	2.7	3.2	2.4	2.5	3.4	3.2	3.0	1.9	3.5	2.4	2.5	1.9	2.2	2.2	4.8	7.4
2. Poor	6.4	8.0	5.0	6.3	6.1	7.9	6.3	5.4	6.7	6.8	5.8	5.3	6.8	7.0	7.7	8.8
3. Fair	25.0	25.7	24.8	25.7	21.4	28.8	26.8	22.1	21.1	24.8	25.5	21.7	28.4	26.7	25.9	16.2
4. Good	36.6	34.3	38.6	37.4	35.3	37.3	36.4	38.4	31.3	37.6	36.6	39.2	36.4	33.0	34.2	33.8
5. Very good	19.8	18.6	20.7	19.1	25.1	13.0	18.4	24.3	24.2	20.3	19.4	24.7	18.2	18.6	15.1	10.3
8. No opinion	9.4	10.3	8.4	9.0	8.3	9.8	9.2	7.8	13.2	8.1	10.2	7.2	8.0	12.6	12.4	23.5
Item 8420 N(Wtd)	3733	1699	1898	2958	411	912	1071	1242	508	1746	1732	1302	1072	446	757	68
A24F: The national news media (TV, magazines, news services)?																
1. Very poor	3.7	4.2	3.3	3.6	2.9	3.7	4.1	2.7	5.1	3.7	3.4	3.2	3.9	1.6	4.5	13.2
2. Poor	7.7	7.9	7.4	8.0	5.3	7.8	8.4	7.6	6.3	8.5	7.2	8.0	9.3	5.4	6.6	2.9
3. Fair	24.1	23.8	24.3	24.6	19.6	21.3	24.6	24.8	26.4	24.6	23.6	24.0	22.5	24.4	27.8	7.4
4. Good	35.2	34.5	36.1	35.9	34.6	38.0	33.9	34.6	34.1	36.0	34.3	35.2	36.4	38.8	31.5	33.8
5. Very good	25.8	26.1	25.4	24.6	32.2	25.7	25.4	26.7	24.8	25.1	26.6	26.2	24.3	26.7	26.0	29.4
8. No opinion	3.6	3.5	3.5	3.3	5.3	3.5	3.7	3.8	3.1	2.2	4.8	3.4	3.5	3.1	3.6	14.7
Item 8430 N(Wtd)	3741	1704	1901	2960	413	916	1072	1245	508	1751	1733	1307	1072	446	759	68
A24G: The President and his administration?																
1. Very poor	10.1	12.8	7.6	10.3	5.3	9.0	11.6	9.9	9.3	9.5	10.7	9.3	9.7	8.7	12.3	10.3
2. Poor	15.8	18.5	13.2	16.7	13.3	15.0	16.9	16.2	14.2	16.9	14.4	13.9	16.6	18.4	17.8	11.8
3. Fair	37.8	35.7	39.9	38.5	35.0	37.3	39.5	35.9	39.9	39.7	36.5	37.7	37.6	35.9	39.7	29.4
4. Good	21.4	21.2	21.6	21.5	22.6	25.5	19.4	20.5	20.2	22.2	20.7	22.2	23.2	19.1	18.3	22.1
5. Very good	4.8	5.2	4.4	4.1	8.7	3.6	3.5	7.4	3.0	3.8	5.1	5.6	4.2	5.4	2.9	10.3
8. No opinion	10.2	6.5	13.4	8.9	15.0	9.7	9.2	10.1	13.6	7.8	12.5	11.3	8.6	12.3	9.0	14.7
Item 8440 N(Wtd)	3737	1699	1901	2957	412	915	1072	1243	506	1751	1732	1306	1071	446	758	68

QUESTIONNAIRE FORM 3 1978	TOTAL	SEX		RACE		REGION				4YR COLLEGE PLANS		ILLICIT DRUG USE: LIFETIME				
		M	F	White	Black	NE	NC	S	W	Yes	No	None	Mari-juana Only	Few Pills	More Pills	Any Her-oin
Weighted No. of Cases:	3778	1711	1917	2973	417	926	1080	1257	516	1758	1748	1313	1078	451	764	68
% of Weighted Total:	100.0	45.3	50.7	78.7	11.0	24.5	28.6	33.3	13.7	46.5	46.3	34.8	28.5	11.9	20.2	1.8
A24H: Congress--that is, the U.S. Senate and House of Representatives?																
1. Very poor	6.3	8.2	4.4	6.1	4.1	6.4	6.5	6.1	5.7	5.0	7.2	5.7	6.2	4.3	8.3	7.4
2. Poor	14.2	18.0	11.1	15.3	10.9	13.4	17.1	12.5	14.0	16.0	12.6	14.1	13.6	16.6	14.5	8.8
3. Fair	37.9	38.7	37.2	38.4	36.3	36.8	38.0	38.5	38.5	40.7	35.3	36.4	39.0	36.6	40.2	38.2
4. Good	21.0	20.7	21.3	21.6	17.4	21.6	19.5	21.8	21.1	22.1	20.1	22.0	23.0	18.4	18.2	17.6
5. Very good	3.7	4.4	3.0	3.0	8.2	4.0	2.7	4.8	2.8	3.3	3.9	4.2	2.9	4.7	2.2	8.8
8. No opinion	16.9	10.1	23.0	15.6	23.0	18.0	16.2	16.5	17.8	12.9	21.0	17.6	15.3	19.3	16.6	17.6
Item 8450 N(Wtd)	3726	1699	1892	2951	413	908	1071	1240	506	1746	1729	1303	1066	445	758	68
A24I: The U.S. Supreme Court?																
1. Very poor	4.1	5.7	2.6	4.1	2.7	5.3	3.7	4.0	2.4	2.4	5.4	3.5	4.5	3.2	4.6	9.0
2. Poor	8.9	10.2	7.6	9.0	7.6	12.0	9.6	6.7	7.2	9.2	8.3	8.9	8.8	7.9	9.3	10.4
3. Fair	30.8	31.6	30.3	31.2	29.1	27.9	33.7	30.2	31.0	30.7	31.0	30.7	30.3	28.8	34.2	20.9
4. Good	28.3	29.8	27.1	29.1	24.0	27.6	28.1	28.5	29.4	32.6	24.5	28.0	29.9	29.3	26.2	28.4
5. Very good	6.6	8.2	5.1	6.1	10.5	6.2	6.2	7.1	7.0	6.5	6.2	7.4	5.0	7.3	6.9	7.5
8. No opinion	21.3	14.5	27.4	20.6	26.4	21.0	18.6	23.3	23.0	18.6	24.6	21.6	21.7	23.8	18.8	25.4
Item 8460 N(Wtd)	3707	1689	1884	2940	409	903	1067	1237	500	1741	1714	1297	1061	441	755	67
A24J: All the courts and the justice system in general?																
1. Very poor	6.8	9.1	4.7	7.1	3.9	9.3	6.8	5.5	5.7	6.5	7.0	5.9	6.2	6.1	8.7	13.2
2. Poor	17.7	20.9	15.0	18.6	12.0	20.5	17.5	16.2	16.6	20.5	15.1	15.9	19.7	15.3	20.5	13.2
3. Fair	36.3	35.6	36.9	36.9	35.0	36.3	37.3	36.0	34.6	36.6	36.0	36.4	37.4	37.5	35.3	23.5
4. Good	21.3	19.9	22.6	21.1	22.2	17.5	22.8	22.9	20.6	21.9	21.5	23.4	19.9	22.5	18.7	13.2
5. Very good	3.6	4.8	2.5	3.0	6.1	4.0	3.1	3.2	4.7	2.7	3.8	3.2	3.2	3.8	3.9	5.9
8. No opinion	14.4	9.7	18.3	13.2	21.0	12.5	12.5	16.2	17.6	11.8	16.6	15.1	13.4	14.8	13.0	29.4
Item 8470 N(Wtd)	3722	1696	1892	2948	409	907	1071	1238	506	1747	1724	1301	1064	445	760	68
A24K: The police and other law enforcement agencies?																
1. Very poor	7.5	9.0	5.7	6.7	9.9	8.6	5.7	8.5	6.7	6.1	8.3	5.0	6.6	7.0	11.7	17.6
2. Poor	14.5	14.6	14.5	13.6	20.1	13.1	17.4	15.5	8.3	14.4	14.5	13.3	14.7	11.7	18.0	13.2
3. Fair	37.0	35.6	38.0	37.3	39.2	37.3	36.3	38.1	35.2	39.4	35.1	34.7	39.4	41.9	34.5	35.3
4. Good	29.6	30.0	29.8	32.0	17.9	29.2	30.2	28.1	32.6	31.4	28.7	34.7	29.3	28.0	24.3	19.1
5. Very good	7.4	7.4	7.6	7.3	6.3	7.5	7.2	6.5	10.3	5.9	9.0	8.9	6.5	7.8	5.8	4.4
8. No opinion	4.0	3.4	4.4	3.1	6.8	4.3	3.4	3.3	6.9	2.8	4.4	3.5	3.4	3.8	5.5	8.8
Item 8480 N(Wtd)	3736	1699	1903	2958	413	915	1071	1244	506	1750	1730	1304	1070	446	760	68
A24L: The U.S. military?																
1. Very poor	2.7	3.7	1.7	2.6	1.7	3.1	3.2	1.9	3.0	3.1	2.3	2.6	1.8	1.6	5.1	3.0
2. Poor	4.4	5.6	3.3	4.4	3.1	4.2	4.9	3.3	6.1	5.8	3.1	3.1	3.8	3.6	7.4	6.0
3. Fair	25.0	24.7	25.0	25.0	26.4	21.2	26.3	25.8	26.9	26.3	23.4	24.8	27.1	26.7	23.0	13.4
4. Good	34.6	36.2	33.5	35.5	30.0	36.5	33.3	36.2	29.7	34.8	35.4	34.5	36.2	33.9	33.0	37.3
5. Very good	18.6	21.9	15.7	18.0	23.5	20.2	16.2	20.4	16.4	15.1	21.7	19.1	17.7	19.1	17.4	19.4
8. No opinion	14.8	7.9	20.7	14.5	15.3	14.9	16.2	12.4	17.8	14.8	14.2	16.0	13.6	15.2	14.2	19.4
Item 8490 N(Wtd)	3728	1696	1897	2950	413	909	1071	1242	505	1745	1730	1302	1067	446	758	67
A25: All things considered, do you think the armed services presently have too much or too little influence on the way this country is run?																
1. Far too little	3.6	4.6	2.4	3.3	5.4	2.6	3.4	5.2	2.0	2.7	4.1	4.3	3.1	3.2	3.3	1.6
2. Too little	18.7	18.8	18.8	19.0	16.7	19.4	14.9	22.4	16.9	16.3	20.9	18.0	16.9	23.2	20.5	17.2
3. About right	66.9	64.7	69.4	67.0	68.4	64.4	70.7	64.6	68.7	68.3	66.6	67.4	69.7	66.5	61.7	71.9
4. Too much	8.7	9.2	7.9	8.8	7.6	10.6	9.3	6.3	9.8	10.5	6.6	8.3	8.7	5.0	11.2	7.8
5. Far too much	2.1	2.7	1.5	1.9	2.0	3.0	1.8	1.5	2.6	2.3	1.8	1.9	1.5	1.8	3.4	3.1
Item 8500 N(Wtd)	3644	1682	1826	2879	408	896	1057	1199	492	1714	1685	1270	1054	436	733	64

QUESTIONNAIRE FORM 3 1978	TOTAL	SEX		RACE		REGION				4YR COLLEGE PLANS		ILLICIT DRUG USE: LIFETIME				
		M	F	White	Black	NE	NC	S	W	Yes	No	None	Mari- juana Only	Few Pills	More Pills	Any Her- oin
Weighted No. of Cases:	3778	1711	1917	2973	417	926	1080	1257	516	1758	1748	1313	1078	451	764	68
% of Weighted Total:	100.0	45.3	50.7	78.7	11.0	24.5	28.6	33.3	13.7	46.5	46.3	34.8	28.5	11.9	20.2	1.8

A26: Do you think the U.S. spends too much or too little on the armed services?

	TOTAL	M	F	White	Black	NE	NC	S	W	Yes	No	None	Marijuana Only	Few Pills	More Pills	Any Heroin
1. Far too little	5.9	9.1	2.6	5.8	5.5	2.8	4.4	9.5	6.0	6.1	5.6	6.4	5.1	5.3	6.2	11.8
2. Too little	24.6	29.2	20.3	25.6	22.6	20.5	21.9	31.3	21.1	25.1	24.6	24.4	24.5	27.0	24.6	22.1
3. About right	45.6	39.7	51.5	45.2	49.4	47.1	48.1	42.7	44.8	41.6	49.6	47.5	46.9	43.7	40.7	44.1
4. Too much	19.3	16.6	21.6	19.1	17.9	23.0	21.2	13.2	23.3	22.0	16.6	18.0	19.3	20.1	21.6	17.6
5. Far too much	4.6	5.2	3.9	4.3	5.0	6.5	4.4	3.3	4.8	5.2	3.6	3.8	4.2	3.9	6.9	4.4
Item 8510 N(Wtd)	3635	1686	1816	2876	403	887	1048	1202	498	1699	1688	1267	1051	437	723	68

A27: Next are some questions which ask about your experiences and attitudes concerning particular drugs. First we want your answers about some drugs that can be bought at a drugstore without a doctor's prescription--sometimes called over-the-counter or non-prescription drugs. DURING THE LAST 12 MONTHS, on how many occasions have you...

A27A: ...used non-prescription drugs which are supposed to relieve pain (such as aspirin, Anacin, Bufferin, or Excedrin)?

	TOTAL	M	F	White	Black	NE	NC	S	W	Yes	No	None	Marijuana Only	Few Pills	More Pills	Any Heroin
1. 0 occasions	8.7	9.9	7.1	6.5	18.4	8.2	9.1	8.8	8.7	7.0	8.9	10.5	8.0	7.6	6.2	8.8
2. 1-2 occasions	16.7	19.6	14.2	14.4	27.7	16.9	14.0	17.4	20.6	14.8	18.5	20.8	15.9	17.0	11.2	8.8
3. 3-5 occasions	18.1	19.9	16.6	18.1	17.2	17.5	17.0	19.6	17.4	18.4	17.9	19.6	19.3	17.9	14.3	14.7
4. 6-9 occasions	15.3	14.8	15.7	15.9	11.2	14.0	14.9	16.4	16.2	15.8	15.5	15.1	16.9	14.8	14.3	8.8
5. 10-19 occasions	18.8	17.7	19.8	20.5	11.9	18.6	20.3	18.5	16.4	19.6	18.3	17.4	19.9	19.5	19.6	17.6
6. 20-39 occasions	10.4	8.9	12.0	11.5	7.3	13.2	10.2	9.7	8.1	12.2	9.2	8.7	9.8	10.5	14.6	16.2
7. 40 or more	11.9	9.1	14.7	13.2	6.3	11.5	14.5	9.6	12.5	12.1	11.7	8.0	10.1	13.0	19.8	26.5
Item 8520 N(Wtd)	3733	1691	1907	2958	412	919	1069	1240	505	1746	1733	1304	1074	447	761	68

A27B: ...used non-prescription drugs that are supposed to help people get to sleep (such as Sleep-Eze, Sominex, or Nytol)?

	TOTAL	M	F	White	Black	NE	NC	S	W	Yes	No	None	Marijuana Only	Few Pills	More Pills	Any Heroin
1. 0 occasions	88.9	89.9	88.3	89.1	90.6	90.4	88.1	88.5	88.7	89.8	88.8	93.9	92.5	85.7	79.6	69.1
2. 1-2 occasions	6.5	5.6	7.3	6.9	4.1	6.0	6.9	6.8	5.7	6.6	6.3	4.1	5.4	10.5	10.4	4.4
3. 3-5 occasions	2.4	2.4	2.3	2.3	1.9	1.6	3.0	2.5	2.4	2.1	2.7	1.2	1.8	2.2	4.9	5.9
4. 6-9 occasions	.9	1.1	.7	.7	1.0	.5	1.0	1.0	1.0	.9	.9	.3	.4	.4	2.5	4.4
5. 10-19 occasions	.7	.7	.7	.7	.2	.7	.3	.6	1.8	.5	.7	.5	-	.2	1.5	7.4
6. 20-39 occasions	.2	.1	.2	.1	.2	.2	.2	.2	.2	.1	.2	-	.1	.2	.5	1.5
7. 40 or more	.3	.4	.4	.2	1.9	.4	.4	.3	.2	.2	.3	.2	-	.4	.4	7.4
Item 8530 N(Wtd)	3724	1690	1901	2953	413	916	1070	1233	506	1747	1726	1301	1074	446	756	68

A27C: ...used non-prescription drugs that are supposed to help people stay awake (such as No-Doz, Wake, or Vivarin)?

	TOTAL	M	F	White	Black	NE	NC	S	W	Yes	No	None	Marijuana Only	Few Pills	More Pills	Any Heroin
1. 0 occasions	89.1	88.1	90.0	89.1	93.0	90.4	87.1	89.6	89.9	90.3	88.5	97.2	94.7	89.7	70.7	57.4
2. 1-2 occasions	4.7	5.1	4.4	5.1	1.7	4.3	5.9	4.1	4.5	4.7	4.5	1.5	3.3	6.5	10.9	7.4
3. 3-5 occasions	2.1	2.5	1.9	2.3	.5	1.2	2.6	2.6	1.4	1.9	2.4	.6	.6	2.0	7.0	4.4
4. 6-9 occasions	1.4	1.8	.8	1.3	1.5	1.5	1.3	1.2	1.6	1.2	1.4	.5	.8	.4	3.4	5.9
5. 10-19 occasions	1.1	1.0	1.2	.8	1.7	.7	1.2	1.4	1.0	.9	1.4	.1	.6	.2	3.0	11.8
6. 20-39 occasions	.8	.5	.9	.7	.2	.8	.9	.6	1.0	.6	.9	-	.1	.7	2.4	7.4
7. 40 or more	.8	.9	.7	.7	1.5	1.2	1.0	.6	.4	.4	1.0	.2	-	.4	2.8	7.4
Item 8540 N(Wtd)	3725	1693	1900	2952	412	917	1068	1234	506	1747	1725	1299	1074	448	760	68

A27D: ...used non-prescription drugs that are supposed to calm people down--keep them from being nervous or in a bad mood (such as Cope, Compoz, Devarex, or Miles Nervine)?

	TOTAL	M	F	White	Black	NE	NC	S	W	Yes	No	None	Marijuana Only	Few Pills	More Pills	Any Heroin
1. 0 occasions	93.4	94.6	92.6	94.2	91.7	93.1	93.4	92.9	94.9	95.0	92.6	97.5	97.7	93.3	83.0	73.5
2. 1-2 occasions	2.3	1.9	2.6	2.0	3.2	2.0	2.3	2.8	1.6	2.1	2.4	1.2	1.2	3.8	4.5	4.4
3. 3-5 occasions	1.9	1.5	2.2	1.9	1.7	2.2	2.1	1.6	1.8	1.3	2.5	.8	.1	1.3	6.6	5.9
4. 6-9 occasions	1.0	1.0	.9	.9	.7	1.6	.2	1.1	.8	1.0	.9	-	.8	.9	2.6	2.9
5. 10-19 occasions	.5	.5	.6	.4	.7	.3	.7	.4	.8	.2	.8	.2	.2	.2	1.6	1.5
6. 20-39 occasions	.4	.4	.3	.2	.7	.1	.5	.6	-	.3	.2	.2	.1	.4	.5	4.4
7. 40 or more	.5	.2	.7	.4	1.2	.7	.6	.5	-	.1	.6	.2	-	.2	1.2	5.9
Item 8550 N(Wtd)	3724	1692	1899	2952	410	916	1067	1234	506	1746	1724	1300	1073	448	759	68

QUESTIONNAIRE FORM 3 1978	TOTAL	SEX		RACE		REGION				4YR COLLEGE PLANS		ILLICIT DRUG USE: LIFETIME				
		M	F	White	Black	NE	NC	S	W	Yes	No	None	Mari- juana Only	Few Pills	More Pills	Any Her- oin
Weighted No. of Cases:	3778	1711	1917	2973	417	926	1080	1257	516	1758	1748	1313	1078	451	764	68
% of Weighted Total:	100.0	45.3	50.7	78.7	11.0	24.5	28.6	33.3	13.7	46.5	46.3	34.8	28.5	11.9	20.2	1.8

A28: Individuals differ in whether or not they disapprove of people doing certain things. Do YOU disapprove of people (who are 18 or older) doing each of the following?

A28A: Smoking one or more packs of cigarettes per day

1. Don't disapprove	33.0	34.3	31.9	33.8	28.7	33.6	36.0	31.9	28.4	24.4	41.3	20.1	33.1	34.7	51.9	52.9
2. Disapprove	34.3	33.3	35.4	34.8	31.1	34.9	34.6	34.7	32.0	36.2	32.8	36.1	35.7	36.0	29.6	19.1
3. Strongly disapprove	32.6	32.4	32.7	31.4	40.2	31.4	29.4	33.4	39.6	39.4	25.9	43.8	31.2	29.3	18.4	29.4
Item 8560 N(Wtd)	3738	1702	1903	2957	415	919	1072	1240	507	1749	1735	1305	1074	450	759	68

A28B: Trying marijuana (pot, grass) once or twice

1. Don't disapprove	66.6	69.8	64.1	68.3	57.5	75.6	66.0	60.5	66.7	66.6	66.8	30.3	85.8	80.6	92.8	88.2
2. Disapprove	16.0	15.2	16.5	15.7	16.4	12.3	17.4	18.1	14.6	17.7	14.0	30.2	9.4	11.4	4.0	5.9
3. Strongly disapprove	17.4	15.2	19.4	16.0	26.3	12.1	16.7	21.3	18.7	15.6	19.2	39.5	4.8	8.2	3.3	5.9
Item 8570 N(Wtd)	3735	1696	1907	2955	414	918	1072	1237	508	1748	1737	1304	1075	449	759	68

A28C: Smoking marijuana occasionally

1. Don't disapprove	56.5	60.9	52.6	58.0	48.8	65.3	56.7	50.1	55.8	55.2	58.0	19.4	71.3	70.9	88.8	91.2
2. Disapprove	19.6	17.7	21.2	19.5	20.1	18.0	20.0	20.1	20.7	21.5	17.6	29.4	19.5	14.3	6.8	2.9
3. Strongly disapprove	23.9	21.4	26.1	22.5	31.3	16.8	23.4	29.9	23.5	23.4	24.3	51.3	9.1	14.8	4.3	5.9
Item 8580 N(Wtd)	3729	1695	1902	2953	412	918	1067	1236	507	1742	1734	1301	1072	447	761	68

A28D: Smoking marijuana regularly

1. Don't disapprove	32.6	38.2	27.2	32.6	28.2	38.6	33.7	27.0	33.0	27.4	36.7	7.4	30.9	38.9	70.7	74.6
2. Disapprove	27.8	27.8	27.6	27.9	27.2	28.4	25.6	29.4	27.2	30.7	25.0	20.7	41.6	30.9	18.2	20.9
3. Strongly disapprove	39.7	34.1	45.2	39.5	44.7	33.0	40.7	43.7	40.0	41.9	38.3	71.9	27.4	30.0	11.1	6.0
Item 8590 N(Wtd)	3726	1697	1899	2954	412	918	1066	1239	503	1743	1732	1304	1071	447	758	67

A28E: Trying LSD once or twice

1. Don't disapprove	14.6	16.7	12.8	14.6	12.1	16.1	16.8	11.7	14.0	13.2	15.9	5.7	7.4	13.8	36.0	66.2
2. Disapprove	23.1	21.9	24.1	23.6	20.5	24.9	24.5	21.8	19.9	21.9	24.4	17.4	26.0	26.9	27.6	13.2
3. Strongly disapprove	62.3	61.4	63.0	61.8	67.4	58.9	58.7	66.5	66.1	64.9	59.7	76.9	66.5	59.3	36.3	20.6
Item 8600 N(Wtd)	3737	1702	1905	2959	414	918	1070	1241	508	1748	1738	1307	1075	450	758	68

A28F: Taking LSD regularly

1. Don't disapprove	3.6	5.2	2.1	2.8	6.7	3.8	4.4	2.9	3.4	2.4	4.4	2.7	2.0	2.7	6.5	20.6
2. Disapprove	14.6	15.9	13.5	14.5	12.8	14.8	16.2	14.0	12.2	11.5	17.5	8.0	11.9	14.3	27.7	41.2
3. Strongly disapprove	81.8	78.8	84.4	82.7	80.2	81.3	79.4	83.2	84.2	86.1	78.0	89.4	86.1	83.0	65.8	38.2
Item 8610 N(Wtd)	3731	1698	1903	2953	415	913	1071	1241	507	1743	1738	1307	1073	448	757	68

A28G: Trying heroin (smack, horse) once or twice

1. Don't disapprove	8.0	8.4	7.6	7.4	9.4	9.2	8.4	7.2	6.7	7.3	8.5	4.8	5.0	6.7	13.9	60.3
2. Disapprove	16.3	16.3	16.6	16.7	13.5	16.4	17.9	16.4	12.4	14.1	18.2	12.8	15.8	18.3	21.1	19.1
3. Strongly disapprove	75.7	75.4	75.7	76.0	77.1	74.5	73.8	76.3	80.7	78.5	73.3	82.5	79.2	75.1	65.0	22.1
Item 8620 N(Wtd)	3735	1700	1904	2957	414	917	1068	1242	507	1748	1736	1308	1071	449	760	68

A28H: Taking heroin occasionally

1. Don't disapprove	3.6	4.3	2.8	2.6	6.8	3.4	3.7	3.6	3.4	2.1	4.5	3.1	2.0	2.2	4.6	29.4
2. Disapprove	12.6	12.3	13.1	12.5	13.1	13.1	13.4	13.0	9.3	10.4	14.7	9.7	10.8	14.7	17.5	27.9
3. Strongly disapprove	83.9	83.4	84.0	84.9	80.1	83.6	82.9	83.4	87.5	87.5	80.8	87.2	87.3	83.1	77.7	44.1
Item 8630 N(Wtd)	3736	1701	1905	2960	413	918	1071	1240	506	1748	1737	1305	1075	450	759	68

QUESTIONNAIRE FORM 3 1978	TOTAL	SEX		RACE		REGION				4YR COLLEGE PLANS		ILLICIT DRUG USE: LIFETIME				
		M	F	White	Black	NE	NC	S	W	Yes	No	None	Mari-juana Only	Few Pills	More Pills	Any Her-oin
Weighted No. of Cases:	3778	1711	1917	2973	417	926	1080	1257	516	1758	1748	1313	1078	451	764	68
% of Weighted Total:	100.0	45.3	50.7	78.7	11.0	24.5	28.6	33.3	13.7	46.5	46.3	34.8	28.5	11.9	20.2	1.8

A28I: Taking heroin regularly

	TOTAL	M	F	White	Black	NE	NC	S	W	Yes	No	None	Mari-juana Only	Few Pills	More Pills	Any Her-oin
1. Don't disapprove	2.3	3.2	1.3	1.4	5.6	2.1	2.3	2.4	2.2	1.3	2.8	2.5	1.3	1.6	2.5	10.4
2. Disapprove	9.0	9.3	8.8	8.6	10.2	8.8	9.4	9.6	6.9	6.7	11.1	7.1	8.5	8.5	12.0	17.9
3. Strongly disapprove	88.8	87.5	89.8	90.0	84.4	89.2	88.3	88.1	90.9	92.0	86.1	90.4	90.2	90.0	85.4	73.1
Item 8640 N(Wtd)	3722	1691	1901	2951	410	913	1069	1233	507	1738	1735	1297	1072	449	759	67

A28J: Trying a barbiturate (downer, goofball, red, yellow, etc.) once or twice

	TOTAL	M	F	White	Black	NE	NC	S	W	Yes	No	None	Mari-juana Only	Few Pills	More Pills	Any Her-oin
1. Don't disapprove	17.6	19.0	16.8	18.2	11.4	22.5	18.0	14.5	15.2	16.0	19.1	5.3	8.4	19.1	47.0	69.1
2. Disapprove	23.3	21.7	24.6	24.2	16.9	23.3	25.0	23.1	20.3	23.6	22.8	18.8	24.0	30.7	26.1	20.6
3. Strongly disapprove	59.1	59.3	58.6	57.6	71.7	54.1	57.0	62.4	64.5	60.4	58.1	75.9	67.6	50.4	26.8	8.8
Item 8650 N(Wtd)	3734	1697	1907	2959	414	918	1070	1239	507	1747	1739	1304	1075	450	760	68

A28K: Taking barbiturates regularly

	TOTAL	M	F	White	Black	NE	NC	S	W	Yes	No	None	Mari-juana Only	Few Pills	More Pills	Any Her-oin
1. Don't disapprove	5.7	6.7	4.7	4.6	9.2	6.7	5.8	5.3	4.6	3.8	6.8	3.1	2.6	2.7	13.5	29.9
2. Disapprove	24.7	24.7	24.7	24.5	23.2	26.9	25.4	24.1	20.4	20.4	28.9	14.8	20.4	31.3	42.4	38.8
3. Strongly disapprove	69.6	68.6	70.6	70.9	67.6	66.4	68.9	70.6	75.0	75.9	64.2	82.1	77.0	66.1	44.0	31.3
Item 8660 N(Wtd)	3728	1699	1903	2958	413	917	1070	1237	504	1744	1739	1308	1074	448	757	67

A28L: Trying an amphetamine (upper, pep pill, bennie, speed) once or twice

	TOTAL	M	F	White	Black	NE	NC	S	W	Yes	No	None	Mari-juana Only	Few Pills	More Pills	Any Her-oin
1. Don't disapprove	25.2	26.6	24.2	25.9	16.0	30.0	26.9	20.4	24.7	21.8	28.5	7.0	12.7	31.9	67.3	75.0
2. Disapprove	23.8	22.1	25.2	24.6	19.4	24.1	23.6	25.0	20.3	24.3	23.2	21.6	29.3	29.0	17.3	16.2
3. Strongly disapprove	51.0	51.2	50.5	49.4	64.8	45.8	49.4	54.5	54.8	53.9	48.4	71.3	58.1	39.3	15.4	8.8
Item 8670 N(Wtd)	3731	1700	1906	2959	412	917	1070	1238	507	1746	1739	1307	1076	448	759	68

A28M: Taking amphetamines regularly

	TOTAL	M	F	White	Black	NE	NC	S	W	Yes	No	None	Mari-juana Only	Few Pills	More Pills	Any Her-oin
1. Don't disapprove	6.5	7.3	5.9	6.1	6.6	8.2	7.1	4.9	6.1	4.4	7.9	2.7	2.1	3.4	18.3	33.8
2. Disapprove	23.2	23.0	23.4	22.6	22.2	26.0	23.1	22.1	21.0	18.7	27.8	13.4	18.2	28.6	43.2	30.9
3. Strongly disapprove	70.3	69.8	70.6	71.4	71.1	65.8	69.8	73.0	72.9	76.9	64.4	83.8	79.5	68.0	38.3	35.3
Item 8680 N(Wtd)	3715	1696	1896	2947	409	912	1063	1235	505	1742	1728	1303	1070	447	754	68

A28N: Trying cocaine once or twice

	TOTAL	M	F	White	Black	NE	NC	S	W	Yes	No	None	Mari-juana Only	Few Pills	More Pills	Any Her-oin
1. Don't disapprove	23.0	26.5	20.1	23.0	19.8	29.7	21.2	18.7	25.5	21.6	23.6	6.6	11.7	28.9	60.6	72.1
2. Disapprove	19.8	18.8	20.6	20.0	17.4	19.6	20.9	20.5	16.4	18.7	20.9	16.2	24.5	24.8	16.6	13.2
3. Strongly disapprove	57.2	54.7	59.3	57.0	63.1	50.8	57.8	60.9	58.1	59.6	55.4	77.2	63.7	46.3	22.8	16.2
Item 8690 N(Wtd)	3725	1700	1899	2955	409	913	1069	1237	506	1743	1736	1306	1073	447	758	68

A28O: Taking cocaine regularly

	TOTAL	M	F	White	Black	NE	NC	S	W	Yes	No	None	Mari-juana Only	Few Pills	More Pills	Any Her-oin
1. Don't disapprove	8.1	10.9	5.4	7.4	8.3	9.5	7.8	7.1	8.3	7.0	8.9	3.1	2.9	5.6	22.7	36.8
2. Disapprove	18.9	19.1	18.5	18.2	20.5	21.4	18.1	17.9	18.2	15.8	21.3	9.8	16.5	20.9	34.1	39.7
3. Strongly disapprove	73.1	70.0	76.1	74.4	71.0	69.1	74.0	75.0	73.5	77.3	69.8	87.2	80.6	73.4	43.2	22.1
Item 8700 N(Wtd)	3688	1682	1880	2932	400	902	1059	1222	505	1728	1716	1293	1057	444	753	68

A28P: Trying one or two drinks of an alcoholic beverage (beer, wine, liquor)

	TOTAL	M	F	White	Black	NE	NC	S	W	Yes	No	None	Mari-juana Only	Few Pills	More Pills	Any Her-oin
1. Don't disapprove	84.4	85.6	83.8	87.2	69.9	90.4	88.5	78.5	79.5	86.1	84.3	68.8	92.6	90.4	96.6	86.8
2. Disapprove	9.9	8.8	10.6	8.3	17.2	6.2	8.0	13.1	12.4	8.9	9.9	18.9	5.4	7.8	2.0	5.9
3. Strongly disapprove	5.7	5.7	5.6	4.5	13.0	3.4	3.6	8.4	7.9	5.1	5.8	12.3	2.0	1.8	1.5	7.4
Item 8710 N(Wtd)	3720	1694	1902	2952	408	914	1067	1233	507	1739	1735	1302	1070	448	756	68

QUESTIONNAIRE FORM 3 1978	TOTAL	SEX		RACE		REGION				4YR COLLEGE PLANS		ILLICIT DRUG USE: LIFETIME				
		M	F	White	Black	NE	NC	S	W	Yes	No	None	Mari-juana Only	Few Pills	More Pills	Any Her-oin
Weighted No. of Cases:	3778	1711	1917	2973	417	926	1080	1257	516	1758	1748	1313	1078	451	764	68
% of Weighted Total:	100.0	45.3	50.7	78.7	11.0	24.5	28.6	33.3	13.7	46.5	46.3	34.8	28.5	11.9	20.2	1.8
A28Q: Taking one or two drinks nearly every day																
1. Don't disapprove	32.3	39.9	25.6	33.2	27.0	34.5	35.5	30.5	26.1	28.2	36.9	18.7	33.1	33.6	50.7	60.6
2. Disapprove	43.0	40.4	45.3	43.5	40.2	44.7	44.1	41.2	42.0	45.2	40.6	42.8	47.0	45.0	38.6	25.8
3. Strongly disapprove	24.7	19.7	29.1	23.3	32.8	20.8	20.4	28.3	31.7	26.6	22.5	38.4	20.1	21.5	10.7	13.6
Item 8720 N(Wtd)	3716	1691	1901	2950	408	910	1068	1234	505	1740	1733	1303	1071	447	756	66
A28R: Taking four or five drinks nearly every day																
1. Don't disapprove	9.8	13.6	6.4	9.2	11.7	10.4	11.6	8.6	7.9	5.5	13.7	4.9	7.9	9.8	17.5	33.8
2. Disapprove	28.9	32.4	25.4	29.6	22.4	29.0	30.7	29.3	24.6	26.8	30.8	20.6	30.7	28.1	39.8	41.2
3. Strongly disapprove	61.3	53.9	68.3	61.2	65.6	60.7	57.7	62.2	67.5	67.8	55.5	74.5	61.4	62.1	42.5	26.5
Item 8730 N(Wtd)	3717	1693	1901	2950	410	908	1070	1234	505	1742	1731	1304	1070	448	753	68
A28S: Having five or more drinks once or twice each weekend																
1. Don't disapprove	43.8	53.3	35.2	46.1	26.9	49.0	46.0	40.3	38.0	39.3	48.2	21.0	47.2	50.8	70.8	75.0
2. Disapprove	25.9	22.9	28.6	26.2	23.1	25.8	26.7	26.6	22.6	27.8	24.1	29.9	28.6	25.7	17.5	8.8
3. Strongly disapprove	30.4	23.8	36.2	27.7	49.8	25.2	27.4	33.1	39.2	32.9	27.7	49.0	24.2	23.5	11.6	16.2
Item 8740 N(Wtd)	3725	1696	1904	2953	412	913	1069	1238	505	1742	1737	1307	1073	447	756	68
A29: During the LAST 12 MONTHS, how often have you been around people who were taking each of the following to get high or for "kicks"?																
A29A: Marijuana (pot, grass) or hashish																
1. Not at all	17.3	13.7	20.8	16.4	21.4	10.6	15.5	22.9	19.6	16.4	17.7	39.2	4.8	9.6	3.4	1.5
2. Once or twice	18.4	17.8	19.1	17.7	23.1	16.5	18.3	19.5	19.2	20.2	17.5	27.9	18.8	15.4	5.1	2.9
3. Occasionally	25.3	25.5	24.6	26.2	22.8	23.3	27.4	25.5	24.3	27.4	23.4	21.5	37.1	25.6	16.0	8.8
4. Often	39.0	43.0	35.5	39.8	32.8	49.6	38.9	31.9	37.2	36.0	41.3	11.4	39.3	49.4	75.5	88.2
Item 20590 N(Wtd)	3725	1697	1904	2954	412	916	1065	1238	506	1743	1737	1305	1072	449	758	68
A29B: LSD																
1. Not at all	81.9	81.3	82.3	80.7	91.2	77.9	80.1	87.7	78.6	81.5	82.5	92.4	88.6	83.0	58.4	23.9
2. Once or twice	11.1	10.8	11.5	12.2	5.3	14.0	11.1	7.8	13.8	11.7	10.5	5.5	8.8	12.1	21.9	31.3
3. Occasionally	5.2	5.7	4.8	5.5	1.5	5.8	5.7	4.1	5.8	5.3	5.0	1.9	2.2	3.8	14.1	25.4
4. Often	1.8	2.3	1.4	1.6	2.0	2.2	3.0	.4	1.8	1.4	2.1	.2	.3	1.1	5.4	19.4
Item 20600 N(Wtd)	3682	1681	1880	2932	399	907	1057	1218	501	1723	1715	1281	1063	447	753	67
A29C: Other psychedelics (mescaline, peyote, PCP, etc.)																
1. Not at all	76.7	74.6	78.3	75.0	90.9	69.9	74.8	84.6	74.1	77.8	76.7	93.5	85.3	71.7	42.4	26.5
2. Once or twice	13.4	14.8	12.5	14.4	4.9	16.0	14.2	9.8	16.2	13.8	12.4	4.6	11.0	18.4	28.3	26.5
3. Occasionally	7.0	7.6	6.5	7.6	2.5	9.3	7.8	4.5	7.3	6.4	7.5	1.5	2.7	8.3	20.5	25.0
4. Often	2.9	3.0	2.6	2.9	1.7	4.8	3.3	1.1	2.4	2.0	3.5	.4	.9	1.8	8.9	22.1
Item 20610 N(Wtd)	3710	1693	1894	2944	408	908	1066	1231	505	1737	1727	1298	1072	446	755	68
A29D: Amphetamines (uppers, pep pills, bennies, speed)																
1. Not at all	60.9	60.8	60.8	57.7	82.2	53.5	58.4	69.5	58.9	63.3	59.2	82.9	68.4	53.7	20.1	20.6
2. Once or twice	18.8	19.5	17.9	20.4	11.0	20.4	18.6	16.9	21.1	19.2	18.2	12.3	21.3	27.4	22.3	14.7
3. Occasionally	13.5	14.8	12.7	14.8	4.6	16.9	15.2	10.1	12.3	12.5	14.5	3.9	8.5	14.9	35.0	30.9
4. Often	6.7	4.8	8.5	7.1	2.2	9.2	7.7	3.7	7.7	5.0	8.2	1.0	1.8	4.0	22.8	35.3
Item 20620 N(Wtd)	3712	1688	1900	2944	409	911	1063	1232	506	1737	1729	1295	1069	449	758	68

QUESTIONNAIRE FORM 3 1978	TOTAL	SEX		RACE		REGION				4YR COLLEGE PLANS		ILLICIT DRUG USE: LIFETIME				
		M	F	White	Black	NE	NC	S	W	Yes	No	None	Mari- juana Only	Few Pills	More Pills	Any Her- oin
Weighted No. of Cases:	3778	1711	1917	2973	417	926	1080	1257	516	1758	1748	1313	1078	451	764	68
% of Weighted Total:	100.0	45.3	50.7	78.7	11.0	24.5	28.6	33.3	13.7	46.5	46.3	34.8	28.5	11.9	20.2	1.8
A29E: Barbiturates (downers, goofballs, reds, yellows, etc.)																
1. Not at all	73.5	72.7	73.9	71.6	86.6	68.2	72.9	77.9	73.5	74.0	73.6	89.9	81.2	71.9	39.0	28.4
2. Once or twice	14.6	16.0	13.3	15.5	9.5	15.9	14.5	13.0	15.9	16.1	13.1	7.3	13.4	18.7	25.4	23.9
3. Occasionally	8.5	8.6	8.7	9.3	2.2	10.7	8.5	7.1	8.2	7.8	9.1	2.2	4.2	7.8	24.7	22.4
4. Often	3.4	2.7	4.1	3.6	1.5	5.2	4.0	2.0	2.4	2.1	4.2	.5	1.0	1.6	10.8	25.4
Item 20630 N(Wtd)	3708	1689	1896	2941	409	910	1063	1233	502	1736	1727	1293	1071	449	756	67
A29F: Tranquilizers (Librium, Valium, Miltown)																
1. Not at all	67.5	69.3	65.6	64.7	85.8	63.7	67.1	70.5	67.9	67.0	67.5	81.5	77.6	58.1	36.3	29.4
2. Once or twice	19.1	18.0	19.9	20.7	8.8	18.9	18.4	19.4	20.0	20.6	17.9	12.8	15.4	29.8	29.2	25.0
3. Occasionally	8.6	9.3	8.2	9.4	2.9	10.9	9.1	6.7	7.9	8.1	9.1	4.0	4.9	7.3	21.5	20.6
4. Often	4.9	3.3	6.4	5.3	2.2	6.5	5.5	3.5	4.2	4.3	5.5	1.5	2.1	4.7	13.1	25.0
Item 20640 N(Wtd)	3711	1691	1896	2945	408	911	1064	1231	505	1734	1732	1293	1071	449	758	68
A29G: Cocaine ("coke")																
1. Not at all	69.8	67.2	72.2	69.3	75.4	61.6	71.2	77.2	63.4	71.2	69.7	88.8	79.5	62.7	32.9	5.9
2. Once or twice	16.3	18.5	14.2	16.6	13.9	20.1	16.3	12.2	19.6	16.1	16.1	7.8	14.9	23.0	27.7	27.9
3. Occasionally	9.3	9.6	9.0	9.5	7.1	11.7	8.6	6.7	12.3	8.8	9.2	2.5	4.5	10.9	25.1	35.3
4. Often	4.6	4.7	4.6	4.5	3.7	6.5	3.9	3.9	4.7	3.9	4.9	.9	1.1	3.1	14.3	30.9
Item 20650 N(Wtd)	3715	1693	1897	2946	410	911	1064	1233	506	1738	1731	1298	1072	448	757	68
A29H: Heroin (smack, horse)																
1. Not at all	91.8	92.3	91.3	92.1	92.0	91.4	91.0	93.4	89.9	92.7	91.5	95.0	95.6	92.4	86.7	26.5
2. Once or twice	5.5	5.4	5.5	5.7	3.7	6.4	5.5	4.6	6.1	5.2	5.5	3.3	3.0	5.8	10.2	30.9
3. Occasionally	1.9	1.7	2.0	1.6	2.2	1.6	1.8	1.6	3.2	1.6	1.9	1.3	.8	.9	2.1	30.9
4. Often	.9	.5	1.2	.6	2.2	.5	1.7	.3	1.0	.5	1.1	.4	.5	1.1	1.1	11.8
Item 20660 N(Wtd)	3714	1693	1897	2945	410	911	1065	1233	505	1736	1732	1295	1073	448	758	68
A29I: Other narcotics (methadone, opium, codeine, paregoric, etc.)																
1. Not at all	81.8	81.4	82.1	81.2	88.7	79.3	80.7	86.3	77.7	83.1	81.0	92.1	91.0	81.3	56.6	22.1
2. Once or twice	11.7	12.6	11.0	12.3	6.6	12.5	12.3	9.4	14.6	12.0	11.0	5.6	6.9	14.3	25.8	36.8
3. Occasionally	4.5	4.0	4.9	4.8	2.5	5.9	3.8	3.4	5.9	3.6	5.3	1.9	1.5	3.1	12.6	22.1
4. Often	2.0	2.0	2.1	1.7	2.2	2.3	3.1	.9	1.8	1.3	2.7	.5	.7	1.3	5.0	19.1
Item 20670 N(Wtd)	3711	1692	1897	2945	407	911	1063	1230	507	1736	1730	1296	1072	448	756	68
A29J: Alcoholic beverages (beer, wine, liquor)																
1. Not at all	5.5	5.3	5.6	4.5	7.0	4.6	4.2	6.2	7.9	5.3	5.1	12.6	1.2	1.6	.8	8.8
2. Once or twice	9.0	7.4	10.3	7.4	14.8	6.3	7.1	11.4	11.7	8.7	9.2	17.5	5.2	6.9	1.7	1.5
3. Occasionally	24.8	23.4	25.8	23.4	35.4	25.3	21.9	26.3	26.1	25.1	24.5	32.7	26.6	21.8	12.0	5.9
4. Often	60.8	63.9	58.3	64.6	42.5	63.8	66.7	56.1	54.3	61.0	61.4	37.3	66.9	69.7	85.4	83.8
Item 20680 N(Wtd)	3725	1697	1905	2955	412	914	1068	1238	506	1745	1734	1306	1071	449	759	68
This section asks for your views and feelings about a number of different things.																
D01: How satisfied are you with your life as a whole these days?																
1. Completely dissatisfied	2.5	2.6	2.3	2.0	4.5	2.6	2.6	2.6	1.5	2.3	2.3	2.8	2.1	2.4	2.8	1.7
2. Quite dissatisfied	9.0	8.9	9.4	8.8	11.6	9.7	8.0	8.9	9.9	8.8	9.2	8.4	9.0	10.5	9.1	10.0
3. Somewhat dissatisfied	13.2	12.7	13.4	12.4	17.9	15.0	12.0	12.6	14.0	12.3	14.2	10.7	12.7	13.4	16.8	20.0
4. Neither, or mixed feelings	12.1	13.5	10.6	11.8	10.8	11.1	12.6	12.4	12.1	11.1	14.7	10.5	12.8	13.4	14.0	8.3
5. Somewhat satisfied	26.0	28.2	24.0	26.6	23.9	26.3	25.5	26.0	26.4	27.6	24.5	24.1	26.7	26.5	28.5	23.3
6. Quite satisfied	32.0	29.4	34.5	33.6	23.0	30.9	33.6	32.1	30.2	35.3	29.0	36.3	32.5	29.1	27.2	25.0
7. Completely satisfied	5.3	4.6	5.9	4.8	8.0	4.4	5.7	5.3	5.9	4.6	5.9	7.1	4.1	4.8	2.7	11.7
Item 6840 N(Wtd)	3501	1587	1825	2854	352	821	1033	1175	473	1712	1685	1236	1017	419	716	60

QUESTIONNAIRE FORM 3 1978	TOTAL	SEX		RACE		REGION				4YR COLLEGE PLANS		ILLICIT DRUG USE: LIFETIME				
		M	F	White	Black	NE	NC	S	W	Yes	No	None	Marijuana Only	Few Pills	More Pills	Any Heroin
Weighted No. of Cases:	3778	1711	1917	2973	417	926	1080	1257	516	1758	1748	1313	1078	451	764	68
% of Weighted Total:	100.0	45.3	50.7	78.7	11.0	24.5	28.6	33.3	13.7	46.5	46.3	34.8	28.5	11.9	20.2	1.8

D02: These questions are about your health during the last MONTH.

D02A: Have you been bothered by shortness of breath when you were not exercising or working hard?

1. Never	73.8	75.9	71.8	74.5	73.6	73.6	71.9	74.2	77.7	77.9	70.8	82.4	76.4	65.1	61.4	63.3
2. Seldom	15.3	14.8	15.7	15.4	11.4	16.0	15.8	15.3	13.0	13.9	16.3	10.7	14.2	17.5	22.1	23.3
3. Sometimes	9.8	8.5	11.1	9.2	12.5	8.7	11.0	9.9	8.9	7.3	12.0	6.1	8.5	15.3	14.8	13.3
4. Often	1.1	.8	1.4	.8	2.3	1.7	1.3	.7	.6	1.1	1.0	.8	.9	1.9	1.5	-
Item 8850 N(Wtd)	3492	1584	1821	2847	352	817	1033	1171	471	1709	1679	1235	1012	418	715	60

D02B: Have you been bothered by your heart beating hard?

1. Never	71.6	75.2	68.0	71.0	75.8	70.5	70.2	71.7	76.8	74.0	69.4	77.0	77.8	65.7	57.6	65.0
2. Seldom	18.3	17.5	19.4	19.1	10.8	19.0	20.4	17.0	15.5	18.0	18.7	14.7	14.3	24.2	27.0	20.0
3. Sometimes	9.0	6.4	11.4	9.0	10.8	9.3	8.4	10.2	6.6	7.2	10.7	7.4	7.0	8.7	13.7	11.7
4. Often	1.1	.9	1.2	.8	2.6	1.2	1.0	1.1	1.1	.8	1.3	.9	.8	1.4	1.5	3.3
Item 8860 N(Wtd)	3486	1581	1817	2843	351	816	1032	1169	470	1705	1678	1236	1010	414	714	60

D02C: Have you had spells of dizziness?

1. Never	58.3	66.2	51.4	57.0	66.3	60.8	54.6	59.6	58.3	60.1	56.7	62.3	63.6	53.2	47.0	50.0
2. Seldom	25.7	22.9	27.9	26.7	15.9	23.9	28.1	24.0	27.4	25.5	25.4	23.5	23.0	29.4	31.4	25.0
3. Sometimes	13.3	9.5	16.6	13.5	15.0	13.1	13.9	13.6	11.7	12.7	13.9	11.9	11.0	14.6	17.3	18.3
4. Often	2.8	1.5	4.1	2.9	2.9	2.0	3.4	2.9	2.6	1.6	3.9	2.1	2.4	2.9	4.2	5.0
Item 8870 N(Wtd)	3471	1573	1811	2832	347	807	1030	1164	470	1695	1674	1232	1008	412	706	60

D02D: Have your hands trembled enough to bother you?

1. Never	78.9	86.0	72.8	79.0	81.5	80.9	77.5	78.1	80.6	81.4	76.6	83.5	82.5	73.5	70.7	63.3
2. Seldom	12.9	9.2	16.2	13.1	9.8	11.9	14.0	12.6	12.6	11.8	13.8	10.7	11.2	16.4	16.1	26.7
3. Sometimes	6.2	3.4	8.4	5.9	6.6	5.8	6.5	6.6	5.3	5.2	7.3	4.1	4.8	8.9	10.1	5.0
4. Often	2.0	1.3	2.5	1.9	1.7	1.4	2.0	2.7	1.3	1.6	2.3	1.7	1.6	1.2	3.2	5.0
Item 8880 N(Wtd)	3474	1577	1811	2837	346	812	1028	1164	470	1702	1670	1230	1005	415	710	60

D02E: Have you been troubled by your hands sweating so that they felt damp and clammy?

1. Never	63.5	66.2	60.9	62.9	69.4	64.4	60.6	63.6	67.5	64.6	61.8	68.2	67.5	54.6	54.6	55.0
2. Seldom	21.6	22.0	21.5	22.4	15.0	21.7	24.1	20.0	20.0	22.7	20.8	20.0	21.0	24.9	24.0	23.3
3. Sometimes	10.8	9.1	12.3	10.9	9.5	10.9	10.9	11.9	8.3	9.3	12.7	8.6	9.1	13.0	15.6	15.0
4. Often	4.1	2.7	5.2	3.7	6.4	3.0	4.4	4.5	4.2	3.4	4.7	3.2	2.5	7.5	5.7	6.7
Item 8890 N(Wtd)	3475	1577	1811	2838	346	810	1029	1166	471	1707	1667	1234	1007	414	707	60

D02F: Have there been times when you couldn't take care of things because you just couldn't get going?

1. Never	52.7	59.2	46.6	51.4	58.1	52.9	49.7	54.9	53.3	53.1	52.2	59.8	57.9	41.4	38.2	46.7
2. Seldom	28.2	26.8	29.4	29.5	19.9	27.1	30.0	26.9	29.3	30.6	25.6	24.0	26.4	34.5	35.9	26.7
3. Sometimes	16.0	12.2	19.8	16.0	18.5	16.1	16.9	16.0	14.2	14.0	18.3	14.0	13.4	21.0	20.6	15.0
4. Often	3.1	1.8	4.2	3.1	3.4	4.0	3.4	2.2	3.0	2.3	3.8	2.2	2.3	3.1	5.3	10.0
Item 8900 N(Wtd)	3475	1573	1816	2833	351	807	1026	1171	471	1704	1669	1234	1010	415	704	60

D03: At any time during the LAST 12 MONTHS, have you felt in your own mind that you should REDUCE or STOP your use of...

QUESTIONNAIRE FORM 3 1978	TOTAL	SEX		RACE		REGION				4YR COLLEGE PLANS		ILLICIT DRUG USE: LIFETIME				
		M	F	White	Black	NE	NC	S	W	Yes	No	None	Mari- juana Only	Few Pills	More Pills	Any Her- oin
Weighted No. of Cases:	3778	1711	1917	2973	417	926	1080	1257	516	1758	1748	1313	1078	451	764	68
% of Weighted Total:	100.0	45.3	50.7	78.7	11.0	24.5	28.6	33.3	13.7	46.5	46.3	34.8	28.5	11.9	20.2	1.8
D03A: Alcohol?																
1. Yes	31.7	35.2	28.2	31.1	38.1	29.4	28.8	35.7	32.2	30.8	32.1	21.4	34.7	34.6	39.5	41.0
2. No	56.4	55.1	57.9	58.4	37.3	63.1	62.5	48.8	49.5	57.3	55.8	48.3	61.0	60.5	59.3	55.7
8. Haven't used in last 12 months	12.0	9.7	13.9	10.5	24.6	7.5	8.7	15.5	18.3	11.9	12.0	30.3	4.3	5.0	1.3	3.3
Item 8910 N(Wtd)	3017	1424	1514	2513	260	704	910	1004	398	1491	1428	940	905	382	683	61
D03B: Cigarettes?																
1. Yes	31.3	29.8	31.9	30.4	34.4	32.2	33.0	33.2	21.3	24.7	37.3	11.3	34.4	40.1	53.3	57.1
2. No	15.1	14.2	16.4	14.7	15.6	15.6	17.0	14.1	13.0	12.0	18.0	9.7	16.4	17.8	19.8	22.2
8. Haven't used in last 12 months	53.6	56.0	51.7	54.9	50.0	52.3	50.0	52.7	65.7	63.3	44.7	79.0	49.2	42.1	26.9	20.6
Item 8920 N(Wtd)	3400	1542	1775	2789	334	788	1020	1132	460	1666	1625	1191	996	404	696	63
D03C: Marijuana?																
1. Yes	22.0	27.5	16.8	21.5	25.4	22.6	23.0	20.6	22.2	22.5	21.0	-	34.0	32.7	35.4	30.0
2. No	28.9	30.5	27.7	29.4	20.9	35.8	27.5	24.8	29.3	24.6	33.5	-	41.6	34.6	52.6	65.0
8. Haven't used in last 12 months	49.1	42.1	55.4	49.1	53.7	41.5	49.5	54.6	48.5	52.9	45.5	100.0	24.4	33.0	12.2	6.7
Item 8930 N(Wtd)	3066	1391	1598	2572	268	738	926	993	410	1534	1435	1081	858	364	666	60
D03D: Psychedelics (LSD, etc.)?																
1. Yes	3.8	4.6	3.1	3.9	-	4.7	4.0	2.5	5.0	3.9	3.7	-	-	.6	17.0	32.2
2. No	3.2	4.7	2.1	2.8	1.9	4.7	3.7	1.8	3.0	2.5	3.7	-	-	2.6	12.2	32.2
8. Haven't used in last 12 months	93.0	90.8	94.8	93.3	98.1	90.6	92.3	95.7	91.9	93.7	92.6	100.0	100.0	96.8	70.9	35.6
Item 8940 N(Wtd)	2986	1332	1577	2508	260	683	911	996	397	1532	1373	1090	915	344	540	59
D03E: Amphetamines (uppers)?																
1. Yes	5.2	5.8	4.8	5.3	1.1	6.6	5.1	3.7	6.7	4.9	5.4	-	-	3.4	24.2	29.8
2. No	8.0	7.5	8.4	8.1	2.3	10.0	8.4	5.4	9.6	5.6	10.2	-	-	3.7	37.7	43.9
8. Haven't used in last 12 months	86.8	86.6	86.7	86.7	97.0	83.4	86.3	90.9	83.7	89.5	84.4	100.0	100.0	92.9	38.1	28.1
Item 8950 N(Wtd)	2915	1325	1516	2445	263	699	864	966	387	1505	1332	1092	917	297	512	57
D03F: Quaaludes?																
1. Yes	1.8	2.3	1.3	1.6	-	2.3	1.3	2.0	1.7	1.6	1.9	-	-	1.4	6.7	18.5
2. No	2.6	3.3	2.1	2.4	1.5	1.8	2.5	3.0	3.0	1.9	2.8	-	-	.3	10.4	29.6
8. Haven't used in last 12 months	95.6	94.5	96.6	96.0	98.5	95.9	96.2	95.1	95.5	96.6	95.2	100.0	100.0	98.6	82.9	51.9
Item 8960 N(Wtd)	3028	1352	1600	2549	265	703	914	1006	404	1539	1406	1089	915	354	578	54
D03G: Barbiturates (downers)?																
1. Yes	2.8	3.1	2.6	2.7	.4	4.0	2.2	2.5	2.5	3.1	2.2	-	-	.9	11.2	32.7
2. No	3.7	3.7	3.8	3.7	1.5	4.0	4.0	3.5	2.8	2.7	4.7	-	-	1.7	15.7	30.8
8. Haven't used in last 12 months	93.5	93.2	93.6	93.6	98.5	92.0	93.9	93.9	94.5	94.1	93.2	100.0	100.0	97.7	73.1	38.5
Item 8970 N(Wtd)	3002	1342	1584	2522	264	704	906	994	398	1532	1390	1091	914	345	562	52
D03H: Cocaine?																
1. Yes	2.4	3.2	1.7	2.2	1.6	3.1	2.1	2.0	2.9	2.4	2.4	-	-	2.0	9.1	21.6
2. No	5.7	7.6	4.1	5.9	1.9	8.5	5.2	3.5	7.4	5.2	5.7	-	-	1.8	23.7	45.1
8. Haven't used in last 12 months	91.9	89.2	94.2	91.9	96.9	88.4	92.8	94.5	89.7	92.4	91.9	100.0	100.0	96.2	67.0	33.3
Item 8980 N(Wtd)	3026	1356	1591	2552	258	709	911	999	407	1549	1394	1089	912	342	594	51
D03I: Heroin?																
1. Yes	.7	.8	.6	.2	2.3	.3	.4	1.1	1.2	.7	.4	-	-	-	-	43.5
2. No	.4	.4	.3	.4	-	.4	.5	.2	.5	.2	.6	-	-	-	-	21.7
8. Haven't used in last 12 months	98.9	98.7	99.1	99.4	97.7	99.3	99.0	98.7	98.3	99.1	98.9	100.0	100.0	100.0	100.0	34.8
Item 8990 N(Wtd)	3037	1356	1604	2562	264	706	917	1004	409	1552	1404	1091	912	355	594	46

QUESTIONNAIRE FORM 3 1978	TOTAL	SEX		RACE		REGION				4YR COLLEGE PLANS		ILLICIT DRUG USE: LIFETIME				
		M	F	White	Black	NE	NC	S	W	Yes	No	None	Mari-juana Only	Few Pills	More Pills	Any Her-oin
Weighted No. of Cases:	3778	1711	1917	2973	417	926	1080	1257	516	1758	1748	1313	1078	451	764	68
% of Weighted Total:	100.0	45.3	50.7	78.7	11.0	24.5	28.6	33.3	13.7	46.5	46.3	34.8	28.5	11.9	20.2	1.8

D03J: Other narcotics?

	TOTAL	M	F	White	Black	NE	NC	S	W	Yes	No	None	Mari-juana Only	Few Pills	More Pills	Any Her-oin
1. Yes	2.1	2.4	1.8	2.0	1.5	2.1	2.4	1.5	2.6	1.6	2.2	-	-	1.5	8.4	26.7
2. No	2.5	2.8	2.4	2.3	1.9	3.7	2.9	1.4	2.6	1.7	3.5	-	-	.9	10.8	31.1
8. Haven't used in last 12 months	95.4	94.8	95.8	95.7	96.5	94.2	94.7	97.0	94.8	96.8	94.3	100.0	100.0	97.9	80.8	42.2
Item 9000 N(Wtd)	2915	1297	1542	2452	259	674	883	974	385	1480	1357	1088	910	335	500	45

D04: How likely is it that you will use marijuana in the next 12 months?

	TOTAL	M	F	White	Black	NE	NC	S	W	Yes	No	None	Mari-juana Only	Few Pills	More Pills	Any Her-oin
1. Definitely will-GO TO Q.D05	20.4	25.1	16.5	21.5	11.4	28.4	20.1	15.4	20.0	18.9	21.6	1.5	19.1	26.2	53.9	65.4
2. Probably will-GO TO Q.D05	14.4	16.0	13.0	14.5	11.4	14.9	16.8	12.1	13.7	13.2	15.8	1.5	26.2	19.9	18.2	21.2
3. Probably will not	20.4	19.7	21.0	20.8	20.5	20.5	19.8	21.4	19.7	23.2	17.5	15.7	30.0	21.9	15.6	1.9
4. Definitely will not	44.8	39.1	49.5	43.2	56.4	36.2	43.4	51.1	46.9	44.7	45.1	81.2	24.7	31.7	12.3	11.5
Item 9010 N(Wtd)	3098	1373	1654	2587	273	712	941	1029	416	1542	1467	1182	890	347	584	52

Here are some reasons people give for not using marijuana, or for stopping use. If you have never used marijuana, or if you have stopped using it, please tell us which reasons are true for you. (Mark all that apply.)

	TOTAL	M	F	White	Black	NE	NC	S	W	Yes	No	None	Mari-juana Only	Few Pills	More Pills	Any Her-oin
A. Concerned about possible psychological damage	57.4	55.9	59.1	58.6	46.9	59.8	56.8	56.2	58.1	61.0	53.4	64.1	47.1	58.2	42.2	71.4
B. Concerned about possible physical damage	58.3	54.5	61.4	58.9	54.5	63.5	55.6	57.6	58.5	62.4	53.8	64.6	47.5	57.6	49.1	14.3
C. Concerned about getting arrested	46.9	52.9	42.9	48.1	38.8	44.4	46.2	51.3	40.4	47.8	45.6	44.5	54.0	52.7	38.5	-
D. Concerned about becoming addicted to marijuana	38.1	35.7	40.6	37.6	40.2	37.3	37.7	40.2	34.9	34.2	42.2	43.9	30.0	37.5	22.4	28.6
E. It's against my beliefs	49.4	47.4	51.4	51.9	36.4	47.2	51.2	48.7	50.4	55.1	43.3	61.0	32.8	38.0	32.9	28.6
F. Concerned about loss of energy or ambition	28.4	29.7	27.5	27.7	30.1	32.0	24.5	28.9	29.8	31.8	24.2	29.6	24.8	26.6	31.1	42.9
G. Concerned about possible loss of control of myself	43.9	39.5	47.6	45.1	39.7	48.0	42.4	44.3	40.1	45.7	42.1	49.9	31.5	45.7	39.8	28.6
H. It might lead to stronger drugs	46.9	45.0	48.7	46.9	50.2	48.6	45.1	50.1	39.7	43.4	50.2	53.8	35.9	44.6	36.0	14.3
I. Not enjoyable, I didn't like it	30.7	30.2	31.0	29.7	35.9	32.0	30.4	30.5	30.1	29.5	31.7	21.2	52.5	32.1	29.8	28.6
J. My parents would disapprove	55.9	54.3	57.3	57.0	48.3	54.3	60.2	54.7	52.6	58.1	53.2	58.5	55.9	55.4	41.0	28.6
K. My husband/wife (or boyfriend/girlfriend) would disapprove	29.6	28.4	30.8	30.0	27.8	25.2	30.2	31.5	29.0	24.5	34.9	29.1	27.5	37.0	31.1	14.3
L. I don't like being with the people who use it	35.8	33.0	38.2	35.9	37.8	29.9	35.6	38.9	36.0	35.4	36.9	44.1	23.7	30.4	23.0	28.6
M. My friends don't use it	27.7	22.6	31.7	29.0	18.7	23.1	28.1	28.0	32.4	31.0	24.3	32.5	22.3	23.4	18.0	28.6
N. I might have a bad trip	16.5	16.4	17.0	16.3	18.2	17.8	16.8	16.6	14.3	14.1	19.1	19.1	11.8	16.3	12.4	28.6
O. Too expensive§	26.0	31.5	22.4	27.1	18.7	26.8	29.2	23.7	24.3	24.9	27.4	24.4	31.3	21.2	26.7	14.3
P. Not available§	4.9	5.2	4.8	4.9	4.3	2.9	5.4	5.2	6.3	4.9	5.0	5.3	4.0	5.4	4.3	-
Q. Don't feel like getting high§	53.0	48.1	56.8	53.9	46.4	61.9	50.2	48.0	60.3	51.5	54.8	54.4	49.8	54.3	50.3	42.9
Item 9020-9180 N(Wtd) ★	1960	775	1138	1601	209	381	576	731	272	1014	894	1106	476	184	161	7

D05A: Has your use of alcohol ever caused any of the following problems for you?

Responses to this set of questions are not included because of complexities in the presentation and interpretation of the data.

Item 9190-9350

D05M: Has your use of marijuana ever caused any of the following problems for you? (Mark all that apply.)

§ = category added in this data collection.   ★ = excludes respondents for whom question was inappropriate.

QUESTIONNAIRE FORM 3 1978	TOTAL	SEX		RACE		REGION				4YR COLLEGE PLANS		ILLICIT DRUG USE: LIFETIME				
		M	F	White	Black	NE	NC	S	W	Yes	No	None	Marijuana Only	Few Pills	More Pills	Any Heroin
Weighted No. of Cases:	3778	1711	1917	2973	417	926	1080	1257	516	1758	1748	1313	1078	451	764	68
% of Weighted Total:	100.0	45.3	50.7	78.7	11.0	24.5	28.6	33.3	13.7	46.5	46.3	34.8	28.5	11.9	20.2	1.8

Responses to this set of questions are not included because of complexities in the presentation and interpretation of the data.

Item 9360-9520

D05O: Has your use of other drugs ever caused any of the following problems for you? (Mark all that apply.)

Responses to this set of questions are not included because of complexities in the presentation and interpretation of the data.

Item 9530-9690

E01: Some people think about what's going on in government very often, and others are not that interested. How much of an interest do you take in government and current events?

	TOTAL	M	F	White	Black	NE	NC	S	W	Yes	No	None	Marijuana Only	Few Pills	More Pills	Any Heroin
5. A very great interest	7.2	10.2	4.8	6.6	9.4	6.8	6.0	8.8	5.9	9.5	4.7	7.7	6.7	5.5	7.8	12.3
4. A lot of interest	16.6	20.0	14.1	16.6	12.8	14.9	16.3	15.4	23.1	21.7	11.1	18.6	15.7	15.7	14.2	21.1
3. Some interest	47.1	47.6	46.0	47.5	47.2	41.5	50.4	48.2	45.7	47.2	47.2	48.0	48.7	44.1	44.6	43.9
2. Very little interest	23.4	17.4	28.7	23.8	24.1	28.8	21.4	22.7	20.3	17.9	28.9	21.4	23.4	29.1	23.9	19.3
1. No interest at all	5.8	4.8	6.4	5.5	6.6	8.0	5.7	4.8	4.6	3.6	8.1	4.3	5.5	5.5	9.3	5.3
Item 6330 N(Wtd)	3270	1446	1741	2688	320	733	998	1101	438	1628	1543	1175	953	381	654	57

E02: Do you agree or disagree that most efforts to prevent (or clean up) pollution...

E02A: ...are just too expensive

	TOTAL	M	F	White	Black	NE	NC	S	W	Yes	No	None	Marijuana Only	Few Pills	More Pills	Any Heroin
1. Disagree	23.9	26.7	21.4	22.9	29.2	26.0	20.9	24.5	25.8	24.8	22.8	22.9	26.5	20.9	24.4	22.0
2. Mostly disagree	24.0	23.2	24.9	25.1	19.7	24.2	22.6	25.0	24.7	28.1	19.9	25.3	22.3	20.9	25.5	30.0
3. Neither	29.5	26.0	32.5	30.7	21.3	26.4	33.7	27.5	30.0	27.6	31.7	28.2	29.6	34.1	29.2	22.0
4. Mostly agree	16.3	16.2	16.2	16.0	17.9	16.7	17.2	16.6	12.3	14.7	18.1	17.7	14.9	17.2	14.8	18.0
5. Agree	6.3	7.9	5.0	5.3	11.6	6.9	5.5	6.3	7.2	4.7	7.5	6.0	6.8	6.9	6.1	6.0
Item 9700 N(Wtd)	3233	1439	1712	2657	319	724	995	1084	430	1610	1528	1168	945	378	643	50

E02B: ...cost more jobs than it's worth

	TOTAL	M	F	White	Black	NE	NC	S	W	Yes	No	None	Marijuana Only	Few Pills	More Pills	Any Heroin
1. Disagree	29.9	30.8	29.0	29.1	34.5	32.4	26.6	31.4	29.3	32.4	27.7	28.1	31.9	25.8	31.5	40.4
2. Mostly disagree	25.5	24.3	26.8	27.8	15.8	25.6	26.2	24.2	27.6	29.2	21.7	28.1	22.4	25.0	27.1	25.0
3. Neither	28.2	28.3	28.1	28.6	21.2	26.4	30.9	26.8	28.8	25.6	31.0	25.6	30.4	28.9	29.4	21.2
4. Mostly agree	11.4	10.9	11.8	10.8	16.1	10.1	12.0	12.3	10.3	9.4	13.5	12.1	11.4	15.3	8.9	5.8
5. Agree	4.9	5.7	4.2	3.7	12.0	5.6	4.3	5.3	4.0	3.3	6.1	6.1	3.9	5.0	3.1	7.7
Item 9710 N(Wtd)	3215	1436	1698	2643	316	716	993	1079	427	1599	1522	1156	939	380	639	52

E02C: ...are proposed by people who usually don't know what they are talking about

	TOTAL	M	F	White	Black	NE	NC	S	W	Yes	No	None	Marijuana Only	Few Pills	More Pills	Any Heroin
1. Disagree	20.4	20.9	20.1	20.3	19.9	22.2	18.8	19.6	23.2	22.6	18.1	19.5	21.4	18.8	21.3	26.0
2. Mostly disagree	23.5	21.6	25.2	24.8	18.6	22.2	25.5	22.3	23.9	27.5	19.0	25.3	24.2	20.6	21.4	16.0
3. Neither	31.1	29.1	32.6	31.6	25.3	31.9	32.3	28.6	33.0	29.5	33.2	29.7	30.0	36.5	32.6	32.0
4. Mostly agree	15.6	16.8	14.5	14.7	19.9	14.5	15.5	18.1	11.7	13.7	17.7	16.4	15.7	15.5	15.1	8.0
5. Agree	9.4	11.6	7.6	8.5	16.3	9.3	8.0	11.4	8.0	6.7	12.0	9.1	8.6	8.6	9.4	18.0
Item 9720 N(Wtd)	3186	1428	1677	2626	312	711	989	1058	427	1591	1505	1150	929	373	635	5

QUESTIONNAIRE FORM 3 1978	TOTAL	SEX		RACE		REGION				4YR COLLEGE PLANS		ILLICIT DRUG USE: LIFETIME				
		M	F	White	Black	NE	NC	S	W	Yes	No	None	Mari-juana Only	Few Pills	More Pills	Any Her-oin
Weighted No. of Cases:	3778	1711	1917	2973	417	926	1080	1257	516	1758	1748	1313	1078	451	764	68
% of Weighted Total:	100.0	45.3	50.7	78.7	11.0	24.5	28.6	33.3	13.7	46.5	46.3	34.8	28.5	11.9	20.2	1.8

E02D: ...will not be enough anyhow

1. Disagree	20.4	19.9	20.8	19.4	24.2	22.1	17.7	20.5	23.6	22.7	17.9	21.0	21.2	18.8	19.0	25.5
2. Mostly disagree	22.5	21.1	23.7	24.3	16.5	21.2	23.1	22.5	23.1	25.0	20.0	24.3	21.9	22.5	20.3	15.7
3. Neither	29.7	28.8	30.6	30.1	26.5	27.8	33.1	28.9	27.4	26.0	34.1	29.5	28.9	30.0	31.2	31.4
4. Mostly agree	19.2	21.1	17.4	19.1	17.7	19.1	20.5	19.1	16.5	19.0	19.6	18.0	19.7	21.7	20.1	17.6
5. Agree	8.2	9.2	7.5	7.2	15.2	9.8	5.6	9.0	9.4	7.3	8.5	7.3	8.3	7.0	9.7	9.8
Item 9730 N(Wtd)	3167	1419	1669	2606	310	706	988	1050	424	1579	1498	1141	921	373	632	51

E02E: ...are useless because this society won't last long enough for such efforts to do any good

1. Disagree	39.4	40.2	38.6	40.8	31.8	41.5	37.9	38.5	41.9	47.2	31.3	40.2	41.6	38.9	36.1	33.3
2. Mostly disagree	21.3	21.1	21.7	22.5	17.0	20.8	24.1	20.1	18.1	23.0	19.5	21.9	21.1	18.9	22.1	21.6
3. Neither	24.7	24.0	25.4	24.5	21.2	23.8	24.8	24.4	26.4	19.4	30.4	23.0	23.6	26.9	27.8	25.5
4. Mostly agree	8.6	8.6	8.5	7.6	14.1	7.6	8.6	9.6	8.0	7.0	10.4	8.4	8.5	8.8	8.8	5.9
5. Agree	6.0	6.1	5.9	4.6	16.1	6.3	4.5	7.4	5.6	3.3	8.4	6.6	5.0	6.1	5.2	13.7
Item 9740 N(Wtd)	3175	1419	1676	2617	311	710	986	1053	425	1580	1503	1144	922	375	634	51

E03: There has been talk about shortages of energy, food, and raw materials in this country. Do you think that in the coming years we will have plenty to meet our needs, a sufficient amount, or will we have to consume less?

1. Plenty to meet our needs	10.9	15.0	7.2	9.8	17.5	8.3	12.3	11.0	11.8	9.1	12.7	10.5	12.5	10.2	8.8	6.1
2. A sufficient amount	42.9	43.8	42.2	42.8	46.0	48.4	40.0	44.4	37.1	40.0	46.1	43.3	44.0	36.2	43.4	59.2
3. Will have to consume less	46.2	41.3	50.6	47.3	36.1	43.4	47.7	44.6	51.1	51.0	41.1	46.2	43.5	53.6	47.8	34.7
Item 9750 N(Wtd)	3109	1369	1661	2573	291	678	968	1048	415	1556	1459	1129	910	362	611	49

E04: The questions in this section deal with population problems. How much do you agree or disagree with each statement?

E04A: Our government should help other countries to control their population

1. Disagree	22.4	26.8	18.3	22.4	24.6	25.3	21.2	21.7	21.8	19.5	25.4	22.3	20.2	21.2	24.2	31.5
2. Mostly disagree	17.5	16.8	17.9	18.1	13.6	19.5	17.8	16.1	17.1	18.7	16.3	17.6	19.1	14.2	17.7	11.1
3. Neither	22.0	19.9	23.9	22.5	16.1	22.5	25.3	19.2	20.6	21.5	22.5	22.3	22.3	22.3	21.6	25.9
4. Mostly agree	23.4	21.1	25.5	23.7	20.8	20.5	23.6	24.8	24.2	24.5	22.3	21.3	23.9	25.8	25.0	22.2
5. Agree	14.8	15.4	14.4	13.2	24.9	12.3	12.0	18.3	16.1	15.8	13.4	16.3	14.3	16.4	11.7	11.1
Item 9760 N(Wtd)	3208	1419	1706	2637	317	697	999	1090	422	1594	1517	1155	936	372	640	54

E04B: Governments should avoid making policy about population and let the individual decide

1. Disagree	14.1	15.9	12.6	12.4	23.3	13.4	12.0	16.1	14.6	14.0	14.0	14.9	14.7	13.6	11.3	14.8
2. Mostly disagree	21.7	21.0	22.7	22.9	16.7	21.2	20.7	21.9	24.4	23.8	20.0	20.4	23.0	21.4	22.5	24.1
3. Neither	24.9	25.0	25.1	25.5	17.9	26.8	25.7	23.0	24.9	25.1	25.1	23.5	26.6	24.4	26.5	22.2
4. Mostly agree	23.3	21.6	24.7	23.7	21.1	21.6	26.3	22.5	20.8	22.0	24.4	24.2	21.6	22.2	24.9	22.2
5. Agree	16.0	16.6	15.0	15.5	20.8	16.7	15.2	16.4	15.3	15.2	16.4	17.1	14.3	18.4	15.0	16.7
Item 9770 N(Wtd)	3185	1408	1695	2616	318	693	996	1078	418	1590	1503	1149	926	369	635	54

E04C: I feel strongly enough about preventing overpopulation that I'd be willing to limit my family to two children

1. Disagree	13.6	14.2	13.3	12.8	21.0	17.2	13.9	11.4	12.6	13.6	13.9	15.2	12.4	12.8	12.9	9.3
2. Mostly disagree	12.1	12.0	12.3	12.0	14.6	12.7	14.4	9.7	12.2	13.8	10.3	12.7	11.0	13.0	12.5	14.8
3. Neither	21.3	22.5	20.2	21.4	14.9	24.9	22.6	19.1	18.4	19.8	22.7	20.2	24.4	17.4	21.6	24.1
4. Mostly agree	23.7	24.0	23.4	23.9	24.1	22.9	23.5	26.0	19.3	23.6	23.5	23.8	24.4	23.9	22.4	20.4
5. Agree	29.3	27.4	30.7	29.9	25.4	22.6	25.7	33.7	37.9	29.2	29.6	28.2	28.0	33.2	30.6	31.5
Item 9780 N(Wtd)	3182	1410	1689	2616	315	687	997	1079	419	1584	1505	1145	930	368	634	54

QUESTIONNAIRE FORM 3 1978	TOTAL	SEX		RACE		REGION				4YR COLLEGE PLANS		ILLICIT DRUG USE: LIFETIME				
		M	F	White	Black	NE	NC	S	W	Yes	No	None	Mari-juana Only	Few Pills	More Pills	Any Her-oin
Weighted No. of Cases:	3778	1711	1917	2973	417	926	1080	1257	516	1758	1748	1313	1078	451	764	68
% of Weighted Total:	100.0	45.3	50.7	78.7	11.0	24.5	28.6	33.3	13.7	46.5	46.3	34.8	28.5	11.9	20.2	1.8

E04D: To help prevent overpopulation, I might decide not to have any children of my own

	TOTAL	M	F	White	Black	NE	NC	S	W	Yes	No	None	Mari.	Few	More	Her.
1. Disagree	52.1	48.1	55.7	52.4	54.0	54.8	51.6	51.6	50.1	54.0	50.1	52.7	54.0	48.8	49.6	58.5
2. Mostly disagree	16.8	17.7	15.8	17.1	13.1	16.7	16.7	17.6	15.1	17.4	16.1	18.5	14.8	17.9	16.6	7.5
3. Neither	16.0	18.6	13.7	16.1	11.5	17.8	16.6	13.8	17.3	15.4	16.7	14.2	17.3	14.9	17.4	18.9
4. Mostly agree	6.8	7.4	6.4	6.2	13.1	4.8	6.7	8.1	6.7	5.8	7.8	6.1	6.4	8.9	7.3	5.7
5. Agree	8.4	8.1	8.4	8.3	8.3	5.8	8.4	8.9	10.6	7.4	9.4	8.3	7.4	9.8	9.3	7.5
Item 9790 N(Wtd)	3172	1402	1688	2613	313	684	995	1076	417	1575	1506	1140	928	369	633	53

E04E: High schools should offer instruction in birth control methods

	TOTAL	M	F	White	Black	NE	NC	S	W	Yes	No	None	Mari.	Few	More	Her.
1. Disagree	5.9	7.0	5.1	5.0	9.4	5.6	5.7	5.4	8.3	5.4	6.4	7.2	5.1	5.6	5.1	1.9
2. Mostly disagree	5.3	6.0	4.6	5.6	3.3	6.2	6.4	5.8	3.3	5.1	5.8	6.6	5.2	3.5	4.1	3.8
3. Neither	12.7	13.9	11.8	13.1	8.1	13.8	14.1	11.2	12.1	11.3	14.6	15.7	13.1	8.6	9.4	21.2
4. Mostly agree	27.3	28.8	25.7	27.8	25.7	26.7	25.4	28.9	29.0	26.7	27.9	27.3	28.8	30.9	23.9	19.2
5. Agree	48.7	44.2	52.7	48.4	53.4	47.9	48.5	50.6	45.7	51.6	45.3	43.3	47.8	51.3	57.6	55.8
Item 9800 N(Wtd)	3163	1391	1691	2608	307	682	985	1076	420	1576	1492	1137	926	372	628	52

E04F: I personally consider most methods of birth control to be immoral

	TOTAL	M	F	White	Black	NE	NC	S	W	Yes	No	None	Mari.	Few	More	Her.
1. Disagree	42.3	37.1	46.7	43.8	33.9	44.4	39.8	42.0	45.1	47.1	37.7	35.0	43.4	43.8	53.3	44.2
2. Mostly disagree	20.0	22.3	18.2	21.3	11.2	21.5	19.1	19.4	21.0	21.1	18.9	22.4	19.9	18.9	17.4	13.5
3. Neither	20.9	22.1	19.8	20.4	22.0	20.7	23.0	20.1	18.6	18.1	24.1	23.9	20.2	20.3	17.8	19.2
4. Mostly agree	8.9	9.7	8.2	7.7	17.8	7.1	9.2	10.3	7.9	7.2	10.7	9.8	9.6	8.6	5.5	13.5
5. Agree	7.9	8.9	7.2	6.8	14.8	6.5	8.8	8.1	7.6	6.5	8.6	9.0	6.8	8.4	6.1	11.5
Item 9810 N(Wtd)	3143	1383	1678	2597	304	680	975	1068	419	1568	1481	1130	923	370	619	52

E04G: The government should make birth control information and services available without cost to anyone who wants them

	TOTAL	M	F	White	Black	NE	NC	S	W	Yes	No	None	Mari.	Few	More	Her.
1. Disagree	6.7	6.9	6.4	6.3	7.9	6.5	6.9	5.5	9.9	6.5	6.8	8.0	7.0	5.1	5.1	3.8
2. Mostly disagree	7.2	7.5	7.0	7.2	5.6	6.2	7.9	7.2	7.0	7.6	6.6	7.7	7.3	6.2	6.9	11.5
3. Neither	13.2	15.6	11.1	13.2	8.5	12.0	15.1	12.7	12.3	11.8	15.0	15.1	13.5	9.5	10.4	21.2
4. Mostly agree	25.5	25.0	26.0	26.4	25.2	26.9	26.6	24.1	23.8	25.9	25.8	27.6	24.0	28.9	23.4	15.4
5. Agree	47.4	44.9	49.6	47.0	52.5	48.3	43.4	50.5	47.1	48.3	45.9	41.7	48.3	50.3	54.1	48.1
Item 9820 N(Wtd)	3134	1374	1680	2583	305	677	977	1065	416	1562	1479	1124	917	370	625	52

E05: What do you think would be the ideal population size for the United States?

	TOTAL	M	F	White	Black	NE	NC	S	W	Yes	No	None	Mari.	Few	More	Her.
1. Much smaller than it is now	10.7	11.5	10.2	10.7	10.8	10.0	11.2	10.2	12.2	10.2	10.6	9.9	9.5	11.1	12.5	21.6
2. Somewhat smaller than it is now	37.8	35.3	39.9	40.4	22.6	41.1	38.5	35.6	37.0	41.0	35.1	36.5	37.9	41.2	39.4	29.4
3. About the same as it is now	44.7	44.8	44.5	44.3	45.6	42.4	45.0	46.0	44.5	44.4	45.2	46.0	47.0	41.5	42.0	41.2
4. Somewhat larger than it is now	4.9	6.0	4.1	3.6	13.4	4.7	4.3	5.6	4.4	3.4	6.4	5.0	4.6	5.4	4.3	2.0
5. Much larger than it is now	1.9	2.4	1.4	1.0	7.5	1.8	1.0	2.7	1.9	1.0	2.8	2.7	1.1	.8	1.8	5.9
Item 9830 N(Wtd)	3123	1370	1673	2577	305	677	972	1063	411	1554	1477	1129	907	369	622	51

E06: What do you think would be the ideal population size for the entire world?

	TOTAL	M	F	White	Black	NE	NC	S	W	Yes	No	None	Mari.	Few	More	Her.
1. Much smaller than it is now	29.4	33.3	26.3	31.5	14.0	28.5	30.7	27.7	32.0	33.0	25.4	28.3	28.3	31.5	31.4	33.3
2. Somewhat smaller than it is now	41.4	39.6	42.8	43.7	27.4	44.3	44.7	37.6	38.8	45.3	38.1	41.3	43.5	40.8	41.3	27.5
3. About the same as it is now	22.1	20.0	23.8	20.9	30.4	21.9	18.1	26.0	21.6	17.6	27.1	22.7	22.6	19.8	21.6	21.6
4. Somewhat larger than it is now	4.3	4.2	4.2	2.8	14.0	3.4	4.3	4.6	5.1	3.1	5.2	4.2	4.1	6.3	3.6	3.9
5. Much larger than it is now	2.7	2.8	2.8	1.1	14.0	1.8	2.1	4.1	2.4	1.0	4.2	3.6	1.8	1.6	2.3	13.7
Item 9850 N(Wtd)	3100	1367	1652	2560	299	670	966	1053	412	1538	1469	1120	904	368	612	51

QUESTIONNAIRE FORM 3 1978	TOTAL	SEX		RACE		REGION				4YR COLLEGE PLANS		ILLICIT DRUG USE: LIFETIME				
		M	F	White	Black	NE	NC	S	W	Yes	No	None	Mari-juana Only	Few Pills	More Pills	Any Her-oin
Weighted No. of Cases:	3778	1711	1917	2973	417	926	1080	1257	516	1758	1748	1313	1078	451	764	68
% of Weighted Total:	100.0	45.3	50.7	78.7	11.0	24.5	28.6	33.3	13.7	46.5	46.3	34.8	28.5	11.9	20.2	1.8
E07: Some people like school very much. Others don't. How do you feel about going to school?																
5. I like school very much	13.6	13.0	14.0	11.7	27.1	10.0	12.6	15.5	17.4	17.8	9.0	18.1	12.9	11.2	7.2	15.4
4. I like school quite a lot	29.7	26.2	32.7	29.9	25.5	25.7	30.2	31.5	30.2	36.5	23.1	37.3	28.1	27.5	21.6	17.3
3. I like school some	37.7	41.8	34.7	38.2	35.9	37.2	38.5	37.6	37.1	34.1	41.3	31.9	41.6	42.2	38.9	44.2
2. I don't like school very much	13.1	13.5	12.5	14.0	7.8	17.0	14.1	10.9	10.2	9.1	17.5	9.9	12.3	15.0	19.4	9.6
1. I don't like school at all	5.9	5.5	6.0	6.2	3.6	10.0	4.7	4.7	5.0	2.5	9.2	2.9	5.2	3.7	12.8	15.4
Item 7630 N(Wtd)	3154	1378	1695	2601	306	681	980	1073	420	1567	1488	1137	918	374	624	52
E08: Did you have a unit on sex education when you were in high school?																
1. No, and I'm glad I didn't	9.0	10.0	8.2	8.7	8.9	7.6	6.8	11.3	10.3	8.6	9.5	10.3	8.8	8.1	6.9	9.6
2. No, and I wish I had	31.2	32.0	30.6	31.1	35.2	29.4	24.7	39.3	28.6	28.1	34.6	32.3	31.3	31.6	28.4	30.8
3. Yes, and it was very worthwhile	22.1	18.1	25.2	19.7	33.6	19.1	23.5	22.2	23.7	21.0	22.9	22.2	23.3	22.4	19.2	21.2
4. Yes, and it was somewhat worthwhile	28.1	27.3	28.7	30.1	17.8	29.9	35.3	20.5	27.6	33.0	23.2	27.8	27.9	27.8	30.7	21.2
5. Yes, but it was not worthwhile at all	9.6	12.5	7.3	10.4	4.9	14.0	9.8	6.8	9.8	9.4	9.7	7.4	8.5	10.0	14.9	17.3
Item 9860 N(Wtd)	3100	1356	1662	2550	304	659	972	1059	409	1538	1467	1115	904	370	610	52
E09: Did you ever study about birth control methods in high school?																
1. No, and I'm glad I didn't	11.9	16.6	8.1	11.6	11.4	11.2	9.7	14.7	10.6	10.8	12.8	15.3	11.1	10.2	7.1	13.5
2. No, and I wish I had	39.4	39.9	38.6	40.3	39.6	39.5	36.4	44.6	33.1	39.1	40.2	38.2	42.1	35.6	40.0	32.7
3. Yes, and it was very worthwhile	23.2	16.8	28.4	20.6	35.6	20.2	23.8	23.8	24.9	22.1	24.2	21.9	23.7	25.4	22.4	30.8
4. Yes, and it was somewhat worthwhile	19.8	19.9	19.8	21.4	10.4	20.4	24.6	13.5	24.7	22.3	17.2	19.6	18.7	22.7	21.2	17.3
5. Yes, but it was not worthwhile at all	5.7	6.8	5.0	6.1	2.7	8.7	5.6	3.4	6.9	5.8	5.5	4.8	4.4	6.1	9.4	3.8
Item 9870 N(Wtd)	3064	1330	1657	2523	298	653	957	1048	405	1523	1451	1102	893	362	608	52
E10: The next questions are about some things which may have happened TO YOU while you were at school (inside or outside or in a schoolbus). During the LAST 12 MONTHS, how often ...																
E10A: Has something of yours (worth under $50) been stolen?																
1. Not at all	64.2	59.8	68.2	62.9	71.7	64.6	62.6	65.5	63.8	60.3	67.9	69.9	63.7	61.7	56.0	63.0
2. Once	23.3	25.4	21.2	24.6	16.9	22.5	25.2	22.9	20.9	25.9	21.0	20.9	23.4	25.0	27.0	16.7
3. Twice	8.9	10.2	7.7	8.9	7.6	8.9	8.2	8.5	11.5	9.9	7.7	6.6	9.8	10.1	11.0	16.7
4. 3 or 4 times	2.9	3.4	2.2	2.8	2.5	2.8	3.9	2.2	2.2	2.7	2.8	2.5	2.6	2.4	4.0	1.9
5. 5 or more times	.8	1.1	.6	.7	1.3	1.2	.2	.7	1.7	1.1	.5	.2	.5	.5	2.2	1.9
Item 9871 N(Wtd)	3173	1397	1692	2606	314	675	991	1090	417	1568	1500	1140	923	376	627	54
E10B: Has something of yours (worth over $50) been stolen?																
1. Not at all	91.9	89.5	94.2	92.9	85.9	91.9	92.5	91.4	91.9	92.3	91.5	94.8	92.8	89.3	89.1	75.9
2. Once	6.5	8.1	4.9	5.8	10.6	6.3	5.3	7.8	6.7	6.4	6.6	4.4	5.9	9.4	7.9	24.1
3. Twice	1.1	1.6	.6	.9	2.9	1.2	1.7	.6	.7	1.0	1.1	.6	1.0	.5	2.4	-
4. 3 or 4 times	.3	.4	.1	.2	.6	.1	.3	.2	.7	.2	.4	.1	.3	.5	.5	-
5. 5 or more times	.2	.2	.1	.1	-	.6	.1	-	.2	.1	.3	.1	.1	.3	.3	-
Item 9872 N(Wtd)	3161	1394	1683	2601	312	669	992	1082	418	1568	1489	1134	922	374	624	54
E10C: Has someone deliberately damaged your property (your car, clothing, etc.)?																
1. Not at all	74.8	67.9	80.5	74.3	78.7	78.0	73.4	75.5	70.8	74.8	74.8	80.0	75.0	69.7	69.1	64.8
2. Once	16.6	20.6	13.2	17.2	12.3	15.4	18.0	15.7	17.5	16.8	16.5	13.5	16.9	20.4	18.7	24.1
3. Twice	6.0	7.9	4.5	5.9	4.5	4.3	6.9	5.3	8.6	6.5	5.3	4.8	6.1	6.2	7.4	11.1
4. 3 or 4 times	2.0	2.7	1.4	2.1	1.9	.7	1.6	2.7	2.6	1.5	2.6	1.3	1.6	2.4	3.5	-
5. 5 or more times	.7	.9	.5	.5	1.9	1.5	.2	.7	.5	.5	.8	.4	.5	1.1	1.3	-
Item 9873 N(Wtd)	3153	1391	1679	2597	310	669	991	1075	418	1562	1488	1130	925	373	621	54

QUESTIONNAIRE FORM 3 1978	TOTAL	SEX		RACE		REGION				4YR COLLEGE PLANS		ILLICIT DRUG USE: LIFETIME				
		M	F	White	Black	NE	NC	S	W	Yes	No	None	Mari-juana Only	Few Pills	More Pills	Any Her-oin
Weighted No. of Cases:	3778	1711	1917	2973	417	926	1080	1257	516	1758	1748	1313	1078	451	764	68
% of Weighted Total:	100.0	45.3	50.7	78.7	11.0	24.5	28.6	33.3	13.7	46.5	46.3	34.8	28.5	11.9	20.2	1.8

E10D: Has someone injured you with a weapon (like a knife, gun, or club)?

	TOTAL	M	F	White	Black	NE	NC	S	W	Yes	No	None	Mari-juana Only	Few Pills	More Pills	Any Her-oin
1. Not at all	95.4	93.1	97.7	96.1	92.9	94.5	96.4	95.4	94.2	96.5	94.7	97.6	97.0	93.0	92.9	74.1
2. Once	3.0	4.4	1.5	2.6	4.5	3.6	2.6	2.9	3.4	2.6	3.2	1.7	2.2	4.0	4.3	16.7
3. Twice	.9	1.4	.4	.7	1.6	1.3	.6	1.0	.7	.5	1.2	.3	.5	2.2	1.6	1.9
4. 3 or 4 times	.5	.5	.3	.3	.3	.3	.3	.3	1.4	.2	.6	.2	—	.8	.5	5.6
5. 5 or more times	.3	.6	–	.3	.6	.3	.2	.4	.2	.1	.3	.2	.3	.3	.5	–
Item 9874 N(Wtd)	3153	1385	1684	2594	311	670	990	1076	416	1564	1486	1133	922	372	622	54

E10E: Has someone threatened you with a weapon, but not actually injured you?

	TOTAL	M	F	White	Black	NE	NC	S	W	Yes	No	None	Mari-juana Only	Few Pills	More Pills	Any Her-oin
1. Not at all	88.4	82.9	93.1	88.8	87.0	88.9	89.8	87.1	87.8	91.3	85.8	93.7	90.1	85.2	81.8	50.9
2. Once	6.8	9.8	4.4	6.8	7.2	7.2	6.2	7.6	6.0	5.8	8.1	4.3	6.4	9.2	10.0	15.1
3. Twice	2.8	3.8	1.7	2.8	2.0	2.1	2.2	3.7	3.1	1.8	3.6	1.2	2.2	3.8	4.4	20.8
4. 3 or 4 times	1.1	2.0	.4	1.0	1.6	1.5	1.0	.7	1.7	.8	1.4	.6	.7	.8	2.6	1.9
5. 5 or more times	.8	1.4	.3	.7	2.6	.6	.7	.9	1.2	.3	1.0	.2	.8	.8	1.3	11.3
Item 9875 N(Wtd)	3142	1383	1676	2587	307	667	987	1071	417	1558	1484	1130	919	371	620	53

E10F: Has someone injured you on purpose without using a weapon?

	TOTAL	M	F	White	Black	NE	NC	S	W	Yes	No	None	Mari-juana Only	Few Pills	More Pills	Any Her-oin
1. Not at all	87.8	85.7	89.8	88.5	85.7	87.6	87.4	87.7	89.1	88.6	87.0	91.8	89.6	83.1	82.4	74.1
2. Once	7.5	9.0	6.1	7.1	9.4	8.1	7.8	8.2	4.6	6.6	8.7	5.5	6.6	9.9	10.2	16.7
3. Twice	2.8	3.1	2.6	2.9	1.6	3.3	3.3	2.0	2.9	2.6	3.2	1.6	1.7	4.8	5.2	5.6
4. 3 or 4 times	1.0	1.2	.8	.9	1.3	.6	1.0	.8	2.2	1.2	.7	.4	1.1	1.3	1.1	1.9
5. 5 or more times	.9	1.0	.8	.7	2.3	.6	.4	1.3	1.4	1.0	.5	.6	.9	1.1	1.5	–
Item 9876 N(Wtd)	3141	1380	1677	2586	307	668	988	1069	414	1558	1481	1131	916	372	618	54

E10G: Has an unarmed person threatened you with injury, but not actually injured you?

	TOTAL	M	F	White	Black	NE	NC	S	W	Yes	No	None	Mari-juana Only	Few Pills	More Pills	Any Her-oin
1. Not at all	80.0	73.0	85.9	79.6	82.4	79.6	82.4	77.7	80.3	80.3	80.0	85.0	81.0	78.4	73.1	40.7
2. Once	10.4	13.1	8.2	10.6	10.1	12.6	8.4	11.8	8.2	11.0	9.9	9.0	10.9	9.4	12.6	20.4
3. Twice	4.2	5.3	3.2	4.4	2.6	3.0	4.0	4.5	5.3	3.9	4.2	3.3	3.8	5.4	5.3	7.4
4. 3 or 4 times	2.4	3.8	1.3	2.5	1.3	2.2	2.5	3.0	1.2	2.0	2.9	1.5	1.5	2.7	4.4	14.8
5. 5 or more times	3.0	4.7	1.6	2.9	3.6	2.4	2.6	3.1	4.8	2.7	3.0	1.3	2.8	4.0	4.7	16.7
Item 9877 N(Wtd)	3139	1379	1676	2584	307	668	988	1067	416	1558	1481	1128	916	371	618	54

E11: Looking toward the future, how important would it be for you to have each of the following things?

E11A: At least one car

	TOTAL	M	F	White	Black	NE	NC	S	W	Yes	No	None	Mari-juana Only	Few Pills	More Pills	Any Her-oin
1. Not important	3.4	4.1	2.6	2.6	7.6	4.2	3.4	3.4	2.2	2.7	3.5	3.1	2.7	4.9	2.8	13.0
2. Somewhat important	18.3	17.1	19.3	17.0	24.2	18.9	17.0	17.9	20.8	20.3	16.0	19.5	17.3	18.6	17.2	16.7
3. Quite important	35.8	34.1	37.4	37.5	27.2	36.3	40.4	32.3	33.2	34.7	37.3	38.1	35.5	33.5	34.6	29.6
4. Extremely important	42.5	44.6	40.7	42.8	41.4	40.5	39.1	46.3	43.8	42.1	43.2	39.3	44.4	43.0	45.5	40.7
Item 13835 N(Wtd)	3118	1371	1665	2570	302	661	980	1065	413	1554	1462	1119	910	370	616	54

E11B: At least two cars

	TOTAL	M	F	White	Black	NE	NC	S	W	Yes	No	None	Mari-juana Only	Few Pills	More Pills	Any Her-oin
1. Not important	52.0	42.7	59.9	51.1	60.9	56.3	51.3	50.4	51.0	53.8	50.0	54.9	51.2	53.3	48.7	40.7
2. Somewhat important	29.2	32.8	26.0	30.7	18.9	25.5	32.1	27.9	31.6	26.6	32.6	28.4	30.6	29.8	27.8	38.9
3. Quite important	13.0	16.0	10.3	13.2	11.1	12.1	12.9	14.1	11.7	14.8	11.0	12.8	12.0	11.3	15.5	9.3
4. Extremely important	5.8	8.4	3.7	5.1	9.1	6.1	3.6	7.6	6.1	4.8	6.5	4.0	6.2	5.8	7.9	11.1
Item 13840 N(Wtd)	3103	1365	1655	2564	297	652	980	1059	412	1551	1450	1112	908	362	618	54

E11C: A large (full-sized) car

	TOTAL	M	F	White	Black	NE	NC	S	W	Yes	No	None	Mari-juana Only	Few Pills	More Pills	Any Her-oin
1. Not important	66.3	58.8	72.6	67.5	60.8	66.5	65.6	64.9	71.6	66.9	65.9	69.8	63.0	69.7	63.5	70.4
2. Somewhat important	20.0	23.3	17.3	20.3	16.9	17.3	22.5	20.4	17.4	19.5	20.7	16.6	25.0	12.9	23.2	14.8
3. Quite important	9.2	11.5	7.3	8.8	10.8	11.1	8.9	8.7	8.3	9.1	9.2	8.9	8.2	12.1	9.0	9.3
4. Extremely important	4.5	6.4	2.8	3.5	11.5	5.1	3.0	6.0	2.9	4.5	4.2	4.7	3.7	5.0	4.4	7.4
Item 13850 N(Wtd)	3084	1354	1648	2553	296	641	976	1059	408	1542	1440	1108	901	363	608	54

QUESTIONNAIRE FORM 3 1978	TOTAL	SEX		RACE		REGION				4YR COLLEGE PLANS		ILLICIT DRUG USE: LIFETIME				
		M	F	White	Black	NE	NC	S	W	Yes	No	None	Mari-juana Only	Few Pills	More Pills	Any Her-oin
Weighted No. of Cases:	3778	1711	1917	2973	417	926	1080	1257	516	1758	1748	1313	1078	451	764	68
% of Weighted Total:	100.0	45.3	50.7	78.7	11.0	24.5	28.6	33.3	13.7	46.5	46.3	34.8	28.5	11.9	20.2	1.8

E11D: A new car every two or three years

	TOTAL	M	F	White	Black	NE	NC	S	W	Yes	No	None	Mari-juana Only	Few Pills	More Pills	Any Her-oin
1. Not important	66.8	59.1	73.8	66.6	70.1	70.1	63.8	65.1	73.0	67.9	66.3	71.5	66.9	64.5	61.0	54.0
2. Somewhat important	21.4	24.4	18.6	22.4	12.6	17.3	23.8	22.1	20.3	20.8	21.7	19.7	20.8	22.3	24.8	20.0
3. Quite important	6.9	9.7	4.6	6.5	7.8	7.9	8.0	6.6	3.5	6.9	7.0	5.4	7.5	7.2	7.4	24.0
4. Extremely important	4.9	6.9	3.0	4.4	9.5	4.6	4.3	6.3	3.2	4.4	5.0	3.4	4.8	6.1	6.7	4.0
Item 13860 N(Wtd)	3070	1353	1636	2539	294	646	974	1047	403	1545	1426	1100	898	363	608	50

E11E: Clothes in the latest style

	TOTAL	M	F	White	Black	NE	NC	S	W	Yes	No	None	Mari-juana Only	Few Pills	More Pills	Any Her-oin
1. Not important	14.3	19.5	10.2	14.5	10.2	14.7	13.7	13.1	18.2	14.0	14.2	16.7	12.4	13.7	11.7	32.7
2. Somewhat important	38.2	36.9	39.9	40.1	27.2	38.7	39.8	37.1	36.5	38.2	38.9	38.8	38.5	37.2	40.2	21.2
3. Quite important	29.9	29.2	29.8	30.1	25.9	29.1	31.9	28.4	30.5	31.1	28.4	29.0	32.4	28.7	28.4	34.6
4. Extremely important	17.6	14.5	20.1	15.3	36.7	17.6	14.6	21.4	14.8	16.6	18.5	15.6	16.8	20.5	19.6	13.5
Item 13870 N(Wtd)	3093	1356	1655	2556	294	652	979	1056	406	1546	1448	1104	905	366	617	52

E11F: A house of my own (instead of an apartment or condominium)

	TOTAL	M	F	White	Black	NE	NC	S	W	Yes	No	None	Mari-juana Only	Few Pills	More Pills	Any Her-oin
1. Not important	17.6	12.7	21.5	17.8	12.8	19.2	18.1	16.7	16.1	17.7	17.4	17.4	16.3	22.5	16.4	25.0
2. Somewhat important	23.6	21.3	25.5	24.8	18.5	23.3	25.2	23.1	22.0	25.1	22.1	24.0	24.4	25.2	22.4	11.5
3. Quite important	27.4	30.7	25.0	28.3	19.9	25.6	29.9	25.1	30.0	27.3	27.6	28.2	28.8	27.1	23.5	28.8
4. Extremely important	31.4	35.5	28.0	29.0	48.8	31.7	26.9	35.1	32.2	29.8	32.9	30.3	30.5	25.2	37.7	36.5
Item 13880 N(Wtd)	3108	1367	1659	1568	297	652	986	1060	410	1555	1451	112	909	369	616	52

E11G: Lots of space around my house, a big yard

	TOTAL	M	F	White	Black	NE	NC	S	W	Yes	No	None	Mari-juana Only	Few Pills	More Pills	Any Her-oin
1. Not important	13.6	10.4	16.1	12.3	20.7	13.4	12.8	13.8	15.2	12.2	15.0	12.5	13.2	19.6	11.9	17.3
2. Somewhat important	26.4	26.2	26.4	26.5	26.2	23.6	26.8	28.0	25.7	27.1	25.4	26.2	27.7	25.6	25.5	38.5
3. Quite important	30.2	32.6	28.6	31.8	20.7	27.4	33.8	27.8	31.9	31.6	29.0	31.3	30.9	26.2	30.2	15.4
4. Extremely important	29.9	30.9	28.9	29.5	32.3	35.6	26.7	30.4	27.2	29.2	30.5	30.1	28.2	28.9	32.4	30.8
Item 13890 N(Wtd)	3101	1364	1655	2563	294	649	983	1060	408	1553	1446	1112	903	367	615	52

E11H: A well-kept garden and lawn

	TOTAL	M	F	White	Black	NE	NC	S	W	Yes	No	None	Mari-juana Only	Few Pills	More Pills	Any Her-oin
1. Not important	11.3	12.4	10.2	10.6	15.3	13.9	10.7	11.5	7.8	10.4	11.9	10.5	11.9	14.0	9.6	19.2
2. Somewhat important	29.0	29.3	29.2	29.9	21.1	29.9	28.7	27.9	30.9	28.2	30.3	25.9	29.5	32.0	32.0	28.8
3. Quite important	33.4	32.9	33.5	34.2	28.6	29.0	36.0	33.7	33.3	35.3	31.7	34.9	33.2	31.1	33.7	19.2
4. Extremely important	26.3	25.5	27.1	25.3	34.7	27.2	24.5	26.9	27.9	26.1	26.0	28.6	25.4	22.6	24.9	32.7
Item 13900 N(Wtd)	3090	1357	1651	2558	294	648	981	1054	408	1549	1440	1110	901	363	615	52

E11I: Major labor-saving appliances (washer, drier, dishwasher, etc.)

	TOTAL	M	F	White	Black	NE	NC	S	W	Yes	No	None	Mari-juana Only	Few Pills	More Pills	Any Her-oin
1. Not important	11.8	11.7	11.9	10.8	14.9	13.5	11.4	11.5	10.8	10.3	13.4	11.4	10.5	14.7	12.6	11.5
2. Somewhat important	32.2	32.5	31.7	33.7	25.3	31.4	34.8	30.1	32.7	32.7	31.6	32.1	33.3	32.7	32.4	34.6
3. Quite important	33.1	34.0	32.6	34.5	24.0	28.8	34.8	33.1	35.9	35.8	30.7	34.6	33.9	29.2	32.2	36.5
4. Extremely important	22.9	21.8	23.8	21.0	35.8	26.3	19.1	25.3	20.6	21.1	24.2	22.7	22.3	23.2	22.9	17.3
Item 13910 N(Wtd)	3086	1357	1648	2550	296	643	976	1059	407	1543	1441	1108	897	367	612	52

E11J: A high-quality stereo

	TOTAL	M	F	White	Black	NE	NC	S	W	Yes	No	None	Mari-juana Only	Few Pills	More Pills	Any Her-oin
1. Not important	17.1	11.8	21.2	15.9	24.7	16.9	16.5	19.0	14.0	15.7	18.5	23.1	14.5	15.3	11.3	17.3
2. Somewhat important	30.2	26.7	33.8	31.4	21.9	27.8	31.7	28.5	34.9	32.2	29.0	35.1	31.1	30.6	22.4	9.6
3. Quite important	27.4	29.1	25.8	28.6	25.3	24.8	29.9	28.2	23.6	29.2	25.5	25.1	30.1	27.3	28.0	25.0
4. Extremely important	25.2	32.3	19.1	24.1	27.7	30.4	21.9	24.3	27.5	22.9	27.1	16.6	24.2	27.0	38.5	48.1
Item 13920 N(Wtd)	3079	1352	1647	2547	292	644	972	1057	407	1540	1440	1106	897	366	611	52

E11K: A vacation house

	TOTAL	M	F	White	Black	NE	NC	S	W	Yes	No	None	Mari-juana Only	Few Pills	More Pills	Any Her-oin
1. Not important	63.1	54.2	70.0	63.7	62.2	58.2	65.8	62.9	64.7	61.5	65.3	67.4	62.0	64.2	57.6	56.9
2. Somewhat important	23.4	29.0	19.3	24.4	16.2	23.7	23.8	23.0	23.0	24.8	21.8	21.7	25.4	21.1	24.7	25.5
3. Quite important	7.6	9.7	5.8	7.0	12.8	9.0	6.3	8.4	6.2	7.9	7.2	6.1	8.1	7.3	9.2	9.8
4. Extremely important	5.9	7.2	4.9	4.9	8.8	9.0	4.0	5.7	5.9	5.7	5.6	4.9	4.6	7.0	8.5	9.8
Item 13930 N(Wtd)	3078	1347	1649	2543	296	641	978	1054	405	1541	1439	1101	898	369	611	51

QUESTIONNAIRE FORM 3 1978	TOTAL	SEX		RACE		REGION				4YR COLLEGE PLANS		ILLICIT DRUG USE: LIFETIME				
		M	F	White	Black	NE	NC	S	W	Yes	No	None	Mari-juana Only	Few Pills	More Pills	Any Her-oin
Weighted No. of Cases:	3778	1711	1917	2973	417	926	1080	1257	516	1758	1748	1313	1078	451	764	68
% of Weighted Total:	100.0	45.3	50.7	78.7	11.0	24.5	28.6	33.3	13.7	46.5	46.3	34.8	28.5	11.9	20.2	1.8

E11L: A motor-powered, recreational vehicle (powerboat, snowmobile)

	TOTAL	M	F	White	Black	NE	NC	S	W	Yes	No	None	Mar	Few	More	Any
1. Not important	58.1	43.9	70.0	56.9	72.2	59.5	56.6	58.7	57.6	59.6	56.7	62.7	60.7	58.4	47.0	51.9
2. Somewhat important	23.7	29.0	19.1	25.0	12.2	20.6	25.9	22.9	25.5	25.0	22.7	22.5	21.6	26.0	28.5	15.4
3. Quite important	10.9	16.4	6.3	11.0	8.8	9.7	12.1	11.1	9.3	10.0	11.8	8.9	10.9	9.3	14.4	17.3
4. Extremely important	7.4	10.6	4.6	7.1	6.8	10.4	5.4	7.2	7.6	5.4	8.8	6.0	7.0	6.6	10.0	17.3
Item 13940 N(Wtd)	3083	1354	1649	2551	295	642	978	1055	408	1543	1442	1107	900	365	613	52

E12: When (if ever) did you FIRST do each of the following things? Don't count anything you took because a doctor told you to.

E12A: Smoke cigarettes on a daily basis

	TOTAL	M	F	White	Black	NE	NC	S	W	Yes	No	None	Mar	Few	More	Any
8. Never	57.1	60.5	54.6	56.9	58.4	53.4	54.0	58.1	68.3	67.7	46.3	85.8	51.4	45.2	26.9	11.5
1. Grade 6 or below	5.7	7.2	4.5	5.7	4.6	6.4	6.5	4.6	5.3	3.9	7.8	1.4	5.3	6.7	11.1	21.2
2. Grade 7 or 8	12.1	10.6	13.2	12.6	6.9	15.7	11.9	11.0	9.5	9.8	14.5	3.7	12.3	13.6	24.5	17.3
3. Grade 9 (Freshman)	8.7	7.7	9.3	8.6	8.8	9.8	8.9	9.2	4.8	6.3	11.1	2.0	10.5	12.1	14.9	15.4
4. Grade 10 (Sophomore)	7.4	5.8	8.6	7.4	8.8	6.7	9.7	6.6	4.2	4.8	9.7	2.6	8.2	10.9	11.5	15.4
5. Grade 11 (Junior)	5.3	5.0	5.5	5.7	5.0	5.1	5.6	5.8	3.9	4.6	5.9	1.9	7.3	5.8	8.1	7.7
6. Grade 12 (Senior)	3.8	3.2	4.4	3.2	8.0	3.0	3.4	4.7	3.9	2.9	4.8	2.6	5.0	5.8	2.7	9.6
Item 5570 N(Wtd)	2814	1227	1510	2335	262	594	909	954	357	1423	1301	999	807	330	583	52

E12B: Try an alcoholic beverage - more than just a few sips

	TOTAL	M	F	White	Black	NE	NC	S	W	Yes	No	None	Mar	Few	More	Any
8. Never	8.0	7.3	8.4	7.0	15.0	5.2	5.9	10.6	11.1	7.5	8.3	21.0	.9	3.1	.5	-
1. Grade 6 or below	9.2	12.5	6.5	8.6	12.6	10.8	10.6	6.6	10.0	7.9	10.5	6.5	7.4	10.5	14.5	13.2
2. Grade 7 or 8	20.7	22.7	18.7	21.7	10.1	25.8	22.0	15.4	22.7	21.4	20.3	10.4	21.8	23.6	32.5	32.1
3. Grade 9 (Freshman)	24.3	26.2	22.7	25.0	15.4	25.3	22.8	25.4	23.8	23.7	24.8	16.1	29.2	25.9	27.8	41.5
4. Grade 10 (Sophomore)	18.4	16.5	19.8	19.5	14.6	16.9	19.4	19.4	15.2	20.1	16.1	16.0	22.5	21.4	16.0	7.5
5. Grade 11 (Junior)	12.6	9.8	15.2	12.5	16.6	9.9	14.0	13.9	10.2	13.0	12.6	17.8	13.3	11.4	5.9	-
6. Grade 12 (Senior)	6.9	5.0	8.7	5.7	15.4	5.9	5.4	8.7	6.9	6.4	7.4	12.3	4.8	4.0	2.9	5.7
Item 5580 N(Wtd)	2832	1260	1495	2375	247	593	905	973	361	1420	1319	927	866	351	594	53

E12C: Try marijuana or hashish

	TOTAL	M	F	White	Black	NE	NC	S	W	Yes	No	None	Mar	Few	More	Any
8. Never	42.4	36.4	47.7	41.7	50.0	34.1	42.1	47.1	43.9	45.2	39.5	100.0	.2	26.1	9.1	-
1. Grade 6 or below	1.7	2.8	.7	1.3	2.3	1.8	1.5	.9	3.6	.8	2.6	-	1.1	2.6	4.4	10.2
2. Grade 7 or 8	10.8	13.0	9.0	11.3	3.8	16.0	9.9	7.9	12.5	10.1	11.7	-	10.1	11.1	29.8	36.7
3. Grade 9 (Freshman)	13.4	14.1	12.5	13.1	14.6	16.5	14.3	11.2	11.9	12.1	14.3	-	18.7	17.3	26.4	34.7
4. Grade 10 (Sophomore)	14.5	15.5	13.4	15.1	9.2	14.7	15.7	14.9	10.4	14.0	14.9	-	26.4	22.6	19.2	14.3
5. Grade 11 (Junior)	10.8	11.1	10.5	11.2	11.9	10.2	10.7	11.1	10.9	11.1	10.7	-	27.2	12.6	7.6	-
6. Grade 12 (Senior)	6.4	7.0	6.2	6.2	8.5	6.6	5.9	6.9	6.8	6.8	6.3	-	16.3	7.6	3.5	6.1
Item 5590 N(Wtd)	2931	1277	1575	2450	260	618	922	1006	385	1493	1341	1080	830	341	594	49

E12D: Try LSD

	TOTAL	M	F	White	Black	NE	NC	S	W	Yes	No	None	Mar	Few	More	Any
8. Never	92.5	90.4	94.1	92.4	97.8	89.9	91.5	95.8	89.7	93.3	91.7	100.0	100.0	93.7	68.9	26.7
1. Grade 6 or below	.2	.5	-	.1	-	-	.3	.1	.8	.1	.4	-	-	.3	.6	6.7
2. Grade 7 or 8	.8	1.1	.6	.9	-	1.1	.6	.4	2.1	.9	.9	-	-	3.9	6.7
3. Grade 9 (Freshman)	2.0	2.0	1.9	1.8	1.1	3.1	2.1	.6	3.1	1.5	2.4	-	-	1.4	7.6	24.4
4. Grade 10 (Sophomore)	1.6	1.9	1.5	1.7	1.1	1.8	2.1	.8	2.6	1.0	2.1	-	-	.6	7.4	13.3
5. Grade 11 (Junior)	1.8	2.4	1.3	1.9	-	2.5	2.3	1.1	1.8	2.0	1.4	-	-	1.7	7.6	13.3
6. Grade 12 (Senior)	1.1	1.7	.6	1.2	-	1.6	1.0	1.4	-	1.3	1.1	-	-	2.0	4.1	8.9
Item 5600 N(Wtd)	2957	1297	1584	2452	278	611	931	1026	390	1512	1347	1096	885	348	543	45

E12E: Try any psychedelic other than LSD

	TOTAL	M	F	White	Black	NE	NC	S	W	Yes	No	None	Mar	Few	More	Any
8. Never	93.3	91.7	94.7	93.2	97.8	91.3	92.0	96.1	92.1	93.6	93.1	100.0	100.0	96.6	68.8	29.3
1. Grade 6 or below	.1	.2	-	*	-	-	.1	.1	.3	.1	.2	-	-	-	.4	2.4
2. Grade 7 or 8	.7	.9	.5	.8	-	1.0	.9	.1	1.3	.5	.9	-	-	.3	3.9	2.4
3. Grade 9 (Freshman)	1.7	2.3	1.3	1.5	1.8	2.4	2.1	.8	2.4	1.5	1.8	-	-	.3	7.3	31.7
4. Grade 10 (Sophomore)	1.8	2.2	1.6	2.0	.4	2.4	2.3	1.2	1.8	1.4	2.3	-	-	.6	9.2	14.6
5. Grade 11 (Junior)	1.6	2.1	1.2	1.8	-	1.9	2.0	1.1	1.6	1.8	1.4	-	-	.9	8.0	9.8
6. Grade 12 (Senior)	.7	.7	.7	.7	-	.9	.7	.8	.5	1.1	.3	-	-	1.5	2.4	9.8
Item 5610 N(Wtd)	2887	1259	1547	2394	279	587	908	1013	379	1472	1320	1097	890	327	490	41

* = less than .05 per cent.

QUESTIONNAIRE FORM 3 1978	TOTAL	SEX		RACE		REGION				4YR COLLEGE PLANS		ILLICIT DRUG USE: LIFETIME				
		M	F	White	Black	NE	NC	S	W	Yes	No	None	Mari-juana Only	Few Pills	More Pills	Any Her-oin
Weighted No. of Cases:	3778	1711	1917	2973	417	926	1080	1257	516	1758	1748	1313	1078	451	764	68
% of Weighted Total:	100.0	45.3	50.7	78.7	11.0	24.5	28.6	33.3	13.7	46.5	46.3	34.8	28.5	11.9	20.2	1.8

E12F: Try amphetamines

	TOTAL	M	F	White	Black	NE	NC	S	W	Yes	No	None	Mari-juana Only	Few Pills	More Pills	Any Her-oin
8. Never	86.0	86.0	85.6	85.2	96.7	84.1	83.9	90.0	83.1	88.3	83.7	100.0	100.0	85.2	28.7	10.3
1. Grade 6 or below	.1	.2	-	.1	-	.2	.1	.1	-	.1	.1	-	-	-	.2	2.6
2. Grade 7 or 8	1.3	1.4	1.2	1.3	-	1.7	.9	.9	2.2	.8	1.9	-	-	.4	6.6	12.8
3. Grade 9 (Freshman)	3.4	3.2	3.6	3.5	1.8	3.5	4.0	2.1	5.6	2.6	4.1	-	-	1.6	16.7	43.6
4. Grade 10 (Sophomore)	3.8	3.3	4.3	4.2	.7	5.2	3.5	3.0	4.5	2.8	4.9	-	-	2.3	21.5	12.8
5. Grade 11 (Junior)	3.4	3.9	3.2	3.6	1.1	4.2	4.5	2.2	2.8	3.4	3.4	-	-	4.3	18.3	5.1
6. Grade 12 (Senior)	2.0	1.9	2.1	2.2	-	1.0	3.1	1.7	1.7	1.9	2.0	-	-	6.3	7.9	10.3
Item 5620 N(Wtd)	2762	1232	1453	2278	276	572	875	959	356	1424	1249	1094	888	256	442	39

E12G: Try quaaludes

	TOTAL	M	F	White	Black	NE	NC	S	W	Yes	No	None	Mari-juana Only	Few Pills	More Pills	Any Her-oin
8. Never	94.4	93.2	95.3	94.4	98.6	93.7	95.7	93.9	93.6	95.2	93.9	100.0	100.0	97.9	76.1	34.1
1. Grade 6 or below	-	-	-	-	-	-	-	-	-	-	-	-	-	-	-	-
2. Grade 7 or 8	.5	.5	.4	.5	-	.5	.3	.6	.5	.3	.8	-	-	-	2.2	7.3
3. Grade 9 (Freshman)	1.5	1.5	1.6	1.3	1.4	1.3	1.3	1.8	1.8	1.3	1.5	-	-	.6	5.3	34.1
4. Grade 10 (Sophomore)	1.5	2.2	.9	1.6	-	2.0	1.3	1.5	1.0	1.1	1.8	-	-	.3	6.9	12.2
5. Grade 11 (Junior)	1.4	1.6	1.2	1.4	-	1.5	1.0	1.4	2.0	1.1	1.5	-	-	.6	6.4	4.9
6. Grade 12 (Senior)	.8	1.2	.5	.7	-	1.3	.2	.9	1.0	1.0	.5	-	-	.9	3.1	7.3
Item 5630 N(Wtd)	2961	1290	1591	2450	283	615	932	1023	391	1505	1365	1098	892	340	547	41

E12H: Try barbiturates

	TOTAL	M	F	White	Black	NE	NC	S	W	Yes	No	None	Mari-juana Only	Few Pills	More Pills	Any Her-oin
8. Never	91.8	91.0	92.3	91.6	97.8	90.3	91.5	93.1	92.0	92.2	91.7	100.0	100.0	94.9	61.6	20.9
1. Grade 6 or below	.2	.2	.1	*	.4	.2	.1	.1	.5	.1	.2	-	-	1.0	.2	2.3
2. Grade 7 or 8	1.1	1.2	1.0	1.1	-	1.3	.8	.8	1.9	.7	1.5	-	-	.6	5.0	9.3
3. Grade 9 (Freshman)	2.2	2.2	2.2	2.2	.4	2.2	2.1	1.9	3.2	2.1	2.3	-	-	.6	10.0	30.2
4. Grade 10 (Sophomore)	2.1	2.2	2.1	2.2	1.8	3.4	2.2	1.5	1.3	1.6	2.3	-	-	.3	10.8	18.6
5. Grade 11 (Junior)	1.7	2.2	1.4	1.9	-	1.8	2.4	1.4	.5	2.2	1.2	-	-	1.3	8.9	7.0
6. Grade 12 (Senior)	.9	1.0	.9	1.0	-	.8	.9	1.0	.5	1.2	.6	-	-	1.0	3.5	11.6
Item 5640 N(Wtd)	2865	1253	1537	2362	279	597	904	989	374	1463	1306	1094	891	314	482	43

E12I: Try tranquilizers

	TOTAL	M	F	White	Black	NE	NC	S	W	Yes	No	None	Mari-juana Only	Few Pills	More Pills	Any Her-oin
8. Never	90.9	91.3	90.5	90.6	97.4	88.2	90.8	92.5	91.4	91.2	90.9	100.0	100.0	87.9	56.0	34.1
1. Grade 6 or below	.3	.3	.3	.3	-	.3	.6	.1	.3	.4	.2	-	-	-	1.8	-
2. Grade 7 or 8	1.1	.7	1.4	1.1	.4	1.6	1.1	.6	1.2	.8	1.4	-	-	1.6	5.3	4.9
3. Grade 9 (Freshman)	2.7	1.7	3.4	2.9	-	3.5	1.9	2.3	4.0	2.4	2.6	-	-	2.7	12.4	31.7
4. Grade 10 (Sophomore)	2.4	2.8	2.2	2.3	1.9	3.5	2.7	1.9	1.4	1.9	2.8	-	-	1.9	12.6	14.6
5. Grade 11 (Junior)	1.8	2.2	1.6	2.1	.4	2.1	1.9	1.9	1.4	2.3	1.5	-	-	3.5	8.9	7.3
6. Grade 12 (Senior)	.8	.8	.8	.8	-	.9	1.0	.6	.6	1.1	.6	-	-	2.3	2.8	7.3
Item 5650 N(Wtd)	2758	1219	1468	2274	270	574	894	943	347	1414	1254	1090	891	257	436	41

E12J: Try cocaine

	TOTAL	M	F	White	Black	NE	NC	S	W	Yes	No	None	Mari-juana Only	Few Pills	More Pills	Any Her-oin
8. Never	90.1	86.8	92.6	90.3	93.8	85.2	90.7	93.0	89.3	90.8	89.9	100.0	100.0	90.4	60.1	21.3
1. Grade 6 or below	.1	.1	-	.2	-	-	-	-	.3	-	.1	-	-	.3	-	2.1
2. Grade 7 or 8	.3	.5	.1	.2	-	.5	.3	.1	.3	.2	.4	-	-	-	1.1	4.3
3. Grade 9 (Freshman)	1.5	2.3	.9	1.6	-	2.6	1.4	.7	2.0	1.4	1.6	-	-	1.5	5.4	21.3
4. Grade 10 (Sophomore)	2.2	2.6	2.0	2.0	2.2	2.7	2.7	1.3	2.3	1.6	2.4	-	-	.3	9.9	17.0
5. Grade 11 (Junior)	3.4	4.3	2.6	3.4	1.8	5.0	2.6	3.0	3.8	3.0	3.8	-	-	4.0	13.5	25.5
6. Grade 12 (Senior)	2.4	3.5	1.7	2.4	1.8	4.0	2.2	2.0	2.0	3.0	1.9	-	-	3.4	9.9	8.5
Item 5660 N(Wtd)	2952	1285	1589	2454	274	620	928	1013	391	1507	1351	1097	890	323	554	47

E12K: Try heroin

	TOTAL	M	F	White	Black	NE	NC	S	W	Yes	No	None	Mari-juana Only	Few Pills	More Pills	Any Her-oin
8. Never	98.8	98.6	99.0	99.1	98.9	98.4	98.8	99.1	98.2	98.9	99.1	100.0	100.0	100.0	100.0	-
1. Grade 6 or below	*	.1	-	-	-	-	-	-	.3	-	.1	-	-	-	-	2.9
2. Grade 7 or 8	.1	.3	-	.1	-	-	.2	-	.5	.1	.1	-	-	-	-	11.4
3. Grade 9 (Freshman)	.2	.2	.2	.2	-	.6	.2	-	.3	.2	.4	-	-	-	-	20.0
4. Grade 10 (Sophomore)	.2	.2	.2	.1	1.1	.2	.6	-	-	.1	.1	-	-	-	-	20.0
5. Grade 11 (Junior)	.3	.4	.2	.3	-	.6	-	.3	.5	.4	.2	-	-	-	-	25.7
6. Grade 12 (Senior)	.2	.2	.2	.1	-	.2	-	.6	-	.4	-	-	-	-	-	20.0
Item 5670 N(Wtd)	3000	1319	1604	2483	284	628	949	1029	395	1520	1385	1096	889	351	586	35

= less than .05 per cent.

QUESTIONNAIRE FORM 3 1978	TOTAL	SEX		RACE		REGION				4YR COLLEGE PLANS		ILLICIT DRUG USE: LIFETIME				
		M	F	White	Black	NE	NC	S	W	Yes	No	None	Mari-juana Only	Few Pills	More Pills	Any Her-oin
Weighted No. of Cases:	3778	1711	1917	2973	417	926	1080	1257	516	1758	1748	1313	1078	451	764	68
% of Weighted Total:	100.0	45.3	50.7	78.7	11.0	24.5	28.6	33.3	13.7	46.5	46.3	34.8	28.5	11.9	20.2	1.8
E12L: Try any narcotic other than heroin																
8. Never	95.9	95.5	96.2	96.2	98.5	94.0	95.2	97.9	95.4	96.9	95.1	100.0	100.0	97.5	81.0	19.2
1. Grade 6 or below	.1	.1	-	-	-	-	.1	-	.3	.1	.1	-	-	.3	.2	3.8
2. Grade 7 or 8	.4	.6	.4	.5	-	.7	.6	.2	.3	.3	.5	-	-	.3	2.0	7.7
3. Grade 9 (Freshman)	1.0	1.2	.9	.9	-	1.4	1.2	.3	1.9	.8	1.3	-	-	-	4.8	26.9
4. Grade 10 (Sophomore)	1.3	1.3	1.4	1.2	1.5	1.4	1.8	.9	1.4	.8	1.8	-	-	.6	5.9	34.6
5. Grade 11 (Junior)	.8	1.1	.5	.7	-	1.7	.7	.4	.5	.5	1.0	-	-	1.0	4.1	-
6. Grade 12 (Senior)	.4	.3	.5	.5	-	.9	.3	.4	.3	.5	.4	-	-	.6	2.0	3.8
Item 5680 N(Wtd)	2824	1231	1518	2331	273	584	893	980	367	1439	1294	1096	887	314	459	26
E12M: Try inhalants																
8. Never	92.2	90.6	93.7	91.8	96.7	90.4	91.5	94.2	91.6	93.9	90.7	99.4	97.2	89.8	74.5	48.8
1. Grade 6 or below	1.1	2.0	.5	1.2	-	1.2	1.7	.5	1.6	.8	1.6	.4	.4	.3	4.2	4.7
2. Grade 7 or 8	2.0	2.3	1.6	2.1	1.1	1.3	2.5	1.8	1.8	1.8	2.2	.1	1.1	2.4	5.5	20.9
3. Grade 9 (Freshman)	1.8	1.8	1.7	1.9	.4	2.7	1.6	1.3	2.6	1.4	2.4	.1	.7	2.1	6.6	9.3
4. Grade 10 (Sophomore)	1.1	1.2	1.0	1.0	1.1	1.5	1.4	.7	.8	.6	1.4	-	.2	.9	4.2	11.6
5. Grade 11 (Junior)	1.1	1.2	1.0	1.2	.4	1.7	.9	1.1	.8	.9	1.3	-	.2	2.4	3.8	4.7
6. Grade 12 (Senior)	.7	.9	.5	.7	.4	1.3	.4	.3	1.0	.8	.4	-	.4	2.1	1.5	2.3
Item 5685 N(Wtd)	2867	1242	1545	2381	269	594	902	990	381	1464	1311	1075	846	332	529	43

QUESTIONNAIRE FORM 4 1978	TOTAL	SEX		RACE		REGION				4YR COLLEGE PLANS		ILLICIT DRUG USE: LIFETIME				
		M	F	White	Black	NE	NC	S	W	Yes	No	None	Mari- juana Only	Few Pills	More Pills	Any Her- oin
Weighted No. of Cases:	3783	1747	1877	2997	411	917	1079	1254	533	1771	1689	1343	1032	467	788	49
% of Weighted Total:	100.0	46.2	49.6	79.2	10.9	24.2	28.5	33.1	14.1	46.8	44.6	35.5	27.3	12.3	20.8	1.3

A01: Taking all things together, how would you say things are these days-would you say you're very happy, pretty happy, or not too happy these days?

	TOTAL	M	F	White	Black	NE	NC	S	W	Yes	No	None	Mari-juana Only	Few Pills	More Pills	Any Heroin
3. Very happy	17.0	15.2	19.0	18.6	10.3	14.5	16.7	17.9	19.5	20.7	13.9	21.0	14.9	15.4	14.3	18.4
2. Pretty happy	70.9	73.5	68.9	71.9	66.0	71.4	73.4	69.1	69.0	69.0	74.3	68.4	74.1	70.2	72.9	71.4
1. Not too happy	12.1	11.3	12.2	9.5	23.7	14.1	9.8	12.9	11.5	10.4	11.9	10.6	10.9	14.3	12.9	10.2
Item 1190 N(Wtd)	3775	1742	1875	2994	409	917	1077	1252	529	1767	1687	1340	1032	467	785	49

A02: Looking ahead to the next five years, do you think that things in this country will get better or worse?

	TOTAL	M	F	White	Black	NE	NC	S	W	Yes	No	None	Mari-juana Only	Few Pills	More Pills	Any Heroin
1. Get much better	2.1	2.1	2.0	1.5	4.9	1.5	2.0	2.5	2.6	1.8	2.2	2.6	1.7	2.4	1.3	4.1
2. Get somewhat better	27.6	30.5	24.2	26.3	36.1	29.4	26.5	27.0	28.0	29.6	25.7	28.0	29.9	21.3	26.5	26.5
3. Stay about the same	26.1	27.1	25.7	28.0	14.9	28.9	26.3	24.4	25.0	27.9	25.1	26.4	29.0	23.2	24.7	24.5
4. Get somewhat worse	37.9	34.7	41.4	38.8	35.6	34.7	40.1	38.0	38.9	35.6	40.5	36.7	34.3	46.9	40.5	36.7
5. Get much worse	6.2	5.6	6.7	5.3	8.8	5.5	4.9	8.1	5.5	5.2	6.6	6.4	5.0	6.5	7.1	8.2
Item 9940 N(Wtd)	3774	1746	1871	2991	410	913	1075	1254	532	1765	1688	1342	1030	465	786	49

A03: Looking ahead to the next five years, do you think that things in the rest of the world will get better or worse?

	TOTAL	M	F	White	Black	NE	NC	S	W	Yes	No	None	Mari-juana Only	Few Pills	More Pills	Any Heroin
1. Get much better	1.8	1.9	1.3	1.2	4.7	1.9	1.2	1.8	2.8	1.6	1.7	2.2	1.4	2.1	1.3	2.1
2. Get somewhat better	20.5	21.2	19.9	19.6	27.2	21.9	19.4	20.3	21.3	22.6	18.8	21.6	21.9	17.8	19.4	16.7
3. Stay about the same	27.4	26.9	28.0	28.5	23.0	29.9	28.9	25.5	24.3	27.5	27.5	26.6	27.7	24.5	30.6	22.9
4. Get somewhat worse	42.5	42.7	42.6	43.6	36.5	38.9	44.0	43.6	42.9	41.3	44.0	41.5	42.2	46.8	41.4	47.9
5. Get much worse	7.8	7.4	8.2	7.1	8.4	7.3	6.4	8.9	8.7	7.0	8.2	8.1	6.8	8.8	7.4	10.4
Item 9950 N(Wtd)	3767	1745	1866	2990	405	912	1075	1249	531	1763	1685	1340	1028	466	785	48

A04: How do you think your own life will go in the next five years-- do you think it will get better or worse?

	TOTAL	M	F	White	Black	NE	NC	S	W	Yes	No	None	Mari-juana Only	Few Pills	More Pills	Any Heroin
1. Get much better	39.7	36.3	42.2	37.9	50.0	41.7	36.5	40.0	41.8	40.3	38.2	35.9	40.7	39.2	44.1	44.7
2. Get somewhat better	48.8	51.8	46.6	50.3	41.5	46.9	52.0	48.2	46.7	49.0	49.4	50.9	49.2	49.7	45.5	46.8
3. Stay about the same	9.5	10.3	8.9	10.1	4.9	9.6	9.6	9.8	8.9	9.4	10.0	11.0	8.3	9.0	8.9	4.3
4. Get somewhat worse	1.7	1.0	2.2	1.5	2.4	1.2	1.7	1.8	2.3	1.2	2.1	1.9	1.4	1.9	1.3	2.1
5. Get much worse	.3	.6	.1	.2	1.2	.7	.3	.2	.2	.2	.4	.1	.6	.6	.1	2.1
Item 9960 N(Wtd)	3770	1739	1875	2989	410	914	1078	1248	531	1765	1686	1337	1030	467	786	47

A05: Some people think a lot about the social problems of the nation and the world, and about how they might be solved. Others spend little time thinking about these issues. How much do you think about such things?

	TOTAL	M	F	White	Black	NE	NC	S	W	Yes	No	None	Mari-juana Only	Few Pills	More Pills	Any Heroin
1. Never	2.1	2.8	1.6	2.3	1.0	4.0	1.3	1.5	1.7	.8	3.4	1.4	1.8	2.8	3.1	4.1
2. Seldom	17.9	18.9	17.3	18.0	16.9	18.6	17.5	16.9	20.2	13.1	22.1	17.1	19.2	15.5	18.6	26.5
3. Sometimes	50.0	49.7	50.1	51.2	43.6	49.2	54.6	47.8	46.9	49.3	51.6	50.7	50.4	51.7	49.2	36.7
4. Quite often	24.5	23.2	25.8	23.7	30.1	23.5	22.2	27.2	24.5	29.1	20.2	25.0	23.3	26.4	23.2	22.4
5. A great deal	5.5	5.4	5.3	4.7	8.6	4.6	4.5	6.5	6.6	7.7	2.7	5.7	5.1	3.6	6.0	8.2
Item 6880 N(Wtd)	3774	1745	1874	2994	408	915	1077	1252	531	1768	1687	1343	1029	466	785	49

A06: These questions are about pollution and the environment. Please mark the circle that shows how much you agree or disagree with each statement below.

A06A: In general, pollution has increased in the U.S. in the last ten years

	TOTAL	M	F	White	Black	NE	NC	S	W	Yes	No	None	Mari-juana Only	Few Pills	More Pills	Any Heroin
1. Disagree	3.9	4.6	3.1	3.3	7.3	4.6	2.8	4.5	3.4	3.5	4.0	3.1	5.1	3.4	3.7	2.0
2. Mostly disagree	6.6	8.1	5.3	6.8	6.1	5.7	7.6	5.3	8.8	7.3	6.2	6.9	6.0	6.7	6.5	10.2
3. Neither	3.8	4.4	3.0	3.8	2.4	3.5	4.3	3.8	3.8	4.4	3.2	3.3	4.1	3.4	4.2	12.2
4. Mostly agree	27.7	26.0	29.2	28.3	24.1	26.8	31.1	25.8	26.5	26.9	28.8	28.6	27.0	27.1	27.8	20.4
5. Agree	58.0	56.7	59.4	57.8	60.0	59.4	54.1	60.4	57.6	58.0	57.8	58.2	57.9	59.1	57.8	55.1
Item 9970 N(Wtd)	3771	1743	1872	2990	410	911	1073	1254	533	1767	1683	1343	1028	465	785	49

QUESTIONNAIRE FORM 4 1978	TOTAL	SEX		RACE		REGION				4YR COLLEGE PLANS		ILLICIT DRUG USE: LIFETIME				
		M	F	White	Black	NE	NC	S	W	Yes	No	None	Marijuana Only	Few Pills	More Pills	Any Heroin
Weighted No. of Cases:	3783	1747	1877	2997	411	917	1079	1254	533	1771	1689	1343	1032	467	788	49
% of Weighted Total:	100.0	46.2	49.6	79.2	10.9	24.2	28.5	33.1	14.1	46.8	44.6	35.5	27.3	12.3	20.8	1.3

A06B: The dangers of pollution are not really as great as government, the media, and environmental groups would like us to believe

1. Disagree	43.5	42.0	45.0	44.4	39.3	50.1	41.4	41.9	39.9	48.0	39.8	43.3	45.8	41.6	42.9	41.7
2. Mostly disagree	24.7	24.3	25.6	26.3	15.0	22.5	29.5	21.3	27.3	27.9	22.4	23.6	25.9	24.5	25.6	27.1
3. Neither	8.5	9.4	7.5	8.0	10.6	7.8	8.0	9.3	8.9	6.6	9.6	7.9	8.7	8.0	8.9	12.5
4. Mostly agree	15.4	16.4	14.3	14.6	20.9	13.1	14.4	18.5	14.3	11.5	19.3	17.7	12.6	15.8	15.1	10.4
5. Agree	7.9	8.0	7.6	6.7	14.3	6.5	6.9	8.8	9.8	6.0	9.0	7.6	7.0	10.0	7.5	6.3
Item 9980 N(Wtd)	3754	1739	1861	2977	407	907	1069	1247	531	1764	1672	1337	1025	461	784	48

A06C: America needs growth to survive, and that is going to require some increase in pollution

1. Disagree	35.5	35.6	35.6	35.7	32.8	35.2	35.5	36.3	34.3	36.5	34.1	36.3	36.6	32.4	35.6	29.2
2. Mostly disagree	24.2	24.5	23.9	26.2	13.8	26.8	24.2	23.0	22.5	28.0	21.6	25.2	25.7	26.8	19.5	25.0
3. Neither	9.7	9.4	10.3	10.2	8.1	9.1	12.1	7.3	11.3	9.3	9.6	9.3	8.3	9.1	11.7	18.8
4. Mostly agree	16.9	16.9	16.9	17.1	17.3	15.5	16.2	18.3	17.5	15.8	17.9	14.9	15.8	19.9	20.1	16.7
5. Agree	13.7	13.6	13.3	10.8	28.1	13.6	12.0	15.2	14.2	10.4	16.7	14.4	13.7	11.9	13.1	10.4
Item 9990 N(Wtd)	3740	1738	1853	2967	405	904	1069	1237	530	1757	1673	1332	1023	463	776	48

A06D: People will have to change their buying habits and way of life to correct our environmental problems

1. Disagree	9.9	11.3	8.3	8.3	16.3	9.4	7.9	12.2	9.2	7.5	11.4	8.9	10.1	8.6	10.7	12.5
2. Mostly disagree	10.5	11.7	9.2	10.9	9.9	10.1	10.2	11.6	9.4	9.2	11.6	10.7	10.6	9.7	10.6	12.5
3. Neither	10.0	10.6	9.0	10.4	8.4	9.1	10.3	9.3	12.4	8.7	11.4	8.9	10.0	11.6	10.2	16.7
4. Mostly agree	32.7	31.7	34.6	34.7	23.9	31.9	36.9	30.9	29.9	34.9	32.0	33.0	33.7	31.6	33.2	25.0
5. Agree	36.9	34.7	39.0	35.6	41.9	39.4	34.7	36.0	39.1	39.7	33.8	38.6	35.6	38.5	35.3	31.3
Item 10000 N(Wtd)	3745	1730	1861	2969	406	903	1070	1241	532	1755	1674	1333	1015	465	782	48

A06E: Government should take action to solve our environmental problems even if it means that some of the products we now use would have to be changed or banned

1. Disagree	4.9	5.5	4.3	3.9	10.3	3.9	4.5	6.0	4.9	3.2	5.8	5.5	5.4	5.0	2.9	6.3
2. Mostly disagree	5.5	7.0	4.0	5.1	7.4	4.5	5.9	5.9	5.3	4.8	5.5	5.4	5.4	5.6	4.9	10.4
3. Neither	8.4	10.2	6.5	8.3	6.6	6.8	10.1	7.6	9.5	6.1	10.1	8.9	7.5	7.1	9.1	6.3
4. Mostly agree	30.3	29.9	31.1	31.6	23.8	28.2	32.1	30.3	30.2	31.6	30.6	32.2	28.2	29.2	30.5	29.2
5. Agree	50.9	47.5	54.1	51.0	52.0	56.7	47.5	50.2	49.9	54.3	47.8	48.1	53.6	53.0	52.6	45.8
Item 10010 N(Wtd)	3754	1738	1864	2979	408	907	1071	1246	529	1760	1679	1338	1026	462	781	48

A06F: Government should place higher taxes on products which cause pollution in their manufacture or disposal, so that companies will be encouraged to find better ways to produce them

1. Disagree	14.6	15.0	13.4	13.1	21.0	13.2	15.8	14.4	15.1	12.4	16.0	14.0	14.6	14.5	15.0	12.5
2. Mostly disagree	10.6	11.4	9.6	10.9	9.4	10.0	11.7	11.2	7.8	9.7	11.4	10.8	11.4	10.0	9.1	12.5
3. Neither	11.1	10.2	12.4	11.8	7.4	10.8	13.2	9.4	11.7	10.3	12.2	9.9	10.9	11.7	13.1	10.4
4. Mostly agree	26.9	27.6	26.6	27.3	23.5	26.1	28.1	25.5	29.5	28.8	25.5	27.6	26.8	27.3	25.6	29.2
5. Agree	36.8	35.8	38.0	36.9	38.8	39.9	31.2	39.6	35.9	38.9	34.8	37.7	36.3	36.6	37.3	33.3
Item 10020 N(Wtd)	3753	1741	1859	2978	405	909	1069	1245	529	1760	1677	1338	1024	462	781	48

A06G: I wish that government would ban throwaway bottles and beverage cans

1. Disagree	18.2	16.6	19.8	17.0	24.6	16.3	16.4	20.5	19.5	15.6	20.2	19.1	18.7	15.1	17.4	17.0
2. Mostly disagree	11.1	10.1	11.6	11.2	11.4	10.0	11.0	12.7	9.5	11.1	11.2	11.8	11.6	10.5	9.3	6.4
3. Neither	18.5	16.9	20.3	18.6	18.7	19.2	19.9	17.7	16.7	19.8	17.8	17.0	18.7	20.6	19.8	29.8
4. Mostly agree	19.4	19.4	19.7	20.7	11.7	21.9	20.5	15.6	21.6	19.9	19.3	19.1	20.7	20.0	17.7	14.9
5. Agree	32.8	37.0	28.6	32.5	33.3	32.5	32.1	33.5	32.6	33.6	31.4	33.1	30.3	33.5	36.0	29.8
Item 10030 N(Wtd)	3737	1738	1847	2964	402	907	1068	1235	528	1754	1672	1327	1023	465	776	47

QUESTIONNAIRE FORM 4 1978	TOTAL	SEX		RACE		REGION				4YR COLLEGE PLANS		ILLICIT DRUG USE: LIFETIME				
		M	F	White	Black	NE	NC	S	W	Yes	No	None	Mari- juana Only	Few Pills	More Pills	Any Her- oin
Weighted No. of Cases:	3783	1747	1877	2997	411	917	1079	1254	533	1771	1689	1343	1032	467	788	49
% of Weighted Total:	100.0	46.2	49.6	79.2	10.9	24.2	28.5	33.1	14.1	46.8	44.6	35.5	27.3	12.3	20.8	1.3
A06H: T.V. commercials stimulate people to buy a lot of things they don't really need																
1. Disagree	4.6	5.0	4.1	4.0	8.8	4.0	4.8	5.2	4.2	3.9	4.9	4.3	4.8	4.5	4.5	10.4
2. Mostly disagree	5.8	6.6	4.9	5.8	5.4	5.2	5.6	6.9	4.7	5.9	5.8	5.2	5.9	5.8	6.3	4.2
3. Neither	5.5	7.4	3.9	5.7	3.9	4.5	6.2	5.6	5.7	6.4	4.5	6.0	5.7	4.3	5.3	8.3
4. Mostly agree	26.2	30.1	22.7	27.3	23.6	24.0	27.8	25.4	28.7	25.5	27.1	26.7	25.8	28.4	26.1	29.2
5. Agree	57.8	50.9	64.4	57.1	58.5	62.3	55.7	56.8	56.9	58.3	57.7	57.8	57.9	56.9	57.9	47.9
Item 10040 N(Wtd)	3753	1732	1867	2975	407	910	1070	1243	529	1760	1677	1337	1024	464	779	48
A06I: T.V. commercials do a lot of good by showing new products that we might not know about otherwise																
1. Disagree	8.9	9.8	8.1	9.2	7.4	10.2	7.1	7.9	13.0	9.8	7.5	8.7	7.9	9.3	10.1	14.6
2. Mostly disagree	12.3	11.7	13.1	13.4	5.9	14.3	12.0	11.1	12.4	14.0	10.9	13.0	12.1	13.2	11.7	4.2
3. Neither	15.7	15.7	16.2	16.8	7.1	16.4	18.3	12.0	18.0	18.2	13.7	14.3	18.3	14.7	16.9	10.4
4. Mostly agree	33.2	32.1	34.6	35.1	24.6	34.1	34.7	32.8	29.5	33.3	34.4	33.9	33.2	31.2	34.1	37.5
5. Agree	29.9	30.8	28.0	25.5	55.0	25.0	28.0	36.2	27.1	24.9	33.5	31.1	28.5	31.6	27.2	31.3
Item 10050 N(Wtd)	3749	1728	1868	2972	407	903	1067	1248	532	1756	1679	1340	1020	462	779	48
A06J: My family and I often buy things we don't really need; we could get along with much less																
1. Disagree	12.7	13.6	11.3	10.3	24.4	13.6	10.3	13.7	13.5	10.3	13.7	11.4	11.6	14.5	13.7	12.5
2. Mostly disagree	12.2	13.3	11.4	12.3	14.9	13.6	12.3	10.8	13.5	12.6	11.4	12.0	12.2	11.3	12.9	20.8
3. Neither	10.2	12.6	7.8	9.8	9.5	10.0	10.9	7.9	14.3	11.0	9.5	9.6	10.7	7.4	11.3	16.7
4. Mostly agree	30.0	29.8	30.2	32.2	19.3	31.1	32.8	28.5	26.3	32.6	28.9	30.1	31.4	31.0	29.0	25.0
5. Agree	34.9	30.6	39.2	35.3	31.7	31.9	33.8	39.3	32.3	33.5	36.5	36.9	33.9	35.7	33.1	25.0
Item 10060 N(Wtd)	3753	1733	1868	2973	410	907	1069	1244	533	1760	1677	1337	1024	462	782	48
A06K: By the year 2000, engineers and scientists will probably have invented devices that will solve our pollution problems																
1. Disagree	11.1	12.7	9.5	11.3	9.3	10.0	12.1	10.6	12.2	11.2	11.1	10.2	11.8	9.9	12.2	10.4
2. Mostly disagree	17.1	16.6	17.6	17.6	14.2	18.3	17.1	16.1	16.8	17.9	16.5	16.6	16.2	17.0	18.9	16.7
3. Neither	23.3	23.6	23.4	24.6	15.9	22.9	23.6	21.5	27.3	23.3	22.8	24.1	21.3	22.6	25.6	22.9
4. Mostly agree	31.6	29.7	33.3	32.2	29.3	31.3	33.9	31.1	28.6	33.1	31.5	31.5	33.8	30.1	29.2	39.6
5. Agree	17.0	17.4	16.3	14.3	31.3	17.4	13.3	20.6	15.1	14.5	18.0	17.4	16.8	20.4	13.9	8.3
Item 10070 N(Wtd)	3759	1737	1867	2979	409	908	1070	1249	531	1761	1681	1341	1022	465	784	48
A07: In your own actions--the things you buy and the things you do-- how much of an effort do you make to conserve energy and protect the environment?																
1. None	5.1	5.8	4.4	4.6	6.6	6.9	4.7	4.5	4.0	4.2	5.8	3.7	5.4	4.5	7.6	8.5
2. A little	24.0	24.7	23.9	23.7	27.4	26.2	22.9	25.4	19.6	23.5	24.4	22.2	26.0	25.0	24.9	23.4
3. Some	56.9	56.3	57.4	58.1	51.6	53.4	60.9	55.2	58.9	58.4	56.1	58.2	56.8	55.2	55.8	51.1
4. Quite a bit	14.0	13.2	14.3	13.5	14.5	13.7	11.5	14.9	17.6	13.8	13.7	15.8	11.9	15.5	11.7	17.0
Item 10080 N(Wtd)	3606	1655	1823	2890	380	878	1036	1191	501	1699	1624	1300	985	444	746	47

The next questions are about work.

A08: Different people may look for different things in their work. Below is a list of some of these things. Please read each one, then indicate how important this thing is for you.

QUESTIONNAIRE FORM 4 1978	TOTAL	SEX		RACE		REGION				4YR COLLEGE PLANS		ILLICIT DRUG USE: LIFETIME				
		M	F	White	Black	NE	NC	S	W	Yes	No	None	Mari- juana Only	Few Pills	More Pills	Any Her- oin
Weighted No. of Cases:	3783	1747	1877	2997	411	917	1079	1254	533	1771	1689	1343	1032	467	788	49
% of Weighted Total:	100.0	46.2	49.6	79.2	10.9	24.2	28.5	33.1	14.1	46.8	44.6	35.5	27.3	12.3	20.8	1.3

A08A: A job where you can see the results of what you do

1. Not important	.9	.8	.8	.8	1.2	.9	.6	.8	1.5	.7	.9	.7	.7	.9	1.0	2.1
2. A little important	5.8	6.6	5.2	5.7	4.9	5.9	6.3	4.9	7.0	5.2	5.8	6.1	5.8	4.8	5.0	10.6
3. Pretty important	32.7	35.0	30.9	34.4	22.4	33.0	36.5	28.9	33.4	33.0	33.6	31.8	32.9	36.3	31.8	42.6
4. Very important	60.6	57.6	63.2	59.1	71.3	60.3	56.7	65.4	58.1	61.1	59.6	61.3	60.7	58.1	62.2	42.6
Item 10090 N(Wtd)	3753	1738	1860	2977	407	914	1069	1243	527	1757	1680	1335	1025	463	783	47

A08B: A job that has high status and prestige

1. Not important	11.5	9.8	13.5	12.6	3.5	13.8	11.3	9.7	12.4	11.8	11.5	12.2	9.6	12.3	12.6	12.8
2. A little important	28.6	28.0	29.6	30.8	17.4	27.8	32.6	23.7	33.2	28.7	28.8	28.6	29.4	27.4	28.6	36.2
3. Pretty important	35.5	38.0	33.5	35.6	37.0	34.7	34.5	37.4	34.5	36.6	34.8	36.9	35.7	36.1	33.9	27.7
4. Very important	24.4	24.3	23.4	21.1	42.2	23.8	21.6	29.1	19.7	22.9	24.9	22.3	25.3	24.0	25.0	23.4
Item 10100 N(Wtd)	3733	1727	1854	2964	403	907	1063	1239	524	1750	1672	1329	1021	463	776	47

A08C: A job which is interesting to do

1. Not important	.4	.6	.3	.2	1.5	.4	.4	.6	.4	.1	.5	.2	.4	.9	.5	-
2. A little important	1.0	1.4	.5	.8	1.5	.9	1.0	.9	1.1	.7	.9	1.1	.8	.7	.9	2.1
3. Pretty important	9.5	10.6	8.5	9.2	10.7	8.7	11.5	7.9	10.7	8.0	10.5	10.3	7.7	8.9	10.9	6.4
4. Very important	89.1	87.4	90.8	89.9	86.0	90.0	87.1	90.6	87.8	91.2	88.1	88.4	91.1	89.8	87.8	91.5
Item 10110 N(Wtd)	3728	1721	1854	2960	401	904	1061	1237	525	1745	1670	1330	1015	459	778	47

A08D: A job where the chances for advancement and promotion are good

1. Not important	1.4	1.6	1.2	1.4	.5	1.8	1.7	1.0	1.0	1.3	1.3	1.7	1.2	1.3	.6	6.4
2. A little important	8.3	7.0	9.5	8.6	6.4	8.9	9.3	6.8	8.6	9.2	6.9	9.6	8.2	8.4	6.1	6.4
3. Pretty important	27.6	24.7	30.8	28.1	20.2	28.6	30.5	23.1	30.8	28.5	27.1	29.3	26.3	30.5	26.3	14.9
4. Very important	62.7	66.7	58.5	61.8	72.8	60.8	58.4	69.1	59.7	60.9	64.8	59.4	64.3	59.7	66.9	70.2
Item 10120 N(Wtd)	3748	1735	1858	2974	405	913	1067	1243	526	1757	1677	1334	1023	462	782	47

A08E: A job that gives you an opportunity to be directly helpful to others

1. Not important	2.8	4.0	1.6	2.8	1.7	3.5	3.4	1.4	3.8	2.9	2.4	2.0	3.2	1.5	4.2	2.1
2. A little important	13.1	18.3	8.0	13.9	6.9	12.2	15.7	9.5	17.8	11.7	14.1	9.9	15.1	12.1	16.1	21.3
3. Pretty important	34.6	41.2	28.8	35.6	27.5	31.6	37.0	34.5	34.8	34.2	35.8	33.7	32.4	33.9	38.8	42.6
4. Very important	49.5	36.4	61.7	47.7	63.9	52.8	43.9	54.5	43.6	51.1	47.7	54.3	49.3	52.3	41.0	31.9
Item 10130 N(Wtd)	3749	1734	1859	2972	407	911	1067	1243	528	1756	1677	1333	1025	463	781	47

A08F: A job which provides you with a chance to earn a good deal of money

1. Not important	1.9	1.8	1.9	2.0	.2	2.9	1.8	1.1	2.5	2.7	1.0	2.0	2.7	.9	1.3	2.1
2. A little important	9.8	7.4	12.3	10.5	6.4	10.4	10.3	9.0	9.6	13.2	6.1	12.6	7.8	9.7	8.1	8.5
3. Pretty important	38.0	35.1	41.4	40.6	24.5	37.3	39.6	35.2	42.3	41.5	36.3	41.5	39.3	39.3	32.8	19.1
4. Very important	50.3	55.7	44.3	46.8	68.9	49.5	48.3	54.7	45.7	42.7	56.6	43.9	50.2	50.1	57.9	72.3
Item 10140 N(Wtd)	3745	1732	1858	2968	408	911	1067	1243	523	1756	1674	1333	1022	463	780	47

A08G: A job where you have the chance to be creative

1. Not important	5.2	5.5	5.0	5.3	5.4	5.4	5.6	4.7	5.5	4.3	6.2	4.7	3.9	6.3	6.5	6.4
2. A little important	21.7	24.6	19.4	21.8	21.7	19.3	24.9	19.9	23.7	21.2	21.4	22.0	21.5	22.2	20.9	17.0
3. Pretty important	35.7	36.0	35.5	36.2	34.6	35.5	36.4	36.4	32.8	34.9	37.7	37.9	35.4	32.6	34.1	40.4
4. Very important	37.4	33.9	40.1	36.7	38.5	39.9	33.2	39.0	37.9	39.8	34.6	35.3	39.3	38.7	38.5	34.0
Item 10150 N(Wtd)	3744	1733	1857	2970	405	910	1062	1244	528	1753	1677	1330	1023	463	781	47

QUESTIONNAIRE FORM 4 1978	TOTAL	SEX		RACE		REGION				4YR COLLEGE PLANS		ILLICIT DRUG USE: LIFETIME				
		M	F	White	Black	NE	NC	S	W	Yes	No	None	Mari-juana Only	Few Pills	More Pills	Any Her-oin
Weighted No. of Cases:	3783	1747	1877	2997	411	917	1079	1254	533	1771	1689	1343	1032	467	788	49
% of Weighted Total:	100.0	46.2	49.6	79.2	10.9	24.2	28.5	33.1	14.1	46.8	44.6	35.5	27.3	12.3	20.8	1.3

A08H: A job where the skills you learn will not go out of date

1. Not important	4.4	4.1	4.6	4.1	4.9	5.1	4.7	3.5	5.0	5.0	3.5	4.7	4.2	2.6	4.3	4.3
2. A little important	12.6	11.3	13.4	13.1	8.9	12.9	14.0	11.0	12.6	14.9	10.1	13.6	12.4	12.8	10.4	14.9
3. Pretty important	30.9	29.6	32.5	32.4	21.7	31.5	36.0	26.0	31.0	31.1	31.8	31.0	30.1	30.0	34.5	19.1
4. Very important	52.2	54.9	49.5	50.4	64.5	50.6	45.4	59.4	51.4	49.0	54.7	50.7	53.3	54.6	50.8	63.8
Item 10160 N(Wtd)	3741	1731	1857	2968	406	909	1068	1240	525	1750	1677	1331	1024	460	782	47

A08I: A job that gives you a chance to make friends

1. Not important	2.1	2.5	1.7	1.5	5.4	3.0	1.3	2.3	2.3	1.8	1.9	2.0	2.3	1.9	2.3	2.1
2. A little important	10.5	12.5	8.2	9.4	15.5	9.2	12.2	9.0	12.5	9.8	10.2	9.8	10.0	10.8	11.0	8.5
3. Pretty important	33.1	38.0	28.8	33.6	28.3	34.7	32.1	30.3	38.9	32.4	34.7	31.7	33.4	33.0	34.4	46.8
4. Very important	54.2	47.1	61.3	55.5	50.7	53.1	54.4	58.4	46.1	56.0	53.2	56.5	54.4	54.0	52.2	42.6
Item 10170 N(Wtd)	3742	1731	1857	2969	406	909	1063	1243	527	1756	1673	1332	1021	463	781	47

A08J: A job which uses your skills and abilities--lets you do the things you can do best

1. Not important	.7	.9	.4	.5	2.2	.2	.6	1.0	.8	.3	.8	.5	.8	.9	.8	2.1
2. A little important	3.2	3.7	2.4	2.5	5.7	3.3	3.6	2.5	4.2	2.7	3.0	3.1	2.1	4.1	3.8	2.1
3. Pretty important	24.6	26.7	23.2	25.3	18.7	25.5	26.9	21.8	25.2	22.9	26.3	23.4	24.3	26.5	25.8	27.7
4. Very important	71.4	68.7	74.0	71.8	73.7	70.9	69.0	74.6	69.6	74.0	69.8	73.1	72.9	68.3	69.5	68.1
Item 10180 N(Wtd)	3746	1735	1859	2974	407	912	1068	1244	523	1757	1676	1333	1022	464	783	47

A08K: A job that is worthwhile to society

1. Not important	3.4	4.6	2.4	3.4	2.8	4.5	3.0	3.2	3.1	2.9	4.0	3.0	3.0	4.1	4.6	6.5
2. A little important	14.3	17.4	11.2	14.9	9.5	14.8	16.8	10.8	16.0	12.3	16.2	11.5	13.0	14.7	19.3	19.6
3. Pretty important	38.9	41.6	36.5	39.5	32.6	37.3	40.7	36.9	42.6	37.1	40.9	38.4	39.4	40.1	39.5	30.4
4. Very important	43.4	36.3	49.9	42.3	55.1	43.2	39.5	49.1	38.4	47.7	38.9	47.1	44.6	40.9	36.7	43.5
Item 10190 N(Wtd)	3719	1722	1847	2955	399	905	1064	1226	524	1741	1669	1321	1012	464	779	46

A08L: A job where you have more than two weeks vacation

1. Not important	23.5	18.4	28.9	24.3	20.1	23.9	23.3	24.0	22.4	25.2	23.0	26.1	22.9	23.8	20.3	18.8
2. A little important	35.6	35.1	35.8	36.3	31.9	33.1	40.6	34.4	32.4	35.4	35.8	36.5	37.5	35.2	32.3	29.2
3. Pretty important	24.7	26.1	23.3	23.9	28.0	24.0	23.5	25.5	26.8	23.6	25.9	23.5	24.8	24.8	27.0	31.3
4. Very important	16.2	20.4	12.0	15.4	19.7	18.9	12.8	16.1	18.4	15.7	15.3	13.9	14.9	16.0	20.3	20.8
Item 10200 N(Wtd)	3743	1732	1857	2967	407	908	1065	1242	527	1755	1675	1332	1022	463	777	48

A08M: A job where you get a chance to participate in decision making

1. Not important	5.1	4.3	5.9	5.1	5.2	5.9	5.9	4.1	4.5	3.6	6.6	4.8	4.7	5.6	6.3	2.1
2. A little important	23.6	22.2	25.1	24.1	18.9	24.0	26.1	20.7	24.6	20.5	26.8	25.2	21.2	26.0	23.0	14.9
3. Pretty important	44.0	43.6	44.1	45.2	41.0	45.3	43.6	45.3	39.4	44.8	43.7	42.2	45.3	43.6	45.2	51.1
4. Very important	27.3	29.9	24.9	25.6	34.9	24.9	24.3	29.9	31.3	31.2	22.9	27.8	28.9	24.7	25.5	29.8
Item 10210 N(Wtd)	3747	1733	1859	2970	407	910	1067	1242	528	1755	1676	1335	1025	461	779	47

A08N: A job which leaves a lot of time for other things in your life

1. Not important	2.3	2.1	2.5	2.0	3.9	3.6	1.6	2.3	1.7	2.7	1.9	2.9	1.8	2.4	2.2	2.1
2. A little important	17.5	13.3	21.4	17.7	19.7	18.8	17.4	17.2	16.1	19.7	15.7	19.6	16.4	15.8	16.6	19.1
3. Pretty important	39.1	37.8	40.5	40.7	32.7	36.4	42.1	37.7	40.8	38.8	40.3	40.8	40.1	37.7	36.0	36.2
4. Very important	41.0	46.8	35.6	39.7	43.7	41.2	38.8	42.8	41.2	38.8	42.2	36.7	41.8	44.0	45.2	42.6
Item 10220 N(Wtd)	3737	1732	1853	2964	407	911	1067	1238	522	1750	1674	1332	1020	461	777	47

QUESTIONNAIRE FORM 4 1978	TOTAL	SEX		RACE		REGION				4YR COLLEGE PLANS		ILLICIT DRUG USE: LIFETIME				
		M	F	White	Black	NE	NC	S	W	Yes	No	None	Mari-juana Only	Few Pills	More Pills	Any Her-oin
Weighted No. of Cases:	3783	1747	1877	2997	411	917	1079	1254	533	1771	1689	1343	1032	467	788	49
% of Weighted Total:	100.0	46.2	49.6	79.2	10.9	24.2	28.5	33.1	14.1	46.8	44.6	35.5	27.3	12.3	20.8	1.3

A08O: A job which allows you to establish roots in a community and not have to move from place to place

	TOTAL	M	F	White	Black	NE	NC	S	W	Yes	No	None	Mari-juana Only	Few Pills	More Pills	Any Her-oin
1. Not important	9.7	8.7	10.5	9.6	8.9	12.5	8.3	8.4	10.8	11.1	8.0	7.5	9.4	10.4	13.4	19.1
2. A little important	18.0	16.6	19.5	18.5	16.0	18.5	18.7	17.5	17.3	21.1	14.9	16.9	17.7	19.7	19.1	23.4
3. Pretty important	33.0	33.6	32.6	33.7	34.7	35.3	35.1	29.9	32.1	35.0	31.5	31.8	35.3	33.9	32.9	25.5
4. Very important	39.2	41.1	37.3	38.3	40.4	33.7	37.8	44.2	39.8	32.8	45.6	43.8	37.6	36.1	34.6	31.9
Item 10230 N(Wtd)	3747	1736	1858	2974	406	910	1067	1243	527	1755	1678	1334	1023	463	781	47

A08P: A job which leaves you mostly free of supervision by others

	TOTAL	M	F	White	Black	NE	NC	S	W	Yes	No	None	Mari-juana Only	Few Pills	More Pills	Any Her-oin
1. Not important	8.6	7.6	9.5	8.2	12.3	7.3	7.8	10.1	9.3	9.3	7.7	10.1	7.8	8.2	7.4	4.3
2. A little important	25.2	21.9	28.7	25.5	23.5	23.0	27.5	24.2	26.5	26.3	24.3	26.7	24.6	28.7	22.3	17.0
3. Pretty important	39.5	39.5	39.4	40.2	35.5	39.6	39.7	39.1	39.6	39.2	40.2	39.9	39.8	37.1	39.4	48.9
4. Very important	26.7	31.0	22.4	26.1	28.7	30.3	25.0	26.6	24.6	25.2	27.7	23.1	27.8	25.9	30.7	29.8
Item 10240 N(Wtd)	3749	1735	1859	2971	408	909	1068	1244	528	1756	1678	1335	1023	464	781	47

A08Q: A job that offers a reasonably predictable, secure future

	TOTAL	M	F	White	Black	NE	NC	S	W	Yes	No	None	Mari-juana Only	Few Pills	More Pills	Any Her-oin
1. Not important	1.2	1.7	.6	.8	1.7	1.8	.8	1.0	1.3	1.3	.8	.8	1.1	1.1	1.7	4.3
2. A little important	5.9	4.4	7.2	5.9	5.9	6.2	6.0	5.6	6.1	6.7	4.4	5.6	5.6	5.0	6.2	12.8
3. Pretty important	29.0	28.5	29.8	30.7	19.1	30.6	31.4	24.5	32.5	30.7	28.7	29.8	26.1	30.2	30.7	27.7
4. Very important	63.8	65.5	62.4	62.6	73.5	61.6	61.7	68.9	60.2	61.4	66.1	63.8	67.5	63.8	61.6	55.3
Item 10250 N(Wtd)	3739	1732	1856	2965	408	909	1065	1242	523	1752	1675	1333	1020	461	779	47

A08R: A job where you can learn new things, learn new skills

	TOTAL	M	F	White	Black	NE	NC	S	W	Yes	No	None	Mari-juana Only	Few Pills	More Pills	Any Her-oin
1. Not important	1.5	1.5	1.5	1.7	.5	2.0	1.4	1.3	1.3	1.8	1.3	1.4	1.4	.9	1.9	-
2. A little important	10.9	12.8	9.4	12.0	5.4	11.3	13.0	8.5	11.3	12.0	10.1	11.5	11.1	10.4	10.1	12.8
3. Pretty important	40.4	43.5	37.9	42.4	29.9	39.2	43.5	37.4	43.6	42.0	39.7	40.3	37.7	44.7	42.8	42.6
4. Very important	47.2	42.3	51.3	44.0	64.2	47.5	42.2	52.9	43.8	44.2	48.9	46.8	49.8	44.0	45.1	44.7
Item 10260 N(Wtd)	3739	1731	1857	2966	408	908	1065	1243	523	1751	1675	1333	1020	461	780	47

A08S: A job where you do not have to pretend to be a type of person that you are not

	TOTAL	M	F	White	Black	NE	NC	S	W	Yes	No	None	Mari-juana Only	Few Pills	More Pills	Any Her-oin
1. Not important	4.8	6.5	2.8	4.2	4.7	5.8	4.9	3.7	5.4	3.7	4.7	4.3	4.5	5.9	4.9	4.2
2. A little important	4.3	5.9	2.7	4.1	5.2	2.9	5.2	4.8	3.6	4.2	4.1	3.5	4.9	3.3	5.0	8.3
3. Pretty important	17.3	23.8	10.9	17.7	15.0	18.3	19.2	14.8	17.6	15.7	18.9	18.2	16.4	16.9	16.9	16.7
4. Very important	73.7	63.8	83.6	74.0	75.4	73.0	70.9	76.7	73.4	76.5	72.2	73.9	74.1	74.0	73.2	70.8
Item 10270 N(Wtd)	3734	1729	1855	2965	406	906	1065	1241	522	1749	1675	1333	1017	461	780	48

A08T: A job that most people look up to and respect

	TOTAL	M	F	White	Black	NE	NC	S	W	Yes	No	None	Mari-juana Only	Few Pills	More Pills	Any Her-oin
1. Not important	5.8	6.8	4.8	5.8	4.7	7.6	5.5	4.4	6.9	4.7	6.3	4.5	6.3	5.4	7.9	6.4
2. A little important	19.4	19.5	19.6	20.5	13.6	20.0	22.0	16.1	20.7	20.1	19.3	18.6	20.5	21.6	18.5	14.9
3. Pretty important	38.1	40.3	36.4	39.9	29.5	39.1	39.4	35.8	39.8	38.5	38.6	39.6	37.6	35.7	39.2	36.2
4. Very important	36.6	33.3	39.2	33.9	52.2	33.2	33.2	43.7	32.7	36.7	35.8	37.4	35.6	37.3	34.4	42.6
Item 10280 N(Wtd)	3732	1728	1854	2965	404	906	1064	1239	523	1750	1672	1330	1019	459	780	47

A08U: A job that permits contact with a lot of people

	TOTAL	M	F	White	Black	NE	NC	S	W	Yes	No	None	Mari-juana Only	Few Pills	More Pills	Any Her-oin
1. Not important	7.4	9.0	5.8	7.3	9.2	6.9	8.3	6.8	7.9	6.6	7.8	6.7	8.2	8.1	7.3	8.7
2. A little important	22.4	27.8	17.0	22.5	23.8	19.6	24.0	21.8	25.1	20.0	23.9	21.7	23.4	21.4	22.2	28.3
3. Pretty important	37.3	38.2	36.9	37.2	35.4	39.2	36.1	37.7	36.0	35.9	39.9	37.1	37.1	38.1	38.8	32.6
4. Very important	32.9	25.0	40.3	33.1	31.7	34.5	31.6	33.7	31.0	37.5	28.4	34.4	31.5	32.5	31.6	32.6
Item 10290 N(Wtd)	3727	1725	1852	2960	404	904	1063	1238	522	1748	1670	1330	1017	459	778	46

QUESTIONNAIRE FORM 4 1978	TOTAL	SEX		RACE		REGION				4YR COLLEGE PLANS		ILLICIT DRUG USE: LIFETIME				
		M	F	White	Black	NE	NC	S	W	Yes	No	None	Mari- juana Only	Few Pills	More Pills	Any Her- oin
Weighted No. of Cases:	3783	1747	1877	2997	411	917	1079	1254	533	1771	1689	1343	1032	467	788	49
% of Weighted Total:	100.0	46.2	49.6	79.2	10.9	24.2	28.5	33.1	14.1	46.8	44.6	35.5	27.3	12.3	20.8	1.3
A08V: A job with an easy pace that lets you work slowly																
1. Not important	27.0	26.4	27.9	27.1	28.6	25.6	25.7	27.4	31.2	31.2	23.2	25.8	29.5	28.6	25.4	23.4
2. A little important	39.0	39.1	38.7	39.8	38.7	38.8	43.3	36.0	38.1	38.4	39.9	38.3	40.4	38.4	38.9	36.2
3. Pretty important	24.5	24.3	25.0	24.5	20.9	25.4	22.3	26.2	23.4	22.7	26.6	25.3	22.0	25.3	26.1	27.7
4. Very important	9.5	10.2	8.4	8.7	11.8	10.1	8.7	10.5	7.5	7.7	10.4	10.5	8.1	7.9	9.7	12.8
Item 10300 N(Wtd)	3729	1726	1852	2959	406	907	1064	1235	522	1746	1671	1332	1017	458	777	47
A08W: A job where most problems are quite difficult and challenging																
1. Not important	16.2	13.4	18.7	16.3	17.0	17.3	14.9	17.3	14.4	12.6	19.5	16.2	15.9	15.9	17.0	10.6
2. A little important	37.3	37.2	37.6	38.3	32.9	36.3	41.3	35.2	35.6	33.6	41.2	36.8	36.3	39.6	38.0	40.4
3. Pretty important	33.2	34.8	32.0	33.9	28.7	33.4	33.0	32.7	34.9	37.7	29.8	33.4	34.9	30.9	33.7	27.7
4. Very important	13.3	14.6	11.8	11.5	21.1	13.0	10.9	14.9	15.1	16.2	9.6	13.5	12.9	13.9	11.3	19.1
Item 10310 N(Wtd)	3731	1728	1854	2961	407	909	1059	1240	522	1752	1670	1330	1019	460	778	47
A09: What kind of work do you think you will be doing when you are 30 years old? Mark the one that comes closest to what you expect to be doing.																
01. Laborer (car washer, sanitary worker, farm laborer)	.4	.6	.2	.4	.6	.5	.7	.2	.4	.1	.8	.6	.4	.2	.1	-
02. Service worker (cook, waiter, barber, janitor, gas station attendant, practical nurse, beautician)	2.6	.8	4.4	2.6	2.8	3.0	3.0	1.7	3.0	.7	4.6	2.5	2.2	3.5	2.7	-
03. Operative or semi-skilled worker (garage worker, taxicab, bus or truck driver, assembly line worker, welder)	2.6	5.1	.2	2.4	2.5	2.2	3.3	2.5	2.2	.2	4.7	2.1	2.9	2.1	2.8	9.1
04. Sales clerk in a retail store (shoe salesperson, department store clerk, drug store clerk)	1.2	.6	1.8	1.2	2.2	.7	1.6	1.2	1.6	.5	1.8	1.2	.8	2.1	1.2	2.3
05. Clerical or office worker (bank teller, bookkeeper, secretary, typist, postal clerk or carrier, ticket agent)	11.3	1.8	19.9	10.7	16.6	9.0	11.3	13.4	10.1	5.3	17.7	12.7	8.6	13.6	10.7	9.1
06. Protective service (police officer, fireman, detective)	2.6	3.9	1.2	2.6	2.2	3.5	2.0	2.4	3.0	2.2	2.8	2.4	4.0	1.8	1.7	2.3
07. Military service	2.2	4.0	.6	1.9	5.2	1.4	1.9	3.0	2.6	1.6	2.9	2.2	2.5	1.2	2.0	6.8
08. Craftsman or skilled worker (carpenter, electrician, brick layer, mechanic, machinist, tool and die maker, telephone installer)	11.2	22.7	.5	10.7	11.0	10.2	13.0	10.5	10.7	2.4	18.9	7.9	13.3	11.1	14.3	9.1
09. Farm owner, farm manager	2.3	3.8	.8	2.5	.6	1.5	3.1	2.5	1.6	1.7	3.0	3.6	1.4	2.1	1.5	-
10. Owner of small business (restaurant owner, shop owner)	5.5	7.7	3.6	5.8	4.1	5.6	5.0	5.1	7.7	4.7	6.5	4.0	5.6	6.7	6.9	13.6
11. Sales representative (insurance agent, real estate broker, bond salesman)	1.8	2.5	1.1	2.0	.8	1.2	2.1	2.0	1.6	2.5	1.2	.9	2.0	2.3	2.8	2.3
12. Manager or administrator (office manager, sales manager, school administrator, government official)	5.8	6.6	5.2	5.7	7.2	5.6	6.2	6.1	5.1	8.8	3.2	5.3	7.2	5.5	5.1	2.3
13. Professional without doctoral degree (registered nurse, librarian, engineer, architect, social worker, technician, accountant, actor, artist, musician)	28.8	23.0	34.1	29.7	28.2	31.9	27.5	29.0	25.9	43.1	14.9	31.1	28.8	25.8	27.9	15.9
14. Professional with doctoral degree or equivalent (lawyer, physician, dentist, scientist, college professor)	10.6	11.9	9.8	10.3	11.0	12.6	7.9	10.8	12.3	19.6	1.1	12.4	10.4	9.9	8.8	6.8
15. Full-time homemaker or housewife	5.1	-	10.1	5.5	1.4	5.2	5.9	4.1	5.9	2.0	8.7	5.8	4.7	5.3	3.7	11.4
16. Don't know-GO TO Q.A13	5.9	5.1	6.5	6.1	3.6	6.3	5.3	5.7	6.9	4.5	7.3	5.1	5.0	6.7	7.7	4.5
Item 10320 N(Wtd)	3517	1622	1769	2839	362	864	991	1167	495	1671	1579	1266	954	434	749	44

QUESTIONNAIRE FORM 4 1978	TOTAL	SEX		RACE		REGION				4YR COLLEGE PLANS		ILLICIT DRUG USE: LIFETIME				
		M	F	White	Black	NE	NC	S	W	Yes	No	None	Marijuana Only	Few Pills	More Pills	Any Heroin
Weighted No. of Cases:	3783	1747	1877	2997	411	917	1079	1254	533	1771	1689	1343	1032	467	788	49
% of Weighted Total:	100.0	46.2	49.6	79.2	10.9	24.2	28.5	33.1	14.1	46.8	44.6	35.5	27.3	12.3	20.8	1.3

A10: How likely do you think it is that you will actually get to do this kind of work?

1. Not very likely	1.5	1.7	1.0	1.2	3.1	1.0	1.7	1.9	1.1	.8	2.1	1.6	1.5	1.7	1.1	-
2. Somewhat likely	7.9	8.8	6.9	7.3	9.4	9.0	8.0	7.6	6.4	8.1	7.6	6.4	7.7	8.6	9.6	8.9
3. Fairly likely	23.6	25.2	22.6	23.4	23.8	23.1	22.7	24.1	25.6	24.5	22.1	21.7	25.9	24.5	25.4	11.1
4. Very likely	42.0	40.9	43.9	43.5	39.8	42.5	43.5	41.3	39.5	47.9	37.4	45.3	39.5	41.6	39.4	53.3
5. Certain	15.7	12.3	18.5	15.2	17.0	15.9	14.4	15.3	18.6	15.3	15.9	16.3	16.0	16.2	14.7	8.9
6. I already do this kind of work	9.2	11.1	7.2	9.2	6.5	8.6	9.6	9.8	8.3	3.4	15.0	8.7	9.3	7.8	9.8	15.6
Item 10330 N(Wtd) ★	3418	1591	1692	2708	382	824	983	1143	468	1634	1510	1227	942	421	696	45

A11: How certain are you that this kind of work is a good choice for you?

1. Not at all certain	3.5	3.1	3.9	3.5	3.1	2.6	3.9	3.8	3.6	3.4	3.2	4.0	3.0	4.2	2.5	4.4
2. Somewhat certain	8.6	9.3	7.7	8.2	11.0	8.8	9.1	8.9	6.5	8.7	7.6	7.7	9.0	9.9	8.0	6.7
3. Fairly certain	32.3	32.7	32.5	33.3	28.3	31.6	33.0	33.4	29.5	34.9	30.9	31.9	31.6	33.0	34.1	40.0
4. Very certain	37.9	36.9	38.6	38.2	34.9	36.4	38.9	36.8	41.3	36.7	39.9	39.0	38.3	35.8	38.1	24.4
5. Completely certain	17.7	17.9	17.3	16.8	22.6	20.6	15.2	17.1	18.9	16.2	18.3	17.5	18.2	17.2	17.2	26.7
Item 10340 N(Wtd) ★	3447	1608	1703	2734	381	833	992	1146	475	1640	1532	1232	949	424	709	45

A12: How satisfying do you think this kind of work will be for you?

1. Not very satisfying	.8	1.0	.4	.8	.5	1.1	.4	.8	1.1	.6	.9	.4	.8	.7	1.0	4.4
2. Somewhat satisfying	6.3	6.5	5.8	5.6	7.1	5.9	7.1	6.0	5.9	4.5	8.1	5.9	6.2	7.8	5.6	6.7
3. Quite satisfying	24.7	26.2	23.5	24.9	24.7	21.7	27.1	26.8	19.9	22.7	26.6	22.1	22.5	27.9	28.9	33.3
4. Very satisfying	40.1	41.2	39.4	41.1	35.4	41.3	41.6	37.6	41.2	39.4	41.5	42.3	42.6	33.8	37.7	37.8
5. Extremely satisfying	28.1	25.1	30.9	27.5	32.3	30.2	23.9	28.8	31.9	32.9	22.8	29.3	27.7	29.6	26.8	20.0
Item 10350 N(Wtd) ★	3436	1603	1697	2725	381	829	989	1144	473	1636	1525	1227	945	423	709	45

A13: To what extent do you think the things listed below will prevent you from getting the kind of work you would like to have?

A13A: Your religion

1. Not at all	90.9	90.5	91.7	92.1	85.9	91.1	91.9	90.3	89.8	92.2	90.2	89.9	91.6	90.7	92.5	92.9
2. Somewhat	4.5	5.1	3.9	4.5	5.5	5.6	3.4	4.5	4.8	4.5	4.5	4.5	4.3	4.9	4.4	2.4
3. A lot	1.1	1.1	1.2	.6	3.1	.8	.9	1.6	1.2	.8	1.3	1.5	.6	.9	1.2	2.4
8. Don't know	3.5	3.4	3.4	2.8	5.7	2.4	3.9	3.6	4.2	2.6	4.0	4.1	3.5	3.5	1.9	4.8
Item 10360 N(Wtd)	3602	1671	1788	2875	383	868	1034	1200	500	1702	1612	1288	982	451	751	42

A13B: Your sex

1. Not at all	77.9	86.7	70.2	78.1	75.2	76.9	75.5	81.2	77.2	77.0	78.8	78.0	78.8	79.4	77.3	71.4
2. Somewhat	16.0	8.6	22.8	16.8	13.3	18.0	17.6	12.7	17.4	17.7	14.8	16.7	15.4	14.2	16.6	16.7
3. A lot	4.0	3.1	4.5	3.4	7.8	3.9	4.6	4.0	2.8	3.6	4.2	3.7	3.8	4.4	3.7	4.8
8. Don't know	2.1	1.6	2.5	1.7	3.7	1.3	2.4	2.2	2.6	1.8	2.1	1.6	2.0	1.8	2.3	7.1
Item 10370 N(Wtd)	3605	1672	1788	2876	383	871	1035	1199	499	1703	1612	1288	981	452	753	42

A13C: Your race

1. Not at all	81.0	80.0	82.9	88.3	38.3	83.4	83.0	77.6	81.1	81.4	83.1	80.2	80.0	82.5	85.5	88.1
2. Somewhat	11.9	12.1	11.2	7.5	38.3	9.6	10.6	14.4	12.9	11.7	10.6	11.7	13.9	11.5	8.0	4.8
3. A lot	4.2	5.3	3.0	2.4	14.8	3.9	3.9	5.1	3.0	4.5	3.5	4.6	3.9	3.1	4.3	2.4
8. Don't know	2.9	2.6	2.9	1.7	8.9	3.0	2.6	2.9	3.0	2.4	2.7	3.5	2.2	2.9	2.3	4.8
Item 10380 N(Wtd)	3600	1673	1785	2872	384	869	1035	1197	498	1702	1611	1290	978	451	751	42

A13D: Your family background

1. Not at all	86.2	86.8	86.3	88.1	78.1	84.7	84.9	87.2	89.2	88.6	85.0	86.1	86.4	85.6	88.5	88.1
2. Somewhat	8.5	8.5	8.3	8.0	10.9	9.6	9.9	7.6	6.0	7.4	9.3	9.2	7.8	9.5	7.2	4.8
3. A lot	2.5	2.3	2.4	2.0	4.7	2.6	2.5	2.6	1.8	1.5	3.2	1.8	3.3	2.0	1.9	2.4
8. Don't know	2.8	2.4	2.9	1.9	6.0	3.0	2.7	2.5	3.0	2.5	2.5	3.0	2.4	3.1	2.4	7.1
Item 10390 N(Wtd)	3602	1673	1785	2873	384	871	1033	1199	499	1703	1610	1286	981	452	751	42

★=excludes respondents for whom question was inappropriate.

QUESTIONNAIRE FORM 4 1978	TOTAL	SEX		RACE		REGION				4YR COLLEGE PLANS		ILLICIT DRUG USE: LIFETIME				
		M	F	White	Black	NE	NC	S	W	Yes	No	None	Mari-juana Only	Few Pills	More Pills	Any Her-oin
Weighted No. of Cases:	3783	1747	1877	2997	411	917	1079	1254	533	1771	1689	1343	1032	467	788	49
% of Weighted Total:	100.0	46.2	49.6	79.2	10.9	24.2	28.5	33.1	14.1	46.8	44.6	35.5	27.3	12.3	20.8	1.3

A13E: Your political views

1. Not at all	81.1	82.2	81.3	83.6	68.6	81.6	82.3	79.3	82.0	82.7	80.9	81.0	82.1	81.5	81.5	78.6
2. Somewhat	10.0	10.6	8.9	8.9	14.0	11.1	9.5	9.6	10.2	9.1	10.4	9.9	9.7	9.5	10.5	9.5
3. A lot	1.8	2.0	1.5	1.4	3.4	1.4	1.6	2.6	1.4	1.8	1.7	1.4	1.7	2.0	1.3	4.8
8. Don't know	7.1	5.1	8.4	6.0	14.0	5.9	6.7	8.5	6.4	6.5	7.0	7.8	6.3	7.3	6.8	7.1
Item 10400 N(Wtd)	3602	1672	1787	2874	385	871	1033	1199	499	1701	1613	1286	979	454	750	42

A13F: Your education

1. Not at all	48.8	48.1	49.9	49.2	50.1	48.4	44.7	51.7	51.3	54.9	43.4	53.7	49.1	46.2	43.1	42.2
2. Somewhat	24.8	24.4	24.7	25.4	19.7	24.9	26.5	23.5	24.2	20.2	29.3	20.3	24.5	30.5	29.0	20.0
3. A lot	23.0	23.4	22.7	22.3	27.0	23.5	25.6	21.2	21.0	21.7	23.7	23.1	23.0	19.7	23.9	26.7
8. Don't know	3.4	4.0	2.7	3.1	3.1	3.1	3.3	3.6	3.6	3.3	3.6	2.9	3.4	3.3	4.0	11.1
Item 10410 N(Wtd)	3599	1672	1785	2872	385	867	1033	1199	499	1704	1606	1284	982	452	749	45

A13G: Lack of vocational training

1. Not at all	52.9	54.2	52.6	54.3	51.4	53.3	47.7	56.4	54.7	59.4	47.1	55.8	52.4	52.8	49.9	45.2
2. Somewhat	26.2	25.7	26.3	26.0	24.0	23.3	29.9	25.6	24.8	21.7	30.8	24.8	25.0	25.9	29.5	26.2
3. A lot	13.2	13.3	12.9	12.8	13.1	13.9	15.4	10.2	14.6	10.8	15.1	11.8	14.5	13.7	13.2	21.4
8. Don't know	7.7	6.8	8.1	6.9	11.2	9.4	7.1	7.8	6.0	8.1	7.0	7.6	8.1	7.8	7.4	7.1
Item 10420 N(Wtd)	3593	1669	1781	2864	383	868	1034	1192	499	1697	1607	1282	980	451	748	42

A13H: Lack of ability

1. Not at all	58.4	59.7	57.1	58.3	57.7	57.8	53.1	60.7	65.0	60.5	55.5	56.7	58.8	63.1	58.7	54.8
2. Somewhat	16.5	15.8	17.1	16.7	15.1	17.2	18.5	15.5	13.1	15.0	18.1	15.8	17.2	13.3	17.7	33.3
3. A lot	21.2	21.1	21.6	21.6	22.1	21.1	24.2	19.9	18.3	21.1	21.9	22.8	20.5	20.1	20.4	11.9
8. Don't know	3.9	3.4	4.2	3.4	5.5	3.9	4.3	3.8	3.6	3.4	4.6	4.7	3.5	3.5	3.1	2.4
Item 10430 N(Wtd)	3593	1671	1780	2865	385	867	1031	1197	497	1696	1610	1281	980	452	751	42

A13I: Not knowing the right people

1. Not at all	44.8	41.2	48.1	44.6	43.0	38.0	42.3	50.3	48.6	41.7	47.9	46.3	43.3	44.8	43.4	45.2
2. Somewhat	37.0	38.1	36.4	38.0	34.3	40.9	38.3	32.9	36.9	40.7	33.8	36.9	37.9	37.3	36.2	35.7
3. A lot	11.9	14.3	9.1	11.8	12.9	13.7	12.9	10.8	8.8	11.7	11.6	9.7	12.1	11.1	15.4	14.3
8. Don't know	6.4	6.4	6.3	5.6	9.8	7.5	6.5	6.0	5.6	5.9	6.7	7.0	6.8	6.9	4.9	7.1
Item 10440 N(Wtd)	3602	1678	1782	2871	388	871	1033	1200	498	1697	1616	1284	984	451	752	42

A13J: Not wanting to work hard

1. Not at all	62.3	59.9	64.0	62.0	62.8	62.0	58.7	62.6	69.0	62.4	61.5	62.0	61.9	62.6	62.9	55.8
2. Somewhat	10.7	12.1	9.6	10.5	12.5	11.2	11.4	10.4	9.5	11.1	10.2	9.9	10.3	11.6	12.3	11.6
3. A lot	24.5	25.6	24.0	25.5	22.1	24.7	27.5	23.9	18.8	24.5	25.7	25.6	25.6	21.6	23.3	20.9
8. Don't know	2.5	2.4	2.4	2.1	2.9	2.1	2.3	3.1	2.4	2.1	2.6	2.5	2.2	4.2	1.5	11.6
Item 10450 N(Wtd)	3587	1670	1776	2860	384	869	1031	1194	494	1692	1609	1280	980	449	747	43

A13K: Not wanting to conform

1. Not at all	52.9	50.4	54.8	52.6	55.4	46.8	52.5	54.7	60.2	51.8	53.9	54.7	53.1	50.3	51.2	57.1
2. Somewhat	22.5	24.7	20.8	23.2	18.7	27.0	22.4	21.1	18.4	24.9	20.6	21.6	23.4	23.8	21.6	21.4
3. A lot	14.2	15.0	14.1	15.0	11.9	15.3	14.4	13.8	13.1	14.9	14.1	14.6	13.3	13.8	15.5	11.9
8. Don't know	10.3	9.9	10.3	9.2	14.0	10.9	10.7	10.4	8.4	8.5	11.5	9.1	10.2	12.0	11.6	11.9
Item 10460 N(Wtd)	3559	1658	1762	2839	379	863	1022	1184	490	1682	1594	1266	975	449	740	42

A14: If you were to get enough money to live as comfortably as you'd like for the rest of your life, would you want to work?

1. I would want to work	81.4	81.7	80.9	80.8	83.7	79.1	81.1	83.9	80.1	85.3	77.5	84.6	81.7	80.6	76.2	76.6
2. I would not want to work	18.6	18.3	19.1	19.2	16.3	20.9	18.9	16.1	19.9	14.6	22.5	15.3	18.2	19.6	23.7	23.4
Item 8100 N(Wtd)	3717	1723	1852	2958	405	903	1066	1232	517	1749	1668	1326	1015	459	780	47

QUESTIONNAIRE FORM 4 1978	TOTAL	SEX		RACE		REGION				4YR COLLEGE PLANS		ILLICIT DRUG USE: LIFETIME				
		M	F	White	Black	NE	NC	S	W	Yes	No	None	Mari-juana Only	Few Pills	More Pills	Any Her-oin
Weighted No. of Cases:	3783	1747	1877	2997	411	917	1079	1254	533	1771	1689	1343	1032	467	788	49
% of Weighted Total:	100.0	46.2	49.6	79.2	10.9	24.2	28.5	33.1	14.1	46.8	44.6	35.5	27.3	12.3	20.8	1.3

A15: How much do you agree or disagree with each statement below?

A15A: One sees so few good or happy marriages that one questions it as a way of life

1. Disagree	31.1	29.8	32.8	33.7	21.7	28.0	34.1	29.9	33.1	33.8	29.8	37.3	29.0	27.7	26.3	23.9
2. Mostly disagree	19.5	19.5	19.9	21.4	10.6	22.8	19.2	17.9	18.6	22.3	17.2	20.2	19.5	20.0	19.7	8.7
3. Neither	17.3	20.6	13.7	16.5	16.1	18.9	17.0	15.7	18.8	15.3	18.3	14.7	18.6	17.2	19.7	17.4
4. Mostly agree	19.1	18.0	19.8	18.3	21.2	18.8	18.4	19.8	19.7	17.2	20.7	15.1	20.8	23.1	20.6	30.4
5. Agree	13.0	12.1	13.8	10.1	30.2	11.6	11.3	16.8	9.9	11.5	14.0	12.9	12.2	11.8	13.6	19.6
Item 10470 N(Wtd)	3703	1715	1845	2952	397	896	1057	1232	517	1750	1659	1315	1018	459	777	46

A15B: It is usually a good idea for a couple to live together before getting married in order to find out whether they really get along

1. Disagree	28.9	20.6	37.0	29.6	25.5	19.7	28.8	34.5	31.6	31.4	28.2	45.0	23.3	26.5	11.6	13.0
2. Mostly disagree	14.3	14.1	14.7	15.3	10.1	15.2	15.4	14.3	12.1	15.5	13.9	14.9	15.0	13.9	12.9	6.5
3. Neither	17.1	19.5	15.2	18.3	11.6	17.8	19.1	15.0	16.5	18.3	16.1	15.5	18.0	20.0	17.8	15.2
4. Mostly agree	19.7	21.6	17.6	19.6	19.8	22.1	20.7	17.4	18.6	18.8	20.6	13.4	22.1	17.8	28.6	17.4
5. Agree	20.2	24.2	15.5	17.2	33.2	25.3	15.9	18.8	23.2	16.1	21.4	11.1	21.4	21.9	28.9	45.7
Item 10480 N(Wtd)	3733	1728	1861	2971	404	905	1067	1239	522	1756	1676	1334	1021	461	782	46

A15C: Having a close intimate relationship with only one partner is too restrictive for the average person

1. Disagree	38.3	31.5	45.2	39.6	36.8	35.9	37.5	40.9	38.2	39.1	38.8	45.0	34.1	41.9	32.7	26.1
2. Mostly disagree	23.6	24.2	23.1	24.6	20.1	27.4	24.4	21.2	21.0	25.7	22.1	21.7	26.4	21.7	25.5	10.9
3. Neither	13.9	17.2	10.9	13.9	11.3	13.4	13.8	13.6	15.4	13.6	13.8	14.4	14.0	10.0	14.6	23.9
4. Mostly agree	13.9	16.0	11.6	12.8	17.8	13.5	14.7	13.6	13.7	12.6	14.3	10.4	14.0	17.1	17.0	19.6
5. Agree	10.3	11.1	9.2	9.0	14.3	9.9	9.6	10.6	11.6	8.9	10.9	8.5	11.4	9.1	10.5	19.6
Item 10490 N(Wtd)	3719	1724	1851	2962	399	903	1064	1234	518	1749	1672	1327	1014	461	781	46

A15D: Having a job takes away from a woman's relationship with her husband

1. Disagree	49.8	38.1	60.5	48.1	60.8	53.3	44.9	50.7	51.3	51.6	48.1	51.2	50.1	50.0	46.8	43.2
2. Mostly disagree	25.7	28.1	23.8	27.5	18.5	26.4	27.9	24.8	22.2	27.2	24.7	26.2	24.4	27.0	26.4	25.0
3. Neither	11.6	15.6	7.8	11.8	7.5	8.8	14.2	11.3	11.9	10.6	12.7	9.9	12.7	10.7	13.5	22.7
4. Mostly agree	8.5	12.2	5.2	8.4	8.5	7.1	9.0	8.9	8.9	7.8	9.0	8.1	8.5	8.0	9.5	4.5
5. Agree	4.4	6.0	2.6	4.2	4.7	4.2	4.0	4.2	5.8	2.8	5.4	4.5	4.5	4.3	3.8	4.5
Item 10500 N(Wtd)	3720	1720	1856	2964	401	904	1062	1234	519	1751	1671	1329	1017	460	780	44

A15E: Having a job gives a wife more of a chance to develop herself as a person

1. Disagree	4.2	5.0	3.2	3.7	5.0	5.0	3.1	3.8	6.4	3.7	4.4	4.5	4.2	3.7	4.0	2.1
2. Mostly disagree	3.9	5.6	2.3	3.9	3.0	4.0	3.8	3.4	5.0	3.5	4.1	3.6	3.7	4.8	4.1	2.1
3. Neither	9.3	13.5	5.4	9.5	4.5	7.4	9.0	9.2	13.9	8.7	9.9	9.8	9.1	9.6	8.7	17.0
4. Mostly agree	28.9	35.5	23.3	30.5	21.5	26.7	32.9	28.4	26.0	28.1	30.3	28.2	28.7	27.0	31.3	38.3
5. Agree	53.6	40.5	65.8	52.3	66.1	57.0	51.3	55.2	48.9	56.1	51.4	54.0	54.1	54.9	52.1	42.6
Item 10510 N(Wtd)	3727	1724	1859	2967	404	905	1064	1238	519	1755	1674	1332	1020	459	780	47

A15F: Being a father and raising children is one of the most fulfilling experiences a man can have

1. Disagree	5.6	5.9	5.1	5.4	7.0	5.9	5.9	5.1	5.5	4.9	5.9	4.3	4.7	8.3	7.9	4.3
2. Mostly disagree	5.8	5.3	6.3	5.6	4.3	5.5	6.7	3.8	9.2	6.1	5.3	4.8	5.5	6.3	6.7	4.3
3. Neither	21.1	20.1	22.6	22.5	11.8	22.7	23.6	17.4	21.6	20.9	21.5	19.1	20.0	19.0	26.9	32.6
4. Mostly agree	30.8	31.7	29.8	31.9	29.3	31.4	32.6	29.9	27.9	31.6	30.7	32.8	30.8	30.6	28.4	21.7
5. Agree	36.8	37.2	36.2	34.5	47.8	34.4	31.3	43.6	35.9	36.4	36.7	38.9	39.0	35.8	30.1	37.0
Item 10520 N(Wtd)	3685	1725	1817	2933	400	895	1051	1226	513	1738	1653	1312	1010	458	772	46

QUESTIONNAIRE FORM 4 1978	TOTAL	SEX		RACE		REGION				4YR COLLEGE PLANS		ILLICIT DRUG USE: LIFETIME				
		M	F	White	Black	NE	NC	S	W	Yes	No	None	Mari-juana Only	Few Pills	More Pills	Any Her-oin
Weighted No. of Cases:	3783	1747	1877	2997	411	917	1079	1254	533	1771	1689	1343	1032	467	788	49
% of Weighted Total:	100.0	46.2	49.6	79.2	10.9	24.2	28.5	33.1	14.1	46.8	44.6	35.5	27.3	12.3	20.8	1.3

A15G: Most mothers should spend more time with their children than they do now

1. Disagree	4.3	3.9	4.6	4.2	4.0	6.7	3.7	2.8	4.8	4.8	3.5	3.0	4.3	4.8	6.4	2.2
2. Mostly disagree	9.1	9.6	8.6	9.9	4.2	11.2	10.3	6.2	10.2	10.7	8.0	8.1	9.1	8.7	11.2	8.7
3. Neither	22.0	29.6	15.2	23.0	13.7	24.2	23.5	17.6	25.4	25.4	18.7	18.3	22.9	20.7	27.3	32.6
4. Mostly agree	31.1	28.7	33.5	32.8	26.9	30.9	32.3	31.2	29.3	30.6	32.6	31.4	32.3	31.4	30.4	26.1
5. Agree	33.5	28.2	38.1	30.0	50.9	27.1	30.2	42.2	30.4	28.4	37.3	39.1	31.3	34.3	24.6	32.6
Item 10530 N(Wtd)	3716	1722	1849	2959	401	904	1059	1233	519	1750	1667	1326	1020	458	779	46

A15H: If a wife works, her husband should take a greater part in housework and child-care

1. Disagree	7.4	8.3	6.4	6.9	7.4	8.3	6.7	7.2	7.7	6.5	7.4	8.6	6.8	5.6	6.1	8.5
2. Mostly disagree	7.3	7.9	6.7	7.4	6.4	7.4	7.4	6.7	8.4	5.9	8.8	6.6	7.5	7.6	8.6	8.5
3. Neither	12.8	14.3	11.3	13.1	7.7	11.7	13.9	10.4	17.9	11.5	13.9	11.0	14.2	12.6	13.7	17.0
4. Mostly agree	35.9	37.6	34.5	37.2	30.2	35.0	38.5	36.2	31.7	36.2	36.5	35.8	36.3	35.1	37.2	34.0
5. Agree	36.6	31.8	41.1	35.4	48.0	37.6	33.6	39.4	34.4	39.8	33.4	38.0	35.2	39.0	34.4	31.9
Item 10540 N(Wtd)	3729	1730	1856	2969	404	904	1064	1240	521	1756	1676	1331	1020	461	782	47

A16: How much TV do you estimate you watch on an average weekday?

1. None	4.9	4.5	5.3	5.3	1.7	5.3	4.3	3.7	8.1	5.4	4.3	4.3	4.8	3.9	6.2	15.2
2. Half-hour or less	11.7	11.3	12.3	12.6	5.7	13.5	10.8	10.2	14.1	14.8	8.6	11.1	9.3	16.4	13.9	8.7
3. About one hour	19.6	21.6	17.8	22.0	6.2	20.7	23.8	15.7	18.2	21.6	18.3	16.2	20.7	20.4	23.9	23.9
4. About two hours	21.3	22.3	20.8	22.4	15.9	21.6	22.4	20.7	19.8	21.7	20.9	20.0	23.4	21.9	20.9	19.6
5. About three hours	17.1	17.7	16.0	16.7	19.6	15.6	18.3	17.1	17.2	15.5	19.1	18.8	16.6	16.2	14.9	17.4
6. About four hours	12.8	12.3	13.1	11.3	20.6	13.1	10.4	14.7	12.6	10.7	14.2	13.3	12.8	10.1	12.7	10.9
7. Five hours or more	12.7	10.3	14.7	9.8	30.3	10.1	10.1	17.9	9.9	10.3	14.7	16.4	12.4	10.9	7.6	4.3
Item 10550 N(Wtd)	3715	1716	1858	2961	403	902	1061	1236	516	1752	1669	1325	1020	457	779	46

A17: In the past year, how many books have you read just because you wanted to--that is, without their being assigned?

1. None	15.7	22.5	9.6	15.8	14.7	15.7	15.8	16.7	13.2	10.0	21.0	13.3	20.0	10.6	16.5	27.1
2. One	12.1	13.6	10.8	12.3	9.6	13.5	11.8	12.0	10.9	9.6	14.5	11.6	12.1	12.3	13.2	8.3
3. Two to five	38.0	38.2	37.9	37.9	39.5	40.0	40.2	36.5	33.8	39.4	36.4	37.3	38.1	42.2	36.8	29.2
4. Six to ten	13.2	11.3	14.8	12.6	16.9	12.9	12.1	14.3	13.2	14.8	11.5	14.7	11.2	14.9	12.5	10.4
5. Ten or more	21.0	14.3	26.9	21.4	19.4	17.9	20.2	20.5	28.9	26.2	16.6	23.0	18.6	19.9	21.1	25.0
Item 10560 N(Wtd)	3741	1730	1871	2982	408	905	1072	1241	523	1758	1683	1337	1028	462	783	48

A18: Some people think about what's going on in government very often, and others are not that interested. How much of an interest do you take in government and current events?

1. No interest at all	4.8	4.4	5.1	4.8	3.7	6.3	4.8	3.6	5.0	2.2	7.2	4.5	4.8	4.3	5.2	8.3
2. Very little interest	19.9	15.3	24.1	18.9	24.7	22.7	19.6	18.7	18.6	13.8	25.2	17.3	22.2	20.1	20.4	22.9
3. Some interest	50.1	48.4	51.7	50.7	47.7	50.5	51.0	49.8	48.4	50.2	50.5	51.5	48.1	50.9	50.6	45.8
4. A lot of interest	18.8	23.8	14.4	19.3	17.6	15.7	20.1	19.9	19.0	23.8	14.5	19.7	19.8	18.6	17.8	10.4
5. A very great interest	6.4	8.2	4.8	6.4	6.4	5.0	4.7	7.9	9.0	10.1	2.4	7.1	5.2	6.1	6.0	12.5
Item 6330 N(Wtd)	3740	1729	1871	2983	409	905	1073	1241	521	1758	1684	1337	1027	462	783	48

A19: Some people think that there ought to be changes in the amount of influence and power that certain organizations have in our society. Do you think the following organizations should have more influence, less influence, or about the same amount of influence as they have now?

QUESTIONNAIRE FORM 4 1978	TOTAL	SEX		RACE		REGION				4YR COLLEGE PLANS		ILLICIT DRUG USE: LIFETIME				
		M	F	White	Black	NE	NC	S	W	Yes	No	None	Mari- juana Only	Few Pills	More Pills	Any Her- oin
Weighted No. of Cases:	3783	1747	1877	2997	411	917	1079	1254	533	1771	1689	1343	1032	467	788	49
% of Weighted Total:	100.0	46.2	49.6	79.2	10.9	24.2	28.5	33.1	14.1	46.8	44.6	35.5	27.3	12.3	20.8	1.3

A19A: Large corporations?

	TOTAL	M	F	White	Black	NE	NC	S	W	Yes	No	None	Mari- juana Only	Few Pills	More Pills	Any Her- oin
1. Much less	9.3	10.8	8.0	10.2	4.0	13.0	9.7	6.2	9.7	12.5	6.3	8.3	9.5	10.0	10.8	8.3
2. Less	35.3	38.4	33.1	38.5	17.2	37.5	36.7	30.8	39.7	40.8	30.5	35.6	36.3	34.1	37.0	25.0
3. Same as now	30.0	30.1	29.8	30.7	29.9	27.4	30.9	32.4	27.6	28.5	32.6	30.1	30.1	31.7	29.3	25.0
4. More	8.5	7.8	9.1	7.1	18.0	7.4	7.1	11.2	6.6	5.5	10.8	8.2	7.7	10.0	7.6	22.9
5. Much more	3.2	3.2	2.7	1.9	9.5	1.9	2.1	4.9	3.3	2.5	3.1	4.1	2.3	3.1	2.2	6.3
8. No opinion	13.7	9.7	17.3	11.7	21.4	12.8	13.6	14.6	13.2	10.2	16.7	13.8	14.0	11.1	13.0	10.4
Item 10570 N(Wtd)	3694	1718	1842	2950	401	891	1063	1226	514	1739	1664	1321	1013	458	776	48

A19B: Major labor unions?

	TOTAL	M	F	White	Black	NE	NC	S	W	Yes	No	None	Mari- juana Only	Few Pills	More Pills	Any Her- oin
1. Much less	11.8	14.4	9.3	13.2	4.0	10.3	13.1	12.1	11.1	16.1	8.0	13.2	12.1	9.2	11.4	14.6
2. Less	26.2	29.0	24.0	29.3	11.1	26.3	27.9	24.8	25.8	31.1	22.1	28.2	25.5	26.6	25.2	20.8
3. Same as now	26.3	26.7	26.6	27.5	20.7	26.7	26.5	25.3	27.8	25.8	27.5	25.4	26.9	23.4	28.8	22.9
4. More	16.8	16.0	17.0	14.1	31.1	18.7	15.5	17.0	16.3	13.5	19.7	14.4	17.2	21.6	16.0	22.9
5. Much more	6.9	6.2	7.1	4.4	18.8	4.5	4.9	9.9	8.2	4.7	8.0	7.0	6.6	8.1	5.8	8.3
8. No opinion	11.9	7.8	15.9	11.5	14.3	13.5	12.2	11.1	11.1	8.8	14.6	11.7	11.8	11.1	12.8	12.5
Item 10580 N(Wtd)	3693	1721	1839	2948	405	890	1061	1227	515	1739	1666	1323	1019	458	771	48

A19C: Churches and religious organizations?

	TOTAL	M	F	White	Black	NE	NC	S	W	Yes	No	None	Mari- juana Only	Few Pills	More Pills	Any Her- oin
1. Much less	4.5	6.1	3.1	4.6	.7	7.0	3.3	2.9	6.2	4.7	3.9	2.4	5.3	3.3	7.6	8.5
2. Less	7.6	8.3	6.8	8.0	5.2	8.0	8.0	5.5	11.0	8.5	6.9	5.4	9.2	7.8	9.3	8.5
3. Same as now	34.8	37.4	32.8	37.2	18.0	38.6	39.1	28.4	34.6	35.2	35.0	31.2	38.2	32.8	37.0	38.3
4. More	27.0	26.0	27.9	27.5	26.4	25.2	27.5	28.0	26.3	28.7	26.0	30.4	25.8	29.1	22.2	17.0
5. Much more	17.3	13.6	20.9	14.9	36.7	11.8	13.5	26.5	13.0	16.6	18.1	22.7	12.4	18.9	13.3	19.1
8. No opinion	8.9	8.7	8.7	7.7	13.3	9.5	8.5	8.8	8.7	6.3	10.1	7.8	9.2	7.8	10.6	12.8
Item 10590 N(Wtd)	3701	1717	1849	2951	406	892	1065	1227	517	1740	1672	1328	1016	460	774	47

A19D: The national news media (TV, magazines, news services)?

	TOTAL	M	F	White	Black	NE	NC	S	W	Yes	No	None	Mari- juana Only	Few Pills	More Pills	Any Her- oin
1. Much less	7.7	7.7	7.5	8.2	4.0	7.6	6.8	8.0	8.9	9.1	6.0	7.1	8.0	9.4	7.6	8.7
2. Less	21.9	22.2	22.1	23.3	15.6	23.1	22.3	20.2	23.5	25.7	19.0	21.7	22.9	20.0	23.1	21.7
3. Same as now	42.4	42.7	42.9	44.0	36.8	40.9	44.0	43.2	40.1	44.9	41.2	44.7	41.2	39.9	42.4	43.5
4. More	15.1	15.4	14.0	14.2	18.8	15.9	16.1	13.9	14.6	11.0	18.5	14.7	15.3	17.0	14.3	10.9
5. Much more	6.3	6.1	6.2	4.7	14.8	5.1	5.0	8.1	6.4	5.0	7.2	6.2	6.6	7.8	4.8	4.3
8. No opinion	6.6	5.7	7.3	5.5	10.1	7.4	5.9	6.7	6.6	4.3	8.2	5.7	6.1	6.3	7.8	10.9
Item 10600 N(Wtd)	3692	1718	1845	2947	405	889	1059	1230	514	1740	1672	1323	1016	459	774	46

A19E: The Presidency and the administration?

	TOTAL	M	F	White	Black	NE	NC	S	W	Yes	No	None	Mari- juana Only	Few Pills	More Pills	Any Her- oin
1. Much less	4.3	5.1	3.5	4.2	5.2	5.3	4.4	4.1	2.7	3.0	5.6	3.3	4.9	4.6	5.3	4.2
2. Less	12.3	13.1	11.7	12.5	10.6	12.0	13.6	10.3	15.5	12.4	11.9	11.0	13.0	12.4	13.6	22.9
3. Same as now	39.6	40.4	40.0	41.8	29.1	39.2	38.8	40.8	39.5	43.4	37.6	40.5	39.2	39.8	41.1	18.8
4. More	20.8	21.0	20.4	22.1	14.3	21.3	22.0	20.3	19.0	22.2	20.1	22.7	19.5	22.4	17.7	27.1
5. Much more	11.9	11.9	11.4	10.1	22.0	11.0	11.1	14.3	9.3	10.9	12.1	11.8	13.1	10.7	10.9	16.7
8. No opinion	11.0	8.5	13.0	9.2	18.5	11.2	10.2	10.3	14.1	8.0	12.7	10.7	10.3	10.2	11.5	10.4
Item 10610 N(Wtd)	3695	1721	1844	2949	405	892	1058	1228	517	1741	1670	1323	1016	460	774	48

A19F: The Congress--that is, the U.S. Senate and House of Representatives?

	TOTAL	M	F	White	Black	NE	NC	S	W	Yes	No	None	Mari- juana Only	Few Pills	More Pills	Any Her- oin
1. Much less	4.3	5.4	3.2	4.4	4.7	5.1	4.0	4.3	3.7	3.3	5.4	3.1	4.3	4.6	6.5	2.1
2. Less	12.1	13.2	11.2	12.6	10.7	11.4	14.4	10.5	12.4	12.2	11.9	10.6	12.9	12.4	13.5	14.6
3. Same as now	39.7	40.1	39.8	41.5	30.0	37.9	39.8	40.9	39.8	42.4	38.0	42.5	37.4	37.4	39.3	43.8
4. More	22.2	22.0	22.2	22.6	20.6	22.6	23.5	21.2	21.3	24.2	20.8	23.4	22.8	24.1	19.4	14.6
5. Much more	9.4	9.8	8.6	8.2	15.4	10.3	7.8	10.8	7.5	8.6	9.8	9.0	10.5	9.6	8.0	8.3
8. No opinion	12.4	9.5	15.0	10.9	18.6	12.8	10.6	12.2	15.5	9.3	14.1	11.4	12.1	12.0	13.5	18.8
Item 10620 N(Wtd)	3692	1721	1840	2948	403	889	1057	1229	517	1739	1669	1326	1010	460	773	48

QUESTIONNAIRE FORM 4 1978	TOTAL	SEX		RACE		REGION				4YR COLLEGE PLANS		ILLICIT DRUG USE: LIFETIME				
		M	F	White	Black	NE	NC	S	W	Yes	No	None	Mari-juana Only	Few Pills	More Pills	Any Her-oin
Weighted No. of Cases:	3783	1747	1877	2997	411	917	1079	1254	533	1771	1689	1343	1032	467	788	49
% of Weighted Total:	100.0	46.2	49.6	79.2	10.9	24.2	28.5	33.1	14.1	46.8	44.6	35.5	27.3	12.3	20.8	1.3

A19G: The U.S. Supreme Court?

1. Much less	3.1	4.1	2.1	3.0	4.0	4.2	3.0	2.9	1.7	2.5	3.6	2.8	2.9	2.6	4.3	-
2. Less	7.0	7.9	6.2	6.9	7.0	7.0	6.8	7.4	6.6	6.4	7.5	5.8	8.1	7.8	7.8	4.2
3. Same as now	43.1	43.0	45.8	45.8	29.6	44.1	44.6	41.3	42.5	46.9	40.1	45.5	41.4	41.4	42.4	47.9
4. More	23.3	23.9	22.8	23.6	22.3	20.4	24.1	24.6	23.1	24.0	23.0	23.9	22.7	25.3	22.2	18.8
5. Much more	11.0	12.0	9.6	9.5	18.5	11.1	9.7	11.7	11.5	10.2	11.5	10.5	11.7	11.8	9.5	16.7
8. No opinion	12.6	9.3	15.6	11.3	18.5	13.2	11.7	11.9	14.6	9.9	14.3	11.7	13.0	11.1	14.0	12.5
Item 10630 N(Wtd)	3680	1718	1832	2944	399	886	1057	1222	515	1739	1658	1320	1011	459	767	48

A19H: All the courts and the justice system in general?

1. Much less	2.9	4.4	1.6	2.8	4.2	3.5	2.7	2.9	1.9	1.8	3.7	2.1	3.6	2.6	3.9	2.1
2. Less	6.7	7.7	5.4	6.8	4.9	7.5	7.5	5.2	7.4	6.9	6.5	5.0	6.9	6.8	9.3	6.3
3. Same as now	41.2	42.9	40.6	27.4	32.6	36.8	43.2	41.7	42.8	43.9	39.4	42.2	40.6	41.2	37.5	
4. More	26.6	25.8	27.7	27.4	23.7	28.6	26.3	25.9	25.6	28.4	25.5	27.6	26.1	31.8	22.7	29.2
5. Much more	10.3	9.8	10.5	9.1	15.6	12.4	8.3	11.1	9.1	10.0	10.5	11.5	10.3	7.8	9.2	16.7
8. No opinion	12.2	9.6	14.4	10.9	19.0	11.2	12.1	12.7	13.2	9.0	14.5	11.6	12.6	9.8	14.2	8.3
Item 10640 N(Wtd)	3695	1723	1842	2950	405	889	1060	1230	516	1741	1671	1326	1013	459	775	48

A19I: The police and other law enforcement agencies?

1. Much less	4.1	5.9	2.5	4.0	3.7	5.3	4.5	3.0	3.9	3.4	4.7	1.7	2.9	3.7	10.1	6.3
2. Less	7.6	8.4	6.7	7.4	9.8	8.5	7.2	8.0	6.2	7.0	8.0	3.6	7.3	10.9	12.3	14.6
3. Same as now	31.7	34.4	29.6	33.0	27.8	30.4	32.6	30.7	34.7	34.8	29.0	28.4	34.2	33.1	34.2	25.0
4. More	29.4	29.0	29.9	31.4	17.4	30.6	31.4	26.6	29.8	32.2	27.6	34.9	28.4	29.2	22.4	20.8
5. Much more	19.8	15.8	23.1	18.1	27.3	18.6	16.8	23.9	18.4	16.6	22.6	25.2	19.6	18.3	11.4	22.9
8. No opinion	7.4	6.5	8.1	6.1	14.0	6.7	7.5	7.9	7.0	5.8	8.0	6.0	7.7	5.0	9.6	10.4
Item 10650 N(Wtd)	3696	1723	1844	2950	407	891	1061	1227	516	1742	1669	1325	1015	459	774	48

A19J: The U.S. military?

1. Much less	4.3	4.8	3.9	4.1	3.0	5.7	4.8	2.7	4.8	4.7	3.8	3.5	3.8	4.1	7.0	2.1
2. Less	8.0	8.7	7.1	7.8	7.6	9.0	8.2	6.2	10.1	9.3	6.5	6.3	8.4	11.8	7.8	16.7
3. Same as now	40.3	40.1	40.7	43.1	29.1	42.6	41.8	37.4	40.3	44.6	37.0	43.2	39.5	39.3	39.0	25.0
4. More	21.1	22.0	20.6	20.7	24.9	20.1	19.8	23.9	18.4	20.7	22.0	20.7	22.2	21.0	20.5	22.9
5. Much more	14.4	16.8	11.9	13.1	19.7	9.6	14.2	18.8	13.2	11.0	17.6	15.3	14.2	12.9	13.1	22.9
8. No opinion	11.8	7.6	15.8	11.0	15.8	12.9	11.2	11.0	13.2	9.8	13.1	11.0	11.9	11.4	12.7	8.3
Item 10660 N(Wtd)	3691	1719	1843	2946	406	890	1060	1224	516	1736	1671	1325	1013	458	772	48

The next questions ask your views about drugs.

A20: Do you think that people (who are 18 or older) should be prohibited by law from doing each of the following?

A20A: Smoking marijuana (pot, grass) in private

1. No	60.6	63.3	58.9	61.2	59.6	66.2	61.1	56.4	60.2	62.3	59.2	35.5	69.0	69.9	85.3	91.8
2. Not sure	14.0	12.3	15.1	13.6	17.2	11.8	15.1	15.3	12.5	13.0	14.3	21.6	14.1	11.3	3.2	2.0
3. Yes	25.4	24.3	26.0	25.2	23.5	22.0	23.8	28.3	27.3	24.7	26.5	42.9	16.9	18.8	11.4	4.1
Item 10780 N(Wtd)	3738	1735	1870	2985	408	904	1072	1242	520	1758	1685	1338	1030	462	784	49

A20B: Smoking marijuana in public places

1. No	22.6	26.5	18.5	21.3	25.4	23.5	24.6	20.6	21.6	19.1	24.8	11.8	19.6	26.2	39.4	59.2
2. Not sure	17.9	19.1	17.2	18.7	14.8	20.6	18.0	15.7	18.5	15.9	20.0	7.6	23.6	22.6	25.3	16.3
3. Yes	59.5	54.3	64.3	60.0	59.6	55.9	57.4	63.7	59.9	65.0	55.1	80.5	56.9	51.4	35.3	22.4
Item 10790 N(Wtd)	3733	1733	1867	2983	406	903	1070	1241	519	1757	1681	1336	1029	461	782	49

QUESTIONNAIRE FORM 4 1978	TOTAL	SEX		RACE		REGION				4YR COLLEGE PLANS		ILLICIT DRUG USE: LIFETIME				
		M	F	White	Black	NE	NC	S	W	Yes	No	None	Marijuana Only	Few Pills	More Pills	Any Heroin
Weighted No. of Cases:	3783	1747	1877	2997	411	917	1079	1254	533	1771	1689	1343	1032	467	788	49
% of Weighted Total:	100.0	46.2	49.6	79.2	10.9	24.2	28.5	33.1	14.1	46.8	44.6	35.5	27.3	12.3	20.8	1.3
A20C: Taking LSD in private																
1. No	25.1	27.5	22.6	23.6	33.6	26.2	26.2	24.3	22.5	20.3	29.1	17.9	22.4	23.2	38.4	63.3
2. Not sure	12.3	11.7	12.6	11.5	15.8	14.3	12.7	11.6	9.6	10.4	14.3	10.2	12.8	15.4	13.5	8.2
3. Yes	62.7	60.9	64.8	64.9	50.6	59.5	61.0	64.1	67.9	69.3	56.6	71.9	64.8	61.4	48.1	28.6
Item 10800 N(Wtd)	3732	1732	1868	2983	405	904	1070	1238	520	1758	1683	1336	1029	461	783	49
A20D: Taking LSD in public places																
1. No	13.5	16.8	9.9	11.7	22.7	12.4	14.0	15.2	10.8	9.2	16.7	12.2	13.3	12.8	14.3	30.6
2. Not sure	5.8	6.3	5.0	5.9	4.2	6.1	7.5	4.7	4.0	3.1	8.5	2.0	4.8	4.3	13.5	8.2
3. Yes	80.7	76.9	85.1	82.5	73.1	81.4	78.6	80.1	85.4	87.7	74.9	85.7	81.9	82.9	72.2	59.2
Item 10810 N(Wtd)	3728	1733	1864	2984	401	903	1068	1237	520	1758	1676	1334	1027	462	783	49
A20E: Taking amphetamines (uppers) or barbiturates (downers) in private																
1. No	30.9	31.6	30.2	30.2	36.0	32.6	31.6	30.1	28.3	26.1	35.5	20.4	26.5	34.9	49.8	65.3
2. Not sure	16.9	16.7	17.0	16.1	19.0	18.8	17.4	15.8	14.8	16.6	17.1	16.2	15.0	19.0	19.4	12.2
3. Yes	52.2	51.7	52.9	53.8	45.1	48.6	50.9	54.0	56.8	57.3	47.4	63.4	58.3	46.1	30.8	20.4
Item 10820 N(Wtd)	3727	1732	1863	2980	406	901	1069	1238	519	1753	1683	1335	1030	458	783	49
A20F: Taking amphetamines or barbiturates in public places																
1. No	15.1	17.8	12.3	13.7	23.6	16.2	15.4	15.3	12.3	10.5	19.1	12.0	13.7	16.3	19.9	28.6
2. Not sure	9.1	9.1	9.0	8.5	10.1	10.0	9.3	8.9	7.7	7.1	10.7	4.3	7.0	10.0	17.9	22.4
3. Yes	75.8	73.1	78.8	77.7	66.3	73.8	75.3	75.8	80.0	82.4	70.2	83.8	79.2	73.7	62.2	49.0
Item 10830 N(Wtd)	3733	1734	1867	2985	407	902	1070	1242	519	1758	1684	1337	1030	460	783	49
A20G: Taking heroin (smack, horse) in private																
1. No	21.6	23.7	19.3	19.5	35.9	20.6	22.7	22.5	19.4	16.5	26.0	17.7	22.2	19.9	25.5	53.1
2. Not sure	9.6	8.5	10.4	8.8	11.6	10.3	9.6	10.1	6.9	7.9	11.1	9.2	8.2	10.8	11.0	12.2
3. Yes	68.8	67.7	70.2	71.7	52.5	69.2	67.7	67.4	73.7	75.6	62.9	73.1	69.6	69.0	63.5	34.7
Item 10840 N(Wtd)	3725	1733	1861	2979	404	899	1068	1237	520	1756	1680	1332	1028	462	781	49
A20H: Taking heroin in public places																
1. No	12.8	15.2	10.0	10.7	25.0	11.6	13.0	14.5	10.5	7.9	16.8	12.4	13.5	13.6	10.2	24.5
2. Not sure	4.7	5.0	4.2	4.7	2.8	4.6	5.1	5.0	3.5	2.6	6.7	1.8	3.7	4.1	10.7	8.2
3. Yes	82.5	79.7	85.8	84.6	72.3	83.9	82.0	80.4	86.0	89.4	76.6	85.8	82.7	82.0	79.2	65.3
Item 10850 N(Wtd)	3715	1723	1861	2976	400	899	1064	1237	516	1750	1677	1335	1019	462	778	49
A20I: Getting drunk in private																
1. No	70.3	71.8	69.6	72.1	62.5	73.1	74.1	66.8	66.0	71.7	69.3	54.2	76.4	77.1	85.4	87.8
2. Not sure	12.3	11.2	13.5	11.9	14.1	10.1	11.7	14.0	13.5	13.3	11.8	21.2	9.4	8.0	4.1	6.1
3. Yes	17.4	17.0	17.0	16.0	23.5	16.7	14.1	19.1	20.6	14.9	18.9	24.7	14.2	14.9	10.5	6.1
Item 10860 N(Wtd)	3728	1733	1863	2981	405	902	1068	1239	520	1753	1683	1333	1028	463	782	49
A20J: Getting drunk in public places																
1. No	29.2	32.0	26.5	29.5	24.3	30.8	34.4	24.4	27.4	25.5	31.6	17.9	30.1	34.3	42.9	42.9
2. Not sure	20.5	21.9	19.3	21.6	14.3	21.1	21.8	19.8	18.0	19.5	22.1	16.5	23.7	23.3	21.8	18.4
3. Yes	50.3	46.1	54.2	48.9	61.5	48.1	43.8	55.8	54.5	55.1	46.3	65.6	46.1	42.5	35.4	36.7
Item 10870 N(Wtd)	3720	1730	1859	2979	400	900	1068	1232	521	1756	1675	1330	1025	463	780	49

QUESTIONNAIRE FORM 4 1978	TOTAL	SEX		RACE		REGION				4YR COLLEGE PLANS		ILLICIT DRUG USE: LIFETIME				
		M	F	White	Black	NE	NC	S	W	Yes	No	None	Mari-juana Only	Few Pills	More Pills	Any Her-oin
Weighted No. of Cases:	3783	1747	1877	2997	411	917	1079	1254	533	1771	1689	1343	1032	467	788	49
% of Weighted Total:	100.0	46.2	49.6	79.2	10.9	24.2	28.5	33.1	14.1	46.8	44.6	35.5	27.3	12.3	20.8	1.3

A20K: Smoking tobacco in certain specified public places

1. No	41.9	41.8	42.1	42.2	41.3	39.1	47.2	40.4	39.4	40.0	43.6	32.9	44.3	43.6	52.5	49.0
2. Not sure	15.9	16.9	15.1	15.6	17.2	14.7	15.7	16.4	16.9	12.8	19.0	16.3	16.3	14.0	15.3	16.3
3. Yes	42.2	41.2	42.8	42.2	41.5	46.2	37.1	43.2	43.8	47.1	37.4	50.8	39.3	42.3	32.2	32.7
Item 10760 N(Wtd)	3734	1736	1868	2985	407	902	1070	1242	520	1759	1684	1338	1030	463	783	49

A21: In particular, there has been a great deal of public debate about whether marijuana use should be legal. Which of the following policies would you favor?

1. Using marijuana should be entirely legal	32.9	37.4	29.1	33.4	26.6	40.1	30.8	28.6	35.5	31.6	33.6	8.4	37.4	42.2	60.6	72.9
2. It should be a minor violation --like a parking ticket-- but not a crime	30.2	29.0	31.3	29.9	33.3	29.6	33.1	28.4	29.9	31.3	29.4	23.5	39.0	35.3	27.9	22.9
3. It should be a crime	22.2	20.9	23.4	23.1	18.2	15.8	21.8	26.8	23.1	23.8	21.7	45.3	9.5	14.1	5.5	2.1
4. Don't know	14.6	12.7	16.2	13.6	21.9	14.5	14.2	16.3	11.8	13.2	15.3	22.8	13.9	8.7	5.8	2.1
Item 10880 N(Wtd)	3721	1730	1865	2979	406	898	1069	1235	519	1754	1679	1335	1027	462	780	48

A22: If it were legal for people to USE marijuana, should it also be legal to SELL marijuana?

1. No	21.8	20.4	23.0	21.5	21.4	20.7	21.3	21.8	24.8	23.5	20.2	35.1	14.5	20.1	10.1	8.3
2. Yes, but only to adults	53.6	56.7	50.9	54.6	49.8	52.5	55.7	54.6	48.9	55.6	51.5	40.5	60.4	60.2	62.9	60.4
3. Yes, to anyone	12.0	12.2	11.6	11.6	13.3	14.0	9.7	11.2	14.9	9.7	13.7	9.9	11.3	9.7	16.8	22.9
4. Don't know	12.6	10.7	14.6	12.3	15.5	12.6	13.3	12.5	11.4	11.2	14.6	14.4	13.7	10.2	10.1	8.3
Item 10890 N(Wtd)	3719	1728	1864	2978	406	902	1069	1232	517	1753	1679	1333	1028	462	779	48

A23: If marijuana were legal to use and legally available, which of the following would you be most likely to do?

1. Not use it, even if it were legal and available	46.4	43.2	49.3	46.2	50.0	38.4	45.0	52.1	49.4	49.3	44.9	85.6	31.7	29.1	12.3	4.1
2. Try it	7.1	5.7	8.4	6.8	10.4	6.7	6.2	8.5	6.6	7.8	6.3	9.1	8.6	4.3	2.8	6.1
3. Use it about as often as I do now	30.9	34.6	28.0	32.4	19.8	39.6	30.6	25.4	29.8	29.8	31.6	.9	39.2	46.2	61.4	61.2
4. Use it more often than I do now	6.3	7.2	5.5	6.7	4.7	5.4	8.3	5.6	4.8	5.4	7.5	.1	7.0	7.8	14.2	20.4
5. Use it less than I do now	2.7	2.8	2.2	1.9	5.9	2.4	2.7	2.4	3.5	2.0	2.9	.6	3.2	5.0	3.7	4.1
6. Don't know	6.7	6.5	6.6	5.9	9.2	7.3	7.2	6.0	5.8	5.9	6.8	3.7	10.2	7.8	5.7	6.1
Item 10900 N(Wtd)	3711	1728	1859	2976	404	900	1066	1229	516	1752	1675	1336	1026	461	775	49

This section asks for your views and feelings about a number of different things.

D01: How satisfied are you with your life as a whole these days?

1. Completely dissatisfied	2.5	2.3	2.6	2.1	4.6	2.8	2.2	2.0	3.7	2.3	2.5	2.6	2.5	2.4	2.1	2.3
2. Quite dissatisfied	9.5	9.7	9.7	9.3	11.2	9.8	9.4	8.8	11.2	10.1	8.4	9.6	11.0	8.2	7.7	11.4
3. Somewhat dissatisfied	12.6	12.2	12.9	12.3	14.1	14.4	12.3	12.2	11.6	11.0	14.1	11.3	14.1	15.8	14.6	11.4
4. Neither, or mixed feelings	13.5	12.5	14.3	13.0	15.6	12.3	12.8	15.9	11.4	12.2	14.9	11.1	11.4	16.2	18.2	18.2
5. Somewhat satisfied	24.8	27.5	22.5	25.1	23.9	24.6	24.4	26.0	23.0	24.3	25.6	23.4	25.6	23.5	27.1	25.0
6. Quite satisfied	32.3	31.3	33.1	34.2	22.8	31.2	35.1	29.4	35.3	35.1	29.8	35.3	34.3	31.1	26.1	25.0
7. Completely satisfied	4.8	4.6	5.0	4.0	8.1	4.9	3.7	5.8	4.1	5.0	4.7	6.6	3.7	2.8	4.1	6.8
Item 6840 N(Wtd)	3448	1585	1786	2845	347	789	1027	1167	465	1711	1612	1268	936	425	727	44

D02: FOR THOSE WHO HAVE A JOB: All things considered, how satisfied are you with your present job?

1. Completely dissatisfied	5.9	5.7	5.9	5.4	8.2	8.7	4.9	5.0	5.7	5.4	6.2	4.9	6.7	5.0	6.2	11.4
2. Quite dissatisfied	10.4	10.1	10.5	9.8	13.3	10.2	10.3	9.8	12.8	11.1	9.3	9.3	12.3	9.2	10.2	17.1
3. Somewhat dissatisfied	15.0	14.1	15.9	14.9	15.8	12.6	14.8	16.1	17.2	14.3	15.7	11.9	13.7	21.3	16.7	17.1
4. Neither, or mixed feelings	14.0	13.8	14.0	13.9	10.8	15.3	15.8	11.4	13.1	14.1	13.4	12.6	15.2	11.7	16.0	14.3
5. Somewhat satisfied	25.5	26.9	23.6	25.8	29.1	24.9	25.9	25.2	26.3	26.5	24.9	28.0	24.5	24.1	24.6	11.4
6. Quite satisfied	22.7	23.2	22.5	23.9	17.7	21.7	23.5	24.7	17.5	21.2	24.5	26.4	21.2	21.6	20.3	28.6
7. Completely satisfied	6.6	6.1	7.4	6.3	5.1	6.8	4.8	7.8	7.7	7.3	5.9	6.9	6.4	7.4	5.6	2.9
Item 10910 N(Wtd) ★	2308	1154	1100	1983	158	531	735	745	297	1091	1138	772	657	282	532	35

★ = excludes respondents for whom question was inappropriate.

QUESTIONNAIRE FORM 4 1978	TOTAL	SEX		RACE		REGION				4YR COLLEGE PLANS		ILLICIT DRUG USE: LIFETIME				
		M	F	White	Black	NE	NC	S	W	Yes	No	None	Mari-juana Only	Few Pills	More Pills	Any Her-oin
Weighted No. of Cases:	3783	1747	1877	2997	411	917	1079	1254	533	1771	1689	1343	1032	467	788	49
% of Weighted Total:	100.0	46.2	49.6	79.2	10.9	24.2	28.5	33.1	14.1	46.8	44.6	35.5	27.3	12.3	20.8	1.3

D03: People have different opinions about world problems. How much do you agree or disagree with each of the following statements?

D03A: I feel that I can do very little to change the way the world is today

1. Disagree	9.2	9.4	9.2	8.0	18.2	8.9	6.8	11.4	9.6	9.8	7.9	9.4	10.1	8.5	7.4	11.6
2. Mostly disagree	20.5	19.0	21.7	20.6	19.7	18.5	20.0	20.9	24.0	26.0	14.7	23.0	18.3	19.6	20.3	14.0
3. Neither	21.9	21.6	22.0	21.9	18.2	21.1	24.2	19.3	24.9	20.6	23.5	22.2	20.7	22.0	22.4	30.2
4. Mostly agree	31.3	30.3	32.3	33.2	20.9	34.2	32.7	29.3	28.4	31.4	32.4	30.8	33.1	30.7	31.0	25.6
5. Agree	17.1	19.7	14.8	16.3	23.2	17.3	16.4	19.1	13.1	12.2	21.6	14.5	17.8	19.1	18.9	16.3
Item 10920 N(Wtd)	3397	1561	1762	2812	340	764	1021	1154	458	1683	1579	1259	919	414	713	43

D03B: It does little good to clean up air and water pollution because this society will not last long enough for it to matter

1. Disagree	45.5	43.9	46.8	46.5	40.2	50.2	42.2	44.5	47.1	54.1	35.7	46.6	47.7	44.8	43.1	23.8
2. Mostly disagree	28.2	28.3	28.0	29.9	18.3	27.1	31.1	27.1	25.9	28.1	29.2	28.9	26.4	25.2	31.5	28.6
3. Neither	13.0	13.5	12.4	12.7	12.7	10.2	14.5	12.8	14.9	8.9	17.4	11.2	12.5	16.5	14.1	26.2
4. Mostly agree	7.5	7.7	7.3	6.7	13.0	6.9	7.2	7.8	8.3	5.2	9.8	7.0	6.6	7.3	8.3	16.7
5. Agree	5.9	6.6	5.5	4.2	15.4	5.8	4.8	7.8	3.7	3.6	8.0	6.3	6.9	6.5	3.0	2.4
Item 10930 N(Wtd)	3385	1553	1757	2805	338	757	1021	1152	456	1677	1572	1254	919	413	708	42

D03C: When things get tough enough, we'll put our minds to it and find a technological solution

1. Disagree	7.1	6.8	7.1	6.8	7.5	7.6	7.1	6.6	7.5	6.4	7.4	6.1	6.6	8.1	8.5	11.9
2. Mostly disagree	10.7	9.7	11.4	11.3	5.7	11.9	10.8	9.9	10.2	10.7	10.6	10.4	8.3	11.5	13.0	16.7
3. Neither	19.8	18.5	21.1	19.9	17.8	19.1	20.8	19.8	18.5	17.4	22.1	17.7	20.3	19.7	22.9	14.3
4. Mostly agree	37.8	38.2	37.4	38.2	36.1	36.0	39.2	36.8	40.2	41.6	34.7	38.4	39.1	37.6	35.5	38.1
5. Agree	24.8	26.8	22.9	23.7	33.1	25.5	22.3	26.9	23.6	23.9	25.3	27.3	25.7	23.1	20.1	16.7
Item 10940 N(Wtd)	3361	1541	1744	2788	332	748	1019	1140	453	1664	1564	1246	911	407	707	42

D03D: When I think about all the terrible things that have been happening, it is hard for me to hold out much hope for the world

1. Disagree	18.4	18.9	17.9	17.9	23.0	18.7	16.5	18.9	20.8	22.5	14.0	20.5	18.1	17.9	16.3	11.9
2. Mostly disagree	28.1	29.5	26.9	30.2	16.1	27.5	29.6	27.8	26.2	32.1	24.2	27.7	31.0	27.2	26.0	16.7
3. Neither	24.2	25.4	23.2	24.2	21.5	28.1	25.8	20.6	23.3	20.9	28.2	22.3	23.9	22.8	28.7	28.6
4. Mostly agree	19.8	17.8	21.3	19.8	19.7	18.6	19.3	20.7	20.8	16.8	22.7	19.3	18.8	22.8	20.6	28.6
5. Agree	9.4	8.4	10.7	7.9	20.0	7.1	8.7	11.9	8.9	7.7	10.9	10.1	8.3	9.3	8.5	14.3
Item 10950 N(Wtd)	3357	1537	1744	2787	330	748	1018	1141	451	1665	1561	1244	911	408	705	42

D03E: I often wonder if there is any real purpose to my life in light of the world situation

1. Disagree	26.1	24.1	27.9	26.2	26.4	27.3	23.5	24.8	33.3	31.5	20.1	29.6	25.9	24.6	21.5	21.4
2. Mostly disagree	22.0	23.2	21.0	22.7	17.8	26.6	22.0	20.8	17.2	24.6	19.7	22.9	24.6	21.1	18.3	19.0
3. Neither	26.1	27.9	24.6	27.3	17.8	21.7	29.9	24.4	28.8	21.9	30.9	24.2	24.0	27.0	32.1	23.8
4. Mostly agree	17.8	17.5	17.9	17.2	19.6	17.4	17.0	20.0	14.5	15.6	20.0	16.4	17.9	16.9	19.8	21.4
5. Agree	8.1	7.3	8.6	6.6	18.4	6.9	7.7	10.1	5.8	6.4	9.4	6.9	7.6	10.4	8.3	14.3
Item 10960 N(Wtd)	3336	1528	1734	2772	326	736	1019	1133	448	1657	1550	1238	905	403	701	42

D03F: My guess is that this country will be caught up in a major world upheaval in the next 10 years

1. Disagree	13.8	15.3	12.4	13.8	16.4	15.9	12.4	14.0	13.0	15.6	11.6	14.3	14.0	13.3	12.9	14.3
2. Mostly disagree	17.3	19.5	15.3	17.9	13.9	18.2	18.5	17.6	12.1	18.9	15.6	17.1	20.0	15.3	16.3	7.1
3. Neither	35.1	32.6	37.3	35.6	31.6	32.8	38.1	33.8	35.8	34.6	36.4	34.3	34.7	36.3	35.8	33.3
4. Mostly agree	21.2	20.6	21.8	21.3	18.3	20.9	20.1	20.2	26.6	20.5	21.7	20.5	20.7	20.6	23.4	26.2
5. Agree	12.6	12.0	13.2	11.4	19.8	12.1	10.9	14.5	12.5	10.5	14.6	13.8	10.5	14.5	11.6	19.0
Item 10970 N(Wtd)	3316	1519	1722	2757	323	729	1010	1131	447	1652	1538	1231	899	399	698	42

QUESTIONNAIRE FORM 4 1978	TOTAL	SEX		RACE		REGION				4YR COLLEGE PLANS		ILLICIT DRUG USE: LIFETIME				
		M	F	White	Black	NE	NC	S	W	Yes	No	None	Mari- juana Only	Few Pills	More Pills	Any Her- oin
Weighted No. of Cases:	3783	1747	1877	2997	411	917	1079	1254	533	1771	1689	1343	1032	467	788	49
% of Weighted Total:	100.0	46.2	49.6	79.2	10.9	24.2	28.5	33.1	14.1	46.8	44.6	35.5	27.3	12.3	20.8	1.3

D03G: Nuclear or biological annihilation will probably be the fate of all mankind, within my lifetime

1. Disagree	21.1	22.5	19.6	22.0	17.5	20.8	20.2	21.8	22.1	26.0	15.8	25.7	21.0	16.9	16.6	4.8
2. Mostly disagree	18.0	20.4	16.0	18.6	13.1	20.9	17.8	17.6	14.6	20.4	15.8	16.7	21.0	15.6	18.3	16.7
3. Neither	32.9	27.9	37.3	32.7	32.2	31.5	34.7	31.8	34.5	30.2	36.2	33.2	30.9	35.0	34.4	31.0
4. Mostly agree	17.4	18.2	16.7	17.2	19.4	15.5	17.6	17.8	18.7	14.9	20.1	14.6	16.8	21.4	20.0	28.6
5. Agree	10.5	10.9	10.3	9.5	17.8	11.3	9.6	11.0	10.1	8.4	12.2	9.8	10.3	11.3	10.8	19.0
Item 10980 N(Wtd)	3300	1517	1710	2747	320	727	1010	1119	444	1647	1528	1225	894	397	694	42

D03H: The human race has come through tough times before, and will do so again

1. Disagree	4.2	5.1	3.3	3.8	6.9	4.5	3.6	4.4	4.5	3.4	4.6	3.3	3.6	5.8	5.3	4.9
2. Mostly disagree	6.9	7.0	6.6	6.5	8.4	8.4	6.4	6.3	6.7	6.2	7.6	7.0	5.7	6.0	8.5	9.8
3. Neither	21.6	21.7	21.5	21.4	20.6	19.2	23.6	20.7	23.1	18.4	25.3	20.8	22.5	21.8	21.8	14.6
4. Mostly agree	36.2	35.6	36.5	37.2	29.3	36.2	39.3	34.5	33.2	39.1	33.6	35.9	34.9	37.3	38.8	24.4
5. Agree	31.2	30.5	32.1	31.1	35.2	31.8	27.0	34.1	32.5	32.9	28.9	33.0	33.3	29.5	25.7	48.8
Item 10990 N(Wtd)	3313	1518	1721	2756	321	730	1013	1125	446	1653	1534	1231	899	400	693	41

The next questions are about alcohol use-- this time asking separately about beer, wine, and hard liquor.

D04: On how many occasions (if any) have you had beer to drink...

D04A: ...in your lifetime?

1. 0 occasions	11.0	7.9	13.8	9.8	17.8	8.2	9.3	14.0	12.3	12.5	9.5	23.8	2.9	5.7	2.6	-
2. 1-2	11.0	6.7	14.8	9.8	22.4	8.1	9.1	14.4	11.3	11.9	10.1	19.9	5.7	8.6	3.8	2.4
3. 3-5	7.1	4.9	8.9	6.6	10.8	9.1	5.5	6.7	8.8	7.1	7.1	11.3	4.9	6.5	3.3	2.4
4. 6-9	7.0	6.2	7.9	6.5	12.2	6.4	8.1	6.0	7.9	6.2	8.0	9.3	7.9	6.3	2.6	-
5. 10-19	11.3	9.5	13.0	11.2	10.5	13.3	10.5	10.4	12.3	12.5	10.1	10.2	15.4	11.5	7.1	2.4
6. 20-39	12.0	11.6	12.4	13.0	5.9	14.5	13.7	9.4	10.4	12.6	11.7	10.2	16.2	12.5	9.9	7.3
7. 40 or more	40.6	53.3	29.1	43.0	20.6	40.4	43.7	39.3	37.0	37.3	43.4	14.3	47.0	48.6	70.6	85.4
Item 11000 N(Wtd)	3199	1475	1656	2699	286	705	982	1080	432	1602	1478	1169	883	383	687	41

D04B: ...during the last 12 months?

1. 0 occasions	23.0	15.8	29.4	20.7	41.4	18.7	19.4	28.2	25.3	25.0	21.0	42.6	11.4	16.6	8.8	2.5
2. 1-2	11.5	7.0	15.3	10.4	20.5	12.6	9.2	11.7	14.4	11.1	12.0	17.5	8.0	12.1	5.3	5.0
3. 3-5	9.2	9.0	9.3	9.2	9.7	10.7	8.5	8.4	10.4	9.8	8.6	11.1	10.8	8.4	5.0	-
4. 6-9	9.6	9.9	9.4	9.8	8.6	10.1	9.8	9.7	8.1	9.4	9.8	8.3	13.2	9.0	7.6	7.5
5. 10-19	14.2	14.0	14.5	14.9	7.6	15.0	16.7	11.7	13.9	15.0	13.3	9.1	18.2	16.4	17.0	10.0
6. 20-39	12.6	14.5	11.0	13.4	6.8	13.3	13.5	12.5	9.7	12.4	12.7	5.9	17.6	14.2	16.3	22.5
7. 40 or more	19.9	29.7	11.0	21.6	5.0	19.7	23.1	17.8	18.1	17.4	22.6	5.3	20.7	23.0	40.0	57.5
Item 11010 N(Wtd)	3165	1461	1639	2676	278	701	972	1060	431	1591	1459	1150	876	379	683	40

D04C: ...during the last 30 days?

1. 0 occasions	37.7	27.0	47.3	34.9	62.5	35.2	31.6	41.6	45.8	40.5	34.8	63.1	24.7	30.5	17.5	5.0
2. 1-2	16.3	15.5	17.0	16.2	16.6	17.1	19.1	14.6	12.7	16.8	15.6	15.6	21.3	17.0	10.5	12.5
3. 3-5	16.7	18.1	15.6	17.5	7.6	16.5	16.3	15.9	19.4	17.2	16.1	10.9	21.0	17.5	20.9	12.5
4. 6-9	13.0	16.4	10.0	14.1	5.8	13.1	13.3	13.8	10.2	13.6	12.3	6.4	17.4	14.6	17.3	17.5
5. 10-19	9.7	12.4	7.1	10.5	5.1	11.4	10.9	8.6	6.9	8.3	11.6	2.9	11.4	11.9	17.4	20.0
6. 20-39	4.2	6.6	2.1	4.3	2.2	4.4	5.6	3.2	3.5	2.4	6.0	1.0	2.9	5.8	10.2	7.5
7. 40 or more	2.4	4.0	1.0	2.5	.7	2.1	3.0	2.4	1.6	1.3	3.6	.1	1.5	3.2	6.0	25.0
Item 11020 N(Wtd)	3159	1461	1633	2673	277	701	970	1056	432	1587	1461	1149	872	377	684	40

D05: Think back over the LAST TWO WEEKS. How many times have you had five or more 12-ounce cans of beer (or the equivalent) in a row?

1. None	64.6	50.1	77.4	62.8	81.6	63.3	60.2	68.2	67.9	70.6	58.4	85.7	57.3	59.3	43.5	25.6
2. Once	10.3	13.0	7.8	11.0	5.4	11.0	10.8	9.9	9.3	10.6	10.0	6.4	14.1	11.7	11.6	12.8
3. Twice	8.9	11.5	6.9	9.3	6.1	8.6	10.5	7.6	9.0	8.1	10.1	3.5	10.6	11.2	14.1	10.3
4. Three to five times	11.0	16.6	6.1	11.9	3.2	12.2	12.0	10.1	9.5	8.5	13.6	3.0	14.0	13.3	19.0	23.1
5. Six to nine times	3.0	5.4	1.1	3.1	1.4	3.0	4.3	2.2	2.4	1.4	4.9	1.0	2.1	1.9	7.7	15.4
6. Ten or more times	2.0	3.6	.6	1.9	1.4	1.7	2.3	2.0	2.1	.8	3.0	.4	2.0	2.4	4.2	12.8
Item 11030 N(Wtd)	3132	1436	1633	2644	277	690	970	1052	421	1576	1441	1151	858	376	674	39

QUESTIONNAIRE FORM 4 1978	TOTAL	SEX		RACE		REGION				4YR COLLEGE PLANS		ILLICIT DRUG USE: LIFETIME				
		M	F	White	Black	NE	NC	S	W	Yes	No	None	Mari- juana Only	Few Pills	More Pills	Any Her- oin
Weighted No. of Cases: % of Weighted Total:	3783 100.0	1747 46.2	1877 49.6	2997 79.2	411 10.9	917 24.2	1079 28.5	1254 33.1	533 14.1	1771 46.8	1689 44.6	1343 35.5	1032 27.3	467 12.3	788 20.8	49 1.3

D06: On how many occasions (if any) have you had wine to drink...

D06A: ...in your lifetime?

1. 0 occasions	12.8	13.1	12.7	11.5	20.1	9.4	10.5	16.2	14.8	11.5	14.2	23.7	7.4	5.5	4.2	12.2
2. 1-2	15.5	15.6	15.4	14.7	22.5	12.6	13.4	19.5	14.8	14.0	16.8	23.0	13.7	12.6	6.9	2.4
3. 3-5	17.0	17.1	16.7	17.5	13.4	16.0	17.9	17.2	16.0	17.8	16.4	18.6	18.6	17.1	13.0	4.9
4. 6-9	15.2	14.7	15.7	15.2	16.5	15.9	14.2	15.2	16.2	14.8	15.5	13.5	17.3	15.7	15.2	19.5
5. 10-19	15.9	15.1	16.8	16.8	10.6	19.9	17.4	12.5	14.4	16.3	15.7	10.4	19.1	18.9	19.9	14.6
6. 20-39	11.2	10.9	11.2	11.8	7.0	10.2	13.7	10.3	9.3	12.0	10.8	5.7	11.8	13.4	19.5	2.4
7. 40 or more	12.5	13.6	11.5	12.4	9.9	16.0	12.8	9.0	14.4	13.7	10.7	5.1	12.0	16.8	21.4	43.9
Item 11040 N(Wtd)	3183	1473	1645	2683	284	705	975	1071	432	1600	1462	1167	874	381	683	41

D06B: ...during the last 12 months?

1. 0 occasions	30.7	31.5	29.9	28.5	49.1	24.0	24.9	38.9	35.0	26.7	34.5	44.9	24.9	21.8	18.9	19.5
2. 1-2	23.1	23.8	22.4	23.5	22.7	22.1	23.2	24.3	21.6	23.0	23.1	26.1	23.9	23.1	17.1	14.6
3. 3-5	18.2	16.8	19.4	19.1	12.1	20.8	21.2	13.9	17.1	19.9	16.6	15.2	20.6	21.2	19.1	19.5
4. 6-9	12.0	12.7	11.5	12.5	7.3	15.5	12.3	10.2	9.6	13.4	10.7	6.3	13.8	14.3	17.7	22.0
5. 10-19	9.1	8.9	9.3	9.5	5.1	8.6	11.7	7.1	8.2	9.9	8.2	5.1	10.8	9.3	13.4	12.2
6. 20-39	4.1	3.0	5.0	4.1	2.2	5.6	4.5	2.6	4.5	4.0	4.3	1.6	3.2	6.4	8.3	4.9
7. 40 or more	2.9	3.3	2.5	2.8	1.8	3.3	2.3	2.9	3.8	3.0	2.7	.8	2.8	4.2	5.4	9.8
Item 11050 N(Wtd)	3125	1453	1610	2639	273	696	965	1038	426	1580	1431	1138	863	377	671	41

D06C: ...during the last 30 days?

1. 0 occasions	62.4	65.2	59.8	61.3	73.1	52.4	59.2	69.8	67.5	58.6	66.2	75.1	58.7	51.6	51.6	47.6
2. 1-2	22.2	20.2	24.0	22.9	16.4	27.9	24.3	17.7	19.3	25.3	19.0	17.7	24.9	28.4	23.6	21.4
3. 3-5	9.0	8.7	9.3	9.4	5.5	10.3	9.9	7.6	8.5	10.1	7.9	4.4	10.7	11.6	13.3	9.5
4. 6-9	4.0	3.5	4.5	4.0	3.3	6.6	4.6	2.1	3.1	3.7	4.5	1.8	4.1	4.2	7.3	14.3
5. 10-19	1.6	1.1	2.0	1.7	.4	2.3	1.7	1.3	1.4	1.7	1.5	.8	.9	2.9	3.1	2.4
6. 20-39	.4	.6	.3	.4	.4	.4	.3	.7	-	.4	.5	.2	.2	.5	.9	2.4
7. 40 or more	.4	.7	.2	.3	.4	-	.2	.8	.5	.3	.4	.2	.6	.8	.4	-
Item 11060 N(Wtd)	3121	1448	1610	2635	275	696	963	1037	425	1578	1430	1135	859	380	670	42

D07: Think back over the LAST TWO WEEKS. How many times have you had five or more 4-ounce glasses of wine in a row (or the equivalent, which is about three-fourths of a bottle)?

1. None	86.5	85.8	87.3	86.2	90.7	85.0	84.6	88.3	89.1	87.4	85.4	94.2	86.0	83.1	76.3	73.0
2. Once	7.4	8.0	6.7	7.5	6.8	7.6	7.8	8.0	4.7	7.9	6.8	4.4	7.4	9.3	11.4	8.1
3. Twice	3.9	4.0	3.9	4.2	1.4	5.2	5.2	1.7	4.3	3.2	5.0	.7	5.0	4.1	7.3	13.5
4. Three to five times	1.7	1.8	1.6	1.8	.7	1.9	2.1	1.3	1.2	1.1	2.3	.7	1.2	2.2	3.7	-
5. Six to nine times	.3	.2	.4	.2	.7	.4	.1	.3	.5	.4	.3	-	.1	1.1	.7	-
6. Ten or more times	.2	.2	.2	.1	-	-	.1	.3	.5	.1	.2	-	.2	-	.4	2.7
Item 11070 N(Wtd)	3122	1432	1627	2634	280	699	958	1042	423	1591	1408	1157	860	367	668	37

These next questions are about hard liquor. (Hard liquor includes whiskey, Scotch, bourbon, gin, vodka, rum, etc., or mixed drinks made with liquor.)

D08: On how many occasions (if any) have you had liquor to drink...

D08A: ...in your lifetime?

1. 0 occasions	15.6	14.5	16.5	12.6	37.1	12.5	12.8	19.1	18.3	16.8	14.4	32.0	6.1	7.0	4.1	2.4
2. 1-2	13.8	12.1	15.4	13.2	22.0	13.0	12.6	15.9	12.9	13.3	14.1	21.7	13.1	11.1	3.4	2.4
3. 3-5	11.5	11.3	11.7	11.6	13.3	12.3	11.4	11.3	11.0	12.7	10.5	13.4	14.1	11.4	5.4	2.4
4. 6-9	11.4	11.3	11.5	11.4	10.1	10.6	13.1	9.9	12.4	11.0	11.7	11.3	14.6	13.2	6.9	7.1
5. 10-19	15.0	16.3	14.0	16.3	5.9	17.2	14.1	13.0	19.0	15.2	14.7	10.7	21.3	17.1	14.0	11.9
6. 20-39	13.4	12.6	14.0	14.3	3.8	12.2	16.5	12.2	11.2	13.4	13.9	5.6	14.6	17.9	22.9	14.3
7. 40 or more	19.3	21.9	16.9	20.7	7.7	22.0	19.7	18.7	15.2	17.7	20.8	5.3	16.2	22.3	43.3	57.1
Item 11080 N(Wtd)	3178	1463	1646	2673	286	705	972	1073	427	1593	1470	1164	870	386	681	42

QUESTIONNAIRE FORM 4 1978	TOTAL	SEX		RACE		REGION				4YR COLLEGE PLANS		ILLICIT DRUG USE: LIFETIME				
		M	F	White	Black	NE	NC	S	W	Yes	No	None	Mari-juana Only	Few Pills	More Pills	Any Her-oin
Weighted No. of Cases:	3783	1747	1877	2997	411	917	1079	1254	533	1771	1689	1343	1032	467	788	49
% of Weighted Total:	100.0	46.2	49.6	79.2	10.9	24.2	28.5	33.1	14.1	46.8	44.6	35.5	27.3	12.3	20.8	1.3

D08B: ...during the last 12 months?

1. 0 occasions	27.6	25.2	29.8	23.5	61.1	25.5	22.3	32.0	32.4	28.0	26.9	49.0	18.8	16.5	8.4	9.5
2. 1-2	16.9	17.7	16.1	17.0	19.3	16.4	18.3	16.8	15.0	16.3	17.2	19.8	19.7	18.4	7.8	7.1
3. 3-5	15.3	16.1	14.6	16.2	7.9	17.0	15.0	12.1	21.1	16.0	14.5	13.9	18.9	15.5	14.0	7.1
4. 6-9	12.0	12.2	11.7	12.6	6.1	10.9	13.9	11.4	10.3	11.8	12.3	8.1	13.7	14.2	15.5	11.9
5. 10-19	14.1	13.6	14.5	15.4	2.5	14.4	15.0	14.2	11.5	15.1	13.3	5.8	16.6	17.1	23.5	16.7
6. 20-39	7.5	7.4	7.5	8.1	1.8	9.5	8.5	6.6	4.0	6.9	8.4	2.2	6.9	11.0	14.9	16.7
7. 40 or more	6.7	7.7	5.8	7.2	1.4	6.3	7.0	6.9	5.6	5.8	7.4	1.2	5.3	7.1	16.0	31.0
Item 11090 N(Wtd)	3141	1454	1620	2643	280	695	962	1057	426	1587	1444	1145	861	381	677	42

D08C: ...during the last 30 days?

1. 0 occasions	51.8	51.1	52.4	49.1	79.2	52.2	46.3	54.0	57.9	52.3	50.7	72.7	44.9	43.4	29.8	26.2
2. 1-2	22.1	23.6	21.0	23.0	12.9	20.3	24.8	19.8	25.0	23.2	21.0	16.4	29.3	23.9	23.0	7.1
3. 3-5	12.1	12.1	12.2	13.0	5.0	12.1	13.9	12.4	7.9	12.4	12.3	5.8	13.3	15.7	19.4	19.0
4. 6-9	7.9	7.4	8.2	8.5	1.8	7.9	8.6	8.0	6.3	7.9	8.1	3.4	7.9	9.8	14.2	19.0
5. 10-19	4.7	4.5	4.8	5.0	.4	6.8	5.0	4.3	1.4	3.4	6.3	1.2	3.7	6.1	10.5	16.7
6. 20-39	.7	.4	1.1	.8	.4	.6	.9	.7	.7	.4	1.1	.1	.7	.5	1.9	7.1
7. 40 or more	.6	.9	.4	.6	.4	.1	.5	.9	.7	.4	.6	.4	.2	.8	1.0	4.8
Item 11100 N(Wtd)	3128	1447	1614	2631	279	695	958	1047	428	1578	1440	1141	860	376	674	42

D09: Think back over the LAST TWO WEEKS. How many times have you had five or more mixed drinks or shot-glasses of hard liquor in a row?

1. None	78.1	75.6	80.4	76.8	92.6	78.3	76.1	77.5	83.9	82.1	73.3	91.5	78.3	70.1	60.0	42.5
2. Once	9.1	9.2	8.6	9.5	3.3	8.3	10.6	9.0	6.7	8.2	9.9	3.3	10.1	13.5	15.4	10.0
3. Twice	6.2	7.1	5.3	6.7	2.9	6.4	6.0	6.6	5.1	5.1	7.7	2.9	6.0	8.1	10.3	20.0
4. Three to five times	4.3	4.8	3.9	4.5	-	5.1	4.5	4.2	2.9	3.1	5.5	1.8	3.2	4.9	9.1	15.0
5. Six to nine times	1.6	1.9	1.3	1.5	.7	1.3	1.9	1.7	1.0	1.1	2.2	.2	1.3	2.4	3.4	7.5
6. Ten or more times	.9	1.4	.4	.9	.4	.4	1.1	1.1	.7	.4	1.3	.4	.8	1.1	1.5	5.0
Item 11110 N(Wtd)	3068	1408	1598	2583	272	686	937	1030	415	1563	1400	1135	843	371	648	40

These next questions ask for your opinions about the military services in the United States.

E01: To what extent do you think the following opportunities are available to people who work in the military services?

E01A: A chance to get ahead

1. To a very little extent	7.6	10.5	5.2	7.6	8.3	5.3	7.9	8.6	8.3	7.8	7.1	6.8	7.1	9.4	8.7	2.5
2. To a little extent	11.5	13.5	9.8	11.7	10.9	9.6	12.9	11.4	11.8	12.0	11.1	12.1	10.5	13.6	11.2	5.0
3. To some extent	47.2	47.7	47.1	48.4	35.3	46.9	50.5	44.7	46.4	47.5	47.0	45.8	48.6	45.0	50.2	42.5
4. To a great extent	23.0	19.0	26.7	22.9	26.0	25.7	20.9	23.0	23.7	23.3	22.7	23.7	23.8	23.8	19.6	22.5
5. To a very great extent	10.6	9.4	11.2	9.3	19.6	12.5	8.0	12.3	9.5	9.2	12.0	11.5	10.0	7.9	10.2	22.5
Item 11120 N(Wtd)	3178	1462	1641	2641	312	674	980	1101	422	1590	1476	1196	858	382	658	40

E01B: A chance to get more education

1. To a very little extent	3.6	4.5	2.8	3.5	5.1	2.7	3.3	4.2	4.0	3.7	3.2	3.2	3.2	4.5	4.0	-
2. To a little extent	7.4	9.8	5.4	7.1	9.0	5.8	7.5	7.9	8.3	8.7	5.8	6.5	7.7	8.7	7.3	10.3
3. To some extent	31.8	33.7	30.4	33.0	22.8	32.2	34.9	28.9	31.6	33.1	30.7	29.6	31.7	32.8	36.7	25.6
4. To a great extent	38.6	36.4	40.6	39.1	36.7	37.9	37.3	39.9	39.7	37.4	40.6	40.5	38.7	36.0	37.3	25.6
5. To a very great extent	18.6	15.5	20.8	17.3	26.7	21.5	17.1	19.1	16.4	17.2	19.8	20.1	18.7	18.1	14.8	38.5
Item 11130 N(Wtd)	3169	1458	1636	2635	311	671	977	1099	421	1589	1470	1194	856	381	656	39

E01C: A chance to advance to a more responsible position

1. To a very little extent	3.7	5.0	2.7	3.6	4.9	2.4	4.2	3.9	4.3	3.3	3.7	3.6	3.2	4.5	3.8	2.6
2. To a little extent	8.2	10.1	6.9	8.8	5.6	9.3	8.4	7.2	8.9	10.3	6.1	6.8	9.7	7.9	9.3	7.9
3. To some extent	32.4	35.9	29.3	33.2	25.6	29.5	36.2	30.7	33.1	31.5	33.1	30.9	32.0	34.9	34.3	28.9
4. To a great extent	39.2	36.4	41.5	39.1	42.0	41.7	35.8	40.9	38.4	40.1	38.9	39.0	40.0	36.8	40.4	28.9
5. To a very great extent	16.5	12.6	19.7	15.3	22.0	17.2	15.5	17.4	15.6	14.8	18.1	19.7	15.3	15.6	12.3	28.9
Item 11140 N(Wtd)	3144	1449	1620	2617	305	667	970	1089	417	1583	1451	1183	848	378	653	38

QUESTIONNAIRE FORM 4 1978	TOTAL	SEX		RACE		REGION				4YR COLLEGE PLANS		ILLICIT DRUG USE: LIFETIME				
		M	F	White	Black	NE	NC	S	W	Yes	No	None	Marijuana Only	Few Pills	More Pills	Any Heroin
Weighted No. of Cases:	3783	1747	1877	2997	411	917	1079	1254	533	1771	1689	1343	1032	467	788	49
% of Weighted Total:	100.0	46.2	49.6	79.2	10.9	24.2	28.5	33.1	14.1	46.8	44.6	35.5	27.3	12.3	20.8	1.3

E01D: A chance to have a personally more fulfilling job

1. To a very little extent	6.6	8.4	5.0	6.5	6.4	4.7	7.1	6.7	8.7	7.6	5.4	5.3	6.4	8.4	8.0	2.6
2. To a little extent	12.1	13.5	11.2	12.7	10.3	12.4	12.8	10.9	13.3	13.6	10.4	10.4	13.4	13.4	14.0	10.3
3. To some extent	37.4	38.8	36.5	39.2	23.7	36.1	40.1	35.9	37.1	40.2	35.1	37.8	36.8	36.4	39.0	35.9
4. To a great extent	30.1	27.8	32.0	29.4	34.3	31.4	28.9	30.6	29.4	28.0	32.7	30.7	29.8	30.1	28.7	33.3
5. To a very great extent	13.7	11.3	15.4	12.2	25.3	15.4	11.2	15.8	11.6	10.6	16.4	15.9	13.6	11.8	10.1	17.9
Item 11150 N(Wtd)	3147	1448	1624	2614	312	662	975	1094	415	1576	1458	1187	845	382	651	39

E01E: A chance to get their ideas heard

1. To a very little extent	16.7	20.9	13.3	17.4	12.4	16.8	16.2	16.1	19.6	20.1	13.2	14.1	17.8	15.7	20.6	20.0
2. To a little extent	21.6	22.2	21.2	22.8	15.7	21.1	20.2	22.3	23.7	25.9	17.4	22.7	19.8	24.2	21.7	17.5
3. To some extent	36.4	35.0	37.8	36.9	32.4	36.5	41.2	33.1	33.3	34.2	39.0	35.3	38.9	34.3	36.7	35.0
4. To a great extent	17.4	15.4	19.0	16.2	23.7	16.8	16.2	19.6	15.2	14.2	20.7	17.8	17.0	20.5	14.3	15.0
5. To a very great extent	7.9	6.6	8.7	6.7	15.7	8.7	6.2	8.8	8.2	5.7	9.6	10.1	6.5	5.1	6.6	15.0
Item 11160 N(Wtd)	3124	1435	1614	2605	299	655	970	1085	414	1565	1452	1172	843	376	649	40

E02: To what extent is it likely that a person in the military can get things changed and set right if he is being treated unjustly by a superior?

1. To a very little extent	21.1	23.0	19.6	21.8	16.7	20.6	22.0	19.8	23.4	24.2	17.7	18.6	21.2	22.0	25.5	10.3
2. To a little extent	29.3	28.7	29.9	30.2	22.2	30.7	29.4	27.7	31.6	31.6	27.2	27.5	32.4	30.6	28.3	33.3
3. To some extent	35.9	34.5	37.6	36.5	34.3	35.8	36.4	37.0	31.9	33.0	38.9	38.7	33.1	36.6	35.2	35.9
4. To a great extent	10.3	10.6	9.7	9.1	16.7	9.9	9.5	11.2	10.7	8.5	12.0	11.5	10.2	7.3	9.2	7.7
5. To a very great extent	3.4	3.2	3.3	2.3	10.5	2.9	2.7	4.6	2.4	2.8	4.1	3.7	3.1	3.8	2.0	10.3
Item 11170 N(Wtd)	3091	1422	1595	2569	306	645	961	1073	411	1545	1436	1169	827	372	640	39

E03: To what extent do you think there is any discrimination against women who are in the armed services?

1. To a very little extent	17.2	18.7	15.6	17.1	18.2	17.1	15.9	17.7	19.0	17.2	16.8	18.0	16.2	16.7	16.3	24.3
2. To a little extent	29.3	29.7	29.1	30.1	24.8	29.2	29.4	29.4	29.0	28.5	30.3	29.0	29.3	29.8	31.4	8.1
3. To some extent	36.9	36.6	37.4	37.3	31.6	36.1	37.7	37.5	34.9	37.8	36.4	36.6	38.7	35.2	36.6	48.6
4. To a great extent	11.6	10.9	12.2	11.2	16.9	12.0	12.9	10.4	11.2	11.5	11.7	11.6	10.3	14.5	10.9	10.8
5. To a very great extent	4.9	4.0	5.7	4.2	8.8	5.8	4.0	4.9	6.1	4.9	4.9	4.8	5.5	3.8	4.8	10.8
Item 11180 N(Wtd)	3076	1409	1593	2555	307	643	958	1066	410	1544	1422	1168	825	372	631	37

E04: To what extent do you think there is any discrimination against black people who are in the armed services?

1. To a very little extent	35.8	37.7	34.3	37.3	28.0	34.9	32.0	39.0	37.6	36.7	35.2	36.2	35.1	35.7	35.7	44.4
2. To a little extent	25.6	25.1	26.0	26.0	21.8	26.3	25.2	25.0	27.5	26.8	24.3	24.9	26.3	25.7	27.4	8.3
3. To some extent	27.9	27.5	28.4	27.8	25.1	28.5	32.0	24.5	26.2	26.2	29.5	28.6	27.7	26.5	28.2	30.6
4. To a great extent	7.0	6.6	7.4	6.1	15.6	6.7	7.1	7.1	6.9	7.0	7.0	6.7	7.2	9.7	4.9	8.3
5. To a very great extent	3.6	3.2	3.9	2.9	9.1	3.6	3.6	4.4	2.0	3.2	4.0	3.5	3.5	2.4	3.8	11.1
Item 11190 N(Wtd)	3058	1413	1575	2540	307	631	955	1068	404	1532	1419	1156	820	373	631	36

E05: Do you personally feel that you would receive more just and fair treatment as a civilian or as a member of the military service?

1. Much more fair in the military service	5.9	7.3	4.7	4.9	11.7	5.2	5.6	7.2	4.1	4.6	7.1	6.4	6.5	4.9	4.0	10.3
2. More fair in the military service	11.9	11.8	12.1	11.7	11.4	11.9	11.6	11.7	12.7	11.0	13.0	11.1	12.9	13.4	11.1	2.6
3. About the same	45.0	41.1	48.3	45.5	43.3	43.9	46.2	44.4	45.9	45.2	44.7	47.6	44.7	42.6	41.7	53.8
4. More fair as a civilian	14.5	17.7	11.8	15.6	9.1	11.8	16.5	14.7	13.7	15.5	13.5	12.4	15.0	18.3	16.3	7.7
5. Much more fair as a civilian	9.3	12.6	6.4	9.4	8.1	9.4	9.1	9.2	9.8	11.1	7.3	8.2	8.9	9.3	11.9	15.4
6. Question not appropriate for me	13.5	9.7	16.8	12.9	16.6	17.7	11.0	13.1	13.7	12.6	14.3	14.5	11.7	11.5	15.1	10.3
Item 11200 N(Wtd)	3071	1410	1590	2555	307	638	952	1071	410	1544	1417	1173	827	366	624	39

QUESTIONNAIRE FORM 4 1978	TOTAL	SEX		RACE		REGION				4YR COLLEGE PLANS		ILLICIT DRUG USE: LIFETIME				
		M	F	White	Black	NE	NC	S	W	Yes	No	None	Marijuana Only	Few Pills	More Pills	Any Heroin
Weighted No. of Cases:	3783	1747	1877	2997	411	917	1079	1254	533	1771	1689	1343	1032	467	788	49
% of Weighted Total:	100.0	46.2	49.6	79.2	10.9	24.2	28.5	33.1	14.1	46.8	44.6	35.5	27.3	12.3	20.8	1.3

E06: If YOU felt that it was necessary for the U.S. to fight in some future war, how likely is it that you would volunteer for military service in that war?

	TOTAL	M	F	White	Black	NE	NC	S	W	Yes	No	None	Marijuana Only	Few Pills	More Pills	Any Heroin
1. I'm sure that I would volunteer	7.9	12.0	4.5	7.2	10.0	7.2	8.0	7.8	9.3	6.7	8.9	6.9	9.6	6.4	7.2	15.8
2. I would very likely volunteer	5.5	7.9	3.1	5.8	4.2	3.9	4.9	6.0	8.4	5.0	6.4	4.7	6.8	7.2	4.8	10.5
3. I would probably volunteer	15.6	21.6	10.2	15.9	11.9	16.3	14.0	16.7	15.0	16.4	14.5	17.1	15.4	15.0	14.3	2.6
4. I would probably NOT volunteer	22.0	21.4	22.3	22.4	21.3	19.1	22.9	23.5	20.4	22.2	21.6	22.9	22.2	20.3	21.0	18.4
5. I would very likely NOT volunteer	9.0	7.4	10.4	9.3	7.4	8.0	9.1	10.3	6.9	10.6	7.4	10.0	8.7	8.3	8.4	2.6
6. I would definitely NOT volunteer	16.2	11.5	20.3	15.5	22.3	16.6	18.7	13.4	16.7	15.6	16.7	17.8	14.5	18.3	14.0	23.7
7. In my opinion, there is no such thing as a "necessary" war	23.9	18.0	29.3	24.0	22.6	29.0	22.4	22.3	23.1	23.5	24.6	20.4	23.0	24.4	30.4	31.6
Item 11220 N(Wtd)	3065	1397	1594	2541	310	638	950	1070	407	1538	1414	1168	826	360	629	38

E07: How closely do your ideas agree with your PARENTS' ideas about ...

Our ideas are...

E07A: What you should do with your life.

	TOTAL	M	F	White	Black	NE	NC	S	W	Yes	No	None	Marijuana Only	Few Pills	More Pills	Any Heroin
1. Very similar	24.6	23.7	24.9	24.0	31.6	22.5	22.8	27.3	24.8	30.6	17.6	29.2	22.1	26.1	19.3	5.1
2. Mostly similar	45.1	45.4	45.2	47.7	30.4	47.5	47.3	41.1	46.8	48.0	43.0	47.6	49.1	41.6	39.9	41.0
3. Mostly different	12.2	12.2	12.1	12.0	10.8	12.6	12.4	12.0	11.2	9.5	15.1	8.6	10.5	15.2	19.1	15.4
4. Very different	9.7	7.8	11.5	8.4	16.8	9.4	8.9	10.8	9.3	6.8	12.8	7.5	9.5	11.7	10.9	23.1
8. Don't know	8.4	10.9	6.4	7.9	10.1	8.1	8.5	8.7	7.9	5.1	11.5	7.1	8.7	5.6	10.6	15.4
Item 11230 N(Wtd)	3177	1439	1665	2633	316	668	992	1098	419	1593	1464	1193	863	375	659	39

E07B: What you do in your leisure time

	TOTAL	M	F	White	Black	NE	NC	S	W	Yes	No	None	Marijuana Only	Few Pills	More Pills	Any Heroin
1. Very similar	9.4	8.0	10.7	8.8	13.2	9.4	8.0	10.1	11.0	8.9	9.3	12.4	9.7	6.1	5.8	2.6
2. Mostly similar	34.0	32.1	36.2	34.6	28.1	35.1	33.9	32.5	35.9	39.9	28.2	42.7	32.8	30.4	23.5	15.4
3. Mostly different	27.4	28.6	25.5	28.4	24.2	25.8	29.1	27.1	26.3	27.6	27.3	24.6	28.9	30.1	28.7	35.9
4. Very different	23.6	23.7	23.6	23.0	25.2	24.3	23.4	24.2	21.5	19.2	28.1	15.2	21.2	30.1	37.1	35.9
8. Don't know	5.7	7.7	4.0	5.2	9.0	5.4	5.6	6.1	5.3	4.4	7.0	5.1	7.3	3.2	4.7	10.3
Item 11240 N(Wtd)	3159	1432	1655	2625	310	663	989	1089	418	1586	1455	1184	859	375	655	39

E07C: How you dress--what clothes you wear

	TOTAL	M	F	White	Black	NE	NC	S	W	Yes	No	None	Marijuana Only	Few Pills	More Pills	Any Heroin
1. Very similar	25.1	20.9	28.6	24.8	28.6	26.2	23.2	25.8	25.6	27.4	22.3	27.3	26.1	24.7	20.6	12.8
2. Mostly similar	44.4	42.1	46.2	46.5	34.4	43.9	47.7	41.5	45.5	47.4	42.3	46.0	44.9	44.8	41.3	43.6
3. Mostly different	14.7	17.8	12.1	15.1	12.9	13.3	14.2	15.7	15.6	13.7	15.7	13.6	13.8	12.9	19.7	12.8
4. Very different	12.4	14.2	11.1	10.9	19.3	13.6	12.3	13.2	9.1	8.6	16.0	10.8	11.3	14.5	14.9	20.5
8. Don't know	3.3	5.1	1.9	2.8	4.8	3.0	2.7	3.9	4.1	2.8	3.7	2.2	4.0	3.2	3.5	7.7
Item 11250 N(Wtd)	3151	1425	1655	2613	311	661	986	1086	418	1585	1446	1184	856	373	651	39

E07D: How you spend your money

	TOTAL	M	F	White	Black	NE	NC	S	W	Yes	No	None	Marijuana Only	Few Pills	More Pills	Any Heroin
1. Very similar	12.0	9.1	14.5	11.0	19.7	10.8	11.5	13.1	12.2	11.6	12.0	14.3	13.3	8.6	7.8	5.4
2. Mostly similar	37.1	31.6	41.9	38.4	28.2	36.1	36.7	37.1	39.3	43.8	31.0	46.2	37.3	32.4	26.0	8.1
3. Mostly different	24.3	27.4	21.7	25.2	21.4	25.6	24.5	24.0	22.1	23.0	26.0	19.4	24.4	28.9	30.6	29.7
4. Very different	22.3	25.7	19.0	21.2	26.5	23.3	22.6	21.7	21.1	18.4	25.5	16.6	20.8	25.4	30.9	43.2
8. Don't know	4.4	6.2	2.8	4.2	3.9	3.9	4.7	4.0	5.0	3.3	5.5	3.5	4.3	4.8	4.8	13.5
Item 11260 N(Wtd)	3146	1422	1653	2613	309	660	982	1088	417	1584	1447	1180	857	374	651	37

E07E: What things are O.K. to do when you are on a date

	TOTAL	M	F	White	Black	NE	NC	S	W	Yes	No	None	Marijuana Only	Few Pills	More Pills	Any Heroin
1. Very similar	15.0	11.9	17.7	14.6	19.4	12.5	15.4	15.2	17.7	16.3	13.8	19.0	14.1	14.2	9.4	7.7
2. Mostly similar	32.9	32.2	33.5	33.8	24.8	31.9	35.3	30.8	34.1	34.9	31.2	39.3	31.6	30.1	26.9	15.4
3. Mostly different	20.5	21.4	19.6	20.9	17.4	20.9	19.4	22.4	17.2	22.1	18.3	17.3	21.7	20.2	24.7	17.9
4. Very different	18.1	16.6	19.3	17.2	22.6	19.5	16.9	18.5	18.2	13.8	22.4	11.8	17.4	24.7	24.8	41.0
8. Don't know	13.5	17.9	9.8	13.5	15.5	15.2	13.0	13.3	12.6	13.0	14.3	12.7	15.2	10.5	14.2	15.4
Item 11270 N(Wtd)	3143	1416	1655	2612	310	656	985	1089	413	1581	1444	1176	860	372	648	39

QUESTIONNAIRE FORM 4 1978	TOTAL	SEX		RACE		REGION				4YR COLLEGE PLANS		ILLICIT DRUG USE: LIFETIME				
		M	F	White	Black	NE	NC	S	W	Yes	No	None	Marijuana Only	Few Pills	More Pills	Any Heroin
Weighted No. of Cases:	3783	1747	1877	2997	411	917	1079	1254	533	1771	1689	1343	1032	467	788	49
% of Weighted Total:	100.0	46.2	49.6	79.2	10.9	24.2	28.5	33.1	14.1	46.8	44.6	35.5	27.3	12.3	20.8	1.3

E07F: Whether it is O.K. to drink

1. Very similar	22.3	18.5	25.3	21.0	29.9	18.5	19.8	24.7	28.1	23.6	20.9	33.6	16.9	17.8	12.2	7.7
2. Mostly similar	32.1	32.3	32.1	33.5	24.0	35.4	32.4	29.3	33.7	34.8	30.0	31.7	32.2	34.1	34.0	12.8
3. Mostly different	17.8	19.1	16.6	19.1	10.1	18.4	19.1	16.9	16.3	18.1	17.7	14.3	19.0	17.3	22.3	30.8
4. Very different	22.5	23.0	22.1	21.8	25.3	22.7	23.7	23.6	16.8	19.5	25.2	14.7	26.2	27.6	27.7	30.8
8. Don't know	5.2	7.0	3.9	4.6	10.7	5.4	5.0	5.6	4.8	4.0	6.4	5.7	5.9	3.2	3.7	15.4
Item 11280　N(Wtd)	3128	1411	1646	2597	308	653	976	1083	416	1571	1439	1172	854	370	650	39

E07G: Whether it is O.K. to use marijuana

1. Very similar	34.2	31.3	36.7	34.3	35.0	26.8	33.6	38.0	37.1	36.5	31.9	62.7	19.1	22.5	10.8	10.3
2. Mostly similar	13.2	12.5	13.9	14.0	8.7	16.3	12.1	11.4	12.7	14.3	12.7	13.9	13.5	13.8	11.4	20.5
3. Mostly different	11.7	13.0	10.6	12.0	10.7	14.3	10.7	11.6	10.1	13.1	9.9	3.9	16.0	13.5	18.8	10.3
4. Very different	32.1	33.2	30.9	32.1	29.4	33.7	33.9	30.8	29.2	29.2	34.8	10.1	42.3	42.2	51.3	46.2
8. Don't know	8.8	10.1	7.8	7.6	16.2	9.0	9.7	8.2	8.0	6.9	10.6	9.3	9.1	8.0	7.6	12.8
Item 11290　N(Wtd)	3136	1420	1645	2605	309	652	982	1086	415	1578	1439	1170	855	377	649	39

E07H: Whether it is O.K. to use other drugs

1. Very similar	50.1	46.1	54.0	51.4	46.9	47.4	49.8	51.6	51.0	56.4	43.8	69.6	49.6	45.5	21.4	5.1
2. Mostly similar	13.3	12.0	14.5	14.2	7.8	13.0	13.6	12.8	14.8	15.2	12.0	13.3	14.7	12.3	13.0	10.3
3. Mostly different	4.9	5.4	4.3	4.6	6.1	5.2	5.0	5.1	3.4	4.1	5.4	1.6	5.3	4.5	9.9	7.7
4. Very different	23.2	26.2	20.2	22.4	23.3	26.5	22.4	21.9	23.8	18.7	27.5	7.5	22.3	28.1	48.1	51.3
8. Don't know	8.5	10.3	7.0	7.4	15.9	8.1	9.2	8.7	7.3	5.7	11.3	7.9	8.1	9.9	7.6	25.6
Item 11300　N(Wtd)	3132	1422	1640	2605	309	654	982	1084	412	1574	1439	1171	855	374	646	39

E07I: What values are important in life

1. Very similar	31.0	27.7	34.3	30.3	39.3	29.0	29.0	33.4	32.9	34.5	27.2	37.6	32.8	29.6	18.7	10.8
2. Mostly similar	42.7	44.5	41.3	44.8	29.9	43.2	44.2	40.8	43.6	44.6	41.5	43.8	44.3	40.7	42.3	29.7
3. Mostly different	12.3	13.2	11.2	12.5	9.1	13.3	13.5	11.8	9.2	10.0	14.6	7.8	10.2	14.8	20.3	37.8
4. Very different	8.2	7.8	8.6	7.2	13.6	9.6	7.7	7.8	8.2	7.1	9.0	5.7	6.5	10.0	12.8	18.9
8. Don't know	5.7	6.8	4.7	5.2	8.1	5.0	5.5	6.0	5.8	3.7	7.8	5.0	6.3	5.1	5.9	5.4
Item 11310　N(Wtd)	3121	1417	1634	2595	308	655	978	1075	413	1577	1427	1174	845	371	646	37

E07J: The value of education

1. Very similar	50.4	48.1	52.2	49.4	61.8	49.8	47.0	53.4	51.2	61.8	37.9	57.0	50.5	50.4	40.2	28.9
2. Mostly similar	35.3	35.4	35.5	36.9	19.7	37.1	37.9	31.1	37.1	30.3	41.5	32.7	36.4	31.2	41.3	31.6
3. Mostly different	6.7	7.6	5.9	6.8	6.6	4.9	7.7	7.6	4.4	4.1	9.0	4.4	6.5	8.2	10.3	13.2
4. Very different	5.5	5.6	5.3	5.1	9.2	6.8	5.1	5.4	4.4	2.7	8.5	4.3	4.0	8.5	6.4	18.4
8. Don't know	2.1	3.2	1.0	1.9	2.6	1.2	2.1	2.2	2.7	1.1	3.0	1.5	2.5	1.9	2.0	5.3
Item 11320　N(Wtd)	3114	1417	1629	2591	304	650	981	1074	410	1575	1423	1171	852	365	642	38

E07K: What are appropriate roles for women

1. Very similar	24.7	17.6	30.8	24.5	27.8	24.1	22.7	25.5	28.5	26.3	22.7	27.9	24.9	24.3	19.4	15.4
2. Mostly similar	42.3	42.1	42.7	44.0	31.1	39.7	45.1	41.9	41.1	44.5	40.7	44.3	41.2	38.1	44.0	33.3
3. Mostly different	12.2	13.5	11.0	12.1	12.9	14.0	12.5	11.0	11.4	11.8	12.4	10.2	12.3	12.8	14.6	20.5
4. Very different	7.6	6.7	8.0	7.0	11.3	9.0	7.0	7.5	6.8	5.7	9.3	6.8	6.2	12.0	8.3	10.3
8. Don't know	13.2	20.1	7.5	12.5	17.2	13.3	12.7	14.0	12.2	11.8	14.9	10.7	15.5	12.8	13.8	20.5
Item 11330　N(Wtd)	3112	1411	1632	2592	302	648	977	1077	411	1568	1432	1175	845	367	639	39

E07L: Conservation and pollution issues

1. Very similar	20.6	20.6	20.6	21.1	18.3	20.7	19.0	20.9	23.3	23.6	17.2	24.5	19.8	19.6	15.6	5.3
2. Mostly similar	36.5	36.6	36.2	38.2	27.5	37.5	36.9	35.7	36.2	39.2	34.4	38.7	35.2	35.4	36.1	44.7
3. Mostly different	9.0	9.6	8.2	8.8	8.2	8.8	9.8	8.3	9.7	9.2	8.7	8.0	9.4	9.0	10.4	13.2
4. Very different	5.8	6.8	4.9	5.2	8.8	4.5	5.8	6.7	5.6	4.5	6.9	5.0	5.0	5.7	6.5	15.8
8. Don't know	28.0	26.4	30.1	26.8	37.6	28.6	28.4	28.4	25.2	23.6	32.8	23.7	30.8	30.0	31.3	21.1
Item 11340　N(Wtd)	3111	1416	1625	2587	306	646	976	1077	412	1568	1428	1174	844	367	642	38

QUESTIONNAIRE FORM 4 1978	TOTAL	SEX		RACE		REGION				4YR COLLEGE PLANS		ILLICIT DRUG USE: LIFETIME				
		M	F	White	Black	NE	NC	S	W	Yes	No	None	Mari-juana Only	Few Pills	More Pills	Any Her-oin
Weighted No. of Cases:	3783	1747	1877	2997	411	917	1079	1254	533	1771	1689	1343	1032	467	788	49
% of Weighted Total:	100.0	46.2	49.6	79.2	10.9	24.2	28.5	33.1	14.1	46.8	44.6	35.5	27.3	12.3	20.8	1.3
E07M: Racial issues																
1. Very similar	23.4	24.1	22.5	22.3	33.0	23.3	21.4	25.4	23.0	26.3	19.7	27.4	24.5	19.2	16.8	25.6
2. Mostly similar	34.3	35.1	33.7	36.0	25.4	31.2	35.2	35.3	34.7	36.2	33.1	36.3	33.5	33.2	33.0	33.3
3. Mostly different	13.5	11.4	15.0	13.7	10.2	15.5	13.6	12.0	13.9	14.1	12.8	12.7	13.1	13.5	16.0	17.9
4. Very different	8.5	7.2	9.6	8.2	7.6	9.8	7.5	8.1	9.5	8.2	8.6	6.0	6.9	15.1	10.7	7.7
8. Don't know	20.3	22.1	19.2	19.7	23.8	20.2	22.1	19.4	19.1	15.2	25.8	17.7	21.9	19.0	23.4	17.9
Item 11350 N(Wtd)	3096	1409	1616	2575	303	644	971	1072	409	1563	1420	1170	841	364	636	39
E07N: Religion																
1. Very similar	35.7	32.8	38.4	34.0	47.7	28.5	34.2	41.1	36.7	38.0	33.2	44.3	34.6	36.8	22.1	23.1
2. Mostly similar	32.5	30.8	34.1	34.3	23.7	34.8	33.5	30.4	31.9	33.8	31.8	30.7	34.6	30.2	35.8	23.1
3. Mostly different	12.5	14.7	10.3	12.9	10.5	14.1	12.1	11.6	12.9	12.6	12.1	10.7	12.5	15.5	13.5	17.9
4. Very different	10.1	10.6	9.6	10.0	9.9	12.2	10.2	9.0	9.2	9.7	10.3	7.6	7.7	11.4	15.9	17.9
8. Don't know	9.2	11.1	7.7	9.0	8.6	10.2	10.0	7.9	9.2	5.9	12.6	6.7	10.6	6.0	12.6	15.4
Item 11360 N(Wtd)	3115	1417	1627	2589	304	646	978	1080	411	1570	1432	1175	843	367	643	39
E07O: Politics																
1. Very similar	14.7	14.6	14.8	14.1	20.5	10.7	14.0	17.1	16.3	15.7	13.5	17.8	14.4	12.3	10.1	10.3
2. Mostly similar	33.2	33.1	33.1	35.4	17.5	32.2	34.7	31.4	35.6	36.1	31.0	35.8	32.2	34.6	30.7	23.1
3. Mostly different	12.3	14.6	9.9	12.2	10.2	14.2	11.8	12.2	10.2	13.4	10.5	10.3	12.0	12.8	14.8	30.8
4. Very different	7.0	7.2	6.6	6.2	10.6	8.9	5.7	7.1	6.6	5.8	8.1	6.2	4.9	9.0	8.7	10.3
8. Don't know	32.9	30.5	35.7	32.0	41.6	34.0	33.6	32.4	31.0	29.2	37.0	29.9	36.6	31.3	35.4	23.1
Item 11370 N(Wtd)	3110	1416	1624	2588	303	642	979	1078	410	1570	1428	1171	845	367	641	39

The next questions ask about how your parents and your friends feel about some of the things we have been asking you about.

E08: How do you think your PARENTS feel (or would feel) about YOU doing each of the following things?

E08A: Smoking one or more packs of cigarettes per day

	TOTAL	M	F	White	Black	NE	NC	S	W	Yes	No	None	Mari-juana Only	Few Pills	More Pills	Any Her-oin
1. Not disapprove	11.3	13.5	9.3	10.9	13.8	10.7	11.7	11.1	11.8	7.7	14.4	6.1	10.4	12.5	18.9	41.0
2. Disapprove	35.0	35.4	34.4	34.9	34.5	37.3	34.2	36.7	28.4	31.6	39.0	28.0	36.8	41.5	40.9	41.0
3. Strongly disapprove	53.7	51.1	56.2	54.1	51.6	52.1	54.1	52.2	59.8	60.8	46.6	65.9	52.8	46.0	40.0	17.9
Item 11380 N(Wtd)	3141	1428	1643	2615	304	655	984	1088	415	1578	1446	1181	850	376	650	39

E08B: Trying marijuana (pot, grass) once or twice

1. Not disapprove	16.8	17.7	15.7	17.0	14.8	19.8	15.1	14.9	21.2	17.9	15.7	5.3	18.7	23.2	29.4	43.6
2. Disapprove	27.9	30.1	26.2	28.1	29.9	30.4	30.0	23.9	29.4	27.6	28.1	20.8	33.8	26.9	32.8	41.0
3. Strongly disapprove	55.3	52.2	58.0	55.0	55.6	49.8	54.9	61.2	49.6	54.5	56.2	73.9	47.5	50.1	37.7	17.9
Item 11390 N(Wtd)	3139	1432	1639	2616	304	657	982	1088	411	1581	1442	1178	851	375	650	39

E08C: Smoking marijuana occasionally

1. Not disapprove	9.2	10.5	7.7	9.0	9.6	12.0	8.1	7.9	11.2	8.7	9.6	2.9	7.8	9.6	19.8	41.0
2. Disapprove	23.6	26.3	21.6	23.3	28.9	25.1	23.1	21.6	27.7	23.5	23.7	14.5	27.7	29.5	30.6	35.9
3. Strongly disapprove	67.1	63.2	70.7	67.7	61.5	62.9	68.8	70.5	61.1	67.8	66.7	82.6	64.6	60.9	49.6	23.1
Item 11400 N(Wtd)	3132	1428	1634	2613	301	658	978	1085	411	1579	1437	1177	847	376	647	39

E08D: Smoking marijuana regularly

1. Not disapprove	4.4	5.9	3.1	4.0	7.3	3.7	4.5	4.4	5.1	3.0	5.8	1.9	2.7	4.0	9.2	26.3
2. Disapprove	17.6	20.0	15.3	16.4	24.1	20.3	16.3	16.1	20.7	15.7	19.0	9.8	18.0	21.0	27.6	39.5
3. Strongly disapprove	78.0	74.1	81.6	79.5	68.6	76.0	79.2	79.5	74.5	81.3	75.3	88.3	79.2	75.0	63.2	34.2
Item 11410 N(Wtd)	3135	1429	1638	2612	303	655	980	1087	411	1580	1440	1179	848	376	649	38

QUESTIONNAIRE FORM 4 1978	TOTAL	SEX		RACE		REGION				4YR COLLEGE PLANS		ILLICIT DRUG USE: LIFETIME				
		M	F	White	Black	NE	NC	S	W	Yes	No	None	Mari- juana Only	Few Pills	More Pills	Any Her- oin
Weighted No. of Cases:	3783	1747	1877	2997	411	917	1079	1254	533	1771	1689	1343	1032	467	788	49
% of Weighted Total:	100.0	46.2	49.6	79.2	10.9	24.2	28.5	33.1	14.1	46.8	44.6	35.5	27.3	12.3	20.8	1.3
E08E: Trying LSD once or twice																
1. Not disapprove	2.5	3.8	1.3	2.1	4.6	1.8	2.5	2.9	2.2	1.8	3.1	2.1	1.4	1.9	3.7	7.7
2. Disapprove	9.0	10.3	7.8	7.7	16.8	8.1	8.5	10.5	8.0	7.1	10.7	7.3	8.8	8.8	10.9	23.1
3. Strongly disapprove	88.4	85.9	90.9	90.2	78.5	90.2	88.9	86.6	89.8	91.1	86.3	90.6	89.7	89.1	85.5	69.2
Item 11420 N(Wtd)	3142	1433	1640	2618	303	656	984	1088	413	1583	1442	1179	852	375	653	39
E08F: Trying an amphetamine (upper, pep pill, bennie, speed) once or twice																
1. Not disapprove	3.3	3.8	2.7	2.9	5.0	2.6	3.3	3.5	4.1	2.3	4.2	2.2	1.8	2.7	6.3	12.8
2. Disapprove	11.5	13.5	9.6	10.6	17.8	9.6	11.5	13.2	9.7	10.4	12.3	8.6	9.2	13.1	17.5	25.6
3. Strongly disapprove	85.2	82.6	87.7	86.5	77.2	87.7	85.2	83.3	86.0	87.3	83.5	89.2	89.1	84.0	76.2	59.0
Item 11430 N(Wtd)	3140	1432	1639	2616	303	656	983	1088	413	1584	1440	1179	851	375	651	39
E08G: Taking one or two drinks nearly every day																
1. Not disapprove	11.1	16.2	6.3	10.2	13.4	8.7	14.4	9.5	11.1	8.0	13.9	7.4	10.2	12.7	16.1	27.5
2. Disapprove	31.6	35.2	28.4	31.6	32.7	34.2	31.8	30.7	29.2	29.6	33.6	27.9	32.7	31.6	36.3	37.5
3. Strongly disapprove	57.4	48.7	65.3	58.2	53.9	57.0	53.8	59.8	59.8	62.3	52.4	64.7	57.0	55.7	47.6	35.0
Item 11440 N(Wtd)	3126	1416	1641	2591	306	647	986	1078	415	1580	1427	1176	845	370	651	40
E08H: Taking four or five drinks nearly every day																
1. Not disapprove	3.7	5.5	2.0	3.0	6.9	1.7	5.0	3.5	4.1	1.9	5.2	2.8	3.8	3.9	3.9	7.5
2. Disapprove	18.4	24.6	12.8	16.9	26.0	15.9	19.4	19.0	18.6	14.8	22.2	15.1	18.4	16.5	23.3	40.0
3. Strongly disapprove	77.9	69.9	85.2	80.1	67.1	82.4	75.6	77.5	77.3	83.3	72.6	82.1	77.9	79.6	72.9	52.5
Item 11450 N(Wtd)	3107	1406	1632	2576	304	643	980	1070	414	1577	1415	1174	841	363	645	40
E08I: Having five or more drinks once or twice each weekend																
1. Not disapprove	17.4	22.4	12.8	17.4	15.4	19.0	20.7	14.2	15.8	15.2	19.5	9.5	17.7	18.9	28.9	30.0
2. Disapprove	27.7	31.4	24.3	27.4	29.2	29.6	29.3	27.2	21.8	26.7	28.7	22.3	32.1	29.9	28.9	50.0
3. Strongly disapprove	54.9	46.2	62.9	55.2	55.4	51.3	50.0	58.7	62.6	58.0	51.9	68.2	50.1	51.2	42.2	22.5
Item 11460 N(Wtd)	3103	1405	1630	2572	305	641	980	1069	412	1574	1413	1170	841	365	644	40
E09: The next questions ask about different places to live and how desirable they might be to you. Please rate each kind of place below using the following terms:																

E09: The next questions ask about different places to live and how desirable they might be to you. Please rate each kind of place below using the following terms:

Not at all acceptable: You would not live in a place like this if you could possibly avoid it.

Somewhat acceptable: You would live in a place like this, but not be very happy about it.

Acceptable: A place like this would be O.K.

Desirable: This is the kind of place where you would really like to live.

Type of area: how would you rate...

E09A: A rural area

	TOTAL	M	F	White	Black	NE	NC	S	W	Yes	No	None	Mari- juana Only	Few Pills	More Pills	Any Her- oin
1. Not at all acceptable	14.5	14.1	14.8	12.5	27.9	12.9	13.5	16.2	14.8	13.9	14.5	12.9	13.0	18.3	16.4	15.0
2. Somewhat acceptable	26.2	23.5	28.8	25.1	31.4	25.7	22.8	29.6	26.0	26.1	26.7	22.4	29.7	28.9	26.9	32.5
3. Acceptable	38.6	39.9	36.9	39.3	32.1	38.9	41.6	36.4	36.7	38.0	39.4	40.9	38.0	34.4	37.5	37.5
4. Desirable	20.8	22.4	19.5	23.0	8.6	22.5	22.2	18.0	22.4	22.1	19.5	23.8	19.2	18.6	19.3	15.0
Item 17860 N(Wtd)	3017	1361	1590	2516	290	614	959	1052	392	1523	1388	1145	822	349	621	40

QUESTIONNAIRE FORM 4 1978	TOTAL	SEX		RACE		REGION				4YR COLLEGE PLANS		ILLICIT DRUG USE: LIFETIME				
		M	F	White	Black	NE	NC	S	W	Yes	No	None	Mari-juana Only	Few Pills	More Pills	Any Her-oin
Weighted No. of Cases: % of Weighted Total:	3783 100.0	1747 46.2	1877 49.6	2997 79.2	411 10.9	917 24.2	1079 28.5	1254 33.1	533 14.1	1771 46.8	1689 44.6	1343 35.5	1032 27.3	467 12.3	788 20.8	49 1.3
E09B: A small town																
1. Not at all acceptable	10.7	9.8	11.4	9.2	21.0	9.8	10.8	10.6	11.9	12.1	8.1	7.7	11.7	11.8	13.0	20.0
2. Somewhat acceptable	21.3	21.0	22.0	19.5	31.3	19.1	22.1	22.2	20.6	22.0	21.0	20.4	19.6	24.2	23.7	17.5
3. Acceptable	46.4	47.4	45.0	47.8	40.2	47.6	45.1	48.6	41.6	43.2	49.9	47.1	48.2	41.3	45.1	47.5
4. Desirable	21.7	21.8	21.6	23.5	7.6	23.5	22.1	18.6	25.9	22.7	21.0	24.8	20.8	22.8	18.2	15.0
Item 17870 N(Wtd)	3031	1364	1600	2526	291	613	965	1058	394	1531	1392	1150	822	356	621	40
E09C: A small city																
1. Not at all acceptable	9.1	9.0	8.9	8.8	11.3	12.4	7.9	8.7	8.2	6.8	11.5	8.2	9.0	9.4	10.1	10.0
2. Somewhat acceptable	27.2	28.6	26.2	26.1	32.9	30.9	26.4	25.8	27.0	26.1	27.7	25.6	26.0	27.8	29.8	42.5
3. Acceptable	47.6	47.9	47.3	48.2	46.2	45.1	48.5	50.0	42.9	48.6	47.1	48.8	49.8	46.3	44.3	40.0
4. Desirable	16.1	14.5	17.6	16.9	9.6	11.4	17.3	15.6	22.2	18.5	13.8	17.4	15.1	16.2	15.8	7.5
Item 17880 N(Wtd)	3013	1358	1588	2509	292	614	955	1052	392	1526	1378	1141	820	352	621	40
E09D: A suburb																
1. Not at all acceptable	19.8	21.5	18.4	19.0	23.7	19.2	18.3	21.4	20.4	12.8	27.0	21.3	18.2	17.4	20.9	17.5
2. Somewhat acceptable	27.3	26.8	27.9	27.1	26.8	27.2	25.1	28.7	28.8	23.9	30.7	29.2	23.5	24.5	28.5	47.5
3. Acceptable	34.1	33.1	34.4	34.6	31.6	34.4	35.6	33.3	31.9	38.8	28.9	31.8	35.6	35.3	36.5	27.5
4. Desirable	18.9	18.5	19.3	19.4	17.9	19.3	21.1	16.6	18.6	24.5	13.3	17.7	22.6	22.8	14.1	7.5
Item 17890 N(Wtd)	3009	1360	1583	2506	291	610	958	1049	392	1521	1380	1140	818	351	622	40
E09E: A large city																
1. Not at all acceptable	47.3	51.8	43.5	50.3	27.6	48.3	49.5	45.0	46.1	41.5	54.0	51.2	45.3	43.9	44.5	45.0
2. Somewhat acceptable	22.5	21.8	23.4	22.2	20.8	22.6	21.0	22.7	25.4	24.5	20.1	22.0	23.0	20.2	24.9	22.5
3. Acceptable	19.9	17.9	21.2	19.0	27.6	19.3	20.2	20.6	17.6	22.3	17.1	17.4	22.2	23.4	19.1	20.0
4. Desirable	10.3	8.6	11.9	8.5	23.9	9.7	9.3	11.7	10.6	11.7	8.8	9.4	9.6	12.3	11.4	12.5
Item 17900 N(Wtd)	3015	1360	1587	2506	293	606	959	1053	397	1530	1376	1142	821	351	622	40
Type of Housing: How would you rate...																
E09F: A single-family home																
1. Not at all acceptable	5.6	6.4	5.0	4.0	14.8	3.5	5.5	6.5	6.9	4.1	6.7	4.6	4.7	5.4	7.4	10.3
2. Somewhat acceptable	10.6	12.0	9.3	9.2	17.2	6.3	12.3	11.8	10.0	6.8	15.0	10.7	10.6	9.5	10.3	25.6
3. Acceptable	22.3	23.5	21.1	21.1	29.7	22.8	21.8	23.0	21.0	18.8	25.3	21.3	24.2	21.8	23.2	12.8
4. Desirable	61.5	58.1	64.6	65.8	37.9	67.7	60.4	58.7	62.1	70.4	52.8	63.5	60.6	63.3	59.3	51.3
Item 17910 N(Wtd)	3006	1359	1579	2502	290	606	958	1052	390	1528	1369	1141	815	349	624	39
E09G: A two-family house																
1. Not at all acceptable	36.8	35.7	37.9	37.6	34.9	32.6	34.6	41.5	35.6	38.0	35.7	37.2	35.4	33.8	39.0	18.9
2. Somewhat acceptable	29.5	30.7	28.8	30.4	24.9	29.3	29.3	30.6	27.0	29.9	29.1	30.3	29.5	29.8	28.4	32.4
3. Acceptable	27.5	27.6	26.9	26.8	28.4	32.3	29.4	23.0	27.8	26.9	27.8	26.6	29.7	26.6	27.0	35.1
4. Desirable	6.2	6.0	6.4	5.2	11.8	5.9	6.5	4.9	9.6	5.1	7.3	5.9	5.3	9.8	5.6	13.5
Item 17920 N(Wtd)	2981	1342	1574	2486	289	598	951	1047	385	1516	1362	1141	811	346	610	37
E09H: A condominium																
1. Not at all acceptable	31.5	35.8	28.0	30.9	36.2	34.6	32.3	30.6	27.3	24.6	38.3	33.6	28.3	33.3	30.9	18.9
2. Somewhat acceptable	25.8	26.6	25.1	25.9	21.6	22.4	28.2	26.4	23.2	26.1	26.1	27.3	26.9	25.2	21.1	40.5
3. Acceptable	30.5	28.2	32.3	31.6	25.2	29.4	28.2	32.8	31.7	35.7	25.1	29.0	33.0	29.6	31.5	21.6
4. Desirable	12.3	9.5	14.6	11.5	16.7	13.9	11.4	10.1	17.8	13.7	10.5	10.1	11.7	12.2	16.5	18.9
Item 17930 N(Wtd)	2966	1332	1568	2478	282	599	950	1029	388	1501	1361	1124	810	345	612	37
E09I: A one- or two-story apartment building																
1. Not at all acceptable	28.8	34.8	23.7	28.5	29.8	32.6	27.0	28.0	29.6	25.0	32.5	31.7	24.4	27.8	30.6	21.6
2. Somewhat acceptable	31.9	33.3	30.6	32.7	27.3	31.6	31.7	32.9	30.1	33.6	30.3	31.8	35.2	29.8	28.9	37.8
3. Acceptalble	30.9	26.1	34.7	31.3	30.1	28.6	32.3	30.6	31.9	34.2	27.3	29.6	31.4	34.7	30.1	29.7
4. Desirable	8.4	5.6	10.9	7.6	12.8	7.5	9.0	8.5	8.3	7.2	9.9	6.9	9.0	7.7	10.4	10.8
Item 17940 N(Wtd)	2989	1350	1573	2492	289	602	955	1047	385	1519	1365	1135	813	352	615	37

QUESTIONNAIRE FORM 4 1978	TOTAL	SEX		RACE		REGION				4YR COLLEGE PLANS		ILLICIT DRUG USE: LIFETIME				
		M	F	White	Black	NE	NC	S	W	Yes	No	None	Marijuana Only	Few Pills	More Pills	Any Heroin
Weighted No. of Cases:	3783	1747	1877	2997	411	917	1079	1254	533	1771	1689	1343	1032	467	788	49
% of Weighted Total:	100.0	46.2	49.6	79.2	10.9	24.2	28.5	33.1	14.1	46.8	44.6	35.5	27.3	12.3	20.8	1.3

E09J: A tall (high-rise) apartment building

1. Not at all acceptable	49.0	52.5	46.1	50.4	39.9	54.2	47.3	46.3	52.8	43.4	55.4	52.5	46.4	50.3	47.4	32.4
2. Somewhat acceptable	24.5	23.6	25.5	24.5	24.4	20.6	25.6	25.0	26.7	28.3	20.7	25.4	25.7	23.9	22.2	27.0
3. Acceptable	19.1	17.2	20.7	18.9	21.0	16.9	19.9	21.3	14.8	21.0	16.9	16.0	21.9	19.8	19.8	29.7
4. Desirable	7.3	6.8	7.7	6.3	14.8	8.5	7.1	7.3	5.7	7.4	7.0	6.2	6.0	6.6	10.7	10.8
Item 17950 N(Wtd)	2991	1346	1578	2492	291	603	954	1048	386	1521	1364	1136	814	348	616	37

The following questions ask you to imagine different kinds of married life that you might have. We want you to think about different ways you might share responsibilities for working, taking care of the home and children. Please indicate how acceptable for you each of the different arrangements would be.

E10: Imagine both you and your spouse are working full-time.

How would you feel about each of these arrangements for doing things like cooking, cleaning, and laundry?

E10A: Wife does all cooking, cleaning, laundry

1. Not at all acceptable	43.8	36.1	50.1	43.2	50.7	46.8	43.1	44.8	38.4	50.1	37.5	43.7	42.1	46.2	45.7	43.9
2. Somewhat acceptable	28.1	30.0	26.8	28.6	26.8	24.6	30.0	27.2	31.0	26.8	29.8	29.5	28.9	26.5	25.9	24.4
3. Acceptable	19.5	21.2	18.2	19.2	18.8	20.1	18.6	19.2	22.1	16.4	22.5	18.4	20.1	18.8	21.0	19.5
4. Desirable	8.5	12.6	4.9	9.0	3.7	8.5	8.3	8.8	8.4	6.8	10.0	8.5	8.9	8.3	7.2	12.2
Item 11560 N(Wtd)	2988	1336	1584	2478	298	601	943	1051	393	1516	1364	1144	806	351	610	41

E10B: Wife does most of it

1. Not at all acceptable	24.4	22.3	25.9	23.7	28.5	26.4	24.0	24.1	23.0	25.4	23.0	23.1	25.7	23.4	25.5	27.5
2. Somewhat acceptable	34.3	33.7	34.7	33.5	41.2	34.9	35.1	34.2	31.4	35.4	33.6	34.6	33.6	38.0	33.2	22.5
3. Acceptable	30.4	30.0	30.8	31.6	24.1	29.0	29.7	30.4	33.9	29.2	31.5	32.4	29.1	27.7	29.8	35.0
4. Desirable	10.9	14.1	8.5	11.3	6.2	9.5	11.2	11.2	11.7	10.0	11.9	10.0	11.8	10.9	11.6	12.5
Item 11570 N(Wtd)	2978	1337	1573	2475	291	599	937	1050	392	1509	1364	1140	807	350	605	40

E10C: Both do it equally

1. Not at all acceptable	6.4	8.3	4.7	6.2	7.8	6.0	5.7	7.5	5.1	5.4	7.1	5.9	5.5	7.5	6.4	17.5
2. Somewhat acceptable	19.5	24.4	15.4	19.8	17.7	17.8	22.8	18.3	17.8	17.8	20.7	18.1	21.8	19.6	19.6	17.5
3. Acceptable	32.9	38.4	28.4	32.2	35.8	31.8	31.8	34.7	32.5	30.9	35.9	32.6	33.5	32.3	34.2	27.5
4. Desirable	41.2	28.9	51.5	41.8	38.9	44.4	39.8	39.6	44.4	45.9	36.3	43.4	39.3	40.6	39.8	37.5
Item 11580 N(Wtd)	2973	1335	1570	2467	293	597	935	1046	394	1507	1358	1136	807	347	608	40

E10D: Husband does most of it

1. Not at all acceptable	63.9	62.9	65.0	64.0	63.4	64.1	63.7	65.7	59.8	63.9	63.6	62.1	66.0	61.8	67.1	51.2
2. Somewhat acceptable	28.0	28.4	27.7	28.8	24.7	27.5	27.5	26.9	32.7	28.6	27.8	29.2	26.5	31.3	26.0	29.3
3. Acceptable	6.1	6.9	5.2	5.8	7.9	6.4	6.5	5.9	5.4	6.2	6.1	6.7	6.1	4.3	5.6	12.2
4. Desirable	2.0	1.8	2.1	1.4	4.1	2.0	2.2	1.6	2.0	1.3	2.6	2.0	1.5	2.6	1.2	4.9
Item 11590 N(Wtd)	2962	1331	1562	2458	292	593	935	1042	391	1506	1353	1131	800	348	605	41

E10E: Husband does all of it

1. Not at all acceptable	88.2	87.1	89.3	89.6	80.5	89.7	87.3	88.0	88.5	90.6	86.0	88.8	88.1	85.4	89.8	87.5
2. Somewhat acceptable	7.2	7.8	6.6	6.8	9.9	5.7	7.8	7.4	7.7	6.1	8.4	7.8	6.7	8.6	6.3	5.0
3. Acceptable	2.8	3.5	2.3	2.5	5.1	2.4	3.1	3.0	2.6	1.7	3.6	2.0	3.6	3.1	2.6	5.0
4. Desirable	1.8	1.7	1.8	1.2	4.4	2.0	1.9	1.5	1.5	1.5	2.0	1.5	1.6	2.6	1.2	2.5
Item 11600 N(Wtd)	2969	1332	1568	2463	293	594	937	1047	391	1508	1358	1132	805	350	605	40

QUESTIONNAIRE FORM 4 1978	TOTAL	SEX		RACE		REGION				4YR COLLEGE PLANS		ILLICIT DRUG USE: LIFETIME				
		M	F	White	Black	NE	NC	S	W	Yes	No	None	Mari-juana Only	Few Pills	More Pills	Any Her-oin
Weighted No. of Cases:	3783	1747	1877	2997	411	917	1079	1254	533	1771	1689	1343	1032	467	788	49
% of Weighted Total:	100.0	46.2	49.6	79.2	10.9	24.2	28.5	33.1	14.1	46.8	44.6	35.5	27.3	12.3	20.8	1.3

E11: Imagine you are married and have one or more pre-school children and both you and your spouse have to work full-time.

How would you feel about each of these arrangements for the day-to-day care of the child(ren) after working hours and on weekends?

E11A: Wife does all of it

	TOTAL	M	F	White	Black	NE	NC	S	W	Yes	No	None	Mari-juana Only	Few Pills	More Pills	Any Her-oin
1. Not at all acceptable	62.7	56.3	68.1	63.1	63.9	64.7	63.2	61.9	60.2	67.8	57.2	63.3	62.3	61.0	64.0	61.5
2. Somewhat acceptable	21.9	24.0	20.1	21.5	23.6	19.1	22.0	22.8	23.0	19.5	24.5	22.5	20.9	20.8	23.2	7.7
3. Acceptable	10.7	12.4	9.2	10.8	9.4	12.2	10.0	10.6	10.3	8.4	13.3	9.4	11.9	12.4	9.2	23.1
4. Desirable	4.8	7.3	2.7	4.7	3.1	4.1	4.7	4.7	6.5	4.4	5.0	4.6	4.9	5.8	3.8	7.7
Item 11610 N(Wtd)	2941	1319	1555	2450	288	592	930	1032	387	1496	1342	1124	796	346	600	39

E11B: Wife does most of it

	TOTAL	M	F	White	Black	NE	NC	S	W	Yes	No	None	Mari-juana Only	Few Pills	More Pills	Any Her-oin
1. Not at all acceptable	31.3	29.9	32.6	31.6	30.0	35.5	31.4	29.2	30.3	31.7	30.3	29.6	33.1	29.3	33.0	38.5
2. Somewhat acceptable	39.4	39.9	38.9	38.6	46.7	35.4	38.2	43.4	37.8	39.9	39.1	39.9	40.0	41.7	37.2	30.8
3. Acceptable	22.4	21.7	23.1	23.2	17.8	24.4	23.1	20.5	23.1	21.7	23.5	23.7	20.0	22.0	24.1	23.1
4. Desirable	6.9	8.4	5.5	6.6	5.6	4.9	7.3	7.0	8.5	6.7	7.0	6.9	7.0	7.0	5.7	7.7
Item 11620 N(Wtd)	2943	1319	1556	2452	287	591	930	1035	386	1499	1342	1124	801	345	597	39

E11C: Both do it equally

	TOTAL	M	F	White	Black	NE	NC	S	W	Yes	No	None	Mari-juana Only	Few Pills	More Pills	Any Her-oin
1. Not at all acceptable	3.8	5.2	2.5	3.5	5.2	3.9	4.0	3.8	2.8	2.9	3.9	3.6	4.1	1.7	4.6	7.7
2. Somewhat acceptable	15.9	19.8	12.4	15.4	17.9	13.3	16.5	16.2	17.0	12.8	18.8	14.1	16.6	16.8	17.4	12.8
3. Acceptable	29.3	35.0	24.5	28.4	35.7	28.1	30.7	29.8	26.3	25.9	33.6	29.2	29.8	32.1	27.0	23.1
4. Desirable	51.1	39.9	60.6	52.6	41.2	54.7	48.7	50.2	53.9	58.4	43.8	53.2	49.5	49.4	50.7	56.4
Item 11630 N(Wtd)	2957	1330	1560	2461	291	594	940	1035	388	1511	1343	1126	806	346	603	39

E11D: Husband does most of it

	TOTAL	M	F	White	Black	NE	NC	S	W	Yes	No	None	Mari-juana Only	Few Pills	More Pills	Any Her-oin
1. Not at all acceptable	56.0	54.3	57.6	55.8	55.1	57.4	56.8	55.2	54.2	57.0	53.8	54.1	58.2	51.2	59.0	56.4
2. Somewhat acceptable	34.0	35.2	33.2	34.9	31.0	31.8	32.7	36.0	35.4	34.0	35.2	36.3	32.4	36.0	32.0	25.6
3. Acceptable	8.5	9.0	7.7	8.2	10.8	9.0	8.9	7.8	8.3	7.9	9.1	8.3	7.6	11.0	8.0	12.8
4. Desirable	1.5	1.4	1.5	1.0	3.1	1.9	1.5	1.1	2.1	1.1	1.9	1.3	1.8	1.7	1.0	5.1
Item 11640 N(Wtd)	2934	1315	1551	2445	287	591	932	1027	384	1501	1334	1117	799	344	597	39

E11E: Husband does all of it

	TOTAL	M	F	White	Black	NE	NC	S	W	Yes	No	None	Mari-juana Only	Few Pills	More Pills	Any Her-oin
1. Not at all acceptable	85.1	83.1	86.8	85.7	79.7	87.0	85.1	84.8	83.3	88.7	81.0	86.8	85.3	78.0	87.3	76.9
2. Somewhat acceptable	10.2	11.3	9.3	10.2	11.7	8.0	10.5	10.8	11.2	7.9	12.8	9.7	10.1	15.3	8.0	12.8
3. Acceptable	2.8	4.0	2.0	2.6	4.8	2.9	2.8	2.9	2.6	2.1	3.7	2.0	2.5	3.8	3.8	7.7
4. Desirable	1.9	1.6	1.9	1.4	3.4	2.2	1.7	1.5	2.9	1.3	2.5	1.4	2.1	2.9	.8	2.6
Item 11650 N(Wtd)	2939	1316	1556	2445	291	591	931	1034	383	1500	1339	1119	800	346	599	39

QUESTIONNAIRE FORM 5 1978	TOTAL	SEX		RACE		REGION				4YR COLLEGE PLANS		ILLICIT DRUG USE: LIFETIME				
		M	F	White	Black	NE	NC	S	W	Yes	No	None	Mari- juana Only	Few Pills	More Pills	Any Her- oin
Weighted No. of Cases:	3770	1844	1762	2955	426	911	1074	1259	527	1768	1748	1274	1012	501	813	71
% of Weighted Total:	100.0	48.9	46.7	78.4	11.3	24.2	28.5	33.4	14.0	46.9	46.4	33.8	26.8	13.3	21.6	1.9

A01: Taking all things together, how would you say things are these days--would you say you're very happy, pretty happy, or not too happy these days?

	TOTAL	M	F	White	Black	NE	NC	S	W	Yes	No	None	Mar.	Few	More	Any
3. Very happy	17.8	17.6	18.3	19.0	12.3	16.1	16.6	19.2	19.7	22.1	14.1	20.5	16.5	16.8	15.9	18.6
2. Pretty happy	70.8	71.4	70.5	72.1	67.7	69.9	73.8	70.4	67.4	68.4	73.5	69.7	73.8	72.9	68.9	68.6
1. Not too happy	11.4	11.0	11.3	8.9	20.0	14.1	9.5	10.4	12.8	9.5	12.4	9.8	9.7	10.2	15.3	12.9
Item 1190 N(Wtd)	3754	1835	1758	2945	424	909	1069	1255	522	1763	1738	1271	1005	499	811	70

A02: Some people think a lot about the social problems of the nation and the world, and about how they might be solved. Others spend little time thinking about these issues. How much do you think about such things?

	TOTAL	M	F	White	Black	NE	NC	S	W	Yes	No	None	Mar.	Few	More	Any
1. Never	1.9	1.9	1.9	2.1	1.2	3.1	2.1	1.1	1.5	1.6	2.0	1.7	1.7	.8	3.2	2.9
2. Seldom	14.5	14.3	14.7	14.8	14.1	16.7	14.6	13.5	13.0	11.6	17.5	12.6	15.6	16.6	15.4	8.6
3. Sometimes	52.9	51.5	54.9	54.2	43.5	53.5	53.4	52.4	52.3	51.7	54.8	54.6	53.2	53.3	50.9	52.9
4. Quite often	25.6	26.6	24.3	25.2	30.1	23.2	24.7	27.3	27.4	28.9	22.5	26.4	24.4	25.5	24.9	31.4
5. A great deal	5.0	5.7	4.1	3.8	11.1	3.6	5.2	5.5	5.7	6.2	3.2	4.8	5.2	3.8	5.5	4.3
Item 6880 N(Wtd)	3757	1835	1758	2946	425	909	1070	1255	522	1762	1741	1270	1007	501	811	70

A03: Of all the problems facing the nation today, how often do you worry about each of the following?

A03A: Chance of nuclear war

	TOTAL	M	F	White	Black	NE	NC	S	W	Yes	No	None	Mar.	Few	More	Any
1. Never	18.8	12.7	24.7	18.0	23.7	20.9	20.4	15.8	19.0	15.6	21.5	21.4	16.5	19.4	16.9	23.2
2. Seldom	30.9	30.0	33.0	31.9	28.5	31.1	33.1	29.0	30.5	32.4	30.1	29.9	32.0	32.7	31.8	27.5
3. Sometimes	34.9	38.1	31.5	36.1	26.4	37.0	33.2	35.4	33.7	36.1	33.9	34.1	33.8	35.7	37.1	37.7
4. Often	15.3	19.2	10.8	14.0	21.3	11.0	13.2	19.7	16.8	15.9	14.4	14.7	17.6	12.2	14.4	11.6
Item 11660 N(Wtd)	3745	1836	1747	2946	417	906	1071	1244	525	1758	1738	1267	1005	499	807	69

A03B: Population growth

	TOTAL	M	F	White	Black	NE	NC	S	W	Yes	No	None	Mar.	Few	More	Any
1. Never	13.5	15.6	11.2	13.5	13.6	17.5	13.0	11.6	12.2	12.4	14.5	13.3	14.2	12.4	13.0	16.2
2. Seldom	36.1	38.5	34.2	37.9	27.8	37.5	37.6	36.7	29.2	36.4	35.9	36.0	36.3	39.1	36.1	23.5
3. Sometimes	35.9	32.8	39.4	36.0	35.1	33.1	36.8	35.8	38.7	36.5	35.6	35.2	36.4	35.3	36.2	38.2
4. Often	14.5	13.1	15.2	12.5	23.2	11.9	12.6	15.8	19.8	14.7	14.0	15.5	13.0	13.2	14.7	22.1
Item 11670 N(Wtd)	3739	1835	1744	2944	413	904	1067	1243	524	1754	1738	1265	1005	499	807	68

A03C: Crime and violence

	TOTAL	M	F	White	Black	NE	NC	S	W	Yes	No	None	Mar.	Few	More	Any
1. Never	1.7	2.2	.9	1.5	2.2	1.9	1.4	1.4	2.7	1.0	2.0	1.2	1.4	1.8	2.2	5.9
2. Seldom	11.8	16.8	6.1	12.3	9.1	12.3	11.8	11.1	12.6	12.3	11.3	10.4	12.7	13.1	11.5	20.6
3. Sometimes	37.9	43.3	32.4	40.5	23.7	37.0	39.5	37.1	37.8	39.1	36.9	36.3	40.1	36.7	39.3	26.5
4. Often	48.7	37.6	60.6	45.7	65.1	48.9	47.3	50.3	46.9	47.6	49.8	52.1	45.7	48.4	46.8	47.1
Item 11680 N(Wtd)	3745	1832	1753	2945	418	906	1067	1248	524	1763	1737	1264	1009	498	809	68

A03D: Pollution

	TOTAL	M	F	White	Black	NE	NC	S	W	Yes	No	None	Mar.	Few	More	Any
1. Never	4.6	5.3	3.8	3.9	9.4	4.9	4.1	5.7	2.9	3.5	5.4	4.2	4.0	6.0	4.2	11.8
2. Seldom	22.6	23.4	21.8	22.2	24.2	21.3	21.4	26.1	18.8	20.8	24.5	21.8	22.0	23.5	24.2	23.5
3. Sometimes	42.4	39.8	45.2	43.2	41.8	42.5	46.8	40.1	38.9	42.0	42.6	43.5	43.6	43.0	40.5	27.9
4. Often	30.4	31.5	29.3	30.6	24.9	31.5	27.6	28.1	39.5	33.7	27.4	30.4	30.5	27.5	31.1	36.8
Item 11690 N(Wtd)	3721	1831	1729	2928	414	902	1059	1237	522	1747	1726	1259	996	498	805	68

A03E: Energy shortages

	TOTAL	M	F	White	Black	NE	NC	S	W	Yes	No	None	Mar.	Few	More	Any
1. Never	4.2	4.3	3.8	3.6	6.8	5.3	3.5	4.1	4.0	3.0	4.8	4.7	3.7	3.4	3.6	7.4
2. Seldom	22.3	22.6	22.0	22.4	18.9	27.0	19.0	19.8	26.8	20.6	24.3	21.1	20.9	24.3	24.9	19.1
3. Sometimes	42.5	41.3	43.7	43.5	37.4	42.4	44.2	40.6	44.0	43.5	41.4	43.6	42.5	40.2	43.4	33.8
4. Often	31.0	31.8	30.5	30.5	36.9	25.4	33.3	35.5	25.2	32.8	29.5	30.7	32.9	32.0	28.1	39.7
Item 11700 N(Wtd)	3743	1834	1747	2950	412	904	1072	1245	523	1758	1738	1262	1008	497	811	68

QUESTIONNAIRE FORM 5 1978	TOTAL	SEX		RACE		REGION				4YR COLLEGE PLANS		ILLICIT DRUG USE: LIFETIME				
		M	F	White	Black	NE	NC	S	W	Yes	No	None	Mari-juana Only	Few Pills	More Pills	Any Her-oin
Weighted No. of Cases:	3770	1844	1762	2955	426	911	1074	1259	527	1768	1748	1274	1012	501	813	71
% of Weighted Total:	100.0	48.9	46.7	78.4	11.3	24.2	28.5	33.4	14.0	46.9	46.4	33.8	26.8	13.3	21.6	1.9
A03F: Race relations																
1. Never	16.4	19.8	12.7	17.0	8.0	18.6	15.9	13.2	20.8	10.6	22.0	14.6	15.5	16.9	19.4	16.2
2. Seldom	34.0	37.6	30.3	37.6	16.5	33.6	37.9	32.2	31.2	33.8	34.9	33.1	33.9	34.9	36.8	27.9
3. Sometimes	29.7	26.3	33.0	29.7	28.8	31.5	29.1	30.2	27.0	32.1	27.1	30.5	32.8	28.2	25.1	29.4
4. Often	19.9	16.4	24.0	15.6	46.2	16.3	17.3	24.4	20.8	23.6	15.9	21.8	17.7	20.0	18.7	26.5
Item 11710 N(Wtd)	3729	1829	1740	2934	413	903	1066	1237	523	1753	1728	1264	998	496	804	68
A03G: Hunger and poverty																
1. Never	8.8	13.0	4.1	9.0	7.2	8.3	9.7	8.0	9.6	7.4	9.9	7.8	9.0	8.6	9.9	8.8
2. Seldom	33.8	42.9	24.7	36.5	17.4	33.6	38.0	30.2	33.8	34.3	33.9	29.5	37.2	38.3	35.1	33.8
3. Sometimes	37.1	32.8	41.7	37.4	37.9	38.6	36.2	37.0	36.7	38.0	35.7	38.2	36.9	35.3	36.8	33.8
4. Often	20.3	11.2	29.4	17.1	37.4	19.4	16.1	24.8	19.9	20.2	20.6	24.6	17.0	17.8	18.3	23.5
Item 11720 N(Wtd)	3737	1833	1742	2942	414	904	1070	1240	523	1756	1732	1262	1002	499	807	68
A03H: Using open land for housing or industry																
1. Never	27.3	27.3	28.0	27.4	32.5	28.2	28.7	28.0	21.3	27.2	27.0	27.2	26.5	32.3	26.1	20.3
2. Seldom	32.5	30.4	34.7	32.1	32.7	29.7	33.5	35.1	29.1	33.1	32.0	32.9	32.7	31.3	32.7	37.7
3. Sometimes	22.6	22.7	22.6	23.3	19.0	22.2	23.2	21.2	25.3	23.9	21.6	24.0	24.7	17.6	21.2	10.1
4. Often	17.6	19.7	14.7	17.2	16.1	19.9	14.5	15.7	24.2	15.8	19.3	15.9	16.0	18.6	19.8	31.9
Item 11730 N(Wtd)	3743	1837	1743	2943	416	908	1069	1242	525	1756	1738	1265	1006	499	807	69
A03I: Urban decay																
1. Never	35.4	33.4	37.8	35.6	38.1	32.1	35.2	38.3	34.7	30.2	41.3	34.7	34.2	38.7	36.5	26.5
2. Seldom	38.0	39.6	37.0	39.4	31.3	33.8	39.5	38.9	39.8	40.1	36.1	40.5	37.7	35.7	37.4	38.2
3. Sometimes	20.0	20.6	19.0	19.7	20.8	25.9	18.4	17.0	20.1	22.3	17.2	18.4	22.1	19.2	19.0	27.9
4. Often	6.6	6.4	6.2	5.4	9.8	8.3	6.8	5.7	5.4	7.4	5.4	6.5	5.9	6.5	7.0	7.4
Item 11740 N(Wtd)	3709	1819	1729	2925	409	900	1057	1233	518	1749	1717	1251	997	496	802	68
A03J: Economic problems																
1. Never	8.5	7.9	9.1	8.5	7.4	8.7	8.2	9.1	7.1	6.0	11.2	7.6	8.1	8.5	9.8	11.8
2. Seldom	30.4	30.8	30.1	31.6	26.3	30.6	32.4	28.9	29.2	28.9	32.2	30.5	29.6	30.7	32.9	20.6
3. Sometimes	42.6	41.9	43.8	43.0	41.6	43.3	41.2	43.8	41.6	43.7	41.3	43.5	43.8	41.0	39.8	47.1
4. Often	18.4	19.5	17.0	16.9	24.4	17.2	18.2	18.1	21.9	21.4	15.2	18.5	18.5	19.8	17.5	19.1
Item 11750 N(Wtd)	3740	1833	1744	2939	418	905	1067	1244	524	1755	1737	1265	1008	495	806	68
A03K: Drug abuse																
1. Never	10.0	13.9	5.5	9.3	12.0	8.8	9.9	9.8	12.7	9.2	10.1	7.8	10.5	9.4	12.7	16.2
2. Seldom	24.5	28.6	20.4	25.8	19.7	24.2	24.7	23.6	26.6	26.8	22.5	22.3	24.9	26.5	26.0	27.9
3. Sometimes	35.2	33.4	37.1	36.6	26.7	37.4	36.4	33.7	32.3	36.1	34.7	37.3	35.2	35.5	33.4	20.6
4. Often	30.3	24.0	37.0	28.3	41.6	29.5	28.9	32.9	28.1	27.9	32.7	32.6	29.4	28.9	28.0	35.3
Item 11760 N(Wtd)	3749	1837	1750	2950	416	908	1068	1248	526	1760	1740	1266	1008	499	811	68
A04: How well do you think your experiences and training (at home, school, work, etc.) have prepared you to be a good...																
A04A: Husband or wife																
1. Poorly	2.3	2.7	1.7	2.2	1.7	2.2	2.6	2.1	2.3	2.0	2.4	2.2	2.1	.6	3.8	3.0
2. Not so well	5.6	6.7	4.6	5.7	5.7	6.0	5.9	4.7	6.4	5.5	5.9	4.5	4.2	6.6	8.0	10.4
3. Fairly well	25.0	30.1	19.6	25.5	19.8	26.1	26.3	21.5	28.8	22.9	26.7	23.3	27.0	24.0	25.2	23.9
4. Well	41.5	40.5	42.6	42.3	36.5	40.6	41.4	44.0	36.8	42.0	41.5	41.6	41.5	42.8	41.5	38.8
5. Very well	25.7	20.1	31.3	24.3	36.0	25.0	23.8	27.8	25.7	27.6	23.4	28.5	25.3	26.0	21.6	22.4
Item 11770 N(Wtd)	3664	1804	1705	2896	405	879	1055	1216	513	1736	1690	1237	986	488	791	67

QUESTIONNAIRE FORM 5 1978	TOTAL	SEX		RACE		REGION				4YR COLLEGE PLANS		ILLICIT DRUG USE: LIFETIME				
		M	F	White	Black	NE	NC	S	W	Yes	No	None	Marijuana Only	Few Pills	More Pills	Any Heroin
Weighted No. of Cases:	3770	1844	1762	2955	426	911	1074	1259	527	1768	1748	1274	1012	501	813	71
% of Weighted Total:	100.0	48.9	46.7	78.4	11.3	24.2	28.5	33.4	14.0	46.9	46.4	33.8	26.8	13.3	21.6	1.9

A04B: Parent

1. Poorly	2.7	3.5	1.9	2.9	1.9	2.5	2.5	3.3	2.3	2.4	3.1	1.8	2.7	1.4	4.4	4.4
2. Not so well	6.9	8.6	5.1	7.2	3.4	8.3	8.8	3.8	8.0	6.4	7.6	5.0	7.7	8.2	7.4	16.2
3. Fairly well	25.1	28.2	21.7	26.1	16.7	24.4	25.8	23.3	28.8	23.9	26.6	23.1	24.4	28.4	27.1	26.5
4. Well	37.5	37.1	38.2	38.6	35.0	36.3	41.1	37.2	33.3	37.1	38.0	39.7	37.9	35.3	36.5	29.4
5. Very well	27.7	22.5	33.1	25.3	42.7	28.6	21.9	32.2	27.8	30.2	24.8	30.4	27.2	26.7	24.7	26.5
Item 11780 N(Wtd)	3689	1810	1721	2910	412	888	1061	1225	514	1747	1701	1245	992	490	797	68

A04C: Worker on a job

1. Poorly	1.2	1.7	.5	1.0	1.9	1.4	1.4	.8	1.3	.9	1.3	.8	1.2	.8	1.7	1.5
2. Not so well	3.1	2.7	3.6	3.2	3.6	4.0	2.4	2.7	3.6	2.5	3.5	2.7	2.6	1.8	5.5	1.5
3. Fairly well	15.2	14.0	16.7	16.0	11.3	16.0	16.1	13.0	17.4	14.1	16.0	15.5	15.9	15.7	14.4	14.7
4. Well	39.8	38.3	41.6	41.1	29.7	40.2	43.6	37.4	37.3	39.3	41.3	38.3	40.8	36.3	41.8	42.6
5. Very well	40.7	43.2	37.7	38.8	53.7	38.5	36.3	46.1	40.5	43.2	37.9	42.8	39.4	45.2	36.4	41.2
Item 11790 N(Wtd)	3730	1830	1738	2938	417	899	1066	1242	523	1755	1726	1259	1004	496	804	68

A05: Apart from the particular kind of work you want to do, how would you rate each of the following settings as a place to work?

A05A: Working in a large corporation

1. Not at all acceptable	7.3	7.1	7.2	7.2	4.1	9.5	5.5	6.7	8.4	7.5	7.2	7.4	5.7	6.4	9.1	10.4
2. Somewhat acceptable	29.3	26.9	31.6	30.5	24.0	28.9	29.4	27.9	32.8	28.9	29.8	30.3	29.0	27.5	28.6	28.4
3. Acceptable	46.5	47.1	45.7	46.3	46.9	44.2	49.0	47.5	42.9	45.2	47.5	47.3	46.3	46.8	45.8	50.7
4. Desirable	17.0	18.9	15.5	15.9	24.8	17.4	16.2	17.9	15.8	18.4	15.5	15.0	19.1	19.3	16.6	11.9
Item 11800 N(Wtd)	3745	1836	1747	2946	416	904	1070	1247	524	1757	1739	1264	1007	498	812	67

A05B: Working in a small business

1. Not at all acceptable	4.6	4.6	4.2	3.0	10.3	4.1	2.8	5.1	7.8	4.2	4.6	3.6	5.7	4.2	4.4	2.9
2. Somewhat acceptable	24.6	25.1	23.7	22.8	35.7	24.5	23.2	26.7	22.5	26.5	21.9	21.4	26.0	27.0	25.2	25.0
3. Acceptable	49.5	48.5	51.4	51.4	41.7	48.3	51.7	48.4	49.4	49.1	50.8	52.2	49.7	47.2	47.8	45.6
4. Desirable	21.4	21.9	20.7	22.9	12.5	23.2	22.3	19.9	20.0	20.3	22.7	22.8	18.6	21.4	22.7	26.5
Item 11810 N(Wtd)	3746	1840	1744	2945	417	905	1069	1247	524	1757	1739	1264	1007	496	812	68

A05C: Working in a government agency

1. Not at all acceptable	22.2	23.8	20.5	22.4	15.5	22.4	22.9	22.3	20.1	16.0	28.4	19.9	21.5	21.2	26.6	30.4
2. Somewhat acceptable	32.0	33.8	30.5	34.1	24.5	30.6	34.0	30.3	34.5	33.8	31.0	32.8	31.6	35.6	31.2	20.3
3. Acceptable	31.4	29.4	33.7	31.6	30.3	32.3	31.4	31.1	30.5	34.8	27.2	32.4	31.5	29.2	30.0	33.3
4. Desirable	14.5	13.1	15.3	11.9	29.5	14.9	11.7	16.4	15.1	15.4	13.4	15.0	15.5	13.8	12.2	14.5
Item 11820 N(Wtd)	3741	1830	1749	2945	413	908	1069	1243	522	1756	1737	1264	1001	500	811	69

A05D: Working in the military service

1. Not at all acceptable	44.8	43.6	46.6	47.3	30.9	44.3	49.1	40.3	47.7	47.2	43.1	41.6	44.3	47.3	51.2	42.4
2. Somewhat acceptable	29.1	28.4	29.3	29.0	30.4	29.3	30.3	28.5	27.7	30.4	27.7	29.7	27.7	30.9	28.4	30.3
3. Acceptable	18.3	18.7	17.7	16.8	24.2	17.5	15.7	21.8	16.8	16.6	19.4	21.0	19.1	14.7	14.4	9.1
4. Desirable	7.8	9.3	6.4	6.8	14.7	9.0	5.0	9.4	7.6	5.8	9.8	7.7	8.9	7.1	5.9	19.7
Item 11830 N(Wtd)	3733	1832	1740	2938	414	903	1067	1240	524	1748	1738	1261	1001	495	812	66

A05E: Working in a school or university

1. Not at all acceptable	28.2	35.8	20.3	28.7	26.6	27.7	27.7	29.8	26.5	18.8	37.3	24.9	29.6	26.5	32.6	27.5
2. Somewhat acceptable	31.4	32.8	30.2	32.0	27.4	32.3	32.6	29.8	31.0	30.0	33.0	29.0	33.3	33.7	31.9	33.3
3. Acceptable	28.0	23.1	32.8	27.3	30.3	27.4	28.3	26.5	31.6	33.1	23.0	31.9	25.8	27.7	24.1	26.1
4. Desirable	12.5	8.3	16.8	12.0	16.0	12.5	11.5	13.9	10.9	18.1	6.6	14.3	11.3	11.8	11.5	13.0
Item 11840 N(Wtd)	3737	1833	1743	2941	413	904	1065	1243	525	1755	1734	1257	1007	498	810	69

QUESTIONNAIRE FORM 5 1978	TOTAL	SEX		RACE		REGION				4YR COLLEGE PLANS		ILLICIT DRUG USE: LIFETIME				
		M	F	White	Black	NE	NC	S	W	Yes	No	None	Mari-juana Only	Few Pills	More Pills	Any Her-oin
Weighted No. of Cases:	3770	1844	1762	2955	426	911	1074	1259	527	1768	1748	1274	1012	501	813	71
% of Weighted Total:	100.0	48.9	46.7	78.4	11.3	24.2	28.5	33.4	14.0	46.9	46.4	33.8	26.8	13.3	21.6	1.9

A05F: Working in a police department or police agency

1. Not at all acceptable	31.4	34.2	28.1	30.1	40.7	30.6	31.0	34.8	25.8	29.9	32.9	27.0	29.7	32.3	39.3	39.7
2. Somewhat acceptable	29.2	30.2	28.5	29.9	26.8	27.2	31.8	28.8	27.9	32.2	26.2	29.6	29.9	31.9	27.2	14.7
3. Acceptable	26.3	23.6	29.1	27.5	18.9	27.4	25.8	24.4	30.0	26.6	26.4	30.6	26.0	23.1	22.3	29.4
4. Desirable	13.1	12.0	14.3	12.5	13.9	15.0	11.5	11.9	16.3	11.3	14.4	13.0	14.3	12.4	11.1	16.2
Item 11850 N(Wtd)	3744	1838	1747	2943	418	903	1070	1248	523	1757	1739	1265	1004	498	812	68

A05G: Working in a social service organization

1. Not at all acceptable	22.5	33.9	10.5	23.9	13.3	21.7	23.9	23.0	20.0	20.2	24.8	20.7	24.3	24.3	22.2	29.4
2. Somewhat acceptable	32.5	37.7	26.8	33.1	29.4	33.1	31.7	32.0	34.4	32.2	33.1	32.1	34.0	31.8	30.6	33.8
3. Acceptable	27.8	22.2	33.8	26.0	36.6	27.7	26.7	28.5	28.4	29.3	26.3	28.9	26.4	25.4	28.4	25.0
4. Desirable	17.2	6.2	29.0	17.1	20.5	17.4	17.7	16.5	17.3	18.4	15.8	18.2	15.3	18.5	18.8	11.8
Item 11860 N(Wtd)	3739	1833	1744	2942	415	902	1072	1244	521	1754	1737	1263	1005	497	810	68

A05H: Working with a small group of partners

1. Not at all acceptable	12.2	11.3	13.1	11.2	18.8	14.0	10.7	12.6	11.3	9.1	15.2	11.9	12.9	13.1	11.1	11.8
2. Somewhat acceptable	26.4	24.9	27.9	25.5	32.2	26.6	27.6	25.9	24.9	24.0	28.6	27.9	26.3	26.3	23.3	35.3
3. Acceptable	41.4	42.6	39.8	42.5	33.4	40.1	43.6	41.1	39.8	45.1	38.3	42.3	42.0	39.8	41.6	27.9
4. Desirable	19.9	21.2	19.1	20.7	15.6	19.4	18.0	20.4	23.8	21.9	17.9	18.0	18.8	20.9	23.9	26.5
Item 11870 N(Wtd)	3743	1834	1747	2944	416	903	1072	1247	522	1756	1739	1266	1005	498	808	68

A05I: Working on your own (self-employed)

1. Not at all acceptable	10.7	6.2	15.5	9.8	16.1	11.2	10.0	10.8	11.4	8.7	13.0	11.2	8.6	13.4	10.9	7.4
2. Somewhat acceptable	17.2	13.7	20.8	17.1	17.5	18.2	16.6	16.7	17.9	17.3	16.8	18.9	19.1	13.2	14.8	10.3
3. Acceptable	28.7	28.4	29.2	29.8	26.4	26.1	32.6	27.7	28.0	30.1	27.6	30.9	30.5	30.5	22.9	19.1
4. Desirable	43.3	51.7	34.5	43.3	40.0	44.6	40.8	44.8	42.7	43.9	42.7	38.9	41.8	42.7	51.4	63.2
Item 11880 N(Wtd)	3749	1841	1746	2950	417	905	1073	1246	525	1760	1741	1265	1007	499	813	68

A06: If you were to get enough money to live as comfortably as you'd like for the rest of your life, would you want to work?

1. I would want to work	82.3	81.0	83.7	82.3	83.0	80.4	83.5	83.0	81.7	84.0	81.2	85.6	83.5	83.7	76.5	65.7
2. I would not want to work	17.7	19.1	16.3	17.7	17.0	19.6	16.5	17.1	18.3	16.0	18.8	14.4	16.5	16.1	23.7	35.8
Item 8100 N(Wtd)	3728	1819	1749	2929	418	899	1068	1242	519	1751	1730	1260	1002	496	807	67

A07: The next questions are about race relations. How much have you gotten to know people of other races...

A07A: In school?

1. Not at all	10.5	10.9	10.1	12.4	1.2	8.7	19.8	3.8	10.1	9.2	11.8	10.8	10.9	9.2	10.6	9.9
2. A little	22.8	22.9	22.9	25.0	13.3	25.0	28.3	16.8	21.9	24.0	22.5	22.4	21.5	25.7	24.7	19.7
3. Some	30.8	32.8	28.9	32.3	21.8	33.8	27.3	32.5	28.6	30.1	31.6	28.6	32.7	29.3	32.9	25.4
4. A lot	33.0	30.2	35.5	26.9	62.6	29.9	19.6	44.9	37.4	34.2	30.8	35.3	32.4	32.3	28.7	39.4
8. Does not apply to me	2.9	3.3	2.6	3.3	1.2	2.5	4.9	1.8	1.9	2.5	3.3	2.8	2.5	3.4	3.2	4.2
Item 11890 N(Wtd)	3749	1837	1750	2944	422	909	1069	1248	524	1755	1742	1264	1008	498	811	71

A07B: In your neighborhood?

1. Not at all	37.2	35.3	39.5	42.0	19.0	35.0	47.5	33.1	29.5	37.7	37.1	36.7	37.6	38.8	38.0	31.9
2. A little	21.9	23.1	20.7	21.6	21.9	23.7	21.3	19.1	26.3	21.3	22.4	19.6	22.6	23.1	24.0	24.6
3. Some	15.8	15.4	15.8	13.6	23.6	17.5	9.4	18.5	19.4	15.3	15.6	16.9	15.3	14.1	14.1	18.8
4. A lot	12.3	12.7	11.2	7.9	29.8	11.4	8.2	14.7	16.2	10.6	13.4	12.7	11.3	14.1	10.1	20.3
8. Does not apply to me	12.9	13.5	12.8	14.9	6.0	12.4	13.7	14.7	8.4	15.1	11.4	14.1	13.1	10.0	13.8	4.3
Item 11900 N(Wtd)	3741	1837	1745	2944	416	906	1069	1242	525	1754	1739	1263	1005	498	811	69

QUESTIONNAIRE FORM 5 1978	TOTAL	SEX M	F	RACE White	Black	REGION NE	NC	S	W	4YR COLLEGE PLANS Yes	No	ILLICIT DRUG USE: LIFETIME None	Marijuana Only	Few Pills	More Pills	Any Heroin
Weighted No. of Cases:	3770	1844	1762	2955	426	911	1074	1259	527	1768	1748	1274	1012	501	813	71
% of Weighted Total:	100.0	48.9	46.7	78.4	11.3	24.2	28.5	33.4	14.0	46.9	46.4	33.8	26.8	13.3	21.6	1.9
A07C: In church?																
1. Not at all	43.1	43.6	43.2	47.1	24.3	46.7	50.0	39.0	32.8	42.2	44.8	38.0	46.3	44.1	48.2	39.1
2. A little	19.2	19.0	19.3	18.4	22.7	16.6	17.8	20.0	24.6	19.6	18.7	20.7	17.2	23.3	15.9	24.6
3. Some	11.5	9.8	13.2	10.3	16.1	10.6	10.3	12.0	14.8	10.1	12.5	13.5	11.3	8.9	9.7	17.4
4. A lot	7.1	6.5	7.2	4.2	20.7	4.8	4.1	9.3	11.7	6.8	6.7	10.5	5.6	5.3	4.2	2.9
8. Does not apply to me	19.1	21.0	17.1	19.9	16.4	21.4	17.8	19.8	16.3	21.4	17.3	17.2	19.4	18.6	22.1	15.9
Item 11910 N(Wtd)	3715	1829	1732	2928	415	898	1065	1230	521	1746	1726	1259	998	494	801	69
A07D: On sports teams?																
1. Not at all	20.6	16.8	25.0	22.8	11.8	22.0	28.9	13.9	17.7	17.5	23.5	20.7	19.8	18.8	23.4	19.1
2. A little	17.5	18.0	17.0	18.6	12.3	17.0	20.8	15.3	17.0	18.6	16.7	17.6	19.6	17.9	14.3	22.1
3. Some	19.9	23.3	16.9	19.6	19.0	20.5	16.2	21.9	21.8	20.5	19.0	17.1	21.9	20.0	22.2	23.5
4. A lot	23.9	28.9	17.5	19.9	44.5	20.3	15.0	32.4	28.1	26.6	20.9	25.5	24.9	23.2	18.7	22.1
8. Does not apply to me	18.1	12.9	23.5	19.1	12.7	20.3	19.3	16.5	15.5	16.8	19.9	19.2	13.9	20.0	21.3	11.8
Item 11920 N(Wtd)	3728	1831	1737	2933	416	902	1063	1239	524	1746	1736	1259	1002	496	807	68
A07E: In clubs?																
1. Not at all	30.0	31.6	28.0	32.9	16.1	30.8	40.7	22.2	25.3	26.4	33.6	28.8	31.8	26.5	33.5	27.5
2. A little	19.4	20.7	18.6	19.9	16.8	18.6	19.0	20.5	19.0	20.7	18.2	17.3	20.4	24.3	19.2	10.1
3. Some	18.3	16.7	20.5	17.5	20.9	17.8	14.1	20.3	23.2	20.9	15.8	21.2	18.8	15.6	14.7	23.2
4. A lot	14.2	11.0	16.9	10.9	31.2	12.1	7.3	21.1	15.7	14.6	13.1	16.2	12.4	14.0	11.8	21.7
8. Does not apply to me	18.0	19.9	16.1	18.9	15.3	20.7	18.9	15.8	17.0	17.3	19.3	16.6	16.6	19.6	20.9	17.4
Item 11930 N(Wtd)	3728	1833	1737	2933	417	899	1066	1241	522	1748	1734	1265	1002	494	804	69
A07F: On a job?																
1. Not at all	17.7	17.8	17.7	20.0	7.4	19.6	24.6	11.7	14.3	16.4	19.0	19.3	19.0	15.5	16.5	10.1
2. A little	15.4	16.2	14.5	16.7	8.6	15.7	16.7	13.1	17.6	14.9	16.0	15.0	14.6	17.5	15.4	11.6
3. Some	24.5	25.3	23.6	24.8	22.3	24.9	25.0	23.6	24.9	23.6	26.0	23.0	25.2	23.7	27.3	23.2
4. A lot	30.4	30.9	29.8	26.6	47.2	25.5	22.1	40.7	31.5	31.3	28.7	26.4	31.4	33.9	30.9	47.8
8. Does not apply to me	12.0	9.9	14.5	12.0	14.6	14.2	11.6	10.9	11.9	13.8	10.5	16.2	9.9	9.2	10.0	8.7
Item 11940 N(Wtd)	3741	1837	1744	2945	417	906	1070	1242	523	1752	1741	1263	1004	498	811	69
A08: Thinking about the country as a whole, would you say relations between white people and black people have been getting better, getting worse, or staying pretty much the same?																
1. Better	24.0	23.5	24.4	24.3	23.9	21.1	22.6	25.0	29.7	25.3	22.3	25.0	22.7	23.7	24.9	13.2
2. A little better	47.9	45.4	50.1	47.2	52.6	47.0	51.6	47.7	42.4	49.6	46.5	47.8	49.5	47.4	46.3	55.9
3. Same	18.9	20.7	17.4	19.6	15.3	22.5	17.8	16.5	20.5	17.6	20.6	18.6	19.5	19.1	18.4	20.6
4. A little worse	6.0	6.2	5.9	5.7	5.4	6.5	5.9	5.9	5.1	5.4	6.6	5.6	5.5	6.8	6.6	4.4
5. Worse	3.2	4.2	2.2	3.2	2.8	2.9	2.0	4.9	2.1	2.2	4.1	2.9	2.8	2.8	3.7	5.9
Item 11950 N(Wtd)	3749	1836	1750	2942	426	906	1071	1246	526	1757	1740	1267	1010	498	808	68

The next questions are about driving.

	TOTAL	M	F	White	Black	NE	NC	S	W	Yes	No	None	Marijuana Only	Few Pills	More Pills	Any Heroin
A09: Do you have a driver's license?																
1. Yes	88.6	93.4	83.8	92.6	63.6	81.8	93.2	90.2	87.4	89.4	88.7	87.1	88.1	89.6	92.5	83.8
2. No, but i soon will-- GO TO Q.A13	9.3	5.9	12.8	6.2	30.6	14.8	5.8	8.0	9.8	8.9	9.1	10.0	9.7	9.0	6.5	16.2
3. No--GO TO Q.A13	2.1	.7	3.4	1.2	6.1	3.4	1.0	1.8	2.8	1.7	2.2	2.9	2.1	1.5	1.0	1.5
Item 11960 N(Wtd)	3589	1787	1660	2904	343	874	1052	1162	501	1711	1651	1200	978	469	786	68
A10: Do you own a car?																
1. Yes	50.3	60.8	36.6	51.0	33.5	39.3	47.9	60.4	49.8	41.2	59.3	46.0	49.9	54.2	52.9	70.7
2. No, but I expect to own one in another year or two	32.1	26.5	39.4	31.0	46.3	38.2	31.1	28.0	34.2	33.1	30.8	31.8	32.4	32.7	33.1	24.1
3. No	17.6	12.8	24.1	18.0	20.2	22.5	21.1	11.7	16.0	25.6	9.9	22.2	17.9	12.9	14.0	5.2
Item 11970 N(Wtd) ★	3183	1669	1392	2691	218	715	983	1047	438	1530	1466	1045	862	419	729	55

★ = excludes respondents for whom question was inappropriate.

	TOTAL	SEX		RACE		REGION				4YR COLLEGE PLANS		ILLICIT DRUG USE: LIFETIME				
QUESTIONNAIRE FORM 5 1978		M	F	White	Black	NE	NC	S	W	Yes	No	None	Mari- juana Only	Few Pills	More Pills	Any Her- oin
Weighted No. of Cases:	3770	1844	1762	2955	426	911	1074	1259	527	1768	1748	1274	1012	501	813	71
% of Weighted Total:	100.0	48.9	46.7	78.4	11.3	24.2	28.5	33.4	14.0	46.9	46.4	33.8	26.8	13.3	21.6	1.9
A11: Are you able to use someone else's car when you want to?																
1. Yes, whenever I wish	29.9	30.5	29.7	31.3	19.1	23.9	31.4	32.6	29.7	31.8	29.3	31.6	29.3	32.2	27.7	32.8
2. Yes, most of the time	45.4	42.3	49.3	45.6	45.1	47.0	48.2	42.2	44.5	46.9	44.0	45.9	46.2	43.7	45.7	39.7
3. Sometimes	17.1	19.1	14.6	16.7	21.9	19.6	13.7	18.1	18.5	15.2	18.3	16.2	17.2	16.0	18.3	17.2
4. Rarely	5.3	6.0	4.5	4.7	11.2	6.8	5.1	5.3	3.9	4.1	6.2	4.0	4.9	5.7	6.8	8.6
5. Never	2.2	2.0	1.7	1.8	3.3	2.8	1.7	1.9	3.2	2.0	2.3	2.4	2.6	2.4	1.5	1.7
Item 11980 N(Wtd) ★	3171	1661	1389	2682	215	710	978	1045	438	1521	1463	1042	860	419	722	58
A12: Do you make an effort to cut down on driving, in order to save gasoline?																
1. Not at all	14.4	16.6	11.8	14.4	12.5	18.2	14.5	12.4	12.8	13.8	15.1	9.9	16.6	11.2	19.6	22.0
2. Not very much	33.8	33.3	34.2	34.9	28.7	32.8	33.5	35.6	31.6	36.6	31.4	27.1	37.7	40.3	35.4	20.5
3. Yes, to some extent	41.0	39.1	43.5	40.8	40.7	39.4	41.5	40.4	43.5	37.2	44.3	49.3	37.0	37.5	36.3	30.5
4. Yes, quite a bit	7.5	7.7	6.8	7.1	10.2	4.6	7.7	8.4	9.6	8.8	6.6	10.4	5.6	8.4	4.8	13.6
8. Don't know	3.4	3.2	3.6	2.8	7.9	5.0	2.6	3.2	2.5	3.7	2.6	3.3	3.1	2.6	3.8	3.4
Item 11990 N(Wtd) ★	3181	1666	1392	2690	216	714	982	1049	437	1531	1463	1045	860	419	728	59
A13: Do you make an effort to cut down on the amount of electricity you use in order to save energy?																
1. Not at all	6.3	7.0	5.3	6.1	7.3	7.5	6.1	5.4	6.7	5.5	6.9	4.9	6.5	5.0	9.0	8.5
2. Not very much	23.5	24.6	22.8	24.7	17.4	25.3	23.4	23.0	22.0	23.5	24.7	21.2	25.0	25.8	25.3	21.1
3. Yes, to some extent	50.5	48.7	53.1	51.4	51.3	50.3	51.8	49.8	50.2	50.9	49.7	52.8	48.3	50.6	50.1	43.7
4. Yes, quite a bit	18.1	17.5	18.2	16.7	20.9	15.1	17.6	19.8	19.9	19.1	16.6	19.4	18.6	16.7	14.4	23.9
8. Don't know	1.6	2.2	.7	1.1	3.1	1.9	1.1	1.9	1.3	1.0	2.1	1.7	1.4	1.8	1.1	4.2
Item 12000 N(Wtd)	3755	1841	1752	2945	425	910	1071	1252	522	1761	1742	1271	1010	496	810	71
A14: In the house or apartment where you live, is an effort made to reduce heat during the winter, in order to save energy?																
1. Not at all	4.6	4.2	4.4	3.5	8.9	4.4	3.7	4.8	6.1	3.8	5.3	4.2	3.6	4.4	6.3	8.7
2. Not very much	15.2	15.2	14.9	13.9	21.8	12.8	15.5	15.9	17.2	14.9	15.1	15.1	14.2	16.2	15.9	18.8
3. Yes, to some extent	43.1	41.8	44.1	43.7	38.3	45.2	43.0	41.4	43.7	41.0	44.5	42.6	44.7	42.5	41.9	37.7
4. Yes, quite a bit	35.4	36.6	35.5	37.7	26.5	36.1	36.8	35.5	30.9	39.3	33.1	36.2	35.9	35.9	34.4	31.9
8. Don't know	1.7	2.3	1.1	1.1	4.7	1.7	1.0	2.4	1.7	1.0	2.0	1.9	1.6	1.0	1.5	2.9
Item 12010 N(Wtd)	3756	1839	1757	2947	426	909	1073	1250	524	1760	1745	1269	1010	499	811	69
A15: How do you feel about each of the following?																
A15A: How much do you enjoy shopping for things like clothes, records, sporting goods, and books?																
1. Not at all	2.2	3.8	.5	2.4	1.2	1.9	2.9	2.2	1.3	1.4	2.8	1.7	2.5	1.2	2.7	4.3
2. Not very much	10.3	16.6	3.5	10.9	4.9	11.7	10.5	9.4	9.9	10.7	9.9	10.0	9.2	13.4	9.9	10.0
3. Pretty much	32.2	43.2	20.5	33.6	19.1	32.1	32.9	30.9	33.9	31.9	32.2	30.4	35.8	28.1	32.6	40.0
4. Very much	55.3	36.4	75.5	53.1	74.6	54.3	53.6	57.6	54.7	55.9	55.1	57.9	52.6	57.1	54.9	44.3
Item 12020 N(Wtd)	3758	1840	1756	2948	425	909	1073	1251	525	1762	1745	1270	1010	499	811	70
A15B: How much do you care about having the latest fashion in your clothes, records, leisure activities, and so on?																
1. Not at all	4.2	6.1	2.2	4.4	1.7	5.4	3.7	3.4	5.1	4.0	4.2	3.1	4.5	4.2	5.1	7.1
2. Not very much	20.6	25.2	16.0	21.1	12.5	21.5	22.2	15.0	28.4	21.4	19.4	23.1	17.1	20.2	20.7	20.0
3. Pretty much	39.5	39.3	39.3	41.2	29.2	39.8	40.3	39.4	38.1	40.1	39.9	40.3	41.4	37.7	38.0	42.9
4. Very much	35.7	29.4	42.6	33.3	56.6	33.3	33.8	42.2	28.2	34.5	36.4	33.5	37.2	37.9	36.4	30.0
Item 12030 N(Wtd)	3756	1839	1755	2947	424	910	1071	1250	525	1760	1745	1270	1008	499	811	70

★ = excludes respondents for whom question was inappropriate.

QUESTIONNAIRE FORM 5 1978	TOTAL	SEX		RACE		REGION				4YR COLLEGE PLANS		ILLICIT DRUG USE: LIFETIME				
		M	F	White	Black	NE	NC	S	W	Yes	No	None	Mari- juana Only	Few Pills	More Pills	Any Her- oin
Weighted No. of Cases:	3770	1844	1762	2955	426	911	1074	1259	527	1768	1748	1274	1012	501	813	71
% of Weighted Total:	100.0	48.9	46.7	78.4	11.3	24.2	28.5	33.4	14.0	46.9	46.4	33.8	26.8	13.3	21.6	1.9

A15C: How much do you care about whether your family has most of the things your friends and neighbors have?

1. Not at all	24.4	22.6	25.8	23.5	26.7	28.4	24.0	20.0	28.8	23.1	24.5	23.8	22.9	22.8	27.4	34.8
2. Not very much	47.9	48.4	48.2	49.7	42.3	47.0	50.0	46.5	48.6	49.1	47.9	48.3	49.2	49.7	45.9	36.2
3. Pretty much	20.6	21.9	19.3	20.9	17.3	18.2	19.2	24.8	17.5	20.8	20.6	20.3	20.0	21.6	20.5	29.0
4. Very much	7.1	7.1	6.7	6.0	13.7	6.4	6.8	8.6	5.1	7.0	6.9	7.6	8.0	5.6	6.4	-
Item 12040 N(Wtd)	3753	1837	1755	2946	423	908	1071	1249	525	1759	1744	1268	1009	499	811	69

A16: When you are older, do you expect to own more possessions than your parents do now, or about the same, or less?

I expect to own...

1. Much less than my parents	1.8	1.7	1.7	1.6	2.6	1.3	1.5	2.3	1.9	1.5	2.1	2.2	1.2	.4	2.7	-
2. Somewhat less than my parents	9.4	8.4	10.4	10.0	6.9	10.0	10.8	7.1	11.1	9.2	9.9	8.8	8.9	10.1	11.1	4.3
3. About as much as my parents	39.8	34.8	45.9	43.6	20.3	39.2	42.6	37.5	41.0	37.7	42.8	45.2	38.8	37.0	34.8	39.1
4. Somewhat more than my parents	35.7	38.7	32.3	33.8	45.2	35.5	33.3	39.3	32.0	36.2	34.7	33.2	37.5	40.1	34.2	33.3
5. Much more than my parents	13.2	16.4	9.7	10.9	25.1	14.0	11.8	13.7	14.0	15.4	10.6	10.7	13.5	12.1	17.3	21.7
Item 12050 N(Wtd)	3731	1826	1749	2934	423	896	1068	1246	522	1755	1730	1265	1004	494	805	69

A17: Compared with your parents, what is the smallest amount that you could be content or satisfied to own?

The least I could be content to own is...

1. Much less than my parents	11.2	9.9	12.8	11.9	7.6	11.1	10.1	11.4	12.8	12.3	10.4	12.1	8.6	11.8	12.4	13.2
2. Somewhat less than my parents	32.9	31.3	35.1	36.6	12.6	31.8	38.0	27.7	37.1	35.2	31.2	32.9	34.4	31.9	33.2	23.5
3. About as much as my parents	40.0	41.5	38.8	39.6	43.0	42.2	37.6	42.9	34.6	38.3	42.4	41.5	40.0	39.8	38.0	45.6
4. Somewhat more than my parents	12.1	13.1	10.3	9.4	27.0	10.9	10.8	14.1	11.8	10.7	12.6	10.9	13.0	12.2	11.2	13.2
5. Much more than my parents	3.8	4.2	3.0	2.6	10.0	4.0	3.5	3.9	3.5	3.6	3.4	2.6	4.0	4.1	5.1	2.9
Item 12060 N(Wtd)	3703	1817	1733	2916	419	889	1057	1240	517	1743	1717	1252	1000	492	797	68

A18: These next questions ask your opinions about a number of different topics. How much do you agree or disagree with each statement below?

A18A: We ought to worry about our own country and let the rest of the world take care of itself

1. Disagree	24.3	20.6	27.8	22.9	32.8	25.3	20.7	26.3	25.2	26.0	21.8	27.5	22.8	23.4	22.0	19.1
2. Mostly disagree	24.4	22.2	27.4	25.8	16.7	23.0	25.8	24.2	24.4	27.3	21.8	25.2	24.2	26.1	24.1	10.3
3. Neither	14.1	13.5	14.8	14.5	11.3	13.8	16.8	10.8	17.2	13.7	14.7	13.0	14.7	12.0	16.3	23.5
4. Mostly agree	25.5	27.9	22.8	25.8	24.8	25.4	27.6	25.0	22.5	23.9	28.1	25.2	25.6	26.3	24.9	32.4
5. Agree	11.7	15.9	7.1	11.0	14.2	12.6	9.1	13.6	10.7	9.1	13.4	9.2	12.8	12.2	12.8	14.7
Item 12070 N(Wtd)	3749	1837	1753	2943	424	905	1072	1248	524	1757	1744	1267	1009	499	810	68

A18B: It would be better if we all felt more like citizens of the world than of any particular country

1. Disagree	11.5	14.2	8.7	12.2	5.9	11.3	11.1	10.7	14.0	10.9	11.9	10.0	12.1	12.9	12.4	5.8
2. Mostly disagree	12.6	13.5	11.5	13.8	5.9	12.7	13.8	12.1	10.9	13.2	11.8	11.6	13.5	11.5	13.2	18.8
3. Neither	17.2	16.2	18.1	18.4	13.0	15.5	20.3	16.5	15.4	17.6	17.0	16.7	16.4	16.7	20.0	13.0
4. Mostly agree	29.5	29.7	29.7	29.8	25.1	28.5	29.9	28.9	31.5	29.1	30.6	31.0	30.9	26.4	26.7	30.4
5. Agree	29.4	26.4	31.9	25.9	50.0	32.1	24.8	31.8	28.0	29.0	28.7	30.7	26.9	32.5	27.8	30.4
Item 12080 N(Wtd)	3736	1831	1747	2936	422	904	1063	1247	521	1754	1736	1262	1006	496	806	69

QUESTIONNAIRE FORM 5 1978	TOTAL	SEX		RACE		REGION				4YR COLLEGE PLANS		ILLICIT DRUG USE: LIFETIME				
		M	F	White	Black	NE	NC	S	W	Yes	No	None	Mari-juana Only	Few Pills	More Pills	Any Her-oin
Weighted No. of Cases:	3770	1844	1762	2955	426	911	1074	1259	527	1768	1748	1274	1012	501	813	71
% of Weighted Total:	100.0	48.9	46.7	78.4	11.3	24.2	28.5	33.4	14.0	46.9	46.4	33.8	26.8	13.3	21.6	1.9
A18C: I find it hard to be sympathetic toward starving people in foreign lands, when there is so much trouble in our own country																
1. Disagree	33.9	22.8	45.6	32.4	41.1	34.4	31.7	34.8	36.0	32.8	34.8	35.7	30.9	37.1	34.6	18.6
2. Mostly disagree	24.5	24.3	24.7	26.2	15.6	25.1	27.8	20.9	24.9	27.7	21.9	25.9	25.3	23.2	23.3	20.0
3. Neither	14.4	17.8	11.4	15.0	10.9	14.4	14.7	14.0	14.9	14.3	14.5	14.2	14.0	13.4	14.2	30.0
4. Mostly agree	15.9	19.3	12.2	16.0	15.4	15.8	15.2	17.3	13.8	16.5	15.2	13.3	17.6	15.8	17.7	17.1
5. Agree	11.3	15.8	6.2	10.3	17.0	10.3	10.7	13.0	10.5	8.5	13.6	10.9	12.3	10.2	10.2	14.3
Item 12090 N(Wtd)	3746	1834	1752	2941	423	904	1071	1248	522	1757	1741	1264	1008	499	810	70
A18D: Maybe some minority groups do get unfair treatment, but that's no business of mine																
1. Disagree	42.1	32.5	52.7	38.5	60.8	42.7	39.5	42.3	46.2	47.0	37.2	46.4	40.5	45.0	36.3	31.4
2. Mostly disagree	28.1	30.2	26.0	30.7	14.2	27.8	31.6	24.8	29.5	30.6	26.5	29.2	29.4	27.0	27.3	21.4
3. Neither	18.0	21.0	14.7	19.3	11.1	18.5	18.8	18.0	16.0	15.4	20.6	14.9	18.0	16.1	23.9	28.6
4. Mostly agree	6.9	9.8	3.8	6.9	6.1	6.1	6.7	8.4	5.0	4.2	9.4	6.2	6.8	7.3	6.6	15.7
5. Agree	4.9	6.4	2.9	4.5	7.6	4.9	3.4	6.6	3.5	2.9	6.4	3.5	5.4	4.6	5.9	4.3
Item 12100 N(Wtd)	3731	1826	1745	2926	423	905	1063	1244	519	1755	1731	1262	1006	496	802	70
A18E: I get very upset when I see other people treated unfairly																
1. Disagree	3.4	3.7	3.1	3.3	2.8	3.1	3.7	3.1	4.0	3.0	3.6	2.5	4.0	3.4	3.3	7.1
2. Mostly disagree	4.5	6.3	2.6	5.0	1.4	6.1	4.6	3.8	2.9	4.0	4.7	2.8	5.9	4.8	5.0	5.7
3. Neither	7.4	10.7	4.2	7.9	4.5	6.1	9.1	6.8	7.5	6.3	8.6	6.2	6.7	7.6	10.5	8.6
4. Mostly agree	32.3	37.7	26.3	33.9	24.4	32.5	33.7	31.7	30.2	31.1	33.0	29.6	34.2	30.7	33.5	47.1
5. Agree	52.5	41.6	63.8	49.9	66.8	52.2	48.9	54.5	55.4	55.5	50.0	58.9	49.4	53.3	47.7	31.4
Item 12110 N(Wtd)	3739	1833	1748	2936	422	902	1068	1247	523	1756	1736	1265	1005	499	807	70
A18F: I would agree to a good plan to make a better life for the poor, even if it cost me money																
1. Disagree	7.4	10.7	3.7	8.1	2.6	8.3	7.6	6.5	7.7	6.8	8.3	5.4	9.2	7.7	8.7	8.7
2. Mostly disagree	11.0	14.1	7.9	11.7	5.9	11.4	12.1	10.0	10.0	10.7	11.3	9.1	10.8	13.9	12.1	7.2
3. Neither	22.2	24.8	20.0	24.0	13.0	21.5	22.5	22.0	23.5	23.0	21.7	18.0	24.0	23.0	26.3	30.4
4. Mostly agree	36.1	32.3	40.0	36.6	34.8	35.0	37.4	35.7	36.0	37.4	35.2	39.6	35.6	35.7	32.7	27.5
5. Agree	23.3	18.0	28.4	19.6	43.6	23.8	20.4	25.9	22.5	22.1	23.6	27.9	20.4	19.8	20.2	26.1
Item 12120 N(Wtd)	3732	1825	1748	2928	422	903	1062	1247	519	1759	1728	1264	1005	496	802	69
A18G: It's not really my problem if others are in trouble and need help																
1. Disagree	40.3	30.7	50.3	38.6	53.0	42.9	36.5	41.3	41.2	42.5	38.2	45.0	36.9	41.5	37.6	26.1
2. Mostly disagree	34.3	37.2	31.9	36.9	23.5	33.8	37.3	33.0	32.4	36.2	33.3	33.1	38.7	32.3	33.7	33.3
3. Neither	14.7	17.1	11.8	15.2	9.3	13.7	16.2	13.7	15.8	13.0	16.1	12.8	15.3	11.8	18.9	20.3
4. Mostly agree	7.3	10.3	3.9	6.6	7.8	6.9	7.0	7.7	7.5	5.6	8.6	6.2	5.6	10.4	7.0	13.0
5. Agree	3.4	4.7	2.1	2.7	6.4	2.7	3.2	4.4	3.1	2.7	3.9	3.0	3.5	4.2	2.6	5.8
Item 12130 N(Wtd)	3735	1825	1751	2938	421	904	1071	1241	519	1758	1732	1261	1008	499	803	69
A18H: Americans could change their eating habits to provide more food for the hungry people in other parts of the world, and at the same time be healthier themselves																
1. Disagree	8.5	12.1	4.5	8.2	9.4	9.0	7.5	9.9	6.7	7.6	9.1	6.3	10.4	8.0	9.0	10.0
2. Mostly disagree	8.7	11.3	5.4	8.6	6.8	7.6	8.9	9.4	8.4	8.1	9.0	8.1	8.8	8.2	9.0	14.3
3. Neither	14.2	17.7	11.0	14.9	10.8	14.4	14.2	13.9	14.7	14.1	14.3	12.8	14.6	13.7	15.3	27.1
4. Mostly agree	29.1	28.8	29.4	29.9	24.1	28.2	32.0	27.9	27.3	29.3	29.1	32.1	27.8	27.3	27.8	25.7
5. Agree	39.6	30.2	49.8	38.4	48.8	40.8	37.5	39.0	43.1	40.9	38.5	40.7	38.4	42.6	38.7	22.9
Item 12140 N(Wtd)	3745	1833	1752	2938	424	904	1069	1247	524	1760	1739	1265	1008	498	808	70

QUESTIONNAIRE FORM 5 1978	TOTAL	SEX		RACE		REGION				4YR COLLEGE PLANS		ILLICIT DRUG USE: LIFETIME				
		M	F	White	Black	NE	NC	S	W	Yes	No	None	Mari- juana Only	Few Pills	More Pills	Any Her- oin
Weighted No. of Cases:	3770	1844	1762	2955	426	911	1074	1259	527	1768	1748	1274	1012	501	813	71
% of Weighted Total:	100.0	48.9	46.7	78.4	11.3	24.2	28.5	33.4	14.0	46.9	46.4	33.8	26.8	13.3	21.6	1.9

A18I: My family and I often buy things we really don't need; we could get along with much less

	TOTAL	M	F	White	Black	NE	NC	S	W	Yes	No	None	Mari- juana Only	Few Pills	More Pills	Any Her- oin
1. Disagree	12.9	13.5	11.8	10.4	24.8	17.6	9.9	12.0	13.2	11.4	13.4	12.5	12.6	13.9	11.8	18.6
2. Mostly disagree	14.8	16.3	13.2	14.4	16.5	15.5	14.9	14.7	13.4	14.5	15.3	14.5	15.3	17.1	12.9	21.4
3. Neither	14.4	17.3	11.5	14.7	11.3	15.0	16.2	12.0	15.1	14.1	13.8	13.8	16.0	13.1	14.0	14.3
4. Mostly agree	30.0	30.7	29.8	32.6	18.9	27.3	31.9	31.0	28.1	33.0	28.2	30.8	30.7	25.5	31.3	24.3
5. Agree	28.0	22.3	33.9	28.0	28.5	24.6	27.0	30.2	30.4	26.9	29.3	28.4	25.3	30.7	30.0	20.0
Item 10060 N(Wtd)	3741	1828	1753	2937	424	905	1068	1245	523	1756	1739	1265	1005	498	808	70

A18J: Most people will have fuller and happier lives if they choose legal marriage rather than staying single, or just living with someone

	TOTAL	M	F	White	Black	NE	NC	S	W	Yes	No	None	Mari- juana Only	Few Pills	More Pills	Any Her- oin
1. Disagree	23.7	21.7	25.7	22.5	28.8	28.6	22.0	21.2	24.5	21.8	25.1	14.4	23.8	26.8	34.6	35.7
2. Mostly disagree	14.8	15.9	13.4	15.1	12.5	16.6	16.6	13.1	12.4	15.1	14.4	11.3	16.5	15.9	18.1	15.7
3. Neither	23.5	24.2	23.3	23.0	23.9	24.6	26.2	19.4	25.8	24.5	22.6	25.3	24.8	21.7	20.0	25.7
4. Mostly agree	16.1	17.6	14.3	17.2	11.3	14.1	17.2	17.3	14.1	15.3	16.8	18.8	15.6	14.1	14.3	7.1
5. Agree	21.9	20.6	23.3	22.1	23.4	16.0	18.1	29.1	22.9	23.2	21.1	30.2	19.2	21.3	13.1	14.3
Item 12150 N(Wtd)	3738	1827	1753	2936	423	901	1069	1245	523	1759	1736	1267	1005	497	807	70

A18K: Parents should encourage just as much independence in their daughters as in their sons

	TOTAL	M	F	White	Black	NE	NC	S	W	Yes	No	None	Mari- juana Only	Few Pills	More Pills	Any Her- oin
1. Disagree	5.8	8.8	2.2	5.3	6.4	5.1	4.5	7.0	7.1	5.2	6.3	5.8	7.5	3.8	4.6	4.3
2. Mostly disagree	8.3	11.7	4.4	8.1	5.9	9.2	7.2	7.9	9.6	8.1	7.9	7.8	9.5	8.0	7.8	5.7
3. Neither	8.6	12.7	4.6	8.3	9.0	8.5	9.1	7.9	9.4	7.7	9.4	9.3	9.2	6.8	7.8	12.9
4. Mostly agree	24.2	28.9	19.6	25.5	16.8	22.9	26.0	22.8	26.0	23.6	25.0	25.7	23.9	23.4	23.3	15.7
5. Agree	53.1	38.0	69.2	52.8	61.8	54.3	53.1	54.5	48.1	55.3	51.4	51.4	49.9	57.9	56.6	61.4
Item 12160 N(Wtd)	3740	1830	1753	2940	422	903	1069	1247	520	1757	1738	1263	1008	499	808	70

A18L: Being a mother and raising children is one of the most fulfilling experiences a woman can have

	TOTAL	M	F	White	Black	NE	NC	S	W	Yes	No	None	Mari- juana Only	Few Pills	More Pills	Any Her- oin
1. Disagree	8.1	5.4	10.6	7.6	10.4	7.5	7.9	7.8	9.8	8.8	7.1	6.2	7.7	7.8	12.3	3.1
2. Mostly disagree	6.7	5.7	7.8	7.0	4.3	7.0	7.7	5.9	6.1	7.2	6.2	5.4	6.7	10.4	7.1	7.7
3. Neither	26.4	37.4	16.0	28.7	15.4	27.2	28.7	22.9	28.9	32.0	21.6	22.9	30.7	25.6	28.2	30.8
4. Mostly agree	25.6	23.1	28.1	26.8	21.0	26.7	26.1	24.3	25.9	24.8	27.3	27.8	25.2	26.0	22.9	26.2
5. Agree	33.1	28.4	37.5	29.9	48.9	31.4	29.6	39.2	29.1	27.1	37.8	37.9	29.7	30.3	29.4	32.3
Item 12170 N(Wtd)	3651	1752	1747	2867	415	881	1049	1212	509	1724	1691	1250	970	489	786	65

A18M: Most fathers should spend more time with their children than they do now

	TOTAL	M	F	White	Black	NE	NC	S	W	Yes	No	None	Mari- juana Only	Few Pills	More Pills	Any Her- oin
1. Disagree	1.5	1.6	1.1	1.3	1.2	1.8	1.2	1.2	2.1	1.1	1.8	1.4	1.0	1.4	2.1	-
2. Mostly disagree	2.7	2.6	2.9	2.7	1.4	3.4	2.5	1.9	3.6	2.5	2.8	2.4	3.0	2.8	4.3	4.3
3. Neither	11.9	13.0	11.0	12.5	8.1	13.2	14.0	8.5	13.2	12.6	11.1	10.1	13.1	10.3	14.9	10.0
4. Mostly agree	33.9	35.1	33.3	36.1	22.7	36.0	34.1	31.9	35.1	35.5	33.3	33.4	34.8	35.9	33.0	31.4
5. Agree	50.0	47.7	51.7	47.4	66.7	45.7	48.1	56.5	46.0	48.3	51.0	52.7	47.9	49.8	47.6	52.9
Item 12180 N(Wtd)	3727	1820	1750	2931	418	900	1068	1237	522	1753	1735	1265	999	496	805	70

A18N: The husband should make all the important decisions in the family

	TOTAL	M	F	White	Black	NE	NC	S	W	Yes	No	None	Mari- juana Only	Few Pills	More Pills	Any Her- oin
1. Disagree	39.0	24.5	54.8	38.4	46.9	42.7	40.1	37.0	35.2	41.6	37.6	40.3	36.6	40.3	41.4	21.7
2. Mostly disagree	20.3	21.1	19.7	21.5	16.8	20.0	21.9	19.5	19.4	20.8	20.2	19.6	21.4	19.2	20.2	34.8
3. Neither	15.5	20.7	10.2	16.0	10.7	17.7	17.2	11.7	17.1	15.9	15.3	15.7	16.8	13.0	15.2	18.8
4. Mostly agree	14.8	18.6	10.5	14.2	14.9	12.4	12.0	18.3	16.3	13.9	15.1	14.2	14.9	17.8	13.0	15.9
5. Agree	10.4	15.1	4.9	9.8	10.7	7.2	8.7	13.6	11.7	7.9	11.8	10.2	10.3	9.4	10.3	7.2
Item 12190 N(Wtd)	3743	1835	1751	2942	422	902	1071	1249	520	1759	1741	1267	1009	499	807	69

QUESTIONNAIRE FORM 5 1978	TOTAL	SEX		RACE		REGION				4YR COLLEGE PLANS		ILLICIT DRUG USE: LIFETIME				
		M	F	White	Black	NE	NC	S	W	Yes	No	None	Marijuana Only	Few Pills	More Pills	Any Heroin
Weighted No. of Cases:	3770	1844	1762	2955	426	911	1074	1259	527	1768	1748	1274	1012	501	813	71
% of Weighted Total:	100.0	48.9	46.7	78.4	11.3	24.2	28.5	33.4	14.0	46.9	46.4	33.8	26.8	13.3	21.6	1.9

A19: Some people think about what's going on in government very often, and others are not that interested. How much of an interest do you take in government and current events?

	TOTAL	M	F	White	Black	NE	NC	S	W	Yes	No	None	Marijuana Only	Few Pills	More Pills	Any Heroin
1. No interest at all	4.1	3.4	4.5	3.7	4.3	5.9	3.7	3.5	2.9	2.3	5.6	3.2	3.2	3.8	6.0	2.9
2. Very little interest	20.1	15.2	25.1	19.8	22.0	24.8	19.0	19.0	16.8	14.4	25.6	18.3	18.3	22.2	23.4	24.3
3. Some interest	50.0	47.5	52.8	50.1	49.4	49.2	53.5	48.3	48.4	49.0	51.3	51.2	51.4	50.3	47.5	42.9
4. A lot of interest	19.3	24.6	14.1	19.9	17.2	15.6	18.2	20.6	25.1	24.7	13.8	21.0	19.7	19.4	16.4	18.6
5. A very great interest	6.5	9.4	3.5	6.5	7.2	4.4	5.6	8.7	6.8	9.5	3.6	6.3	7.6	4.2	6.7	11.4
Item 6330 N(Wtd)	3734	1828	1750	2938	419	903	1069	1245	517	1754	1736	1267	1006	495	806	70

A20: If you have at least an average income in the future, how likely is it that you will contribute money to the following organizations? If you have already contributed, mark the last circle only. Are you likely to contribute to...

A20A: The United Fund or other community charities?

	TOTAL	M	F	White	Black	NE	NC	S	W	Yes	No	None	Marijuana Only	Few Pills	More Pills	Any Heroin
1. Definitely not	4.5	6.2	2.4	4.1	4.6	4.2	4.0	4.0	6.8	3.0	5.5	3.6	4.1	4.1	5.5	8.8
2. Probably not	15.3	18.4	12.1	16.3	9.6	15.5	15.7	13.9	17.8	13.7	16.8	11.6	16.9	17.8	18.2	16.2
3. Don't know	41.3	41.4	41.0	40.5	44.8	38.3	39.8	43.5	43.9	39.4	43.5	41.3	39.7	41.6	43.4	33.8
4. Probably will	26.9	24.2	30.0	26.8	30.7	29.2	25.8	27.2	24.2	30.4	23.5	31.3	27.0	25.2	20.6	27.9
5. Definitely will	3.3	2.6	4.0	3.1	5.0	3.8	3.7	3.1	2.3	4.1	2.7	4.0	3.0	2.4	2.9	5.9
6. Already have	8.8	7.2	10.5	9.3	5.3	9.0	10.9	8.3	5.3	9.3	8.0	8.2	9.2	8.9	9.5	5.9
Item 12200 N(Wtd)	3705	1821	1736	2920	417	888	1064	1240	512	1739	1733	1254	1000	493	801	68

A20B: International relief organizations (CARE, UNICEF, etc.)?

	TOTAL	M	F	White	Black	NE	NC	S	W	Yes	No	None	Marijuana Only	Few Pills	More Pills	Any Heroin
1. Definitely not	4.5	6.2	2.5	4.3	4.6	4.0	4.3	4.3	6.0	3.6	5.1	3.4	4.6	4.3	5.5	7.2
2. Probably not	12.8	16.4	9.3	13.7	8.0	11.6	13.1	12.0	15.8	12.3	13.1	10.8	14.3	14.5	14.0	14.5
3. Don't know	30.0	33.7	25.3	30.2	28.9	26.1	30.2	31.2	33.5	27.3	32.9	32.8	29.4	25.5	29.6	21.7
4. Probably will	33.3	29.8	37.5	33.3	34.9	32.3	33.1	35.7	29.8	34.9	31.8	33.7	32.3	34.6	32.0	40.6
5. Definitely will	6.8	4.4	8.9	4.9	16.1	7.2	6.0	7.6	5.6	7.1	6.1	7.5	6.4	6.9	5.5	5.8
6. Already have	12.7	9.5	16.4	13.5	7.7	18.9	13.1	9.2	9.1	14.9	11.0	11.9	13.1	14.5	13.5	10.1
Item 12210 N(Wtd)	3709	1821	1740	2924	415	893	1065	1237	514	1741	1734	1255	1002	491	802	69

A20C: Minority group organizations (NAACP, SCLS, etc.)?

	TOTAL	M	F	White	Black	NE	NC	S	W	Yes	No	None	Marijuana Only	Few Pills	More Pills	Any Heroin
1. Definitely not	12.4	17.6	7.1	13.9	4.3	12.0	10.4	14.4	12.7	12.6	12.2	10.4	14.5	12.4	12.5	19.1
2. Probably not	26.7	28.5	25.4	30.7	7.2	24.1	28.4	26.9	26.9	29.3	25.3	25.1	27.2	27.0	30.3	20.6
3. Don't know	39.8	36.9	42.7	41.5	25.8	41.4	43.3	34.9	41.7	35.9	43.8	42.8	37.2	40.6	39.1	35.3
4. Probably will	15.3	11.9	18.5	11.8	33.8	15.9	14.2	16.5	13.6	15.3	14.5	15.2	14.7	15.0	14.0	16.2
5. Definitely will	4.2	3.5	4.8	1.5	21.0	4.5	2.6	5.5	3.7	5.1	3.0	5.3	4.2	3.4	2.6	7.4
6. Already have	1.6	1.6	1.4	.6	7.7	2.1	1.1	1.8	1.4	1.8	1.2	1.1	2.2	1.8	1.5	1.5
Item 12220 N(Wtd)	3700	1816	1736	2920	414	885	1064	1238	513	1736	1733	1249	1002	493	800	68

A20D: Church or religious organizations?

	TOTAL	M	F	White	Black	NE	NC	S	W	Yes	No	None	Marijuana Only	Few Pills	More Pills	Any Heroin
1. Definitely not	5.4	6.8	3.6	5.4	2.4	7.6	5.0	2.4	9.4	4.9	5.8	2.4	5.2	6.7	8.6	11.9
2. Probably not	9.0	10.0	8.0	9.6	5.1	10.0	8.5	7.0	13.3	7.9	9.9	6.2	9.3	8.2	14.0	11.9
3. Don't know	13.6	14.5	12.2	13.3	11.5	16.6	12.4	11.3	16.7	11.8	15.3	10.9	12.6	15.7	16.8	22.4
4. Probably will	23.9	25.1	22.6	23.7	24.4	24.9	24.6	23.9	20.8	22.1	25.4	23.7	24.9	24.1	22.4	22.4
5. Definitely will	14.0	13.7	14.2	13.1	21.8	11.8	12.4	18.0	12.0	15.5	12.8	17.6	14.8	10.6	9.6	9.0
6. Already have	34.0	29.8	39.4	34.9	35.0	29.2	37.1	37.4	27.5	37.7	30.8	39.2	33.2	34.7	28.7	20.9
Item 12230 N(Wtd)	3700	1816	1736	2921	409	893	1066	1231	510	1741	1723	1254	1000	490	799	67

QUESTIONNAIRE FORM 5 1978	TOTAL	SEX		RACE		REGION				4YR COLLEGE PLANS		ILLICIT DRUG USE: LIFETIME				
		M	F	White	Black	NE	NC	S	W	Yes	No	None	Mari-juana Only	Few Pills	More Pills	Any Her-oin
Weighted No. of Cases:	3770	1844	1762	2955	426	911	1074	1259	527	1768	1748	1274	1012	501	813	71
% of Weighted Total:	100.0	48.9	46.7	78.4	11.3	24.2	28.5	33.4	14.0	46.9	46.4	33.8	26.8	13.3	21.6	1.9

A20E: Political parties or organizations?

	TOTAL	M	F	White	Black	NE	NC	S	W	Yes	No	None	Mari-juana Only	Few Pills	More Pills	Any Her-oin
1. Definitely not	17.9	19.7	15.9	17.0	21.2	23.4	14.8	15.7	19.8	14.8	21.3	13.6	17.6	22.5	20.9	33.3
2. Probably not	27.8	26.3	29.7	28.8	20.9	31.8	28.4	23.5	29.7	27.4	28.9	27.3	27.9	28.2	29.3	23.2
3. Don't know	33.8	31.9	35.4	33.8	36.2	30.0	36.1	36.0	30.7	32.9	34.8	37.9	35.6	29.4	29.5	17.4
4. Probably will	13.5	14.5	12.6	13.4	16.0	9.4	13.7	16.6	12.3	16.0	10.2	14.7	12.1	12.3	12.6	17.4
5. Definitely will	3.3	3.7	2.7	3.3	3.2	2.6	3.1	4.0	3.3	4.3	1.9	2.9	3.3	2.9	3.7	7.2
6. Already have	3.8	3.9	3.6	3.7	2.2	2.8	3.8	4.3	4.1	4.6	3.0	3.6	3.6	4.5	4.0	-
Item 12240 N(Wtd)	3679	1804	1728	2905	406	881	1059	1228	511	1732	1719	1241	998	489	793	69

A20F: Citizen lobbies (Common Cause, Public Citizen, etc.)?

	TOTAL	M	F	White	Black	NE	NC	S	W	Yes	No	None	Mari-juana Only	Few Pills	More Pills	Any Her-oin
1. Definitely not	10.7	12.4	8.9	10.6	11.2	11.5	10.2	9.3	13.5	10.0	11.4	9.2	11.9	9.2	11.6	16.2
2. Probably not	24.9	23.4	26.6	26.1	17.7	23.8	25.1	23.9	28.6	24.6	25.5	25.6	25.8	25.3	23.0	25.0
3. Don't know	44.7	43.3	46.6	45.4	42.2	43.4	47.5	43.7	43.3	45.1	44.2	47.5	44.3	43.3	43.8	35.3
4. Probably will	15.3	15.5	14.6	14.4	20.9	16.6	14.0	17.1	11.0	15.9	14.5	13.6	13.7	18.0	17.3	14.7
5. Definitely will	2.5	3.0	2.0	2.0	4.6	2.8	1.9	3.0	2.0	3.1	2.0	2.3	2.5	1.2	3.4	2.9
6. Already have	2.0	2.5	1.2	1.4	3.4	1.7	1.4	2.8	1.6	1.4	2.4	1.8	1.8	2.9	1.1	4.4
Item 12250 N(Wtd)	3690	1811	1732	2912	412	889	1060	1231	510	1733	1723	1245	998	490	800	68

A20G: Charities to help fight diseases (cancer, heart disease, etc.)?

	TOTAL	M	F	White	Black	NE	NC	S	W	Yes	No	None	Mari-juana Only	Few Pills	More Pills	Any Her-oin
1. Definitely not	1.6	2.5	.5	1.4	1.7	1.9	1.5	.8	3.3	1.0	2.1	1.9	1.4	1.2	1.2	1.4
2. Probably not	2.9	4.6	1.0	3.0	2.2	2.7	3.4	2.4	3.5	1.6	3.7	1.7	2.8	3.0	4.6	5.8
3. Don't know	9.3	12.1	6.4	9.4	8.1	7.4	10.0	8.9	12.1	8.6	10.3	8.6	9.2	9.3	10.0	20.3
4. Probably will	36.2	40.6	30.8	35.8	36.4	34.0	35.7	37.3	38.3	35.8	35.9	35.9	38.2	32.5	37.3	24.6
5. Definitely will	28.4	24.0	33.5	27.5	35.6	29.7	26.8	29.2	27.0	29.2	28.2	29.3	29.1	32.1	23.6	24.6
6. Already have	21.6	16.3	27.7	22.9	16.3	24.2	22.6	21.4	15.8	23.9	19.9	22.6	19.2	22.0	23.4	23.2
Item 12260 N(Wtd)	3710	1819	1741	2922	418	891	1067	1240	512	1741	1734	1255	1003	492	802	69

A20H: Organizations concerned with population problems (Planned Parenthood, ZPG, etc.)?

	TOTAL	M	F	White	Black	NE	NC	S	W	Yes	No	None	Mari-juana Only	Few Pills	More Pills	Any Her-oin
1. Definitely not	7.3	10.2	4.0	6.8	7.9	8.5	6.2	6.5	8.9	7.1	7.3	6.5	8.1	6.3	7.2	10.1
2. Probably not	17.0	19.4	15.0	18.3	12.7	17.3	18.0	16.4	15.9	17.3	17.0	17.4	18.0	15.6	16.9	15.9
3. Don't know	40.6	43.3	37.6	41.9	35.7	38.5	45.6	38.9	37.7	40.4	41.4	41.8	41.3	39.1	39.6	34.8
4. Probably will	25.1	20.5	29.4	24.2	26.6	24.6	22.0	27.3	27.2	25.6	24.2	25.9	23.4	27.4	24.2	26.1
5. Definitely will	8.4	5.3	11.7	7.1	15.8	9.4	6.0	9.7	8.2	8.3	8.0	7.6	7.9	9.7	9.2	5.8
6. Already have	1.7	1.2	2.4	1.6	1.0	1.9	2.1	1.2	1.9	1.3	2.0	.8	1.4	1.6	3.0	7.2
Item 12270 N(Wtd)	3706	1816	1743	2921	417	892	1062	1238	515	1741	1733	1253	1002	493	801	69

A20I: Organizations concerned with environmental problems (Sierra Club, Friends of Earth, etc.)?

	TOTAL	M	F	White	Black	NE	NC	S	W	Yes	No	None	Mari-juana Only	Few Pills	More Pills	Any Her-oin
1. Definitely not	7.0	8.1	5.9	6.5	9.6	7.2	5.6	6.7	10.3	6.0	8.1	6.5	6.3	7.5	7.9	5.8
2. Probably not	15.2	13.5	17.2	15.8	14.4	14.9	17.8	14.7	11.7	13.6	17.4	15.1	16.1	14.6	15.5	13.0
3. Don't know	37.7	35.9	39.5	37.6	40.1	33.0	41.1	39.3	35.0	34.0	41.0	40.9	37.5	35.0	34.9	36.2
4. Probably will	25.0	26.8	23.3	25.3	22.6	26.4	23.1	25.9	24.5	27.9	22.5	24.9	24.4	29.4	24.4	11.6
5. Definitely will	12.1	12.4	11.9	11.9	11.8	15.4	10.0	10.7	14.0	14.9	9.1	10.1	12.5	11.5	14.5	23.2
6. Already have	2.9	3.4	2.2	3.0	1.4	3.0	2.3	2.7	4.5	3.5	1.9	2.6	3.2	2.0	2.8	7.2
Item 12280 N(Wtd)	3702	1816	1739	2918	416	887	1063	1238	514	1741	1729	1253	1001	494	799	69

Now we have a different kind of question.

A21: How satisfied are you with your life as a whole these days?

	TOTAL	M	F	White	Black	NE	NC	S	W	Yes	No	None	Mari-juana Only	Few Pills	More Pills	Any Her-oin
1. Completely dissatisfied	1.5	1.4	1.7	1.2	2.9	1.1	1.3	1.9	1.7	1.3	1.8	1.7	1.5	1.2	1.7	1.4
2. Quite dissatisfied	6.1	4.9	7.0	6.4	5.3	6.0	6.5	5.5	6.9	5.7	5.9	5.8	6.2	7.0	6.6	4.3
3. Somewhat dissatisfied	9.8	10.0	9.6	9.2	11.5	10.5	9.2	9.2	10.8	8.8	10.0	7.2	9.2	11.2	12.9	14.5
4. Neither, or mixed feelings	13.8	13.3	14.9	13.2	15.0	15.1	14.2	12.5	14.1	12.5	15.1	12.8	14.4	15.1	14.4	14.5
5. Somewhat satisfied	28.4	30.0	26.7	28.3	29.6	28.6	30.0	28.3	24.7	27.2	29.8	26.9	28.7	28.9	28.5	37.7
6. Quite satisfied	33.6	34.0	33.1	35.4	27.0	31.9	33.5	34.4	34.9	37.6	30.4	36.3	33.7	31.5	31.7	21.7
7. Completely satisfied	6.9	6.5	7.0	6.4	8.8	6.9	5.4	8.1	6.9	6.8	6.5	9.2	6.5	5.0	4.2	5.8
Item 6840 N(Wtd)	3728	1828	1750	2941	419	901	1064	1245	518	1759	1728	1269	1007	498	807	69

QUESTIONNAIRE FORM 5 1978	TOTAL	SEX		RACE		REGION				4YR COLLEGE PLANS		ILLICIT DRUG USE: LIFETIME				
		M	F	White	Black	NE	NC	S	W	Yes	No	None	Marijuana Only	Few Pills	More Pills	Any Heroin
Weighted No. of Cases:	3770	1844	1762	2955	426	911	1074	1259	527	1768	1748	1274	1012	501	813	71
% of Weighted Total:	100.0	48.9	46.7	78.4	11.3	24.2	28.5	33.4	14.0	46.9	46.4	33.8	26.8	13.3	21.6	1.9

A22: These questions are about whether you think women are discriminated against in each of the following areas. To what extent are women discriminated against...

A22A: In getting a college education?

	TOTAL	M	F	White	Black	NE	NC	S	W	Yes	No	None	Mari- juana Only	Few Pills	More Pills	Any Her- oin
1. Not at all	45.5	50.4	40.6	45.8	44.4	44.8	44.7	46.9	45.3	44.4	46.6	45.0	48.0	42.6	44.7	53.7
2. Very little	30.0	25.8	35.2	32.6	18.1	30.9	33.1	27.1	28.9	34.5	26.7	32.2	28.5	30.1	31.1	13.4
3. Some	12.8	10.6	14.6	12.2	15.5	13.7	11.4	13.5	12.6	13.4	12.5	12.9	11.5	12.9	13.4	22.4
4. A good deal	2.2	1.8	2.5	1.8	3.1	1.7	2.5	2.3	2.3	1.4	2.8	1.7	2.7	3.6	1.1	3.0
5. A great deal	2.0	1.9	1.9	.9	6.9	1.8	1.2	2.8	2.1	1.3	2.0	2.1	1.8	2.0	1.5	1.5
8. Don't know	7.4	9.5	5.3	6.7	11.9	7.3	7.0	7.3	8.5	5.1	9.4	6.1	7.5	8.8	8.1	7.5
Item 12290 N(Wtd)	3717	1820	1748	2934	419	896	1062	1243	516	1756	1726	1264	1006	498	805	67

A22B: In gaining positions of leadership over men and women?

	TOTAL	M	F	White	Black	NE	NC	S	W	Yes	No	None	Mari- juana Only	Few Pills	More Pills	Any Her- oin
1. Not at all	6.4	9.0	3.5	5.9	7.9	4.2	5.1	9.3	6.2	5.2	7.1	6.5	6.7	6.3	4.9	13.4
2. Very little	14.2	16.9	11.1	14.7	11.8	13.0	14.1	14.3	16.2	11.8	16.9	13.2	14.5	15.5	14.8	14.9
3. Some	34.5	35.4	33.9	37.0	24.5	33.6	37.6	33.4	31.7	37.0	31.4	36.3	33.2	32.1	34.6	40.3
4. A good deal	25.3	22.7	28.4	25.6	24.0	29.5	25.8	22.0	24.6	28.5	22.6	24.8	27.9	25.0	24.2	16.4
5. A great deal	13.5	8.8	18.2	11.4	22.3	13.0	11.7	14.8	14.5	12.9	14.4	13.3	12.3	15.1	14.6	7.5
8. Don't know	6.2	7.2	4.9	5.4	9.6	6.6	5.7	6.2	6.6	4.6	7.7	6.0	5.3	6.0	7.0	7.5
Item 12300 N(Wtd)	3715	1818	1747	2932	417	898	1060	1241	517	1756	1722	1266	1005	496	803	67

A22C: In obtaining executive positions in business?

	TOTAL	M	F	White	Black	NE	NC	S	W	Yes	No	None	Mari- juana Only	Few Pills	More Pills	Any Her- oin
1. Not at all	7.1	8.3	5.5	6.4	9.3	5.9	5.0	9.0	8.7	5.2	8.5	7.9	6.4	7.0	5.8	16.4
2. Very little	14.7	15.7	14.1	14.9	12.4	12.5	14.7	14.9	18.1	13.4	16.1	13.0	15.7	13.7	16.4	19.4
3. Some	31.4	32.2	30.8	33.0	25.4	33.8	32.6	30.4	27.6	32.6	29.7	31.4	32.8	32.3	29.1	28.4
4. A good deal	25.8	25.4	26.1	27.1	21.3	26.6	28.8	24.3	22.1	28.5	23.9	25.8	25.9	23.9	27.2	25.4
5. A great deal	13.1	9.5	17.0	11.8	19.1	14.6	10.9	13.8	13.0	13.6	12.8	13.9	12.4	14.7	12.8	6.0
8. Don't know	7.9	9.0	6.3	6.9	12.4	6.6	8.0	7.7	10.5	6.8	9.0	8.0	6.8	8.6	8.7	6.0
Item 12310 N(Wtd)	3714	1818	1748	2931	418	897	1062	1240	515	1752	1725	1263	1006	498	804	67

A22D: In obtaining top jobs in the professions?

	TOTAL	M	F	White	Black	NE	NC	S	W	Yes	No	None	Mari- juana Only	Few Pills	More Pills	Any Her- oin
1. Not at all	10.2	12.2	7.9	9.7	11.4	9.6	8.0	12.1	11.3	8.5	11.6	11.2	9.3	11.5	8.5	18.2
2. Very little	18.9	20.0	17.7	19.7	13.5	15.5	18.7	20.5	20.8	18.3	19.3	18.2	18.8	17.5	20.7	19.7
3. Some	29.3	29.8	28.9	30.5	24.9	30.3	30.9	28.4	26.5	30.2	28.6	28.8	30.2	29.2	29.6	22.7
4. A good deal	21.9	19.9	24.0	22.3	19.6	24.2	23.6	19.3	20.2	23.3	20.4	21.6	22.6	21.4	21.8	22.7
5. A great deal	12.7	9.2	16.1	11.1	21.7	13.6	11.2	13.8	11.1	13.4	12.2	13.6	11.9	13.3	11.7	9.1
8. Don't know	7.2	8.9	5.5	6.7	9.2	6.7	7.6	5.9	10.1	6.2	7.9	6.6	7.2	6.9	7.7	7.6
Item 12320 N(Wtd)	3706	1816	1743	2929	414	895	1059	1238	514	1750	1723	1261	1005	496	802	66

A22E: In getting skilled labor jobs?

	TOTAL	M	F	White	Black	NE	NC	S	W	Yes	No	None	Mari- juana Only	Few Pills	More Pills	Any Her- oin
1. Not at all	9.0	11.0	6.8	8.3	9.2	8.6	7.0	10.0	11.1	7.7	10.1	9.2	9.2	10.2	7.3	13.4
2. Very little	17.3	17.9	16.7	18.1	12.8	16.4	19.0	16.4	17.2	17.6	17.0	16.4	18.4	16.9	18.4	13.4
3. Some	31.7	30.8	32.6	32.8	25.7	34.0	31.1	30.4	32.4	32.4	31.3	31.3	30.9	29.7	34.8	34.3
4. A good deal	20.3	20.2	20.3	21.3	17.7	20.6	22.4	19.5	17.2	21.1	19.4	20.3	19.8	22.6	19.1	23.9
5. A great deal	11.4	9.8	12.8	9.6	22.3	10.3	8.9	14.3	11.5	10.6	11.9	11.6	11.6	11.4	10.4	9.0
8. Don't know	10.4	10.3	10.7	9.9	12.6	10.1	11.5	9.5	10.7	10.6	10.2	11.2	10.3	9.1	10.1	7.5
Item 12330 N(Wtd)	3696	1807	1740	2919	413	894	1057	1232	513	1751	1714	1259	1002	492	799	67

A22F: In getting elected to political office?

	TOTAL	M	F	White	Black	NE	NC	S	W	Yes	No	None	Mari- juana Only	Few Pills	More Pills	Any Her- oin
1. Not at all	5.9	8.4	2.8	5.3	6.7	5.9	4.7	6.9	6.2	4.5	7.0	5.6	6.3	5.8	5.2	11.9
2. Very little	11.9	15.4	8.1	12.0	9.1	11.0	10.5	13.5	12.3	11.8	11.3	11.7	13.2	12.1	10.1	11.9
3. Some	25.0	26.9	23.4	25.9	21.3	22.5	25.1	26.0	26.7	26.0	24.4	25.6	24.2	23.8	26.0	28.4
4. A good deal	24.3	23.4	25.8	25.2	18.7	27.5	25.3	22.7	21.8	27.7	21.5	24.8	24.8	25.0	23.5	22.4
5. A great deal	26.5	18.0	35.4	25.2	34.1	26.6	27.6	25.8	25.5	25.4	27.4	26.3	26.0	27.2	27.1	20.9
8. Don't know	6.4	8.0	4.5	5.6	9.8	6.5	6.9	5.6	7.4	4.5	8.4	6.0	5.7	6.0	8.1	4.5
Item 12340 N(Wtd)	3711	1819	1744	2929	417	898	1061	1240	513	1750	1724	1260	1006	496	804	67

QUESTIONNAIRE FORM 5 1978	TOTAL	SEX		RACE		REGION				4YR COLLEGE PLANS		ILLICIT DRUG USE: LIFETIME				
		M	F	White	Black	NE	NC	S	W	Yes	No	None	Mari- juana Only	Few Pills	More Pills	Any Her- oin
Weighted No. of Cases:	3770	1844	1762	2955	426	911	1074	1259	527	1768	1748	1274	1012	501	813	71
% of Weighted Total:	100.0	48.9	46.7	78.4	11.3	24.2	28.5	33.4	14.0	46.9	46.4	33.8	26.8	13.3	21.6	1.9
A22G: In getting equal pay for equal work?																
1. Not at all	14.7	20.2	8.8	14.5	12.9	15.0	12.9	15.7	15.1	12.9	16.0	13.7	16.0	14.9	13.8	26.9
2. Very little	19.9	20.5	19.7	21.1	16.8	17.7	20.9	20.0	21.1	21.8	18.1	21.0	20.0	19.1	19.8	20.9
3. Some	25.8	25.0	26.8	27.3	19.4	27.5	25.6	25.4	24.4	27.2	25.0	25.7	25.9	25.7	25.7	26.9
4. A good deal	17.6	16.0	19.6	17.7	17.3	19.7	18.2	15.9	16.5	18.8	17.0	16.5	17.7	19.3	18.7	9.0
5. A great deal	16.4	11.0	21.1	14.3	25.7	15.5	15.5	18.8	14.3	14.3	17.7	17.7	14.9	15.1	16.2	13.4
8. Don't know	5.7	7.3	4.0	5.1	7.7	4.6	6.9	4.2	8.5	5.0	6.1	5.4	5.5	5.8	6.0	3.0
Item 12350 N(Wtd)	3716	1820	1747	2933	417	898	1061	1242	516	1753	1726	1263	1006	498	804	67

A23: The next questions ask for your opinions on the effects of using certain drugs and other substances. First, how much do you think people risk harming themselves (physically or in other ways), if they...

A23A: Smoke one or more packs of cigarettes per day

	TOTAL	M	F	White	Black	NE	NC	S	W	Yes	No	None	Mari- juana Only	Few Pills	More Pills	Any Her- oin
1. No risk	1.5	1.6	1.0	.9	4.3	1.5	.7	2.2	1.2	.8	1.7	1.3	1.4	1.2	1.0	5.7
2. Slight risk	8.0	7.8	7.8	7.7	5.8	8.2	8.0	8.6	6.4	4.4	11.0	6.6	7.2	8.2	9.9	11.4
3. Moderate risk	30.1	30.7	30.1	31.3	24.5	27.1	34.3	30.9	24.3	27.3	33.2	24.9	30.3	31.7	36.9	37.1
4. Great risk	59.0	58.0	60.1	59.3	60.1	62.1	56.2	56.2	66.6	66.7	52.0	64.9	60.4	58.1	51.1	45.7
5. Can't say, drug unfamiliar	1.5	1.9	1.0	.7	5.5	1.1	.9	2.2	1.6	.9	2.0	2.2	.7	.6	1.1	–
Item 12360 N(Wtd)	3722	1828	1745	2936	416	904	1061	1241	515	1756	1728	1267	1005	499	808	70

A23B: Try marijuana (pot, grass) once or twice

	TOTAL	M	F	White	Black	NE	NC	S	W	Yes	No	None	Mari- juana Only	Few Pills	More Pills	Any Her- oin
1. No risk	54.6	58.0	51.3	57.4	39.1	65.9	55.4	45.6	55.0	56.7	53.0	23.0	68.3	65.1	81.0	70.0
2. Slight risk	24.9	22.2	28.2	24.8	26.6	19.2	28.0	27.1	23.2	25.4	24.8	36.2	22.0	22.6	12.1	20.0
3. Moderate risk	8.8	8.0	9.8	8.6	8.9	8.7	6.8	10.7	8.8	8.0	9.7	16.1	5.8	4.6	3.8	5.7
4. Great risk	8.1	8.1	7.8	7.0	15.0	4.0	7.5	11.0	9.6	7.5	8.4	18.3	2.3	3.6	2.2	2.9
5. Can't say, drug unfamiliar	3.5	3.7	3.0	2.1	10.1	2.1	2.2	5.7	3.5	2.3	4.1	6.2	1.6	3.8	.7	1.4
Item 12370 N(Wtd)	3715	1823	1746	2935	414	904	1060	1238	513	1754	1724	1267	1000	499	807	70

A23C: Smoke marijuana occasionally

	TOTAL	M	F	White	Black	NE	NC	S	W	Yes	No	None	Mari- juana Only	Few Pills	More Pills	Any Her- oin
1. No risk	32.4	36.6	28.3	33.9	27.2	39.8	32.8	28.1	29.2	31.5	33.2	6.3	36.7	40.1	61.3	64.3
2. Slight risk	30.8	30.0	31.8	31.0	26.7	30.9	32.0	28.9	32.9	32.9	29.0	26.2	40.4	34.7	24.6	24.3
3. Moderate risk	21.2	17.3	25.4	22.2	17.7	18.4	22.7	22.0	21.4	22.0	21.2	35.6	16.4	16.4	9.1	4.3
4. Great risk	12.4	12.6	11.8	10.9	21.1	9.0	10.8	15.8	13.6	11.5	12.9	26.3	5.3	5.4	4.3	5.7
5. Can't say, drug unfamiliar	3.1	3.4	2.6	2.0	7.5	1.8	1.6	5.3	2.9	2.1	3.7	5.5	1.2	3.4	.7	–
Item 12380 N(Wtd)	3715	1825	1741	2934	412	902	1061	1237	514	1753	1725	1263	1004	499	806	70

A23D: Smoke marijuana regularly

	TOTAL	M	F	White	Black	NE	NC	S	W	Yes	No	None	Mari- juana Only	Few Pills	More Pills	Any Her- oin
1. No risk	13.0	15.7	9.8	12.7	13.9	14.1	12.8	13.0	11.3	10.2	15.3	2.3	10.1	14.0	29.2	48.5
2. Slight risk	22.3	24.0	21.0	23.6	14.8	27.6	24.3	17.7	19.9	22.6	22.5	7.4	27.0	29.1	36.3	25.0
3. Moderate risk	26.5	26.6	26.3	27.4	21.9	26.3	26.4	24.7	31.4	29.9	23.4	20.9	36.1	30.3	21.5	19.1
4. Great risk	34.9	30.2	39.9	34.2	41.8	29.7	34.5	39.4	34.4	35.1	34.8	63.5	25.0	23.8	11.9	7.4
5. Can't say, drug unfamiliar	3.3	3.6	2.9	2.1	7.8	2.3	1.9	5.3	3.1	2.1	4.0	5.9	1.8	2.8	1.1	–
Item 12390 N(Wtd)	3712	1824	1742	2935	411	902	1060	1238	512	1753	1721	1261	1005	499	808	68

A23E: Try LSD once or twice

	TOTAL	M	F	White	Black	NE	NC	S	W	Yes	No	None	Mari- juana Only	Few Pills	More Pills	Any Her- oin
1. No risk	5.2	5.5	4.5	4.9	5.6	5.4	6.3	4.3	4.7	3.4	6.5	2.4	2.6	3.8	11.4	27.1
2. Slight risk	17.1	15.6	19.1	18.6	10.4	19.5	19.1	14.0	16.6	17.1	17.4	11.7	14.8	18.5	27.7	27.1
3. Moderate risk	24.4	21.6	27.6	25.8	16.7	25.7	28.0	22.2	20.3	26.0	23.3	23.3	24.4	24.6	26.8	28.6
4. Great risk	42.7	46.2	39.1	42.0	49.0	38.8	36.5	48.3	49.0	45.2	40.5	52.4	44.8	40.3	28.0	17.1
5. Can't say, drug unfamiliar	10.5	11.1	9.7	8.7	18.4	10.5	10.1	11.3	9.4	8.3	12.4	10.1	13.3	12.5	6.0	1.4
Item 12400 N(Wtd)	3715	1821	1746	2933	414	902	1062	1240	512	1752	1727	1266	1007	496	806	70

QUESTIONNAIRE FORM 5 1978	TOTAL	SEX		RACE		REGION				4YR COLLEGE PLANS		ILLICIT DRUG USE: LIFETIME				
		M	F	White	Black	NE	NC	S	W	Yes	No	None	Mari- juana Only	Few Pills	More Pills	Any Her- oin
Weighted No. of Cases:	3770	1844	1762	2955	426	911	1074	1259	527	1768	1748	1274	1012	501	813	71
% of Weighted Total:	100.0	48.9	46.7	78.4	11.3	24.2	28.5	33.4	14.0	46.9	46.4	33.8	26.8	13.3	21.6	1.9
A23F: Take LSD regularly																
1. No risk	1.5	1.9	.7	.8	4.6	1.4	1.2	2.0	1.0	.7	1.9	1.3	1.4	1.2	1.2	4.3
2. Slight risk	1.1	1.4	.7	1.2	.2	.4	1.6	1.1	.8	.7	1.2	.2	.3	.4	3.2	8.6
3. Moderate risk	6.4	5.4	7.7	7.0	2.9	6.3	8.3	5.5	4.7	5.0	7.4	2.8	4.1	5.2	14.5	24.3
4. Great risk	81.1	80.9	81.7	82.8	74.8	81.9	79.3	80.8	84.4	85.7	78.1	86.7	81.9	80.8	74.5	60.0
5. Can't say, drug unfamiliar	9.9	10.5	9.0	8.1	17.4	9.8	9.5	10.5	9.1	7.9	11.4	8.9	12.4	12.2	6.2	1.4
Item 12410 N(Wtd)	3707	1818	1741	2927	413	902	1056	1236	514	1751	1721	1257	1005	499	805	70
A23G: Try heroin (smack, horse) once or twice																
1. No risk	2.9	2.9	2.6	2.1	6.2	2.9	2.8	3.4	2.1	1.7	3.7	2.2	2.0	2.8	3.0	25.0
2. Slight risk	11.2	9.4	13.1	11.8	9.8	10.2	14.3	10.6	7.8	10.2	12.1	9.9	9.8	9.4	14.6	27.9
3. Moderate risk	21.9	20.3	24.0	23.6	12.5	22.6	25.4	18.5	21.4	23.4	20.8	22.8	19.5	22.9	23.8	20.6
4. Great risk	52.9	56.3	49.9	53.3	52.3	52.8	47.3	55.2	59.6	55.8	50.6	54.9	55.5	51.6	50.0	22.1
5. Can't say, drug unfamiliar	11.0	11.2	10.5	9.2	18.9	11.5	10.0	12.3	9.2	8.9	12.8	10.1	12.9	13.3	8.6	4.4
Item 12420 N(Wtd)	3717	1824	1745	2934	417	902	1061	1240	513	1755	1725	1266	1007	498	806	68
A23H: Take heroin occasionally																
1. No risk	1.5	1.8	.9	.8	5.5	1.4	.9	2.2	1.6	.8	1.8	1.4	1.2	1.2	1.4	7.1
2. Slight risk	1.7	1.2	2.2	1.6	1.7	.9	2.3	2.0	1.0	1.3	2.1	1.6	1.0	1.0	2.2	8.6
3. Moderate risk	14.7	12.4	17.6	15.5	13.4	15.2	17.7	13.7	10.4	13.7	16.0	14.7	12.8	13.9	17.0	28.6
4. Great risk	71.4	73.9	69.0	73.3	60.9	71.4	69.5	70.2	78.5	75.7	67.8	72.5	72.5	72.0	71.1	50.0
5. Can't say, drug unfamiliar	10.6	10.7	10.2	8.8	18.5	11.0	9.5	12.0	8.6	8.4	12.3	9.9	12.5	11.9	8.3	5.7
Item 12430 N(Wtd)	3712	1821	1743	2930	417	900	1062	1238	512	1750	1725	1265	1004	497	805	70
A23I: Take heroin regularly																
1. No risk	1.5	1.8	.7	.8	4.9	1.3	1.1	2.0	1.0	.6	1.9	1.5	1.3	1.0	1.2	4.3
2. Slight risk	.2	.2	.2	.2	.2	.1	.3	.2	.4	-	.5	.3	.1	-	.2	1.4
3. Moderate risk	1.7	1.4	2.1	1.5	1.7	1.4	2.3	1.6	1.0	1.4	1.8	1.8	.8	1.6	2.0	7.2
4. Great risk	86.6	86.2	87.6	89.2	75.7	87.2	87.6	84.2	89.6	90.3	84.1	87.4	86.0	85.5	88.7	81.2
5. Can't say, drug unfamiliar	10.0	10.4	9.3	8.3	17.5	10.0	8.7	11.9	8.0	7.7	11.7	9.0	11.8	11.9	7.9	5.8
Item 12440 N(Wtd)	3697	1814	1737	2922	412	897	1056	1233	510	1749	1715	1260	1001	495	802	69
A23J: Try barbiturates (downers, goofballs, reds, yellows, etc.) once or twice																
1. No risk	8.3	7.6	8.5	8.4	5.8	9.8	8.7	7.2	7.6	6.4	9.8	2.5	4.2	8.4	20.1	35.7
2. Slight risk	22.4	22.7	22.4	24.5	12.3	23.4	24.6	20.5	20.7	23.4	21.9	16.2	18.5	26.7	34.9	28.6
3. Moderate risk	27.1	24.2	30.2	28.4	18.6	29.6	28.6	25.1	24.6	29.1	25.4	28.6	27.3	27.3	25.2	12.9
4. Great risk	31.3	34.9	28.1	29.9	41.4	26.3	28.3	34.4	38.8	32.3	30.5	39.8	36.9	26.7	14.5	21.4
5. Can't say, drug unfamiliar	10.9	10.6	10.8	8.8	21.9	10.9	9.9	12.8	8.6	8.8	12.3	12.9	13.1	10.8	5.3	1.4
Item 12450 N(Wtd)	3716	1825	1744	2934	415	900	1062	1240	513	1754	1727	1265	1005	498	807	70
A23K: Take barbiturates regularly																
1. No risk	1.7	2.3	.8	1.1	4.4	2.0	1.2	2.3	1.0	.5	2.4	1.4	1.2	1.4	2.2	5.8
2. Slight risk	3.2	3.1	3.5	3.3	1.2	3.8	3.4	3.3	1.8	2.4	4.1	.5	1.2	1.6	9.6	21.7
3. Moderate risk	15.9	15.7	15.9	17.1	10.0	16.9	18.2	13.8	14.6	13.6	18.6	9.6	11.5	19.0	29.6	26.1
4. Great risk	68.4	68.5	69.4	69.7	63.0	67.5	67.2	67.5	74.6	75.4	62.5	76.3	73.0	67.8	52.9	43.5
5. Can't say, drug unfamiliar	10.7	10.5	10.5	8.8	21.3	9.8	9.9	13.2	8.2	8.1	12.3	12.3	13.2	10.1	5.7	1.4
Item 12460 N(Wtd)	3696	1823	1728	2924	408	898	1059	1227	512	1744	1719	1256	1003	494	804	69
A23L: Try amphetamines (uppers, pep pills, bennies, speed) once or twice																
1. No risk	11.4	11.6	10.9	11.9	7.0	13.4	12.3	9.1	11.7	9.1	13.6	3.2	5.7	11.2	29.2	42.0
2. Slight risk	22.9	22.3	23.8	25.1	11.4	23.8	25.8	20.8	20.4	23.5	22.6	15.8	18.2	30.5	36.6	18.8
3. Moderate risk	26.0	23.9	28.5	27.0	20.1	28.2	27.2	24.4	23.5	28.2	24.2	28.1	29.8	26.5	18.1	23.2
4. Great risk	29.9	32.4	27.4	28.4	40.7	25.9	25.8	33.8	35.8	31.2	28.9	40.8	34.4	23.8	11.7	13.0
5. Can't say, drug unfamiliar	9.7	9.7	9.4	7.5	21.1	8.7	8.9	11.8	8.4	7.9	10.8	11.9	12.0	7.8	4.5	1.4
Item 12470 N(Wtd)	3713	1826	1741	2935	413	900	1061	1238	514	1753	1726	1264	1006	499	805	69

QUESTIONNAIRE FORM 5 1978	TOTAL	SEX		RACE		REGION				4YR COLLEGE PLANS		ILLICIT DRUG USE: LIFETIME				
		M	F	White	Black	NE	NC	S	W	Yes	No	None	Mari- juana Only	Few Pills	More Pills	Any Her- oin
Weighted No. of Cases:	3770	1844	1762	2955	426	911	1074	1259	527	1768	1748	1274	1012	501	813	71
% of Weighted Total:	100.0	48.9	46.7	78.4	11.3	24.2	28.5	33.4	14.0	46.9	46.4	33.8	26.8	13.3	21.6	1.9

A23M: Take amphetamines regularly

1. No risk	2.2	2.4	1.6	1.5	5.9	2.6	1.5	2.8	1.4	.7	3.1	1.4	1.3	1.2	4.0	9.0
2. Slight risk	4.8	4.7	4.8	5.0	1.7	5.2	5.4	4.2	4.1	3.0	6.4	.8	2.4	3.6	13.4	25.4
3. Moderate risk	15.6	16.3	14.6	17.1	7.8	16.0	17.9	13.6	14.8	13.9	17.5	9.1	11.1	19.7	28.9	28.4
4. Great risk	67.1	66.5	69.0	68.3	63.4	67.0	66.3	66.6	70.1	74.1	61.5	76.6	72.8	66.2	48.3	35.8
5. Can't say, drug unfamiliar	10.3	10.0	10.0	8.0	21.2	9.1	8.9	12.6	9.4	8.2	11.5	12.0	12.4	9.3	5.3	1.5
Item 12480 N(Wtd)	3704	1817	1740	2931	410	898	1060	1234	512	1751	1719	1262	1006	497	804	67

A23N: Try cocaine once or twice

1. No risk	13.6	16.6	10.2	13.9	8.8	16.6	13.7	11.0	14.1	12.6	14.6	2.7	6.8	13.3	36.4	47.1
2. Slight risk	19.1	19.1	19.2	20.0	15.3	21.4	20.5	17.1	17.3	20.0	18.2	12.4	19.0	25.4	25.4	27.1
3. Moderate risk	24.1	21.2	27.6	25.2	19.0	23.4	26.3	23.5	22.5	25.6	23.6	28.0	24.6	26.8	16.7	15.7
4. Great risk	33.2	33.3	33.2	32.6	38.7	28.8	30.2	37.2	37.3	34.0	32.3	45.1	37.8	26.0	15.9	7.1
5. Can't say, drug unfamiliar	9.9	9.9	9.8	8.3	18.5	9.7	9.2	11.2	8.8	7.8	11.4	11.7	11.9	8.5	5.5	2.9
Item 12490 N(Wtd)	3702	1817	1740	2928	411	898	1058	1236	510	1750	1719	1260	1002	497	806	70

A23O: Take cocaine regularly

1. No risk	3.4	4.4	2.1	3.0	5.6	2.9	3.5	3.7	3.3	2.3	4.3	1.6	1.5	1.8	7.8	20.9
2. Slight risk	5.2	6.2	3.9	5.2	2.5	7.4	4.5	4.1	5.1	4.6	5.5	.8	2.3	3.8	15.1	22.4
3. Moderate risk	13.6	15.3	11.9	14.5	7.4	15.5	14.9	11.5	13.1	13.8	13.5	5.5	12.2	17.8	25.0	28.4
4. Great risk	68.2	64.6	72.6	69.0	68.6	64.9	68.3	69.8	69.6	71.9	65.2	81.3	72.7	67.9	46.0	23.9
5. Can't say, drug unfamiliar	9.6	9.5	9.5	8.3	15.9	9.5	8.8	10.8	8.8	7.3	11.5	10.8	11.4	8.7	6.1	3.0
Item 12500 N(Wtd)	3688	1814	1730	2919	408	892	1056	1229	510	1748	1710	1254	1002	495	800	67

A23P: Try one or two drinks of an alcoholic beverage (beer, wine, liquor)

1. No risk	59.8	62.2	57.9	63.4	36.9	66.2	62.7	53.6	57.5	61.2	59.6	39.9	67.5	67.6	77.9	62.9
2. Slight risk	28.3	26.9	29.5	27.2	37.9	25.7	28.1	30.8	27.3	28.4	27.6	39.3	26.2	24.9	15.3	27.1
3. Moderate risk	7.7	6.8	8.2	6.4	14.3	5.2	6.2	9.9	9.7	7.1	8.3	12.8	4.4	4.8	4.8	8.6
4. Great risk	3.4	3.4	3.5	2.7	7.3	2.9	2.5	4.1	4.7	2.9	3.7	6.7	1.4	2.0	2.0	1.4
5. Can't say, drug unfamiliar	.8	.7	.7	.3	3.4	.1	.7	1.5	.8	.5	.9	1.4	.5	.6	-	1.4
Item 12510 N(Wtd)	3708	1818	1743	2931	412	900	1061	1234	513	1752	1719	1261	1004	497	806	70

A23Q: Take one or two drinks nearly every day

1. No risk	11.8	14.9	8.3	12.2	7.8	11.4	11.4	12.9	10.7	8.3	15.0	6.1	13.6	13.0	16.5	27.1
2. Slight risk	30.3	32.7	27.7	30.9	24.8	31.1	31.7	30.2	26.2	29.0	31.5	24.6	33.0	29.5	35.5	34.3
3. Moderate risk	37.1	34.7	40.0	38.0	36.0	38.8	38.3	34.9	37.1	39.1	35.8	41.4	37.4	38.3	30.9	22.9
4. Great risk	19.6	16.3	23.2	18.3	27.3	18.3	17.9	19.7	25.6	23.1	16.3	26.4	14.9	17.8	16.8	14.3
5. Can't say, drug unfamiliar	1.2	1.4	.7	.6	4.1	.6	.7	2.3	.6	.5	1.3	1.4	1.1	1.4	.2	1.4
Item 12520 N(Wtd)	3706	1823	1738	2932	411	895	1062	1237	512	1751	1722	1259	1004	499	805	70

A23R: Take four or five drinks nearly every day

1. No risk	3.6	4.8	1.9	2.7	6.3	3.2	3.3	4.8	1.9	1.7	4.9	2.3	3.7	2.8	5.0	10.1
2. Slight risk	8.0	9.6	6.0	8.4	4.1	6.5	8.1	9.7	6.4	5.7	10.1	4.6	9.2	9.2	10.3	15.9
3. Moderate risk	24.0	27.0	20.9	25.3	16.3	23.2	25.7	24.7	20.1	21.5	26.9	19.4	23.2	23.8	31.8	27.5
4. Great risk	63.1	57.0	70.4	62.9	68.5	66.4	62.5	58.3	70.6	70.7	56.6	72.3	62.8	62.7	52.4	44.9
5. Can't say, drug unfamiliar	1.3	1.5	.8	.6	4.8	.7	.5	2.6	1.0	.6	1.4	1.4	1.1	1.4	.6	1.4
Item 12530 N(Wtd)	3712	1824	1744	2936	416	896	1062	1241	513	1752	1726	1265	1005	499	806	69

A23S: Have five or more drinks once or twice each weekend

1. No risk	13.3	16.8	9.2	13.3	10.4	14.4	15.8	11.8	9.8	10.7	15.5	6.2	13.9	13.3	22.5	28.6
2. Slight risk	21.5	25.0	17.7	22.9	13.3	22.2	20.3	22.4	20.4	21.1	21.9	13.5	24.2	26.3	28.0	22.9
3. Moderate risk	29.4	27.5	31.9	30.9	21.4	30.8	30.8	28.4	26.6	29.1	30.6	29.7	29.4	32.1	27.4	30.0
4. Great risk	34.5	29.7	40.1	32.5	50.6	32.1	32.1	35.1	42.5	38.5	30.7	49.2	31.4	26.5	21.6	14.3
5. Can't say, drug unfamiliar	1.2	1.1	1.0	.5	4.6	.4	.9	2.3	.8	.7	1.2	1.3	1.2	1.8	.4	2.9
Item 12540 N(Wtd)	3714	1827	1742	2937	415	900	1062	1240	511	1755	1725	1264	1007	498	806	70

QUESTIONNAIRE FORM 5 1978	TOTAL	SEX		RACE		REGION				4YR COLLEGE PLANS		ILLICIT DRUG USE: LIFETIME				
		M	F	White	Black	NE	NC	S	W	Yes	No	None	Mari-juana Only	Few Pills	More Pills	Any Her-oin
Weighted No. of Cases:	3770	1844	1762	2955	426	911	1074	1259	527	1768	1748	1274	1012	501	813	71
% of Weighted Total:	100.0	48.9	46.7	78.4	11.3	24.2	28.5	33.4	14.0	46.9	46.4	33.8	26.8	13.3	21.6	1.9

This section asks for your views and feelings about a number of different things.

D01: Do you agree or disagree with each of the following?

D01A: I take a positive attitude toward myself

	TOTAL	M	F	White	Black	NE	NC	S	W	Yes	No	None	Mari-juana Only	Few Pills	More Pills	Any Her-oin
1. Disagree	2.1	1.6	2.4	1.5	4.9	3.0	1.3	2.2	1.9	1.4	2.7	2.1	1.6	2.3	2.5	-
2. Mostly disagree	6.0	3.9	8.4	6.3	4.4	7.4	6.4	4.9	5.5	5.6	6.4	5.0	5.6	7.8	7.5	1.6
3. Neither	9.2	9.4	9.0	9.6	5.8	10.2	10.3	7.7	9.1	7.2	11.2	9.3	8.7	10.7	9.1	6.3
4. Mostly agree	48.6	47.0	49.9	50.7	33.2	50.1	49.9	46.3	48.5	47.0	50.7	47.3	48.7	45.7	51.4	52.4
5. Agree	34.1	38.2	30.4	31.9	51.9	29.2	32.2	38.9	35.1	38.9	29.0	36.5	35.2	33.5	29.3	39.7
Item 12550 N(Wtd)	3501	1703	1693	2837	364	826	1032	1173	470	1736	1665	1206	940	477	755	63

D01B: Good luck is more important than hard work for success

	TOTAL	M	F	White	Black	NE	NC	S	W	Yes	No	None	Mari-juana Only	Few Pills	More Pills	Any Her-oin
1. Disagree	37.1	33.2	41.0	36.5	43.8	33.6	34.1	42.3	36.5	37.1	36.5	39.1	36.8	39.6	33.6	30.2
2. Mostly disagree	36.6	38.4	35.2	39.5	20.8	37.5	39.7	32.6	38.0	38.7	35.2	35.7	37.5	37.9	37.5	31.7
3. Neither	15.9	17.1	14.3	16.1	10.2	18.5	18.1	11.9	16.6	16.1	15.8	14.5	16.5	13.5	18.5	19.0
4. Mostly agree	7.5	8.5	6.4	6.2	13.6	8.8	6.3	8.1	6.2	5.6	9.5	7.1	6.5	6.1	8.4	12.7
5. Agree	3.0	2.8	3.1	1.7	11.6	1.7	1.6	5.1	3.0	2.5	3.0	3.6	2.6	2.7	2.1	6.3
Item 12560 N(Wtd)	3492	1699	1690	2830	361	822	1031	1170	469	1732	1661	1203	937	475	753	63

D01C: I feel I am a person of worth, on an equal plane with others

	TOTAL	M	F	White	Black	NE	NC	S	W	Yes	No	None	Mari-juana Only	Few Pills	More Pills	Any Her-oin
1. Disagree	1.5	1.5	1.4	1.2	3.1	1.7	1.1	1.6	1.7	1.1	1.9	1.2	1.2	1.9	1.7	3.2
2. Mostly disagree	3.5	3.1	4.0	3.5	3.1	4.9	4.4	2.2	2.3	3.5	3.4	2.8	3.1	5.1	4.2	-
3. Neither	8.8	9.0	8.2	8.9	5.6	9.4	9.0	8.0	11.3	6.3	11.3	8.1	9.5	8.0	9.5	3.2
4. Mostly agree	41.2	41.2	41.4	42.8	28.1	43.9	43.0	40.0	35.8	40.0	43.3	41.8	40.5	41.2	40.5	50.8
5. Agree	45.0	45.2	45.1	43.5	60.3	40.1	42.6	48.2	50.7	49.2	40.0	46.2	45.6	43.8	44.0	41.3
Item 12570 N(Wtd)	3484	1693	1688	2824	360	820	1027	1168	469	1727	1657	1201	934	473	754	63

D01D: I am able to do things as well as most other people

	TOTAL	M	F	White	Black	NE	NC	S	W	Yes	No	None	Mari-juana Only	Few Pills	More Pills	Any Her-oin
1. Disagree	1.3	.8	1.5	.8	3.6	1.6	.7	1.6	1.3	.9	1.8	1.6	1.0	1.3	.8	1.6
2. Mostly disagree	2.2	1.6	2.7	1.9	2.2	2.1	2.8	1.5	2.8	1.3	3.0	1.7	1.6	3.6	2.5	1.6
3. Neither	5.8	5.4	6.5	5.9	4.5	7.2	5.7	5.3	4.9	5.2	6.6	5.8	5.7	7.0	5.4	3.2
4. Mostly agree	43.5	40.7	46.5	44.8	35.7	42.3	46.6	42.5	41.0	40.3	46.7	42.3	45.0	39.3	45.9	47.6
5. Agree	47.2	51.5	42.7	46.6	54.0	46.8	44.1	49.1	50.2	52.5	41.9	48.5	46.8	49.0	45.3	46.0
Item 12580 N(Wtd)	3479	1689	1689	2822	359	818	1029	1166	466	1727	1654	1202	932	471	753	63

D01E: Every time I try to get ahead, something or somebody stops me

	TOTAL	M	F	White	Black	NE	NC	S	W	Yes	No	None	Mari-juana Only	Few Pills	More Pills	Any Her-oin
1. Disagree	19.8	19.6	19.8	19.6	21.6	19.7	17.2	20.0	25.0	23.6	15.9	20.7	21.7	19.0	18.0	12.9
2. Mostly disagree	32.8	33.0	33.3	35.1	19.7	33.0	34.7	30.6	33.4	38.9	27.1	32.6	35.4	30.2	32.8	27.4
3. Neither	23.5	23.8	23.4	24.2	18.8	26.4	23.7	21.3	23.5	21.6	25.2	22.8	24.0	26.4	22.1	21.0
4. Mostly agree	17.0	16.9	17.2	15.8	24.2	14.8	16.9	19.7	14.7	12.1	21.8	16.1	14.1	17.1	20.2	25.8
5. Agree	6.9	6.8	6.3	5.4	15.4	6.1	7.5	8.3	3.7	3.8	9.9	7.7	4.8	7.2	6.9	11.3
Item 12590 N(Wtd)	3473	1687	1684	2820	356	819	1027	1163	464	1724	1651	1196	931	474	751	62

D01F: Planning only makes a person unhappy since plans hardly ever work out anyway

	TOTAL	M	F	White	Black	NE	NC	S	W	Yes	No	None	Mari-juana Only	Few Pills	More Pills	Any Her-oin
1. Disagree	30.4	29.5	31.6	30.6	31.3	26.7	29.7	31.3	36.2	34.8	25.3	34.3	31.2	27.8	26.8	17.7
2. Mostly disagree	32.2	32.2	32.3	33.9	20.6	32.7	34.7	29.3	32.8	35.6	28.9	32.5	31.6	34.5	30.9	40.3
3. Neither	15.5	18.0	13.2	15.6	14.9	18.6	15.3	13.8	15.2	13.6	17.6	15.3	15.4	13.1	16.8	21.0
4. Mostly agree	14.4	13.9	14.8	14.0	17.5	13.7	14.6	16.9	9.4	10.4	18.4	11.1	13.9	18.7	17.0	9.7
5. Agree	7.4	6.4	8.1	6.0	15.8	8.4	5.7	8.8	6.4	5.5	9.6	6.8	7.9	5.9	8.4	9.7
Item 12600 N(Wtd)	3470	1681	1688	2820	355	813	1022	1168	467	1723	1649	1193	929	475	754	62

QUESTIONNAIRE FORM 5 1978	TOTAL	SEX		RACE		REGION				4YR COLLEGE PLANS		ILLICIT DRUG USE: LIFETIME				
		M	F	White	Black	NE	NC	S	W	Yes	No	None	Mari-juana Only	Few Pills	More Pills	Any Her-oin
Weighted No. of Cases:	3770	1844	1762	2955	426	911	1074	1259	527	1768	1748	1274	1012	501	813	71
% of Weighted Total:	100.0	48.9	46.7	78.4	11.3	24.2	28.5	33.4	14.0	46.9	46.4	33.8	26.8	13.3	21.6	1.9

D01G: People who accept their condition in life are happier than those who try to change things

1. Disagree	20.3	19.9	20.5	20.0	22.4	20.7	18.6	21.0	21.5	23.5	16.9	20.1	19.8	18.6	21.9	24.6
2. Mostly disagree	25.5	26.6	25.0	27.1	18.4	28.8	26.6	21.8	26.8	30.7	20.1	23.6	26.6	29.7	25.6	14.8
3. Neither	19.7	20.4	19.1	20.1	16.4	19.8	22.0	17.6	19.5	18.6	20.9	17.4	21.3	18.8	21.5	19.7
4. Mostly agree	20.1	20.5	19.8	20.0	18.7	17.6	20.4	22.8	17.4	15.2	25.3	22.0	18.2	21.1	17.8	26.2
5. Agree	14.4	12.6	15.7	12.8	24.4	13.2	12.4	16.8	14.8	11.9	16.8	16.8	13.9	11.8	13.1	13.1
Item 12610 N(Wtd)	3450	1667	1683	2804	353	805	1016	1164	466	1719	1635	1189	928	474	741	61

D01H: On the whole, I'm satisfied with myself

1. Disagree	3.5	2.9	3.8	3.1	4.8	3.7	3.1	4.0	2.8	3.0	4.1	2.8	3.3	3.6	4.7	3.3
2. Mostly disagree	7.0	6.5	7.5	6.9	7.4	7.3	7.9	6.5	5.4	6.7	7.1	4.6	6.7	10.4	9.0	8.3
3. Neither	9.5	10.5	8.5	9.6	6.3	10.5	9.8	8.2	10.2	9.0	9.8	9.5	8.6	8.3	11.3	8.3
4. Mostly agree	40.6	39.5	42.3	41.7	31.3	42.1	40.0	39.8	40.8	39.4	42.4	40.1	40.1	38.3	42.5	50.0
5. Agree	39.4	40.6	37.9	38.7	50.3	36.3	39.1	41.3	40.6	41.9	36.6	43.0	41.4	39.4	32.4	31.7
Item 12620 N(Wtd)	3456	1673	1682	2813	352	807	1020	1167	463	1716	1643	1194	928	472	744	60

D01I: People like me don't have much of a chance to be successful in life

1. Disagree	56.0	52.9	59.0	55.9	63.1	53.4	53.6	58.4	59.4	64.1	47.2	57.0	57.2	54.4	54.0	59.7
2. Mostly disagree	27.3	28.3	26.3	28.9	17.3	27.8	30.1	24.9	25.8	25.1	30.0	27.5	25.6	30.5	27.2	22.6
3. Neither	10.0	11.1	8.8	9.7	7.4	12.1	10.1	9.3	8.0	6.9	13.1	8.9	10.2	8.9	11.5	11.3
4. Mostly agree	4.1	4.7	3.5	3.6	6.3	4.4	4.6	3.7	3.9	2.2	6.2	3.8	3.8	4.0	5.0	3.2
5. Agree	2.7	3.0	2.3	2.0	6.3	2.2	1.7	3.7	3.0	1.7	3.4	2.9	3.2	2.1	2.3	3.2
Item 12630 N(Wtd)	3449	1670	1679	2804	352	801	1022	1165	461	1717	1635	1192	925	472	742	62

D01J: When I make plans, I am almost certain that I can make them work

1. Disagree	2.8	2.3	3.2	2.3	5.7	2.4	2.9	3.4	1.9	1.8	4.0	3.3	1.6	2.1	3.9	3.2
2. Mostly disagree	6.9	6.2	7.6	6.9	6.3	6.6	8.4	6.5	5.2	6.0	8.1	5.6	6.4	9.1	8.5	3.2
3. Neither	16.0	16.3	15.7	16.1	11.9	18.5	16.0	14.8	14.9	15.1	16.7	15.5	16.3	14.8	16.8	17.7
4. Mostly agree	47.1	45.3	49.2	48.9	41.5	46.6	46.8	48.2	45.7	48.0	46.5	47.3	47.5	47.7	45.6	53.2
5. Agree	27.1	29.8	24.3	25.8	34.9	26.0	25.8	27.0	32.1	29.2	24.6	28.2	28.0	26.1	25.3	22.6
Item 12640 N(Wtd)	3446	1671	1675	2804	352	801	1020	1162	464	1714	1636	1192	920	472	744	62

D01K: A lot of times I feel lonely

1. Disagree	17.2	19.1	14.8	16.4	19.5	18.3	15.8	16.6	19.3	16.2	17.7	16.0	19.2	16.7	17.1	11.1
2. Mostly disagree	28.3	28.4	28.4	30.8	16.1	28.9	30.6	26.3	27.8	30.3	26.8	28.8	30.1	27.4	27.3	19.0
3. Neither	17.6	20.1	15.0	18.8	10.8	19.8	18.4	14.0	21.5	18.5	16.8	17.7	18.0	18.6	15.4	27.0
4. Mostly agree	24.3	22.5	27.0	23.7	26.9	23.7	24.5	25.6	22.1	23.6	25.2	23.4	22.7	27.4	26.1	27.0
5. Agree	12.5	9.9	14.8	10.4	26.6	9.3	10.8	17.5	9.5	11.3	13.6	14.0	10.1	10.0	14.3	15.9
Item 12650 N(Wtd)	3437	1674	1658	2790	353	792	1017	1166	461	1700	1629	1191	924	468	733	63

D01L: I feel I do not have much to be proud of

1. Disagree	44.4	43.4	45.7	44.5	47.1	45.1	43.3	44.6	45.4	49.2	39.2	45.4	49.3	42.1	39.9	40.3
2. Mostly disagree	32.8	34.4	31.0	34.4	23.7	31.5	33.8	33.0	32.0	33.3	33.0	32.8	28.9	35.7	35.6	29.0
3. Neither	9.0	9.5	8.6	8.9	6.3	10.0	8.9	7.5	10.9	6.4	11.2	8.7	8.2	9.0	9.8	11.3
4. Mostly agree	9.9	9.3	10.5	9.1	13.1	9.2	10.7	10.4	8.0	8.0	11.7	8.8	9.9	10.5	10.4	14.5
5. Agree	4.0	3.4	4.2	3.2	9.7	4.3	3.2	4.6	3.7	3.1	4.9	4.3	3.7	2.8	4.4	4.8
Item 12660 N(Wtd)	3429	1670	1654	2787	350	790	1016	1162	460	1695	1626	1188	923	468	731	62

D01M: There is always someone I can turn to if I need help

1. Disagree	4.0	5.2	2.4	3.2	7.4	2.3	3.4	5.5	4.1	3.8	4.0	3.3	4.5	2.3	5.1	12.9
2. Mostly disagree	6.2	7.6	4.9	6.2	5.7	5.2	7.5	6.0	5.7	6.9	5.2	5.6	5.0	7.0	8.1	4.8
3. Neither	5.6	6.6	4.7	5.6	3.4	7.0	5.8	4.1	6.8	5.9	5.2	5.8	5.3	4.1	6.6	4.8
4. Mostly agree	29.9	33.0	26.6	30.4	25.7	31.2	30.5	28.1	31.2	30.2	29.8	27.2	30.6	32.8	32.3	27.4
5. Agree	54.3	47.7	61.3	54.5	57.7	54.3	52.7	56.3	52.3	53.2	55.8	58.1	54.7	53.9	48.0	50.0
Item 12670 N(Wtd)	3417	1661	1653	2778	350	786	1015	1158	459	1689	1620	1185	916	469	727	62

QUESTIONNAIRE FORM 5 1978	TOTAL	SEX		RACE		REGION				4YR COLLEGE PLANS		ILLICIT DRUG USE: LIFETIME				
		M	F	White	Black	NE	NC	S	W	Yes	No	None	Marijuana Only	Few Pills	More Pills	Any Heroin
Weighted No. of Cases:	3770	1844	1762	2955	426	911	1074	1259	527	1768	1748	1274	1012	501	813	71
% of Weighted Total:	100.0	48.9	46.7	78.4	11.3	24.2	28.5	33.4	14.0	46.9	46.4	33.8	26.8	13.3	21.6	1.9

D01N: Sometimes I think that I am no good at all

1. Disagree	30.8	33.5	27.9	29.2	44.4	28.1	27.0	34.6	34.4	32.4	29.3	31.6	33.3	30.1	26.9	35.5
2. Mostly disagree	24.6	25.3	24.1	26.1	17.9	27.5	25.3	22.6	23.5	25.8	23.7	24.5	26.0	23.5	25.2	19.4
3. Neither	17.5	18.2	16.6	18.3	11.0	17.3	19.0	16.7	16.8	16.8	18.2	17.4	15.9	18.6	18.0	21.0
4. Mostly agree	15.3	14.0	17.1	15.4	11.8	16.0	16.8	14.0	14.4	14.7	16.1	15.1	14.4	16.2	15.8	11.3
5. Agree	11.7	8.9	14.3	11.0	15.0	11.0	12.0	12.2	10.9	10.2	12.7	11.2	10.3	11.3	14.2	12.9
Item 12680 N(Wtd)	3408	1658	1647	2772	347	779	1013	1157	459	1682	1619	1183	912	468	726	62

D01O: I often feel left out of things

1. Disagree	19.4	21.1	17.3	18.6	23.1	20.5	17.3	19.3	22.5	18.4	20.3	18.1	20.8	17.2	21.2	16.1
2. Mostly disagree	27.0	26.7	27.4	28.2	17.1	26.2	28.2	26.3	27.4	30.9	23.1	26.1	30.9	25.2	24.7	30.6
3. Neither	19.6	21.0	18.8	20.7	14.5	19.8	23.0	17.0	18.4	20.1	19.2	20.3	18.1	19.6	20.4	24.2
4. Mostly agree	23.0	22.5	23.8	23.0	24.3	24.8	22.8	22.5	21.9	21.7	24.5	23.1	20.8	28.0	23.6	12.9
5. Agree	11.0	8.6	12.7	9.5	20.8	8.9	8.6	14.9	9.8	9.0	12.7	12.4	9.4	10.3	10.2	16.1
Item 12690 N(Wtd)	3397	1647	1648	2767	346	779	1006	1156	457	1680	1612	1183	906	465	725	62

D01P: I believe a person is master of his/her own fate

1. Disagree	5.0	5.4	4.4	4.7	5.9	3.7	3.9	6.8	4.6	4.0	5.7	6.4	3.7	5.0	3.6	4.8
2. Mostly disagree	6.5	6.4	6.6	6.9	4.4	7.0	7.1	6.1	5.7	7.3	5.7	6.3	6.7	8.0	6.0	3.2
3. Neither	17.9	15.7	20.4	18.4	12.6	22.5	18.8	15.0	15.2	16.9	18.8	17.6	18.7	16.5	18.0	24.2
4. Mostly agree	35.4	35.7	35.6	37.3	24.6	34.5	39.0	34.1	32.5	36.8	35.0	35.0	33.9	35.9	39.4	24.2
5. Agree	35.2	36.8	33.1	32.6	52.5	32.3	31.3	38.0	41.8	35.0	34.7	34.7	37.0	34.8	33.0	41.9
Item 12700 N(Wtd)	3386	1645	1641	2759	341	774	1006	1151	455	1674	1608	1179	899	462	728	62

D01Q: There is usually someone I can talk to, if I need to

1. Disagree	3.1	3.6	2.4	2.2	8.1	2.2	2.6	4.2	2.4	3.1	3.1	2.6	4.2	1.7	2.8	4.8
2. Mostly disagree	5.5	7.1	4.0	5.6	4.9	6.7	3.9	5.7	6.3	6.1	4.7	5.2	3.7	6.0	7.9	6.5
3. Neither	5.3	6.7	3.8	5.1	4.4	5.5	6.6	3.8	5.6	4.7	5.6	5.7	5.3	3.7	5.7	8.1
4. Mostly agree	29.5	33.4	25.8	30.7	21.3	29.3	32.1	26.9	30.6	29.5	29.6	26.5	28.2	32.6	34.2	32.3
5. Agree	56.6	49.2	64.0	56.4	62.0	56.3	54.5	59.3	55.2	56.5	57.0	59.9	58.8	55.9	49.5	50.0
Item 12710 N(Wtd)	3404	1653	1649	2773	347	778	1014	1154	458	1684	1614	1187	910	463	725	62

D01R: I feel that I can't do anything right

1. Disagree	45.0	47.2	42.8	44.6	52.2	45.1	42.6	45.7	48.1	49.9	39.9	44.4	48.0	43.8	42.7	52.5
2. Mostly disagree	28.8	27.6	30.4	30.8	18.8	30.5	31.5	25.7	28.0	29.9	28.1	30.0	27.1	28.7	30.2	18.6
3. Neither	14.1	12.3	15.8	14.1	10.7	12.5	16.8	13.5	12.3	11.2	16.8	13.1	13.3	15.3	15.7	15.3
4. Mostly agree	8.3	8.9	7.6	7.7	11.6	8.4	6.9	9.8	7.2	6.3	10.5	9.2	7.7	8.9	7.5	6.8
5. Agree	3.8	4.0	3.5	2.8	7.0	3.4	2.2	5.3	4.4	2.7	4.7	3.2	4.0	3.5	4.0	6.8
Item 12720 N(Wtd)	3386	1644	1641	2758	345	774	1011	1145	457	1677	1603	1184	904	463	719	59

D01S: I often wish I had more good friends

1. Disagree	15.2	13.2	16.7	15.1	15.5	16.1	14.6	13.9	18.0	16.3	14.1	16.2	15.0	15.0	13.9	21.1
2. Mostly disagree	14.9	14.6	15.5	15.2	14.6	16.2	15.7	14.3	12.7	16.5	13.3	13.3	15.1	16.5	17.4	7.0
3. Neither	16.8	19.0	15.3	17.5	11.7	17.8	18.8	14.4	16.7	16.2	17.5	16.2	17.5	15.7	16.5	24.6
4. Mostly agree	28.0	29.7	26.0	29.2	22.2	27.0	29.0	27.9	27.5	28.0	28.1	28.6	26.6	28.8	27.9	26.3
5. Agree	25.1	23.5	26.5	23.1	35.7	22.7	22.0	29.4	25.3	23.0	26.9	25.6	25.8	24.2	24.3	22.8
Item 12730 N(Wtd)	3379	1641	1638	2756	342	770	1008	1148	455	1673	1600	1178	902	466	720	57

D01T: Planning ahead makes things turn out better

1. Disagree	4.1	3.0	4.9	2.9	9.9	4.0	2.5	5.8	3.8	2.7	5.8	4.8	3.7	2.4	4.1	5.3
2. Mostly disagree	6.8	6.0	7.7	6.7	5.8	9.0	7.3	5.2	5.7	4.8	9.0	4.6	6.2	10.2	8.7	3.5
3. Neither	19.5	18.2	20.9	20.2	13.4	23.5	19.8	17.8	16.6	18.6	21.0	14.8	21.3	20.8	23.0	26.3
4. Mostly agree	38.9	38.5	39.2	40.2	33.5	36.9	41.4	38.9	36.4	42.6	34.9	41.5	36.7	40.1	37.6	29.8
5. Agree	30.7	34.3	27.3	30.0	37.3	26.5	28.9	32.4	38.0	31.4	29.4	34.2	32.1	26.5	26.6	33.3
Item 12740 N(Wtd)	3381	1640	1641	2756	343	769	1009	1149	453	1678	1598	1185	900	461	723	57

188   MONITORING THE FUTURE

QUESTIONNAIRE FORM 5 1978	TOTAL	SEX M	F	RACE White	Black	REGION NE	NC	S	W	4YR COLLEGE PLANS Yes	No	ILLICIT DRUG USE: LIFETIME None	Mari- juana Only	Few Pills	More Pills	Any Her- oin
Weighted No. of Cases:	3770	1844	1762	2955	426	911	1074	1259	527	1768	1748	1274	1012	501	813	71
% of Weighted Total:	100.0	48.9	46.7	78.4	11.3	24.2	28.5	33.4	14.0	46.9	46.4	33.8	26.8	13.3	21.6	1.9

D01U: I feel that my life is not very useful

	TOTAL	M	F	White	Black	NE	NC	S	W	Yes	No	None	Mari- juana Only	Few Pills	More Pills	Any Her- oin
1. Disagree	50.4	51.3	49.0	49.7	57.4	50.2	46.1	52.3	55.7	55.1	45.5	51.9	54.5	48.4	46.2	39.7
2. Mostly disagree	28.6	29.8	28.0	30.1	22.4	27.7	31.5	27.7	26.2	27.7	30.1	28.7	26.1	30.4	30.5	25.9
3. Neither	12.4	11.4	13.6	12.5	9.1	13.3	13.8	11.3	10.1	10.4	14.3	11.6	10.6	13.7	13.9	22.4
4. Mostly agree	6.1	5.5	6.5	5.8	5.6	5.9	7.3	5.8	4.4	4.9	7.1	5.5	6.3	6.1	6.8	5.2
5. Agree	2.5	2.0	2.9	1.9	5.9	2.9	1.3	2.9	3.5	1.9	3.1	2.3	2.5	1.5	2.6	8.6
Item 12750 N(Wtd)	3380	1644	1637	2759	340	769	1007	1150	454	1678	1597	1183	904	461	721	58

D01V: I usually have a few friends around that I can get together with

	TOTAL	M	F	White	Black	NE	NC	S	W	Yes	No	None	Mari- juana Only	Few Pills	More Pills	Any Her- oin
1. Disagree	4.3	3.6	4.6	3.6	6.7	4.0	4.1	4.0	6.2	3.9	4.7	4.6	4.1	3.7	4.4	7.0
2. Mostly disagree	4.7	4.7	4.6	4.4	5.0	4.9	3.7	5.5	4.6	4.6	4.8	5.7	4.4	4.1	3.7	1.8
3. Neither	6.5	7.1	6.0	6.3	7.0	7.0	7.6	5.3	6.4	6.4	6.7	7.6	4.9	7.8	5.4	12.3
4. Mostly agree	34.8	33.5	36.3	36.2	27.4	33.8	37.9	33.4	33.2	35.2	34.6	34.8	34.2	34.6	36.4	36.8
5. Agree	49.7	50.9	48.5	49.5	53.9	50.3	46.7	51.9	49.9	49.8	49.2	47.3	52.5	50.1	49.9	42.1
Item 12760 N(Wtd)	3391	1645	1645	2766	343	770	1011	1155	455	1680	1606	1185	907	463	723	57

These next questions ask your views about different lifestyles that have been in the news lately.

D02: A man and a woman who live together without being married are...

	TOTAL	M	F	White	Black	NE	NC	S	W	Yes	No	None	Mari- juana Only	Few Pills	More Pills	Any Her- oin
1. Experimenting with a worth-while alternative lifestyle	20.4	20.6	20.1	20.8	21.4	24.6	22.1	16.7	19.2	21.3	18.9	13.6	21.6	22.5	29.5	18.2
2. Doing their own thing and not affecting anyone else	52.8	54.8	51.1	52.2	53.7	57.9	54.2	49.1	50.0	49.2	57.0	47.8	56.9	55.4	53.0	65.5
3. Living in a way that could be destructive to society	6.8	7.0	6.6	6.9	7.4	5.1	7.2	8.2	5.1	7.3	6.3	9.6	5.7	5.5	4.1	3.6
4. Violating a basic principle of human morality	14.0	11.8	15.8	14.3	10.1	5.7	10.8	19.8	19.7	15.2	12.8	22.5	10.9	12.9	5.8	5.5
8. None of the above	6.0	5.8	6.4	5.8	7.4	6.8	5.4	6.2	6.0	7.0	5.1	6.5	5.1	3.9	7.5	5.5
Item 12770 N(Wtd)	3332	1620	1616	2720	337	749	996	1136	452	1661	1568	1164	890	457	711	55

D03: A man and a woman who decide to have and raise a child out of wedlock are...

	TOTAL	M	F	White	Black	NE	NC	S	W	Yes	No	None	Mari- juana Only	Few Pills	More Pills	Any Her- oin
1. Experimenting with a worth-while alternative lifestyle	7.9	8.5	6.5	7.0	11.3	9.3	7.7	7.3	7.4	7.8	7.8	5.7	8.1	8.1	9.8	14.8
2. Doing their own thing and not affecting anyone else	31.3	33.2	29.6	29.0	43.8	36.9	31.0	27.8	31.0	29.6	33.5	26.0	32.7	29.7	38.0	42.6
3. Living in a way that could be destructive to society	24.8	24.4	25.7	26.0	20.8	22.4	28.0	24.4	22.3	25.2	23.7	24.7	26.2	26.9	22.6	22.2
4. Violating a basic principle of human morality	23.0	21.6	24.6	24.8	11.6	16.2	20.4	28.1	27.0	24.1	22.0	30.6	21.8	22.0	14.2	13.0
8. None of the above	13.1	12.4	13.7	13.2	12.8	15.0	12.8	12.5	12.1	13.3	13.0	13.0	11.3	13.4	15.5	7.4
Item 12880 N(Wtd)	3302	1595	1611	2700	336	740	986	1128	448	1644	1559	1150	887	454	705	54

D04: These next questions ask how you feel about your present financial situation and your future financial security.

D04A: I feel that I have enough money to get along pretty well

	TOTAL	M	F	White	Black	NE	NC	S	W	Yes	No	None	Mari- juana Only	Few Pills	More Pills	Any Her- oin
1. Never	9.5	7.4	10.6	7.6	21.4	7.9	9.1	11.4	8.1	8.1	10.5	10.4	8.5	10.1	8.6	7.1
2. Seldom	19.5	17.8	21.8	19.2	18.7	19.9	20.3	16.4	24.9	18.5	20.7	17.4	18.5	21.8	22.7	17.9
3. Sometimes	33.4	33.3	34.0	33.6	33.2	36.7	33.1	32.6	30.9	31.3	35.2	31.8	35.0	34.1	33.0	42.9
4. Often	28.0	29.8	26.2	29.1	22.6	25.6	27.5	30.1	27.1	29.7	26.6	30.0	28.3	23.3	27.8	23.2
5. Always	9.6	11.7	7.4	10.5	4.5	9.9	9.9	9.4	9.0	12.4	6.9	10.4	9.6	11.0	8.1	7.1
Item 12990 N(Wtd)	3308	1602	1609	2700	337	738	995	1128	446	1650	1558	1156	883	455	701	56

QUESTIONNAIRE FORM 5 1978	TOTAL	SEX		RACE		REGION				4YR COLLEGE PLANS		ILLICIT DRUG USE: LIFETIME				
		M	F	White	Black	NE	NC	S	W	Yes	No	None	Marijuana Only	Few Pills	More Pills	Any Heroin
Weighted No. of Cases:	3770	1844	1762	2955	426	911	1074	1259	527	1768	1748	1274	1012	501	813	71
% of Weighted Total:	100.0	48.9	46.7	78.4	11.3	24.2	28.5	33.4	14.0	46.9	46.4	33.8	26.8	13.3	21.6	1.9

D04B: I get very concerned about how I am going to be able to pay my next bills

	TOTAL	M	F	White	Black	NE	NC	S	W	Yes	No	None	Marijuana Only	Few Pills	More Pills	Any Heroin
1. Never	25.8	23.3	28.1	25.2	36.0	27.5	21.1	27.5	29.8	29.4	22.1	30.5	24.3	24.6	22.5	19.6
2. Seldom	26.8	27.9	25.9	27.8	17.8	24.8	30.1	24.5	28.6	27.2	26.3	26.8	25.4	29.5	26.0	30.4
3. Sometimes	26.9	27.6	26.0	27.6	21.1	27.1	27.9	27.2	23.2	25.4	28.0	23.6	31.5	23.2	28.6	25.0
4. Often	14.0	14.7	13.3	13.2	14.8	15.0	14.7	13.2	12.5	13.0	15.2	11.6	12.8	15.8	17.7	16.1
5. Always	6.5	6.4	6.8	6.2	10.6	5.5	6.3	7.6	5.9	4.9	8.3	7.3	6.2	6.7	5.2	7.1
Item 13000 N(Wtd)	3275	1589	1592	2677	331	726	991	1118	440	1630	1550	1144	874	448	699	56

D04C: I worry whether I will have any job at all in a few months

	TOTAL	M	F	White	Black	NE	NC	S	W	Yes	No	None	Marijuana Only	Few Pills	More Pills	Any Heroin
1. Never	35.6	36.8	34.9	37.2	30.9	33.3	35.0	36.5	38.5	39.4	31.7	34.7	40.9	35.8	32.7	28.3
2. Seldom	25.3	28.9	21.8	26.6	13.9	26.4	27.0	24.7	21.1	26.4	24.3	23.8	23.5	25.6	29.4	30.2
3. Sometimes	18.1	15.9	20.1	17.3	23.6	18.0	17.4	18.6	18.1	17.4	18.8	20.0	16.3	19.6	16.2	11.3
4. Often	13.7	13.5	13.7	13.1	15.8	15.5	14.3	11.7	14.5	12.4	15.1	13.6	12.7	12.4	14.6	22.6
5. Always	7.3	4.9	9.5	5.8	15.8	6.7	6.4	8.4	7.7	4.5	10.1	8.0	6.5	6.7	7.3	7.5
Item 13010 N(Wtd)	3265	1582	1589	2672	330	721	987	1116	441	1623	1546	1136	872	450	698	53

D04D: I feel sure that I could go out and get a new job (with decent pay) whenever I want one

	TOTAL	M	F	White	Black	NE	NC	S	W	Yes	No	None	Marijuana Only	Few Pills	More Pills	Any Heroin
1. Never	9.2	6.2	11.9	7.3	21.8	11.4	6.8	10.9	7.1	7.5	10.6	12.0	7.5	8.8	6.7	9.1
2. Seldom	20.0	15.2	24.6	19.7	20.8	23.9	22.3	15.7	19.0	20.0	20.0	19.0	17.8	23.0	22.1	20.0
3. Sometimes	34.7	32.7	36.8	35.8	26.3	34.2	37.6	31.7	36.4	33.1	36.7	35.0	37.4	28.9	35.2	27.3
4. Often	23.2	27.9	19.0	24.0	18.7	19.6	22.5	26.2	22.9	25.6	20.5	22.0	24.8	23.6	23.2	23.6
5. Always	13.0	17.8	7.7	13.2	12.1	11.0	10.7	15.5	14.6	13.9	12.2	12.1	12.5	15.5	12.6	20.0
Item 13020 N(Wtd)	3262	1589	1581	2669	331	719	987	1119	437	1620	1545	1137	867	453	697	55

FOR THOSE WHO HAVE A JOB:

D04E: I feel sure I that can keep working steadily with my present employer as long as I want to

	TOTAL	M	F	White	Black	NE	NC	S	W	Yes	No	None	Marijuana Only	Few Pills	More Pills	Any Heroin
1. Never	5.7	5.2	5.9	4.9	10.1	4.6	5.0	7.0	6.0	4.1	7.1	6.5	3.0	7.6	6.4	9.8
2. Seldom	5.2	5.5	4.5	4.5	10.7	4.6	5.2	5.4	5.3	4.8	5.5	5.0	5.0	6.7	4.5	4.9
3. Sometimes	12.8	10.8	14.9	12.4	15.4	14.7	13.3	9.9	16.3	10.8	15.0	14.1	9.9	12.8	13.7	14.6
4. Often	26.7	26.7	26.6	27.2	21.9	30.1	26.4	26.5	21.6	27.5	26.5	27.0	25.4	22.6	28.9	31.7
5. Always	49.6	51.7	48.1	51.1	42.0	45.7	50.1	51.2	51.1	52.8	45.9	47.4	56.6	50.2	46.7	36.6
Item 13030 N(Wtd) ★	2227	1175	985	1893	169	495	694	756	282	1059	1102	703	606	327	512	41

D04F: I worry about getting fired or laid-off from my job

	TOTAL	M	F	White	Black	NE	NC	S	W	Yes	No	None	Marijuana Only	Few Pills	More Pills	Any Heroin
1. Never	59.3	57.3	62.5	60.5	56.4	57.6	59.9	59.9	59.5	60.4	58.1	57.3	61.3	63.5	61.1	51.2
2. Seldom	24.8	25.8	23.7	25.2	16.4	25.8	24.8	23.7	26.2	26.9	23.1	24.9	23.3	23.0	26.4	29.3
3. Sometimes	10.2	10.6	9.0	9.8	13.3	9.9	10.1	10.1	10.8	9.2	11.3	11.8	8.8	9.8	9.0	7.3
4. Often	3.5	4.1	2.8	3.1	7.3	3.4	4.3	3.2	2.2	2.6	4.3	3.6	4.1	2.5	2.0	7.3
5. Always	2.2	2.2	2.2	1.5	6.7	3.0	1.0	3.1	1.4	.9	3.1	2.3	2.6	1.2	1.4	2.4
Item 13040 N(Wtd) ★	2213	1168	976	1884	165	493	690	750	279	1055	1093	694	604	326	511	41

D05: Which best describes the law IN YOUR STATE regarding marijuana? Possession in private of an ounce or less of marijuana (by an adult) is...

	TOTAL	M	F	White	Black	NE	NC	S	W	Yes	No	None	Marijuana Only	Few Pills	More Pills	Any Heroin
1. A criminal offense, carrying a possible jail sentence	25.6	27.8	23.6	26.1	25.2	23.2	24.9	31.1	17.4	25.0	25.6	27.9	24.1	23.3	25.3	25.9
2. A criminal offense, carrying a possible fine but not a jail sentence	20.5	23.2	18.0	20.4	22.4	24.5	18.4	20.5	18.8	20.0	20.7	14.7	22.4	26.6	24.3	20.4
3. A non-criminal offense - like a traffic ticket - carrying a small fine and no criminal record at all	11.9	14.1	9.0	11.4	11.8	14.0	11.5	7.1	21.9	12.3	11.2	7.8	11.0	15.3	16.2	14.8
4. I don't know if the offense is criminal, but I know it only carries a fine	11.0	10.0	12.3	10.8	10.5	11.7	13.1	8.5	11.4	10.6	11.7	8.7	13.0	9.5	13.0	16.7
5. Not a legal offense at all	3.3	3.7	2.9	3.0	5.4	4.0	2.7	3.0	4.4	2.6	3.9	2.0	3.7	3.2	4.6	1.9
6. I just don't know	27.7	21.3	34.1	28.3	24.3	22.8	29.6	29.8	26.0	29.4	26.9	38.8	25.6	22.3	16.5	18.5
Item 13050 N(Wtd)	3213	1549	1570	2641	313	707	973	1102	430	1597	1514	1115	860	443	691	54

★=excludes respondents for whom question was inappropriate.

QUESTIONNAIRE FORM 5 1978	TOTAL	SEX		RACE		REGION				4YR COLLEGE PLANS		ILLICIT DRUG USE: LIFETIME				
		M	F	White	Black	NE	NC	S	W	Yes	No	None	Marijuana Only	Few Pills	More Pills	Any Heroin
Weighted No. of Cases:	3770	1844	1762	2955	426	911	1074	1259	527	1768	1748	1274	1012	501	813	71
% of Weighted Total:	100.0	48.9	46.7	78.4	11.3	24.2	28.5	33.4	14.0	46.9	46.4	33.8	26.8	13.3	21.6	1.9

The next questions ask about characteristics which some people associate with the use of particular drugs. First, we want to know what you think.

E01: Do YOU think that people who smoke marijuana several times a week tend to be...

E01A: More creative than average

	TOTAL	M	F	White	Black	NE	NC	S	W	Yes	No	None	Mari. Only	Few Pills	More Pills	Any Her.
1. No	53.5	53.6	53.3	55.1	39.6	53.1	56.5	48.8	59.0	60.5	46.8	63.4	58.6	47.5	38.5	20.4
2. Yes	18.1	20.3	15.7	17.2	23.5	18.7	16.4	20.8	14.4	15.5	20.7	7.0	14.3	23.0	33.5	63.0
3. Not sure, no opinion	28.4	26.1	31.0	27.7	37.2	28.2	27.1	30.4	26.7	24.0	32.5	29.6	27.1	29.5	27.8	18.5
Item 13060 N(Wtd)	3264	1577	1592	2678	328	712	1000	1113	439	1623	1539	1134	877	444	701	54

E01B: Less sensible than average

1. No	35.7	38.3	33.2	36.4	32.0	37.1	37.4	35.5	30.0	36.2	35.7	18.2	38.6	41.0	53.7	77.8
2. Yes	43.2	42.4	44.4	44.1	35.7	42.8	43.7	40.8	48.9	45.8	40.7	57.6	41.7	38.1	28.4	18.5
3. Not sure, no opinion	21.1	19.4	22.4	19.5	32.3	20.1	18.9	23.5	21.1	18.0	23.7	24.2	19.7	21.2	17.8	3.7
Item 13070 N(Wtd)	3249	1568	1586	2665	328	706	998	1109	436	1618	1530	1131	871	444	696	54

E01C: More interesting people than average

1. No	58.4	57.2	59.7	60.9	41.0	61.4	58.9	53.9	64.0	64.2	53.1	68.9	62.7	52.3	43.9	27.8
2. Yes	19.5	21.6	17.7	18.8	23.9	19.0	19.8	21.1	15.8	16.8	22.4	6.0	17.4	27.6	35.6	61.1
3. Not sure, no opinion	22.1	21.1	22.7	20.3	35.5	19.6	21.4	25.0	20.2	19.0	24.6	25.1	19.8	20.1	20.5	13.0
Item 13080 N(Wtd)	3247	1572	1582	2663	327	705	997	1109	436	1617	1530	1131	872	442	694	54

E01D: Less hard-working than average

1. No	36.6	37.2	36.2	37.1	32.6	39.7	37.9	34.9	32.9	35.9	37.4	21.0	37.3	41.3	55.2	67.3
2. Yes	44.3	45.3	42.8	45.2	35.7	43.3	44.2	42.8	49.7	46.5	42.1	52.9	43.0	46.9	32.7	25.5
3. Not sure, no opinion	19.2	17.5	21.0	17.7	31.4	17.0	17.9	22.3	17.2	17.6	20.5	26.2	19.8	11.8	12.1	7.3
Item 13090 N(Wtd)	3248	1574	1578	2661	328	706	997	1110	435	1614	1534	1131	874	441	694	55

E01E: More independent than average

1. No	43.7	42.4	45.3	44.5	38.0	44.6	42.0	41.9	51.3	45.3	42.2	48.0	42.9	46.3	38.8	24.5
2. Yes	33.8	37.0	30.8	34.3	26.9	33.7	36.7	33.8	27.4	33.8	34.3	24.2	34.0	37.6	44.8	58.5
3. Not sure, no opinion	22.4	20.7	23.9	21.2	35.2	21.6	21.4	24.4	21.1	20.9	23.6	27.8	23.1	16.1	16.6	17.0
Item 13100 N(Wtd)	3231	1565	1573	2652	324	698	989	1108	435	1610	1520	1126	870	441	688	53

E01F: More emotionally unstable than average

1. No	34.3	36.9	31.8	34.9	30.2	37.1	34.3	34.3	29.6	34.8	33.6	17.4	37.6	40.6	51.9	61.8
2. Yes	45.1	43.5	46.7	45.2	44.0	42.7	43.9	46.2	48.6	46.6	43.7	58.0	42.4	44.0	30.4	18.2
3. Not sure, no opinion	20.6	19.6	21.4	19.8	26.2	20.2	21.8	19.5	21.8	18.6	22.8	24.6	20.0	15.4	17.8	18.2
Item 13110 N(Wtd)	3245	1568	1581	2660	325	703	995	1110	436	1616	1527	1132	874	441	690	55

E01G: More concerned about other people than average

1. No	62.4	62.1	62.8	64.7	48.0	64.1	63.6	59.3	65.4	67.9	57.1	68.0	65.2	63.1	52.0	32.1
2. Yes	13.6	16.0	11.4	12.9	16.3	14.2	12.7	15.2	10.6	10.8	16.5	5.1	12.3	15.7	25.5	47.2
3. Not sure, no opinion	24.0	21.9	25.8	22.4	35.7	21.7	23.7	25.6	23.8	21.2	26.4	26.8	22.5	21.2	22.4	20.8
Item 13120 N(Wtd)	3228	1558	1577	2649	325	696	991	1107	433	1611	1517	1129	870	439	686	53

E01H: More weak-willed than average

1. No	35.4	38.0	32.7	36.6	25.6	39.9	37.1	32.5	31.3	35.5	35.0	17.6	37.8	44.3	53.8	60.0
2. Yes	40.2	39.3	41.1	39.5	43.2	37.7	39.6	40.5	45.2	41.9	38.4	52.8	40.0	32.5	26.6	21.8
3. Not sure, no opinion	24.4	22.7	26.2	23.8	31.5	22.4	23.3	27.0	23.4	22.6	26.6	29.4	22.1	23.2	19.6	16.4
Item 13130 N(Wtd)	3226	1558	1574	2647	324	697	991	1106	431	1607	1519	1128	867	440	684	55

QUESTIONNAIRE FORM 5 1978	TOTAL	SEX		RACE		REGION				4YR COLLEGE PLANS		ILLICIT DRUG USE: LIFETIME				
		M	F	White	Black	NE	NC	S	W	Yes	No	None	Marijuana Only	Few Pills	More Pills	Any Heroin
Weighted No. of Cases:	3770	1844	1762	2955	426	911	1074	1259	527	1768	1748	1274	1012	501	813	71
% of Weighted Total:	100.0	48.9	46.7	78.4	11.3	24.2	28.5	33.4	14.0	46.9	46.4	33.8	26.8	13.3	21.6	1.9

E01I: More criminal than average

1. No	42.0	43.1	41.1	43.3	34.8	48.0	41.8	40.4	37.0	42.1	42.0	19.8	47.0	49.7	65.0	71.7
2. Yes	34.3	37.1	31.6	34.3	32.3	29.6	33.6	35.2	41.2	35.1	33.2	49.3	30.1	30.1	19.9	13.2
3. Not sure, no opinion	23.7	19.9	27.3	22.4	32.9	22.5	24.5	24.3	21.8	22.8	24.7	30.8	22.9	20.3	15.1	15.1
Item 13140 N(Wtd)	3222	1554	1574	2646	322	692	991	1107	432	1605	1516	1127	869	439	682	53

Next we want to ask you how you think most of the people you know would answer the same questions.

E02: Do you think that MOST OF THE PEOPLE YOU KNOW feel that individuals who smoke marijuana several times a week tend to be...

E02A: More creative than average

1. No	51.3	52.1	51.0	53.5	35.6	52.1	53.7	47.0	55.0	55.5	47.5	57.6	53.7	46.5	43.8	26.9
2. Yes	24.5	25.4	23.3	23.7	30.6	25.3	23.0	27.7	18.4	23.1	25.6	14.0	23.0	33.3	35.4	55.8
3. Not sure, no opinion	24.2	22.4	25.7	22.8	33.8	22.5	23.2	25.2	26.4	21.4	26.9	28.4	23.3	20.0	20.9	15.4
Item 13190 N(Wtd)	3157	1522	1542	2591	317	672	977	1085	424	1579	1480	1111	849	430	664	52

E02B: Less sensible than average

1. No	38.1	37.7	38.1	38.5	32.7	41.4	36.2	37.8	37.9	37.9	38.2	25.5	39.5	42.2	52.3	74.5
2. Yes	41.7	43.4	41.0	43.1	37.1	40.6	45.0	41.0	38.1	44.9	38.4	50.4	40.7	39.1	32.8	17.6
3. Not sure, no opinion	20.2	18.9	20.9	18.5	30.5	18.2	18.9	21.2	24.3	17.2	23.4	24.1	20.0	18.5	15.1	7.8
Item 13200 N(Wtd)	3142	1515	1534	2578	315	665	976	1081	420	1574	1473	1111	841	427	662	51

E02C: More interesting people than average

1. No	51.3	52.3	50.7	54.1	34.7	52.9	52.5	49.6	50.1	54.7	48.3	56.0	54.0	49.1	44.1	31.4
2. Yes	27.1	28.1	26.1	26.1	31.8	28.1	25.9	28.0	26.1	25.7	28.5	17.3	23.7	33.6	40.6	54.9
3. Not sure, no opinion	21.6	19.6	23.1	19.8	33.4	18.9	21.5	22.4	24.0	19.6	23.2	26.7	22.3	17.1	15.4	13.7
Item 13210 N(Wtd)	3139	1514	1534	2580	314	665	975	1078	421	1571	1471	1107	844	426	662	51

E02D: Less hard-working than average

1. No	37.3	37.5	37.2	38.2	31.6	41.3	35.0	37.6	35.2	37.1	37.3	26.3	39.3	39.2	50.6	60.8
2. Yes	42.0	43.9	40.0	42.5	38.7	41.4	42.9	42.8	38.3	44.5	39.2	47.3	40.0	43.4	36.1	27.5
3. Not sure, no opinion	20.7	18.6	22.8	19.3	30.0	17.2	22.1	19.5	26.6	18.4	23.5	26.4	20.9	17.2	13.3	11.8
Item 13220 N(Wtd)	3138	1514	1532	2581	310	669	972	1079	418	1567	1476	1108	843	424	662	51

E02E: More independent than average

1. No	41.8	42.1	41.7	42.5	37.5	41.7	41.4	41.6	43.3	42.3	41.7	41.9	41.7	45.7	40.8	24.0
2. Yes	33.7	35.4	32.0	34.2	27.5	35.3	33.6	33.8	31.0	34.6	32.5	28.1	34.1	34.1	40.7	60.0
3. Not sure, no opinion	24.5	22.5	26.2	23.2	35.0	23.0	24.9	24.7	25.7	23.1	25.9	30.1	24.1	20.1	18.5	14.0
Item 13230 N(Wtd)	3131	1509	1531	2577	309	666	970	1074	420	1568	1468	1105	842	422	661	50

E02F: More emotionally unstable than average

1. No	37.3	38.1	36.4	38.3	30.3	43.3	35.2	36.7	33.7	37.5	36.6	25.3	40.5	40.2	50.2	58.8
2. Yes	40.3	40.4	40.6	40.4	41.3	37.6	41.3	40.9	40.6	42.1	38.9	48.0	37.5	40.9	32.4	23.5
3. Not sure, no opinion	22.5	21.5	23.0	21.3	28.4	19.1	23.4	22.4	25.7	20.4	24.5	26.7	22.0	19.1	17.4	17.6
Item 13240 N(Wtd)	3130	1505	1533	2572	310	665	971	1073	421	1571	1463	1106	840	423	660	51

E02G: More concerned about other people than average

1. No	59.6	60.0	59.5	62.1	43.2	60.2	61.8	56.6	60.9	64.5	54.9	62.8	59.9	61.2	56.1	37.3
2. Yes	14.8	16.5	13.2	14.1	20.1	16.3	13.2	16.7	11.3	12.9	16.8	8.5	13.5	17.2	22.5	43.1
3. Not sure, no opinion	25.6	23.5	27.4	23.8	36.7	23.3	24.9	26.7	27.8	22.6	28.3	28.7	26.4	21.6	21.4	17.6
Item 13250 N(Wtd)	3118	1499	1527	2566	308	661	971	1070	417	1564	1460	1104	836	425	654	51

QUESTIONNAIRE FORM 5 1978	TOTAL	SEX		RACE		REGION				4YR COLLEGE PLANS		ILLICIT DRUG USE: LIFETIME				
		M	F	White	Black	NE	NC	S	W	Yes	No	None	Marijuana Only	Few Pills	More Pills	Any Heroin
Weighted No. of Cases:	3770	1844	1762	2955	426	911	1074	1259	527	1768	1748	1274	1012	501	813	71
% of Weighted Total:	100.0	48.9	46.7	78.4	11.3	24.2	28.5	33.4	14.0	46.9	46.4	33.8	26.8	13.3	21.6	1.9

E02H: More weak-willed than average

1. No	36.5	39.0	33.9	36.8	31.6	43.4	32.9	36.5	34.2	38.0	34.7	24.3	38.5	41.8	48.9	66.0
2. Yes	38.9	38.9	39.5	39.0	40.3	33.8	41.2	39.6	39.7	40.5	37.5	47.2	37.6	35.9	30.3	22.0
3. Not sure, no opinion	24.6	22.1	26.6	24.2	28.1	23.0	25.9	23.8	26.1	21.4	27.9	28.3	23.9	22.5	20.8	12.0
Item 13260 N(Wtd)	3131	1508	1529	2574	310	662	973	1078	418	1564	1471	1105	841	426	659	50

E02I: More criminal than average

1. No	40.0	39.9	40.4	41.0	34.0	47.8	37.0	38.8	37.4	40.3	39.7	26.5	43.9	43.9	54.2	60.0
2. Yes	37.3	39.7	34.9	37.6	34.9	30.3	38.9	39.5	39.3	39.4	35.4	44.8	33.8	35.7	31.2	28.0
3. Not sure, no opinion	22.7	20.4	24.7	21.4	30.8	21.9	24.1	21.7	23.3	20.4	24.9	28.7	22.3	20.7	14.6	12.0
Item 13270 N(Wtd)	3130	1508	1529	2573	312	663	971	1079	417	1562	1471	1105	843	426	657	50

The next questions are similar, but ask about illegal drugs other than marijuana-- like psychedelics, barbiturates, narcotics, and amphetamines.

E03: Do YOU think that people who use illegal drugs (other than marijuana) several times a week tend to be...

E03A: More creative than average

1. No	60.7	61.0	60.7	62.5	43.9	62.2	63.1	56.7	63.4	66.9	54.7	66.3	59.5	59.4	57.6	39.6
2. Yes	11.0	10.8	11.4	10.4	16.5	11.9	9.9	12.2	9.0	9.5	12.7	6.4	8.1	12.3	17.4	45.3
3. Not sure, no opinion	28.3	28.3	28.0	27.1	39.3	25.7	27.0	31.2	27.8	23.7	32.5	27.4	32.2	28.3	25.0	13.2
Item 13330 N(Wtd)	3072	1478	1505	2530	303	645	959	1059	410	1545	1433	1084	825	424	639	53

E03B: Less sensible than average

1. No	15.0	15.9	14.1	14.3	17.3	16.5	13.8	16.7	11.0	12.6	17.4	11.7	13.3	16.1	20.4	28.3
2. Yes	61.5	60.1	63.5	64.1	46.5	64.4	63.5	56.8	65.0	68.9	54.2	65.2	59.5	61.1	59.7	62.3
3. Not sure, no opinion	23.5	24.0	22.5	21.6	36.2	19.1	22.7	26.6	24.0	18.6	28.4	23.0	27.3	23.0	20.1	11.3
Item 13340 N(Wtd)	3066	1474	1501	2524	301	643	959	1057	408	1538	1433	1082	822	422	638	53

E03C: More interesting people than average

1. No	62.3	60.8	64.2	64.7	42.2	65.6	62.8	58.6	65.2	69.1	56.0	67.7	60.9	64.3	57.1	39.2
2. Yes	10.7	11.4	9.9	9.9	17.9	10.5	10.6	12.3	7.1	8.8	12.7	5.6	7.6	10.9	20.4	47.1
3. Not sure, no opinion	27.0	27.8	25.9	25.5	39.9	23.9	26.5	29.1	27.5	22.1	31.2	26.8	31.5	24.8	22.6	13.7
Item 13350 N(Wtd)	3058	1474	1496	2518	301	640	954	1056	408	1536	1428	1078	820	423	637	51

E03D: Less hard-working than average

1. No	18.0	16.7	19.4	18.1	17.9	22.3	17.9	16.7	14.5	16.3	19.6	14.8	14.4	20.7	24.8	33.3
2. Yes	56.4	57.9	54.9	57.8	43.2	56.4	56.8	54.5	60.6	61.8	51.1	58.8	55.9	56.5	54.4	45.1
3. Not sure, no opinion	25.6	25.4	25.7	24.2	38.9	21.3	25.3	28.8	24.9	22.0	29.4	26.4	29.7	22.8	20.9	21.6
Item 13360 N(Wtd)	3055	1473	1493	2515	301	640	952	1056	406	1535	1427	1078	819	421	636	51

E03E: More independent than average

1. No	46.7	45.6	48.3	48.1	37.9	47.8	47.0	44.7	50.0	49.8	43.8	48.9	45.6	48.1	45.5	37.3
2. Yes	24.7	26.7	22.6	24.9	21.6	26.6	24.3	25.1	21.9	25.3	23.9	22.0	21.4	26.5	31.1	37.3
3. Not sure, no opinion	28.6	27.7	29.3	27.1	40.9	25.7	28.8	30.2	28.3	25.0	32.3	29.1	33.0	25.4	23.4	27.5
Item 13370 N(Wtd)	3053	1470	1494	2516	301	638	952	1056	406	1535	1423	1077	821	422	633	51

E03F: More emotionally unstable than average

1. No	13.9	14.5	13.2	13.6	15.0	14.8	12.7	15.3	11.8	11.8	15.9	12.0	11.3	13.1	20.3	25.5
2. Yes	62.5	60.3	64.9	64.2	50.3	64.8	62.8	60.1	64.0	69.5	55.7	64.5	60.7	65.5	60.4	60.8
3. Not sure, no opinion	23.6	25.2	21.8	22.2	34.7	20.5	24.5	24.4	24.3	18.7	28.4	23.5	28.1	21.4	19.3	15.7
Item 13380 N(Wtd)	3055	1471	1495	2515	300	640	951	1056	408	1535	1425	1077	821	420	636	51

QUESTIONNAIRE FORM 5 1978	TOTAL	SEX		RACE		REGION				4YR COLLEGE PLANS		ILLICIT DRUG USE: LIFETIME				
		M	F	White	Black	NE	NC	S	W	Yes	No	None	Mari-juana Only	Few Pills	More Pills	Any Her-oin
Weighted No. of Cases:	3770	1844	1762	2955	426	911	1074	1259	527	1768	1748	1274	1012	501	813	71
% of Weighted Total:	100.0	48.9	46.7	78.4	11.3	24.2	28.5	33.4	14.0	46.9	46.4	33.8	26.8	13.3	21.6	1.9

E03G: More concerned about other people than average

1. No	65.7	66.2	66.0	68.1	49.8	68.7	66.6	62.5	67.5	71.5	60.0	67.8	63.9	68.7	65.0	52.9
2. Yes	6.5	6.5	6.2	5.7	11.0	6.4	4.9	8.3	5.7	5.1	8.1	4.4	4.6	6.9	9.4	31.4
3. Not sure, no opinion	27.7	27.4	27.8	26.2	39.5	24.9	28.4	29.2	26.8	23.4	31.8	27.8	31.4	24.2	25.7	15.7
Item 13390 N(Wtd)	3048	1470	1490	2511	299	638	950	1054	406	1532	1424	1078	819	422	631	51

E03H: More weak-willed than average

1. No	16.5	16.4	16.5	16.4	15.0	21.9	15.7	15.7	12.3	15.5	17.7	12.7	14.0	17.3	24.5	31.4
2. Yes	57.0	56.5	57.9	57.6	52.5	54.2	56.8	57.3	61.2	62.8	51.1	60.7	56.3	58.4	51.8	51.0
3. Not sure, no opinion	26.4	27.1	25.5	26.0	32.6	23.9	27.5	27.0	26.4	21.8	31.1	26.6	29.6	24.2	23.7	17.6
Item 13400 N(Wtd)	3054	1472	1493	2515	301	640	953	1057	405	1531	1427	1077	824	421	633	51

E03I: More criminal than average

1. No	18.6	16.7	20.8	19.2	15.9	24.7	19.6	16.3	12.6	18.1	19.2	14.1	15.3	17.6	29.5	39.2
2. Yes	55.1	57.7	53.1	56.4	48.2	50.4	54.3	56.2	61.6	59.3	51.2	59.6	54.9	57.7	47.8	43.1
3. Not sure, no opinion	26.2	25.6	26.1	24.4	35.9	24.7	26.1	27.6	25.6	22.7	29.5	26.3	29.8	24.7	22.7	15.7
Item 13410 N(Wtd)	3052	1470	1492	2511	301	639	952	1056	406	1529	1425	1078	823	421	630	51

E04: Do you think that MOST OF THE PEOPLE YOU KNOW feel that individuals who use illegal drugs (other than marijuana) several times a week tend to be...

E04A: More creative than average

1. No	55.6	55.5	55.9	57.4	42.8	55.7	59.1	52.4	55.4	61.5	49.9	58.4	55.2	56.0	54.0	39.2
2. Yes	14.6	14.4	14.8	13.7	19.4	15.9	12.6	16.0	13.1	12.8	16.3	10.7	12.0	17.1	20.1	41.2
3. Not sure, no opinion	29.8	30.0	29.3	28.8	37.5	28.2	28.2	31.5	31.5	25.6	34.0	30.9	32.8	27.1	25.9	19.6
Item 13490 N(Wtd)	3008	1447	1474	2476	299	627	941	1043	397	1512	1402	1078	805	409	617	51

E04B: Less sensible than average

1. No	18.1	17.6	18.5	17.5	19.7	19.8	16.5	18.7	17.8	16.2	20.4	14.9	15.7	20.8	22.3	36.7
2. Yes	55.3	55.0	55.8	57.6	42.8	57.3	58.3	52.2	53.0	62.1	48.5	58.5	54.1	53.8	55.5	44.9
3. Not sure, no opinion	26.6	27.4	25.7	24.9	37.5	22.9	25.3	29.1	29.1	21.7	31.1	26.6	30.2	25.4	22.1	20.4
Item 13500 N(Wtd)	3007	1444	1475	2474	299	625	942	1041	398	1510	1403	1075	804	409	620	49

E04C: More interesting people than average

1. No	56.1	55.6	57.0	57.9	43.6	56.3	59.2	53.8	54.6	61.1	51.6	57.5	56.7	56.7	55.3	38.8
2. Yes	14.7	14.9	14.3	14.6	15.2	16.2	12.9	15.5	14.2	13.3	16.3	11.7	10.7	15.8	21.1	40.8
3. Not sure, no opinion	29.2	29.4	28.8	27.6	41.2	27.3	27.8	30.7	31.2	25.6	32.1	30.7	32.5	27.5	23.4	20.4
Item 13510 N(Wtd)	2993	1434	1473	2470	296	623	938	1038	394	1506	1394	1074	802	404	615	49

E04D: Less hard-working than average

1. No	20.1	18.7	21.8	20.1	20.8	23.8	18.2	20.4	18.2	18.2	22.2	17.1	17.1	20.4	27.0	40.0
2. Yes	51.6	52.8	50.3	53.0	41.6	51.3	53.7	50.2	51.3	57.0	46.4	54.0	50.9	53.1	50.4	38.0
3. Not sure, no opinion	28.2	28.4	27.9	26.9	37.6	24.9	28.1	29.4	30.8	24.8	31.5	28.9	32.1	26.5	22.8	22.0
Item 13520 N(Wtd)	2994	1435	1470	2463	298	622	936	1039	396	1507	1395	1073	800	407	615	50

E04E: More independent than average

1. No	43.7	43.2	44.6	44.8	36.5	42.8	45.4	43.1	42.4	45.8	41.8	44.5	39.8	45.2	48.0	42.9
2. Yes	25.3	26.5	23.7	25.5	22.2	28.5	23.8	24.8	25.0	26.1	24.4	24.0	24.6	26.8	26.5	32.7
3. Not sure, no opinion	31.0	30.2	31.7	29.7	41.3	28.8	30.7	32.1	32.6	28.1	33.9	31.6	35.6	28.3	25.4	26.5
Item 13530 N(Wtd)	2988	1436	1465	2466	293	621	938	1032	396	1504	1391	1073	801	403	614	49

QUESTIONNAIRE FORM 5 1978	TOTAL	SEX		RACE		REGION				4YR COLLEGE PLANS		ILLICIT DRUG USE: LIFETIME				
		M	F	White	Black	NE	NC	S	W	Yes	No	None	Marijuana Only	Few Pills	More Pills	Any Heroin
Weighted No. of Cases:	3770	1844	1762	2955	426	911	1074	1259	527	1768	1748	1274	1012	501	813	71
% of Weighted Total:	100.0	48.9	46.7	78.4	11.3	24.2	28.5	33.4	14.0	46.9	46.4	33.8	26.8	13.3	21.6	1.9

E04F: More emotionally unstable than average

1. No	16.8	16.8	16.7	16.9	14.8	20.1	14.7	17.4	14.8	14.1	19.5	13.8	13.8	17.2	23.6	35.3
2. Yes	55.6	54.7	56.9	57.0	46.1	56.2	57.2	54.2	54.8	62.1	49.3	58.2	54.6	57.9	53.7	45.1
3. Not sure, no opinion	27.6	28.6	26.4	26.1	38.7	23.9	28.1	28.5	30.2	23.8	31.2	28.1	31.6	25.1	22.8	19.6
Item 13540 N(Wtd)	2989	1436	1467	2462	297	623	933	1035	398	1507	1394	1073	798	406	615	51

E04G: More concerned about other people than average

1. No	60.4	60.3	61.0	63.0	45.1	60.5	63.3	58.0	60.0	66.0	54.9	62.9	58.4	60.9	61.3	51.0
2. Yes	8.6	9.1	8.1	7.8	13.1	9.8	6.4	10.1	7.6	6.8	10.8	6.4	7.0	10.3	10.9	26.5
3. Not sure, no opinion	31.0	30.7	30.8	29.2	41.8	29.5	30.3	31.9	32.4	27.2	34.3	30.7	34.7	28.5	27.9	22.4
Item 13550 N(Wtd)	2989	1434	1469	2462	297	621	935	1037	395	1506	1391	1070	802	407	613	49

E04H: More weak-willed than average

1. No	18.4	18.3	18.6	18.5	14.7	24.6	16.5	16.8	17.1	16.7	20.5	16.7	15.8	16.9	24.5	36.7
2. Yes	51.8	51.1	52.3	52.9	46.3	47.8	54.5	52.5	49.2	56.9	46.3	53.5	50.4	55.1	49.8	46.9
3. Not sure, no opinion	29.9	30.6	29.1	28.6	38.7	27.7	28.8	30.6	33.7	26.4	33.2	29.9	34.0	27.7	25.8	16.3
Item 13560 N(Wtd)	2996	1439	1470	2465	300	621	937	1041	398	1506	1396	1073	806	408	612	49

E04I: More criminal than average

1. No	19.3	17.6	21.2	19.7	15.4	25.1	17.8	18.6	16.2	18.5	20.3	16.6	16.0	19.7	28.1	22.4
2. Yes	52.0	54.2	50.1	53.4	45.5	47.4	54.3	52.1	53.3	57.1	47.2	53.6	52.5	52.6	48.1	55.1
3. Not sure, no opinion	28.7	28.2	28.6	26.9	39.1	27.7	27.9	29.3	30.6	24.4	32.5	29.8	31.5	27.8	23.8	20.4
Item 13570 N(Wtd)	2995	1440	1468	2464	299	622	936	1040	396	1506	1393	1071	807	407	613	49

E05: Some people like school very much. Others don't. How do you feel about going to school?

5. I like school very much	14.4	14.9	13.8	13.3	23.2	9.3	13.1	17.8	16.4	18.5	10.1	20.4	13.7	10.9	8.1	7.3
4. I like school quite a lot	28.6	27.9	29.0	28.4	28.6	26.6	29.3	27.1	33.4	33.5	23.5	35.9	28.5	27.0	18.2	18.2
3. I like school some	36.6	37.0	36.0	36.6	35.9	39.9	36.9	34.6	36.0	34.5	38.6	32.4	39.1	38.6	39.1	38.2
2. I don't like school very much	13.7	13.6	14.2	14.9	8.3	15.9	13.1	14.5	9.6	9.6	18.2	8.2	13.2	17.1	19.8	21.8
1. I don't like school at all	6.8	6.7	6.9	6.8	4.1	8.5	7.5	6.0	4.7	3.8	9.6	3.0	5.6	6.2	14.8	14.5
Item 7630 N(Wtd)	3158	1510	1554	2589	315	659	982	1090	428	1569	1480	1120	842	433	655	55

E06: How important is each of the following for being looked up to or having high status in your school?

E06A: Coming from the right family

1. No importance	14.4	15.2	13.5	13.1	17.9	18.0	12.7	11.9	19.4	13.6	15.6	13.2	14.6	14.1	15.6	24.1
2. Little importance	21.7	22.4	21.4	22.6	15.0	26.8	18.6	19.5	26.8	23.2	20.3	20.7	22.7	21.2	23.3	14.8
3. Moderate importance	32.1	31.2	32.9	33.8	22.1	33.9	35.0	30.9	25.6	33.2	31.2	31.9	32.4	37.2	29.7	27.8
4. Great importance	17.3	16.9	17.4	17.2	19.5	10.7	19.3	19.3	17.3	16.2	17.9	18.2	16.6	15.0	17.8	16.7
5. Very great importance	14.5	14.2	14.9	13.4	25.4	10.5	14.4	18.3	11.1	13.7	15.0	15.9	13.7	12.4	13.6	16.7
Item 13580 N(Wtd)	3111	1485	1533	2550	307	646	967	1076	422	1553	1451	1102	837	419	647	54

E06B: Being a leader in student activities

1. No importance	9.6	10.1	8.9	8.9	10.2	14.6	9.3	6.6	10.2	6.4	13.1	6.4	9.2	10.7	14.1	18.5
2. Little importance	15.6	16.7	14.4	15.7	15.1	17.9	15.4	13.8	16.9	13.9	16.9	12.9	16.8	15.5	18.1	18.5
3. Moderate importance	32.3	34.1	30.8	32.7	28.9	33.2	32.5	31.2	33.0	33.2	31.7	33.5	34.1	29.3	30.2	20.4
4. Great importance	28.6	26.2	31.2	29.4	25.0	24.8	29.4	31.0	26.4	32.6	24.7	31.2	27.0	31.0	25.7	27.8
5. Very great importance	13.9	13.0	14.7	13.4	20.7	9.3	13.3	17.3	13.3	13.9	13.6	15.9	12.8	13.6	11.9	14.8
Item 13590 N(Wtd)	3107	1482	1531	2551	304	642	969	1076	421	1554	1447	1101	834	420	646	54

QUESTIONNAIRE FORM 5 1978	TOTAL	SEX		RACE		REGION				4YR COLLEGE PLANS		ILLICIT DRUG USE: LIFETIME				
		M	F	White	Black	NE	NC	S	W	Yes	No	None	Marijuana Only	Few Pills	More Pills	Any Heroin
Weighted No. of Cases:	3770	1844	1762	2955	426	911	1074	1259	527	1768	1748	1274	1012	501	813	71
% of Weighted Total:	100.0	48.9	46.7	78.4	11.3	24.2	28.5	33.4	14.0	46.9	46.4	33.8	26.8	13.3	21.6	1.9

E06C: Having a nice car

1. No importance	19.3	16.7	21.3	16.8	32.7	23.6	17.4	18.6	18.3	17.2	21.4	21.3	19.1	19.1	15.2	24.1
2. Little importance	25.0	23.2	27.0	26.2	19.8	26.7	26.6	23.7	22.1	26.2	24.3	27.2	25.1	26.3	21.1	9.3
3. Moderate importance	31.5	33.6	30.0	32.9	20.8	31.8	32.8	28.6	35.1	34.3	28.9	30.1	34.6	28.5	32.4	29.6
4. Great importance	15.6	17.0	14.1	16.0	13.2	11.9	15.3	17.7	16.8	14.5	16.4	13.7	14.1	18.2	19.4	16.7
5. Very great importance	8.6	9.4	7.6	8.0	13.5	6.1	7.7	11.4	7.7	7.8	8.9	7.6	7.2	7.7	11.9	18.5
Item 13600 N(Wtd)	3100	1479	1528	2547	303	641	969	1074	416	1548	1447	1099	832	418	645	54

E06D: Getting good grades

1. No importance	4.8	5.6	4.1	5.1	1.7	7.2	4.3	3.4	6.0	3.8	5.6	2.7	5.2	5.3	7.0	7.7
2. Little importance	14.9	16.0	14.0	15.8	5.3	16.6	15.5	12.3	17.9	15.5	14.1	13.2	14.0	18.6	17.2	15.4
3. Moderate importance	34.1	34.5	34.2	37.1	14.0	33.3	36.0	31.3	38.4	35.8	32.2	33.1	36.1	33.9	35.7	23.1
4. Great importance	28.5	27.4	29.5	28.2	32.7	28.1	29.4	30.0	23.6	27.9	29.6	28.9	29.8	27.0	26.2	26.9
5. Very great importance	17.6	16.7	18.2	13.7	46.3	15.0	14.8	23.1	14.1	16.8	18.4	22.2	14.9	15.3	13.8	25.0
Item 13610 N(Wtd)	3094	1477	1526	2542	300	640	970	1065	419	1550	1439	1095	833	419	645	52

E06E: Being a good athlete

1. No importance	9.3	7.9	10.9	8.2	16.1	10.8	9.3	8.9	8.3	6.2	12.4	7.1	9.4	8.6	12.4	22.6
2. Little importance	12.2	10.8	13.5	12.5	11.8	13.7	12.1	11.8	10.5	9.7	15.0	11.5	10.7	12.6	15.3	15.1
3. Moderate importance	24.7	24.7	24.6	24.6	21.3	24.5	23.2	25.5	26.4	24.5	24.6	25.1	23.5	25.2	24.6	22.6
4. Great importance	29.7	33.4	26.6	30.9	22.3	33.9	30.4	27.5	27.1	33.6	25.9	30.1	33.6	27.9	26.3	18.9
5. Very great importance	24.1	23.2	24.3	23.8	28.5	17.2	24.9	26.1	27.6	26.0	22.1	26.2	22.8	25.7	21.5	20.8
Item 13620 N(Wtd)	3102	1480	1528	2546	305	641	969	1073	420	1550	1447	1098	833	420	647	53

E06F: Knowing a lot about intellectual matters

1. No importance	12.2	12.2	12.3	12.4	13.6	16.1	11.9	10.2	12.7	10.7	13.7	8.9	13.4	14.4	15.2	14.8
2. Little importance	27.4	26.5	29.1	29.5	11.6	29.5	28.1	25.2	28.1	28.3	26.5	28.7	28.6	26.1	26.6	20.4
3. Moderate importance	36.8	36.6	37.0	38.1	30.2	34.6	38.2	36.8	36.9	38.3	35.0	37.8	37.2	35.2	35.2	37.0
4. Great importance	15.3	16.7	14.0	14.1	21.6	14.1	16.5	15.4	13.9	15.5	15.5	16.0	15.0	16.0	13.5	14.8
5. Very great importance	8.3	7.9	7.7	6.0	22.9	5.5	5.4	12.5	8.4	7.1	9.3	8.6	5.9	8.1	9.6	13.0
Item 13630 N(Wtd)	3094	1482	1518	2544	301	638	967	1071	417	1549	1444	1095	831	418	644	54

E06G: Planning to go to college

1. No importance	14.7	15.8	13.2	14.6	13.4	16.8	14.9	13.8	13.8	9.0	20.6	12.8	14.6	14.8	17.7	18.5
2. Little importance	22.2	21.9	23.0	23.6	13.4	21.6	21.8	21.7	25.1	19.6	25.3	21.1	21.0	22.5	26.4	25.9
3. Moderate importance	31.4	30.8	31.7	33.1	20.0	35.4	32.6	27.5	31.7	34.8	27.7	33.6	31.9	30.6	29.1	24.1
4. Great importance	17.8	17.8	18.0	17.6	20.3	14.6	19.8	18.3	16.9	20.7	15.0	17.5	20.1	16.7	15.2	13.0
5. Very great importance	13.9	13.5	14.1	11.1	32.8	11.6	10.8	18.7	12.2	16.0	11.4	15.0	12.4	15.3	11.6	18.5
Item 13640 N(Wtd)	3093	1479	1520	2536	305	638	968	1068	419	1549	1438	1093	830	418	645	54

E07: How about using drugs (other than marijuana or alcohol)--does that cause a student to be looked up to or looked down on?

E07A: Among the majority of students in my school, such drug use is...

1. Looked down on a lot	17.3	20.3	14.4	17.3	19.9	13.4	17.1	19.1	19.6	19.3	15.5	20.7	18.6	16.1	11.7	9.8
2. Looked down on some	21.0	20.4	21.4	22.2	16.3	19.2	20.4	22.3	22.3	21.2	20.6	22.1	21.1	23.4	19.4	5.9
3. Neither, or mixed	49.9	48.0	52.2	50.2	44.2	53.8	51.0	46.7	49.2	48.9	51.1	46.7	48.9	48.9	55.6	52.9
4. Looked up to some	9.1	8.9	9.5	8.3	13.3	10.4	9.1	8.9	7.3	8.4	9.5	7.7	8.2	10.2	11.4	17.6
5. Looked up to a lot	2.7	2.5	2.5	2.0	6.3	3.5	2.3	3.0	1.7	2.3	3.4	2.8	3.1	1.4	2.0	15.7
Item 13650 N(Wtd)	3069	1464	1511	2521	301	636	964	1056	413	1539	1427	1075	828	423	640	51

QUESTIONNAIRE FORM 5 1978	TOTAL	SEX		RACE		REGION				4YR COLLEGE PLANS		ILLICIT DRUG USE: LIFETIME				
		M	F	White	Black	NE	NC	S	W	Yes	No	None	Mari-juana Only	Few Pills	More Pills	Any Her-oin
Weighted No. of Cases:	3770	1844	1762	2955	426	911	1074	1259	527	1768	1748	1274	1012	501	813	71
% of Weighted Total:	100.0	48.9	46.7	78.4	11.3	24.2	28.5	33.4	14.0	46.9	46.4	33.8	26.8	13.3	21.6	1.9

E07B: Among my own group of friends, such drug use is...

	TOTAL	M	F	White	Black	NE	NC	S	W	Yes	No	None	Mari-juana Only	Few Pills	More Pills	Any Her-oin
1. Looked down on a lot	35.6	34.7	36.2	36.2	33.7	30.0	35.4	37.0	40.8	41.5	29.2	55.3	33.1	30.5	12.7	5.9
2. Looked down on some	18.5	17.9	19.0	18.9	16.0	19.7	18.9	17.7	17.5	19.0	18.4	20.0	19.4	18.6	15.5	5.9
3. Neither, or mixed	35.4	36.5	34.9	35.1	35.7	37.5	35.0	34.8	35.0	31.7	39.2	21.4	38.4	41.3	50.3	41.2
4. Looked up to some	7.7	8.0	7.4	7.3	11.7	10.2	8.0	6.9	5.3	6.2	9.2	2.6	7.2	7.9	14.4	27.5
5. Looked up to a lot	2.8	2.9	2.6	2.6	3.3	2.7	2.6	3.7	1.2	1.6	4.0	.7	1.8	1.7	7.1	21.6
Item 13660 N(Wtd)	3062	1464	1506	2516	300	630	963	1058	412	1540	1419	1075	828	419	638	51

E07C: My own feelings about such drug use is that...

	TOTAL	M	F	White	Black	NE	NC	S	W	Yes	No	None	Mari-juana Only	Few Pills	More Pills	Any Her-oin
1. I look down on it a lot	45.1	43.4	46.5	45.4	42.0	42.1	44.4	45.3	50.7	50.6	39.5	71.4	41.2	35.4	16.5	9.8
2. I look down on it some	18.8	19.4	18.4	18.6	21.0	19.0	18.4	18.9	19.2	17.3	20.6	14.5	21.9	21.4	20.8	9.8
3. Neither, or mixed	30.1	31.2	29.2	30.0	31.0	32.1	31.7	28.9	26.5	28.1	31.8	13.4	32.8	34.4	49.8	47.1
4. I look up to it some	4.9	4.9	4.8	4.9	4.7	6.0	4.6	5.0	3.6	3.3	6.4	.6	3.7	8.1	9.9	21.6
5. I look up to it a lot	1.1	1.1	1.1	1.0	1.3	1.0	.9	1.8	-	.7	1.6	.2	.4	.5	3.0	13.7
Item 13670 N(Wtd)	3063	1461	1509	2518	300	630	963	1058	412	1543	1416	1078	827	421	636	51

E08: How often have you been around people who were taking each of the following to get high or for "kicks"?

E08A: Marijuana (pot, grass) or hashish

	TOTAL	M	F	White	Black	NE	NC	S	W	Yes	No	None	Mari-juana Only	Few Pills	More Pills	Any Her-oin
1. Never	13.6	11.2	15.6	12.8	17.9	9.2	14.2	14.5	16.8	13.5	13.9	30.7	3.2	7.3	3.2	-
2. Once or twice	20.2	18.9	21.7	20.9	18.2	17.7	19.5	22.3	20.7	20.1	20.7	35.7	16.3	13.6	5.8	3.8
3. Occasionally	29.5	30.2	28.7	29.0	32.1	28.0	29.3	30.7	28.8	28.5	30.5	24.7	42.1	32.2	20.1	20.8
4. Often	36.7	39.8	33.9	37.3	32.1	45.2	37.1	32.6	33.4	37.8	34.9	8.9	38.3	46.6	71.0	75.5
Item 8750 N(Wtd)	3093	1479	1518	2536	308	640	966	1072	416	1550	1438	1082	833	425	652	53

E08B: LSD

	TOTAL	M	F	White	Black	NE	NC	S	W	Yes	No	None	Mari-juana Only	Few Pills	More Pills	Any Her-oin
1. Never	75.3	75.4	75.2	74.2	87.9	71.6	73.9	78.3	76.1	77.3	73.4	89.5	84.3	73.9	45.4	19.2
2. Once or twice	15.0	14.4	15.6	15.8	6.4	17.1	16.2	13.1	14.2	14.8	15.3	8.2	11.4	20.7	26.9	21.2
3. Occasionally	7.0	7.3	6.7	7.2	5.1	8.5	7.0	6.0	7.2	6.1	8.0	2.0	2.6	3.8	20.9	34.6
4. Often	2.7	3.0	2.4	2.9	1.0	2.8	2.8	2.6	2.2	1.8	3.2	.4	1.7	1.4	7.0	26.9
Item 8760 N(Wtd)	3063	1470	1498	2520	297	633	958	1057	415	1534	1429	1072	822	421	647	52

E08C: Other psychedelics (mescaline, peyote, PCP, etc.)

	TOTAL	M	F	White	Black	NE	NC	S	W	Yes	No	None	Mari-juana Only	Few Pills	More Pills	Any Her-oin
1. Never	74.8	71.9	78.0	73.4	90.1	68.5	73.1	79.1	77.2	75.8	74.3	91.9	82.4	70.3	43.3	15.4
2. Once or twice	14.0	15.3	12.2	14.7	4.3	17.2	14.8	11.8	12.3	15.6	12.1	5.9	12.3	19.9	25.4	21.2
3. Occasionally	8.5	9.4	7.7	9.2	4.6	11.8	9.0	6.3	8.0	6.2	10.9	1.6	3.7	8.6	24.2	34.6
4. Often	2.7	3.3	2.2	2.9	1.0	2.4	3.1	2.8	2.2	2.4	2.8	.6	1.6	1.2	7.1	28.8
Item 8770 N(Wtd)	3072	1467	1509	2522	304	634	959	1066	413	1541	1427	1077	828	417	649	52

E08D: Quaaludes (quads, methaqualone)

	TOTAL	M	F	White	Black	NE	NC	S	W	Yes	No	None	Mari-juana Only	Few Pills	More Pills	Any Her-oin
1. Never	77.3	75.9	78.7	75.7	90.3	73.2	79.6	75.8	81.4	78.3	76.8	93.8	84.1	73.6	47.1	23.1
2. Once or twice	13.2	13.8	12.3	14.1	5.7	14.4	12.6	13.7	11.1	13.2	12.9	5.1	11.0	18.8	25.3	26.9
3. Occasionally	7.1	7.4	6.8	7.5	3.3	9.4	6.1	7.3	5.3	6.8	7.3	1.1	3.3	5.7	20.8	25.0
4. Often	2.5	2.9	2.1	2.6	.7	2.9	1.7	3.1	1.9	1.8	3.0	.1	1.6	1.7	6.7	23.1
Item 8780 N(Wtd)	3055	1467	1495	2507	300	631	953	1059	413	1535	1417	1066	824	420	643	52

E08E: Barbiturates (downers, goofballs, reds, yellows, etc.)

	TOTAL	M	F	White	Black	NE	NC	S	W	Yes	No	None	Mari-juana Only	Few Pills	More Pills	Any Her-oin
1. Never	66.8	66.8	66.6	65.1	79.5	61.3	67.3	67.7	71.3	68.4	64.8	83.8	76.1	60.2	34.1	15.1
2. Once or twice	20.3	20.9	19.7	21.5	11.9	22.5	21.5	19.0	17.6	21.3	19.6	12.7	18.1	29.0	30.1	28.3
3. Occasionally	9.5	8.8	10.2	10.0	5.9	13.0	7.9	9.8	7.5	8.0	11.2	2.5	4.5	8.2	26.5	34.0
4. Often	3.4	3.5	3.5	3.4	2.3	3.2	3.2	3.5	3.6	2.3	4.5	.9	1.3	2.6	9.5	22.6
Item 8790 N(Wtd)	3069	1471	1504	2519	303	631	961	1062	415	1541	1425	1077	827	417	645	53

QUESTIONNAIRE FORM 5 1978	TOTAL	SEX		RACE		REGION				4YR COLLEGE PLANS		ILLICIT DRUG USE: LIFETIME				
		M	F	White	Black	NE	NC	S	W	Yes	No	None	Mari-juana Only	Few Pills	More Pills	Any Her-oin
Weighted No. of Cases:	3770	1844	1762	2955	426	911	1074	1259	527	1768	1748	1274	1012	501	813	71
% of Weighted Total:	100.0	48.9	46.7	78.4	11.3	24.2	28.5	33.4	14.0	46.9	46.4	33.8	26.8	13.3	21.6	1.9

E08F: Tranquilizers (Librium, Valium, Miltown)

	TOTAL	M	F	White	Black	NE	NC	S	W	Yes	No	None	Mari-juana Only	Few Pills	More Pills	Any Her-oin
1. Never	66.7	68.2	64.8	65.2	77.2	63.2	69.6	63.7	73.4	67.7	65.9	82.4	74.5	61.7	36.3	21.2
2. Once or twice	18.9	18.4	19.7	20.0	12.2	19.4	18.4	20.8	14.3	20.1	17.5	12.8	17.9	24.6	27.1	21.2
3. Occasionally	10.3	9.3	11.3	10.9	7.6	13.4	7.9	11.5	7.7	9.6	11.2	4.0	5.8	9.6	25.5	30.8
4. Often	4.1	4.0	4.2	4.0	3.0	4.1	4.1	4.0	4.6	2.7	5.4	.9	1.8	4.1	11.1	25.0
Item 8800 N(Wtd)	3066	1470	1502	2515	303	628	960	1065	413	1541	1425	1077	827	418	642	52

E08G: Cocaine ("coke")

	TOTAL	M	F	White	Black	NE	NC	S	W	Yes	No	None	Mari-juana Only	Few Pills	More Pills	Any Her-oin
1. Never	68.9	65.9	71.7	68.5	77.6	62.5	68.9	73.0	68.3	69.1	68.9	89.8	76.4	57.2	36.3	7.5
2. Once or twice	17.0	18.6	15.7	16.8	12.2	20.6	16.6	14.9	17.4	18.5	15.9	7.8	16.5	29.8	25.0	18.9
3. Occasionally	9.7	10.7	8.9	10.4	5.9	12.1	9.8	8.3	10.2	9.2	10.1	1.5	5.7	9.9	27.3	32.1
4. Often	4.3	4.9	3.8	4.2	4.0	4.8	4.7	3.8	4.1	3.2	5.2	.9	1.4	3.1	11.5	39.6
Item 8810 N(Wtd)	3068	1473	1501	2518	303	630	961	1064	413	1540	1426	1076	828	416	645	53

E08H: Heroin (smack, horse)

	TOTAL	M	F	White	Black	NE	NC	S	W	Yes	No	None	Mari-juana Only	Few Pills	More Pills	Any Her-oin
1. Never	87.9	87.8	88.1	88.2	90.1	87.4	87.8	87.3	90.6	90.1	85.9	91.7	92.1	88.9	81.6	13.2
2. Once or twice	8.8	8.3	9.2	8.6	6.6	9.2	9.0	8.8	8.0	7.6	10.0	7.1	5.7	8.9	12.9	45.3
3. Occasionally	2.2	2.4	2.1	2.1	3.6	2.5	2.3	2.5	1.0	1.8	2.7	1.0	1.2	1.7	3.6	26.4
4. Often	1.0	1.4	.6	1.0	-	.6	.9	1.5	.7	.5	1.4	.1	1.0	.7	1.9	15.1
Item 8820 N(Wtd)	3060	1471	1495	2509	303	629	957	1060	414	1534	1424	1077	823	416	641	53

E08I: Other narcotics (methadone, opium, codeine, paregoric, etc.)

	TOTAL	M	F	White	Black	NE	NC	S	W	Yes	No	None	Mari-juana Only	Few Pills	More Pills	Any Her-oin
1. Never	79.4	77.9	80.9	78.3	90.1	75.7	78.8	81.0	82.9	80.1	78.6	91.9	86.8	76.6	55.1	19.2
2. Once or twice	13.7	14.2	13.1	14.5	6.3	16.8	14.4	12.0	11.6	14.4	12.9	6.6	10.0	17.9	26.8	32.7
3. Occasionally	5.2	5.9	4.5	5.5	2.0	6.3	5.1	5.2	3.6	4.4	6.3	1.1	1.7	4.3	14.5	32.7
4. Often	1.7	2.0	1.4	1.7	1.3	1.1	1.8	1.9	1.7	1.0	2.2	.4	1.6	1.2	3.7	13.5
Item 8830 N(Wtd)	3064	1469	1500	2515	302	630	960	1060	414	1538	1423	1076	827	419	641	52

E08J: Inhalants (glue, laughing gas, snappers, etc.)

	TOTAL	M	F	White	Black	NE	NC	S	W	Yes	No	None	Mari-juana Only	Few Pills	More Pills	Any Her-oin
1. Never	78.9	76.4	81.4	78.7	85.8	77.6	79.7	78.3	80.7	80.3	77.4	87.6	81.3	77.1	63.9	54.7
2. Once or twice	15.1	16.5	13.9	15.3	10.3	16.5	14.6	15.1	14.5	15.1	15.3	10.0	13.1	18.6	24.1	17.0
3. Occasionally	4.4	5.2	3.4	4.3	3.3	4.8	4.3	4.8	3.1	3.6	5.3	1.7	3.8	3.6	8.9	18.9
4. Often	1.6	1.9	1.4	1.6	.7	1.1	1.6	1.9	1.7	1.1	2.0	.6	1.7	.7	3.1	9.4
Item 8835 N(Wtd)	3066	1472	1499	2516	302	629	959	1063	414	1540	1422	1075	825	420	643	53

E08K: Alcoholic beverages (beer, wine, liquor)

	TOTAL	M	F	White	Black	NE	NC	S	W	Yes	No	None	Mari-juana Only	Few Pills	More Pills	Any Her-oin
1. Never	7.6	6.9	7.8	6.1	16.4	7.6	6.6	7.7	9.7	7.2	8.3	12.7	7.2	3.1	2.3	-
2. Once or twice	7.7	7.4	7.5	7.1	12.2	7.0	5.6	8.0	12.6	7.9	7.5	14.4	4.1	5.0	2.5	1.9
3. Occasionally	24.5	22.8	26.4	24.3	27.6	23.9	25.0	24.3	24.9	24.4	24.8	36.4	21.5	19.0	13.6	13.2
4. Often	60.2	62.9	58.3	62.5	43.8	61.8	62.7	60.0	52.9	60.5	59.4	36.5	67.1	72.9	81.6	84.9
Item 8840 N(Wtd)	3079	1475	1510	2528	304	633	963	1069	414	1546	1430	1080	831	421	645	53

Cross-Time Index of Questionnaire Items, 1975-1978

Introduction to the Indexing Conventions

This cross-time index of question locations is organized in numerical sequence according to item reference number, which is the unique numerical identifier assigned to each question in the study.

The Content Index may be used in two major ways:

1. **Locating a Question Across Years.** Having located a question of interest in the Descriptive Results section, the reader may determine in what other years that same question has appeared simply by looking it up here under its unique item reference number. The Index will show all years in which that item has appeared and also show its location each year (by questionnaire form, section, and item number). All items will retain their unique reference numbers in future years as well, and thus may be located in exactly the same way in subsequent volumes in this series.

EXAMPLE: A reader interested in a particular item about enjoying the fast pace of today's life would find that it has been assigned item Reference Number 1210. The index entry for item 1210 shows that this item has appeared in Section A of questionnaire Form 1 in all annual surveys in the series. Its question number was 4B in 1975 and 2B thereafter. By looking up the same item reference number in the index of any other volume of interest, the reader can ascertain the page location in that volume for the descriptive results on the same question.

2. **Locating Questions by Subject Area.** Given an interest in some particular subject area, one can quickly scan the Index to locate all questions dealing with that area. Table 3 shows the 19 general subject areas into which all items are classified, along with the alphabetical code assigned each area. (Category A, Drugs, is further subdivided into numerically identified subcategories.)

EXAMPLE: A reader interested in items dealing with religion should first locate the relevant code in Table 3: Code G, "Religion." The second step is to scan all pages of the item index looking for entries in Column G under the heading Subject Area, noting for every item showing a G, its item reference number and page location in this volume. The reader may or may not find the abbreviated description of the item (given in the third column of the index and further described below) helpful in deciding whether to look up a particular item in the Descriptive Results section. Some of these descriptions are rather clear as to their meaning, but others are less so.

Definitions of the Column Headings

The definitions of column headings, and the conventions used for the entries in each column, are given below under the numbers indicated in the following key.

① **Item Reference Number.** A unique identification number is assigned to each question for the duration of this research and reporting series. It appears below that question in the Descriptive Results section, as well as in this index and the indices of all other volumes in the series.

② **Page Location.** The second column of the Question Index gives the page number of the present volume on which a verbatim statement of the question may be found along with this year's descriptive results.

③ **Item Description (Abbreviated).** This is a brief mnemonic description — up to 16 characters in length — which attempts to characterize the content of the question. Originally developed for question identification on OSIRIS computer files, it may in many cases allow one to determine the relevance of the question to one's own interest and thus reduce the number of irrelevant questions which must be looked up in the Descriptive Results section.

④ **Questionnaire Location by Year.** An entry is provided for every year in which an item appeared in one of the study's questionnaire forms. The six (or fewer) characters comprising the entry indicate the form in which the question appeared, the section of that form, and the question number. Take as an example the questionnaire location 1A004A. This location code indicates that the question appeared in Form 1, Section A, and was labeled as Question 4a.

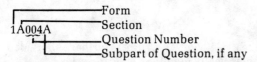

Occasionally an entry will be enclosed in parentheses. This indicates that there was a change (usually minor) in the wording of the question and/or the answer alternatives in subsequent years.

A form number (ranging from 1 to 5) is usually shown in the first character location. However, two substitute characters will replace the form number at times:

+ A plus sign indicates that the item appeared in all five forms that year and that it appeared in the same location on all forms.
* An asterisk indicates that the item appeared in four forms (Forms 2 through 5) and in the same location on all forms.

⑤ **Subject Area.** Table 3 shows the subject content areas which have been distinguished here and gives the alphabetical code assigned to each of them. Every question item in the index has been classified into one or more of the subject areas, and the alphabetical codes for those subject areas are printed in the appropriate column(s) next to each item under the general heading "Subject Area." A separate column has been assigned to each subject area code to facilitate rapid scanning. (Note that area A, dealing with drugs, has been given numerically identified subcategories because there were so many questions dealing with this general subject area.)

Figure 2

Guide to Cross-Time Index

①	②	③	④				⑤	
ITEM REFERENCE NUMBER	PAGE LOCATION (IN THIS VOLUME)	ITEM DESCRIPTION (ABBREVIATED)	QUESTIONNAIRE LOCATION BY YEAR (FORM, SECTION, AND QUESTION NUMBER)				SUBJECT AREA	
			1975	1976	1977	1978	A	B C D E F G H I J K L M N O P Q R S
10	16	R'S BIRTH YEAR		+C001	+C001	+C001		R
20	16	R'S BIRTH MONTH		+C002	+C002	+C002		R
30	16	R'S SEX		+C003	+C003	+C003		R
40	16	R'S RACE		+C004	+C004	+C004		R
50	16	R SPD >TIM R-URB		+C005	+C005	+C005		R
60	17	R NOT MARRIED		+C006	+C006	+C006		D R
80	17	R'S HSHLD ALONE		+C007A	+C007A	+C007A		M R
90	17	R'S HSHLD FATHER		+C007B	+C007B	+C007B		M R
100	17	R'S HSHLD MOTHER		+C007C	+C007C	+C007C		M R
110	17	R'S HSHLD BR/SR		+C007D	+C007D	+C007D		M R
120	17	R'S HSHLD GRPRNT		+C007E	+C007E	+C007E		M R
130	17	R'S HSHLD SPOUSE		+C007F	+C007F	+C007F		M R
140	17	R'S HSHLD CHLDRN		+C007G	+C007G	+C007G		M R
150	17	R'S HSHLD RELTVS		+C007H	+C007H	+C007H		M R
160	17	R'S HSHLD NONRLT		+C007I	+C007I	+C007I		M R
310	17	FATHR EDUC LEVEL		+C008	+C008	+C008		B R
320	17	MOTHR EDUC LEVEL		+C009	+C009	+C009		B R
330	17	MOTH PD JB R YNG		+C010	+C010	+C010		C R
340	18	R'S POLTL PRFNC		+C011	+C011	+C011		H R
350	18	R'POL BLF RADCL		+C012	+C012	+C012		H R
360	18	R'S RELGS PRFNC		+C013A	+C013A	+C013A		G R
370	18	R'ATTND REL SVC		+C013B	+C013B	+C013B		G R
380	18	RLGN IMP R'S LF		+C013C	+C013C	+C013C		G R
390	19	WHEN R XPCT GRAD		+C014	+C014	+C014		B R
400	19	R'S HS PROGRAM		+C015	+C015	+C015		B R
410	19	RT SF SCH AB>AVG		+C016	+C016	+C016		R
420	19	RT SF INTELL>AVG		+C017	+C017	+C017		R
430	19	#DA/4W SC MS ILL		+C018A	+C018A	+C018A		B
440	19	#DA/4W SC MS CUT		+C018B	+C018B	+C018B		B
450	20	#DA/4W SC MS OTH		+C018C	+C018C			
460	20	#DA/4W SKP CLASS		+C019				
470	20	R HS GRADE/D=1		+C02				R
480	20	R WL DO VOC/TEC						R
490	20	R WL DO ARMD FC						
500	20	R WL DO 2YR CLG						
510	21	R WL DO 4YR CLG						
520	21	R WL DO GRD/PR						
530	21	R WNTR						

Table 3

Subject Area Key
(Referenced by letter in the Question Index)

A. **Drugs.** Drug use and related attitudes and beliefs, drug availability and exposure, surrounding conditions and social meaning of drug use. Views of significant others regarding drugs.

    A01 Use of Drugs
                A01A — . . . in lifetime
                A01B — . . . in the last 12 months
                A01C — . . . in the last 30 days
                A01D — Quantity used
                A01E — How high? (How often?)
                A01F — How long high?
                A01G — Incidence of first use
                A01H — Use with other drugs
                A01I — Try to stop?
                A01J — . . . on doctor's orders?
                A01K — Bad trip?
                A01L — Kinds of drugs

    A02 Exposure to Drug Use
                A02A — Friends' use of drugs
                A02B — Exposure to users

    A03 Availability of Drugs

    A04 Expected Future Use

    A05 Conditions of Use
                A05A — Alone
                A05B — With others
                A05C — Settings
                A05D — Mode of drug administration

    A06 Reasons for Use, Abstention, and Stopping

    A07 Problems with Drugs

    A08 Sources of Help regarding Drugs

    A09 Parental Awareness of Use

    A10 Drug Education

    A11 Own Attitudes regarding Drugs and Drug Users
                A11A — For adults
                A11C — For own children
                A11D — Perception of drug users

    A12 Others' Attitudes regarding Drugs and Drug Users
                A12A — Parents
                A12B — Friends
                A12C — Students in school
                A12D — Perception of Drug Users

Table 3 (continued)

A13   Legal Issues regarding Drugs
          A13A — Preferred legality for adults
          A13C — Own response to legalization
          A13D — Knowledge of marijuana laws

A14   Risk of Drug Harm
          A14A — To self
          A14B — To others

B.   **Education.** Educational lifestyle, values, experiences, and environments. Media usage.

C.   **Work and Leisure.** Vocational values, meaning of work and leisure, work and leisure activities, preferences regarding occupational characteristics and type of work setting.

D.   **Sex Roles and Family.** Values, attitudes, and expectations about marriage, family structure, sex roles, and sex discrimination.

E.   **Family Plans and Population Concerns.** Values, attitudes, and expectations about personal family plans. Views on sexual mores and concerns about overpopulation.

F.   **Conservation, Materialism, Equity, Etc.** Values, attitudes, and expectations related to conservation, pollution, materialism, equity, and the sharing of resources. Preferences regarding type of dwelling and urbanicity.

G.   **Religion.** Religious affiliation, practices, and views.

H.   **Politics.** Political affiliation, activities, and views.

I.   **Social Change.** Values, attitudes, and expectations about social change.

J.   **Social Problems.** Concern with various social problems facing the nation and the world.

K.   **Major Social Institutions.** Confidence in and commitment to various major social institutions (business, unions, branches of government, press, organized religion, military, etc.).

L.   **Military.** Views about the armed services and the use of military force. Personal plans for military service.

M.   **Interpersonal Relationships.** Qualitative and quantitative characteristics of cross-age and peer relationships. Interpersonal conflict.

N.   **Race Relations.** Attitudes toward and experiences with other racial groups.

O.   **Concern for Others.** Radius of concern for others, voluntary and charitable activities.

P.   **Happiness.** Happiness and life satisfaction, overall and in specific life domains.

Q.   **Other Personality Variables.** Attitudes about self (including self-esteem), locus of control, loneliness, optimism, trust in others, somatic symptoms, importance placed on various life goals, counter-culture orientation.

R.   **Background and School.** Demographic and family background characteristics, curriculum and grades in high school, victimization in school.

S.   **Deviant Behavior and Victimization.** Delinquent behaviors, driving violations and accidents, violations and accidents under the influence of drugs, victimization experiences.

ITEM REFERENCE NUMBER	PAGE LOCATION (IN THIS VOLUME)	ITEM DESCRIPTION (ABBREVIATED)	QUESTIONNAIRE LOCATION BY YEAR (FORM, SECTION, AND QUESTION NUMBER) 1975	1976	1977	1978	SUBJECT AREA A	B	C	D	E	F	G	H	I	J	K	L	M	N	O	P	Q	R	S
10	16	R'S BIRTH YEAR		+C001	+C001	+C001																		R	
20	16	R'S BIRTH MONTH		+C002	+C002	+C002																		R	
30	16	R'S SEX		+C003	+C003	+C003																		R	
40	16	R'S RACE		+C004	+C004	+C004																		R	
50	16	R SPD >TIM R-URB		+C005	+C005	+C005																		R	
60	17	R NOT MARRIED		+C006	+C006	+C006				D														R	
80	17	R'S HSHLD ALONE		+C007A	+C007A	+C007A													M					R	
90	17	R'S HSHLD FATHER		+C007B	+C007B	+C007B													M					R	
100	17	R'S HSHLD MOTHER		+C007C	+C007C	+C007C													M					R	
110	17	R'S HSHLD BR/SR		+C007D	+C007D	+C007D													M					R	
120	17	R'S HSHLD GRPRNT		+C007E	+C007E	+C007E													M					R	
130	17	R'S HSHLD SPOUSE		+C007F	+C007F	+C007F													M					R	
140	17	R'S HSHLD CHLDRN		+C007G	+C007G	+C007G													M					R	
150	17	R'S HSHLD RELTVS		+C007H	+C007H	+C007H													M					R	
160	17	R'S HSHLD NONRLT		+C007I	+C007I	+C007I													M					R	
310	17	FATHR EDUC LEVEL		+C008	+C008	+C008		B																R	
320	17	MOTHR EDUC LEVEL		+C009	+C009	+C009		B																R	
330	17	MOTH PD JB R YNG		+C010	+C010	+C010			C															R	
340	18	R'S POLTL PRFNC		+C011	+C011	+C011								H										R	
350	18	R'POL BLF RADCL		+C012	+C012	+C012								H										R	
360	18	R'S RELGS PRFNC		+C013A	+C013A	+C013A							G											R	
370	18	R'ATTND REL SVC		+C013B	+C013B	+C013B							G											R	
380	18	RLGN IMP R'S LF		+C013C	+C013C	+C013C							G											R	
390	19	WHEN R XPCT GRAD		+C014	+C014	+C014		B																R	
400	19	R'S HS PROGRAM		+C015	+C015	+C015		B																R	
410	19	RT SF SCH AB>AVG		+C016	+C016	+C016																		R	
420	19	RT SF INTELL>AVG		+C017	+C017	+C017																		R	
430	19	#DA/4W SC MS ILL		+C018A	+C018A	+C018A		B																	
440	19	#DA/4W SC MS CUT		+C018B	+C018B	+C018B		B																	
450	20	#DA/4W SC MS OTH		+C018C	+C018C	+C018C		B																	
460	20	#DA/4W SKP CLASS		+C019	+C019	+C019		B																	
470	20	R HS GRADE/D=1		+C020	+C020	+C020																		R	
480	20	R WL DO VOC/TEC		+C021A	+C021A	+C021A		B	C															R	
490	20	R WL DO ARMD FC		+C021B	+C021B	+C021B		B										L						R	
500	20	R WL DO 2YR CLG		+C021C	+C021C	+C021C		B																R	
510	21	R WL DO 4YR CLG		+C021D	+C021D	+C021D		B																R	
520	21	R WL DO GRD/PRF		+C021E	+C021E	+C021E		B																R	
530	21	R WNTDO VOC/TEC		+C022A	+C022A	+C022A		B	C															R	
540	21	R WNTDO ARMD FC		+C022B	+C022B	+C022B		B										L						R	
550	21	R WNTDO 2YR CLG		+C022C	+C022C	+C022C		B																R	
560	21	R WNTDO 4YR CLG		+C022D	+C022D	+C022D		B																R	
570	21	R WNTDO GRD/PRF		+C022E	+C022E	+C022E		B																R	
580	21	R WNTDO NONE		+C022F	+C022F	+C022F		B																R	
590	21	HRS/W WRK SCHYR		+C023	+C023	+C023			C																
600	21	R$/AVG WEEK JOB		+C024A	+C024A	+C024A																		R	
610	22	R$/AVG WEEK OTH		+C024B	+C024B	+C024B																		R	
620	22	#X/AV WK GO OUT		+C025	+C025	+C025			C										M						
630	22	#X DATE 3+/WK		+C026	+C026	+C026			C										M						
640	22	DRIVE>200 MI/WK		+C027	+C027	+C027						F													
650	22	#X/12MO R TCKTD		+C028	+C028	+C028	A07A																		S
660	23	#TCKTS AFT DRNK		+C029A	+C029A	+C029A	A07A																		S
670	23	#TCKTS AFT MARJ		+C029B	+C029B	+C029B	A07A																		S
680	23	#TCKTS AFT OTDG		+C029C	+C029C	+C029C	A07A																		S
690	23	#ACCIDNTS/12 MO		+C030	+C030	+C030	A07A																		S
700	23	#ACDTS AFT DRNK		+C031A	+C031A	+C031A	A07A																		S
710	23	#ACDTS AFT MARJ		+C031B	+C031B	+C031B	A07A																		S
720	24	#ACDTS AFT OTDG		+C031C	+C031C	+C031C	A07A																		S
730	24	R'S BRANCH SERV		+C032	+C032	+C032												L						R	
740	24	R XPCTS B OFFCR		+C033	+C033	+C033												L						R	
750	24	R XPCTS MLTR CR		+C034	+C034	+C034												L						R	
760	24	EVR SMK CIG,REGL	1A018 *B01	+B001	+B001	(+B001)	A01A A01A																			
780	41 24	#CIGS SMKD/30DAY	1A020 *B02	1B003 *B02	1B003 *B02	1B003 *B02	A01C A01C																			
790	25	EVER DRINK	1A026 *B03	*B03	*B03	*B03	A01A A01A																			

ITEM REFERENCE NUMBER	PAGE LOCATION (IN THIS VOLUME)	ITEM DESCRIPTION (ABBREVIATED)	QUESTIONNAIRE LOCATION BY YEAR (FORM, SECTION, AND QUESTION NUMBER)				SUBJECT AREA	
			1975	1976	1977	1978	A	B C D E F G H I J K L M N O P Q R S
810	42	#X DRNK/LIFETIME	1A028A	1B007A	1B007A	1B007A	A01A	
	25		*B04A	*B04A	*B04A	*B04A	A01A	
820	42	#X DRNK/LAST12MO	1A028B	1B007B	1B007B	1B007B	A01B	
	25		*B04B	*B04B	*B04B	*B04B	A01B	
830	42	#X DRNK/LAST30DA	1A028C	1B007C	1B007C	1B007C	A01C	
	25		*B04C	*B04C	*B04C	*B04C	A01C	
840	25	#X DRK ENF FL HI	*B05	*B05	*B05	*B05	A01E	
850	44	5+DRK ROW/LST 2W	1A035	1B012	1B012	1B012	A01D	
	25		*B06	*B06	*B06	*B06	A01D	
860		#XMJ+HS/LIFETIME	1A044A				A01A	
	26		*B07A	*B07A	*B07A	*B07A	A01A	
870		#XMJ+HS/LAST12MO	1A044B				A01B	
	26		*B07B	*B07B	*B07B	*B07B	A01B	
880		#XMJ+HS/LAST30DA	1A044C				A01C	
	26		*B07C	*B07C	*B07C	*B07C	A01C	
890	50	#X LSD/LIFETIME	1A057A	1B029A	1B029A	1B029A	A01A	
	26		*B08A	*B08A	*B08A	*B08A	A01A	
900	50	#X LSD/LAST 12MO	1A057B	1B029B	1B029B	1B029B	A01B	
	27		*B08B	*B08B	*B08B	*B08B	A01B	
910	50	#X LSD/LAST 30DA	1A057C	1B029C	1B029C	1B029C	A01C	
	27		*B08C	*B08C	*B08C	*B08C	A01C	
920	53	#X PSYD/LIFETIME	1A071A	1B038A	1B038A	1B038A	A01A	
	27		*B09A	*B09A	*B09A	*B09A	A01A	
930	53	#X PSYD/LAST12MO	1A071B	1B038B	1B038B	1B038B	A01B	
	27		*B09B	*B09B	*B09B	*B09B	A01B	
940	53	#X PSYD/LAST30DA	1A071C	1B038C	1B038C	1B038C	A01C	
	27		*B09C	*B09C	*B09C	*B09C	A01C	
950	69	#X COKE/LIFETIME	1A144A	1B076A	1B076A	1B076A	A01A	
	28		*B10A	*B10A	*B10A	*B10A	A01A	
960	69	#X COKE/LAST12MO	1A144B	1B076B	1B076B	1B076B	A01B	
	28		*B10B	*B10B	*B10B	*B10B	A01B	
970	69	#X COKE/LAST30DA	1A144C	1B076C	1B076C	1B076C	A01C	
	28		*B10C	*B10C	*B10C	*B10C	A01C	
980	55	#X AMPH/LIFETIME	1A087A	1B043A	1B043A	1B043A	A01A	
	28		*B11A	*B11A	*B11A	*B11A	A01A	
990	55	#X AMPH/LAST12MO	1A087B	1B043B	1B043B	1B043B	A01B	
	28		*B11B	*B11B	*B11B	*B11B	A01B	
1000	55	#X AMPH/LAST30DA	1A087C	1B043C	1B043C	1B043C	A01C	
	29		*B11C	*B11C	*B11C	*B11C	A01C	
1010	59	#X QUAD/LIFETIME	1A102A	1B053A	1B053A	1B053A	A01A	
	29		*B12A	*B12A	*B12A	*B12A	A01A	
1020	59	#X QUAD/LAST12MO	1A102B	1B053B	1B053B	1B053B	A01B	
	29		*B12B	*B12B	*B12B	*B12B	A01B	
1030	59	#X QUAD/LAST30DA	1A102C	1B053C	1B053C	1B053C	A01C	
	29		*B12C	*B12C	*B12C	*B12C	A01C	
1040	60	#X BRBT/LIFETIME	1A116A	1B057A	1B057A	1B057A	A01A	
	29		*B13A	*B13A	*B13A	*B13A	A01A	
1050	60	#X BRBT/LAST12MO	1A116B	1B057B	1B057B	1B057B	A01B	
	30		*B13B	*B13B	*B13B	*B13B	A01B	
1060	60	#X BRBT/LAST30DA	1A116C	1B057C	1B057C	1B057C	A01C	
	30		*B13C	*B13C	*B13C	*B13C	A01C	
1070	64	#X TRQL/LIFETIME	1A131A	1B067A	1B067A	1B067A	A01A	
	30		*B14A	*B14A	*B14A	*B14A	A01A	
1080	65	#X TRQL/LAST12MO	1A131B	1B067B	1B067B	1B067B	A01B	
	30		*B14B	*B14B	*B14B	*B14B	A01B	
1090	65	#X TRQL/LAST30DA	1A131C	1B067C	1B067C	1B067C	A01C	
	30		*B14C	*B14C	*B14C	*B14C	A01C	
1100	73	#X "H"/LIFETIME	1A158A	1B085A	1B085A	1B085A	A01A	
	31		*B15A	*B15A	*B15A	*B15A	A01A	
1110	73	#X "H"/LAST 12MO	1A158B	1B085B	1B085B	1B085B	A01B	
	31		*B15B	*B15B	*B15B	*B15B	A01B	
1120	74	#X "H"/LAST 30DA	1A158C	1B085C	1B085C	1B085C	A01C	
	31		*B15C	*B15C	*B15C	*B15C	A01C	
1130	78	#X NARC/LIFETIME	1A173A	1B095A	1B095A	1B095A	A01A	
	31		*B16A	*B16A	*B16A	*B16A	A01A	
1140	78	#X NARC/LAST12MO	1A173B	1B095B	1B095B	1B095B	A01B	

ITEM REFERENCE NUMBER	PAGE LOCATION (IN THIS VOLUME)	ITEM DESCRIPTION (ABBREVIATED)	1975	1976	1977	1978	A	B	C	D	E	F	G	H	I	J	K	L	M	N	O	P	Q	R	S
	31		*B16B	*B16B	*B16B	*B16B	A01B																		
1150	78	#X NARC/LAST30DA	1A173C	1B095C	1B095C	1B095C	A01C																		
	32		*B16C	*B16C	*B16C	*B16C	A01C																		
1160	32	#X INHL/LIFETIME		*B17A	*B17A	*B17A	A01A																		
1170	32	#X INHL/LAST12MO		*B17B	*B17B	*B17B	A01B																		
1180	32	#X INHL/LAST30DA		*B17C	*B17C	*B17C	A01C																		
1190	*	VRY HPY THS DAYS		+A001	+A001	+A001																P	Q	R	
1200	33	US NEEDS PLANNG	1A004A	1A002A	1A002A	1A002A									I										
1210	33	ENJOY FAST PACE	1A004B	1A002B	1A002B	1A002B									I								Q		
1220	33	THG CHG 2 QUICK	1A004D	1A002C	1A002C	1A002C									I								Q		
1230	33	X AHEAD TOUGHER	1A004G	1A002D	1A002D	1A002D									I								Q		
1240	33	TM SPT ADLT MST	1A006	1A003	1A003	1A003														M						
1250	34	LK MR TM ADLT	1A007	1A004	1A004	1A004														M						
1260	34	LK MR TM YG CHD	1A008	1A005	1A005	1A005														M						
1270	34	SAT PRESENT JOB	1A009A	1A006A	1A006A	1A006A			C														P			
1280	34	SAT NEIGHBORHOD	1A009B	1A006B	1A006B	1A006B																	P			
1290	34	SAT PRSNL SAFTY	1A009C	1A006C	1A006C	1A006C																	P			
1300	35	SAT OWN PROP SF	1A009D	1A006D	1A006D	1A006D																	P			
1310	35	SAT EDUC EXPRNCS	1A009E	1A006E	1A006E	1A006E		B															P			
1320	35	SAT OWN FRIENDS	1A009F	1A006F	1A006F	1A006F														M			P			
1330	35	SAT GT ALNG PRNT	1A009G	1A006G	1A006G	1A006G														M			P			
1340	35	SAT YOURSELF	1A009H	1A006H	1A006H	1A006H																	P	Q		
1350	35	SAT STD OF LVG	1A009I	1A006I	1A006I	1A006I						F											P			
1360	36	SAT TIME FR THGS	1A009J	1A006J	1A006J	1A006J																	P			
1370	36	SAT SPD LEISR	1A009K	1A006K	1A006K	1A006K			C														P			
1380	36	SAT LIFE AS WHLE	1A009L	1A006L	1A006L	1A006L																	P			
1390	36	SAT GOVT OPRTNG		1A006M	1A006M	1A006M								H			K								
1400	36	SAT AMT OF FUN		1A006N	1A006N	1A006N																	P	Q	R	
1410	36	IMP B SUCCSS WK		1A007A	1A007A	1A007A			C															Q		
1420	37	IMP GD MRRG&FAM		1A007B	1A007B	1A007B				D														Q		
1430	37	IMP LOTS OF $		1A007C	1A007C	1A007C						F												Q		
1440	37	IMP TM RCRN&HBY		1A007D	1A007D	1A007D			C															Q		
1450	37	IMP STRG FRDSHP		1A007E	1A007E	1A007E														M				Q		
1460	37	IMP STEADY WORK		1A007F	1A007F	1A007F			C															Q		
1470	37	IMP CNTRBTN SOC		1A007G	1A007G	1A007G																O		Q		
1480	37	IMP LDR COMUNTY		1A007H	1A007H	1A007H														M				Q		
1490	37	IMP CHLD BTR OPP		1A007I	1A007I	1A007I																		Q		
1500	38	IMP LIV CLS PRNT		1A007J	1A007J	1A007J														M				Q		
1510	38	IMP GT AWY AREA		1A007K	1A007K	1A007K																		Q		
1520	38	IMP CRRCT INEQL		1A007L	1A007L	1A007L																O		Q		
1530	38	IMP NEW XPRNCE		1A007M	1A007M	1A007M																		Q		
1540	38	IMP FND PRPS LF		1A007N	1A007N	1A007N																		Q		
1550	38	PPL CAN B TRSTD	1A010	1A008	1A008	1A008																		Q		
1560	38	PPL TRY B HLPFL	1A011	1A009	1A009	1A009																		Q		
1570	39	PPL TRY BE FAIR	1A012	1A010	1A010	1A010																		Q		
1580	39	-OBY LW=-GD CTZN		1A011A	1A011A	1A011A								H												
1590	39	GD CTZN ALG GOVT		1A011B	1A011B	1A011B								H												
1600	39	GD CTZN CHG GOVT	1A013B	1A011C	1A011C	1A011C								H												
1610	39	VOTE->MAJ IMPCT		1A011D	1A011D	1A011D								H	I											
1620	39	CTZN GRP HV EFCT		1A011E	1A011E	1A011E								H	I											
1630	40	OUR SYST ST BS	1A013C	1A011F	1A011F	1A011F								H												
1640	40	US NEEDS GROWTH	1A013E	1A011G	1A011G	1A011G						F														
1650	40	LV THNGS TO GOD	1A004C	1A011H	1A011H	1A011H									I											
1660	40	GO SCH ENJY XPR	1A013I	1A011I	1A011I	1A011I		B																		
1670	40	DO WL SC IMP/JB	1A013H	1A011J	1A011J	1A011J		B	C																	
1680	41	SMK CIG DLY/12G	1A019	1B002	1B002	(1B002)	A01G																			
1690	41	*TRY STP SMK&FL	1A021	1B004	1B004	1B004	A01I																			
1700	41	*WNT STP SMK NW	1A022	1B005	1B005	1B005	A01I																			
1710	41	NO SMK IN 5 YR	1A023	1B006	1B006	1B006	A04A																			
1720	42	#X/YR ALC ALONE		1B008A	1B008A	1B008A	A05A																			
1730	42	#X/YR ALC-2 PPL		1B008B	1B008B	1B008B	A05B																			
1740	43	#X/YR ALC@PARTY		1B008C	1B008C	1B008C	A05C																			
1750	43	#X/YR ALC-DT/SP		1B008D	1B008D	1B008D	A05B																			
1760	43	#X/YR ALC-ADLTS		1B008E	1B008E	1B008E	A05B																			
1770	43	#X/YR ALC-DATIM		1B008F	1B008F	1B008F	A05C																			
1780	43	#X/YR ALC@HOME		1B008G	1B008G	1B008G	A05C																			

* Descriptive results for Forms 1, 2, 3, 4, and 5, respectively, can be found on pages 33, 88, 116, 143, and 170.

ITEM REFERENCE NUMBER	PAGE LOCATION (IN THIS VOLUME)	ITEM DESCRIPTION (ABBREVIATED)	QUESTIONNAIRE LOCATION BY YEAR (FORM, SECTION, AND QUESTION NUMBER)				SUBJECT AREA	
			1975	1976	1977	1978	A	B C D E F G H I J K L M N O P Q R S
1790	43	#X/YR ALC@SCHL		1B008H	1B008H	1B008H	A05C	
1810	43	#X/YR ALCIN CAR		1B008I	1B008I	1B008I	A05C	
1820	44	ALC EXPERIMENT		1B009A	1B009A	1B009A	A06A	
1830	44	ALC RELAX	1A032A	1B009B	1B009B	1B009B	A06A	
1840	44	ALC GET HIGH	1A032B	1B009C	1B009C	1B009C	A06A	
1850	44	ALC SEEK INSGHT	1A032C	1B009D	1B009D	1B009D	A06A	
1860	44	ALC GD TM FRNDS	1A032D	1B009E	1B009E	1B009E	A06A	
1870	44	ALC FIT IN GRP	1A032E	1B009F	1B009F	1B009F	A06A	
1880	44	ALC GET AWY PRB	1A032F	1B009G	1B009G	1B009G	A06A	
1890	44	ALC BOREDOM	1A032G	1B009H	1B009H	1B009H	A06A	
1900	44	ALC ANGR&FRSTRN	1A032H	1B009I	1B009I	1B009I	A06A	
1910	44	ALC GT THRU DAY	1A032J	1B009J	1B009J	1B009J	A06A	
1920	44	ALC INCRS EF DR	1A032K	1B009K	1B009K	1B009K	A06A	
1930	44	ALC DECRS EF DR	1A032L	1B009L	1B009L	1B009L	A06A	
1940	44	ALC GET SLEEP		1B009M	1B009M	1B009M	A06A	
1950	44	ALC TASTES GOOD	1A032N	1B009N	1B009N	1B009N	A06A	
1960	44	ALC I AM HOOKED	1A032M	1B009O	1B009O	1B009O	A06A	
1970	44	#X DRK ENF FL 4	1A033	1B010	1B010	1B010	A01E	
1980	44	DRK AL,HI24+HR	1A034	1B011	1B011	1B011	A01F	
1990	45	#X/2W,3-4 DR RW	1A036	1B013	1B013	1B013	A01D	
2000	45	#X/2WK,2 DRK RW	1A037	1B014	1B014	1B014	A01D	
2010	45	#X/2WK,JST 1DRK	1A038	1B015	1B015	1B015	A01D	
2020	45	*TRY STP ALC&FL	1A039	1B016	1B016	1B016	A01D	
2030	45	NO ALC IN 5 YR	1A040	1B017	1B017	1B017	A04A	
2040	46	#X HASH/LIFETIM		1B018A	1B018A	1B018A	A01A	
2050	46	#X HASH/LAST12M		1B018B	1B018B	1B018B	A01B	
2060	46	#X HASH/LAST30D		1B018C	1B018C	1B018C	A01C	
2070	46	#X MARJ/LIFETIME		1B019A	1B019A	1B019A	A01A	
2080	46	#X MARJ/LAST12MO		1B019B	1B019B	1B019B	A01B	
2090	46	#X MARJ/LAST30DA		1B019C	1B019C	1B019C	A01C	
2100	47	#X/YR MJ ALONE	1A045	1B020A	1B020A	1B020A	A05A	
2110	47	#X/YR MJ-2 PPL		1B020B	1B020B	1B020B	A05B	
2120	47	#X/YR MJ@PARTY		1B020C	1B020C	1B020C	A05C	
2130	47	#X/YR MJ-DT/SP		1B020D	1B020D	1B020D	A05B	
2140	47	#X/YR MJ-ADLTS		1B020E	1B020E	1B020E	A05B	
2150	47	#X/YR MJ-DATIME		1B020F	1B020F	1B020F	A05C	
2160	48	#X/YR MJ@HOME		1B020G	1B020G	1B020G	A05C	
2170	48	#X/YR MJ@SCHL		1B020H	1B020H	1B020H	A05C	
2190	48	#X/YR MJIN CAR		1B020I	1B020I	1B020I	A05C	
2200	48	#X OVL MJ+ ALC		1B021	1B021	1B021	A06A	
2210	48	MJ EXPERIMENT	1A049A	1B022A	1B022A	1B022A	A06A	
2220	48	MJ RELAX	1A049B	1B022B	1B022B	1B022B	A06A	
2230	48	MJ GET HIGH	1A049C	1B022C	1B022C	1B022C	A06A	
2240	48	MJ SEEK INSIGHT	1A049D	1B022D	1B022D	1B022D	A06A	
2250	48	MJ GD TM FRNDS	1A049E	1B022E	1B022E	1B022E	A06A	
2260	48	MJ FIT IN GRP	1A049F	1B022F	1B022F	1B022F	A06A	
2270	48	MJ GET AWY PRB	1A049G	1B022G	1B022G	1B022G	A06A	
2280	48	MJ BOREDOM	1A049H	1B022H	1B022H	1B022H	A06A	
2290	48	MJ ANGR&FRUSTRN	1A049I	1B022I	1B022I	1B022I	A06A	
2300	48	MJ GET THRU DAY	1A049K	1B022J	1B022J	1B022J	A06A	
2310	48	MJ INCRS EF DRG	1A049L	1B022K	1B022K	1B022K	A06A	
2320	48	MJ DECRS EF DRG	1A049M	1B022L	1B022L	1B022L	A06A	
2330	48	MJ I AM HOOKED		1B022M	1B022M	1B022M	A06A	
2340	49	MJ/HSH,VRY HIGH	1A050	1B023	1B023	1B023	A01E	
2350	49	MJ/HSH,HI 24+HR	1A051	1B024	1B024	1B024	A01F	
2360	49	JOINT/DA LST MO		1B025	1B025	1B025	A01D	
2370	49	OZS.MJ LST MO/6		1B026	1B026	1B026	A01D	
2380	49	*TRY STP MJ &FL	1A052	1B027	1B027	1B027	A01I	
2390	49	NO MJ/HSH IN5YR	1A053	1B028	1B028	1B028	A04A	
2400	50	#X/YR LSD ALONE		1B030A	1B030A	1B030A	A05A	
2410	50	#X/YR LSD-2 PPL		1B030B	1B030B	1B030B	A05B	
2420	51	#X/YR LSD@PARTY		1B030C	1B030C	1B030C	A05C	
2430	51	#X/YR LSD-DT/SP		1B030D	1B030D	1B030D	A05B	
2440	51	#X/YR LSD-ADLTS		1B030E	1B030E	1B030E	A05B	
2450	51	#X/YR LSD-DATIM		1B030F	1B030F	1B030F	A05C	
2460	51	#X/YR LSD@HOME		1B030G	1B030G	1B030G	A05C	

ITEM REFERENCE NUMBER	PAGE LOCATION (IN THIS VOLUME)	ITEM DESCRIPTION (ABBREVIATED)	QUESTIONNAIRE LOCATION BY YEAR (FORM, SECTION, AND QUESTION NUMBER)				SUBJECT AREA	
			1975	1976	1977	1978	A	B C D E F G H I J K L M N O P Q R S
2470	51	#X/YR LSD@SCHL		1B030H	1B030H	1B030H	A05C	
2490	51	#X/YR LSDIN CAR		1B030I	1B030I	1B030I	A05C	
2500	52	#X OVL LSD+ ALC		1B031A	1B031A	1B031A	A01H	
2510	52	#X OVL LSD+ MJ		1B031B	1B031B	1B031B	A01H	
2520	52	LSD EXPERIMENT	1A062A	1B032A	1B032A	1B032A	A06A	
2530	52	LSD RELAX	1A062B	1B032B	1B032B	1B032B	A06A	
2540	52	LSD GET HIGH	1A062C	1B032C	1B032C	1B032C	A06A	
2550	52	LSD SEEK INSGHT	1A062D	1B032D	1B032D	1B032D	A06A	
2560	52	LSD GD TM FRNDS	1A062E	1B032E	1B032E	1B032E	A06A	
2570	52	LSD FIT IN GRP	1A062F	1B032F	1B032F	1B032F	A06A	
2580	52	LSD GT AWY PRB	1A062G	1B032G	1B032G	1B032G	A06A	
2590	52	LSD BOREDOM	1A062H	1B032H	1B032H	1B032H	A06A	
2600	52	LSD ANGR&FRSTRN	1A062I	1B032I	1B032I	1B032I	A06A	
2610	52	LSD GT THRU DAY	1A062K	1B032J	1B032J	1B032J	A06A	
2620	52	LSD INCRS EF DR	1A062L	1B032K	1B032K	1B032K	A06A	
2630	52	LSD DCRS EF DRG	1A062M	1B032L	1B032L	1B032L	A06A	
2640	52	LSD I AM HOOKED		1B032M	1B032M	1B032M	A06A	
2650	52	LSD,GET VERY HI	1A063	1B033	1B033	1B033	A01E	
2660	52	LSD,HIGH 24+ HR	1A064	1B034	1B034	1B034	A01F	
2670	53	1+ BAD TRIP LSD	1A065	1B035	1B035	1B035	A01K	
2680	53	*TRY STP LSD&FL	1A066	1B036	1B036	1B036	A01I	
2690	53	NO LSD IN 5 YRS	1A067	1B037	1B037	1B037	A04A	
2700	54	PSYD,GT VERY HI	1A077	1B039	1B039	1B039	A01E	
2710	54	PSYD,HI 24+ HRS	1A078	1B040	1B040	1B040	A01F	
2720	54	TKN YR,MESCALIN	1A079A	1B041A	1B041A	1B041A	A01L	
2730	54	TKN YR,PEYOTE	1A079B	1B041B	1B041B	1B041B	A01L	
2740	54	TKN YR,PSILOCYB	1A079C	1B041C	1B041C	1B041C	A01L	
2750	54	TKN YR,PCP		1B041D	1B041D	1B041D	A01L	
2760	54	TKN YR,CNCT THC	1A079D	1B041E	1B041E	1B041E	A01L	
2770	54	TKN YR,OTH PSYD	1A079E	1B041F	1B041F	1B041F	A01L	
2780	54	TKN YR,DK NAME	1A079F	1B041G	1B041G	1B041G	A01L	
2790	54	DR TOLD TK AMPH	1A085	1B042	1B042	1B042	A01J	
2800	55	#X/YR AMPH ALNE		1B044A	1B044A	1B044A	A05A	
2810	55	#X/YR AMPH-2PPL		1B044B	1B044B	1B044B	A05B	
2820	56	#X/YR AMPH@PRTY		1B044C	1B044C	1B044C	A05C	
2830	56	#X/YR AMPH-DT/S		1B044D	1B044D	1B044D	A05B	
2840	56	#X/YR AMPH-ADLT		1B044E	1B044E	1B044E	A05B	
2850	56	#X/YR AMPH-DATM		1B044F	1B044F	1B044F	A05C	
2860	56	#X/YR AMPH@HOME		1B044G	1B044G	1B044G	A05C	
2880	56	#X/YR AMPH@SCHL		1B044H	1B044H	1B044H	A05C	
2890	56	#X/YR AMPH@CAR		1B044I	1B044I	1B044I	A05C	
2900	57	#X OVL AMPH+ALC		1B045A	1B045A	1B045A	A01H	
2910	57	#X OVL AMPH+MJ		1B045B	1B045B	1B045B	A01H	
2920	57	#X OVL AMPH+LSD		1B045C	1B045C	1B045C	A01H	
2930	57	#X OVL AMPH+PSY		1B045D	1B045D	1B045D	A01H	
2940	57	AMPH EXPERIMENT	1A092A	1B046A	1B046A	1B046A	A06A	
2950	57	AMPH RELAX	1A092B	1B046B	1B046B	1B046B	A06A	
2960	57	AMPH GET HIGH	1A092C	1B046C	1B046C	1B046C	A06A	
2970	57	AMPH SK INSIGHT	1A092D	1B046D	1B046D	1B046D	A06A	
2980	57	AMPH GD TM FRND	1A092E	1B046E	1B046E	1B046E	A06A	
2990	57	AMPH FIT IN GRP	1A092F	1B046F	1B046F	1B046F	A06A	
3000	57	AMPH GT AWY PRB	1A092G	1B046G	1B046G	1B046G	A06A	
3010	57	AMPH BOREDOM	1A092H	1B046H	1B046H	1B046H	A06A	
3020	57	AMPH ANGR&FRSTN	1A092I	1B046I	1B046I	1B046I	A06A	
3030	57	AMPH GT THRU DA	1A092K	1B046J	1B046J	1B046J	A06A	
3040	57	AMPH INCR EF DR	1A092L	1B046K	1B046K	1B046K	A06A	
3050	57	AMPH DCRS EF DR	1A092M	1B046L	1B046L	1B046L	A06A	
3060	57	AMPH STAY AWAKE	1A092N	1B046M	1B046M	1B046M	A06A	
3070	57	AMPH GET>ENERGY	1A092O	1B046N	1B046N	1B046N	A06A	
3080	57	AMPH LOSE WGHT	1A092P	1B046O	1B046O	1B046O	A06A	
3090	57	AMPH I AM HOOKD	1A092Q	1B046P	1B046P	1B046P	A06A	
3100	58	AMPH,GT VERY HI	1A093	1B047	1B047	1B047	A01E	
3110	58	AMPH,HI 24+ HRS	1A094	1B048	1B048	1B048	A01F	
3120	58	TKN YR,BENZDRIN	1A095A	1B049A	1B049A	1B049A	A01L	
3130	58	TKN YR,DEXEDRIN	1A095B	1B049B	1B049B	1B049B	A01L	
3140	58	TKN YR,METHDRIN	1A095C	1B049C	1B049C	1B049C	A01L	

ITEM REFERENCE NUMBER	PAGE LOCATION (IN THIS VOLUME)	ITEM DESCRIPTION (ABBREVIATED)	QUESTIONNAIRE LOCATION BY YEAR (FORM, SECTION, AND QUESTION NUMBER)				SUBJECT AREA	
			1975	1976	1977	1978	A	B C D E F G H I J K L M N O P Q R S
3150	58	TKN YR,RITALIN	1A095D	1B049D	1B049D	1B049D	A01L	
3160	58	TKN YR,PRELUDIN	1A095E	1B049E	1B049E	1B049E	A01L	
3170	58	TKN YR,DEXAMYL	1A095F	1B049F	1B049F	1B049F	A01L	
3180	58	TKN YR,METHAMPH	1A095G	1B049G	1B049G	1B049G	A01L	
3190	58	TKN YR,OTH AMPH	1A095H	1B049H	1B049H	1B049H	A01L	
3200	58	TKN YR,DNT KN N	1A095I	1B049I	1B049I	1B049I	A01L	
3210	58	MTHD AMPH-MOUTH		1B050A	1B050A	1B050A	A05D	
3220	58	MTHD AMPH-INJCT		1B050B	1B050B	1B050B	A05D	
3230	58	MTHD AMPH-OTHER		1B050C	1B050C	1B050C	A05D	
3240	58	*TRY STP AMP&FL	1A096	1B051	1B051	1B051	A01I	
3250	58	NO AMPH IN 5YR	1A097	1B052	1B052	1B052	A04A	
3260	59	QUAD GT VERY HI	1A108	1B054	1B054	1B054	A01E	
3270	60	QUAD,HI 24+ HRS	1A109	1B055	1B055	1B055	A01F	
3280	60	DR TOLD TK BARB	1A114	1B056	1B056	1B056	A01J	
3290	61	#X/YR BRBT ALNE		1B058A	1B058A	1B058A	A05B	
3300	61	#X/YR BRBT-2PPL		1B058B	1B058B	1B058B	A05C	
3310	61	#X/YR BRBT@PRTY		1B058C	1B058C	1B058C	A05C	
3320	61	#X/YR BRBT-DT/S		1B058D	1B058D	1B058D	A05B	
3330	61	#X/YR BRBT-ADLT		1B058E	1B058E	1B058E	A05B	
3340	61	#X/YR BRBT-DATM		1B058F	1B058F	1B058F	A05C	
3350	62	#X/YR BRBT@HOME		1B058G	1B058G	1B058G	A05C	
3360	62	#X/YR BRBT@SCHL		1B058H	1B058H	1B058H	A05C	
3380	62	#X/YR BRBT@CAR		1B058I	1B058I	1B058I	A05C	
3390	62	#X OVL BARB+ALC		1B059A	1B059A	1B059A	A01H	
3400	62	#X OVL BARB+MJ		1B059B	1B059B	1B059B	A01H	
3410	62	#X OVL BARB+LSD		1B059C	1B059C	1B059C	A01H	
3420	62	#X OVL BARB+PSY		1B059D	1B059D	1B059D	A01H	
3430	63	#X OVL BARB+AMP		1B059E	1B059E	1B059E	A01H	
3440	63	#X OVL BARB+QUA		1B059F	1B059F	1B059F	A01H	
3450	63	BARB EXPERIMENT	1A121A	1B060A	1B060A	1B060A	A06A	
3460	63	BARB RELAX	1A121B	1B060B	1B060B	1B060B	A06A	
3470	63	BARB GET HIGH	1A121C	1B060C	1B060C	1B060C	A06A	
3480	63	BARB SK INSIGHT	1A121D	1B060D	1B060D	1B060D	A06A	
3490	63	BARB GD TM FRND	1A121E	1B060E	1B060E	1B060E	A06A	
3500	63	BARB FIT IN GRP	1A121F	1B060F	1B060F	1B060F	A06A	
3510	63	BARB GT AWY PRB	1A121G	1B060G	1B060G	1B060G	A06A	
3520	63	BARB BOREDOM	1A121H	1B060H	1B060H	1B060H	A06A	
3530	63	BARB ANGR&FRSTN	1A121I	1B060I	1B060I	1B060I	A06A	
3540	63	BARB GT THRU DA	1A121K	1B060J	1B060J	1B060J	A06A	
3550	63	BARB INCR EF DR	1A121L	1B060K	1B060K	1B060K	A06A	
3560	63	BARB DCRS EF DR	1A121M	1B060L	1B060L	1B060L	A06A	
3570	63	BARB GET SLEEP	1A121N	1B060M	1B060M	1B060M	A06A	
3575	63	BARB RLV PHYS PN				1B060N	A06A	
3580	63	BARB I AM HOOKD	1A121O	1B060N	1B060N	1B060O	A06A	
3590	63	BARB,GT VERY HI	1A122	1B061	1B061	1B061	A01E	
3600	63	BARB,HI 24+ HRS	1A123	1B062	1B062	1B062	A01F	
3610	64	TKN YR,PHNOBARB	1A124A	1B063A	1B063A	1B063A	A01L	
3620	64	TKN YR,SECONAL	1A124B	1B063B	1B063B	1B063B	A01L	
3630	64	TKN YR,TUINAL	1A124C	1B063C	1B063C	1B063C	A01L	
3640	64	TKN YR,NEMBUTAL	1A124D	1B063D	1B063D	1B063D	A01L	
3650	64	TKN YR,LUMINAL	1A124E	1B063E	1B063E	1B063E	A01L	
3660	64	TKN YR,DESBUTAL	1A124F	1B063F	1B063F	1B063F	A01L	
3670	64	TKN YR,AMYTAL	1A124G	1B063G	1B063G	1B063G	A01L	
3680	64	TKN YR,ADRNOCAL	1A124H	1B063H	1B063H	1B063H	A01L	
3690	64	TKN YR,OTH BRBT	1A124I	1B063I	1B063I	1B063I	A01L	
3700	64	TKN YR,DNT KNOW	1A124J	1B063J	1B063J	1B063J	A01L	
3710	64	TRY STP BARB&FL	1A125	1B064	1B064	1B064	A01I	
3720	64	NO BARB IN 5YR	1A126	1B065	1B065	1B065	A04A	
3730	64	DR TOLD TK TRNQ	1A129	1B066	1B066	1B066	A01J	
3740	65	#X/YR TRQL ALNE		1B068A	1B068A	1B068A	A05A	
3750	65	#X/YR TRQL-2PPL		1B068B	1B068B	1B068B	A05B	
3760	65	#X/YR TRQL@PRTY		1B068C	1B068C	1B068C	A05C	
3770	66	#X/YR TRQL-DT/S		1B068D	1B068D	1B068D	A05B	
3780	66	#X/YR TRQL-ADLT		1B068E	1B068E	1B068E	A05B	
3790	66	#X/YR TRQL-DATM		1B068F	1B068F	1B068F	A05C	
3800	66	#X/YR TRQL@HOME		1B068G	1B068G	1B068G	A05C	

ITEM REFERENCE NUMBER	PAGE LOCATION (IN THIS VOLUME)	ITEM DESCRIPTION (ABBREVIATED)	QUESTIONNAIRE LOCATION BY YEAR (FORM, SECTION, AND QUESTION NUMBER)				SUBJECT AREA	
			1975	1976	1977	1978	A	B C D E F G H I J K L M N O P Q R S
3810	66	#X/YR TRQL@SCHL		1B068H	1B068H	1B068H	A05C	
3830	66	#X/YR TRQL@CAR		1B068I	1B068I	1B068I	A05C	
3840	67	#X OVL TRQL+ALC		1B069A	1B069A	1B069A	A01H	
3850	67	#X OVL TRQL+MJ		1B069B	1B069B	1B069B	A01H	
3860	67	#X OVL TRQL+LSD		1B069C	1B069C	1B069C	A01H	
3870	67	#X OVL TRQL+PSY		1B069D	1B069D	1B069D	A01H	
3880	67	#X OVL TRQL+AMP		1B069E	1B069E	1B069E	A01H	
3890	67	#X OVL TRQL+QUA		1B069F	1B069F	1B069F	A01H	
3900	67	#X OVL TRQL+BRB		1B069G	1B069G	1B069G	A01H	
3910	68	TRNQ EXPERIMENT	1A136A	1B070A	1B070A	1B070A	A06A	
3920	68	TRNQ RELAX	1A136B	1B070B	1B070B	1B070B	A06A	
3930	68	TRNQ GET HIGH	1A136C	1B070C	1B070C	1B070C	A06A	
3940	68	TRNQ SK INSIGHT	1A136D	1B070D	1B070D	1B070D	A06A	
3950	68	TRNQ GD TM FRND	1A136E	1B070E	1B070E	1B070E	A06A	
3960	68	TRNQ FIT IN GRP	1A136F	1B070F	1B070F	1B070F	A06A	
3970	68	TRNQ GT AWY PRB	1A136G	1B070G	1B070G	1B070G	A06A	
3980	68	TRNQ BOREDOM	1A136H	1B070H	1B070H	1B070H	A06A	
3990	68	TRNQ ANGR&FRSTN	1A136I	1B070I	1B070I	1B070I	A06A	
4000	68	TRNQ GT THRU DA	1A136K	1B070J	1B070J	1B070J	A06A	
4010	68	TRNQ INCR EF DR	1A136L	1B070K	1B070K	1B070K	A06A	
4020	68	TRNQ DCRS EF DR	1A136M	1B070L	1B070L	1B070L	A06A	
4030	68	TRNQ GET SLEEP	1A136N	1B070M	1B070M	1B070M	A06A	
4035	68	TRNQ RLV PHYS PN				1B070N	A06A	
4040	68	TRNQ I AM HOOKD	1A136O	1B070N	1B070N	1B070O	A06A	
4050	68	TRNQ,GT VERY HI	1A137	1B071	1B071	1B071	A01E	
4060	68	TRNQ,HI 24+ HRS	1A138	1B072	1B072	1B072	A01F	
4070	68	TKN YR,LIBRIUM		1B073A	1B073A	1B073A	A01L	
4080	68	TKN YR,VALIUM		1B073B	1B073B	1B073B	A01L	
4090	68	TKN YR,MILTOWN		1B073C	1B073C	1B073C	A01L	
4100	68	TKN YR,EQUANIL		1B073D	1B073D	1B073D	A01L	
4110	68	TKN YR,MEPRBMTE		1B073E	1B073E	1B073E	A01L	
4120	68	TKN YR,SERAX		1B073F	1B073F	1B073F	A01L	
4130	68	TKN YR,ATARAX		1B073G	1B073G	1B073G	A01L	
4140	68	TKN YR,TRANXENE		1B073H	1B073H	1B073H	A01L	
4150	68	TKN YR,VISTARIL		1B073I	1B073I	1B073I	A01L	
4160	68	TKN YR,DNT KNW		1B073J	1B073J	1B073J	A01L	
4170	69	*TRY STP TRQ&FL	1A139	1B074	1B074	1B074	A01I	
4180	69	NO TRNQ IN 5YR	1A140	1B075	1B075	1B075	A04A	
4190	70	#X/YR COKE ALNE		1B077A	1B077A	1B077A	A05A	
4200	70	#X/YR COKE-2PPL		1B077B	1B077B	1B077B	A05B	
4210	70	#X/YR COKE@PRTY		1B077C	1B077C	1B077C	A05C	
4220	70	#X/YR COKE-DT/S		1B077D	1B077D	1B077D	A05B	
4230	70	#X/YR COKE-ADLT		1B077E	1B077E	1B077E	A05B	
4240	70	#X/YR COKE-DATM		1B077F	1B077F	1B077F	A05C	
4250	70	#X/YR COKE@HOME		1B077G	1B077G	1B077G	A05C	
4260	71	#X/YR COKE@SCHL		1B077H	1B077H	1B077H	A05C	
4280	71	#X/YR COKE@CAR		1B077I	1B077I	1B077I	A05C	
4290	71	#X OVL COKE+ALC		1B078A	1B078A	1B078A	A01H	
4300	71	#X OVL COKE+MJ		1B078B	1B078B	1B078B	A01H	
4310	71	#X OVL COKE+LSD		1B078C	1B078C	1B078C	A01H	
4320	71	#X OVL COKE+PSY		1B078D	1B078D	1B078D	A01H	
4330	71	#X OVL COKE+AMP		1B078E	1B078E	1B078E	A01H	
4340	72	#X OVL COKE+QUA		1B078F	1B078F	1B078F	A01H	
4350	72	#X OVL COKE+BRB		1B078G	1B078G	1B078G	A01H	
4360	72	#X OVL COKE+TRN		1B078H	1B078H	1B078H	A01H	
4370	72	COKE EXPERIMENT	1A149A	1B079A	1B079A	1B079A	A06A	
4380	72	COKE RELAX	1A149B	1B079B	1B079B	1B079B	A06A	
4390	72	COKE GET HIGH	1A149C	1B079C	1B079C	1B079C	A06A	
4400	72	COKE SK INSIGHT	1A149D	1B079D	1B079D	1B079D	A06A	
4410	72	COKE GD TM FRND	1A149E	1B079E	1B079E	1B079E	A06A	
4420	72	COKE FIT IN GRP	1A149F	1B079F	1B079F	1B079F	A06A	
4430	72	COKE GT AWY PRB	1A149G	1B079G	1B079G	1B079G	A06A	
4440	72	COKE BOREDOM	1A149H	1B079H	1B079H	1B079H	A06A	
4450	72	COKE ANGR&FRSTN	1A149I	1B079I	1B079I	1B079I	A06A	
4460	72	COKE GT THRU DA	1A149K	1B079J	1B079J	1B079J	A06A	
4470	72	COKE INCR EF DR	1A149L	1B079K	1B079K	1B079K	A06A	

ITEM REFERENCE NUMBER	PAGE LOCATION (IN THIS VOLUME)	ITEM DESCRIPTION (ABBREVIATED)	QUESTIONNAIRE LOCATION BY YEAR (FORM, SECTION, AND QUESTION NUMBER)				SUBJECT AREA	
			1975	1976	1977	1978	A	B C D E F G H I J K L M N O P Q R S
4480	72	COKE DCRS EF DR	1A149M	1B079L	1B079L	1B079L	A06A	
4490	72	COKE STAY AWAKE		1B079M	1B079M	1B079M	A06A	
4500	72	COKE GET>ENERGY	1A149N	1B079N	1B079N	1B079N	A06A	
4510	72	COKE I AM HOOKD	1A149O	1B079O	1B079O	1B079O	A06A	
4520	72	COK,GET VERY HI	1A150	1B080	1B080	1B080	A01E	
4530	73	COK,HIGH 24+ HR	1A151	1B081	1B081	1B081	A01F	
4540	73	*TRY STP COK&FL	1A152	1B082	1B082	1B082	A01I	
4550	73	MTHD COKE SNORT	1A153A	1B083A	1B083A	1B083A	A05D	
4560	73	MTHD COKE-SMOKE	1A153B	1B083B	1B083B	1B083B	A05D	
4570	73	MTHD COKE-INJCT	1A153C	1B083C	1B083C	1B083C	A05D	
4580	73	MTHD COKE-MOUTH	1A153D	1B083D	1B083D	1B083D	A05D	
4590	73	MTHD COKE-OTHER	1A153E	1B083E	1B083E	1B083E	A05D	
4600	73	NO COKE IN 5YR	1A154	1B084	1B084	1B084	A04A	
4610	74	#X/YR HER ALONE		1B086A	1B086A	1B086A	A05B	
4620	74	#X/YR HER-2 PPL		1B086B	1B086B	1B086B	A05C	
4630	74	#X/YR HER@PARTY		1B086C	1B086C	1B086C	A05C	
4640	74	#X/YR HER-DA/SP		1B086D	1B086D	1B086D	A05B	
4650	74	#X/YR HER-ADULT		1B086E	1B086E	1B086E	A05B	
4660	75	#X/YR HER-DATIM		1B086F	1B086F	1B086F	A05C	
4670	75	#X/YR HER@HOME		1B086G	1B086G	1B086G	A05C	
4680	75	#X/YR HER@SCHL		1B086H	1B086H	1B086H	A05C	
4700	75	#X/YR HER@CAR		1B086I	1B086I	1B086I	A05C	
4710	75	#X OVL HER +ALC		1B087A	1B087A	1B087A	A01H	
4720	75	#X OVL HER +MJ		1B087B	1B087B	1B087B	A01H	
4730	76	#X OVL HER +LSD		1B087C	1B087C	1B087C	A01H	
4740	76	#X OVL HER +PSY		1B087D	1B087D	1B087D	A01H	
4750	76	#X OVL HER +AMP		1B087E	1B087E	1B087E	A01H	
4760	76	#X OVL HER +QUA		1B087F	1B087F	1B087F	A01H	
4770	76	#X OVL HER +BRB		1B087G	1B087G	1B087G	A01H	
4780	76	#X OVL HER +TRN		1B087H	1B087H	1B087H	A01H	
4790	76	#X OVL HER +COK		1B087I	1B087I	1B087I	A01H	
4800	77	HERIN EXPERMENT	1A163A	1B088A	1B088A	1B088A	A06A	
4810	77	HERIN RELAX	1A163B	1B088B	1B088B	1B088B	A06A	
4820	77	HERIN GET HIGH	1A163C	1B088C	1B088C	1B088C	A06A	
4830	77	HERIN SK INSIGT	1A163D	1B088D	1B088D	1B088D	A06A	
4840	77	HERIN GD TM FRN	1A163E	1B088E	1B088E	1B088E	A06A	
4850	77	HERIN FT IN GRP	1A163F	1B088F	1B088F	1B088F	A06A	
4860	77	HERIN GT AWY PB	1A163G	1B088G	1B088G	1B088G	A06A	
4870	77	HERIN BOREDOM	1A163H	1B088H	1B088H	1B088H	A06A	
4880	77	HERIN ANGR&FRST	1A163I	1B088I	1B088I	1B088I	A06A	
4890	77	HERIN GT THR DA	1A163K	1B088J	1B088J	1B088J	A06A	
4900	77	HERIN INC EF DG	1A163L	1B088K	1B088K	1B088K	A06A	
4910	77	HERIN DEC EF DG	1A163M	1B088L	1B088L	1B088L	A06A	
4920	77	HERIN I AM HOOK	1A163N	1B088M	1B088M	1B088M	A06A	
4930	77	HER,GT VERY HI	1A164	1B089	1B089	1B089	A01E	
4940	77	HER,HI 24+ HRS	1A165	1B090	1B090	1B090	A01F	
4950	77	TRY STP HER& FL	1A166	1B091	1B091	1B091	A01I	
4960	77	METHD HRN SNORT	1A167A	1B092A	1B092A	1B092A	A05D	
4970	77	METHD HRN-SMOKE	1A167B	1B092B	1B092B	1B092B	A05D	
4980	77	METHD HRN-INJCT	1A167C	1B092C	1B092C	1B092C	A05D	
4990	77	METHD HRN-MOUTH	1A167D	1B092D	1B092D	1B092D	A05D	
5000	77	METHD HRN-OTHER	1A167E	1B092E	1B092E	1B092E	A05D	
5010	78	NO HER IN 5 YR	1A168	1B093	1B093	1B093	A04A	
5020	78	DR TOLD TK NARC	1A171	1B094	1B094	1B094	A01J	
5030	79	#X/YR NARC ALNE		1B096A	1B096A	1B096A	A05A	
5040	79	#X/YR NARC-2PPL		1B096B	1B096B	1B096B	A05B	
5050	79	#X/YR NARC@PRTY		1B096C	1B096C	1B096C	A05C	
5060	79	#X/YR NARC-DT/S		1B096D	1B096D	1B096D	A05B	
5070	79	#X/YR NARC-ADLT		1B096E	1B096E	1B096E	A05B	
5080	80	#X/YR NARC-DATM		1B096F	1B096F	1B096F	A05C	
5090	80	#X/YR NARC@HOME		1B096G	1B096G	1B096G	A05C	
5100	80	#X/YR NARC@SCHL		1B096H	1B096H	1B096H	A05C	
5120	80	#X/YR NARC @CAR		1B096I	1B096I	1B096I	A05C	
5130	80	#X OVL NARC+ALC		1B097A	1B097A	1B097A	A01H	
5140	80	#X OVL NARC+MJ		1B097B	1B097B	1B097B	A01H	
5150	81	#X OVL NARC+LSD		1B097C	1B097C	1B097C	A01H	

ITEM REFERENCE NUMBER	PAGE LOCATION (IN THIS VOLUME)	ITEM DESCRIPTION (ABBREVIATED)	QUESTIONNAIRE LOCATION BY YEAR (FORM, SECTION, AND QUESTION NUMBER)				SUBJECT AREA	
			1975	1976	1977	1978	A	B C D E F G H I J K L M N O P Q R S
5160	81	#X OVL NARC+PSY		1B097D	1B097D	1B097D	A01H	
5170	81	#X OVL NARC+AMP		1B097E	1B097E	1B097E	A01H	
5180	81	#X OVL NARC+QUA		1B097F	1B097F	1B097F	A01H	
5190	81	#X OVL NARC+BRB		1B097G	1B097G	1B097G	A01H	
5200	81	#X OVL NARC+TRN		1B097H	1B097H	1B097H	A01H	
5210	81	#X OVL NARC+COK		1B097I	1B097I	1B097I	A01H	
5220	82	#X OVL NARC+HER		1B097J	1B097J	1B097J	A01H	
5230	82	NARC EXPERIMENT	1A178A	1B098A	1B098A	1B098A	A06A	
5240	82	NARC RELAX	1A178B	1B098B	1B098B	1B098B	A06A	
5250	82	NARC GET HIGH	1A178C	1B098C	1B098C	1B098C	A06A	
5260	82	NARC SK INSIGTS	1A178D	1B098D	1B098D	1B098D	A06A	
5270	82	NARC GD TM FRND	1A178E	1B098E	1B098E	1B098E	A06A	
5280	82	NARC FIT IN GRP	1A178F	1B098F	1B098F	1B098F	A06A	
5290	82	NARC GT AWY PBM	1A178G	1B098G	1B098G	1B098G	A06A	
5300	82	NARC BOREDOM	1A178H	1B098H	1B098H	1B098H	A06A	
5310	82	NARC ANGR&FRSTN	1A178I	1B098I	1B098I	1B098I	A06A	
5320	82	NARC GT THRU DA	1A178K	1B098J	1B098J	1B098J	A06A	
5330	82	NARC INC EF DG	1A178L	1B098K	1B098K	1B098K	A06A	
5340	82	NARC DEC EF DG	1A178M	1B098L	1B098L	1B098L	A06A	
5350	82	NARC GET SLEEP		1B098M	1B098M	1B098M	A06A	
5360	82	NARC SBST HERIN	1A178O	1B098N	1B098N	1B098N	A06A	
5363	82	NARC RLV PHYS PN				1B098O	A06A	
5366	82	NARC RLV COUGHNG				1B098P	A06A	
5370	82	NARC I AM HOOKD	1A178N	1B098O	1B098O	1B098Q	A06A	
5380	82	NARC,GT VERY HI	1A179	1B099	1B099	1B099	A01E	
5390	82	NARC,HI 24+ HRS	1A180	1B100	1B100	1B100	A01F	
5400	82	NARC TKN MTHDNE	1A181A	1B101A	1B101A	1B101A	A01L	
5410	82	NARC TKN OPIUM	1A181B	1B101B	1B101B	1B101B	A01L	
5420	82	NARC TKN MRPHNE	1A181C	1B101C	1B101C	1B101C	A01L	
5430	82	NARC TKN CODEIN	1A181D	1B101D	1B101D	1B101D	A01L	
5440	82	NARC TKN DEMROL	1A181E	1B101E	1B101E	1B101E	A01L	
5450	82	NARC TKN PARGRC	1A181F	1B101F	1B101F	1B101F	A01L	
5460	82	NARC TKN TALWIN	1A181G	1B101G	1B101G	1B101G	A01L	
5470	82	NARC TKN LDANUM	1A181H	1B101H	1B101H	1B101H	A01L	
5480	82	NARC TKN OTHER	1A181I	1B101I	1B101I	1B101I	A01L	
5490	82	NARC TKN DNT KN	1A181J	1B101J	1B101J	1B101J	A01L	
5500	83	TRY STP NARC&FL	1A182	1B102	1B102	1B102	A01I	
5510	83	METH NARC SNORT	1A183A	1B103A	1B103A	1B103A	A05D	
5520	83	METH NARC SMOKE	1A183B	1B103B	1B103B	1B103B	A05D	
5530	83	METH NARC INJCT	1A183C	1B103C	1B103C	1B103C	A05D	
5540	83	METH NARC MOUTH	1A183D	1B103D	1B103D	1B103D	A05D	
5550	83	METH NARC OTHER	1A183E	1B103E	1B103E	1B103E	A05D	
5560	83	NO NARC IN 5YR	1A184	1B104	1B104	1B104	A04A	
5570	83	GR 1ST SMOK DLY	1A019	1B105A	1B105A	1B105A	A01G	
	140				3E12A	3E12A	A01G	
5580	83	GR 1ST TRY ALC	1A027	1B105B	1B105B	1B105B	A01G	
	140				3E12B	3E12B	A01G	
5590	83	GR 1ST TRY MJ	1A043	1B105C	1B105C	1B105C	A01G	
	140				3E12C	3E12C	A01G	
5600	84	GR 1ST TRY LSD	1A056	1B105D	1B105D	1B105D	A01G	
	140				3E12D	3E12D	A01G	
5610	84	GR 1ST TRY PSY	1A070	1B105E	1B105E	1B105E	A01G	
	140				3E12E	3E12E	A01G	
5620	84	GR 1ST TRY AMP	1A086	1B105F	1B105F	1B105F	A01G	
	141				3E12F	3E12F	A01G	
5630	84	GR 1ST TRY QUA	1A101	1B105G	1B105G	1B105G	A01G	
	141				3E12G	3E12G	A01G	
5640	84	GR 1ST TRY BRB	1A115	1B105H	1B105H	1B105H	A01G	
	141				3E12H	3E12H	A01G	
5650	84	GR 1ST TRY TRN	1A130	1B105I	1B105I	1B105I	A01G	
	141				3E12I	3E12I	A01G	
5660	85	GR 1ST TRY COK	1A143	1B105J	1B105J	1B105J	A01G	
	141				3E12J	3E12J	A01G	
5670	85	GR 1ST TRY HER	1A157	1B105K	1B105K	1B105K	A01G	
	141				3E12K	3E12K	A01G	
5680	85	GR 1ST TRY NRC	1A172	1B105L	1B105L	1B105L	A01G	

ITEM REFERENCE NUMBER	PAGE LOCATION (IN THIS VOLUME)	ITEM DESCRIPTION (ABBREVIATED)	QUESTIONNAIRE LOCATION BY YEAR (FORM, SECTION, AND QUESTION NUMBER)				SUBJECT AREA																		
			1975	1976	1977	1978	A	B	C	D	E	F	G	H	I	J	K	L	M	N	O	P	Q	R	S
	142				3E12L	3E12L	A01G																		
5685	142	GR 1ST TRY INHAL				3E12M	A01G																		
5690	98	US GO WAR FR OTH	2A38B	2A18B	2A18B	2A18B								H				L							
5700	85	*SC WRK NVR MNG		1D002	1D002	1D002		B																	
5710	85	*MST COUR V DUL		1D003	1D003	1D003		B																	
5720	86	*LRN SCH NT IMPT		1D004	1D004	1D004		B																	
5730	86	LOT CMPTN GRADE		1D005	1D005	1D005		B																	
5740	86	STDTS DSLK CHTG		1D006	1D006	1D006		B																	
5750	86	ST -LK PROV TCH		1D007	1D007	1D007		B																	
5760	86	FRD NCG/TCH -LK		1D008	1D008	1D008		B																	
5770	86	R IN WK-STDY PG		1D009	1D009	1D009		B	C																
5780	87	#X/YR COUNS IND		1D010	1D010	1D010		B											M						
5790	87	#X/YR COUNS GRP		1D011	1D011	1D011		B											M						
5800	87	R LK C COUNS MR		1D012	1D012	1D012		B											M						
5810	87	CSLNG VRY HLPFL		(1D013)	1D013	1D013		B											M						
5820	88	DALY WATCH TV		2A02A	2A02A	2A02A		B	C																
5830	88	DALY GO TO MOVIE		2A02B	2A02B	2A02B		B	C																
5840	88	DALY ART,MSC,PLA		2A02C	2A02C	2A02C		B	C																
5850	88	DALY RIDE FORFUN			2A02D	2A02D			C																
5860	88	DALY CMNTY AFFRS		2A02E	2A02E	2A02E			C												O				
5870	89	DALY PLA MSC,SNG		2A02F	2A02F	2A02F			C																
5880	89	DALY CREAT WRTNG		2A02G	2A02G	2A02G			C																
5890	89	DALY ACTV SPORTS		2A02H	2A02H	2A02H			C																
5900	89	DALY ART/CRAFTS		2A02I	2A02I	2A02I			C																
5910	89	DALY WRK HSE,CAR		2A02J	2A02J	2A02J			C																
5920	89	DALY VIST W/FRDS		2A02K	2A02K	2A02K			C										M						
5930	89	DALY GO SHOPPING		2A02L	2A02L	2A02L			C			F													
5940	90	DALY ALONE LEISR		(2A02M)	2A02M	2A02M			C																
5950	90	DALY READ BK,MAG		2A02N	2A02N	2A02N		B	C																
5960	90	DALY GO TO BARS		2A02O	2A02O	2A02O			C																
5970	90	DALY GO TO PARTY		2A02P	2A02P	2A02P			C																
5980		DALY GO CHURCH		2A02D					C				G												
5990	90	US 2 MUCH PROFIT	2A23J	2A03A	2A03A	2A03A						F									O				
6000	90	2MUCH CNCRN MTRL	2A23K	2A03B	2A03B	2A03B						F													
6010	91	ENCOURG PPL BUY>	2A23L	2A03C	2A03C	2A03C						F													
6020	91	-WRNG ADVERTISNG	2A23M	2A03D	2A03D	2A03D						F													
6030	91	MOR SHORTGS FUTR	2A23N	2A03E	2A03E	2A03E						F													
6040	91	APRV PETITIONS	2A21A	2A04A	2A04A	2A04A								H	I										
6050	91	APRV BOYCOTT	2A21B	2A04B	2A04B	2A04B								H	I										
6060	91	APRV LWFL DMSTN	2A21C	2A04C	2A04C	2A04C								H	I										
6070	92	APRV OCCUPY BLDG	2A21D	2A04D	2A04D	2A04D								H	I										
6080	92	APRV WLDCAT STRK	2A21E	2A04E	2A04E	2A04E								H	I										
6090	92	APRV BLK TRAFFIC	2A21F	2A04F	2A04F	2A04F								H	I										
6100	92	APRV DAMAG THING	2A21G	2A04G	2A04G	2A04G								H	I										
6110	92	APRV PSNL VIOLNC	2A21H	2A04H	2A04H	2A04H								H	I										
6120	92	DFNTLY PRFR MATE	2A10	2A05	2A05	2A05				D															
6130	92	THINK WILL MARRY	2A11	2A06	2A06	2A06				D															
6140	93	LIKLY STAY MARRD	2A12A	2A07A	2A07A	2A07A				D															
6150	93	LIKLY HAVE KIDS	2A12B	2A07B	2A07B	2A07B				D	E														
6160	93	-CHL,HB WK1.,W=0	2A15A	2A08A	2A08A	2A08A			C	D															
6170	93	-CHL,HB WK1.,W.5	2A15B	2A08B	2A08B	2A08B			C	D															
6180	93	-CHL,HB&WF WK 1.	2A15C	2A08C	2A08C	2A08C			C	D															
6190	94	-CHL,HB&WF WK .5	2A15D	2A08D	2A08D	2A08D			C	D															
6200	94	-CHL,W WK 1.,H.5	2A15E	2A08E	2A08E	2A08E			C	D															
6210	94	-CHL,W WK 1.,H=0	2A15F	2A08F	2A08F	2A08F			C	D															
6220	94	PSCH,HB WK1.,W=0	2A16A	2A09A	2A09A	2A09A			C	D															
6230	94	PSCH,HB WK1.,W.5	2A16B	2A09B	2A09B	2A09B			C	D															
6240	94	PSCH,HB&WF WK 1.	2A16C	2A09C	2A09C	2A09C			C	D															
6250	94	PSCH,HB&WF WK .5	2A16D	2A09D	2A09D	2A09D			C	D															
6260	95	PSCH,WF WK1.,H.5	2A16E	2A09E	2A09E	2A09E			C	D															
6270	95	PSCH,WF WK1.,H=0	2A16F	2A09F	2A09F	2A09F			C	D															
6280	95	H WK,W -WK,W CCR	2A17A	2A10A	2A10A	2A10A				D															
6290	95	H WK,W -WK,W>CCR	2A17B	2A10B	2A10B	2A10B				D															
6300	95	H WK,W -WK,=CHCR	2A17C	2A10C	2A10C	2A10C				D															
6310	95	H WK,W -WK,H>CCR	2A17D	2A10D	2A10D	2A10D				D															
6320	95	H WK,W -WK,H CCR	2A17E	2A10E	2A10E	2A10E				D															

ITEM REFERENCE NUMBER	PAGE LOCATION (IN THIS VOLUME)	ITEM DESCRIPTION (ABBREVIATED)	1975	1976	1977	1978	A	B	C	D	E	F	G	H	I	J	K	L	M	N	O	P	Q	R	S
6330	96	INTEREST IN GOVT	2A31	2A11	2A11	2A11								H										Q		
	134		4A29	3E01	3E01	3E01								H										Q		
	153		5A40	4A18	4A18	4A18								H										Q		
	179			5A19	5A19	5A19								H										Q		
6340	96	GOVT PPL -DSHNST	2A32	2A12	2A12	2A12								H			K								
6350	96	GOVT DSNT WASTE$	2A33	2A13	2A13	2A13								H			K								
6360	96	NEVER TRUST GOVT	2A34	2A14	2A14	2A14								H			K								
6370	96	GVT PPL DK DOING	2A35	2A15	2A15	2A15								H			K								
6380	97	GOVT RUN FOR PPL	2A36	2A16	2A16	2A16								H			K								
6390	97	DO OR PLN VOTE	2A37A	2A17A	2A17A	2A17A								H	I										
6400	97	DO OR PLN WRITE	2A37B	2A17B	2A17B	2A17B								H	I										
6410	97	DO OR PLN GIVE $	2A37C	2A17C	2A17C	2A17C								H	I										
6420	97	DO OR PLN WK CPG	2A37D	2A17D	2A17D	2A17D								H	I										
6430	97	DO OR PLN DEMNST	2A37E	2A17E	2A17E	2A17E								H	I										
6440	97	DO OR PLN BOYCOT	2A37F	2A17F	2A17F	2A17F								H	I										
6450	98	US SHD DISARM	2A38A	2A18A	2A18A	2A18A								H				L							
6460	98	US WAR PRTCT ECN	2A38C	2A18C	2A18C	2A18C								H				L							
6470	98	US ONLY WAR DFNS	2A38D	2A18D	2A18D	2A18D								H				L							
6480	98	-US MIL PWR>USSR	2A38E	2A18E	2A18E	2A18E								H				L							
6490	98	US NEED>PWR OTHS	2A38F	2A18F	2A18F	2A18F								H				L							
6500	99	US FRN PLCY NRRW	2A38G	2A18G	2A18G	2A18G								H				L							
6510	99	SRVCMEN SHD OBEY	2A38H	2A18H	2A18H	2A18H												L							
6520	99	FRQ FIGHT PARNTS	2A39A	2A19A	2A19A	2A19A													M						S
6530	99	FRQ HIT SUPRVISR	2A39B	2A19B	2A19B	2A19B													M						S
6540	99	FRQ FGT WRK/SCHL	2A39C	2A19C	2A19C	2A19C		B	C																S
6550	99	FRQ GANG FIGHT	2A39D	2A19D	2A19D	2A19D																			S
6560	100	FRQ HURT SM1 BAD	2A39E	2A19E	2A19E	2A19E																			S
6570	100	FRQ THREAT WEAPN	2A39F	2A19F	2A19F	2A19F																			S
6580	100	FRQ STEAL <$50	2A39G	2A19G	2A19G	2A19G																			S
6590	100	FRQ STEAL >$50	2A39H	2A19H	2A19H	2A19H																			S
6600	100	FRQ SHOPLIFT	2A39I	2A19I	2A19I	2A19I																			S
6610	100	FRQ CAR THEFT	2A39J	2A19J	2A19J	2A19J																			S
6620	101	FRQ STEAL CAR PT	2A39K	2A19K	2A19K	2A19K																			S
6630	101	FRQ TRESPAS BLDG	2A39L	2A19L	2A19L	2A19L																			S
6640	101	FRQ ARSON	2A39M	2A19M	2A19M	2A19M																			S
6650	101	FRQ DMG SCH PPTY	2A39N	2A19N	2A19N	2A19N		B																	S
6660	101	FRQ DMG WK PRPTY	2A39O	2A19O	2A19O	2A19O			C																S
6670	101	FRQ TRUBL POLICE	2A39P	2A19P	2A19P	2A19P																			S
6680	102	SM1 ROB YRS <$50		2A20A	2A20A	2A20A																			R	S
6690	102	SM1 ROB YRS >$50		2A20B	2A20B	2A20B																			R	S
6700	102	SM1 DMG YR PRPTY		2A20C	2A20C	2A20C																			R	S
6710	102	SM1 INJR U W/WPN		2A20D	2A20D	2A20D																			R	S
6720	102	SM1 THRTN U W/WP		2A20E	2A20E	2A20E																			R	S
6730	102	SM1 INJR YU -WPN		2A20F	2A20F	2A20F																			R	S
6740	102	SM1 THRT U W/INJ		2A20G	2A20G	2A20G																			R	S
6750	103	EASY GT MARIJUAN	2A40A	2A21A	2A21A	2A21A	A03A																			
6760	103	EASY GT LSD	2A40B	2A21B	2A21B	2A21B	A03A																			
6770	103	EASY GT PSYDELIC	2A40C	2A21C	2A21C	2A21C	A03A																			
6780	103	EASY GT AMPHTMNS	2A40D	2A21D	2A21D	2A21D	A03A																			
6790	103	EASY GT BBTUATES	2A40F	2A21E	2A21E	2A21E	A03A																			
6800	103	EASY GT TRANQLIZ	2A40G	2A21F	2A21F	2A21F	A03A																			
6810	104	EASY GT COCAINE	2A40H	2A21G	2A21G	2A21G	A03A																			
6820	104	EASY GT HEROIN	2A40I	2A21H	2A21H	2A21H	A03A																			
6830	104	EASY GT NARCOTIC	2A40J	2A21I	2A21I	2A21I	A03A																			
6840	104	CMP SATFD W/LIFE		2D01	2D01	2D01																	P	Q	R	
	130			3D01	3D01	3D01																	P	Q	R	
	157			4D01	4D01	4D01																	P	Q	R	
	180			5A21	5A21	5A21																	P	Q	R	
6850	104	HOW GD AS SPOUSE	2A19A	2D02A	2D02A	2D02A				D														Q		
6860	104	HOW GD AS PARENT	2A19B	2D02B	2D02B	2D02B				D														Q		
6870	105	HOW GD AS WORKER	2A19C	2D02C	2D02C	2D02C			C															Q		
6880	105	THK ABT SOC ISSU	*A06	2D03	2D03	2D03										J								Q		
	116			3A02	3A02	3A02										J								Q		
	143			4A05	4A05	4A05										J								Q		
	170			5A02	5A02	5A02										J								Q		
6890	105	DHNSTY LARG CORP	2A20A	2D04A	2D04A	2D04A											K								

ITEM REFERENCE NUMBER	PAGE LOCATION (IN THIS VOLUME)	ITEM DESCRIPTION (ABBREVIATED)	QUESTIONNAIRE LOCATION BY YEAR (FORM, SECTION, AND QUESTION NUMBER)				SUBJECT AREA																		
			1975	1976	1977	1978	A	B	C	D	E	F	G	H	I	J	K	L	M	N	O	P	Q	R	S
6900	105	DHNSTY LBR UNION	2A20B	2D04B	2D04B	2D04B												K								
6910	105	DHNSTY COLL&UNIV	2A20C	2D04C	2D04C	2D04C		B										K								
6920	105	DHNSTY PBLC SCHL	2A20D	2D04D	2D04D	2D04D		B										K								
6930	106	DHNSTY CHURCHES	2A20E	2D04E	2D04E	2D04E							G					K								
6940	106	DHNSTY NEWS MDIA	2A20F	2D04F	2D04F	2D04F		B										K								
6950	106	DHNSTY PRES&ADMN	2A20G	2D04G	2D04G	2D04G								H				K								
6960	106	DHNSTY CONGRESS	2A20H	2D04H	2D04H	2D04H								H				K								
6970	106	DHNSTY SUPRM CRT	2A20I	2D04I	2D04I	2D04I								H				K								
6980	106	DHNSTY JUSTC SYS	2A20J	2D04J	2D04J	2D04J								H				K								
6990	107	DHNSTY POLICE	2A20K	2D04K	2D04K	2D04K												K								
7000	107	DHNSTY MILITARY	2A20L	2D04L	2D04L	2D04L												K	L							
7010	107	2MCH COMPTN SCTY	2A23C	2D05A	2D05A	2D05A																		Q		
7020	107	2MANY YNG SLOPPY	2A23H	2D05B	2D05B	2D05B																		Q		
7030	107	2MUCH HARD ROCK	2A23I	2D05C	2D05C	2D05C																		Q		
7040	107	SHD DO OWN THING	2A23A	2D05D	2D05D	2D05D																		Q		
7050	108	KICK DO DANGR TH		2D05E	2D05E	2D05E																		Q		
7060	108	LIKE RISK SOME X		2D05F	2D05F	2D05F																		Q		
7070	108	ALL FRD SMK CIGS	2A41A	2D06A	2D06A	2D06A	A02A																			
7080	108	ALL FRD SMK MARJ	2A41B	2D06B	2D06B	2D06B	A02A																			
7090	108	ALL FRD TAKE LSD	2A41C	2D06C	2D06C	2D06C	A02A																			
7100	108	ALL FRD TK PSYDL	2A41D	2D06D	2D06D	2D06D	A02A																			
7110	109	ALL FRD TK AMPH	2A41E	2D06E	2D06E	2D06E	A02A																			
7120	109	ALL FRD TK QUALD	2A41F	2D06F	2D06F	2D06F	A02A																			
7130	109	ALL FRD TK BARBT	2A41G	2D06G	2D06G	2D06G	A02A																			
7140	109	ALL FRD TK TRNQL	2A41H	2D06H	2D06H	2D06H	A02A																			
7150	109	ALL FRD TK COKE	2A41I	2D06I	2D06I	2D06I	A02A																			
7160	109	ALL FRD TK HERON	2A41J	2D06J	2D06J	2D06J	A02A																			
7170	109	ALL FRD TK NARC	2A41K	2D06K	2D06K	2D06K	A02A																			
7180	110	ALL FRD TK INHL	2A41L	2D06L	2D06L	2D06L	A02A																			
7190	110	ALL FRD DRK ALCL	2A41M	2D06M	2D06M	2D06M	A02A																			
7200	110	ALL FRD GT DRUNK	2A41N	2D06N	2D06N	2D06N	A02A																			
7210		FBD CHLD CIG RGL			2E01A		A11C																			
7220		FBD CHLD MJ OCCS			2E01B		A11C																			
7230		FBD CHLD MJ RGLY			2E01C		A11C																			
7240		FBD CHLD LSD OCC			2E01D		A11C																			
7250		FBD CHLD AMPH OC			2E01E		A11C																			
7260		FBD CHLD BARB OC			2E01F		A11C																			
7270		FBD CHLD COKE OC			2E01G		A11C																			
7280		FBD CHLD HRN OCC			2E01H		A11C																			
7290		FBD CHLD DRNK OC			2E01I		A11C																			
7300		FBD CHLD DRNK RG			2E01J		A11C																			
7310		FBD CHLD DRUNKOC			2E01K		A11C																			
7320		RSK/OT CIG1+PK/D		2E01A			A14B																			
7330		RSK/OT MJ 1-2 X		2E01B			A14B																			
7340		RSK/OT MJ OCSNLY		2E01C			A14B																			
7350		RSK/OT MJ REGLY		2E01D			A14B																			
7360		RSK/OT LSD 1-2 X		2E01E			A14B																			
7370		RSK/OT LSD REGLY		2E01F			A14B																			
7380		RSK/OT 'H' 1-2 X		2E01G			A14B																			
7390		RSK/OT 'H' OCSNL		2E01H			A14B																			
7400		RSK/OT 'H' REGLY		2E01I			A14B																			
7410		RSK/OT BARB 1-2X		2E01J			A14B																			
7420		RSK/OT BARB REGY		2E01K			A14B																			
7430		RSK/OT AMPH 1-2X		2E01L			A14B																			
7440		RSK/OT AMPH REG		2E01M			A14B																			
7450		RSK/OT COKE 1-2X		2E01N			A14B																			
7460		RSK/OT COKE REG		2E01O			A14B																			
7470		RSK/OT 1-2 DRINK		2E01P			A14B																			
7480		RSK/OT 1-2 DR/DA		2E01Q			A14B																			
7490		RSK/OT 4-5 DR/DA		2E01R			A14B																			
7500		RSK/OT 5+DR/WKND		2E01S			A14B																			
7510	110	PRNT THK U DRINK			2E02	2E01	A09A																			
7520	110	PRNT THK U SM MJ			2E03	2E02	A09A																			
7530	110	PRNT THK USE DRG			2E04	2E03	A09A																			
7540		TRN FA/MO DRG HP			2E05A		A08A																			
7550		TRN SR/BR DRG HP			2E05B		A08A																			

ITEM REFERENCE NUMBER	PAGE LOCATION (IN THIS VOLUME)	ITEM DESCRIPTION (ABBREVIATED)	1975	1976	1977	1978	A	B	C	D	E	F	G	H	I	J	K	L	M	N	O	P	Q	R	S
7560		TRN RLTVS DRG HP			2E05C		A08A																			
7570		TRN FRND DRG HP			2E05D		A08A																			
7580		TRN DOCTR DRG HP			2E05E		A08A																			
7590		TRN CLINC DRG HP			2E05F		A08A																			
7600		TRN CNSLR DRG HP			2E05G		A08A																			
7610		TRN TCHR DRG HP			2E05H		A08A																			
7620		TRN MNSTR DRG HP			2E05I		A08A																			
7630	85	R LIKES SCHOOL		1D001	1D001	1D001		B															Q		
	113			2E02	2E06	2E06		B															Q		
	137			3E08	3E07	3E07		B															Q		
	194			4E10	5E05	5E05		B															Q		
				5E04				B															Q		
7640	113	HRS/WK SPND HMWK		2E03	2E07	2E07		B																	
7650	113	PRCL INFL SCL RN		2E04A	2E08A	2E08A		B																	
7660	113	TCHR INFL SCL RN		2E04B	2E08B	2E08B		B																	
7670	113	STDS INFL SCL RN		2E04C	2E08C	2E08C		B																	
7680	114	PRTS INFL SCL RN		2E04D	2E08D	2E08D		B																	
7690	114	HAD DRUG EDUCATN		2E05	2E09	2E09	A10A																			
7700		NOW OWN HAIR DRY		2E09A									F												R	
7710		NOW OWN WT/S SKI		2E09B								F												R	
7720		NOW OWN CAMERA		2E09C								F												R	
7730		NOW OWN WATCH		2E09D								F												R	
7740		NOW OWN HKG BKPK		2E09E								F												R	
7750		NOW OWN CK RADIO		2E09F								F												R	
7760		NOW OWN EL SHAVR		2E09G								F												R	
7770		NOW OWN TENIS RQ		2E09H								F												R	
7780		NOW OWN TV SET		2E09I								F												R	
7790		NOW OWN BICYCLE		2E09J								F												R	
7800		NOW OWN CAR		2E09K								F												R	
7810		NOW OWN TAPE REC		2E09L								F												R	
7820		NOW OWN ELT CALC		2E09M								F												R	
7830		NOW OWN BT/SNMBL		2E09N								F												R	
7840	114	DG ED,>DG INTRST		2E06	2E10	2E10	A10A																			
7850	114	DG ED,SPC COURSE		2E07A	2E11A	2E11A	A10A																			
7860	114	DG ED,IN REG CRS		2E07B	2E11B	2E11B	A10A																			
7870	114	DG ED,NT REG CRS		2E07C	2E11C	2E11C	A10A																			
7880	114	DG ED,SPC DISCUS		2E07D	2E11D	2E11D	A10A																			
7890	114	DG ED,GRT VALUE		2E08	2E12	2E12	A10A																			
7900	114	16YR+,TEST->DIPL			2E13A	2E13A		B																	
7910	115	14YR+,TEST->DIPL			2E13B	2E13B		B																	
7920	115	ALL STD H.S.TEST			2E13C	2E13C		B																	
7930	116	MEN&WOMN/=$,=WRK	3A17A	3A03A	3A03A	3A03A			C	D															
7940	116	CNSDR WMN/HI JOB	3A17B	3A03B	3A03B	3A03B				D				H											
7950	116	WMN SHD =JOB OPP	3A17C	3A03C	3A03C	3A03C			C	D															
7960	116	WMN SHD =ED OPP	3A17D	3A03D	3A03D	3A03D		B		D															
7970	117	MN=ACHV/WMN=HOME	3A17H	3A03E	3A03E	3A03E				D															
7980	117	CHL SUFF W WK MO	3A17I	3A03F	3A03F	3A03F				D															
7990	117	WK MO AS WRM REL	3A17J	3A03G	3A03G	3A03G			C	D															
8000	117	POLLUT INCREASED	3A31A	3A04A	3A04A	3A04A						F													
8010	117	GOVT DEAL ENV PR	3A31D	3A04B	3A04B	3A04B						F		H											
8020	117	MR$ FR LASTG THG	3A31E	3A04C	3A04C	3A04C						F													
8030	118	USE BYC/MAS TRAN	3A31F	3A04D	3A04D	3A04D						F													
8040	118	EAT DIF->FD STRV	3A31G	3A04E	3A04E	3A04E						F									O				
8050	118	LIK WRK CAN FRGT	3A08D	3A05A	3A05A	3A05A			C																
8060	118	WRK=ONLY MK LVNG	3A08E	3A05B	3A05B	3A05B			C																
8070	118	WRK CNTRL PRT LF	3A08G	3A05C	3A05C	3A05C			C																
8080	118	OVTM 2DO BST JOB	3A08H	3A05D	3A05D	3A05D			C																
8090	119	SAME JOB MST LIF	3A08I	3A05E	3A05E	3A05E			C																
8100	119	ENUF$,NT WNT WRK	3A10	3A06	3A06	3A06			C																
	151		4A09A	4A14	4A14	4A14			C																
	173		5A11	5A06	5A06	5A06			C																
8110	119	DES FRND OTH RC	3A19A	3A07A	3A07A	3A07A														N					
8120	119	DES SUPVR DIF RC	3A19B	3A07B	3A07B	3A07B			C											N					
8130	119	DES FAM NX DF RC	3A19C	3A07C	3A07C	3A07C														N					
8140	120	DES CHL FD SM RC	3A19D	3A07D	3A07D	3A07D														N					
8150	120	DES CHL FD OT RC	3A19E	3A07E	3A07E	3A07E														N					

ITEM REFERENCE NUMBER	PAGE LOCATION (IN THIS VOLUME)	ITEM DESCRIPTION (ABBREVIATED)	QUESTIONNAIRE LOCATION BY YEAR (FORM, SECTION, AND QUESTION NUMBER)				SUBJECT AREA																		
			1975	1976	1977	1978	A	B	C	D	E	F	G	H	I	J	K	L	M	N	O	P	Q	R	S
8160	120	DES AL WKS SM RC	3A19F	3A08A	3A08A	3A08A			C												N					
8170	120	DES SO WKS DF RC	3A19G	3A08B	3A08B	3A08B			C												N					
8180	120	DES MS WKS DF RC	3A19H	3A08C	3A08C	3A08C			C												N					
8190	120	DES AL NGB SM RC	3A19I	3A09A	3A09A	3A09A															N					
8200	120	DES SO NGB OT RC	3A19J	3A09B	3A09B	3A09B															N					
8210	121	DES MS NGB OT RC	3A19K	3A09C	3A09C	3A09C															N					
8220	121	DES AL CHL SM RC	3A19L	3A10A	3A10A	3A10A		B													N					
8230	121	DES SM CHL OT RC	3A19M	3A10B	3A10B	3A10B		B													N					
8240	121	DES MS CHL OT RC	3A19N	3A10C	3A10C	3A10C		B													N					
8250	121	FRNDS AL OT RC	3A22	3A11	3A11	3A11															N				R	
8260	121	NGBHD AL OT RC	3A23	3A12	3A12	3A12															N				R	
8270	121	ELEMSCH AL OT RC	3A21	3A13	3A13	3A13															N				R	
8280	122	HISCH AL OT RC	3A20	3A14	3A14	3A14															N				R	
8290	122	WRKRS AL OT RC		3A15	3A15	3A15															N					
8300	122	DO LOT THG OT RC	3A24	3A16	3A16	3A16															N					
8310	122	VRY GD EXP OT RC	3A25	3A17	3A17	3A17															N					
8320	122	MARRD OR ENGAGED	3A41	3A18	3A18	3A18					E														R	
8330	122	WHN WANT GT MARR	3A42	3A19	3A19	3A19					E															
8340	123	THGT LOT HAV CHL	3A43	3A20	3A20	3A20					E															
8350	123	# CHLDN WANT(6+)	3A44	3A21	3A21	3A21					E															
8360	123	IF -POP, MR CHLD	3A45	3A22	3A22	3A22					E															
8370	123	WHN 1ST CHL(5+Y)	3A46	3A23	3A23	3A23					E								M							
8380	123	GD JB LARG CORPS	3A27A	3A24A	3A24A	3A24A											K									
8390	124	GD JB LBR UNIONS	3A27B	3A24B	3A24B	3A24B											K									
8400	124	GD JB COLLG&UNIV	3A27C	3A24C	3A24C	3A24C		B									K									
8410	124	GD JB PBLC SCHOL	3A27D	3A24D	3A24D	3A24D		B									K									
8420	124	GD JB CHURCHES	3A27E	3A24E	3A24E	3A24E							G				K									
8430	124	GD JB NEWS MEDIA	3A27F	3A24F	3A24F	3A24F		B									K									
8440	124	GD JB PRES&ADMIN	3A27G	3A24G	3A24G	3A24G								H			K									
8450	125	GD JB CONGRESS	3A27H	3A24H	3A24H	3A24H								H			K									
8460	125	GD JB SUPRM CRT	3A27I	3A24I	3A24I	3A24I								H			K									
8470	125	GD JB JUSTC SYST	3A27J	3A24J	3A24J	3A24J								H			K									
8480	125	GD JB POLICE	3A27K	3A24K	3A24K	3A24K											K									
8490	125	GD JB MILITARY	3A27L	3A24L	3A24L	3A24L											K	L								
8500	125	MIL TOO MCH INFL	3A28	3A25	3A25	3A25												L								
8510	126	US TOO MCH$ MILT	3A29	3A26	3A26	3A26												L								
8520	126	12MO,#OCC PAINRF	3A48A	3A27A	3A27A	3A27A	A01B																			
8530	126	12MO,#OCC SLP PL	3A48B	3A27B	3A27B	3A27B	A01B																			
8540	126	12MO,#OCC AWK PL	3A48C	3A27C	3A27C	3A27C	A01B																			
8550	126	12MO,#OCC CALM P	3A48D	3A27D	3A27D	3A27D	A01B																			
8560	127	DAP SMK 1PCK CIG	(3A53A)	3A28A	3A28A	3A28A	A11A																			
8570	127	DAP TRY MRJ 1-2T	(3A53B)	3A28B	3A28B	3A28B	A11A																			
8580	127	DAP SMK MRJ OCCS	(3A53C)	3A28C	3A28C	3A28C	A11A																			
8590	127	DAP SMK MRJ REGL	(3A53D)	3A28D	3A28D	3A28D	A11A																			
8600	127	DAP TRY LSD 1-2T	(3A53E)	3A28E	3A28E	3A28E	A11A																			
8610	127	DAP TKG LSD REGL	(3A53F)	3A28F	3A28F	3A28F	A11A																			
8620	127	DAP TRY HRN 1-2T	(3A53G)	3A28G	3A28G	3A28G	A11A																			
8630	127	DAP TKG HRN OCCS	(3A53H)	3A28H	3A28H	3A28H	A11A																			
8640	128	DAP TKG HRN REGL	(3A53I)	3A28I	3A28I	3A28I	A11A																			
8650	128	DAP TRY BRB 1-2T	(3A53J)	3A28J	3A28J	3A28J	A11A																			
8660	128	DAP TKG BRB REGL	(3A53K)	3A28K	3A28K	3A28K	A11A																			
8670	128	DAP TRY AMP 1-2T	(3A53L)	3A28L	3A28L	3A28L	A11A																			
8680	128	DAP TKG AMP REGL	(3A53M)	3A28M	3A28M	3A28M	A11A																			
8690	128	DAP TRY COC 1-2T	(3A53N)	3A28N	3A28N	3A28N	A11A																			
8700	128	DAP TKG COC REGL	(3A53O)	3A28O	3A28O	3A28O	A11A																			
8710	128	DAP TRY DRK ALCL	(3A53P)	3A28P	3A28P	3A28P	A11A																			
8720	129	DAP 1-2 DRK/DAY	(3A53Q)	3A28Q	3A28Q	3A28Q	A11A																			
8730	129	DAP 4-5 DRK/DAY	(3A53R)	3A28R	3A28R	3A28R	A11A																			
8740	129	DAP 5+ DRK WKNDS	(3A53S)	3A28S	3A28S	3A28S	A11A																			
8750	196	OFT W PL TK MARJ	3A55A	5E07A	5E08A	5E08A	A02B																			
8760	196	OFT W PL TK LSD	3A55B	5E07B	5E08B	5E08B	A02B																			
8770	196	OFT W PL TK PSYC	3A55C	5E07C	5E08C	5E08C	A02B																			
8780	196	OFT W PL TK QUAL	3A55D	5E07D	5E08D	5E08D	A02B																			
8790	196	OFT W PL TK BARB	3A55E	5E07E	5E08E	5E08E	A02B																			
8800	197	OFT W PL TK TRQL	3A55F	5E07F	5E08F	5E08F	A02B																			
8810	197	OFT W PL TK COKE	3A55G	5E07G	5E08G	5E08G	A02B																			

ITEM REFERENCE NUMBER	PAGE LOCATION (IN THIS VOLUME)	ITEM DESCRIPTION (ABBREVIATED)	QUESTIONNAIRE LOCATION BY YEAR (FORM, SECTION, AND QUESTION NUMBER)				SUBJECT AREA	
			1975	1976	1977	1978	A	B C D E F G H I J K L M N O P Q R S
8820	197	OFT W PL TK HRN	3A55H	5E07H	5E08H	5E08H	A02B	
8830	197	OFT W PL TK NARC	3A55I	5E07I	5E08I	5E08I	A02B	
8835	197	OFT W PL TK INHL	3A55J	5E07J	5E08J	5E08J	A02B	
8840	197	OFT W PL TK ALCL	3A55K	5E07K	5E08K	5E08K	A02B	
8850	131	OFTN SHRTNS BRTH		(3D02A)	3D02A	3D02A		Q
8860	131	OFTN HEART BEATG		(3D02B)	3D02B	3D02B		Q
8870	131	OFTN SPLLS DZZNS		(3D02C)	3D02C	3D02C		Q
8880	131	OFTN HNDS TRMBLE		(3D02D)	3D02D	3D02D		Q
8890	131	OFTN HNDS SWEATG		(3D02E)	3D02E	3D02E		Q
8900	131	OFTN CDNT GT GNG		(3D02F)	3D02F	3D02F		Q
8910	132	12MO REDUCE ALCL		3D03A	3D03A	3D03A	A01I	
8920	132	12MO REDUCE CIG		3D03B	3D03B	3D03B	A01I	
8930	132	12MO REDUCE MARJ		3D03C	3D03C	3D03C	A01I	
8940	132	12MO REDUCE PSYC		3D03D	3D03D	3D03D	A01I	
8950	132	12MO REDUCE AMPH		3D03E	3D03E	3D03E	A01I	
8960	132	12MO REDUCE QUAL		3D03F	3D03F	3D03F	A01I	
8970	132	12MO REDUCE BARB		3D03G	3D03G	3D03G	A01I	
8980	132	12MO REDUCE COKE		3D03H	3D03H	3D03H	A01I	
8990	132	12MO REDUCE HRN		3D03I	3D03I	3D03I	A01I	
9000	133	12MO REDUCE NARC		3D03J	3D03J	3D03J	A01I	
9010	133	NXT 12MOS USE MJ			3D04	3D04	A01B	
9020	133	CNCRN PSYCH DAMG		3D04A	3D04A	3D04A	A06A	
9030	133	CNCRN PHYSCL DMG		3D04B	3D04B	3D04B	A06A	
9040	133	CNCRN GT ARRESTD		3D04C	3D04C	3D04C	A06A	
9050	133	CNCRN BECOM ADCT		3D04D	3D04D	3D04D	A06A	
9060	133	AGST MY BELIEFS		3D04E	3D04E	3D04E	A06A	
9070	133	CNCRN LEGY&AMBTN		3D04F	3D04F	3D04F	A06A	
9080	133	CNCRN LOSS CNTRL		3D04G	3D04G	3D04G	A06A	
9090	133	MJ ->STRNGR DRGS		3D04H	3D04H	3D04H	A06A	
9100	133	MJ NOT ENJOYABLE		3D04I	3D04I	3D04I	A06A	
9110	133	PRNTS DISAPPROVE		3D04J	3D04J	3D04J	A06A	
9120	133	HS/WF DISAPPROVE		3D04K	3D04K	3D04K	A06A	
9130	133	DONT LIKE USERS		3D04L	3D04L	3D04L	A06A	
9140	133	FRNDS DNT USE IT		3D04M	3D04M	3D04M	A06A	
9150	133	PSSBLY BAD TRIP		3D04N	3D04N	3D04N	A06A	
9160	133	TOO EXPENSIVE			3D04O	3D04O	A06A	
9170	133	NOT AVAILABLE			3D04P	3D04P	A06A	
9180	133	NOT WNT GET HIGH			3D04Q	3D04Q	A06A	
9190	133	AL CS BEHV REGRT		3D05A	3D05A	3D05A	A07A	
9200	133	AL HURT REL PRNT		3D05A	3D05A	3D05A	A07A	
9210	133	AL HURT REL SPSE		3D05A	3D05A	3D05A	A07A	
9220	133	AL HURT REL FRND		3D05A	3D05A	3D05A	A07A	
9230	133	AL HURT REL TCHR		3D05A	3D05A	3D05A	A07A	
9240	133	AL INV PL BD INF		3D05A	3D05A	3D05A	A07A	
9250	133	AL HURT PERF JOB		3D05A	3D05A	3D05A	A07A	
9260	133	AL CAUS<INTERSTD		3D05A	3D05A	3D05A	A07A	
9270	133	AL CS<STABL EMTN		3D05A	3D05A	3D05A	A07A	
9280	133	AL CS HAV<ENERGY		3D05A	3D05A	3D05A	A07A	
9290	133	AL INTF THNK CLR		3D05A	3D05A	3D05A	A07A	
9300	133	AL BD PSYCH EFCT		3D05A	3D05A	3D05A	A07A	
9310	133	AL CS HEALTH BAD		3D05A	3D05A	3D05A	A07A	
9320	133	AL CS DRIV UNSAF		3D05A	3D05A	3D05A	A07A	
9330	133	AL GT TRBL W POL		3D05A	3D05A	3D05A	A07A	
9340	133	AL CS NO PROBLEM			3D05A	3D05A	A07A	
9350	133	AL NEVER USED DG			3D05A	3D05A	A07A	
9360	133	MJ CS BEHV REGRT		3D05M	3D05M	3D05M	A07A	
9370	133	MJ HURT REL PRNT		3D05M	3D05M	3D05M	A07A	
9380	133	MJ HURT REL SPSE		3D05M	3D05M	3D05M	A07A	
9390	133	MJ HURT REL FRND		3D05M	3D05M	3D05M	A07A	
9400	133	MJ HURT REL TCHR		3D05M	3D05M	3D05M	A07A	
9410	133	MJ INV PL BD INF		3D05M	3D05M	3D05M	A07A	
9420	133	MJ HURT PERF JOB		3D05M	3D05M	3D05M	A07A	
9430	133	MJ CAUS<INTERSTD		3D05M	3D05M	3D05M	A07A	
9440	133	MJ CS<STABL EMTN		3D05M	3D05M	3D05M	A07A	
9450	133	MJ CS HAV<ENERGY		3D05M	3D05M	3D05M	A07A	
9460	133	MJ INTF THNK CLR		3D05M	3D05M	3D05M	A07A	

ITEM REFERENCE NUMBER	PAGE LOCATION (IN THIS VOLUME)	ITEM DESCRIPTION (ABBREVIATED)	1975	1976	1977	1978	A	B	C	D	E	F	G	H	I	J	K	L	M	N	O	P	Q	R	S
9470	133	MJ BD PSYCH EFCT		3D05M	3D05M	3D05M	A07A																		
9480	133	MJ CS HEALTH BAD		3D05M	3D05M	3D05M	A07A																		
9490	133	MJ CS DRIV UNSAF		3D05M	3D05M	3D05M	A07A																		
9500	133	MJ GT TRBL W POL		3D05M	3D05M	3D05M	A07A																		
9510	133	MJ CS NO PROBLEM			3D05M	3D05M	A07A																		
9520	133	MJ NEVER USED DG			3D05M	3D05M	A07A																		
9530	134	OT CS BEHV REGRT		3D05O	3D05O	3D05O	A07A																		
9540	134	OT HURT REL PRNT		3D05O	3D05O	3D05O	A07A																		
9550	134	OT HURT REL SPSE		3D05O	3D05O	3D05O	A07A																		
9560	134	OT HURT REL FRND		3D05O	3D05O	3D05O	A07A																		
9570	134	OT HURT REL TCHR		3D05O	3D05O	3D05O	A07A																		
9580	134	OT INV PL BD INF		3D05O	3D05O	3D05O	A07A																		
9590	134	OT HURT PERF JOB		3D05O	3D05O	3D05O	A07A																		
9600	134	OT CAUS<INTERSTD		3D05O	3D05O	3D05O	A07A																		
9610	134	OT CS<STABL EMTN		3D05O	3D05O	3D05O	A07A																		
9620	134	OT CS HAV<ENERGY		3D05O	3D05O	3D05O	A07A																		
9630	134	OT INTF THNK CLR		3D05O	3D05O	3D05O	A07A																		
9640	134	OT BD PSYCH EFCT		3D05O	3D05O	3D05O	A07A																		
9650	134	OT CS HEALTH BAD		3D05O	3D05O	3D05O	A07A																		
9660	134	OT CS DRIV UNSAF		3D05O	3D05O	3D05O	A07A																		
9670	134	OT GT TRBL W POL		3D05O	3D05O	3D05O	A07A																		
9680	134	OT CS NO PROBLEM			3D05O	3D05O	A07A																		
9690	134	OT NEVER USED DG			3D05O	3D05O	A07A																		
9700	134	PRVNT POL TOO >$		3E02A	3E02A	3E02A						F													
9710	134	PRVNT POL CST JB		3E02B	3E02B	3E02B						F													
9720	134	PRVNT POL PPL DK		3E02C	3E02C	3E02C						F													
9730	135	PRVNT POL -ENUF		3E02D	3E02D	3E02D						F													
9740	135	PRVNT POL USELSS		3E02E	3E02E	3E02E						F													
9750	135	FUTR,HAV2 CNSUM<		3E03	3E03	3E03						F													
9760	135	GOV HP PRB POPL	3A32N	3E04A	3E04A	3E04A					E			H											
9770	135	GOV NO POP PLCY	3A32A	3E04B	3E04B	3E04B					E			H											
9780	135	STR OVPOP,LMT FM	3A32B	3E04C	3E04C	3E04C					E														
9790	136	PRV OVPOP,NO CHL	3A32C	3E04D	3E04D	3E04D					E														
9800	136	HISCH INS BRTH C	3A32E	3E04E	3E04E	3E04E		B			E														
9810	136	BRTH CNT IMMORAL	3A32I	3E04F	3E04F	3E04F					E														
9820	136	GOV BRTHC NO CST	3A32M	3E04G	3E04G	3E04G					E			H											
9830	136	US POP SZ LRGER	3A34	3E06	3E05	3E05					E														
9840		GVNG FOOD O CNTY	3A33	3E05							E										O				
9850	136	WRLD POP SZ LRGR	3A35	3E07	3E06	3E06					E														
9860	137	HAD SEX ED IN HS		3E09	3E08	3E08				D	E														
9870	137	STUDY BC IN HS		3E10	3E09	3E09				D	E														
9871	137	SM1 SCL ROB <$50		4E11A	3E10A	3E10A																		R	S
9872	137	SM1 SCL ROB >$50		4E11B	3E10B	3E10B																		R	S
9873	137	SM1 SCL DMG PRTY		4E11C	3E10C	3E10C																		R	S
9874	138	SM1 SCL IN U W/W		4E11D	3E10D	3E10D																		R	S
9875	138	SM1 SCL TH U W/W		4E11E	3E10E	3E10E																		R	S
9876	138	SM1 SCL IN U -WP		4E11F	3E10F	3E10F																		R	S
9877	138	SM1 SCL TH U W/I		4E11G	3E10G	3E10G																		R	S
9880		DK DO W LEISR TM			3E11A				C																
9890		TM QUIK/LEIS HRS			3E11B				C																
9900		WASTE LEIS TIME			3E11C				C																
9910		ENUF TIME FR THG			3E11D				C																
9920		R WL VOTE IN '76		3E11										H											
9940	143	FUTR CNTRY WORSE	4A01	4A02	4A02	4A02									I										
9950	143	FUTR WORLD WORSE	4A02	4A03	4A03	4A03									I										
9960	143	FUTR R LIFE WRSE	4A03	4A04	4A04	4A04									I										
9970	143	PLLTN INCR IN US	4A22A	4A06A	4A06A	4A06A						F													
9980	144	PLLTN NT SO DANG	4A22B	4A06B	4A06B	4A06B						F													
9990	144	PLLTN NEC 4 GRTH	4A22C	4A06C	4A06C	4A06C						F													
10000	144	INDVL RESP 4 ENV	4A22D	4A06D	4A06D	4A06D						F													
10010	144	GOVT RESP 4 ENV	4A22E	4A06E	4A06E	4A06E						F		H											
10020	144	GOVT TAX PLLTRS	4A22F	4A06F	4A06F	4A06F						F		H											
10030	144	GOVT BAN DSPSBLE	4A22G	4A06G	4A06G	4A06G						F		H											
10040	145	TV COMM CRT NDS	4A22H	4A06H	4A06H	4A06H		B				F													
10050	145	TV COMMRCLS GOOD	4A22I	4A06I	4A06I	4A06I		B				F													
10060	145	FAM BUYS THG -ND	4A22L	4A06J	4A06J	4A06J						F													

ITEM REFERENCE NUMBER	PAGE LOCATION (IN THIS VOLUME)	ITEM DESCRIPTION (ABBREVIATED)	1975	1976	1977	1978	A	B	C	D	E	F	G	H	I	J	K	L	M	N	O	P	Q	R	S
	178			5A18I	5A18I	5A18I						F													
10070	145	POL SLVD BY 2000	4A22M	4A06K	4A06K	4A06K						F													
10080	145	R EFRT 2 HLP ENV	4A23	4A07	4A07	4A07						F													
10090	146	JOB IMPC SE RSLT	4A08A	4A08A	4A08A	4A08A			C																
10100	146	JOB IMPC STATUS	4A08B	4A08B	4A08B	4A08B			C																
10110	146	JOB IMPC INTRSTG	4A08C	4A08C	4A08C	4A08C			C																
10120	146	JOB IMPC ADVNCMT	4A08D	4A08D	4A08D	4A08D			C																
10130	146	JOB IMPC HLP OTH	4A08E	4A08E	4A08E	4A08E			C													O				
10140	146	JOB IMPC EARN $	4A08F	4A08F	4A08F	4A08F			C			F													
10150	146	JOB IMPC CREATVY	4A08G	4A08G	4A08G	4A08G			C																
10160	147	JOB IMPC UTILITY	4A08H	4A08H	4A08H	4A08H			C																
10170	147	JOB IMPC MK FRND	4A08I	4A08I	4A08I	4A08I			C										M						
10180	147	JOB IMPC USE SKL	4A08J	4A08J	4A08J	4A08J			C																
10190	147	JOB IMPC WRTHWLE	4A08K	4A08K	4A08K	4A08K			C													O				
10200	147	JOB IMPC VACATN	4A08L	4A08L	4A08L	4A08L			C																
10210	147	JOB IMPC MK DCSN	4A08M	4A08M	4A08M	4A08M			C																
10220	147	JOB IMPC FRE TIM		4A08N	4A08N	4A08N			C																
10230	148	JOB IMPC NO MVNG	4A08O	4A08O	4A08O	4A08O			C																
10240	148	JOB IMPC NO SPRV	4A08P	4A08P	4A08P	4A08P			C																
10250	148	JOB IMPC SECURTY	4A08Q	4A08Q	4A08Q	4A08Q			C																
10260	148	JOB IMPC LRNING	4A08R	4A08R	4A08R	4A08R		B	C																
10270	148	JOB IMPC BE SELF	4A08S	4A08S	4A08S	4A08S			C																
10280	148	JOB IMPC RESPECT	4A08T	4A08T	4A08T	4A08T			C																
10290	148	JOB IMPC CNTC PL	4A08U	4A08U	4A08U	4A08U			C										M						
10300	149	JOB IMPC EZ PACE		4A08V	4A08V	4A08V			C																
10310	149	JOB IMPC HRD PRB		4A08W	4A08W	4A08W			C																
10320	149	KIND OF WORK @30	4A09	4A09	4A09	4A09			C																
10330	150	R SURE GT THS WK		4A10	4A10	4A10			C																
10340	150	R SURE WK GD CHC		4A11	4A11	4A11			C																
10350	150	R THNK WK BE SAT		4A12	4A12	4A12			C														P			
10360	150	JOB OBSTC RELGN		4A13A	4A13A	4A13A			C				G												
10370	150	JOB OBSTC SEX		4A13B	4A13B	4A13B			C	D															
10380	150	JOB OBSTC RACE		4A13C	4A13C	4A13C			C											N					
10390	150	JOB OBSTC BKGRND		4A13D	4A13D	4A13D			C															R	
10400	151	JOB OBSTC POL VW		4A13E	4A13E	4A13E			C					H											
10410	151	JOB OBSTC EDUCTN		4A13F	4A13F	4A13F		B	C																
10420	151	JOB OBSTC -VOC T		4A13G	4A13G	4A13G			C																
10430	151	JOB OBSTC -ABLTY		4A13H	4A13H	4A13H			C															R	
10440	151	JOB OBSTC - PULL		4A13I	4A13I	4A13I			C															R	
10450	151	JOB OBSTC -WK HD		4A13J	4A13J	4A13J			C														Q		
10460	151	JOB OBSTC -CONFM		4A13K	4A13K	4A13K			C														Q		
10470	152	FEW GD MAR, ? IT	4A11A	4A15A	4A15A	4A15A				D															
10480	152	GD LIV TG BF MRG	4A11B	4A15B	4A15B	4A15B				D	E														
10490	152	1 PRTNR=RSTRCTVE	4A11C	4A15C	4A15C	4A15C				D	E														
10500	152	JB INTFR REL HBD	4A11E	4A15D	4A15D	4A15D			C	D															
10510	152	JB DVLP WF PERSN	4A11G	4A15E	4A15E	4A15E			C	D															
10520	152	RS CHLD + FR MAN	4A11H	4A15F	4A15F	4A15F				D															
10530	153	MO SH B W CHL>TM	4A11I	4A15G	4A15G	4A15G				D															
10540	153	WF WK,HBD SHD>HW	4A11K	4A15H	4A15H	4A15H			C	D															
10550	153	#HRS TV/DAY/5+		4A16	4A16	4A16		B																	
10560	153	#BKS LAST YR/10+		4A17	4A17	4A17		B																	
10570	154	>INFLC LARG CORP	4A14A	4A19A	4A19A	4A19A												K							
10580	154	>INFLC LBR UNION	4A14B	4A19B	4A19B	4A19B												K							
10590	154	>INFLC CHURCHES	4A14C	4A19C	4A19C	4A19C							G					K							
10600	154	>INFLC NEWS MDIA	4A14D	4A19D	4A19D	4A19D		B										K							
10610	154	>INFLC PRES&ADMN	4A14E	4A19E	4A19E	4A19E								H				K							
10620	154	>INFLC CONGRESS	4A14F	4A19F	4A19F	4A19F								H				K							
10630	155	>INFLC SUPRM CRT	4A14G	4A19G	4A19G	4A19G								H				K							
10640	155	>INFLC JUSTC SYS	4A14H	4A19H	4A19H	4A19H								H				K							
10650	155	>INFLC POLICE	4A14I	4A19I	4A19I	4A19I												K							
10660	155	>INFLC MILITARY	4A14J	4A19J	4A19J	4A19J												K	L						
10760	157	LAW 4 SMK TOBPUB			4A20K	4A20K	A13A																		
10770		ILGL AD SMK CIG		4A20A			A13A																		
10780	155	ILGL AD MRJ PRIV		4A20B	4A20A	4A20A	A13A																		
10790	155	ILGL AD MRJ PUBL		4A20C	4A20B	4A20B	A13A																		
10800	156	ILGL AD LSD PRIV		4A20D	4A20C	4A20C	A13A																		

ITEM REFERENCE NUMBER	PAGE LOCATION (IN THIS VOLUME)	ITEM DESCRIPTION (ABBREVIATED)	1975	1976	1977	1978	A	B	C	D	E	F	G	H	I	J	K	L	M	N	O	P	Q	R	S
10810	156	ILGL AD LSD PUBL		4A20E	4A20D	4A20D	A13A																		
10820	156	ILGL AD AMP PRIV		4A20F	4A20E	4A20E	A13A																		
10830	156	ILGL AD AMP PUBL		4A20G	4A20F	4A20F	A13A																		
10840	156	ILGL AD HRN PRIV		4A20H	4A20G	4A20G	A13A																		
10850	156	ILGL AD HRN PUBL		4A20I	4A20H	4A20H	A13A																		
10860	156	ILGL AD DRNK PRV		4A20J	4A20I	4A20I	A13A																		
10870	156	ILGL AD DRNK PBL		4A20K	4A20J	4A20J	A13A																		
10880	157	CRIME 2 USE MARJ	4A32	4A21	4A21	4A21	A13C																		
10890	157	LEGAL 2 SELL MRJ	4A33	4A22	4A22	4A22	A13C																		
10900	157	USE<MJ IF LEGAL	4A34	4A23	4A23	4A23	A13C																		
10910	157	CMP SATFD W/JOB		4D02	4D02	4D02			C														P			
10920	158	I CNT CHNG WORLD	4A28A	4D03A	4D03A	4D03A									I	J								Q		
10930	158	SOCTY WONT LAST	4A28B	4D03B	4D03B	4D03B						F				J										
10940	158	THG TUF,TCHN SLV	4A28C	4D03C	4D03C	4D03C									I	J								Q		
10950	158	NO HOPE 4 WORLD	4A28D	4D03D	4D03D	4D03D										J								Q		
10960	158	WNDR PURPS 2 LIF	4A28E	4D03E	4D03E	4D03E										J								Q		
10970	158	WRLD UPHVL 10 YR	4A28F	4D03F	4D03F	4D03F										J								Q		
10980	159	ANNIHLTN IN LFTM	4A28G	4D03G	4D03G	4D03G										J								Q		
10990	159	HMN RCE RSILIENT	4A28H	4D03H	4D03H	4D03H										J								Q		
11000	159	#X BEER/LIFETIME		4D04A	4D04A	4D04A	A01A																		
11010	159	#X BEER/LAST12MO		4D04B	4D04B	4D04B	A01B																		
11020	159	#X BEER/LAST30DA		4D04C	4D04C	4D04C	A01C																		
11030	159	5+BR/LST2WK,10+X		4D05	4D05	4D05	A01D																		
11040	160	#X WINE/LIFETIME		4D06A	4D06A	4D06A	A01A																		
11050	160	#X WINE/LAST12MO		4D06B	4D06B	4D06B	A01B																		
11060	160	#X WINE/LAST30DA		4D06C	4D06C	4D06C	A01C																		
11070	160	#X 20OZ+ WN/2 WK		4D07	4D07	4D07	A01D																		
11080	160	#X LIQR/LIFETIME		4D08A	4D08A	4D08A	A01A																		
11090	161	#X LIQR/LAST12MO		4D08B	4D08B	4D08B	A01B																		
11100	161	#X LIQR/LAST30DA		4D08C	4D08C	4D08C	A01C																		
11110	161	#X 5+LIQ/LST 2WK		4D09	4D09	4D09	A01D																		
11120	161	MLTRY GET AHEAD		4E01A	4E01A	4E01A												L							
11130	161	MLTRY MORE ED		4E01B	4E01B	4E01B		B										L							
11140	161	MLTRY ADVNC RESP		4E01C	4E01C	4E01C												L							
11150	162	MLTRY >FLFLLG JB		4E01D	4E01D	4E01D			C									L							
11160	162	MLTRY IDEAS HERD		4E01E	4E01E	4E01E												L							
11170	162	EXTNT MLTRY JSTC		4E02	4E02	4E02												L							
11180	162	MLTRY DSCRM WOMN		4E03	4E03	4E03				D								L							
11190	162	MLTRY DSCRM BLKS		4E04	4E04	4E04												L		N					
11200	162	>FAIR MLTRY CVLN		4E05	4E05	4E05												L							
11210		-MLTRY COUP U.S.		4E06	4E06										H			L							
11220	163	NT VOL 4 NEC WAR		4E07	4E07	4E06												L							
11230	163	P'IDEA OF DO LIF	4A27A	4E08A	4E08A	4E07A													M						
11240	163	P'IDEA OF LSR TM	4A27B	4E08B	4E08B	4E07B			C										M						
11250	163	P'IDEA OF CLTHES	4A27C	4E08C	4E08C	4E07C													M						
11260	163	P'IDEA OF SPND $	4A27D	4E08D	4E08D	4E07D													M						
11270	163	P'IDEA OF DATE	4A27E	4E08E	4E08E	4E07E													M						
11280	164	P'IDEA OF OK DRK	4A27F	4E08F	4E08F	4E07F													M						
11290	164	P'IDEA OF OK MRJ	4A27G	4E08G	4E08G	4E07G													M						
11300	164	P'IDEA OF OK DRG	4A27H	4E08H	4E08H	4E07H													M						
11310	164	P'IDEA OF VALUES	4A27I	4E08I	4E08I	4E07I													M						
11320	164	P'IDEA OF EDUC	4A27J	4E08J	4E08J	4E07J		B											M						
11330	164	P'IDEA OF SX RLS	4A27K	4E08K	4E08K	4E07K				D									M						
11340	164	P'IDEA OF ECLOGY	4A27L	4E08L	4E08L	4E07L						F							M						
11350	165	P'IDEA OF RCL IS	4A27M	4E08M	4E08M	4E07M													M	N					
11360	165	P'IDEA OF RLGION	4A27N	4E08N	4E08N	4E07N							G						M						
11370	165	P'IDEA OF PLTICS	4A27O	4E08O	4E08O	4E07O								H					M						
11380	165	PRNT DAP CIGS	4A35A	4E09A	4E09A	4E08A	A12A																		
11390	165	PRNT DAP TRY MRJ	4A35B	4E09B	4E09B	4E08B	A12A																		
11400	165	PRNT DAP MJ OCC	4A35C	4E09C	4E09C	4E08C	A12A																		
11410	165	PRNT DAP MJ REG	4A35D	4E09D	4E09D	4E08D	A12A																		
11420	166	PRNT DAP TRY LSD	4A35E	4E09E	4E09E	4E08E	A12A																		
11430	166	PRNT DAP TRY AMP	4A35F	4E09F	4E09F	4E08F	A12A																		
11440	166	PRNT DAP 1-2DR/D	4A35G	4E09G	4E09G	4E08G	A12A																		
11450	166	PRNT DAP 4-5DR/D	4A35H	4E09H	4E09H	4E08H	A12A																		
11460	166	PRNT DAP 5+DR/WE	4A35I	4E09I	4E09I	4E08I	A12A																		

ITEM REFERENCE NUMBER	PAGE LOCATION (IN THIS VOLUME)	ITEM DESCRIPTION (ABBREVIATED)	1975	1976	1977	1978	A	SUBJECT AREA (B–S)
11470		FRD DAP CIGS			4E10A		A12B	
11480		FRD DAP TRY MARJ			4E10B		A12B	
11490		FRD DAP MJ OCC			4E10C		A12B	
11500		FRD DAP MJ REG			4E10D		A12B	
11510		FRD DAP TRY LSD			4E10E		A12B	
11520		FRD DAP TRY AMP			4E10F		A12B	
11530		FRD DAP 1-2DR/DA			4E10G		A12B	
11540		FRD DAP 4-5DR/DA			4E10H		A12B	
11550		FRD DAP 5+DR/WKD			4E10I		A12B	
11560	168	H&W WK,WF AL HWK			4E11A	4E10A		D
11570	168	H&W WK,WF MS HWK			4E11B	4E10B		D
11580	168	H&W WK,DO = HWRK			4E11C	4E10C		D
11590	168	H&W WK,HB MS HWK			4E11D	4E10D		D
11600	168	H&W WK,HB AL HWK			4E11E	4E10E		D
11610	169	H&W WK+CH,W CHCR			4E12A	4E11A		D
11620	169	H&W WK+CH,W>CHCR			4E12B	4E11B		D
11630	169	H&W WK+CH,=CHCAR			4E12C	4E11C		D
11640	169	H&W WK+CH,H>CHCR			4E12D	4E11D		D
11650	169	H&W WK+CH,H CHCR			4E12E	4E11E		D
11660	170	WR/NT NUCLER WAR	5A04A	5A03A	5A03A	5A03A		J
11670	170	WR/NT POP GROWTH	5A04B	5A03B	5A03B	5A03B		E J
11680	170	WR/NT CRIME&VLNC	5A04C	5A03C	5A03C	5A03C		J
11690	170	WR/NT POLLUTION	5A04D	5A03D	5A03D	5A03D		F J
11700	170	WR/NT ENRGY SHRT	5A04E	5A03E	5A03E	5A03E		F J
11710	171	WR/NT RACE RELTN	5A04F	5A03F	5A03F	5A03F		J N
11720	171	WR/NT HNGR&PVRTY	5A04G	5A03G	5A03G	5A03G		F J
11730	171	WR/NT USE OPN LD	5A04H	5A03H	5A03H	5A03H		F J
11740	171	WR/NT URBN DECAY	5A04I	5A03I	5A03I	5A03I		J
11750	171	WR/NT ECON PRBLM	5A04J	5A03J	5A03J	5A03J		J
11760	171	WR/NT DRUG ABUSE	5A04K	5A03K	5A03K	5A03K		J
11770	171	XPRC MK R GD SPS		5A04A	5A04A	5A04A		D
11780	172	XPRC MK R GD PRT		5A04B	5A04B	5A04B		D
11790	172	XPRC MK R GD WKR		5A04C	5A04C	5A04C		C
11800	172	PLC WRK LG CORPN	5A09A	5A05A	5A05A	5A05A		C
11810	172	PLC WRK SM BSNSS	5A09B	5A05B	5A05B	5A05B		C
11820	172	PLC WRK GVT AGCY	5A09C	5A05C	5A05C	5A05C		C H
11830	172	PLC WRK MLTY SVC	5A09D	5A05D	5A05D	5A05D		C L
11840	172	PLC WRK SCH/UNIV	5A09E	5A05E	5A05E	5A05E		B C
11850	173	PLC WRK PLC DEPT	5A09F	5A05F	5A05F	5A05F		C
11860	173	PLC WRK SOC SVCS	5A09G	5A05G	5A05G	5A05G		C O
11870	173	PLC WRK SML GRP	5A09H	5A05H	5A05H	5A05H		C
11880	173	PLC WRK SLF EMPL	5A09I	5A05I	5A05I	5A05I		C
11890	173	RCL CNTCT SCHOOL		5A07A	5A07A	5A07A		B N
11900	173	RCL CNTCT NGHBHD		5A07B	5A07B	5A07B		N
11910	174	RCL CNTCT CHURCH		5A07C	5A07C	5A07C		G N
11920	174	RCL CNTCT SPORTS		5A07D	5A07D	5A07D		N
11930	174	RCL CNTCT CLUBS		5A07E	5A07E	5A07E		N
11940	174	RCL CNTCT JOB		5A07F	5A07F	5A07F		C N
11950	174	B/W RLTNS WRSE	5A15	5A08	5A08	5A08		N
11960	174	DNT HV DRVR LCNS	5A22	5A09	5A09	5A09		F
11970	174	DONT OWN CAR	5A23	5A10	5A10	5A10		F
11980	175	NEVR USE OTHS CR	5A24	5A11	5A11	5A11		F
11990	175	R CUT DRIVING		5A12	5A12	5A12		F
12000	175	R CUT ELECTRICTY		5A13	5A13	5A13		F
12010	175	RDCE HEAT R'S HM		5A14	5A14	5A14		F
12020	175	ENJOY SHOPPING	5A35A	5A15A	5A15A	5A15A		F
12030	175	CARE LATST FASHN	5A35B	5A15B	5A15B	5A15B		F
12040	176	CR FAM HV NBR HV	5A35C	5A15C	5A15C	5A15C		F
12050	176	XPCT 2 OWN>PRNTS	5A36	5A16	5A16	5A16		F
12060	176	LST CNT OWN>PRNT	5A37	5A17	5A17	5A17		F
12070	176	WRRY ABT OW CTRY	5A19A	5A18A	5A18A	5A18A		O
12080	176	BTTR IF CTZ WRLD	5A19C	5A18B	5A18B	5A18B		O
12090	177	-SYMP TWD STARVG	5A19E	5A18C	5A18C	5A18C		F O
12100	177	MNRTY NT MY BSNS	5A19F	5A18D	5A18D	5A18D		N O
12110	177	UPST PL TR -FAIR	5A19G	5A18E	5A18E	5A18E		O
12120	177	HELP POOR W MY $	5A19I	5A18F	5A18F	5A18F		O

ITEM REFERENCE NUMBER	PAGE LOCATION (IN THIS VOLUME)	ITEM DESCRIPTION (ABBREVIATED)	1975	1976	1977	1978	A	B	C	D	E	F	G	H	I	J	K	L	M	N	O	P	Q	R	S
12130	177	-MY PRB OT ND HP	5A19K	5A18G	5A18G	5A18G																O				
12140	177	RB CHNG ETG HABT		5A18H	5A18H	5A18H											K					O				
12150	178	FULLR LVS IF MRY	5A12A	5A18J	5A18J	5A18J				D																
12160	178	ENCRG=INDP DT/SN	5A12B	5A18K	5A18K	5A18K				D																
12170	178	BNG MOTH V FULFL	5A12D	5A18L	5A18L	5A18L				D																
12180	178	FTHR>TIME W CHLD	5A12G	5A18M	5A18M	5A18M				D																
12190	178	HSB MAK IMP DCSN	5A12H	5A18N	5A18N	5A18N				D																
12200	179	CTB TO UNTD FUND	5A20A	5A20A	5A20A	5A20A																O				
12210	179	CTB TO INTL RELF	5A20B	5A20B	5A20B	5A20B																O				
12220	179	CTB TO MNRTY GRP	5A20C	5A20C	5A20C	5A20C														N	O				
12230	179	CTB TO RELGS ORG	5A20D	5A20D	5A20D	5A20D							G									O				
12240	180	CTB TO PLTCL PTY	5A20E	5A20E	5A20E	5A20E								H								O				
12250	180	CTB TO CTZN LBBY	5A20F	5A20F	5A20F	5A20F								H	I							O				
12260	180	CTB TO VS DISEAS	5A20G	5A20G	5A20G	5A20G																O				
12270	180	CTB TO POP PRBMS	5A20H	5A20H	5A20H	5A20H					E											O				
12280	180	CTB TO ENVIR PBM	5A20I	5A20I	5A20I	5A20I						F										O				
12290	181	DSCM WN COLLG ED	5A21A	5A22A	5A22A	5A22A		B		D																
12300	181	DSCM WN LDRSHP	5A21B	5A22B	5A22B	5A22B				D																
12310	181	DSCM WN EXEC/BSN	5A21C	5A22C	5A22C	5A22C			C	D																
12320	181	DSCM WN TOP/PRFN	5A21D	5A22D	5A22D	5A22D			C	D																
12330	181	DSCM WN SKL LABR	5A21E	5A22E	5A22E	5A22E			C	D																
12340	181	DSCM WN PLTCL OF	5A21F	5A22F	5A22F	5A22F				D				H												
12350	182	DSCM WN=PAY=WK	5A21G	5A22G	5A22G	5A22G			C	D																
12360	182	RSK OF CIG1+PK/D	5A41A	5A23A	5A23A	5A23A	A14A																			
12370	182	RSK OF MJ 1-2 X	5A41B	5A23B	5A23B	5A23B	A14A																			
12380	182	RSK OF MJ OCSNLY	5A41C	5A23C	5A23C	5A23C	A14A																			
12390	182	RSK OF MJ REGLY	5A41D	5A23D	5A23D	5A23D	A14A																			
12400	182	RSK OF LSD 1-2 X	5A41E	5A23E	5A23E	5A23E	A14A																			
12410	183	RSK OF LSD REGLY	5A41F	5A23F	5A23F	5A23F	A14A																			
12420	183	RSK OF 'H' 1-2 X	5A41G	5A23G	5A23G	5A23G	A14A																			
12430	183	RSK OF 'H' OCSNL	5A41H	5A23H	5A23H	5A23H	A14A																			
12440	183	RSK OF 'H' REGLY	5A41I	5A23I	5A23I	5A23I	A14A																			
12450	183	RSK OF BARB 1-2X	5A41J	5A23J	5A23J	5A23J	A14A																			
12460	183	RSK OF BARB REGY	5A41K	5A23K	5A23K	5A23K	A14A																			
12470	183	RSK OF AMPH 1-2X	5A41L	5A23L	5A23L	5A23L	A14A																			
12480	184	RSK OF AMPH REG	5A41M	5A23M	5A23M	5A23M	A14A																			
12490	184	RSK OF COKE 1-2X	5A41N	5A23N	5A23N	5A23N	A14A																			
12500	184	RSK OF COKE REG	5A41O	5A23O	5A23O	5A23O	A14A																			
12510	184	RSK OF 1-2 DRINK	5A41P	5A23P	5A23P	5A23P	A14A																			
12520	184	RSK OF 1-2 DR/DA	5A41Q	5A23Q	5A23Q	5A23Q	A14A																			
12530	184	RSK OF 4-5 DR/DA	5A41R	5A23R	5A23R	5A23R	A14A																			
12540	184	RSK OF 5+DR/WKND	5A41S	5A23S	5A23S	5A23S	A14A																			
12550	185	POS ATT TWD SELF	5A39A	5D01A	5D01A	5D01A																		Q		
12560	185	LUCK>IMP HRD WRK	5A39B	5D01B	5D01B	5D01B																		Q		
12570	185	AM PRSN OF WORTH	5A39C	5D01C	5D01C	5D01C																		Q		
12580	185	DO WELL AS OTHRS	5A39D	5D01D	5D01D	5D01D																		Q		
12590	185	TRY GT AHD,STOPD	5A39E	5D01E	5D01E	5D01E																		Q		
12600	185	PLNNG MKS UNHPPY	5A39F	5D01F	5D01F	5D01F																		Q		
12610	186	ACPT LIFE->HAPPR	5A39G	5D01G	5D01G	5D01G																		Q		
12620	186	SATISFD W MYSELF	5A39H	5D01H	5D01H	5D01H																	P	Q		
12630	186	PPL LK ME -CHANC	5A39I	5D01I	5D01I	5D01I																		Q		
12640	186	MY PLANS DO WORK			5D01J	5D01J																		Q		
12650	186	OFTN FEEL LONELY			5D01K	5D01K													M					Q		
12660	186	-MUCH TO B PROUD			5D01L	5D01L																		Q		
12670	186	ALWYS SM1 HELP R			5D01M	5D01M													M					Q		
12680	187	I AM NO GOOD			5D01N	5D01N																		Q		
12690	187	OFTN FL LEFT OUT			5D01O	5D01O													M					Q		
12700	187	PPL MASTER FATE			5D01P	5D01P																		Q		
12710	187	USLY SM1 TALK TO			5D01Q	5D01Q													M					Q		
12720	187	I DO WRONG THING			5D01R	5D01R																		Q		
12730	187	OFT WSH MOR FRND			5D01S	5D01S													M					Q		
12740	187	PLANS->BTR RSLTS			5D01T	5D01T																		Q		
12750	188	MY LIFE NT USEFL			5D01U	5D01U																		Q		
12760	188	USLY FRDS BE WTH			5D01V	5D01V													M					Q		
12770	188	LV TGTH=BD MRLTY		5D05	5D02	5D02				D																
12780	188	PSN TKG MJ/AMBTS		5D02A			A12D																			

ITEM REFERENCE NUMBER	PAGE LOCATION (IN THIS VOLUME)	ITEM DESCRIPTION (ABBREVIATED)	QUESTIONNAIRE LOCATION BY YEAR (FORM, SECTION, AND QUESTION NUMBER)				SUBJECT AREA	
			1975	1976	1977	1978	A	B C D E F G H I J K L M N O P Q R S
12790		PSN TKG MJ/-SOCL		5D02B			A12D	
12800		PSN TKG MJ/CNFMG		5D02C			A12D	
12810		PSN TKG MJ/CRMNL		5D02D			A12D	
12820		PSN TKG MJ/-STBL		5D02E			A12D	
12830		PSN TKG MJ/INTRS		5D02F			A12D	
12840		PSN TKG MJ/RBLS		5D02G			A12D	
12850		PSN TKG MJ/SNSBL		5D02H			A12D	
12860		PSN TKG MJ/SX PR		5D02I			A12D	
12870		PSN TKG MJ/WKWLD		5D02J			A12D	
12880	188	FAM-MAR=BD MRLTY		5D06	5D03	5D03	D	
12890		PSN TKG DG/AMBTS		5D03A			A12D	
12900		PSN TKG DG/-SOCL		5D03B			A12D	
12910		PSN TKG DG/CNFMG		5D03C			A12D	
12920		PSN TKG DG/CRMNL		5D03D			A12D	
12930		PSN TKG DG/-STBL		5D03E			A12D	
12940		PSN TKG DG/INTRS		5D03F			A12D	
12950		PSN TKG DG/RBLS		5D03G			A12D	
12960		PSN TKG DG/SNSBL		5D03H			A12D	
12970		PSN TKG DG/SX PR		5D03I			A12D	
12980		PSN TKG DG/WKWLD		5D03J			A12D	
12990	188	I HAVE ENOUGH $			5D04A	5D04A	C	
13000	189	I LACK $ FR BILL			5D04B	5D04B	C	
13010	189	I WRY @-FINDG JOB			5D04C	5D04C	C	
13020	189	I CAN FIND JOB			5D04D	5D04D	C	
13030	189	I CAN KEEP MY JOB			5D04E	5D04E	C	
13040	189	I WRY @ LOSS MY JOB			5D04F	5D04F	C	
13050	189	R'S STATE LAW/MJ		5D04	5D05	5D05	A13D	
13060	190	I/MJ USR,>CREATV			5E01A	5E01A	A11D	
13070	190	I/MJ USR,<SENSBL			5E01B	5E01B	A11D	
13080	190	I/MJ USR,>INTRST			5E01C	5E01C	A11D	
13090	190	I/MJ USR,<HRDWKG			5E01D	5E01D	A11D	
13100	190	I/MJ USR,>INDPND			5E01E	5E01E	A11D	
13110	190	I/MJ USR,>UNSTBL			5E01F	5E01F	A11D	
13120	190	I/MJ USR,>CNCRND			5E01G	5E01G	A11D	
13130	190	I/MJ USR,>WKWLD			5E01H	5E01H	A11D	
13140	191	I/MJ USR,>CRMNL			5E01I	5E01I	A11D	
13150		FAM+REL GD/CHILD		5E01A			D	M
13160		FAM+REL GD/PARNT		5E01B			D	M
13170		FAM+REL GD/GRPNT		5E01C			D	M
13180		FAM+REL,R LIK/PT		5E01D			D	M
13190	191	PPL/MJUSR>CREATV			5E02A	5E02A	A12D	
13200	191	PPL/MJUSR<SENSBL			5E02B	5E02B	A12D	
13210	191	PPL/MJUSR>INTRST			5E02C	5E02C	A12D	
13220	191	PPL/MJUSR<HRDWKG			5E02D	5E02D	A12D	
13230	191	PPL/MJUSR>INDPND			5E02E	5E02E	A12D	
13240	191	PPL/MJUSR>UNSTBL			5E02F	5E02F	A12D	
13250	191	PPL/MJUSR>CNCRND			5E02G	5E02G	A12D	
13260	192	PPL/MJUSR>WKWLD			5E02H	5E02H	A12D	
13270	192	PPL/MJUSR>CRMNL			5E02I	5E02I	A12D	
13280		FAM+CPL GD/CHILD		5E02A			D	
13290		FAM+CPL GD/PARNT		5E02B			D	
13300		FAM+CPL GD/GRPNT		5E02C			D	
13310		FAM+CPL,LIK/PRNT		5E02D			D	
13320		FAM+CPL,LIK/-CHD		5E02E			D	
13330	192	I/DG USR,>CREATV			5E03A	5E03A	A11D	
13340	192	I/DG USR,<SENSBL			5E03B	5E03B	A11D	
13350	192	I/DG USR,>INTRST			5E03C	5E03C	A11D	
13360	192	I/DG USR,<HRDWKG			5E03D	5E03D	A11D	
13370	192	I/DG USR,>INDPND			5E03E	5E03E	A11D	
13380	192	I/DG USR,>UNSTBL			5E03F	5E03F	A11D	
13390	193	I/DG USR,>CNCRND			5E03G	5E03G	A11D	
13400	193	I/DG USR,>WKWLD			5E03H	5E03H	A11D	
13410	193	I/DG USR,>CRMNL			5E03I	5E03I	A11D	
13420		CPL+OTH +CHD MAR		5E03A			D	
13430		CPL+OTH +CHD DVC		5E03B			D	
13440		CPL+OTH +MAR CPL		5E03C			D	

ITEM REFERENCE NUMBER	PAGE LOCATION (IN THIS VOLUME)	ITEM DESCRIPTION (ABBREVIATED)	1975	1976	1977	1978	A	B	C	D	E	F	G	H	I	J	K	L	M	N	O	P	Q	R	S
13450		CPL+OTH+DIV PRT		5E03D						D															
13460		CPL+OTH+UNMARRD		5E03E						D															
13470		CPL+OTH,LK,MR PT		5E03F						D															
13480		CPL+OTH,LK,DVC P		5E03G						D															
13490	193	PPL/DGUSR>CREATV			5E04A	5E04A	A12D																		
13500	193	PPL/DGUSR<SENSBL			5E04B	5E04B	A12D																		
13510	193	PPL/DGUSR>INTRST			5E04C	5E04C	A12D																		
13520	193	PPL/DGUSR<HRDWKG			5E04D	5E04D	A12D																		
13530	193	PPL/DGUSR>INDPND			5E04E	5E04E	A12D																		
13540	194	PPL/DGUSR>UNSTBL			5E04F	5E04F	A12D																		
13550	194	PPL/DGUSR>CNCRND			5E04G	5E04G	A12D																		
13560	194	PPL/DGUSR>WKWLD			5E04H	5E04H	A12D																		
13570	194	PPL/DGUSR>CRMNL			5E04I	5E04I	A12D																		
13580	194	STS SCH RT FAMLY		5E05A	5E06A	5E06A		B																R	
13590	194	STS SCH LDS STU		5E05B	5E06B	5E06B		B											M						
13600	195	STS SCH NIC CAR		5E05C	5E06C	5E06C		B				F													
13610	195	STS SCH HI GRDE		5E05D	5E06D	5E06D		B																	
13620	195	STS SCH GD ATHLT		5E05E	5E06E	5E06E		B																	
13630	195	STS SCH INTLCTL		5E05F	5E06F	5E06F		B																	
13640	195	STS SCH PLN CLG		5E05G	5E06G	5E06G		B																	
13650	195	DRG USE+,MAJ STD		5E06A	5E07A	5E07A	A12C																		
13660	196	DRG USE+,MY FRND		5E06B	5E07B	5E07B	A12B																		
13670	196	DRG USE+,MY FLGS			5E07C	5E07C	A11D																		
08780	196	OFT W PL TK QUAL		5E07D	5E08D	5E08D	A02B																		
08835	197	OFT W PL TK INHL		5E07J	5E08J	5E08J	A02B																		
13700		BY SOON HAIR DRY		2E10A								F													
13710		BY SOON WT/S SKI		2E10B								F													
13720		BY SOON CAMERA		2E10C								F													
13730		BY SOON WATCH		2E10D								F													
13740		BY SOON HKG BKPK		2E10E								F													
13750		BY SOON CK RADIO		2E10F								F													
13760		BY SOON EL SHAVR		2E10G								F													
13770		BY SOON TENIS RQ		2E10H								F													
13780		BY SOON TV SET		2E10I								F													
13790		BY SOON BICYCLE		2E10J								F													
13800		BY SOON CAR		2E10K								F													
13810		BY SOON TAPE REC		2E10L								F													
13820		BY SOON ELT CALC		2E10M								F													
13830		BY SOON BT/SNMBL		2E10N								F													
13835	138	IMP HAV 1 CAR		3E12A		3E11A						F													
13840	138	IMP HAV 2 CARS		3E12B		3E11B						F													
13850	138	IMP HAV LARG CAR		3E12C		3E11C						F													
13860	139	IMP HAV NW CR OF		3E12D		3E11D						F													
13870	139	IMP HAV NW CLTHS		3E12E		3E11E						F													
13880	139	IMP HAV OWN HSE		3E12F		3E11F						F													
13890	139	IMP HAV BIG YARD		3E12G		3E11G						F													
13900	139	IMP HAV NEAT LWN		3E12H		3E11H						F													
13910	139	IMP HAV APPLINCS		3E12I		3E11I						F													
13920	139	IMP HAV G STEREO		3E12J		3E11J						F													
13930	139	IMP HAV VAC HSE		3E12K		3E11K						F													
13940	140	IMP HAV REC VEH		3E12L		3E11L						F													
16320	111	EFCTV WRIT OFCLS				2E04A								H	I										
16330	111	EFCTV WRK PL CPN				2E04B								H	I										
16340	111	EFCTV VOTING				2E04C								H	I										
16350	111	EFCTV PETITIONS				2E04D								H	I										
16360	111	EFCTV BOYCOTT				2E04E								H	I										
16370	111	EFCTV LWFL DMSTN				2E04F								H	I										
16380	111	EFCTV OCPY BLDGS				2E04G								H	I										
16390	112	EFCTV WLDCT STRK				2E04H								H	I										
16400	112	EFCTV BLK TRAFIC				2E04I								H	I										
16410	112	EFCTV DAMAG THNG				2E04J								H	I										
16420	112	EFCTV PSNL VLNC				2E04K								H	I										
16430	112	SAT EVB CAR POOL				2E05A						F									O				
16440	112	SAT EAT<BEEF>GRN				2E05B						F									O				
16450	113	SAT TAX FR ECLGY				2E05C						F													
17860	166	DESRD LVG RURAL				4E09A						F													

ITEM REFERENCE NUMBER	PAGE LOCATION (IN THIS VOLUME)	ITEM DESCRIPTION (ABBREVIATED)	QUESTIONNAIRE LOCATION BY YEAR (FORM, SECTION, AND QUESTION NUMBER)				SUBJECT AREA	
			1975	1976	1977	1978	A	B C D E F G H I J K L M N O P Q R S
17870	167	DESRD LVG SM TWN				4E09B		F
17880	167	DESRD LVG SM CTY				4E09C		F
17890	167	DESRD LVG SUBURB				4E09D		F
17900	167	DESRD LVG LG CTY				4E09E		F
17910	167	DSRD HSG 1 FAMLY				4E09F		F
17920	167	DSRD HSG 2 FAMLY				4E09G		F
17930	167	DSRD HSG CNDMINM				4E09H		F
17940	167	DSRD HSG APT BLD				4E09I		F
17950	168	DSRD HSG HI RISE				4E09J		F
20590	129	12MO NR OTH MARJ		3A29A	3A29A	3A29A	A02B	
20600	129	12MO NR OTH LSD		3A29B	3A29B	3A29B	A02B	
20610	129	12MO NR OTH PSYC		3A29C	3A29C	3A29C	A02B	
20620	129	12MO NR OTH AMPH		3A29D	3A29D	3A29D	A02B	
20630	130	12MO NR OTH BARB		3A29E	3A29E	3A29E	A02B	
20640	130	12MO NR OTH TRQL		3A29F	3A29F	3A29F	A02B	
20650	130	12MO NR OTH COKE		3A29G	3A29G	3A29G	A02B	
20660	130	12MO NR OTH HRN		3A29H	3A29H	3A29H	A02B	
20670	130	12MO NR OTH NARC		3A29I	3A29I	3A29I	A02B	
20680	130	12MO NR OTH ALCL		3A29J	3A29J	3A29J	A02B	

Appendix A
Sampling Error Estimates and Tables

All of the percentages reported in this volume are really *estimates* of the response percentages that would have been obtained if, instead of using a sample survey, we had asked all high schools throughout the United States to participate, and in all schools that agreed to participate we had invited the whole senior class to fill out the questionnaires. The question naturally arises: How accurate are the present percentage estimates based on a limited number of schools and seniors? For any particular percentage resulting from a sample survey we cannot know exactly how much error has resulted from sampling, but we can make reasonably good estimates of "confidence intervals" — ranges within which the "true" population value is very likely to fall. The word "true" in this context is defined quite narrowly; it refers only to the value that would be found if we had set out to survey the total population — all high school seniors in the United States. Thus this concept of "true" population value does *not* take account of biases that might occur due to refusals, distortion of responses, faulty question wording, and other factors. Each of these sources of possible error is discussed in the "Representativeness and Validity" section of the Introduction to this volume. The reader is urged to review this material and take it into account along with the sampling error estimates included in this appendix.

The estimation of confidence intervals in surveys involving complex samples can be a highly complicated combination of statistical science plus informed judgment. It is an area in which there is no single "right answer" or "best approach." We suspect that many of those using this volume will not be especially interested in *how* we have chosen to solve the problems involved in estimating confidence intervals, so long as we provide guidelines

that can be applied in a fairly simple and straightforward manner. This appendix is designed to accomplish that. Appendix B provides a more extensive discussion of how we obtained the confidence intervals shown here, and it also provides guidelines for computing specific confidence intervals for a wider range of possible applications than can be covered in the tables provided in this appendix.

A very rough example of a confidence interval can be stated in these terms: For percentages based on the total sample (all five questionnaire forms), the "true" values are rarely more than 1.5 percent higher or lower than the percentage estimates reported in this volume. How rarely? The chances are much lower than 1 in 20. Indeed, many of the percentages reported for the total sample are accurate to within one percent.

Of course, most of the data reported here are based on items included only in one or another of the five questionnaire forms. Since such percentages are based on only one-fifth of the total sample, they are somewhat less accurate. The loss in accuracy is less than might be imagined, however, for reasons spelled out in Appendix B. For present purposes, it is enough to say that percentages based on 3,000 or more seniors responding to one questionnaire form are rarely (less than 1 in 20) farther than 2.4 percent away from the "true" value.

We have thus far provided two very rough illustrations of confidence intervals — a range of ±1.5 percent for percentages based on the total sample, and a range of ±2.4 percent for percentages based on the number of seniors responding to one questionnaire form. While these two intervals provide some notion of the overall range of accuracy of the sample, they fall short of our needs in a number of respects. We need to be able to assign confidence intervals for subgroups such as males, females, those who plan to complete college, and so forth, all of which involve smaller numbers of cases and thus some reduction in accuracy. We also need to take account of the fact that, other things equal, confidence intervals grow smaller when one moves from the middle of the scale (percentages near 50 percent) to the extremes (e.g., 4 percent or 96 percent). Further, we need to provide guidelines for evaluating the *difference* between two percentages; for example, we may wish to know whether the difference between male and female percentages in response to a particular question is large enough so that it is not likely to be merely the result of sampling error. Another type of difference of considerable interest is that between percentages from two different years; for example, we may wish to know whether an increase in the percentage of daily marijuana users from one year to the next is large enough to be considered a statistically significant change.

Each of the requirements mentioned above is taken into account in the tables of confidence intervals which follow.

Confidence Intervals for Single Percentages

Table A-1 provides confidence intervals for single percentages that are reasonably good approximations for most *variables* and for most *subgroups* (as well as for the total sample). The table entries slightly underestimate the confidence intervals for regional subgroups and for blacks. These underestimates can be corrected reasonably well by multiplying the entries in Table A-1 by a factor of 1.1 for data based on a single form and by a factor of 1.33 for data based on all five forms. A more serious problem is that the table entries substantially underestimate the confidence intervals for certain variables which tend to be somewhat homogeneous within schools, as well as other factors likely to show clustering according to geographical area or socioeconomic level. A discussion of some of these variables is provided at the end of this appendix.

Table A-1 accommodates various numbers of cases (presented as different columns in the table), and various percentages (presented as different rows in the table). The table entries, when added to and subtracted from the observed percentage, establish the 95 percent confidence interval (calculated as 1.96 sampling errors). Thus, for example, to determine the accuracy of a result of 67.4 percent based on a sample of 1,632 cases, one should first look for the closest values in the table (in this case, about 70 percent and a number of cases approximately equal to 1,500); next determine the values to be added to and subtracted from

the observed percentage (in this case the values would be +2.8 percent and -2.9 percent); and then compute the confidence interval around the observed percentage of 67.4 percent (in this case an interval ranging from 64.5 percent to 70.2 percent). This procedure yields an interval such that, for most variables, the chances are 95 in 100 that if all high school seniors in the country had been asked to participate in the survey the resulting percentage would fall within the interval.

Confidence Intervals for Differences between Two Percentages

Table A-2 provides confidence intervals for differences between certain percentages. Specifically, the table can be used for *comparisons* between males and females, between those who do and do not plan to complete four years of college, and between those falling into different categories of the five-level index of drug usage. The above comparisons are appropriate for data from any single year (e.g., male seniors in 1976 compared with female seniors in 1976, or the "marijuana only" seniors in 1977 compared with the "no illicit drugs" seniors in 1977). Table A-2 is also useful in assessing *one-year* trends for any of the above subgroups as well as for the total sample. For example, one may be interested in a confidence interval (or significance level) for the difference between the percentage of female seniors in 1977 who used marijuana and the percentage of female seniors in 1978 who did so. The values in Table A-2 are appropriate for confidence intervals across adjacent years (e.g., 1976 compared with 1977), provided the same subgroup (e.g., females) is being considered both years. The confidence intervals for comparisons across non-adjacent years (e.g., 1976 compared with 1978), are slightly larger.

With appropriate corrections, the entries in Table A-2 can be used for trends covering more than one year and for trends or comparisons involving regional subgroups and blacks. Each of these applications requires some upward adjustment of the table entries; guidelines for such adjustments are provided in the notes accompanying Table A-2.

For information on the derivation of Table A-2 and for guidelines to be used in computing confidence intervals not covered in that table, the reader is referred to Appendix B.

In order to find the appropriate confidence interval in Table A-2, one must first locate that portion of the table which deals with percentage values closest to the two percentages being compared (for example, if one wished to compare a value of 28.1 percent with one of 35.4 percent, the "p = 30 percent or 70 percent" portion of the table would be closest). The next step is to locate the specific table entry which corresponds most closely to the numbers of cases involved in the two percentages being compared (e.g., if those numbers were 1,478 and 1,563 for 28.1 percent and 35.4 percent, the correct table entry would be 3.9 percent). That table entry, when added to and subtracted from the difference between the two percentages, yields the 95 percent confidence interval for the difference. (In the above illustration that would be 7.3 percent ±3.9 percent or an interval from 3.4 percent to 11.2 percent.) The chances are only 1 in 20 that the "true" difference between two percentages lies outside of this interval.

Another use of Table A-2 is to test whether a difference between two percentages is "statistically significant." If the table entry is smaller than the difference between the two percentages (as is true in the above illustration), then the difference is statistically significant at the 95 percent level (sometimes indicated as p<.05).

Some Cautions

The tables provided here are based on averages of large numbers of sampling errors computed across a wide range of the variables which appear in this volume, as well as across all of the subgroups for which data are reported here. We are confident that the values in the tables are reasonably accurate for most purposes, but we must repeat the caution that the tables slightly underestimate confidence intervals for the following groups and comparisons:

Blacks

Regions (Northeast, North Central, South, West)

Comparisons among regions

Comparisons across non-adjacent years (e.g., 1976 vs. 1978)

A more important problem is that the tables substantially underestimate the confidence intervals for certain variables that, for various reasons, show greater than average homogeneity within schools. After an extensive, but by no means exhaustive, sampling of the kinds of variables which might show such clustering by school, we can provide the following examples of the kinds of variables for which Tables A-1 and A-2 substantially underestimate the confidence intervals.

Variables Related to Educational Background and Aspirations. The questionnaire items dealing with father's education, mother's education, high school curriculum (college preparatory versus all other), and plans for completing four years of col-

lege, all show an appreciable amount of clustering by school. Accordingly, for such variables the confidence intervals provided in the tables should be doubled.

Other items dealing with plans for technical/vocational schooling, a two-year college program, or graduate/professional study, also require adjustment. The confidence intervals in the tables should be multiplied by a factor of 1.5 in order to be applicable to these variables.

It seems clear that the common factor underlying these particular variables is the tendency for family socioeconomic level to be somewhat homogeneous within school districts — some schools serve wealthier populations than others. That makes the form of sampling we use somewhat less efficient for measuring those variables (like those listed above) which are closely associated with family socioeconomic level. Therefore, we urge the reader to treat with caution any variables which are likely to be strongly linked to socioeconomic factors. In the absence of more specific computations of sampling errors, a good rule of thumb for dealing with such variables would be to double the confidence intervals provided in Tables A-1 and A-2.

Variables Related to Geographic Location. Another category of variables which are somewhat homogeneous within schools and school districts consists of those things which reflect differences in region and/or urbanicity. An obvious example is a background question asking where the respondent grew up; the response category "on a farm" shows a very high degree of clustering within schools. One would have to more than double the confidence intervals in the tables to deal with such a measure. Similarly high clustering was found for some responses about religious preference; for example, those whose preference is Baptist are located primarily in the South (and probably heavily in rural areas), whereas those whose preference is Jewish are located primarily in the Northeast (especially in larger cities). The confidence intervals in Tables A-1 and A-2 should be multiplied by a factor as large as 3 in order to be applicable to such variables.

Other variables which show some greater than average homogeneity within schools include such ideologically related dimensions as frequency of attending religious services, importance of religion, and political preference. Still other variables showing high homogeneity, probably because of their association with urbanicity, include driving (percentage who usually do not drive at all), working (percentage with no job), and household composition (percentage with father not living in the home). For each of the variables mentioned in this paragraph, the confidence intervals shown in Tables A-1 and A-2 should be multipled by a factor of about 1.5.

Variables Involving Use of Alcohol and Marijuana. Extensive work has been done to compute sampling errors and confidence intervals for the drug use measures included in this volume (see Johnston, Bachman, and O'Malley, 1977, 1979, especially Appendix B). Most drug use variables show sampling errors which lie within the range of those provided in Tables A-1 and A-2. Usage levels for alcohol and marijuana, however, show some degree of homogeneity within schools, thus requiring that the table levels be adjusted. For items dealing with alcohol use, the table entries should be multiplied by a factor of 1.6; for items dealing with marijuana use, the correction factor is 1.35.

As noted earlier, this appendix has presented guidelines for using the tables of confidence intervals provided herein. Those readers interested in learning more about the rationale underlying such tables, the procedures used to derive the particular tables presented here, and guidelines for further computations of confidence intervals may consult Appendix B of this volume.

Notes to Table A-1

Caution: The entries in this table systematically underestimate confidence intervals for regional subgroups and for blacks. In order to correct these underestimates, the table entries should be multiplied by a factor of 1.10 for data from a single form and by a factor of 1.33 for data based on five forms. Further cautions and corrections are required for some specific variables which relate to educational background and aspirations, geographic location, and the use of alcohol and marijuana (see discussion in the final sections of Appendix A).

The values in this table, when added to and subtracted from an observed percentage, establish the 95 percent confidence interval around that percentage, incorporating a design effect. Table values were calculated using the following formula (adapted from Hays, 1973, p. 379):

$$\text{lower limit} = p - \frac{2N'p + (1.96)^2 - 1.96\sqrt{4N'p\,(1-p) + (1.96)^2}}{2[N' + (1.96)^2]}$$

$$\text{upper limit} = \frac{2N'p + (1.96)^2 + 1.96\sqrt{4N'p\,(1-p) + (1.96)^2}}{2[N' + (1.96)^2]} - p$$

where p = the percentage, and N' is the "effective N," N' = N/(1.3 + .00015N). (See Appendix B for a discussion of the concept of "effective N.")

Table A-1

Confidence Intervals (95% Level) around Percentage Values

									Number of Cases									
	100	200	300	400	500	700	1000	1500	2000	2500	3000	3500	4000	5000	7000	10000	15000	20000
99% +	0.9	0.8	0.7	0.7	0.6	0.6	0.5	0.5	0.4	0.4	0.4	0.4	0.3	0.3	0.3	0.3	0.3	0.2
−	5.6	3.2	2.4	1.9	1.7	1.3	1.1	0.8	0.7	0.6	0.6	0.6	0.5	0.5	0.4	0.4	0.3	0.3
97% +	2.1	1.8	1.6	1.4	1.3	1.2	1.0	0.9	0.8	0.8	0.7	0.7	0.6	0.6	0.6	0.5	0.5	0.5
−	6.6	4.1	3.2	2.6	2.3	1.9	1.6	1.3	1.1	1.0	0.9	0.9	0.8	0.8	0.7	0.6	0.6	0.5
95% +	3.1	2.5	2.2	2.0	1.8	1.6	1.4	1.2	1.1	1.0	0.9	0.9	0.9	0.8	0.7	0.7	0.6	0.6
−	7.4	4.7	3.7	3.1	2.7	2.3	1.9	1.5	1.4	1.2	1.1	1.1	1.0	0.9	0.8	0.8	0.7	0.7
90% +	4.9	3.8	3.3	2.9	2.7	2.3	2.0	1.7	1.5	1.4	1.3	1.3	1.2	1.1	1.0	0.9	0.9	0.8
−	8.8	5.8	4.6	4.0	3.5	2.9	2.5	2.0	1.8	1.6	1.5	1.4	1.4	1.3	1.1	1.0	0.9	0.9
85% +	6.6	4.8	4.1	3.6	3.3	2.9	2.5	2.1	1.9	1.7	1.6	1.5	1.5	1.4	1.2	1.1	1.0	1.0
−	9.7	6.6	5.3	4.5	4.0	3.4	2.9	2.4	2.1	1.9	1.8	1.7	1.6	1.5	1.3	1.2	1.1	1.1
80% +	7.4	5.6	4.7	4.2	3.8	3.3	2.8	2.4	2.1	2.0	1.8	1.7	1.7	1.5	1.4	1.3	1.2	1.1
−	10.3	7.1	5.7	4.9	4.4	3.7	3.1	2.6	2.3	2.1	2.0	1.8	1.8	1.6	1.5	1.3	1.2	1.2
70% +	9.1	6.8	5.6	5.0	4.5	3.9	3.3	2.8	2.5	2.3	2.1	2.0	1.9	1.8	1.6	1.5	1.4	1.3
−	11.1	7.7	6.3	5.5	4.9	4.2	3.5	2.9	2.6	2.4	2.2	2.1	2.0	1.8	1.7	1.5	1.4	1.3
50% +	11.0	7.9	6.5	5.7	5.1	4.4	3.7	3.1	2.8	2.5	2.4	2.2	2.1	2.0	1.8	1.6	1.5	1.4
−	11.0	7.9	6.5	5.7	5.1	4.4	3.7	3.1	2.8	2.5	2.4	2.2	2.1	2.0	1.8	1.6	1.5	1.4
30% +	11.1	7.7	6.3	5.5	4.9	4.2	3.5	2.9	2.6	2.4	2.2	2.1	2.0	1.8	1.7	1.5	1.4	1.3
−	9.1	6.8	5.6	5.0	4.5	3.9	3.3	2.8	2.5	2.3	2.1	2.0	1.9	1.8	1.6	1.5	1.4	1.3
20% +	10.3	7.1	5.7	4.9	4.4	3.7	3.1	2.6	2.3	2.1	2.0	1.8	1.8	1.6	1.5	1.3	1.2	1.2
−	7.4	5.6	4.7	4.2	3.8	3.3	2.8	2.4	2.1	2.0	1.6	1.7	1.7	1.5	1.4	1.3	1.2	1.1
15% +	9.7	6.6	5.3	4.5	4.0	3.4	2.9	2.4	2.1	1.9	1.8	1.7	1.6	1.5	1.3	1.2	1.1	1.1
−	6.3	4.8	4.1	3.6	3.3	2.9	2.5	2.1	1.9	1.7	1.6	1.5	1.5	1.4	1.2	1.1	1.0	1.0
10% +	8.8	5.8	4.6	4.0	3.5	2.9	2.5	2.0	1.8	1.6	1.5	1.4	1.4	1.3	1.1	1.0	0.9	0.9
−	4.9	3.8	3.3	2.9	2.7	2.3	2.0	1.7	1.5	1.4	1.3	1.3	1.2	1.1	1.0	0.9	0.9	0.8
5% +	7.4	4.7	3.7	3.1	2.7	2.3	1.9	1.5	1.4	1.2	1.1	1.1	1.0	0.9	0.8	0.8	0.7	0.7
−	3.1	2.5	2.2	2.0	1.8	1.6	1.4	1.2	1.1	1.0	0.9	0.9	0.9	0.8	0.7	0.7	0.6	0.6
3% +	6.6	4.1	3.2	2.6	2.3	1.9	1.6	1.3	1.1	1.0	0.9	0.9	0.8	0.8	0.7	0.6	0.6	0.5
−	2.1	1.8	1.6	1.4	1.3	1.2	1.0	0.9	0.8	0.8	0.7	0.7	0.6	0.6	0.6	0.5	0.5	0.5
1% +	5.6	3.2	2.4	1.9	1.7	1.3	1.1	0.8	0.7	0.6	0.6	0.6	0.5	0.5	0.4	0.4	0.3	0.3
−	0.9	0.8	0.7	0.7	0.6	0.6	0.5	0.5	0.4	0.4	0.4	0.4	0.3	0.3	0.3	0.3	0.3	0.2

Notes to Table A-2

The entries in this table (which appear on the next two pages) are appropriate for *comparisons* between (a) males and females, (b) those who do and do not plan four years of college, and (c) those falling into different categories of the five-level index of drug usage. The table entries are also appropriate for *one-year trends* for the total sample and any of the subgroups except region. Most other trends and subgroup comparisons require that the table entries be multiplied by an adjustment factor, given below.

Outline of Steps to Follow (see text of appendix for illustrations)

1. Locate the portion of the table with "p" values closest to the two percentages being compared.

2. Locate the specific entry closest to the weighted Ns for the two percentages.

3. Multiply that entry by any necessary adjustment factor (see below).

4. That table value (or adjusted table value), when added to and subtracted from the difference between the two percentages, yields the 95 percent confidence interval for the difference.

5. Also, if the table value (or adjusted table value) is smaller than the difference between the two percentages, then the difference may be described as "statistically significant at the 95 percent level."

	Adjustment Factor (to be multiplied by table entry)
Adjustment Factors	
For comparisons between blacks and whites	
based on single form data	*
based on five form data	1.25
For comparisons between any two regions	
based on single form data	1.15
based on five form data	1.50
For one-year trends involving any region	
based on single form data	*
based on five form data	1.25
For trends over two or more years involving any region	
based on single form data	*
based on five form data	1.35
For trends over two or more years involving all other groups	
based on single form data	*
based on five form data	1.15

*indicates that no adjustment is necessary for category shown

NOTE: The table entries were calculated using the following formula: $1.96\sqrt{p(1-p)\dfrac{1+1}{N_1'\ N_2'}}$

where $N_1' = N_1/DEFF$, and $N_2' = N_2/DEFF$, $DEFF = 1.3 + .000075\left[\dfrac{N_1\ N_2}{N_1 + N_2}\right]$

Table A-2

Confidence Intervals (95% Confidence Level) for Differences Between Two Percentages

	N₁=100	200	300	400	500	700	1000	1500	2000	3000	4000	5000	7000	10000	15000	20000
N₂= 100	3.2															
200	2.7	2.2														
300	2.6	2.0	1.8													
400	2.5	1.9	1.7	1.6												
500	2.4	1.9	1.6	1.5	1.4											
700	2.4	1.8	1.6	1.4	1.3	1.2										
1000	2.3	1.7	1.5	1.3	1.2	1.1	1.0									
1500	2.3	1.7	1.4	1.3	1.2	1.0	0.9	0.8								
2000	2.3	1.7	1.4	1.2	1.1	1.0	0.9	0.8	0.7							
3000	2.3	1.6	1.4	1.2	1.1	1.0	0.8	0.7	0.7	0.6						
4000	2.3	1.6	1.4	1.2	1.1	0.9	0.8	0.7	0.7	0.6	0.6					
5000	2.3	1.6	1.3	1.2	1.1	0.9	0.8	0.7	0.6	0.6	0.5	0.5				
7000	2.3	1.6	1.3	1.2	1.1	0.9	0.8	0.7	0.6	0.5	0.5	0.5	0.4			
10000	2.2	1.6	1.3	1.2	1.0	0.9	0.8	0.7	0.6	0.5	0.5	0.5	0.4	0.4		
15000	2.2	1.6	1.3	1.2	1.0	0.9	0.8	0.6	0.6	0.5	0.5	0.4	0.4	0.4	0.4	
20000	2.2	1.6	1.3	1.1	1.0	0.9	0.8	0.6	0.6	0.5	0.5	0.4	0.4	0.4	0.3	0.3

$p = 1\%$ or 99%

	N₁=100	200	300	400	500	700	1000	1500	2000	3000	4000	5000	7000	10000	15000	20000
N₂= 100	5.4															
200	4.7	3.8														
300	4.4	3.5	3.1													
400	4.3	3.3	2.9	2.7												
500	4.2	3.2	2.8	2.6	2.4											
700	4.1	3.1	2.7	2.4	2.3	2.1										
1000	4.0	3.0	2.5	2.3	2.1	1.9	1.8									
1500	4.0	2.9	2.4	2.2	2.0	1.8	1.6	1.5								
2000	3.9	2.9	2.4	2.1	1.9	1.7	1.5	1.4	1.3							
3000	3.9	2.8	2.3	2.1	1.9	1.7	1.5	1.3	1.2	1.1						
4000	3.9	2.8	2.3	2.0	1.9	1.6	1.4	1.2	1.1	1.0	0.9					
5000	3.9	2.8	2.3	2.0	1.8	1.6	1.4	1.2	1.1	1.0	0.9	0.9				
7000	3.9	2.8	2.3	2.0	1.8	1.6	1.4	1.2	1.0	0.9	0.9	0.8	0.8			
10000	3.9	2.8	2.3	2.0	1.8	1.5	1.3	1.1	1.0	0.9	0.8	0.8	0.7	0.7		
15000	3.8	2.7	2.3	2.0	1.8	1.5	1.3	1.1	1.0	0.9	0.8	0.7	0.7	0.6	0.6	
20000	3.8	2.7	2.3	2.0	1.8	1.5	1.3	1.1	1.0	0.9	0.8	0.7	0.7	0.6	0.6	0.6

$p = 3\%$ or 97%

Table A-2 (continued)

p = 5% or 95%

$N_1=$	100	200	300	400	500	700	1000	1500	2000	3000	4000	5000	7000	10000	15000	20000
$N_2=100$	6.9															
200	6.0	4.9														
300	5.6	4.5	4.0													
400	5.5	4.3	3.8	3.5												
500	5.4	4.1	3.6	3.3	3.1											
700	5.2	3.9	3.4	3.1	2.9	2.7										
1000	5.1	3.8	3.2	2.9	2.7	2.5	2.2									
1500	5.1	3.7	3.1	2.8	2.6	2.3	2.1	1.9								
2000	5.0	3.6	3.1	2.7	2.5	2.2	2.0	1.7	1.6							
3000	5.0	3.6	3.0	2.6	2.4	2.1	1.9	1.6	1.5	1.4						
4000	5.0	3.6	3.0	2.6	2.4	2.1	1.8	1.6	1.4	1.3	1.2					
5000	4.9	3.6	2.9	2.6	2.3	2.0	1.8	1.5	1.4	1.2	1.2	1.1				
7000	4.9	3.5	2.9	2.6	2.3	2.0	1.7	1.5	1.3	1.2	1.1	1.0	1.0			
10000	4.9	3.5	2.9	2.5	2.3	2.0	1.7	1.4	1.3	1.1	1.1	1.0	0.9	0.9		
15000	4.9	3.5	2.9	2.5	2.3	2.0	1.7	1.4	1.3	1.1	1.0	1.0	0.9	0.8	0.8	
20000	4.9	3.5	2.9	2.5	2.3	1.9	1.7	1.4	1.3	1.1	1.0	0.9	0.9	0.8	0.7	0.7

p = 10% or 90%

$N_1=$	100	200	300	400	500	700	1000	1500	2000	3000	4000	5000	7000	10000	15000	20000
$N_2=100$	9.5															
200	8.2	6.7														
300	7.8	6.2	5.5													
400	7.5	5.9	5.2	4.8												
500	7.4	5.7	4.9	4.6	4.3											
700	7.2	5.4	4.7	4.3	4.0	3.7										
1000	7.1	5.2	4.5	4.0	3.7	3.4	3.1									
1500	7.0	5.1	4.3	3.8	3.5	3.2	2.8	2.6								
2000	6.9	5.0	4.2	3.7	3.4	3.0	2.7	2.4	2.2							
3000	6.9	4.9	4.1	3.6	3.3	2.9	2.6	2.2	2.1	1.9						
4000	6.8	4.9	4.1	3.6	3.3	2.8	2.5	2.2	2.0	1.8	1.7					
5000	6.8	4.9	4.0	3.6	3.2	2.8	2.4	2.1	1.9	1.7	1.6	1.5				
7000	6.8	4.9	4.0	3.5	3.2	2.8	2.4	2.0	1.8	1.6	1.5	1.4	1.3			
10000	6.8	4.8	4.0	3.5	3.2	2.7	2.3	2.0	1.8	1.6	1.4	1.4	1.3	1.2		
15000	6.8	4.8	4.0	3.5	3.1	2.7	2.3	2.0	1.8	1.5	1.4	1.3	1.2	1.1	1.1	
20000	6.8	4.8	4.0	3.5	3.1	2.7	2.3	1.9	1.7	1.5	1.4	1.3	1.2	1.1	1.0	1.0

Table A-2 (continued)

p = 15% or 85%

	N₁=100	200	300	400	500	700	1000	1500	2000	3000	4000	5000	7000	10000	15000	20000
N₂=100	11.3															
200	9.8	8.0														
300	9.3	7.3	6.6													
400	9.0	7.0	6.2	5.7												
500	8.8	6.7	5.9	5.4	5.1											
700	8.6	6.5	5.6	5.1	4.8	4.4										
1000	8.4	6.2	5.3	4.8	4.5	4.0	3.7									
1500	8.3	6.1	5.1	4.6	4.2	3.8	3.4	3.0								
2000	8.2	6.0	5.0	4.5	4.1	3.6	3.2	2.9	2.7							
3000	8.2	5.9	4.9	4.3	3.9	3.5	3.0	2.7	2.5	2.2						
4000	8.1	5.8	4.9	4.3	3.9	3.4	2.9	2.6	2.3	2.1	2.0					
5000	8.1	5.8	4.8	4.2	3.8	3.3	2.9	2.5	2.3	2.0	1.9	1.8				
7000	8.1	5.8	4.8	4.2	3.8	3.3	2.8	2.4	2.2	1.9	1.8	1.7	1.6			
10000	8.1	5.8	4.8	4.2	3.8	3.2	2.8	2.4	2.1	1.9	1.7	1.6	1.5	1.4		
15000	8.1	5.7	4.7	4.1	3.7	3.2	2.7	2.3	2.1	1.8	1.7	1.6	1.4	1.3	1.3	
20000	8.0	5.7	4.7	4.1	3.7	3.2	2.7	2.3	2.1	1.8	1.6	1.5	1.4	1.3	1.2	1.2

p = 20% or 80%

	N₁=100	200	300	400	500	700	1000	1500	2000	3000	4000	5000	7000	10000	15000	20000
N₂=100	12.7															
200	11.0	9.0														
300	10.4	8.2	7.4													
400	10.0	7.8	6.9	6.4												
500	9.8	7.5	6.6	6.1	5.7											
700	9.6	7.2	6.2	5.7	5.3	4.9										
1000	9.4	7.0	6.0	5.4	5.0	4.5	4.1									
1500	9.3	6.8	5.7	5.1	4.7	4.2	3.8	3.4								
2000	9.2	6.7	5.6	5.0	4.6	4.0	3.6	3.2	3.0							
3000	9.1	6.6	5.5	4.9	4.4	3.9	3.4	3.0	2.8	2.5						
4000	9.1	6.5	5.4	4.8	4.3	3.8	3.3	2.9	2.6	2.4	2.2					
5000	9.1	6.5	5.4	4.7	4.3	3.7	3.2	2.8	2.6	2.3	2.1	2.0				
7000	9.1	6.5	5.4	4.7	4.2	3.7	3.2	2.7	2.5	2.2	2.0	1.9	1.8			
10000	9.0	6.5	5.3	4.7	4.2	3.6	3.1	2.7	2.4	2.1	1.9	1.8	1.7	1.6		
15000	9.0	6.4	5.3	4.6	4.2	3.6	3.1	2.6	2.3	2.0	1.9	1.7	1.6	1.5	1.4	
20000	9.0	6.4	5.3	4.6	4.2	3.6	3.1	2.6	2.3	2.0	1.8	1.7	1.6	1.5	1.4	1.3

Table A-2 (continued)

	N₁=100	200	300	400	500	700	1000	1500	2000	3000	4000	5000	7000	10000	15000	20000
N₂= 100	14.5															
200	12.6	10.3														
300	11.9	9.4	8.4													
400	11.5	8.9	7.9	7.3												
500	11.3	8.6	7.6	7.0	6.6		p= 30% or 70%									
700	11.0	8.3	7.2	6.5	6.1	5.6										
1000	10.8	8.0	6.8	6.2	5.7	5.2	4.7									
1500	10.6	7.8	6.6	5.9	5.4	4.8	4.3	3.9								
2000	10.6	7.7	6.4	5.7	5.2	4.6	4.1	3.7	3.4							
3000	10.5	7.6	6.3	5.6	5.1	4.4	3.9	3.4	3.2	2.9						
4000	10.4	7.5	6.2	5.5	5.0	4.3	3.8	3.3	3.0	2.7	2.5					
5000	10.4	7.5	6.2	5.4	4.9	4.3	3.7	3.2	2.9	2.6	2.4	2.3				
7000	10.4	7.4	6.1	5.4	4.9	4.2	3.6	3.1	2.8	2.5	2.3	2.2	2.1			
10000	10.4	7.4	6.1	5.3	4.8	4.2	3.6	3.0	2.7	2.4	2.2	2.1	1.9	1.8		
15000	10.3	7.4	6.1	5.3	4.8	4.1	3.5	3.0	2.7	2.3	2.1	2.0	1.8	1.7	1.6	
20000	10.3	7.4	6.1	5.3	4.8	4.1	3.5	3.0	2.6	2.3	2.1	2.0	1.8	1.7	1.6	1.5

	N₁=100	200	300	400	500	700	1000	1500	2000	3000	4000	5000	7000	10000	15000	20000
N₂= 100	15.8															
200	13.7	11.2														
300	13.0	10.3	9.2													
400	12.6	9.8	8.6	8.0												
500	12.3	9.4	8.2	7.6	7.2		p= 35% to 65%									
700	12.0	9.0	7.8	7.1	6.7	6.1										
1000	11.8	8.7	7.5	6.7	6.2	5.6	5.1									
1500	11.6	8.5	7.2	6.4	5.9	5.3	4.7	4.3								
2000	11.5	8.4	7.0	6.2	5.7	5.1	4.5	4.0	3.7							
3000	11.4	8.2	6.9	6.1	5.5	4.8	4.3	3.7	3.4	3.1						
4000	11.4	8.2	6.8	6.0	5.4	4.7	4.1	3.6	3.3	3.0	2.8					
5000	11.3	8.1	6.7	5.9	5.4	4.7	4.1	3.5	3.2	2.8	2.7	2.5				
7000	11.3	8.1	6.7	5.9	5.3	4.6	4.0	3.4	3.1	2.7	2.5	2.4	2.2			
10000	11.3	8.1	6.7	5.8	5.3	4.5	3.9	3.3	3.0	2.6	2.4	2.3	2.1	2.0		
15000	11.3	8.0	6.6	5.8	5.2	4.5	3.8	3.3	2.9	2.5	2.3	2.2	2.0	1.9	1.8	
20000	11.3	8.0	6.6	5.8	5.2	4.5	3.8	3.2	2.9	2.5	2.3	2.1	2.0	1.8	1.7	1.6

Appendix B
Procedures Used to Derive Design
Effects and Sampling Errors

Appendix A provided a very brief and relatively nontechnical explanation of sampling error estimates, accompanied by two tables of confidence intervals which can be used to ascertain the accuracy of most percentages reported in this volume. The present appendix is intended to provide some background concerning the strategy and rationale involved in computing these confidence intervals. It also offers guidance for those wishing to make sampling computations beyond those contained in Appendix A.

This appendix, like the first, is intended to be readable and usable by the nonstatistician. For that reason, we take the time to outline (albeit briefly) a number of relatively elementary factors involved in estimating confidence intervals.

Factors Influencing the Size of Confidence Intervals

The most straightforward types of samples, from a statistical standpoint at least, are simple random samples. In such samples the confidence limits for a proportion are influenced by the size of the sample or subgroups being considered and also by the size of the proportion. For example, the 95 percent confidence interval for a proportion p based on a simple random sample of N cases is approximated by: $p \pm 1.96 \sqrt{p(1-p)/N}$. In a complex probability sample such as the present one, there are a number of other factors which influence the size of confidence limits. This section lists all of the factors which have been taken into account in calculating confidence intervals for use with the data in this volume, beginning with the most simple factors and then proceeding to the more complex.

Number of Cases (N). Other things equal, the larger a sample (or subgroup within a sample), the smaller or more precise will be the confidence interval for a percentage based on that sample. One of the factors determining the size of the confidence interval is $1/\sqrt{N}$. Thus, for example, if all other things were equal, a sample of 400 would have confidence intervals half as large (or twice as precise) as a sample of 100, because $1/\sqrt{400}$ is half as large as $1/\sqrt{100}$.

Size of Percentage. Other things equal, percentage values around 50 percent have larger confidence intervals than higher or lower percentage values. This is because another of the factors determining the size of the confidence interval is $\sqrt{p(1-p)}$ where p is a proportion ranging from 0 to 1.0 (or, to put it in percentage terms, the factor is $\sqrt{x\%(100-x\%)}$). Thus, for example, a proportion of either .1 or .9 (a percentage of either 10 percent or 90 percent) will have a confidence interval only three-fifths as large as the confidence interval around a proportion of .5 (or 50 percent), because $\sqrt{.1(1-.1)}$ is three-fifths as large as $\sqrt{.5(1-.5)}$.

Design Effects in Complex Samples. Under conditions of simple random sampling, a confidence interval can be determined solely on the basis of the number of cases and the percentage value involved. More complex samples such as the one used in the present study make use of stratification and clustering and often differential weighting of respondent scores, and these all influence sampling error. While stratification tends to heighten the precision of a sample, the effects of clustering and weighting reduce precision (compared with a simple random sample of the same size). Therefore, it is not appropriate to apply the standard, simple random sampling formulas to such complex samples in order to obtain estimates of sampling errors, because they would almost always underestimate the actual sampling errors.

Methods exist for correcting for this underestimation, however. Kish (1965, p. 258) defines a correction term called the design effect (DEFF), where:

$$DEFF = \frac{\text{actual sampling variance}}{\substack{\text{expected sampling variance} \\ \text{from a simple random sample} \\ \text{with same number of elements}}}$$

Thus, if the actual sampling variance in a complex sample is four times as large as the expected sampling variance from a simple random sample with the same number of cases, the DEFF is 4.0. Since confidence intervals are proportionate to the square root of variance, the confidence intervals for such a sample would be twice as large (because the square root of 4 is 2) as the confidence interval for a simple random sample with the same number of cases. A fairly simple and straightforward way of applying the concept of design effect may be to note that an increase in design effect has the same impact on precision as a reduction in the number of cases in a simple random sample. For example, a sample of 16,000 cases with a design effect of 4.0 would have the same degree of precision (the same size confidence intervals around various percentages) as a simple random sample of 4,000.

In principle, every different statistic resulting from a complex sample can have its own design effect, and different statistics in the same sample may have quite different design effects. However, it is not feasible to compute every design effect, nor would it be feasible to report every one. Thus, in practice, design effects are averaged across a number of statistics and these average values are used to estimate the design effects for other statistics based on the same sample. Sometimes a single design effect is applied to all statistics of a given type (e.g., percentages) for a given sample. In the present study, however, a rather extensive exploration of design effects revealed a number of systematic differences. These systematic differences have to do with the particular measures being examined, the subgroups involved, and the question of whether a trend over time is being considered. The most consistent difference involves the number of cases in the group or subgroup for which the design effect is computed.

The Relationship between Subgroup Size and Design Effects. Kish et al. (1976) have observed that design effects tend to be smaller for subgroups than for total samples; moreover, the smaller the

subgroup the smaller the design effect is likely to be. The explanation for this widespread phenomenon is that the average number of cases in each sampling cluster is an important factor in determining the size of the design effect, and as subgroup size decreases so does this average number of cases per cluster. This point is illustrated by several subgroups treated in the present volume — males, females, those planning four years of college, and those not planning four years of college. All (or virtually all) of the schools in the sample have both male and female students, as well as some students who plan four years of college and others who do not. Thus, each of these four subgroups is spread more or less evenly across the full number of clusters (schools). Since each of these subgroups includes roughly half of the total sample, the average number of cases per cluster is about half as large as for the total sample, and this leads to a smaller design effect than is found for the total sample. Other subgroups involving different patterns of drug use are also distributed more or less evenly across all clusters and thus are subject to the same phenomenon of smaller design effects because of the smaller number of cases per cluster.

One very important exception to the pattern of smaller design effects for subgroups involves the four geographic region subgroups presented in this volume. These subgroups do not cut across all clusters; instead, regions have been described as "segregated" subgroups, in contrast to the "cross-class" subgroups discussed above. For such segregated subgroups the average number of cases per cluster is about the same as is found in the total sample, and thus the design effects are not lower than those for the total sample (Kish et al., 1976). Another subgroup which is in some respects similar to regional subgroups is the category of blacks. Black respondents are not found equally across high schools throughout the United States. There are, of course, regional differences in proportions of blacks, and these contribute substantially to this lack of equal distribution. In addition, there are patterns of segregation in housing which continue to be reflected in the unequal distribution of blacks in high schools. The net effect of these several factors is that the black subgroup in our sample is "partially segregated" in a sampling sense as well as in the more usual usage of that word. For that reason, the design effects for blacks are somewhat larger than for other subgroups of approximately similar size.

Because the subgroups consisting of blacks and the four regional groups all have larger design effects than other subgroups of the same size, it is necessary to adjust the confidence intervals for these subgroups as indicated in Appendix A. (At a later point in the present appendix we will say more about these adjustment factors.)

One other kind of "subgroup" must be noted in this discussion of the relationship beteen subgroup size and design effects. One-fifth of the total sample filled out each of the five separate questionnaire forms, and thus the respondents to each of these forms may be viewed as a "cross-class" subgroup of the total sample. The average cluster size for a single form is exactly 20 percent of the average cluster size for the total sample. That means, of course, that the single form samples (which are the basis for the large majority of the data presented in this volume) are distinctly more "efficient" than the sample based on all five forms. Accordingly, single form data have much smaller design effects (as displayed later in this appendix).

Design Effects for Comparisons between Subgroups. We noted above that a number of subgroups treated in this volume can be described as "cross-class" subgroups, meaning that members of the subgroup are distributed more or less evenly across sampling clusters. For these kinds of subgroups, it turns out that *comparisons* are relatively efficient, from a sampling standpoint. The technical explanation for this phenomenon is that there is a higher degree of covariance between such subgroup pairs than would be the case in a comparison of independent subgroups. Now let us offer a fairly nontechnical illustration to indicate why this is so. Suppose that a researcher interested in use of marijuana during the senior year of high school obtained data from five high schools concerning female seniors' marijuana use and data from five other high schools concerning male seniors' marijuana use. Suppose that the percentage values for marijuana use during senior year were as follows:

Female seniors (five schools): 60%, 20%,
  65%, 30%, 50%

Male seniors (five other schools): 40%,
  80%, 25%, 70%, 60%

Even though there is a difference of ten percentage points between males and females (if the five schools in each case are averaged), there is still so much variability among schools that one would not conclude with very much confidence that females in general are less likely than males to use marijuana during the senior year of high school. Suppose, on the other hand, that the researcher had obtained data from a total of only five schools and had obtained data concerning both male and female seniors in each school as follows:

	Females	Males
School A	60%	70%
School B	20%	25%
School C	65%	80%
School D	30%	40%
School E	50%	60%

The same group of percentages, this time based on five pairings of males and females rather than independent observations, are much more strongly suggestive of systematic differences between the sexes.

A process analogous to that illustrated above is involved when "cross-class" subgroups are compared, and the increased accuracy or sampling efficiency is reflected in relatively small sampling errors and design effects.

Design Effects for Trends. Thus far this discussion of factors influencing design effects and confidence intervals has focused only on groups and subgroups within a single year. But one of the central purposes of the Monitoring the Future project is to monitor trends over time; indeed, the study procedures have been standardized across years insofar as possible in order to provide the opportunity for sensitive measurement of change. One of the factors designed to produce an added degree of consistency from one year to the next is the use of each school for two data collections, which means that for any two successive years half of the sample of schools is the same. This, plus the fact that the other half of the school sample in a given year is from the same primary sampling units as the half sample it replaced, means that there is a good deal of consistency in the sampling and clustering of the sample from one year to the next. As a result, when cross-year comparisons are made (say, between 1976 and 1977), the design effects are appreciably smaller (i.e., the efficiency is greater) than if completely independent samples of schools had been drawn each year. In other words, the 1976 and 1977 samples are not independent; on the contrary, there is a considerable degree of covariance between them. A similar level of covariance occurs between any pair of adjacent-year samples (e.g., 1977 and 1978), because about half of the schools in both samples were the same. This covariance, or partial "matching," reduces the design effect for differences observed between adjacent years, compared to what they would have been with totally independent samples.

It follows from the discussion above that a trend over an interval greater than one year (e.g., a comparison between 1976 and 1978 which involves totally non-overlapping school samples) is likely to have a design effect which is larger than that for a comparison between adjacent-year samples.

Variables with Unusually Large Design Effects. Kish et al. (1976) stress the importance of computing sampling errors for many kinds of variables, and they point out that they have found "very wide ranges in values of sampling errors (standard errors and design effects) between diverse variables within the same survey" (p. 21). Our own experience has been that, among most variables, the variation in sampling errors and design effects seems more random than consistent, and thus we are reasonably comfortable with the use of averaging procedures (described below) in order to derive a set of general purpose tables. There are some important exceptions to the above generalization, however. Variables which are likely to be grouped according to geographical area (region and/or urbanicity), as well as variables that may differ systematically from one school to another, show much higher than usual amounts of homogeneity within sample clusters. It follows necessarily that such variables also have much higher than usual design effects. The variables in the Monitoring the Future study which seem most likely to show such high design effects tend to be grouped into the questionnaire segment dealing with background factors and educational aspirations (Section C of all questionnaire forms). These variables were excluded from the process of computing overall design effects and the confidence intervals provided in Tables A-1 and A-2. Appendix A provides a further discussion of some of these variables and offers some suggestions for adjusting the confidence interval tables to deal with them.

Procedures Used in Deriving Design Effects and Tables of Confidence Intervals

Having taken some pains to review the several factors which can influence design effects and confidence intervals, it is now a fairly simple matter for us to summarize the steps followed to compute the tables of confidence intervals shown in Appendix A. We were heavily influenced in this effort by the work of Kish and his colleagues (Kish, 1965; Kish et al., 1976) in two ways. First, we followed their recommendation that sampling errors be computed and averaged across a goodly number of variables and subgroups. Second, we paid particular attention to their observation that design effects tend to be smaller for subgroups than for total samples (a point discussed earlier in this appendix).

Confidence Intervals for Single Percentages. Our procedure was to compute sampling errors and design effects for most of the variables which are common to all five forms (those in the C sections of all questionnaires, and those in the B sections of Forms 2 through 5), and for every twentieth varia-

ble in the A, D, and E sections of Forms 2 through 5. (Form 1 was omitted because most of this form is comprised of drug-related items, and such items involve high proportions of missing data because respondents are instructed to skip over many questions which are not applicable to them). Design effects were computed for each of the subgroups reported in this volume, as well as for the total sample. Design effects for each subgroup and for the total were averaged across variables for the C section material (all five forms), the B section material (drug use measures, all five forms), and the sampling of variables from the A, D, and E sections (single form data). As noted earlier, the variables which showed unusually high levels of homogeneity within sample clusters were excluded from the C section variables when they were averaged. The 1977 data were used for this analysis. Later replication using 1976 data provided nearly identical values.

The averaging process consisted of taking a mean of the *square roots* of the design effects. Kish and his colleagues (1976) refer to the design effect as DEFF, and to the square root of the design effect as DEFT; thus, $\sqrt{\text{DEFF}}$ = DEFT. We will find it useful to use this terminology in what follows. The rationale for computing means of DEFT rather than DEFF is that the former value is directly proportionate to the size of confidence intervals. A further reason for doing so is that the values of DEFT approximate a normal distribution much more closely than the values of DEFF, which are skewed upward. (A comparison of mean DEFTs and median DEFTs showed them to be quite similar, something which certainly is not true of mean and median DEFFs).

Bearing in mind that design effects tend to be smaller for subgroups than for total samples, and bearing in mind also that confidence intervals are directly proportionate to DEFT and to $\sqrt{N}$, we plotted the mean DEFT values for the total sample and for all subgroups, in each case relating DEFT to $\sqrt{N}$. The results are shown in Figure B-1. Note that distinctions are made between "cross-class" and "segregated" subgroups, and between mean DEFTs based on five forms and those based on single forms (the $\sqrt{N}$ values for the latter are, of course, much smaller).*

Setting aside the "segregated" subgroups (regions and blacks) for the moment, it is clear that the rest of the mean DEFTs in Figure B-1 show a very clear and consistent pattern: the higher the value $\sqrt{N}$ the higher the mean DEFT. It turns out that these mean DEFT values are very closely approximated by the function DEFT =

*The five form data consisted of C section material, excluding those variables related to region, urbanicity, and/or socioeconomic level.

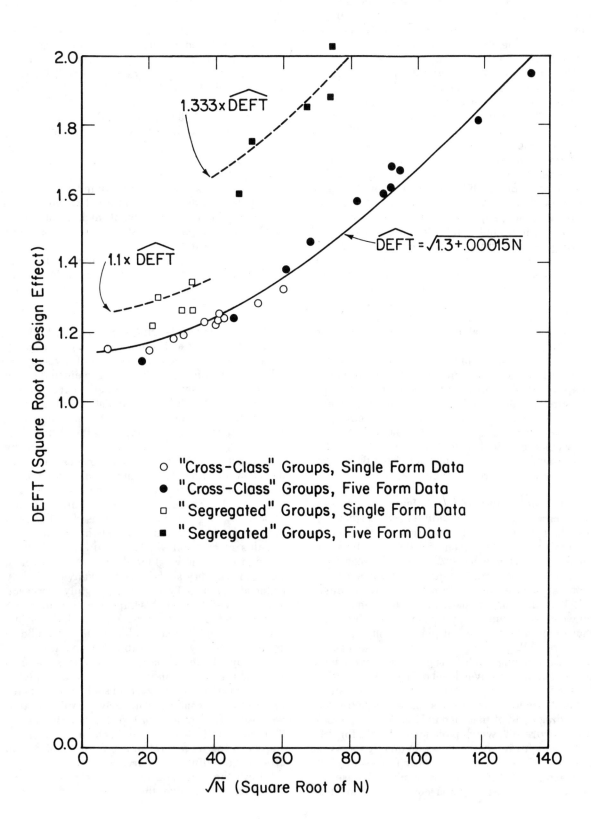

Figure B-1
Design Effects for Single Percentages

$\sqrt{1.3 + .00015N}$, as shown by the solid line in the figure. (The function can also be stated as DEFF = 1.3 + .00015N.) The particular parameters in that function were derived empirically, but the basic function (i.e., DEFT $= \sqrt{a + bN}$) was adapted directly from the work of Kish et al. (1976).

Given the above function that fitted the mean DEFT values for the total sample and the "cross-class" subgroups, we returned to the problem of assigning DEFT values for the "segregated" subgroups. The simplest solution was to select two adjustment factors which could be multiplied by the confidence interval values in Table A-1. These adjustment factors are shown by the dashed lines in Figure B-1; they correspond to multiplying the "standard" DEFT (solid line) by a factor of 1.1 for single form data and by a factor of 1.33 for five form data. These adjustments, which were selected on empirical grounds, yield design effects for the "segregated" subgroups which are approximately equal to the design effects for the total sample (treating single form and five form data separately, of course). This is reassuring, since Kish et al. (1976) have reported that "segregated" subgroups can in general be expected to show design effects approximately equivalent to the design effects for the total sample.

After the data in Figure B-1 were plotted and the form of the main function (indicated by the solid line) was determined, DEFT values for drug use measures (material in Section B of all forms) were checked. It was found that the DEFTs for only two drug categories, alcohol and marijuana, exceeded the values indicated by the function; accordingly, adjustment factors were developed for these two drugs (1.6 and 1.35, respectively).

Confidence Intervals for Differences between Two Percentages. Our procedure here was directly parallel to that followed in determining confidence intervals for single percentages. DEFT values for the differences between 1977 and 1976 percentages were computed using virtually the same set of items as used earlier. Also computed were mean DEFT values for comparisons in the same year between subgroups such as males and females, those who did and did not plan to complete four years of college, blacks and whites, pairings of regions, and pairings of drug use groups. It was found that, for any given level of N, the mean DEFT values for subgroup comparisons were quite similar to the mean DEFT values for one-year trends; accordingly, all of these mean DEFTs were included in Figure B-2, which plots mean DEFTs for differences between percentages. In this figure, as in Figure B-1, the strong relationship was evident between mean DEFTs and the numbers of cases in the two groups being compared. This relationship

can be verly closely approximated by the function DEFT $= \sqrt{1.3 + .000075N}$ (which can also be stated DEFF = 1.3 + .000075N), where N $= 2N_1N_2/N_1 + N_2$.

It was expected on grounds of sampling theory that as we found earlier, the function which fit most differences between percentages would not fit differences involving regions and differences involving blacks. In fact, the data indicated that some adjustment is necessary for black-white comparisons using data from all five forms, and also for comparisons as well as trends involving any region. We have not tried to show those adjustments in Figure B-2, but the several values involved are shown in the guidelines to Table A-2.

It was also expected on the grounds of sampling theory that trends across an interval of two or more years would show somewhat higher values of DEFT than one-year trends. It turned out that this was true only for data from all five forms; data based on one form only did not show significantly higher values. The adjustment factors for trends involving five forms over two or more years are shown in Table A-2.

Use of Weighted Numbers of Cases in Entering Confidence Interval Tables. We should mention in passing that the recommendations for using the tables in Appendix A indicate that *weighted* N values should be used. The computer program which generated our design effect statistics makes use of weights in calculating percentages and actual sampling variances. But in computing the DEFF ratio, defined as the actual sampling variance divided by the expected sampling variance from a simple random sample with the same number of elements, the program makes use of the *unweighted* numbers of cases to determine "the same number of elements." Since the mean weights used in the 1975, 1976, and 1977 data tables are slightly lower than 1.0, this means that when entering the tables in Appendix A with weighted data from those years, one is being very slightly "conservative" (slightly reduced risk of a Type 1 error, slightly increased risk of a Type 2 error). It is important to realize that if one took the trouble to make corrections for this "conservatism," the correction would rarely be as great as multiplying the Table A-1 and Table A-2 entries by a factor of .95; and in the large majority of cases the correction would involve multiplying by a factor of about .98. We find such discrepancies to be trivially small, particularly when compared with what Kish et al. (1976, p. 12) describe as the "heroic simplifications" required in some of the steps leading to general purpose tables of design effects and confidence intervals.

Before the 1978 data tables were produced we had come to realize the advantages in having

Figure B-2
Design Effects for Differences Between Percentages

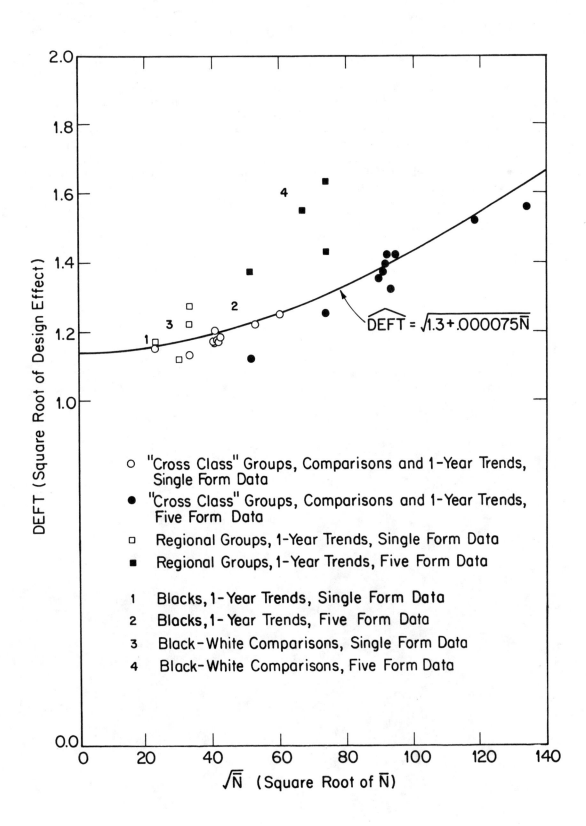

weighted values which averaged 1.0; accordingly, beginning with the 1978 data, the weighted N values in the tables do approximate the actual numbers of cases quite closely. But it was impractical to redo the 1975 through 1977 data tables to incorporate this refinement. Another alternative would have been to employ slightly different versions of Tables A-1 and A-2, containing slightly different confidence intervals for each of those three years; however, we felt that such an approach could introduce confusion when cross-year comparisons were made. Thus, we opted for the solution which seems to us to be most simple and manageable, even though it involves the slight degree of "conservatism" noted above. For readers who find this solution undesirable, we have included Tables B-1 and B-2, which present weighted and unweighted Ns for the various subgroups for each year. Table B-1 contains Ns for all five forms (except for 1975 which shows Ns for Forms 2 through 5), and Table B-2 contains approximate Ns for a single form. Thus, readers who wish to avoid the slight "conservatism" (and also to be more precise for subgroups in 1978 and later whose average weight is not exactly 1.0) may determine the unweighted Ns. Some correction for missing data should be made in this case; this can be accomplished by calculating the percentage of missing data (using the weighted Ns from the data table and the weighted N from Table B-1 or B-2) and adjusting the unweighted N accordingly. These adjusted unweighted Ns can then be used in Appendix A.

Table B-1

Sample Sizes (Unweighted and Weighted) in Subgroups by Year

	Number of Cases							
	Class of 1975[a]		Class of 1976		Class of 1977		Class of 1978	
	Unwtd.	Wtd.	Unwtd.	Wtd.	Unwtd.	Wtd.	Unwtd.	Wtd.
Total Sample	12627	12108	16678	15138	18436	15830	18924	18916
Sex:								
Male	5799	5571	7999	7241	8449	7358	8603	8779
Female	6371	6100	7924	7257	9188	7850	9416	9266
Race:								
White	b	b	12933	11796	13818	12240	14663	14847
Black	b	b	1806	1716	2500	1938	2205	2096
Region:								
Northeast	3014	2695	4034	3570	4760	3959	4841	4607
North Central	3951	3832	5098	4687	5697	4758	5576	5411
South	3366	3857	4177	4597	4908	4820	5566	6292
West	2296	1724	3369	2284	3071	2294	2941	2605
College Plans:								
Complete 4 yrs	b	b	7963	6994	8933	7407	9264	8844
None or under 4 yrs	b	b	7179	6877	7764	7048	7857	8413
Illicit Drug Use:								
None	4329	4400	6532	6091	6672	5878	6400	6595
Marijuana Only	2044	1894	3950	3457	4955	4050	5354	5214
Few Pills	1163	1113	1942	1736	2173	1813	2329	2304
More Pills	2157	1989	3427	2987	3857	3266	3906	3885
Any Heroin	231	216	319	268	321	280	289	302

[a] The number of cases shown for 1975 is based on Forms 2 through 5 only, because the data from Form 1 are intentionally-not included in tabulations based on drug and demographic items which appeared in all forms.

[b] Missing data problems were severe for race and college plans in 1975; accordingly, these data have been excluded from all tables in the 1975 report.

Table B-2

Sample Sizes (Unweighted and Weighted) in Subgroups by Year
for Questions on a Single Form

| | Number of Cases | | | | | | | |
| | Class of 1975 | | Class of 1976 | | Class of 1977 | | Class of 1978 | |
	Unwtd.	Wtd.	Unwtd.	Wtd.	Unwtd.	Wtd.	Unwtd.	Wtd.
Total Sample	3157	3027	3336	3028	3687	3166	3785	3783
Sex:								
Male	1450	1393	1600	1488	1690	1472	1721	1756
Female	1371	1525	1585	1451	1838	1570	1883	1853
Race:								
White	a	a	2587	2359	2764	2448	2933	2969
Black	a	a	361	343	500	388	441	419
Region:								
Northeast	754	674	807	714	952	792	968	921
North Central	988	958	1020	937	1139	952	1115	1082
South	842	964	835	919	982	964	1113	1258
West	574	431	674	457	614	459	588	521
College Plans:								
Complete 4 yrs	a	a	1593	1399	1787	1481	1853	1769
None or under 4 yrs	a	a	1436	1375	1553	1410	1571	1683
Illicit Drug Use:								
None	1082	1100	1306	1218	1334	1176	1280	1319
Marijuana Only	511	474	790	691	991	810	1071	1043
Few Pills	291	278	388	347	435	363	466	461
More Pills	539	497	685	597	771	653	781	777
Any Heroin	58	54	64	54	64	56	58	60

[a] Missing data problems were severe for race and college plans in 1975; accordingly, these data have been excluded from all tables in the 1975 report.

Further Applications of these Design Effects and Sampling Errors

One of the reasons for providing the above review of the factors influencing design effects and confidence intervals, and the procedures used in computing our confidence interval tables, is to provide sufficient background and data to permit the interested reader to go beyond the material provided in Appendix A. In this section we consider two specific extensions, the calculation of levels of "statistical significance" higher than 95 percent and the computation of means and their confidence intervals.

Calculating Confidence Intervals for Higher Levels of Statistical Significance. The entries contained in Tables A-1 and A-2 provide the 95 percent confidence level (also referred to as the .05 level of significance). These entries were computed by multiplying the standard error (square root of sample variance) by a factor of 1.96. The 99 percent confidence interval (.01 level of significance) uses a factor of 2.58 standard errors, and the 99.9 percent confidence interval (.001 level of significance) uses a factor of 3.29 standard errors. To convert the entries in Tables A-1 and A-2 to these higher levels, it is necessary only to multiply the entries by the appropriate constant shown below (keeping in mind that any other adjustments required in the tables must also be applied):

Confidence Interval	Significance Level	Multiply entries in Tables A-1 and A-2 by the following:
99%	.01	2.58/1.96 = 1.32
99.9%	.001	3.29/1.96 = 1.68

Computing Means and Their Confidence Intervals. Many of the questionnaire items included in this volume have ordinal response scales (e.g., agree, agree mostly, neither, disagree mostly, disagree), and it is often the case that a survey analyst will be willing to treat such scales as if they involved equal intervals. In such cases, means and standard deviations are more "efficient" in their use of information than are dichotomies which yield a single percentage or a pair of percentages (e.g., those who respond "agree" or "agree mostly," versus all others). It is a relatively straightforward matter to compute means and standard deviations for the total sample or any of the subgroups treated in this volume. The problem, then, is to be able to

specify confidence intervals for the means, or for the differences between pairs of means. In the case of simple random samples, one needs only the means, standard deviations (or variances), and numbers of cases in order to compute confidence intervals. But in complex samples such as the present one, it is also necessary to take account of design effects. If an estimate of design effect is available, one of the simplest procedures to follow is to divide the actual numbers of cases by the design effect (thereby "depreciating" the actual number to its equivalent value in simple random sample terms) and then employ the standard statistical procedures which have been developed for application to simple random samples. Thus, for example, if the design effect (DEFF) for a sample of 18,000 were 4.0, then one could divide the 18,000 by 4.0 and the result, 4,500, could be entered as the value of "N" in statistical tables and formulas designed for use with simple random samples. To take another example, if one were comparing means based on two subgroups, each involving about 9,000 cases, and if DEFF (for both subgroups) was 2.0, then one could compute the significance of the difference between the two means as if the N for each group were 4,500 (i.e., 9,000 divided by 2.0)

In short, the strategy involves dividing the actual number of cases by the appropriate DEFF in order to get a "simple random sampling equivalent N" or, more simply, an "effective N" for use in statistical procedures designed for random samples.

Design Effects for Use in Computing "Effective Ns." In order to employ the strategy outlined above, one must have estimates of design effects which are judged to be appropriate for one's purposes. In the case of means based on the percentages reported in this volume, we are confident (based on personal communications with Kish) that it is appropriate to use the same DEFF values as were used in developing Tables A-1 and A-2. For other, more complex statistics, we cannot make the same assertion, although it is generally the case that design effects for such statistics are not larger than those for means and percentages (Kish and Frankel, 1970; Frankel, 1971).

In Table B-3 we provide guidelines for computing DEFF values for single percentages (or means) and for differences between two percentages (or means). For reasons discussed elsewhere in this appendix, we must provide for different (and somewhat higher) DEFFs for "segregated" subgroups (regional subgroups and sometimes also blacks), and for trends over two or more years (in contrast to one-year trends). And in all instances, of course, the DEFF values are very much influenced by the average size of sampling clusters, which is always dependent on the number of cases

Table B-3
Guidelines for Computing Design Effects (DEFFs) for Percentages
and Means Derived from Monitoring the Future Samples

DEFINITIONS

$$\text{DEFF (design effect)} = \frac{\text{(estimated) sampling variance}}{\begin{array}{c}\text{expected sampling variance from simple}\\ \text{random sample with same number of elements}\end{array}}$$

N = number of respondents on whom a single percentage or mean is based

$\overline{N} = 2N_1 N_2 / (N_1 + N_2)$, for use in comparisons of two percentages or means, based on two groups of sizes N_1 and N_2.

DESIGN EFFECT FORMULAS

1. For single percentages or means involving . . .
   a. regional subgroups or blacks
      DEFF for single form data .... $(1.3 + .00015N)\,(1.21)$
      DEFF for five form data .... $(1.3 + .00015N)\,(1.78)$

   b. all other subgroups or total sample
      DEFF for single form or five form data .... $1.3 + .00015N$

2. For comparisons between . . .
   a. any two regions
      DEFF for single form data .... $(1.3 + .000075\overline{N})\,(1.32)$
      DEFF for five form data .... $(1.3 + .000075\overline{N})\,(2.25)$

   b. blacks and whites
      DEFF for single form data .... $1.3 + .000075\overline{N}$
      DEFF for five form data .... $(1.3 + .000075\overline{N})\,(1.56)$

   c. genders, college plans groups, or any two "drug use" subgroups
      DEFF for single form or five form data .... $1.3 + .000075\overline{N}$

3. For one-year trends involving . . .
   a. any region
      DEFF for single form data .... $1.3 + .000075\overline{N}$
      DEFF for five form data .... $(1.3 + .000075\overline{N})\,(1.56)$
   b. all other subgroups or total sample
      DEFF for single form or five form data .... $1.3 + .000075\overline{N}$

4. For trends over two or more years involving . . .
   a. any region
      DEFF for single form data .... $1.3 + .000075\overline{N}$
      DEFF for five form data .... $(1.3 + .000075\overline{N})\,(1.82)$
   b. all other subgroups or total sample
      DEFF for single form data .... $1.3 + .000075\overline{N}$
      DEFF for five form data .... $(1.3 + .000075\overline{N})\,(1.32)$

(N). Accordingly, all of the design effect formulas in Table B-3 require computations which take account of N. (It should also be noted that the formulas in Table B-3 correspond exactly to the values of design effects and adjustment factors used in Tables A-1 and A-2 in Appendix A.)

A **Concluding Note.** In their very useful paper dealing with sampling errors for fertility surveys, Kish et al. (1976) commented that some of the methods they used ". . . emerged after several false starts." They went on to say that the volume and diversity of the data they were dealing with ". . . presented new challenges and opportunities." And they added, "Our methods are subject to further developments and modifications, and we invite participation and suggestions" (p. 10). Our own attempts to apply the methods of Kish and his colleagues to the data reported in this volume have been challenged by the diversity of the data, have involved several false starts, and we hope are subject to further developments and modifications. We invite readers to offer their suggestions, and we also encourage readers to inquire about further work that we and/or others may carry out during the coming months and years.

Appendix C
Questionnaire Covers, Instructions, and Sample Page

monitoring the future

a continuing study of the lifestyles and values of youth

This questionnaire is part of a nationwide study of high school seniors, conducted each year by the University of Michigan's Institute for Social Research. The questions ask your opinions about a number of things--the way things are now and the way you think they ought to be in the future. In a sense, many of your answers on this questionnaire will count as "votes" on a wide range of important issues.

If this study is to be helpful, it is important that you answer each question as thoughtfully and frankly as possible. All your answers will be kept strictly confidential, and will never be seen by anyone who knows you.

This study is completely voluntary. If there is any question that you or your parents would find objectionable for any reason, just leave it blank.

In a few months, we would like to mail each of you a summary of the nationwide results from this study. Also, in about a year we would like to mail another questionnaire to some of you, asking about how your plans have worked out and what's happening in your lives.

In order to include you in these mailings, we ask for your name and address on a special form at the end of this questionnaire. This form is to be torn out and handed in separately. Once the address form and the questionnaire have been separated, there is no way they can be matched again, except by using a special computer tape at the University of Michigan. The only purpose for that tape is to match a follow-up questionnaire with this one.

Other seniors have said that these questionnaires are very interesting and that they enjoy filling them out. We hope you will too. Be sure to read the instructions on the other side of this cover page before you begin to answer. Thank you very much for being an important part of this project.

INSTITUTE FOR SOCIAL RESEARCH
THE UNIVERSITY OF MICHIGAN
ANN ARBOR, MICHIGAN

251

INSTRUCTIONS

1.   This is not a test, so there are no right or wrong answers; we would like you to work fairly quickly, so that you can finish.

2.   All of the questions should be answered by marking one of the answer spaces. If you don't always find an answer that fits exactly, use the one that comes closest. If any question does not apply to you, or you are not sure of what it means, just leave it blank.

3.   Your answers will be read automatically by a machine called an optical mark reader. Please follow these instructions carefully:

     • Use only the black lead pencil you have been given.

     • Make heavy black marks inside the circles.

     • Erase cleanly any answer you wish to change.

     • Make no other markings or comments on the answer pages, since they interfere with the automatic reading. (If you want to add a comment about any question, please use the space provided below.)

These kinds of markings will work: ● ● ◕

These kinds of markings will NOT work: ⊙ ✦ ○

(THIS SPACE FOR WRITTEN COMMENTS)

WHY YOUR NAME AND ADDRESS?

As we told you earlier, we'd like to send you a summary of the nationwide results of the present study, and in about a year we want to mail a shorter questionnaire to some of you. In order to include you in these follow-ups, we would like to have an address where information will be sure to reach you during the coming year.

HOW IS CONFIDENTIALITY PROTECTED?

- The information on this page will be used ONLY for mailing, and will always be kept separate from your answers. A special Grant of Confidentiality from the U.S. government protects all information gathered in this research project.

- The questionnaire and address pages will be collected separately, sealed immediately in separate envelopes, and sent to two different cities for processing.

- Once a questionnaire and address page have been separated, there is no way they can be matched, except by using a special computer tape at the University of Michigan. That tape contains the two DIFFERENT numbers that appear on the back of this address page and on the back of the questionnaire. These numbers will be used ONLY to match a follow-up questionnaire with this one.

> Before filling out this address page, please separate it from the rest of the questionnaire by FOLDING ALONG THE PERFORATED LINE AND TEARING CAREFULLY.

Please **PRINT** your name and the address where you can most likely be reached during the coming year.

Mr.
Miss
Ms. _____
Mrs.   FIRST NAME   INITIAL   LAST NAME

STREET _____

CITY _____

STATE _____ ZIP_____

TELEPHONE NO.   (   ) — _____
                      AREA

In case we should have trouble getting mail to you, if you move, please **PRINT** the name and address of one other person (with a different address than your own) who will know where to reach you in the future. (Examples of such a person: aunt or uncle, older sister or brother, or close friend.)

Mr.
Miss
Ms. FIRST NAME   INITIAL   LAST NAME
Mrs.

STREET _____

CITY _____

STATE _____ ZIP_____

TELEPHONE NO.   (   ) — _____
                      AREA

THANK YOU AGAIN FOR YOUR HELP

PART A

* **BEFORE BEGINNING BE SURE YOU HAVE READ THE INSTRUCTIONS ON THE COVER.**

1. Taking all things together, how would you say things are these days--would you say you're very happy, pretty happy, or not too happy these days?

   ○ Very happy
   ○ Pretty happy
   ○ Not too happy

2. Some people think a lot about the social problems of the nation and the world, and about how they might be solved. Others spend little time thinking about these issues. How much do you think about such things?

   ① Never
   ② Seldom
   ③ Sometimes
   ④ Quite often
   ⑤ A great deal

3. Of all the problems facing the nation today, how often do you worry about each of the following? (Mark one circle for each line.)

	Never	Seldom	Sometimes	Often
a. Chance of nuclear war	①	②	③	④
b. Population growth	①	②	③	④
c. Crime and violence	①	②	③	④
d. Pollution	①	②	③	④
e. Energy shortages	①	②	③	④
f. Race relations	①	②	③	④
g. Hunger and poverty	①	②	③	④
h. Using open land for housing or industry	①	②	③	④
i. Urban decay	①	②	③	④
j. Economic problems	①	②	③	④
k. Drug abuse	①	②	③	④

4. How well do you think your experiences and training (at home, school, work, etc.) have prepared you to be a good. . .

	Poorly	Not So Well	Fairly Well	Well	Very Well
a. ...husband or wife?	①	②	③	④	⑤
b. ...parent?	①	②	③	④	⑤
c. ...worker on a job?	①	②	③	④	⑤

5. Apart from the particular kind of work you want to do, how would you rate each of the following settings as a place to work? (Mark one circle for each line.)

	Not At All Acceptable	Somewhat Acceptable	Acceptable	Desirable
a. Working in a large corporation	①	②	③	④
b. Working in a small business	①	②	③	④
c. Working in a government agency	①	②	③	④
d. Working in the military service	①	②	③	④
e. Working in a school or university	①	②	③	④
f. Working in a police department or police agency	①	②	③	④
g. Working in a social service organization	①	②	③	④
h. Working with a small group of partners	①	②	③	④
i. Working on your own (self-employed)	①	②	③	④

6. If you were to get enough money to live as comfortably as you'd like for the rest of your life, would you want to work?

   ① I would want to work
   ② I would not want to work

(Base Year & Follow-up: Form 5—Part A)

References

Adelson, J. "What Generation Gap?" *New York Times Magazine*. January 18, 1970, pp. 1-11.

Adelson, J. "Adolescence and the Generation Gap." *Psychology Today*, September 1979, pp. 33-37.

Bachman, J.G.; O'Malley, P.M.; and Johnston, J. Youth in Transition, Volume VI: *Adolescence to Adulthood — A Study of Change and Stability in the Lives of Young Men*. Ann Arbor: Institute for Social Research, 1978.

Bachman, J. G., and Johnston, L. D. *The Monitoring the Future Project Design and Procedures*. Ann Arbor: Institute for Social Research, 1978.

Frankel, M. R. *Inference from Survey Samples:* An Empirical Investigation. Ann Arbor: Institute for Social Research, 1971.

Golladay, M. *The Condition of Education*. National Center for Education Statistics, Washington, D.C.: U.S. Government Printing Office, 1976.

Golladay, M. *The Condition of Education*. National Center for Education Statistics, *Volume 3, Part 1*. Washington, D.C.: U.S. Government Printing Office, 1977.

Hays, William L. *Statistics for the Social Sciences* (2nd ed.). New York: Holt, Rinehart, & Winston, 1973.

Johnston, L. D. *Drugs and American Youth*. Ann Arbor: Institute for Social Research, 1973.

Johnston, L. D.; Bachman, J. G.; and O'Malley, P. M. *Drug Use Among American High School Students 1975-1977* (National Institute on Drug Abuse). Washington, D.C.: U.S. Government Printing Office, 1977.

Johnston, L. D.; Bachman, J. G.; and O'Malley, P. M. *Drugs and the Class of 1978: Behaviors, Attitudes, and Recent National Trends* (National Institute on Drug Abuse). Washington, D.C.: U.S. Government Printing Office, 1979.

Johnston, L. D.; O'Malley, P. M.; and Eveland, L. K. *Some Preliminary Results from Drugs and American Youth II: A Longitudinal Resurvey*. (Interim report to the National Institute on Drug Abuse.) Ann Arbor: Institute for Social Research, 1975.

Kish, L., and Frankel, M. R. "Balanced Repeated Replication for Standard Errors." *Journal of the American Statistical Association*, 65 (1970): 1071-1094.

Kish, L.; Groves R.M.; and Krotki, K.P. *Sampling Errors for Fertility Surveys* (Occasional Papers Series No. 17). Voorburg, Netherlands: International Statistical Institute, 1976.

U. S. Bureau of the Census. *Current Population Reports*, Series P-20, No. 319. School enrollment — social and economic characteristics of students: October 1976. Washington, D.C.: U.S. Government Printing Office, 1978.

Inferences about one variance

Procedure	Assumptions	Advantages	Limitations	Section
Inferences about a variance based on a chi-square distribution	Random sample from a Gaussian distribution	Inferences are based on exact probabilities obtained from a chi-square distribution.	Procedure is not robust to deviations from the Gaussian assumption.	14-1

Inferences about two variances

Procedure	Assumptions	Advantages	Limitations	Section
Inferences about two variances based on an F distribution	Two independent random samples from Gaussian distributions	Inferences are based on exact probabilities obtained from an F distribution.	Procedure is not robust to deviations from the Gaussian assumption.	14-2
Levene's modified test for equality of two or more variances	Two independent random samples	Procedure is robust to deviations from Gaussian observations.	Probabilities are approximate.	14-4

Inferences about three or more variances

Procedure	Assumptions	Advantages	Limitations	Section
Bartlett's test for equality of variances	Independent random samples from Gaussian distributions	The procedure is well known.	Procedure is not robust to deviations from the Gaussian assumption.	14-3
Levene's modified test for equality of two or more variances	Two or more independent random samples	Procedure is robust to deviations from Gaussian observations.	Probabilities are approximate.	14-4

Inferences about a linear correlation coefficient

Procedure	Assumptions	Advantages	Limitations	Section
Parametric test that a linear correlation coefficient equals zero	Random sample of pairs of observations from a bivariate normal (or Gaussian) distribution	Procedure is well known and easy to use.	Probabilities depend on all the assumptions being satisfied.	15-2
Nonparametric test for independence of two quantitative variables	Random sample of pairs of observations	We need not assume Gaussian observations.	Procedure is less powerful than the parametric procedure when the assumptions for the parametric procedure are satisfied.	15-3